ON THE DANGEROUS EDGE

The Maple Leaf
Our Emblem Dear
The Maple Leaf Forever
God Save Our Queen and Heaven Bless
The Maple Leaf Forever

I am the very toughest of the very tough Canadians
I'm one of those all ready for – the – early – morning raid – y – uns:
I'm always on the parapet a-dying to leap over it,
And when the opportunity arrives I praise Jehovah it!
I do not mind the Huns at all, I always like to strafe at them,
And when I've my smoke helmet on, and in the trench
I roam about – roam about – roam about -
I'm telling you, d'ye get me kid? I'm something to write home about.

Another Garland From the Front, Christmas 1916/New Year 1917

On the Dangerous Edge

British and Canadian Trench Raiding on the Western Front 1914-1918

Kenneth Radley

Helion & Company

Helion & Company Limited
Unit 8 Amherst Business Centre
Budbrooke Road
Warwick
CV34 5WE
England
Tel. 01926 499 619
Fax 0121 711 4075
Email: info@helion.co.uk
Website: www.helion.co.uk
Twitter: @helionbooks
Visit our blog http://blog.helion.co.uk/

Published by Helion & Company 2018
Designed and typeset by Mach 3 Solutions Ltd (www.mach3solutions.co.uk)
Cover designed by Paul Hewitt, Battlefield Design (www.battlefield-design.co.uk)
Printed by Lightning Source, Milton Keynes, Buckinghamshire

ISBN 978-1-912390-75-5

British Library Cataloguing-in-Publication Data.
A catalogue record for this book is available from the British Library.

Contents

List of Plates

List of Maps, Sketches and Diagrams

List of Abbreviations

2IC	Second in Command
BEF	British Expeditionary Force
BGGS	Brigadier General General Staff
BM	Brigade Major
CB	Companion of the Order of the Bath
CBE	Commander of the Order of the British Empire
CEF	Canadian Expeditionary Force
CGS	Chief of the General Staff
CIGS	Chief of the Imperial General Staff
C-in-C	Commander-in-Chief
CMG	Companion of the Order of St. Michael and St. George
CMR	Canadian Mounted Rifles
CO	Commanding Officer
CRA	Commander Royal Artillery
CRE	Commander Royal Engineers
CSM	Company Sergeant-Major
CT	Communication Trench
DCM	Distinguished Conduct Medal
DMGO	Divisional Machine-Gun Officer
DSO	Distinguished Service Order
DTMO	Divisional Trench Mortar Officer
FGCM	Field General Court-Martial
FOO	Forward Observation Officer
FSR	Field Service Regulations
GHQ	General Headquarters
GOC	General Officer Commanding
GOCRA	General Officer Commanding Royal Artillery
GSO1	General Staff Officer (1st Grade)
GSO2	General Staff Officer (2nd Grade)
GSO3	General Staff Officer (3rd Grade)
HE	High Explosive
KOYLI	King's Own Yorkshire Light Infantry
KRRC	King's Royal Rifle Corps
LOB	Left Out of Battle
MC	Military Cross

MGGS	Major General General Staff
MM	Military Medal
MO	Medical Officer
MSD	Map, Sketch, Diagram
NCO	Non-Commissioned Officer
OC	Officer Commanding
OR	Other Rank
psc	passed staff college
QMG	Quartermaster General
RAP	Regimental Aid Post
RCHA	Royal Canadian Horse Artillery
RCR	Royal Canadian Regiment
RCS of I	Royal Canadian School of Infantry
RE	Royal Engineers
Recce	Reconnaissance
RSM	Regimental Sergeant-Major
RND	Royal Naval Division
RV	Rendezvous
VC	Victoria Cross

Acknowledgements

It has again been a pleasure to work with Helion, a publisher ever helpful, patient and encouraging.

I also wish to thank my wife, Lillian, for her reading (twice) of the manuscript, her diligent search for errors, typographical or otherwise, and for their correction. Two of the Indexes are her work, for which I am very grateful. Any errors are the responsibility of the author.

Introduction

> The strafe sounded a lot heavier than usual ... the force of [it] like the blow of a club ... incredibly brutal noise ... Very Lights ... a flattening of the screech [of artillery] told him they had gone over to the support line ... Time to move ... to the Lewis gun post.
>
> Raymond Chandler, "Trench Raid"

Unfortunately, Chandler's recollection of his service with 7th Canadian Battalion never went beyond one paragraph, but the fragment above does show that he knew how a raid usually developed: first, the heavy fire on the forward trenches, then the fire fading as it shifted rearward, the SOS put up by the defenders and then the frantic scramble to weapons posts to meet the imminent infantry assault. That his only writing on the war concerned a raid also tells us that such an enterprise had made a very strong impression upon him. The same is true of Sir Douglas Haig, who in his initial despatches made special mention of raids because of their very nature.

The subject of this book is trench raiding, a perilous and often costly endeavour that featured strongly during certain periods on the Western Front. Specifically, to borrow one of Robert Browning's lines, our interest is "on the dangerous edge of things." This is not to suggest that the "things" (ordinary trench warfare) were not dangerous for they surely were, but Haig accorded raiding a particular edge:

> which not only provided the greatest excitement, but which tested to the highest possible degree the bravery and nerve of the troops taking part ... The character of these operations ... the penetration of the enemy's trenches, the hand-to-hand fighting in the darkness ... the uncertainty as to the strength of the opposing force, gives special scope to the gallantry, dash and quickness of decision of the troops engaged, and much skill and daring are frequently displayed in these operations.[1]

On his first raid Private John Becker of 75th Canadian Battalion, having seen many of his comrades cut down before reaching the enemy trench, on entering it discovered that "I was alone. I could hear bombing further down but as far as I could figure out at the moment I was representing the Empire in that particular trench." Here we see not the shoulder to shoulder type of courage, what the Germans called the "feel of cloth" kind, but what Napoleon thought

1 Robert F. Moss (ed.), *Raymond Chandler: A Literary Reference* (New York: Carroll and Graf Publishers, 2002), p.33. At pages 34-38 are Chandler's Attestation and Casualty Form. Lieut.-Colonel J.H. Boraston, *Sir Douglas Haig's Despatches (December 1915-April 1919)* (London: J.M. Dent & Sons, 1920), pp. 3-4.

the rarest form of courage, the "two o'clock in the morning" kind. The necessity to repeatedly demonstrate it was surely one of the most wearing aspects of raiding. Still, soldiers could find some humour as men of 5th Canadian Battalion did when in imitation of Gilbert and Sullivan they came up with the rollicking "raid – y – uns" that opened this book. As for Chandler, he and others of 7th Canadian Battalion, together with men of the 5th, would late in 1915 pull off a cracker of a raid, its size and success unprecedented and its planning and execution so solid that it set the pattern and the standard for the British Expeditionary Force (BEF). According to the British Official Historian, this "model" raid defined what raid meant. Afterward, as expectations shifted, success and its antonym – failure – would often prove more difficult to define and assess. In fact, the very definition of raid would sometimes change to suit circumstances.[2]

Chandler is at rest now, as are the 5th and the 7th Canadian Battalions and, indeed, all the officers and men of the BEF and those who knew them. Ask someone today to name a major battle of the Great War and the Briton would probably respond with "Somme", while the Canadian would likely say "Vimy." But mention of raids would draw silence and a curious look. Ask about raids during the Second World War and the response would almost certainly be "Dieppe" if one was asking a Canadian. That particular raid has become legend, made so by its spectacular and costly nature and by periodic debate and dismay about its cost.

Readers more conversant with the Great War usually have strong (and differing) views as to why raids were even thought worthwhile, this a recurrent aspect of debate among military historians of the war. An earlier, and more important and meaningful argument, arose among those in the BEF who had to do the raiding. Consensus at that time proved elusive since the perspectives inherent in rank and appointment, and in the minds of planners and participants, determined one's conclusions. Viewpoints often overlapped and were multifaceted, and even inconsistent. When it comes to raids, the ambiguity of contemporary definition and terminology, and the wide range of opinions about the efficacy, impact and value of raids, make one think of George Orwell's notion of "double think."[3] But then the basic colour of history is grey.

The aim of this present study is to examine the nature, purposes, mechanics, execution and value of trench raiding by the BEF. Of necessity, the study is limited to British and Canadian raiding, but the enemy is not forgotten since as surely as night follows day when raided he retaliated. It seems reasonable to assume that he who beat off German raids applied what he learned during that process to his own raiding. For the officers and men engaged in either or both it was a case of good and bad, or as Kipling said, mixed sun and shadow.[4]

Raids (and patrols) shared other characteristics besides danger and uncertainty. Such "minor enterprises," as the former became known, involved a relatively limited number of participants in any particular sortie. The rhythm of these enterprises became that of a seemingly endless cycle. The large number of raids – over 800 by the BEF – and a myriad of patrols saw to that.

2 Brigadier-General J.E. Edmonds, *Military Operations France and Belgium, 1916: Sir Douglas Haig's Command to the 1st July: Battle of the Somme* (London: Macmillan, 1932), p. 156.

3 George Orwell, *Nineteen Eighty-Four* (London: Penguin Books, 1987), p. 223. Double Think in Newspeak was the ability to hold two contradictory beliefs in the mind simultaneously and accept both.

4 Rudyard Kipling, 'Shadow and Sun', in Thomas Pinney (ed.), *The Cambridge Edition of the Poems of Rudyard Kipling Volume III. The Uncollected Poems* (Cambridge: Cambridge University Press, 2013), p. 2070.

In addition, when patrol encountered patrol and when raiders encountered defenders or raiders, severe and vicious struggle ensued: drama, high drama, indeed. Such characteristics do enliven (and complicate) the history of Great War raiding.

After Waterloo the Duke of Wellington wrote that the history of a battle is not unlike the history of a ball. Writing about raiding, given the enormous mass of material available on the subject, not least of which is the War Diaries of Canadian and British units and formations, is not unlike describing hundreds of dancers whirling about different ballrooms simultaneously, or nearly that, in widely separated locations. Given this, it soon became obvious that a strictly chronological account would not do; for one thing, much of what is relevant to a raid – policy, for example – occurs before and well away from any particular raid. In the end, a combination, thematic and chronological, seemed wisest. Consequently, this study begins with a topical examination of raids, and to lesser extent patrols, the vehicle of discussion being Kipling's six honest serving-men. This approach also makes the answers to Kipling's six queries stand out sharply in measured pace. What this enables is discussed below in conjunction with this book's objectives. The answers are also related to specific examples of actual raids. More detailed examples follow in the second part of the book which presents a chronological survey year by year of raiding. But the account is not a comprehensive one; not every raid is reported upon, such a rendering being impossible and even near completion would turn book into catalogue. In lieu, this study offers raids that have some specific and peculiar character that merit attention and emphasis, say a larger and more dramatic aspect, successful or otherwise, while not neglecting the progression of raiding expertise, wisdom and lessons within contextual narrative. What this comes down to is selection. The reader may well think that this or that raid should have been included, but choices had to be made from the hundreds of raids. On this point see also the introduction to Chapter 9.

Whenever possible accounts of any raid in unit and/or formation War Diaries and in other official documents were necessarily compared against the relevant accounts in published works such as books and journal articles. Thucydides observed that "Not that even so the truth was easy to discover: different eye-witnesses gave different accounts of the same events, speaking out of partiality … or else from imperfect memories."[5] The comparison sought not only corroboration of the events reported upon, but to enliven the bald official accounts with the colour and perspective of the more intimate accounts of officers and men in their recollections and to lesser extent in unit/formation histories and in general histories. All of these sources have their own strengths and weaknesses that must be carefully assessed.

In many accounts the location of a raid is described only in general terms referring to the nearest centre of population or to a prominent feature. This may strike some readers as rather nebulous, but it must be realized that aside from the really dramatic raids that feature maps in archival documents or published materials, maps or sketches are not always available, or are often illegible, or offer no details. This means that location can often only be described geographically, not tactically, nor would it be useful to tell readers that "x" battalion's objective, in the grid system in use at the time, was C.5a.1.9.[6] Fortunately, some high-quality maps and

5 Thucydides, *History of the Peloponnesian War*, Rex Warner (trans.) (Harmondsworth: Penguin Books Ltd., 1954), p. 48.

6 Those interested in the development of map grids and reading maps of the time would find the following useful: Shelford Bidwell and Dominick Graham, *Firepower: British Army Weapons and Theories of War 1904–1945* (London: George Allen & Unwin, 1982), Chapter 6.

sketches are extant and a number are included. The overall focus in reporting upon a raid has been its planning, preparation and execution, the reasons why it succeeded or failed and what lessons the raiders and the planners absorbed.

Illustrations, when it comes to raids, are in short supply. Most impressions we have of raids are artistic conceptions; for example, H.J. Mowat's sketch "Trench Raid" which portrays a raiding party leaving its home trench. We have no photographs of the vicious struggles in the night in enemy trenches. Photographs of raids usually show raiders going out or just returning, or they portray individual raiders after a raid; for example, the photograph of Lance-Corporal Frank Cox, 10th Canadian Battalion, on the cover of this book. Some other individuals also appear in this book, as do some of the weapons and activities that supported raids: grenades (bombs), rifle grenades, machine-guns, Lewis guns and mortars. One problem with official photographs can be erroneous captions and/or absence of unit and time information or misinterpretation of same.[7]

As for the objectives of this book, they are six in number. First, the book shows why raids warrant close and serious study, and this to a degree well beyond what "minor enterprises" suggests. The second is to examine the concept, policy and purposes of raids, and the rationale for raiding as prescribed by higher commanders and as implemented by their subordinates. The influence of the former is central to assessment. Third, the book highlights the terminology (and the differences thereof) of raids and patrols, their essential elements and their ever-increasing sophistication, the learning curve presented and the impact on larger operations. It is a fact that we learn wisdom from failure much more than from success; moreover, "we often discover what will do by finding out what will not do; and probably he who never made a mistake never made a discovery."[8] Fourth, *On The Dangerous Edge* examines the planning of raids including fire planning, selection of raid objectives (how set and on what criteria), allocation of men and resources, training and co-ordination and the vital pre-raid activity called reconnaissance. The last is a significant element in this study, just as it was before, during and after actual raids. Reconnaissance, for obvious reasons, was a word constantly and necessarily used in connection with trench raiding. Word and deed could hardly be avoided or neglected. Reconnaissance is emphasized since those who planned and those who experienced raiding often described it as the secret of success, a conclusion in line with that expressed in a manual written a decade and more before the outbreak of war: "Time spent in recce is seldom wasted."[9]

7 The photograph of Lance-Corporal Cox receiving the Distinguished Conduct Medal (DCM) for his work during a raid was mis-identified as to image, caption and negative number at some point in its early life. The errors were corrected at the instigation of this present military historian who after seeing a version of the photograph on the cover of the 15 April 1916 issue of *The War Illustrated* compared it to the photograph at Library and Archives Canada (LAC). Those interested in war photography can read a very interesting account of a photograph identification problem in *Stand To!*, 3 (Winter 1981), 'Evidence in Camera: A Cautionary Tale by Dr. A.J. Peacock', and 4 (Spring 1982), 'Unknown Raiders? Or, Not Every Picture Tells a Story', by W. Alex Frame. Frame states that the raiders in the photos in the article have not yet been identified, nor is it known where or when the raid described actually took place. See also Major General Sir Ernest Swinton (ed.), *Twenty Years After: The Battlefields of 1914-18: Then and Now*. A George Newnes Publication, Part 25, p. 876.

8 Brigadier-General J.J. Collyer, *The Campaign in German South West Africa 1914-1915* (Pretoria: Government Printer, 1937), Preface.

9 *Combined Training (Provisional.)* (London: War Office, 1902), p. 23. This manual is often neglected and should not be for it is highly relevant to the Great War.

Reconnaissance was and is a long word, which is why it came to be shortened to "recce." Recce quickly became common usage verbally and in operational writing, a shorthand convenient as well as appropriate. It remained in use after the war and is still the usage in the Commonwealth. Some non-Commonwealth Armies prefer "recon" instead. This present study adheres to BEF and Commonwealth usage and hereinafter reconnaissance is recce.

Fifth, the book assesses how raids were conducted, including the reasons for them and the consequence of success or failure and the impact on morale and leadership. This is crucial since raids (and most patrols) were led by Subalterns, sometimes by Captains, and less frequently by field officers. This book describes what was expected of infantry officers, how they did and the impact of officer casualties during raids. Loss of many middle-ranking officers in 1915/16, often the best and the bravest, reduced the availability of candidates for field officer and above in 1917/18.[10] Finally, *On The Dangerous Edge* examines the conflicting viewpoints that on the one hand see raids as valuable and on the other hand see them as waste and of little value. Here questions of inevitability and historical continuity arise. An aspect of this is how raids were reported: what happened, who did what, decisions good and bad, and events real and supposed, as related initially and subsequently. Here the sources available to the military historian who studies raids are assessed.

Raids are of interest for several reasons. Curiously, one experienced soldier and the author of the history of the 33rd British Division, reported how it was:

> decided that the 'Grey Rats' on the other side of No-Man's Land must constantly be dug from their holes, and irritated by personal contact with the British soldier. A new [sic] tactical operation was therefore introduced, an operation, which, by the way, became an exceedingly popular one with our troops. This was known as 'The Raid.'[11]

Ignoring for a time the claim about popularity, this was quite forgetting that the history of raids goes back well before 1914. The Vikings, for example, were noted for their swift assaults from the sea. It is generally agreed that their smash and grab at Lindisfarne in 793 AD marked the start of the Viking Age. Over time, the Vikings became better organized, more confident and more ambitious. In the end, they became landed, to go raiding no more. In times closer to our own, good accounts of raids are common, some occurring, for example, during the War for Southern Independence when Confederate raiders raised hell. By 1864 some sharpshooter battalions of the Confederate States Army had become efficient raiders, their speciality being capture of prisoners to obtain information, a vital task for a smaller force. One Confederate, Major Thomas Wooten, 18th North Carolina, won renown in 1864 for scooping up Yankee "fish" by what he called "seine-hauling." As his brigade commander described this tactic, Wooten would lead his raiders in two columns toward the enemy line, the men, depending on the distance between

10 Junior officers were Captains and Lieutenants. A Subaltern was an officer below the rank of Captain. A field officer was an officer in the rank of Major and Lieutenant-Colonel. The first two terms are often confused, which is unfortunate and paints a false picture since initially a Captain commanded a rifle company while a Subaltern commanded a platoon. The difference is in experience, which is always crucial.

11 Lieutenant-Colonel Graham Seton Hutchison, DSO, MC, *The Thirty-Third Division in France and Flanders 1915-1919* (Uckfield, East Sussex: Naval and Military Press, n.d.), p. 6.

the lines, crawling forward until reaching a point past the Yankee line where Wooten would halt them and direct the columns into line left and right until the last man of each column was immediately at either side of him. Then the return homeward would be at a run, the men hauling in left and right every Yankee encountered. In one splendid coup Wooten swept up not only the whole of a picquet line, but its reserve as well.[12]

After 1918 other wars had their raids, some successful, some not so much. Dieppe has already been mentioned. Some of the questions raised were old ones: Was the raid necessary? Was it worth the price paid? Who was responsible? Was planning adequate? Answers to the last two queries were not always conducive to one's career. The Korean War also offers examples of raids and fighting patrols, the accounts of these similar to reports on Great War endeavours. The more things change the more they stay the same! It is obvious that some of the lessons about raiding failed to traverse the gap between 1918 and 1950. This should not surprise since it is not just politicians who have short memories.

Another reason, in fact two, for the interest in raids and, indeed, in military history in general, is simply that men, soldier or civilian, are always keen to know how an Army works (or not) and how its various components (Arms and Services) come together. It is an unusual man who at some point in his life has not wished himself a soldier. Comprehensive descriptions of the various sections of the orchestra of war help the reader grasp how a battle (or a raid) is waged and make the profession of arms more understandable. When the explanation is bolstered by participant accounts then it springs to life highlighting the fact that whatever the organization and technology war is a collective human endeavour. Raids demanded not merely a trio or a quartet, but a complete orchestra in miniature. Raids also appeal because they can be very dramatic; as Cyril Falls wrote "So long as men who took part in the war [were] alive the subject of raids [was] likely to crop up whenever two or three were together." We can be sure that one of the main discussion points concerned who made the first raid, a question seemingly straightforward, but the answer, as later discussion will show, is rather hedged about.[13]

Leadership, good, bad or indifferent, is always of interest, too. Leadership was critical when it came to raids, a capability reflected time and again in raid reports and assessments. One British brigade commander describing a raid by one of his battalions put the requirement like this: "The raid … showed the need of good, coolheaded officers."[14] Such attributes had to be present during each and every raid. Good leadership revealed itself, to mention just a few ways, in sound decision making, firm control and appropriate allocation of resources. Even before 1915, however, "the most alarming reality was that attrition was taking place not just at senior level, but also

12 Fred L. Roy, *Shock Troops of the Confederacy: The Sharpshooter Battalions of the Army of Northern Virginia* (Asheville: CFS Press, 2006), pp. 213-19. One Confederate raid preceded by thorough recce by the two officers who would lead the raid struck along a divisional boundary, achieved complete surprise and made off with 37 prisoners at a cost of one man wounded.

13 Cyril Falls, *The History of the 36th (Ulster) Division* (London: M'Caw, Stevenson & Orr Ltd., 1922), p. 71. Arms kill the enemy. In 1914 the Arms were infantry, artillery and cavalry. Engineers, known as Sappers, were also considered an Arm because they were as far forward as the infantry and often became involved in combat. The Services supplied all that the Arms needed to fight.

14 The National Archives (TNA) WO 95/2557: 38th British Division War Diary, May 1916, raid reports by 114th Brigade and 10th and 14th Battalions, The Welsh Regiment.

extensively at the level of middle-ranking officers."[15] Eventually restrictions had to be placed on the level of rank of officers participating in raids.

The uncertainly of life on the edge also heightens interest. By their very nature any raid large or small, even with the most careful planning, could go wrong. For one thing, leaping into a strange trench in the dark of night, or even in broad daylight, for that matter, was a highly exciting undertaking. For another, the enemy always has his say and that could be decisive. Moreover, neglect of some seemingly innocuous detail could be the fatal flaw, one that meant additional casualties and sometimes disaster, the cause of which might never be known in those cases where no one returned from a raid. Chance, too, could be decisive. Time and again when it came to raids (and patrols) success or failure, life, death or capture, could hinge on something as trivial as a turn to left or right, or, in the case of one German raid in September 1917, the raid commander's chance observance, at a junction of two French trenches, of a large cooking pot with a ladle in it; trifling objects, to be sure, but the memory of these stuck in his mind, this saving him and his men 20 minutes or so later. Forced to hurriedly seek an exit as French defenders closed in, he again spotted the pot that marked the direction of escape. As for the raid's result, once lost in the French trenches the raiders failed to secure a prisoner. Nevertheless, and quite unusually, the raiding party all received 14 days leave. *Leutnant* Ernst Junger, 73rd Hanoverian Fusiliers, later wrote a detailed and fascinating account of raiding German style.[16]

Other characteristics of raids that increase their appeal as a subject fall loosely into eight categories: material (sources), scope, number, simplicity, pattern, focus, impact and their role in national stories. Suffice it to say for now that the available source material is wide-ranging, in considerable volume and highly informative, fortunately so, since raids were a multi-facetted initiative involving at times most levels of command. Such an extensive paper trail presents a daunting challenge, but also a gratifying one. Scope, the second characteristic, means that in size and intent raids make a clear picture of their doctrine, tactics and preparation fairly easily evident. Small scale also highlights the lessons and the readily discernible learning curve that marked the course of raiding. Furthermore, each battalion had a distinctive personality reflected, success or not, in the unit reports that reveal unit pride and a state of mind in which it could be said, without exaggeration, that "the battalion thinks," or "the battalion feels."[17]

15 Peter E. Hodgkinson, *British Infantry Battalion Commanders in the First World War* (Farnham: Ashgate Publishing Limited, 2015), p. 49.

16 Ernst Junger, *The Storm of Steel* (London: Chatto and Windus, 1929; reprint, London: Constable, 1994), pp. 195-201. This book and his *Copse 125: A Chronicle From the Trench Warfare of 1918* (London: Chatto and Windus, 1930; reprint, n.p. Zimmermann and Zimmermann, 1985), celebrate *Fronterlebnis,* the front line experience of the combat officer. Junger served four years on the Western Front. Among his many decorations was the German equivalent of the Victoria Cross, the *Pour le Merite,* which he won while commanding a rifle company. Wounded 14 times, he suffered his last injury in August 1918. Junger also served in the *Wehrmacht* during the Second World War. Born 29 March 1895, he died on 17 February 1998, age 102. Junger's regiment in the Great War perpetuated one of the three Hanoverian battalions that served under General Eliott during the Siege of Gibraltar that ended in 1783. King George III awarded the three battalions the cuff title GIBRALTAR. A fairly recent biography is Thomas Nevin's *Ernst Junger and Germany: Into the Abyss, 1914-1945* (Durham: Duke University Press, 1996).

17 Henry (Jo) Gullet, *Not As a Duty Only: An Infantryman's War* (Melbourne: University Press, 1976), p. 9.

Finally, smaller scale also makes for easier comparison of raids and determination of why one failed and another succeeded.

As for simplicity, it is a supposed characteristic of raids. One of the most intriguing things about raids is how simple they appear at first sight, but how quickly that premise must be disavowed, for what Clausewitz said about war applies equally well to raids: "Everything looks simple; the knowledge required does not look remarkable, the ... options are so obvious." But he goes on to say that the simplest thing can be exceedingly difficult to accomplish. As the difficulties mount, they add to the friction known as the "fog" of war.[18] Thus, the apparently simple and easy formulation of explanation is neither. As raids, like war, became more sophisticated they also became highly complex, requiring careful co-ordination and precise planning. Likewise, objectives grew apace with expectation and requirement, many becoming highly problematic. Obviously, simplicity related directly to the size of the venture. A raid could be a one-man show; for example, a Non-Commissioned Officer (NCO) of the 25th Royal Welsh Fusiliers in mid-1918 entered an enemy trench and while the sole occupant, a sentry, had his back turned, quietly picked up a machine-gun and left: "an unpleasant and uncanny surprise for the sentry" and one difficult to explain. A Canadian pulled off a similar "stunt" in February 1917. In another instance an NCO in 42nd British Division on his own hook took two men into enemy trenches and returned quietly, no fuss, with four prisoners and a small trench mortar; a simple, no cost, night's work.[19] On the other hand, a raid could be a major endeavour, say four infantry companies, plus artillery, engineers, an engineer tunnelling company, 20 officers and 640 Other Ranks (ORs) in all, the case in point being a raid in early 1917 by 47th British Division.[20] When it comes to the relationship between words such as simple and complex and difficult and easy an article useful in the study of raids can be read in the *British Army Review:* "insight ... reduces complex problems to simple ones; skill is what makes difficult problems easy." For the officer training brings skill, while insight comes from the critical study of military history.[21]

Still, when all is said and done, there was a pattern to raids, large and small, a similarity remarked upon in many sources; for example:

> They are very similar, these raids. A small party or a large one waiting; the opening crash of a hurricane bombardment; lights shooting up from the German lines, throwing a shimmering brilliance over the dark broken, tumbled strip of No Man's Land in which men suddenly appear as small black shadows moving swiftly in the mystery of the revealed night – revealed by tossed-up balls of dazzling white, mingled with red lights, green lights strings of lights, showers of golden rain: on the horizon flickering flash of guns; ear-splitting din;

18 Carl von Clausewitz, *On War*. Michael Howard and Peter Paret (ed. and trans.) (Princeton: Princeton University Press, 1976), p. 119.

19 Major C.H. Dudley Ward, *The 74th Yeomanry Division in Syria and France* (Uckfield, East Sussex: Naval and Military Press, n.d.), pp. 210-11; LAC, MG30E100 (Currie Papers), 27 February 1918, letter to Sir Edward Kemp; Frederick P. Gibbon, *The 42nd (East Lancashire) Division 1914-1918* (London: "Country Life," 1920), p. 94. The 74th made a habit of such raids in July and August 1918, pulling off several, all successful and in most cases at very low cost.

20 Alan H. Maude, *The History of the 47th (London) Division 1914-1919* (London: Amalgamated Press Ltd., 1922), p. 89.

21 Spartacus, 'Simplicity', *British Army Review*, 98 (August 1991), pp. 48-52.

> whistles blown; men returning, fumbling into the trench, panting, crouching against the parapet for protection against retaliation.[22]

But similar does not mean identical:

> no two [raids] were exactly alike; some were dummy ones, some were subtle, silent ones, some were proclaimed by a previous bombardment, others ... with an Artillery box-barrage; but the most prolific ones were those in the nature of a surprise ... for instance, the Canadians conceived the unusual idea of raiding the same place twice in one night, and the second one, being unexpected, was by far the most successful.[23]

The encore might seem to contradict the German military maxim that says *Zweimal ist nicht einmal noch* (twice does not mean once again), but certainly doubles must be counted as scarce. A number of raids related in this book may well be unique and a surprising number could be considered unusual.

As for focus, when it comes to raids junior officers were that, and more, they became central. The historian of the 9th (Scottish) Division recalled how when Loos battered the division, its exceptionally heavy casualties including the General Officer Commanding (GOC), eight of 12 battalion commanders and grave loss of Majors and Captains, the task of rebuilding fell to the Subalterns who generally had little experience and no automatic knowledge of how things should be done. At one point in late 1915 the situation was such that the period became "notable as the reign of the Second Lieutenant," every company in one brigade being commanded by one and this the case in many other battalions in the division. This posed great difficulties for the GOC, Major-General W.T. Furse, it being a fact that

> youth and gallantry do not form a complete substitute for knowledge and experience; but the apprenticeship and training in responsibility, which these months brought to the young officers, supplied them with a large body of keen, confident, and efficient leaders who were later to demonstrate their value at the Battle of the Somme.

The divisional schools, which sought "to fortify youth and keenness with knowledge and practice," offered a partial solution to his problem.[24] Practice included command of raiding parties. Around this time platoons and platoon commanders became the critical element for it was they and their men who bore the brunt of the fighting, who were most closely engaged and who endured the savage fighting in the enemy trenches, closer than battle sight range, range being in inches, not yards, and the fighting often savage beyond imagination. Such circumstances gave special importance to gallantry, dash and quickness of decision by the young officers, many of

22 Major C.H. Dudley Ward (comp.), *Regimental Records of the Royal Welsh Fusiliers (23rd Foot)*. Volume III. *1914-1918 France and Flanders* (London: Forster Groom & Co., Ltd., 1929), p. 314, describing a raid in October 1916.

23 Brigadier-General A.H. Hussey and Major D.S. Inman, *The Fifth Division in the Great War* (London: Nisbet and Co., Ltd., 1921), p. 142.

24 John Ewing, *The History of the Ninth (Scottish) Division 1914-1919* (Uckfield, East Sussex: Naval and Military Press, n.d.), p. 66.

them still in their teens, who led the raids and the patrols that presented a chance to shine, to make their mark, to learn the responsibilities of an officer and, in the words of one Subaltern, to realize the decorations, the "book of glory," that accompanied high risk.[25] Clearly, for both sides raids had pronounced impact on officers and men; "minor" enterprises, yes, but usually and truly ugly affairs and the consuming focus of life immediately before and during each raid. Raids also had significant impact on major operations since they were attacks in miniature and as such they demanded the same careful attention as the big "shows" did. What was learned in the planning and conduct of a raid carried over into the same activities before and during major operations. This is evident in the tactical and training manuals in the SS series of publications.

Finally, there are the national stories. It would hardly do for a former Canadian Army officer and now soldier-historian to ignore the exploits (and the failings) of his countrymen when it comes to raids. While Canadians did not invent raids, they came to be seen as expert raiders and to some extent they gave rise to an "anything you can do … ." spirit. Kipling described Dominion troops as "always inquisitive and seldom idle [and] the enemy suffered." Lieutenant W.N. Hodgson, 9th Devons, wrote in error that raids began with the Canadians, their highly successful raid in November 1915 "recalling, by the audacity of the conception and the cool daring of its execution [some] heroic stroke of Nelson's navy." Captain James Dunn, the Medical Officer of the 2nd Royal Welsh Fusiliers, observed how this particular raid became the "mode" and "Every self-respecting battalion will want to raid, the others will be ordered."[26]

Senior commanders became keen on tapping the expertise of those who planned the Canadian "war parties." Stephen Graham, a Private in the Guards, was told by one of his chums that Canadians had gotten the idea of war parties from "North American Indians."[27] The French, who had distributed the report on the Canadian raid of November widely throughout their army, began in early 1916 sending parties of officers and men to train with Canadian raiders. Australians and New Zealanders also sought guidance before mounting their first raids, the former borrowing Canadian officers for this purpose.[28] The Welsh Guards, recognizing in July 1917 the "good raids done by the Canadians" borrowed Lieutenant-Colonel R.D. Davies, Commanding Officer (CO) of the 44th Battalion (4th Canadian Division), who "had recently carried out some conspicuously successful raids with his Battalion." Davies' "Detailed Sequence for Raid Preparation" subsequently circulated widely within the BEF. Finally, in June 1918 2nd Canadian Division staged a series of demonstrations in the art of patrolling and raiding

25 Stuart Cloete, *A Victorian Son: An Autobiography 1897-1922* (London: Collins, 1972), p. 197.

26 Rudyard Kipling, *The Irish Guards in the Great War: The First Battalion* (New York: Sarpedon, 1997), p. 252; Lieut. William Noel Hodgson, 'The Raid', in *Verse and Prose in Peace and War* (London: John Murray, 1917), p. 92. Hodgson was killed in action on 1 July 1916, the first day of the Somme. Captain J.C. Dunn, *The War the Infantry Knew 1914-1919: A Chronicle of Service in France and Belgium* (London: Jane's Publishing Company, 1987), p. 192. Dunn, who wore the Distinguished Service Order (DSO), Military Cross (MC) and Bar and DCM, was a remarkable officer in a remarkable battalion. Both Siegfried Sassoon and Robert Graves served with it, as did Private Frank Richards.

27 Larry Worthington, *Amid the Guns Below* (Toronto: McClelland and Stewart, 1965), pp. 40-41; Stephen Graham, *A Private in the Guards* (London: Macmillan, 1919), p. 263.

28 C.E.W. Bean, *The Official History of Australia in the War of 1914-1918. Volume III. The AIF in France 1916* (St. Lucia: University of Queensland Press, 1982), p. 46; Christopher Pugsley, 'Learning from the Canadian Corps on the Western Front', *Canadian Military History,* 15 (Winter 2006), p. 7.

in daylight, this having become something of a Canadian speciality. By all accounts audiences were impressed with the demonstrations.[29]

One other introductory matter remains. Its concern, the historiography of the subject of raids, is as important as the history itself. The experienced military historian wanting to make best use of his time, begins with recce to see what is out there on his chosen subject; that is, what has been done and what could or should be done. Research, if it is to be comprehensive, must be an all-source search since each source contributes, some obviously more than others.

Looking first at general accounts of the military history of the Great War most at the very least mention raids. Some offer only a sentence or two, even a paragraph or two, less frequently a page or two if a raid was in strength or so dramatic that it merited such attention. Even in the briefest of mentions one can sometimes find a useful snippet or two on some forgotten or neglected aspect of trench raids and patrols. While an accumulation of such information can be helpful, such a package cannot tell the story of raids. One book, now somewhat dated, that offers more is Ashworth's *Trench Warfare 1914-1918* (1980). It provides a fairly comprehensive examination of several aspects of raiding, including concept, policy and performance, for example, but as one reviewer put it, the context is thick with "crusty layers of sociological analysis" that goes nowhere, as such texts routinely do, and serves only to obscure. Moreover, his picture of the relationship between front line units and higher command is skewed, so much so that it almost puts the latter in the enemy camp, an exaggeration that led to several misapprehensions about the nature and development of operations minor and major.[30] Some useful colour and insight can also be gained from fictional accounts and from war poetry provided the reader has knowledge of what raids involved and how they were carried out and provided the reader keeps in mind that the account is fictional. Some poetry conveys the flavour of raids, thanks to the author's experience of raids and/or patrols. Caution is necessary here, too. Interesting in its portrayal of the anxieties of raiding is Herbert Read's *The Raid* (1927), which is really a study in fear, defining it and suggesting what might alleviate it. W.N. Hodgson's "The Raid" and "The Patrol" relate a Subaltern's experience of both. Fictional accounts are uncommon. Three that come to mind – Philip MacDonald's *Patrol,* Vernon Bartlett's *No Man's Land* and Humphrey Cobb's *Paths of Glory* (book and film) – are all now decades out of print. The latter two use raids and patrols simply to set the scene after which they pursue other matters. R.C. Sherriff's play *Journey's End* (1929) concerns a raid that costs six men and the officer most trusted by the company commander, all this to satisfy the brigadier's ambitions (a later chapter looks at this motive for ordering raids).[31]

29 Major C.H. Dudley Ward, *History of the Welsh Guards* (London: The London Stamp Exchange Ltd., 1988), p. 59; TNA: WO 95/1297: 2nd British Division General Staff, War Diary, 13 July 1917. The raids referred to took place on 3, 10 and 13 February 1917. Lt. Col. Cuthbert Headlam, *History of the Guards Division in the Great War 1915-1918: Volume 2* (Uckfield, East Sussex: Naval and Military Press, n.d.), p. 103.

30 Obturator [pseud.], 'Garrison Library', *Stand To!,* 1 (Spring 1981), p.13.The reviewer summarized Ashworth's book as "The most disappointing of 1980."

31 Poems (in various sources) that relate to raids and patrols include Sassoon's 'The Stunt' and 'Trench Duty', Edmund Blunden's 'Trench Raid Near Hooge', Arthur Graeme West's 'Night Patrol' and Eric Cooper's 'Night Attack.' See Herbert Read, *Annals of Innocence and Experience* (London: Faber and Faber Ltd.,1956), pp. 150-58. Brief descriptions of the novels and the play are in Cyril Falls, *War Books: An Annotated Bibliography of Books About the Great War* (London: Greenhill Books, 1989).

The Bibliography lists a considerable number of journal articles on particular raids and survey articles on raids in general. The latter do not discuss raiding in any great detail. After all, these are articles and they are constrained in length. This is not to say that they are not useful, but usually there is little to choose between them. Occasionally some forgotten fact or clever anecdote that makes a useful point is found. *Stand To!*, the journal of the Western Front Association, is by far the best source of original articles on many Great War topics including raiding.

The Bibliography also includes a wide range of contemporary Army manuals, most being essential reading in any study of raids. It is a mystery why these are so often ignored since they resulted from experience and were widely circulated and studied by those who had to plan and lead raids. These manuals, being works in progress, were not infallible, but they were the basis upon which to build. A survey of raiding that is oblivious to, for example, *SS 107 Notes on Minor Enterprises*, is ignoring not only a valuable guide to raiding, but a valuable guide to writing about raiding.[32] The same can be said about the volumes of the British Official History, which are useful on raiding policy as the war progressed and how policy came about. While the series has its faults it cannot be ignored, especially in the absence of a comprehensive Canadian account.

Trench journals (Canadian only) were also consulted. All told, over 100 such journals appeared in the BEF during the war, most consisting of only five or fewer issues before they folded. The largest Canadian series is 7th Battalion's *The Listening Post* which began at four pages per issue, soon expanding to and remaining at 10 pages thereafter. It is striking that in this journal the word "raid" does not appear even once, nor does anything pertaining to raids. Of the other five Canadian journals that lasted an appreciable length of time only one issue mentions "raids" and then only once, the "raid – y – uns" that opened this book. Perhaps raids were considered too serious a matter for humour, or the subject was prohibited or no one wanted to talk about them.[33] Nor do "raids" appear in the famous *Wipers Times*.

Then, of course, we have the vast number of reminiscences, memoirs, private diaries and compilations of letters. Often the time between actual experience and publication is very long, causing reviewers to remark "waited too long to publish" or comment in similar vein. Still, these sources are invaluable for they do bring to life other categories of material. Caution is warranted, however, since the content of such narratives cannot always be corroborated and verified and what is offered is only as good as the writer's memory. Moreover, exaggeration, personal foible, imagination and a desire to excuse or harm can colour what is offered. Nevertheless, such

32 A lengthy list of the Central Distribution Section (CDS) and Stationary Services (SS) series of manuals pertaining to trench warfare is in Peter T. Scott, 'The CDS/SS Series of Manuals and Instructions: A Numerical Checklist', *The Great War 1914-1918* 1 (1988). The University of Birmingham's Centre for War Studies list of these publications (compiled by Peter Hodgkinson, Simon Justice and Tony Bell) is similar, but it is likely that neither list is complete. It should be noted that manuals did not appear in any great number until after Loos in September 1915, experience before that being insufficient to compile manuals of much value. Wisdom comes from experience! A book purporting to tell the story of Canadian training in 1914-15, for example, would be a curiously stilted account since the relationship between training and experience and technology and development of doctrine could not be explored, nor could much be offered on the audit of training. Moreover, such a book would likely give rise to misapprehensions about how the training cycle worked, training content and exaggeration of the value of "barrack" training since precious little could be said about "field" training.

33 Kenneth Radley, *Get Tough, Stay Tough: Shaping the Canadian Corps 1914-1918* (Solihull: Helion & Company Limited, 2014), pp. 245-47.

accounts play a critical role in amplifying content, offering new or forgotten perspectives on such complicated matters as morale, discipline and numerous other aspects of the profession of arms. Obviously, the value of any particular book depends very much upon the author's service experience and his rank. The world of an OR being as narrow as the small span of trench in which he fought means he cannot offer a wider view or much by way of corroboration of experience. Private Fraser, whose *Journal* is one of the very best by an OR, admitted that he could not follow the actions of others, nor could he verify incidents he had heard about. These he could only offer as "part of trench gossip." Similarly, an Irish Guardsman described he and his chums as "fleas in a blanket" and quite unable to see very far.[34] Officer accounts widen the horizon, but here, too, caution is necessary since the writers are concerned with matters such as personal and unit reputation and comments about personalities and competence of superiors may be less than frank, or conversely may be exaggerated or hagiographic.

Before looking at unit and formation histories, which are an extremely valuable reservoir for the military historian, whatever his topic, brief mention of the regimental system is appropriate for the idea of regiment could and did influence reportage by the historians of battalions and divisions. The French and German Armies (and some others) of the time were organized in regiments which fought as regiments within their parent divisions. In the BEF brigades, not regiments, were the tactical entities that did the fighting. Each Canadian brigade consisted of four infantry battalions (see Appendix I), reduced to three in British brigades in early 1918. To make up a brigade as many as four regiments could have contributed a battalion; for example, 10th British Brigade (4th Division) in 1914 consisted of a battalion from each of the Royal Warwickshire Regiment, the Seaforth Highlanders, the Royal Irish Fusiliers and the Royal Dublin Fusiliers. Conversely, 113th British Brigade (38th Division) consisted of four battalions of the Royal Welsh Fusiliers. There are examples in between of two or three battalions from one regiment making up a brigade's four battalions. As well as distinctive cap badges, regiments also share distinct customs and traditions. The key to the regimental system is cap badge, the great talisman. In short, battalions were regimental family, brigades were not. Not surprisingly reportage often reflects that.[35]

The simple fact is that a book about raids could not be done without study of unit and formation histories. Unit histories, by which is meant infantry battalions, and regimental histories, which relate the histories of the battalions of a regimental family, vary considerably in utility and worth. What should be kept in mind when using these as sources about raids is that an account of a one or two battalion regiment will be far more detailed and comprehensive than a single volume history of a regiment that fielded many battalions; for example, the list of battalions of the Royal Fusiliers fills two pages in Brigadier James' *British Regiments*. A single volume purporting to tell the story of the battalions of that regiment would have very little to say about raids since the space available would have to focus on major events if it was to be of any use at all. Otherwise, as Cyril Falls said, "the result [would tend] to be a catalogue." Conversely, the

34 Reginald H. Roy, *The Journal of Private Fraser 1914–1918: Canadian Expeditionary Force* (Victoria: Sono Nis Press, 1985), p. 19; Kipling, *The Irish Guards in the Great War: The First Battalion*, p. 154.

35 Kenneth Radley, *We Lead Others Follow: First Canadian Division 1914–1918* (St. Catharines: Vanwell Publishing Limited, 2006), pp. 40, 51n19. This is still the only published account of a Canadian division.

account of a two-battalion regiment such as the Civil Service Rifles has "room to make it full."[36] The picture for Canadian infantry battalions is simpler. Each battalion history concerns only that battalion. Not every battalion had an historian and, consequently, no published history exists for every battalion; for example, of the 12 battalions in 1st Division only eight are the subject of a published history. For the other three Canadian divisions even fewer battalion histories exist. This makes other categories of sources even more important.

Most formation histories are of divisions. Only a few brigade histories are available. Of the 66 British divisions that were on active service, 45 are the subject of a published history, some being multi-volume accounts.[37] In preparation of this present study each of the 45 were carefully reviewed (some more than once) and notes were made on every raid by and against each division, a time-consuming and exhaustive process, but a necessary one since accounts of raids in these histories had to be weighed against all other sources including the War Diaries and appended orders, instructions and reports. Often these published histories amplify the War Diaries by adding detail on raid participants and events. On the other hand, they just as often are thinner in content than the War Diaries and important information is not there. Something to bear in mind is that some of the authors of these divisional histories, often former or serving officers, can and do exhibit a tendency to smooth over unpleasant or embarrassing matters. Readers should not expect to see much by way of dirty linen since a division, like a regiment, is a family, albeit a large one, and secrets usually remain secrets. Only infrequently do they present pointed and direct instances of failure or weak leadership and they are very careful of reputation, individual and family. What one often sees is discrete vagueness. But careful reading can often penetrate the fog to a useful degree. If the reader has appreciable military service and sufficient experience to recognize military probability, soldierly logic and military common sense much useful and important information can be gleaned since knowing how an Army works (or does not) can provide the key to the nuances. What the Russians call *intonatsiya,* reading between the lines, helps too. Often the authors of the divisional histories reveal a good deal in what they do not say; for example, no mention in a lengthy account of a particular raid or of a certain officer or CO can tell an informed reader a good deal. Given their smaller scale, this applies even more so to battalion histories.

Obviously, the quality of the divisional histories varies. Some are very good, some are very bad and some are excellent such as Cyril Falls' account of the 36th (Ulster) Division and Boraston's history of the 8th British Division, the latter very finely crafted including impressive Appreciations that even today signal a work of exacting analysis. One should be careful not to apply the word "dated" *totus porcus* to these histories; a few are indeed that, but even these frequently offer pertinent information about raids that appears nowhere else. While some of the authors were reluctant to assign blame where it was due, or thought to lay it elsewhere, many do say what went right or wrong and that alone is value added. Nor should it be forgotten that Canadian units and formations were inevitably flanked by British units and formations and co-ordination and co-operation were necessary when it came to raids. In fact, joint raids were

36 Brig. E.A. James, *British Regiments 1914-1918* (Uckfield, East Sussex: Naval and Military Press, 1988), pp. 49-50; Falls, *War Books,* pp. 96, 121.

37 The section entitled 'Histories: Formations and Units' in Falls' invaluable *War Books* lists only three brigade histories. Since publication of Falls' book only two or three other brigade histories have been published.

not uncommon. These facts mean relevant accounts must be compared. Not to fish these waters is myopic and reflects inadequate research.

Archival documents, British and Canadian, such as War Diaries and their appendices feature strongly, of necessity, in this study. Correlation of these primary sources with the secondary sources is a must. A good place to start any consideration of these critical sources is with a definition of War Diary:

> An account of the daily activities of a military unit or formation. The diary was to record all important orders, despatches, reports, instructions and telegrams issued and received, and decisions taken as well as the daily situation, important administrative matters, changes in establishment or strength, meteorological notes and the description of field works … Appendices … include orders, reports, telegrams, sketches, maps and tabular statements.[38]

To use a modern term, War Diaries are the "vital ground" in this present study. One key to reading them is that a clear idea about any raid requires not only careful study of the diary of the battalion involved, but also the diaries of the parent brigade and division. This is necessary because these usually offer more information on the course of the raid from conception and order for the raid, why it was thought necessary in the higher commander's view, the cycle and sequence of preparation and the post-raid assessment up the chain of command. When things went wrong brigade and division War Diaries come into their own because it is there that we see how Corps often asked difficult questions about raids that had to be answered. The questions and answers tell us a great deal about raids and senior commanders. Collation is always a challenge since the levels of command have different perspectives and their War Diaries do not always agree. Other cautions regarding the use of War Diaries are discussed later.

The War Diaries in question are those of the 48 battalions of the 12 brigades of the four divisions of the Canadian Corps, plus the Corps, division and brigade headquarters. The British War Diaries are those of the over 700 infantry battalions of the 180 brigades of the 60 plus divisions of the BEF and the relevant headquarters. The first, while a challenge to completely review, can be done in a reasonable period, but the time it would take to manage the whole of the second set would be prohibitive. What this means is that a process of selection had to be undertaken. This began with a close reading of the published histories of the Canadian battalions and the British divisions. Descriptions of raids in these books were then compared with War Diary descriptions of the same raids. These "accompanied" accounts of raids, that is to say published book plus War Diary, also routinely provided information on raids executed by other formations and units that to date have not been the subject of published books. These markers directed one to the relevant War Diaries and from there comparisons with accounts in general works, personal memoirs and other sources could be made. War Diaries of "unaccompanied" divisions and battalions, that is to say no published source accounts, did bring to light some raids not described elsewhere, but most of these did not warrant inclusion primarily because of the absence of sufficient detail, or because they were very minor and insignificant, or the raid had accomplished little or nothing and thus was of very little interest. As a general rule, a division or battalion account that dismissed a raid in one or two sentences, or a thin paragraph, indicated

38 LAC, RG9IIID3, Volume 4866.

that the War Diary version would likely be similar. There were exceptions, of course. A raid damaging to reputations, personal or institutional, for example, might not have been thought appropriate to publication. Such cases often offered lessons and other material that gained them inclusion in this study. Raids that received extensive space in a published history almost invariably occupied equal space in the War Diaries. Some provided a plethora of operational documents, details on what went wrong and why and numerous lessons, questions and subsequent inquiries, all in appendices to the actual dairy.

Selection was the next step. Obviously, the extent of extant material on a raid was a primary factor in whether or not a raid would be included in this book. A raid that featured in both published accounts and War Diaries had an advantage, but a balance had also to be struck, British and Canadian, raid size and type and success or failure. Selection also depended upon characteristics such as adherence (or not) to what were considered raid "essentials" like thorough recce, training and thorough planning; participants and strength of raids, individual exploits and nature of the raid, be it "ordinary," unusual or especially noteworthy in some aspect. Lessons and why a raid failed were primary concerns. Material once selected was then marked for inclusion either in discussion of Kipling's six honest men or chronologically.

What made life easier during the process was knowing what to look for and what to focus on, an ability stemming from personal background, training and experience. This soldier-historian, a long-serving Canadian Army (Regular) officer and Staff College graduate, found himself immediately familiar and comfortable with the military writing and Staff Duties of the time, the first impression being how little operational writing including Operation Orders and Instructions, Appreciations, reports, preliminary orders and staff papers has changed over the decades since 1918. While certain terms and headings in documents differ, their intent is clear and their format so similar to today that one can move along at a good pace. This state did not pertain initially, of course, but as the war went on staff officers learned and demonstrated increasing confidence and competence, achieving even excellence in a good many instances. The process of collection and correlation outlined above caused several bouts of severe eye strain and consumed paper and printer ink cartridges at an alarming rate, but it resulted in a treasure of material. Not all that resides in the War Diaries could be set in time and place, then assessed and included here, but what is offered is a balanced and detailed picture, one well beyond what has heretofore been available. At the risk of being immodest, it is as complete as any one man can reasonably make it.

War Diaries do have several inherent shortcomings. First, a War Diary entry cannot offer the measured account that a later one can, which is not surprising considering that War Diaries are written under very different and often very difficult conditions. Arthur Crookenden, the historian of the Cheshire Regiment, in relating his experience with War Diaries, thought the diaries of "little value" in telling the story since even if such an account is available it seldom corresponds with the accounts of other battalions. Moreover, in his opinion "the severer the action, the worse the account." This is so, it often being the case that the junior officer writing the daily diary entry was usually tired, even exhausted, over-excited often, certainly distracted. In most, if not in all cases, he was also probably writing hurriedly. Composition suffered accordingly. In addition, he probably thought he knew what had happened, and perhaps he could have got it down right immediately after the events he had to describe, but quite often days would pass before he could pen an account:

> On occasions when a 2nd/Lieut., hardly joined, brings the remnant of a battalion out of action, he cannot be blamed for not writing up the story. In the first place, he probably does not know that there is such a thing as a War Diary. In the second place, he does not know anything of the superior plan and little of the role allotted to the Battalion.

Time plays its tricks, too. Sir Frederick Ponsonby, historian of the Grenadier Guards, described how initially the War Diary was kept with "meticulous accuracy," but eventually it contained "less and less." Crookenden thought brigade War Diaries even worse, but divisional diaries the best even though "they were very hard to reconcile" with brigade and battalion diaries. In similar vein, Canada's official historian of the Second World War thought that providing a "division's log is available, you can write the history of the division with confidence."[39]

Veracity is another problem with War Diaries. *Notes for Commanding Officers* said the CO had to see "that the War Diary is written up to date, and initial entries to it daily … in order that it may later on form the basis for the historical records of the Battalion." We may take these initials by a CO as an indication that what he wanted entered in the diary was, and what he did not was not. One CO, Lieutenant-Colonel William Fraser, added from experience "the story is never really as one writes it – one couldn't write it as it is."[40] This present study includes a number of examples where such initials were very important for they might be the only means of establishing the departure of a CO and the arrival of his successor. When it came to writing the reports that were usually appended to a War Diary, Lord Moran, serving as Medical Officer of an infantry battalion, described the process thus:

> In the Colonel's dug-out it is difficult to move, everyone wishes to report to him at once, but he is busy with his account of the raid which the Brigade must have immediately. They want something that they can improve upon and serve up to the Division, who in turn will pass it on to the Corps adding a little extra colouring. The little that I know is quickly told: thirty-one men were brought back across no-man's-land [sic]: not a single wounded man was left behind. These fellows have played the game. I shall not wait for Colonel who will be a long time over his report. He is an indifferent journalist and has not been instructed in his youth in the art of making much out of little.

It is not surprising to see that "extra" colour could become concerted fiction; for example, after one raid in May 1916 during which uncut wire and strong enemy opposition prevented entry to the enemy trenches the General Headquarters (GHQ) communique reported the raid thus:

39 Col. Arthur Crookenden, *The History of the Cheshire Regiment in the Great War* (Uckfield, East Sussex: Naval and Military Press, n.d.), p. v; The Right Hon. Sir Frederick Ponsonby, *The Grenadier Guards in the Great War of 1914-1918*. Volume I. (London: Macmillan, 1920), p. x; C.P. Stacey, *A Date With History* (Ottawa: Deneau, 1983), p. 230.

40 *Notes for Commanding Officers* (Aldershot: Gale and Polden, 1918), p. 361; David Fraser (ed.), *In Good Company: The First World War Letters and Diaries of The Hon. William Fraser, Gordon Highlanders* (Salisbury: Michael Russell, 1990), p. 321. A modern example of creative military writing was the daily situation report sent from UN HQ Cyprus to the "non-combatants" in New York. It, and the report meant for local consumption, were very different. The first was always very much shorter and not just because it was meant for a higher HQ.

> At Mametz we raided hostile trenches. Our party *entered without difficulty* [!!!] and maintained a spirited bombing fight, and finally withdrew at the end of twenty-five minutes.

Siegfried Sassoon described such reportage as "the truth which is (less than) half a truth!"

It must also be said that no CO was likely to approve an entry in his War Diary that put the battalion in a bad light. Douglas Jerrold cautioned that it was best to read War Diaries in a suspicious frame of mind since "There are few limits … to our powers of self-deception and none whatever to those … whose careers are at stake."[41] This applied equally well to formation War Diaries, Sir James Edmonds, the British Official Historian, bluntly saying he "had no great faith in [them] … in one celebrated case … a general made away with [them] because they revealed too much and sent in a narrative" instead. Regarding another case Tim Travers points out that the evidence suggests that 1st Canadian Division "probably" kept a War Diary at Second Ypres, but it was "replaced" by a narrative of events.[42]

Despite their faults, War Diaries of each level of command cannot be ignored. As the compiler of the history of the Devonshire Regiment points out, historians should be thankful for the "tolerably full and lucid accounts" managed by most units and formations.[43]

What is not in War Diaries can be very revealing and dramatic; for example, as a matter of routine diary entries included the activities of all officers: going on leave, on course, on other external duties and their return, their deaths, wounds or absences missing in action and their postings and the arrival of their replacements, the arrival of visitors and their departure and any attachments or detachments of officers. But a CO who was relieved of command and became "de gommy" simply disappeared: no diary entry and the situation as if he had never existed. The only indication that he had gone was a line introducing the new CO and a change in CO initials (see above). Removal seems not to have been a matter for entry at any level. Said one CO "a good many Battalion Commanders have been un-gummed that I know of." Nor were brigade commanders immune.[44] Several striking instances of removals related to raids feature in a later chapter. When it comes right down to it, some things, like the removal of a CO, did not belong in a War Diary. If certain other matters detrimental to reputation had to be entered for some reason they received only the barest mention. Sometimes "delinquencies set in motion a long chain of … Colonels and Generals … all in some way concerned." Where a War Diary left off, the process could turn to inquiry, formal or informal, allocation of responsibility and punishment. Consequently, one must look beyond War Diaries for detail and denouement.[45]

41 Lord Moran, *The Anatomy of Courage* (London: Constable, 1945), pp. 149-50; Rupert Hart-Davis (ed.), *Siegfried Sassoon Diaries 1915-1918* (London: Faber and Faber Limited, 1923), pp. 65-67; Douglas Jerrold, *Georgian Adventure* (New York: Charles Scribner's Sons, 1938), p. 218.

42 Ian Beckett (ed.), *The Memoirs of Sir James Edmonds* (Brighton: Tom Donovan Editions, 2013), pp. 322-23; Tim Travers, 'Currie and 1st Canadian Division at Second Ypres, April 1915: Controversy, Criticism and Official History', *Canadian Military History*, 5.2 (Autumn 1996), p. 14.

43 C.T. Atkinson (comp.), *The Devonshire Regiment* (Exeter: Eland, 1926), pp. ix-x.

44 Edward Fraser and John Gibbons, *Soldier and Sailor Words and Phrases* (London: George Routledge and Sons Ltd., 1925), p. 294, ungummed = unstuck, dismissed (degommy); Rowland Feilding *War Letters to a Wife: France and Flanders, 1915-1919* (London: The Medici Company, 1929), p. 319.

45 Wyn Griffith, *Up to Mametz* (London: Faber and Faber Limited, 1931), pp. 180-81. A new edition, *Up to Mametz and Beyond,* includes additional Griffith papers. Edited by Jonathan Riley it was published in 2010.

Finally, a very small category of published books have in their titles the word "raid" or a derivative. Tony Spagnoly's *The Anatomy of a Raid* (1991) is a detailed, interesting and fine account of the Australian raid on Celtic Wood in the Ypres Salient in late 1917, but is not further mentioned since it is outside the scope of this present study.

A more recent work is Anthony Saunders' *Raiding on the Western Front* (2012). Unfortunately, this book suffers from several shortcomings, not least of which is that it is inadequately researched, a fact immediately obvious on turning to the sparse and somewhat curious bibliography. A mere three journal articles are listed and of the 41 published books only two accounts of British battalions and only two accounts of British divisions, both on the same division, are offered. Given the ready availability of paperback editions of the British divisional histories this is really paying lip service, if that. Ten of the 41 books listed are general accounts, none of which offer much beyond reiteration. One is a compilation of essays, an excellent work, but one that does not include an essay on raids. Of the 41 books a half-dozen or so are soldier accounts and several others are American publications, most circa 1917-18. A number of entries strike one as illusory; for example, one lists the British Official History as simply "France and Belgium (1925-47)." Are we to assume that each and every volume in the series was actually used? The text says otherwise. Instead of attribution of quoted material throughout there is only a two-page rendering set out by chapter. The 43 footnotes for the entire book are rather grandiloquently entitled "Notes." Few offer much of anything.

As for the text, three of the chapters concern Australian and, to lesser extent, New Zealand raids. One of these chapters examines Celtic Wood. Canada and South Africa share a short chapter: one page devoted to German raids on Canadians, 1.5 pages on the South African Brigade and the balance of the chapter (8.5 pages) on the four Canadian divisions. Given the Canadian record of raiding such coverage seems somewhat grudging and inadequate. Saunders reminds readers – twice – that the Canadian Corps was only a "small component" of the BEF, the only smaller component being the South African brigade. It is true that the Canadian Corps was only one of the 23 Corps of the BEF, but a Corps was not an insignificant contribution by a nation whose population at the time was less than eight million. Curiously, neither the New Zealanders nor the Australians are tagged with the "small" diminutive. As one reads along a sense grows that almost every mention of a Canadian raid, regardless of size or success, is qualified and diminished; for example, of 69 raids by Canadians in one three month period, 61 or 91 percent entered enemy trenches, this being the basis of Saunders' definition of success. This means the Canadian failure rate was nine percent, not the 20 percent he claims. Such basic errors shatter credibility. It is impossible to see his book as a serious study. However, it does serve to introduce the business of raiding.

It remains, then, to say that whether one was commencing a raid, or returning from it, raiding was a three-step affair. Having left the *terra firma* of home trench, one traversed no man's land and then, all going well, entered the enemy trench on "murderous business bent."[46] Having survived whatever ensued there, one returned to home trenches. These trenches, and the life within them, are the subject of the next chapter.

46 Brendan Moorhouse, *Forged by Fire: The Battle Tactics and Soldiers of a World War One Battalion: The 7th Somerset Light Infantry (*Staplehurst: Spellmount Limited, 2003), p. 225. The phrase was part of a line of poetry written in July 1918 by an anonymous member of a raiding party.

1

"Holes and Ditches"

When all is said and done the war was mainly a matter of holes and ditches.
Siegfried Sassoon

Sassoon's "holes and ditches" could be described as short and long trenches, the former usually dug by high explosive, artillery, mortar or mine, and the latter, being etched and improved by man, were more sophisticated, increasingly so as the months passed. Raids began and ended in trenches. Separating the two sets of digging, the enemy's and ours, lay that bit of ground, be it wide or narrow, that came to be called no man's land. This real estate, the abode of the unburied dead, or parts thereof, of both sides, featured a myriad of shell holes, some filled with water in which a careless or unlucky man could drown, and belts of wire and other obstacles, natural and man-made. The earnest concern of commanders at every level, as one of the tactical manuals stressed, was "complete command of No Man's Land [it being] of special importance ... for cultivating an offensive spirit." "Grey Rats," as some tagged the Germans, and the "Brown Rats" of the BEF were set to that task.[1] In the opposing trenches, and in the gap between, Death watched, always ready to augment his domain:

Death whining down from heaven,
Death roaring from the ground,
Death stinking in the nostril,
Death shrill in every sound.[2]

A primary contributor to the general mayhem and misery was artillery, the word "Ubique" (everywhere) on the gunner cap badge being no idle boast. As Kipling said, "There's nothing

1 *SS 135 Instructions for the Training of Divisions for Offensive Action* (London: HMSO, December 1916), p. 52. This manual was one of the most important manuals of the war. Its main lessons apply not just to divisional operations, but to any offensive action: close co-operation between infantry and artillery, careful planning and preparation, increasing use of bombs (hand grenades), importance of infantry support weapons (Lewis gun, Stokes mortar and rifle grenades) and the critical role of platoon commanders.

2 William Noel Hodgson, 'Back to Rest', in *Verse and Prose in Peace and War*, p. 40. The poem was written shortly after Loos in 1915. Hodgson was killed in action on 1 July 1916.

this side 'Eaven or 'Ell Ubique doesn't mean." It is hard to dispute the claim that the Great War was an artillery war given that the guns, together with mortars, caused more than half of all casualties: "artillery was the killer; artillery was the terrifier. Artillery followed the soldier to the rear, sought him out in his billet, found him on the march."[3] One estimate says that 100 million 18-pounder shells and 25 million 4.5-inch howitzer shells were fired during the war. Over five million tons of artillery ammunition were shipped to France. By June 1918 the BEF had over 6,700 guns, an increase of more than 6,000 in four years. Artillery strength had also grown dramatically, rising from just over 93,000 officers and men in 1914 to almost 550,000 in 1918.[4] It is noteworthy that a century before a certain Corsican, one Napoleon Bonaparte, in testimony of the importance he attached to his guns, especially the famous 12-pounders, always referred to them as his "cherished daughters."

The aim of this chapter is to describe the trenches on the Western Front and the establishment of that "systematic and orderly trench routine [that was] a process of great educational value" in trench to trench warfare. As one New Zealand officer so aptly said, "The art of warfare is the cultivation of domestic virtues."[5] Learning any routine can be wearisome, but the toil is always necessary for as John Ruskin wrote "a man should know at least three things – first, where he is; second, where he is going; and third, what he had best do under the circumstances."

Mastery of trench routines contributed greatly to the trench or battle discipline that meant survival. In holes and in ditches the careless or unobservant officer or man could suddenly be propelled into eternity in a wide variety of ways. Reading it today an entry published in 3rd Canadian Battalion Routine Orders in mid-1916 could be seen as sound advice or as fatalism, or both: "in view of the fact that … the life of a soldier is of uncertain tenure the making of a will should be impressed on all." As casualties mounted so did cynicism; for example, a sign in a trench in 1916 echoes a recruiting poster: "Keep your head down. Your King and Country need you." Ever present and ever alert were the snipers of both sides whose accuracy, patience and score were legendary. Sniper H. Norwest, MM (Military Medal), 50th Canadian Battalion, for example, on 28 April 1918 "accounted for his hundredth German, and before night had added another to the score, a record enjoyed by few, if any other snipers." By 28 July Norwest

3 Rudyard Kipling, 'Ubique' in George and Christopher Newark (comps.), *Kipling's Soldiers* (Romford: The Pompadour Gallery, 1993), p. 48; John Terraine, *The Smoke and the Fire: Myths and Anti-Myths of War 1861-1945* (London: Sidgwick & Jackson, 1980), p. 132.

4 Julian Thompson, *The 1916 Experience: Verdun and the Somme* (London: Sevenoaks, 2009), p. 42, attributes 58.5 percent of casualties to artillery and mortars, 39 percent to rifles and machine-guns, 2.2 percent to bombs and grenades and 0.3 percent to bayonets. Ronald Clifton, 'What is an Artillery Brigade?', *Stand To!*, 31 (Spring 1991), p. 34; 'What is a Heavy Battery!', *Stand To!, 35* (Summer 1992), p. 32; Hugh M. Urquhart, *The History of the 16th Battalion (The Canadian Scottish Regiment) Canadian Expeditionary Force in the Great War 1914-1919* (Toronto: Macmillan, 1932), p. 117, describes the primary difference between a gun and a howitzer thus: "A gun gives scant warning but can be avoided by getting behind some impenetrable object. You hear the report of a howitzer and when you have presently forgotten about it something drops from the sky with a sickening thud. In short, howitzer fire falls on you." *Statistics of the Military Effort of the British Empire During the Great War 1914-1920* (London: HMSO, March 1922), pp. 162, 484, 487.

5 C.T. Atkinson, *The Seventh Division, 1914-1918* (London: John Murray, 1927), pp. 131-32; Kevin Fewster, *Gallipoli Correspondent: The Frontline Diary of C.E.W. Bean* (Sydney: George Allen & Unwin, 1983), p. 139.

had upped his tally to 107. But on 18 August a German sniper shot and killed him.[6] Routine also included attrition which ate away at strength and fighting spirit of even the best troops, the "wastage percent per month" standing in 1916 and 1917 at 10 percent for the infantry.[7]

Part of the "Holes and Ditches" story is how trench warfare came about. After a short period of "open" warfare featuring cavalry engagements, infantry manoeuvre and then a lengthy retreat from Mons, the war turned static. On 15 September 1914 the Commander-in-Chief (C-in-C) of the BEF, Sir John French, issued Operation Order 26, its single page a recognition of stark reality: "The Commander-in-Chief wishes the line now held by the Army to be strongly entrenched, and it is his intention to assume a general offensive at the first opportunity."[8] By mid-November the trenches ran in two belts along the whole distance from the North Sea to the Swiss border, a front that until mid-1917 remained essentially static. In the north, the Belgian Army held a 15-mile sector from Nieuport to just short of Ypres. From there the BEF held 85 miles from Ypres to the River Somme. The French Army manned the line southward.

In the autumn of 1914 the first of the Canadian divisions formed and began training at Valcartier, Quebec. What training was done was very basic, drill occupying much of the time with route marching and musketry making up the rest. Tactics hardly saw the light of day, the only exercises, a total of two, featuring outpost duties at night. Even if the officers had possessed the new manual, *Infantry Training (4-Company Organization). 1914,* and even if the nascent battalions had been in four companies, instead of the old style eight, the type of war they were going to would be foreign to all, including the somewhat colourful but erratic Sam Hughes, Minister of Militia, who on one memorable occasion ordered a unit to "Form Square". An ancient former Corporal, recalling something of this manoeuvre, did manage to carry out the spirit of the order, if not the letter of it. Canadians would not again perform such a ballet.[9]

Instead, the Canadian Tommy, like all the infantry of the Empire, would fight "in the trenches," a term that before long would be familiar throughout most of the world, even in some neutrals, one such boasting that its people were too proud to fight. The day's business became the acquisition of the trench discipline that is a fundamental concern of this chapter. Nothing in the pre-war manuals, official and semi-official, prepared officers and men for trench warfare, nor did those that came out in early 1915. None offered much since sufficient experience had yet to accrue to enable a solid body of guidance.[10]

6 LAC, RG9IIIC3, Volume 4040, Folder 14, Books 3-4, Routine Orders, 23 June 1916; Major D.J. Goodspeed, *Battle Royal: A History of the Royal Regiment of Canada, 1862-1962* (Toronto: The Royal Regiment of Canada Association, 1962), p. 137; LAC, 50th Battalion War Diary, April, July and August 1918.

7 Radley, *We Lead Others Follow,* pp. 260-61, 275, describe the Canadian reinforcement system.

8 Brigadier-General J.E. Edmonds, *Military Operations France and Belgium, 1914: Mons, The Retreat to the Seine, The Marne and the Aisne August-October 1914* (London: Macmillan, 1933), Appendix 46, p. 569.

9 Daniel G. Dancocks, *Welcome to Flanders Fields: The First Canadian Battle of the Great War: Ypres, 1915* (Toronto: McClelland & Stewart, 1988), p. 60; Lt.-Col. A.A. Hanbury-Sparrow, 'Discipline or Enthusiasm', *British Army Review,* 20 (April 1965), p. 8, recalled forming square once in 1911.

10 The most important of the pre-war and early war manuals are included in the Bibliography. Two of the most significant ones were these: Brig.-General R.C.B. Haking, CB, psc., *Company Training* (London: Hugh Rees Limited, 1915) and Captain A.P. Birchall, *Rapid Training of a Company for War* (London: Gale and Polden, 1915). Neither had much to say about trenches, but Haking more so in the sense of general usefulness to new officers since his book offered 450 pages. Birchall's

New formations and units, Canadian and British, going into the line for the first time, had everything to learn, usually the hard way, and everything had initially to be improvised from trench mortars to grenades to simple things like duckboards for the bottom of the trenches. At first, unit Adjutants were especially burdened since they were charged with battalion "interior economy," the purpose of which was maintenance of efficiency and well-being: "Mr. Holt, the Adjutant," wrote Sergeant Bagnall of the 14th Canadian Battalion, "was very busy adjusting routines to suit war conditions." Likewise, brigade and divisional staffs and their commanders. All ranks had quickly to adjust for in the forward trenches "Mateship was everything if one was to survive … A loner had to be of particularly strong character to survive."[11]

Just as it took a London cabbie time and earnest focus to acquire "The Knowledge," the soldier, too, had his work cut out for him. It also took time for Regulars to realize that New Army, Territorial and Dominion Battalions, all brand new, both officers and men, could not be regarded or treated like an old battalion which possessed history, experience and that family spirit that develops over the years.[12] Second Ypres, which marked a beginning for Canadians, offered a severe challenge, but also one that focussed the minds of officers and men wonderfully on acquiring trench discipline. Variously described as one of the most dangerous places on earth, and as an evil abode where death waited at one's shoulder, soldiers came to dread the Ypres Salient. Said one Canadian Tommy it was

> At all times stormy and every battalion … there returns … very much attenuated … it was a byword that one was not a soldier unless he had served on the Ypres front … Here have fallen thousands of our best manhood … The Germans themselves have a dread of [it] … Ypres conveyed a sort of horror … sinister forebodings of death … within a fortnight I was smashed up … But everyone gets it at Ypres.[13]

Going into the line at Ypres, or anywhere else, always meant coming out with fewer men, sometimes appallingly fewer. Officers were especially vulnerable: "The life of an infantry officer … was very short … fatal or non-fatal wounds came quickly to a junior officer in a line regiment."[14] Casualties meant units starting again, a cycle of learn and re-learn, acquire and re-acquire "The Knowledge."

contribution was 145 pages (page size three inches by four). Birchall noted in his preface that he had been ill for the early months of the war, which causes one to ask if he was aware of the reality of 1915. His manual does not reflect that.

11 R.C. Fetherstonhaugh, *The Royal Montreal Regiment 14th Battalion C.E.F. 1914-1925* (Montreal: The Gazette Publishing Co. Limited, 1927), pp. 5, 70-71. Lieutenant A.P. Holt, Canadian Grenadier Guards, was appointed Adjutant when the 14th formed in Montreal. Christopher Pugsley, *On the Fringe of Hell: New Zealanders and Military Discipline in the First World War* (Auckland: Hodder & Stoughton, 1991), p. 105.

12 Robert Maxwell, *Villiers-Stuart Goes to War* (Edinburgh: The Pentland Press Ltd., 1990), p. 73. Villiers-Stuart was CO 9th KRRC, 14th British Division, until October 1915.

13 Peter Barton, *The Battlefields of the First World War* (London: Constable In Association With the Imperial War Museum, 2005), p. 115; Roy (ed.), *The Journal of Private Fraser*, pp. 144-45. Fraser served with the 31st Canadian Battalion of 2nd Division. Passchendaele was his last battle, severe wounds putting him out of the "Great Adventure", as he called it.

14 Griffith, *Up to Mametz*, pp. 109-10.

The Somme, too, devastated some units, like the 3rd and 4th Canadian Battalions which together lost over 700 out of 1,100 all ranks at Regina Trench in October 1916. G.M. Hughes, commanding 1st Brigade, told his battalion commanders "You must take every opportunity to build your battalion up to what it was ... before we suffered our losses." This put additional, but inevitable pressure on the "old officers and men." In Hughes' overall message we also hear echoes of John Ruskin (see earlier): "See that they [the men] know where they are, where the enemy is and what is to be done."[15] The British Official History said, in truth, that after the Somme "There remained ... few battalions possessed of the deep grounded knowledge and battle discipline which react instinctively to an unexpected situation and deal effectively with it." After every battle reconstitution, training and the cultivation of "ingenuity and forethought, resolution and determination, steadfastness and devotion," the qualities required for trench warfare, began anew.[16]

The description of the trenches that follows is based upon *SS 101 Notes for Infantry Officers on Trench Warfare* and *Revised Diagrams* and are typical layouts, which adhered to a general pattern with considerable variation in detail and in distances.[17] Essentially the trench system consisted of four trench lines roughly parallel to each other. The first two were the fire trench (the fire line) and very close (20 or so yards) behind it the command trench. The fire trench followed the lie of the ground, curving and bending as it dictated. Where it was straight every 20-30 feet traverses about nine feet wide were dug so that an enemy soldier who had gotten into the trench could not throw a grenade any further than the adjacent fire bay, this limiting the number of casualties he might cause. Traverses usually jutted behind the firing line, but they could be dug forward of it instead. In either case, their purpose was to protect against blast and enfilade fire and they made constructing a barrier or block across a trench easier should the enemy enter the trench. A block sealed intruders off leaving time and space for preparing a counter-attack. The number of men in each firing bay depended on the situation. During a relief (see later in this chapter) the bays could be thick with men. When the enemy was inactive, no raid or patrols being made, a soldier might go weeks without seeing anything of the enemy, perhaps just "A thread of blue smoke from his trenches at breakfast time when you, too, were cooking bacon."[18]

As he stood in his position in a firebay the soldier saw to his front and looming above him the parapet, four or five feet of thrown-up earth reinforced with and topped by sandbags. To his

15 LAC, RG9IIIC3, Volume 4074, Folder 2, File 6, 26 October 1916; MG30E8 (Creelman Papers), 11 July 1916; MG 30E236 (Villiers Papers), Volume 4, Folder 7, Diary, Volume 2, pp. 19-20. Hughes did not have Arthur Currie's confidence, to some degree because of the hostility between his father, Sir Sam Hughes, Minister of Militia, and Currie, but also because Hughes as Brigade Major (BM) of 3rd Canadian Brigade at Second Ypres had not impressed Currie. Currie's assessment was probably somewhat unfair. Major Paul Villiers, for a time Hughes' BM, thought Hughes a very good brigade commander, as did artillery Colonel John Creelman who called Hughes "a really good soldier, even if he was shoved on too fast." Hughes had not commanded a battalion before getting a brigade.

16 Captain Wilfred Miles, *Military Operations France and Belgium, 1916: 2nd July 1916 to the End of the Battles of the Somme* (London: Macmillan, 1938), pp. 451, 471.

17 *SS 101 Notes for Infantry Officers on Trench Warfare* and *Revised Diagrams* (London: HMSO, 1916), p. 9. This important and early manual had five chapters: special characteristics of trench warfare, siting and construction of trenches, occupation and relief of trenches and general trench routine, organization of trench lines and action in case of attack and notes on the attack in trench warfare. Training is a central theme throughout the manual.

18 Charles Edmonds [Charles Carrington], *A Subaltern's War* (London: Peter Davies Ltd., 1929), p. 25.

rear was the parados, sandbagged with a mound of banked earth designed to shield against the blast of shells exploding to the rear of the trench. A man in such a trench, which was at least deep enough for him to walk upright, required a firestep upon which to stand so he could see to fire. Under his feet were slatted wood platforms known as duck boards. The enemy trenches were similar. Upon capturing a trench the immediate task was constructing a firestep on the parados side. If this was not done, an immediate counter-attack by the just ejected enemy could catch the intruders without the ability to easily defend themselves. The result would be loss of the trench they had just taken.

The narrow command trench, which lacked traverses, and the Communication Trenches (CTs) that ran forward to the fire trench, enabled commanders to move quickly along the length of the fire trench. Depending upon ground and situation frontage for a company was 100 to 250 yards, for a battalion 500 to 1,000 yards, for a brigade 1,000 to 2,000 yards and for a division 2,000 to 4,000 yards. Off the command trench were dug-outs, one for each company headquarters and somewhere centrally along the line one for battalion headquarters. When the CO had to be well forward he worked from this dug-out. Other dug-outs, mostly rudimentary "funk-holes," provided some shelter for the men. The use of any deeper and more solidly constructed dug-outs was initially forbidden because as Ex-Private X says:

> Keep men in open trenches and they will endure shell-fire with equanimity, but they will emerge from a safe dugout … with the air of intelligent dogs who have heard the word 'bath' … We acquired the well-known dugout disease. It was really unpleasant to leave the complete safety of that underground haven for the open trench.[19]

Experience said it was no easy task to get sleeping men out of the dug-outs quickly, even more so at night. What could and did happen is not surprising. In December 1915 a German raiding party took prisoner 19 men found asleep in a cellar in 18th British Division lines. In spring 1916 the enemy visited that battalion area again, but this time the battalion stood to in spite of the shelling and refused to seek shelter. The Germans got only two men and lost two of their own.[20]

Lieutenant-Colonel A. A. Hanbury-Sparrow, as did many officers, questioned the wisdom of denying men the use of dug-outs thinking this "very doubtful, for it imposed a great strain on the troops … [their] nerves … so worn by this continual exposure in the open that it is questionable if their resistance was any greater, whilst it is certain their casualties were very much higher." Nevertheless, it was a fact that both sides lost thousands of prisoners because of dug-out use. In the BEF officers responsible for defence of the trenches eventually lost confidence in the ability of NCOs to get the men out quickly enough to man the firing line against oncoming attackers. Hanbury-Sparrow, despite his earlier doubts, wondered if the NCOs had "enough authority to

19 Ex-Private X [Alfred McClelland Burrage], *War is War* (London: Victor Gollancz Ltd., 1930), pp. 171-72; Major D.J. Corrigall, *The History of the Twentieth Canadian Battalion (Central Ontario Regiment), Canadian Expeditionary Force in the Great War, 1914-1918* (Toronto: Stone & Cox Limited, 1935), p. 38. Funk-holes were simply ledges cut into the side of the trench wall, bed linen being sandbags. *Notes on Trench Routine and Discipline by a Second in Command* (London: Forster Groom & Co., Ltd., 1916), p. 6; Jerrold, *Georgian Adventure*, p. 132.

20 Captain G.H.F. Nichols, *The 18th Division in the Great War* (London: William Blackwood and Sons, 1922), pp. 23-24.

get the men out the instant the barrage lifted." He was not alone in this, the consensus being that many NCOs simply did not. As officer casualties mounted – a grim statistic revealed that one in every four Subalterns died on active service – more and more NCOs, the better ones, of course, were commissioned. This, and heavy casualties, had decimated the NCO Corps, the result being less capable NCOs, increasing doubt about their abilities in general and a general perception that they were a weak link. NCO shortcomings forced officers to step in, and in addition to their own duties, do tasks that NCOs should have been able to handle.[21] Exhaustion spelled more officer casualties: "thousands of promising young officers were killed doing [NCO] work … the consequence of this unnecessary slaughter was reflected in a lack of skill in leading which caused hideous casualties."[22] The impact of what became a vicious cycle shows here:

> No digging or wiring party ever goes without an officer, that is the way to get the men along. If one takes out a party of men somewhere they don't know – in the open probably – to dig they'll go like lambs as long as they've got an officer with them … The other night … I had some men and had to get somewhere I'd never been to before … it wasn't difficult and we had ample directions, so before we started I was told to send the men with a Sergeant. Said the Sergeant to me: 'I wish you were coming, sir, I don't know the way.' I said, 'My dear man, nor do I.' To which he made this astounding reply, 'Very likely not, sir, but the men will think you do and they know I don't.'[23]

The Germans had been aware that men remained in the open in British trenches: "Even after they had been captured, the English retained their strict discipline. Up to the end of 1916 they were accustomed to be without shelter even at night. An iron discipline, maintained by a severe code of punishments, was in their very blood." Henry Dundas, an officer of the Scots Guards, offered testimony to that in December 1916 saying that while the Germans were sick of the discomfort of the trenches this "isn't half of what our people go through (who ever saw a British dug-out?)." But dug-outs were in general use in many divisions well before that and they remained in use thereafter, this continuing to worry commanders even into 1918, one CO summing up the dilemma thus: "The problem of keeping troops alive during heavy enemy bombardment calls for solution. When men go down into deep dug-outs they lose touch with the situation, are sometimes buried and always difficult to get out. If they 'Stand To' in the trenches the whole garrison may be wiped out." The difficulty in getting men out quickly enough to man their positions remained. One suggestion was that dug-outs function in threes, the first

21 Lt.-Col. A.A. Hanbury-Sparrow, *The Land-Locked Lake* (London: Arthur Barker Ltd., 1932), p. 222; Adrian de Wiart, *Happy Odyssey* (London: Jonathan Cape, 1950), p. 72; L. Housman (ed.), *War Letters of Fallen Englishmen* (London: Victor Gollancz, 1930), p. v; Kenneth Radley, *Get Tough, Stay Tough* (Solihull: Helion & Company Limited, 2014), pp. 48, 313. About one of every eight Canadian Expeditionary Force CEF) officers died due to enemy action.

22 Hanbury-Sparrow, *The Land-Locked Lake,* p. 212.

23 Andy Simpson, *Hot Blood and Cold Steel: Life and Death in the Trenches of the First World War* (Staplehurst: Spellmount, 2002), pp. 122-23; Christopher Duffy, *Through German Eyes: The British and the Somme 1916* (London: Weidenfeld and Nicolson, 2006), p. 68. Why an officer was supervising digging and wiring puzzled the Germans. One prisoner was also "very much astounded" by the idea of an officer going out on patrol, the German concept being why buy a dog if you intend to do the barking yourself?

out would be responsible for getting occupants of the other two out. Another idea involved tunnelling through traverses, the tunnels to shelter troops while at the same time allowing them to "readily emerge to man the trench." Given the enormous demand for labour, and the already staggering burden of work, one wonders to what extent such a solution could have been implemented and for how long.[24]

From the command trench CTs ran a hundred yards or more rearward to the support trench which had no command trench and was not always traversed, but had some deep dug-outs. Support trenches did what the name says. From a support trench CTs ran, depending on ground, 400-600 yards back to the reserve trenches where troops stood ready to reinforce forward trenches as necessary. Between these lines, fire, support and reserve, lay mutually supporting strong points with garrisons of 10-100 men as required. All trenches were named, usually by the first occupants.[25] Fire and support trenches were protected by barbed wire anchored by pickets. In many areas two, three or more belts of wire strengthened the obstacles. Narrow lanes left open allowed patrols to come and go easily. Saps dug forward of the fire trench were manned by two or three men to watch and give early warning; listening posts, outposts, in a word.

The above is the ideal, of course, a well-constructed and well-sited defensive system occupied for a considerable time. In reality, trenches often amounted to very much less, requiring great improvement if they were to be occupied for very long. Bad weather and poorly maintained trenches reinforced the enemy called mud and misery.

Of the German trenches, there are as many descriptions as there are describers. For both sides the extent, conformation and construction of trenches and dugouts depended on terrain, situation and time available for work. Obviously, British and German trenches shared many features; after all, a trench is a trench. Lord Moran, a Battalion Medical Officer, saw this for himself when he accompanied a raiding party in September 1916: "And this is the Boche trench. Now that we are actually in it we are a little surprised to find it so like our own."[26] Actual trench location determined the style of construction to large degree. While "the hazards of war do not always permit an enemy to select the terrain on which it will fight" the Germans were at some advantage when it came to trenches since more often than not they were the defender. Also, those studying captured documents at the time read about their "elaborate geological staff [that] prepared and distributed instructions on siting of trenches, dugouts and other defence works." These specialists assessed the problems of entrenchment on the Somme and in Flanders, two regions where the soils are in sharp contrast, the chalk of the former and the clay of the latter where "unfathomable" mud posed serious difficulties.[27]

As early as May 1915 German trenchmanship impressed those officers and men of the BEF who had occasion to visit German trenches. That month Major E.W. Hermon, then

24 Colonel W. Nicolai, *The German Secret Service,* George Renwick (trans.) (London: Stanley Paul & Co., Ltd., 1924), p. 188; R.N. Dundas (ed.), *Henry Dundas Scots Guards: A Memoir* (Edinburgh: William Blackwood and Sons, 1921), p. 103.

25 Peter Chasseaud, *Rats Alley: Trench Names of the Western Front 1914-1918* (Stroud: Spellmount, 2006). This book contains a useful gazetteer, one of many reasons to consider it a gem.

26 Lord Moran, *The Anatomy of Courage,* p. 146.

27 Douglas Wilson Johnson, *Battlefields of the World War, Western and Southern Fronts: A Study in Military Geography* (New York: Oxford University Press, 1921), pp. 22-23, 117-20. Of particular relevance is the section 'Relation of Geological Structure to Trench and Dugout Locations.'

commanding a cavalry squadron and touring old German trenches, thought a "badger sett … about the only equivalent of the German trench system. Their trenches are a complete and complicated underground town and they fairly want some digging out. They are much better than we are at digging."[28] Certain features of the German trenches posed serious problems for raiders as 51st (Highland) Division learned while raiding in April 1916:

> These raids … brought to light certain facts concerning German trench construction. The German trenches did not resemble the small ditch-like trenches commonly seen at schools … and training grounds. They can better be compared to the marker's gallery in a rifle range. They were 10-12 feet deep, with the sides for the most part revetted with planks. To get into them was not easy; to get out of them still less easy; while evacuating the wounded from them was a matter of very considerable difficulty. In fact, in the case of [one] raid, it is doubtful if the wounded could have been brought back to our lines at all had not a sally-port through which the more severely wounded were carried been discovered.[29]

A significant feature of the deep German dug-outs came to light in the summer of 1916. A report by engineers of 49th British Division described enemy dug-outs having passages that allowed escape to a flank, or rapid counter-attack, unless exits were found and guarded. Raiders, who operated within tight time limits, could not always find such exits and, consequently,

> It is desirable to bomb dug-outs which are known to be occupied. A Stokes mortar bomb rolled down the entrance is recommended. But the fact that no sounds can be heard after bombs have been exploded in a dug-out does not prove that all occupants have been killed. They may have withdrawn by underground passage to another at a safe distance. It is necessary to detail a garrison to clear dug-outs and to prevent the arrival of fresh troops by this practice.[30]

Raids by 51st (Highland) Division) in early 1917 brought out other lessons for raiders and, indeed, for any attackers:

> It had become clear that the blind leap into a trench was not a sound policy. Not only were the German trenches in many places of a great depth, but they also contained many straight lengths of trench covered by a machine-gun mounted on the top step or a dug-out cut in the side of a traverse. These machine-guns were sited so as to fire straight along the trench as soon as any attacking party had leapt into it.

Assessment of enemy tactics against raiders showed that the enemy had men in open trenches throwing bombs against the raiders while men in the dug-outs fired or threw bombs at

28 Anne Nason (ed.), *For Love and Courage: The Letters of Lieutenant-Colonel E. W. Hermon from the Western Front 1914-1917* (London: Preface Publishing, 2008), p. 35. Hermon was killed in action on 9 April 1917 while CO 24th Northumberland Fusiliers.

29 Major F.W. Bewsher, *The History of the Fifty First (Highland) Division 1914-1918* (Uckfield, East Sussex: Naval and Military Press, n.d.), p. 64.

30 Peter Barton, Peter Doyle and Johan Vaudewalle, *Beneath Flanders Fields: The Tunneller's War 1914-1918* (Stroud: Spellmount Limited, 2004), p. 255.

raiders passing dug-out entrances. Because raiders could not see these until abreast of them nasty surprises had resulted. This drove several changes in training, one exercise designed to have men come up onto the enemy parapet properly extended from where they could shoot and bomb any visible enemy before entering the trench. Subsequently, raiders practised this repeatedly before conducting raids. Another lesson prescribed that dug-outs had to be blasted with larger charges, Mills bombs (grenades) having proven inadequate for the task.[31] R.B. Talbot Kelly, a Forward Observation Officer (FOO) for a raiding party of the Scottish Rifles (9th (Scottish) Division) in January 1917, described how very effective the Stokes bombs were in dug-out blasting especially when accompanied by a "P" (phosphorus) bomb (grenade) which usually set fire to dugouts.[32] Thereafter large charges of ammonal or other explosive served as bunker-busters.

These cities, for that is what the trenches became, required regulations just like other cities. Even courtesy became part of regulations; *viz.* "Trench Manners. Small parties stand aside for large parties. Lay over to the right."[33] General discipline, often referred to as barrack or parade-square discipline, had its codes in the form of *King's Regulations* and the *Manual of Military Law*. These accompanied officers and men into the trenches, but whilst in them they also obeyed the law of the trenches as laid down in procedures variously titled Standing Orders, Standing Orders for Trenches or Trench Orders. All began life as a couple of pages, or even just a single typed or hand-written sheet in which units set out what would be done and how and what would not be done. Their purpose was to inculcate and maintain good trench routines in order to save time, prevent misunderstandings and avoid constant repetition of orders. They also served as a guide and a check list for commanders. Useful, too, were the semi-official publications that began to appear; for example, in 1916 many officers invested 6d in a copy of *Notes on Trench Routine and Discipline by a Second in Command,* based, said the Preface, "on standing orders … and experience in the trenches."[34]

Starting in 1915 the Canadian Corps issued trench orders, these doubling in size between the initial and the 1917 edition as experience, lessons, knowledge gained from other formations and technological advances were incorporated.[35] An officer posted from 76th British Brigade, for example, to 4th Canadian Division, took with him the former's Standing Orders, a document, no doubt, helpful to him in his new role with one of the brigades in the 4th Division. While such orders were similar since "one sector was very much like another so far as the general trend of trench warfare was concerned" valuable comparisons as to content and composition

31 Bewsher, *Fifty First (Highland) Division*, pp. 143, 147.

32 R.B. Talbot Kelly, *A Subaltern's Odyssey: A Memoir of the Great War 1915-1917* (London: William Kimber, 1980), p. 137. The raiders (300 officers and men) took 46 prisoners. The cost was one man killed and wounded.

33 LAC, RG9IIIC3, Volume 4031, Folder 26, File 7, GOC 1st Canadian Brigade to battalions, 3 March 1917.

34 This was published in London in 1916 by Forster Groom and Co.

35 *Canadian Corps Trench Orders* (London: HMSO, October 1915), *Canadian Corps Trench Orders* (Army Printing and Stationary Services, July 1916) and *Canadian Corps Standing Trench Orders* (Army Printing and Stationary Services, July 1917). The 1915 and 1916 editions were 12 pages each, the 1917 edition double that. All have similar content: duties, sentries, care and use of weapons, sanitation, work parties, action on attack, rum issue, reliefs and patrols.

were possible and useful.[36] One of the most impressive divisional standing orders found during research for this present study was 19th British Division's second edition. The main part of these is appropriately and logically laid out in three sections corresponding to how a division would move into the line: procedure before taking over trenches, procedure on taking over trenches and duties having taken them over. Several appendices detail precautions against gas, duties of officers and men, artillery liaison and communications. All in all, this set is a model of what such an order should look like.[37]

As for battalion standing orders, Louis Lipsett, the first CO of the 8th Canadian Battalion, was one of the first Canadian battalion commanders to issue such orders. Coming very soon after his battalion's first battle (Second Ypres), they were modest, just one page of 10 instructions, five prescribing equipment that each man had to have on his person for most of every day. A sixth concerned relief. Another warned that no man was to leave the trench unless he had a pass signed by an officer, this, no doubt, in consequence of the straggling at Second Ypres. Security is the most significant element in Lipsett's orders, it having become clear early on that considerable woe would be the lot of any CO whose standing orders did not include clear and decisive instructions about what to do in case of attack. Lipsett's concern shows in his direction in regard to "Stand to Arms," "Stand To," as it became better known, which became a twice daily ritual and discipline.

Morning Stand To, an hour or less depending on the light, came before dawn. All officers and men took up their positions on the *qui vive,* since this time of day was then seen as the most likely time for the enemy to attack, although less so as experience accrued. Stand To lasted until the enemy parapet could be clearly seen: "All ranks saw the sun-rise grey turning to silver, silver to gold – and the watch is over. Another day has begun."[38] Most BEF units then doled out, under the supervision of an officer, the rum ration of half a gill (1/4 pint) per man, although frequently less than that since the rum had passed through many hands on its way forward to the trenches. Breakfast followed and then rest for those not on duty. Rifle and machine-gun fire often accompanied Stand To, this fire being known as the "morning hate." Things then quieted down, everyone hoping the artillery would not start something that would provoke retaliation. In that event all the infantry could do was launch "a shower of rifle grenades and call on their artillery and trench mortars for further retaliation, trusting devoutly that the latter action [would] not bring additional trouble on their heads."[39]

36 LAC, MG 30E54 (Phelan Papers), Folder 3, 'Standing Orders for Trenches'. This 12-page order consists of 30 sections of guidance, orders and procedures for reliefs, sentries, watch duties, Stand To, gas attacks, counter-attacks, fixing of bayonets, mines, firing by day and by night, work, discipline, sniping, artillery support, SOS signals, medical officer, rations, prisoners and returns. Another example of brigade standing orders is at Mark Adkin, *The Western Front Companion* (London: Aurum Press, 2013), pp. 462-63. This example has 12 sections, several of like material having been combined. Content is similar. Everard Wyrall, *The Fiftieth Division 1914-1919* (Uckfield, East Sussex: Naval and Military Press, n.d.), p. 109.

37 TNA: WO 95/2056: 19th Division General Staff War Diary, 'Standing Orders for Trenches (Second Edition)', February 1918, Appendix 37.

38 LAC, War Diary, 8th Battalion, May 1915; Corrigall, *Twentieth Canadian Battalion,* p. 38.

39 Lieut.-Colonel C. Beresford Topp, *The 42nd Battalion, C.E.F., Royal Highlanders of Canada* (Montreal: Gazette Printing Co., Limited, 1931), p. 24.

Men soon learned what distinguished the various German instruments of retaliation and there grew up a kind of trench onomatopoeia about them. Their 5.9-inch howitzer, said one soldier, exploded with a crash like dishes being broken, followed by a kind of cheering noise like that at a football game. One type of German field gun shell whizzed as it approached, the bang of the explosion almost simultaneous, hence "whizz-bang." Yet another type of shell (not further identified) arrived "with the sound of a woman with a hare-lip trying to whistle."[40]

After its introduction in late 1914 the *Minenwerfer* bombs became known as "Minnies" (they were about the size of a two-gallon oil drum). In 1916 the 24cm *Minenwerfer* shell in flight was thought to resemble "fat aunts turning slow somersaults in mid-air." One soldier thought the Minnie made a woof-woof sound as it advanced. Stephen Graham considered it more like "a row of houses rushing down," probably a more apt description of an explosion massively loud and destructive. Lieutenant-Colonel J.L. Jack, in September 1916 commanding the 2nd West Yorkshires, found the Minnies intensely disagreeable, but he recalled that a man stood a good choice of avoiding them: "One may see them coming high in the air … and [can] dodge them by a display of agility if there is time to run around a traverse." Inattention or distraction sometimes spelled doom for he also remembered a firebay where one Minnie had killed four men and in another three more, all victims of a second Minnie. In Captain F.C. Hitchcock's unit, 2nd Battalion The Leinster Regiment, a sentry with a whistle in each platoon kept watch on the sky, likewise in 2nd Royal Welsh Fusiliers. On hearing the whistle men looked up to see where the Minnie was wobbling, assessed its most likely destination and went the opposite way posthaste. Wrong call could be last call. In one instance a Minnie coming down on the unit completely obliterated a firebay and all its unfortunate occupants. Edmund Blunden, a Subaltern of the Royal Sussex Regiment, learned that Minnies also made large holes in the nerves. At first sight of a descending Minnie he thought it merely a large rifle grenade, but he quickly realized the truth of it and like everyone else scuttled out of its path. Guy Chapman, a Royal Fusiliers Subaltern, was a very lucky survivor of a close encounter with a Minnie:

> As I ran, I heard one coming very close, caught a glimpse of it … and at that moment slipped. I picked myself up, but before I could reach my full height, the Minnie burst. A furious hot whirlwind rushed down, seized me and flung me violently back against the earth. I lay half-stunned while a rain of earth … patterned down on me, followed by something which whizzed viciously and struck quivering in the trench wall; it was a piece of jagged steel eighteen inches long.

In February 1916 Captain Charlie May, 22nd Manchesters, had a similar experience, thereafter concluding that "Close acquaintance with trench mortars is not recommended. I do not like trench mortars at all."[41]

40 Ex-Private X [Burrage], *War is War*, pp. 78-79; Lieut.-Colonel H.R. Sandilands, *The 23rd Division 1914-1919 (*Edinburgh: William Blackwood And Sons, 1925), pp. 57-58; Lt.-Col. C.N.F. Broad, 'The Development of Artillery Tactics, 1914-1918', *Journal of the Royal Artillery*, 39 (October 1922), pp. 66-67, describes the 5.9-inch howitzer as a big surprise in that it outranged British field guns and howitzers.

41 Ex-Private X [Burrage], *War is War*, p 79; Graham, *A Private in the Guards*, p. 199; John Terraine (ed.), *General Jack's Diary 1914-1918: The Trench Diary of Brigadier-General J.L. Jack, D.S.O*, (London:

Initially the BEF, with nothing comparable, made do with crude homemade tubes of one sort or another, these usually more dangerous to the operators than to the enemy, and devices such as West Spring Gun. The Stokes "gun," as it was commonly called, first issued in August 1915, became in the words of one military historian, the "outstanding invention" of the war and "the epitome of simplicity and effectiveness." Liddell Hart, for another, thought it the "outstanding and ubiquitous trench weapon of the war." Even so, not everyone wished to serve in a Trench Mortar Battery. Some officers saw such a posting to one as banishment and a dead-end career wise. When in May 1916 the Stokes entered service with the Welsh Guards Second Lieutenant H.S. Stokes knew his destination "for no other reason" than that of his name. He was not happy with his lot.[42]

A graphic example of what the Stokes could do occurred during 47th British Division's attack on High Wood on 15 September 1916, a day that marked the first use of tanks. This proved an inauspicious beginning for none of the tanks allotted to the 47th reached the enemy trenches. Their movement, in fact, may have warned the enemy of the impending attack and also restricted the artillery covering fire on the German trenches. When, "as a result of the tanks failure," the 140th Brigade stalled due to machine-gun fire the 140th Trench Mortar Battery prepared to put down hurricane fire on the enemy. At 1013 the battery commander, Captain George Goodes, unleashed a terrific "stonk" by his eight tubes, 750 bombs landing in 15 minutes, the result being, as 140th Brigade again advanced, the surrender of large numbers of the enemy. By noon High Wood was secured.[43] By January 1917 2nd Canadian Brigade was emphasizing "the great importance attaching to the employment of mortars … No troops can come through a proper trench mortar barrage, and no trenches under continuous bombardment by them, can long remain tenable."[44]

Cassell, 2003), pp.156, 166; Dunn, *The War the Infantry Knew,* p. 177; Captain F.C. Hitchcock, *"Stand To": A Diary of the Trenches 1915-1918* (Norwich: Gliddon Books, 1988), pp. 193, 198; Edmund Blunden, *Undertones of War* (Harmondsworth: Penguin Books Ltd., 1982), p. 46; Guy Chapman, *A Passionate Prodigality* (New York: Holt, Rinehart and Winston, 1965), p. 54; Gerry Harrison (ed.), *To Fight Alongside Friends: The First World War Diaries of Charlie May* (London: William Collins, 2014), p. 105; Adkin, *The Western Front Companion,* p. 242. Initially the *Minenwerfer* inventory consisted of heavy mortars (26cm calibre, shell weight 207 pounds, rate of fire 20 rounds per hour); medium (17cm, 109 pounds, 30-35 rounds per hour); and light (7.6cm, 10 pounds, 20 rounds per minute). Improved versions entered service in 1916 together with a new 24cm calibre version with a shell weight of 220 pounds. Eventually each German division had a *Minenwerfer* company of four heavy and 16 light weapons. By war's end there were just over 700 such companies on the German establishment.

42 Saunders, *Raiding on the Western Front,* pp. 124-25; Captain B.H. Liddell Hart, *The Real War 1914-1918* (Toronto: Little, Brown and Company, 1930), p. 128; Peter T. Scott, 'Mr. Stokes and His Educated Drainpipe', *The Great War 1914-1918,* 2 (May 1990), p. 90; Dudley Ward, *History of the Welsh Guards,* p. 79.

43 Miles, *2nd July 1916 to the End of the Battles of the Somme,* pp. 332, 335; TNA: WO 95/2701: 47th British Division General Staff War Diary, 'Report on Operations 15th/19th September 1916'; WO 95/2727: 140th Brigade 'Report on Operations September 15/20, 1916'. Adkin, *The Western Front Companion,* pp. 241-42, states that Stokes production in 1915 was 945, more than half of that in the last quarter of the year. Stokes bomb production, 400,000 in 1915, increased to just over a million in 1916. By the Armistice 1,700 Stokes were in service with the BEF. The 3-inch mortar of the Second World War and today's 81mm mortar are refinements of the Stokes.

44 LAC, War Diary, 2nd Canadian Brigade, January 1917.

At the end of 1915 the Stokes was joined by the 2-inch mortar. Its distinctive bombs because of their shape became known as footballs or toffee apples. A 4-inch Stokes entered service at about the same time. Production of this Stokes was never in large quantity, only a thousand or so being produced during the war. It did useful service firing smoke, gas and specialized chemical shells and incendiaries. By the end of 1916 the 9.45-inch heavy mortar with its 150 pound bomb joined the BEF. Six months later the Newton medium mortar, a development based upon the Stokes, replaced the 2-inch mortar.[45]

At first, all mortars were considered infantry weapons, but by June 1916 medium and heavy mortars had been given to the artillery, only the Stokes remaining with the infantry, but under brigade, not battalion control. By May 1916 each Canadian brigade had one Stokes battery of eight tubes. Shortly before that (March) each Canadian division had three medium mortar batteries and one heavy battery.[46]

Major N. Hudson provided a good summary of mortar characteristics and employment in a journal article written soon after the war. In it he described the advantageous characteristics of mortars as cheapness of weapon and ammunition, great destructive power and simplicity of training. He categorized mortars as to their function according to weapon and ammunition weights: the heavies immobile and having the primary task of demolition; the mediums not suitable to accompany infantry in the assault, their primary object being destruction of wire and trenches; and the light mortar with a high rate of fire and relatively mobile, able to accompany the infantry. Its primary function was killing.[47]

Returning now to trench routines the evening Stand To came before dusk preceding the "pregnant hours, wherein anything [could] happen."[48] It lasted a half-hour or more, the guide for stand down being when the enemy fired flares at their usual frequency. Night activities then began: relief, if it was due; re-supply and arrival of mail, oh, so important mail; and work, ever more work, such as repair and improvement of trenches and dug-outs, filling and toting endless numbers of sandbags, revetting trenches and saps, laying and replacing duckboards on the bottom of the trenches, erecting new wire obstacles and thickening old ones, pumping out water and standing the usual sentry duty. The endless work and periodic incoming enemy fire set in motion "Fear, boredom, fear – we swung from one to the other, with a growing fatigue ... and our minds became as muddied as our clothes." Senior commanders could be very critical of the results of work programmes. One Canadian brigadier in mid-1917 considered the results of one unit's work unsatisfactory due to poor organization and insufficient

45 Scott, "Mr. Stokes and His Educated Drainpipe," pp. 91-92.

46 F.W. Perry, *History of the Great War: Order of Battle of Divisions Part 5A. The Divisions of Australia, Canada and New Zealand and those in East Africa* (Newport, Gwent: Ray Westlake, 1992); Radley, *We Lead Others Follow,* p. 100, describes the adverse reaction of several Canadian senior commanders to light mortars being under brigade rather than battalion control.

47 Major N. Hudson, 'Trench Mortars in the Great War', *Journal of the Royal Artillery,* 47 (April 1920), pp. 17, 19-21. The figures are as follows: 9.45-inch heavy mortar, 3,500 pounds and 152 pounds; 2-inch medium, 500 pounds and 52 pounds; 6-inch medium, 375 pounds and 48 pounds; and Stokes 100 pounds and 11 pounds. The ranges in yards of each type were: 9.45-inch 1,140, rising to 2,300 by 1917; 2-inch medium 540; 6-inch medium 1,800 and Stokes, 430, rising to 800 in 1917.

48 *The Dead Horse Corner Gazette* 2 (December 1915), p. 23, the trench journal of 4th Canadian Battalion.

supervision, an assessment that meant trouble for those doing the supervising and more work for the workers.[49]

Enemy flares having just been mentioned it should be said that references to these abound in most division and battalion histories and in other accounts. D.W.J. Cuddeford, Scots Guards, credited the enemy with being much better at "illumination," their lights "far superior to ours" and some very attractive: "bursting into a most beautiful shower of golden or silver rain … [or] red or green balls of fire, or … a succession of different coloured flares." He also relates what many sources do not – the purposes of these pretty pyrotechnics:

> Every different coloured light, or combination of lights, conveyed a signal back to his rear; either an SOS calling for a barrage on us, or to his artillery to lengthen range; or maybe signalling an infantry relief complete and so on. They used a different code of signals on the various army Corps fronts, and these again were frequently changed so that we might not get to know the meaning of them. Nevertheless, from the information gathered from prisoners and other sources, our Corps Intelligence was kept pretty well up to date.

Cuddeford recalled one intelligence warning before the battalion returned to the trenches that the German SOS signal for the day and for a period thereafter was a light breaking into four red balls. Sure enough that night the four red balls appeared, the battalion's movement forward having been observed and within two minutes the enemy launched a "hellish" barrage. Major-General Sir Arthur Scott remembered how at times when the enemy was "extra anxious their front line assumed the appearance of a benefit at the Crystal Palace." Captain D.V. Kelly, MC, Leicestershire Regiment, also described the German system of lights as "much superior", as did many Canadian officers. These lights were also one of several German measures employed against raids. Others are described in a later chapter.[50]

Lights were beautiful. Work was not, nor did it affect just those in the fire trench. New arrivals were struck by the great hive of activity behind the front:

> No sooner had darkness fallen than these roads seethed with humanity; battalions relieving, or being relieved; working parties, wiring parties, ration parties, going or returning … with seemingly little order, tramping along with hardly a word, save a muttered curse as someone tripped … The confusion was made worse by strings of ration carts and waggons, which, in some parts, came surprisingly close to the front line. These rattled along … advertising to all their existence and their route. Indeed, the enemy often sprayed the roads with streams of machine-gun bullets, or dropped a shell at intervals on some likely place.[51]

49 Griffith, *Up to Mametz*, p. 61; LAC, MG30E15 (Griesbach Papers), Volume 3, File 16A, Book of Wisdom, Volume II, 9 September 1917.

50 D.W.J. Cuddeford, *And All For What?* (London: Heath Cranton Limited, 1933), p. 70; Major-General Sir Arthur B. Scott (ed.), *The History of the 12th (Eastern) Division in the Great War 1914-1918* (London: Nisbet & Co. Ltd., 1923), p. 77; D.V. Kelly, *39 Months With the" Tigers" 1915-1918* (London: Ernest Benn Limited, 1930), p. 40.

51 Major W.E. Grey, *The 2nd City of London Regiment (Royal Fusiliers) in the Great War (1914-19)* (London: Published from the Headquarters of the Regiment, 1929), pp. 25-26.

Men in the support and reserve trenches furnished large working parties nightly: "For the soldier in France was not merely a fighting man, he was also navvy and road mender, labourer and engineer, messenger and scavenger and, very frequently, an effective substitute for the pack-mule."[52] Everything required to live, work and fight had to be carried forward. An officer of the South Staffordshire Regiment recalled one particularly hard night when 80 petrol tins of water, 2,000 sandbags, planks, nails, ammunition, corrugated iron, barbed wire with stakes and staples and other trench stores had to be taken forward. The next night his battalion also had to tote rations for 800 men into the line. Another officer, after supervising an exhausting all-night trench dig, waxed poetic:

> If all the troops with all the tools
> Should dig for half a year
> 'Do you suppose,' the Colonel asked,
> 'That we should then be clear?'
> 'I doubt it,' said the Adjutant,
> 'Knowing the Brigadier.'[53]

Units adopted a quick means of allocating night work. When men numbered off in their sections even numbers might be sentries while odd numbers worked. Some units numbered off one, two, three, one, two, three – ones on sentry, twos working, threes resting. Sentries would be on until morning Stand To, standing head and shoulders above the parapet so they could see and be less likely to be surprised. Some work was done during daylight, but on a shift basis so that men could get some sleep. Care had always to be taken that the work did not attract enemy attention.

Officers and men who got six hours rest in every 24, were very lucky, the usual being much less that that. Sleep became the most precious thing of all because lack of it, or repeated interruptions of it, reduced awareness. This could mean death. Still, humour about the rigours of the trenches were not uncommon, an excellent example appearing in the *Dead Horse Corner Gazette:*

> I think I may as well give you an outline of a day's doings in order that you will be able to see for yourself what a grand time we have out here – not forgetting to mention the little personal comforts such as hot and cold water connections in the front trenches, electric cookers, warm baths … a double rum issue every night and morning, and the unrestricted use of stilts when the mud rises higher than the waist-line … Believe me, my boy, we're having one hell of a time.[54]

52 Major H.C. Singer, *History of the 31st Canadian Battalion, C.E.F.* (Calgary: privately printed [1939], p. 231; Brigadier-General A.W. Pagan, *Infantry: An Account of the 1st Gloucestershire Regiment During the War 1914-1918* (Aldershot: Gale & Polden Ltd., 1951), p. 61.

53 Committee of Officers Who Served With the Battalion, *The War History of the Sixth Battalion The South Staffordshire Regiment (T.F.)* (London: William Heinemann Ltd., 1924), pp. 59-60, 72. Trench digging was often supervised by an engineer officer. To check the depth of the digging he carried a long rod with which to measure depth. Most sappers were wise to the infantry trick of digging a small hole in the new trench and then when the sapper was doing his measurement guiding the rod into the small hole where it would register the required depth. Only the newest of sapper officers fell for this dodge.

54 *The Dead Horse Corner Gazette,* 3 (December 1915), 'Trench Routine'.

Reality said otherwise, but it also said that dull routine filled more days than violent attack or desperate defence. What routine meant depended to a great deal upon rank and appointment. For a CO a typical routine, one applicable to most of his peers in any unit of the BEF, might have looked like this:

> Dawn – Wake, tea, cigarette or pipe
> 0600 – Breakfast. Receive reports, prepare reports
> 0800 – Tour battalion trenches until 1300
> 1300 – Lunch. Rest
> 1500 – Prepare Daily Situation Report
> 1600 – Dinner. Paperwork until midnight

Company commanders followed a similar routine. Platoon commanders observed a routine that included assigning and checking work tasks, inspecting men, equipment, weapons and trenches, censoring letters and visiting sentries and listening posts at night. The usual practice in companies had two Subalterns going round the line while two slept with a change-over at midnight. Of course, four Subalterns were not always present; as Brigadier-General A.W. Pagan later wrote "If the number of officers in a company was small – at times there were only two – their duty was strenuous." In 4th Canadian Battalion the system worked like this: two officers in company trenches at all times, shifts of six hours each: "You did a six-hour tour, had 12 hours rest, did another six hour tour, had only six hours off, and so on." In 8th Canadian Battalion the shift was eight hours:

> My watch was 12 to 4 a.m. and p.m. Work that out with Stand To in the morning and also in the evening and you will see that consecutive sleep is not easy! On paper 6-12 (midnight) looks good; but, then remember, dinner at 7 or 7.30 according to the fire, while you may have to turn out at any time if you are being shelled at all. For instance, one night I was just turning in … when a mine went up … and general strafing kept me out until 9.30, after which I couldn't sleep. So at midnight I was tired when I started my four hours, turned in at 4, out again for Stand To, 8 breakfast, 9 rifle inspection, and so it goes.[55]

After morning Stand To one officer per company was on duty. NCOs were assigned tasks by their platoon commanders as required. The private soldier's days and nights were filled with Stand To morning and evening, getting meals, work, sentry duty and some rest.

One Subaltern of the Sixth South Staffordshires remembered well his night time tours of the company trenches: "The trudging and slithering along muddy tracks … pausing to stand by the sentry, gaze into the black night, and help him in his endless task of keeping awake by talking to him; turning into the mess dugout for half an hour or so … then turning out again to do the

55 James H. Pedley, *Only This: A War Retrospect* (Ottawa: Graphic Publishers, 1927), pp. 74-85; Bernard Adams, *Nothing of Importance: A Record of Eight Months at the Front With a Welsh Battalion, October 1915 to June 1916.* (London: Methuen, 1917; reprint ed., Uckfield, East Sussex: Naval and Military Press, n.d.), p. 28; Pagan, *Infantry*, p. 27; LAC, MG 30E60 (Matthews Papers), Volume 3, Folder 12, 'Standing Orders'. The title of Adams' book is misleading. It is a detailed, painstaking and important account of trench warfare and discipline.

round once more." But sometimes humour surfaced. One company commander of the Sixth on return from one of his rounds found four strangers at his company headquarters. After a quick meal he:

> ordered two of the Strangers to sleep for half the night while the other two accompanied him on his rounds. The night was vile, wet overhead, wet underfoot, and black as ink. The Strangers enjoyed the supper more than the trips round the trenches. The less they enjoyed them, the more holes the company commander found for them to fall in, the more wire to trip over. Thus throughout the night the four Strangers either tumbled or tried to get sleep! In due course breakfast was served. Imagine the surprise of this Company Commander and his Subalterns, all of whom had treated the Strangers kindly but firmly, when they appeared for the meal, less their trench-coats, and were shown by their badges to be Field Officers![56]

Another version of 8th Battalion's trench orders, issued in October 1915 by H.H. Matthews, who replaced Louis Lipsett when he left to command a brigade, includes two pages on trenches and three pages common to trenches and billets when out of the line at rest. Matthews' version pretty much echoes Lipsett's, with some additions reflecting the latest experience.[57] One concern at this time was fire discipline which was not notably good. What usually happened was a nervous sentry would fire at what he imagined was enemy movement whereupon others joined in, then the enemy added his bit, making the chorus of fire swell to symphonic proportions along the width or more of the battalion. Usually new units or soldiers caused the clamour, they being "windy" (nervous, over anxious), according to old soldiers, who quite forgot they once did the same. Deciding whether to fire or not was tricky, as the following example shows:

> There had been two unfortunate cases of sentries mistaking wiring parties … for the enemy … no one was hurt … but a good deal of fuss was made about it, our new Brigadier blaming the men who did the shooting – his own men – and saying so pretty forcibly. When I first heard of this I thought that a mistake had been made – if for no other reason than that there would for a time … be a disinclination on the part of the sentry to shoot promptly, which might prove dangerous.

And so it proved. Two sentries, hearing movement, but hesitant to fire, challenged instead, receiving in return a shower of grenades. Despite severe wounds they beat off the enemy raiders, for which the unit received not praise, but severe criticism for allowing the enemy within bombing range! Such things happen in every Army.[58]

Fire discipline could not be perfected in billets behind the line. Two attempts by the 8th Canadian Battalion tried to solve the problem of when to fire. First, no firing was to commence

56 Committee of Officers, *Sixth South Staffordshire Regiment,* pp. 53, 102.
57 LAC, MG 30E60 (Matthews Papers), Volume 3, Folder 12, 26 October 1915.
58 Feilding, *War Letters to a Wife,* p. 247. Feilding was CO 6th Connaught Rangers (47th British Brigade, 16th (Irish) Division). The 'new Brigadier', H.G. Gregorie, DSO, arrived in early December 1917 and commanded the 47th Brigade until April 1918. Gregorie replaced G.E. Pereira, an officer Feilding (pp. 236, 240) much admired: 'one of the best men that ever breathed.'

except upon the order of an officer. It was also thought that officer direction of firing would maximize its effectiveness. Second, night sentries were posted in pairs, experience saying it was less likely that two men would get the wind up. What also had to be tightly controlled was the firing of flares which "windy" men were prone to do. On occasion firing just erupted, as Lieutenant Wyn Griffith, Royal Welsh Fusiliers, discovered when he accompanied his brigadier on an inspection. As they approached a Lewis gun post the gunner fired a drum of ammunition. The gunner did not recognize the brigadier who asked:

> 'Was it you firing, then?'
> 'Yes.'
> 'What were you firing at?'
> 'Don't know.'
> 'Then why did you fire?'
> 'Just to bloody well amuse myself.'

To Griffith's relief the brigadier just laughed. The gunner was lucky in his brigadier.[59]

Unless an enemy attack was imminent a division would usually deploy with two of its brigades in the line and the third in reserve. Each of the forward brigades would have two battalions in the fire trenches, relieved at regular intervals by the other two battalions, but never on the same night. The intervals, four to eight days, generally depended on the state of the trenches, weather and commander preference. Each forward battalion had two companies in the fire trenches, one in support and one in reserve. The two forward companies had two platoons in the fire trenches and two in the support trench. Sometimes a division would deploy all three of its brigades forward, each with two battalions forward, one in support and one in reserve. This meant that six of the division's 13 battalions (the thirteenth was the divisional pioneer battalion) held the divisional line. Each forward battalion had two companies up and two in support. Each forward company had three platoons in the fire trenches and one in the command trench. In such a deployment the six forward battalions were holding the front "with about thirty-six platoon posts and since a platoon could rarely put more than thirty men on duty, we may conclude that the divisional front was held by 1,000 of its, say, 10,000 infantrymen."[60]

Clearly, no one set of men could always be in the line since right from the time of arrival they were moving toward a state at which their effectiveness would be much reduced. Lieutenant Griffith thought four days in the line enough to initiate a "rapid fall along the slope of vitality into a stupor of weariness; on the path, some sharp crest of fear, but the end was overwhelming fatigue."[61]

Consequently, units and formations had to be relieved. The system of relief was fairly complicated. For one thing, the cycle was not always the same. Most units rotated through fire trenches, support line and reserve line, but others had a four-stage cycle: fire trenches, immediate support, main support and reserve. Second, a unit or formation could be in two stages simultaneously:

59 LAC, MG 30E60 (Matthews Papers), Volume 3, Folder 12, October 1915; Griffith, *Up to Mametz*, p. 125.
60 The two-brigade deployment is described in Falls, *36th (Ulster) Division*, p. 31; John Ellis, *Eye-Deep in Hell: The Western Front, 1914-1918* (London: Croom Helm, 1975), p. 27.
61 Griffith, *Up to Mametz*, p. 59.

for example, consider a brigade deployed two battalions in the line, one in support a mile back and the fourth resting in a village two or three miles back. This fourth battalion, still quite close to the line, also formed the brigade reserve. Location permitted it to get more rest, but it had to be ready to move forward quickly. Its location, still within artillery range, meant casualties had to be expected. On the other hand, if enemy artillery was inactive, and the enemy could not observe the area, then more comfort and rest was possible. One Subaltern recorded how after a time in the line his brigade marched back 20 miles to rest. While he does not say so, the distance meant that the brigade may well have been in reserve to higher formation.[62] What makes terms such as in trenches, in support and in reserve more meaningful is tying their use to size and function. A company in support, for example, was well forward. A battalion in support occupied the reserve line or behind it.

The length of time spent in any one set of trenches depended on the level of command involved and upon higher command decision. 8th Canadian Battalion's "Ten Commandments" reminded all ranks to "Honour thy Army Staff, that thy days may be long in the Corps Reserve, to which they may possibly send thee." One British officer looked back with great fondness to the time his division (the 34th) had been "grazing in the pastures of G.H.Q. Reserve." Another British officer (29th Division) noted in his diary in November 1916 that the "Staff fixed the number of days to be spent in the front at three, for support three and seven in reserve."[63]

In February 1915 the Guards Brigade, then with 1st British Division (the Guards Division did not form until August) had experimented with a system of 48 hours relief: "48 hours in trenches and 48 hours rest in billets."[64] This system "enabled [battalions] to do more in a given time than battalions who went in four days at a stretch, as a man could carry two days' rations on him without drawing on the fatigue parties, and the knowledge that he would be relieved at the end of the time kept his edge." However, this system presented serious disadvantages. For one thing, it seriously disrupted training and rest and for another it hindered the accumulation of knowledge about the trenches and the enemy, two days being inadequate for gaining much insight into enemy habits. The 1st Gloucestershire Regiment, also in 1st British Division, also did 48 hours in and 48 out, but with a variation: "The system of early morning reliefs was purely regimental and was discontinued … it had certain good points but was infinitely more fatiguing than the ordinary routine: relief soon after dark, or, if possible, in the afternoon in daylight." The 48 and 48 also posed some risk in that during each relief a little knowledge might not get passed on, or might fail to be absorbed by the relieving unit.[65] Nevertheless, the Guards retained their system during the winter of 1916/17, but during the next winter each battalion did, in turn, four days in the line, four in support and four in reserve.[66]

Other battalion accounts relate different systems adopted by choice or necessity. The Sixth South Staffordshire Regiment, for example, because of depleted strength during the spring of

62 Edmonds [Carrington], *A Subaltern's War,* pp. 25-26.
63 LAC, MG30E60 (Matthews Papers), Volume 3, Folder 12; Maude, *47th (London) Division,* p. 50; Hitchcock, *"Stand To,"* p. 207. G.H.Q. was Headquarters of the BEF.
64 Ponsonby, *The Grenadier Guards,* Volume I, p. 212.
65 Kipling, *The Irish Guards in the Great War: The First Battalion,* p. 105; Pagan, *Infantry,* pp. 6-7.
66 Headlam, *Guards Division,* Volume I, p.192; Volume II, p.30; Carroll Carstairs, *A Generation Missing* (London: William Heinemann Ltd., 1930; reprint ed., Stevenage, Herts: The Strong Oak Press Ltd., 1989), p. 163.

1916 averaged 15 days in trenches followed by five in reserve. In the autumn of 1916 after the Somme the 35th British Division, the famous Bantam Division, while in the Arras sector for almost three months, had all three brigades in the line. Brigadier-General A.H. Marindin, GOC 105th Brigade, deployed three battalions in the line, units rotating by what the division's historian called the "rolling stone" method whereby each battalion had a long period in and a short period out of the line. The fourth battalion relieved each in turn. This method apparently ensured that "battalions took great interest in the improvement of the trenches."[67] In one Canadian unit, 4CMR, a Subaltern described his unit's cycle thus:

> Two companies in the front line and they would be in six days. Then they would be moved back six days to the immediate support trench. Then the whole battalion would move back six days into the main support trench. That meant 18 days in this world of stealth, and then six days out at the waggon lines in the village which was your base. Six days to refit and do a little drilling and try to be soldiers again.[68]

That same winter (1916/17) 6th Royal West Kent Regiment existed on a weekly basis: a week in the line, a week in reserve and a week in billets, all in all "a comfortable way of getting used to the Western Front. Instead of coming up against [it] with a bump, one slid into it." Brigade commanders were not always so amenable. Victor Odlum, GOC 11th Canadian Brigade from June 1916 onward, rotated not on a battalion basis, but by companies, the result being battalions were half in and half out of the line all the time. The negative impact on training for the assault on Vimy Ridge is obvious; quite naturally battalion commanders tended to focus on the half of their battalion that was in the line. Another, and a more telling reason as to why 4th Division did not do as well as the other Canadian divisions at Vimy was the disastrous raid on 1 March involving 1,700 men, half from 11th Brigade. It cost nearly 700 casualties, including many officers, among them two of Odlum's battalion commanders, both killed in action. The course and results of this Canadian raid, which shook 4th Division, is examined in detail in Chapter 12.[69]

Despite the additional work and planning involved for everyone relief was essential to morale and efficiency. Many units carefully noted where they had been and for how long, not just to satisfy curiosity, but also to see how they had fared in distribution of the load. The 31st Canadian Battalion, for example, reported spending its first 258 days in France like this: 124 in the line, 62 in brigade reserve, 62 in division reserve and 10 in corps reserve. During this time it suffered 630 casualties. The 7th Canadian Battalion in the last issue of its trench journal, *The Listening Post,* included a chart depicting where it had spent all of its days from 15 February 1915 to 8 January 1919. About 70 percent were sent in trenches. Major Paul Villiers, BM 3rd Canadian

67 Committee of Officers, *Sixth South Staffordshire Regiment,* pp. 124, 66. A year earlier the unit being at near full strength the routine had been six days in trenches, six in support, six in trenches and then six at rest. Lieutenant-Colonel H.M. Davson, *The History of the 35th Division in the Great War* (London: Sifton Praed & Co. Ltd., 1926), pp. 3, 58. Bantams were men not less than 60 inches tall and not more than 63 inches.

68 LAC, RG 41, CBC Interviews, Lieutenant Gregory Clark, 4 CMR.

69 Alan Thomas, *A Life Apart* (London: Victor Gollancz Ltd., 1968), p. 61; Jack Sheldon, *The German Army on Vimy Ridge 1914-1917* (Barnsley: Pen & Sword, 2008), pp. x-xi, 238-39.

Brigade, compiled a similar list showing where the battalions of the brigade spent (on average) the year 27 October 1916-26 October 1917: 85 days in trenches, 128 in support and 152 days in division or corps reserve. Hugh Urquhart, who had been a CO of the 16th Canadian Battalion and was its postwar historian, compiled a meticulous record showing where the battalion had spent every one of its days from 17 February 1915 to 11 November 1918, in all 1,363 days: 347 in trenches, 295 in brigade support or reserve, 598 in division or corps reserve, 104 in Army reserve, and 19 days in the paradise of GHQ Reserve. Charles Carrington, a British Subaltern, recalled that is 1916 he spent 65 days in fire trenches and 36 more in close support, "that is, 101 days which may be described as under fire." In addition, he was 120 days in reserve and 73 days out in rest. The remaining 72 days were spent at schools, in hospital, on leave, at base depot and travelling. During its 16 tours in the trenches his battalion was in action four times in attacks or raids. "This must," he said, "be a typical experience shared by many hundreds of infantrymen who spent a year continuously at the front."[70]

Whatever the system of relief, the subject usually took up a large portion, often as many as six or more pages, in unit and formation standing orders. 76th British Brigade's orders, which were the basis of 11th Canadian Brigade's orders, filled three pages with the procedure to be followed during relief. 19th British Division's orders had only one page on procedures before and during taking over trenches, but included a two-page appendix detailing the information that had to be handed over at relief (see below). By February 1918 (the date of the second edition of the orders) reliefs were very "old hat." This is not to suggest any general slippage in execution. For one thing, an Operation Order had to be written for every relief and a careless or poorly written one would surely have been remarked upon by the BM. That could spell trouble for a battalion.[71]

Consequently, the seemingly simple and, in time, routine business of relief received careful attention since it almost always took place at night, which increased the chances of something going awry, especially when it involved green troops. Lieutenant-Colonel W.D. Croft, 9th (Scottish) Division, described relieving another division as a "loathsome business." Stanley Spencer, KRRC, expressing a little less distaste, simply described relief as "tiring and tedious … made worse in winter by the pitch darkness of the nights."[72] Inadequate planning, a forgotten detail, flaws in procedure or in an Operation Order, could cause delays that led to congested trenches and profitable targets for enemy fire. Navigation could also be a problem. 10th Canadian Brigade's War Diary for 26 October 1916 reported: "relieved by 12th Brigade. Much delay … due to a company of 78th Battalion getting lost. Much trouble has been caused by the constant misleading of parties in every direction. No landmarks and nights very dark."[73] Undue bustle and noise could alert the enemy that something was up and down would come fire, or

70 Singer, *31st Battalion,* p. 116; *The Listening Post* 33 (March 1919); LAC, MG 30E236 (Villiers Papers), Volume 4, Folder 7, Volume 38 of Diary, 18 November 1917; Urquhart, *16th Battalion,* p. 416; Edmonds [Carrington], *A Subaltern's War,* pp. 120-21. Carrington served with the Royal Warwickshire Regiment.

71 LAC, MG 30E54 (Phelan Papers), Folder 3, 'Standing Orders for Trenches', November 1915; TNA: WO 95/2056: 19th British Division General Staff War Diary, February 1918, 'Standing Orders for Trenches (Second Edition)'.

72 Lieut.-Colonel W.D. Croft, *Three Years With the Ninth (Scottish) Division* (London: John Murray, 1919), p. 27; Tony Spencer, ed., *Stanley Spencer's Great War Diary: 1915-1918* (Barnsley: Pen & Sword, 2008), p. 118.

73 LAC, War Diary, 10th Canadian Brigade, October 1916.

even a raid if the enemy could quickly crank up a sortie. Sometimes prisoners (either side) would reveal an imminent relief of their unit, but such information had to be timely to be useful. Short notice meant that raids could not always be mounted, but in lieu trench mortars, artillery and machine-guns could be asked to fire on enemy CTs and roads leading forward from the reserve area. The result of such speculative fire was seldom known.

A raid during a relief could prove as dangerous as an attack delivered astride a unit or formation boundary; no better time to raid during the in-and-out bustle of a relief where responsibility could be confused in the minds of some, where the newcomers were unfamiliar with the trenches and where the departing troops were distracted by the anticipation of heading for a rest, hot meals and better shelter from the elements. Lieutenant James Pedley, 4th Canadian Battalion, called relief the "most vulnerable moment in trench warfare" and a time of "particular nervousness." Major R.T. Rees, Loyal North Lancashire Regiment, recalled his sinking heart when at the very time his battalion was being relieved, with men of both units still in the trenches, the enemy raided. To his great relief it quickly fizzled out. In another instance, 3rd Battalion Grenadier Guards, while relieving a French unit had to beat off 40-50 raiders. The only loss was one French machine-gun. The battalion historian thought "the arrival of a fresh battalion in the line was likely to be observed … and therefore a raid was highly probable." This may also have been the case in May 1916 when a brigade relief in 34th British Division started at 0800. At 1230 an intense enemy bombardment began, brigade getting a heavy dose that interfered with communications. Things got "pretty warm." In the middle of this, the right forward battalion reported enemy in its trenches and brigade ordered reinforcements forward, but the battalion then advised that the enemy had been rejected, leaving behind one prisoner. The division commander thought the battalion being relieved had done very well.[74]

The enemy during a relief was just as vulnerable. 7th East Yorkshires (17th British Division), raiding on the Arras front on 28/29 July, made what the divisional historian called the division's most successful raid during a three-month period. The 16 prisoners taken revealed that "a relief was actually in progress [which] accounts for the extraordinary number of enemy in the trenches and the stubborn fight."[75]

A battalion of the Cameronians during a relief in early 1918 experienced the impact of neglect of procedure during a relief. When the outgoing battalion (not identified) left its listening posts unmanned in came enemy raiders who overran part of C Company of the Cameronians, killed three men, wounded three others and then withdrew with 13 prisoners. "The raid," according to the Cameronian account, "was a complete surprise." Enemy success stemmed from inattention to standing orders, or perhaps inadequate orders that lacked some crucial direction such as "No man of the relieved unit must quit his post until his relief arrives, and then only on order of an officer." Not least of the questions that begged answers were these: Did the outgoing unit brief the Cameronians on the number and location of the listening posts? Did the Cameronians ask?

74 Pedley, *Only This,* p. 36; Major R.T. Rees, *A Schoolmaster at War* (London: Haycock Press, 1936), p. 77; Ponsonby, *Grenadier Guards,* Volume II, p. 155; Volume III, p. 2; Lieut.-Colonel J. Shakespear, *The Thirty-Fourth Division 1915-1919* (London: H.F. & G. Witherby, 1921), p. 26.

75 Hilliard A. Atteridge, *A History of the 17th (Northern) Division* (Uckfield, East Sussex: Naval and Military Press, n.d.), p. 243; TNA, WO 95/2003: 50th Brigade War Diary, British 17th Division, report of Lieutenant-Colonel G. East King, CO 7th East Yorkshires, July 1917.

What did the outgoing battalion's orders say regarding vacating outposts? Were there no control points where withdrawing men could be checked through by an officer?[76]

Sometimes, if relief occurred in a quiet sector, the prevailing sentiment of the incoming unit was more irritation than anxiety:

> 5 p.m. Arrival in trenches. Temper normal. Half an hour spent trying to appear interested while the outgoing officer explains the enormous amount of work he has done during his time here.
>
> 5:30 p.m. Outgoing officer departs. Half an hour spent commenting with your own officers on the utter and complete absence of any sign of work whatever having been done since you were there last.[77]

And yet more irritation! One Subaltern complained that other battalions always left an untidy mess and, worse, "You work hard repairing the trenches: the relieving regiment you find on your return has done damn all."[78] One CO called a New Army battalion in September 1916 the worst he had ever relieved: "their guides were late; the wire, trenches and men's dugouts were in a shocking state while the officers' dugouts were pretty good – a bad sign. They handed over none of the usual maps, defence orders, or store inventories, and gave us no help of any kind."[79]

Speaking of wire, one company commander, on relieving a company of a battalion new to the front, discovered just what lack of experience and training meant. The outgoing company commander told him that a lot of work had been put into strengthening the wire and invited him to look at it through his periscope: "So we did, and saw the new wire clearly, but in front of the German trench! Our friends … had merely … rolled the wire out without fastening it down. Fritz had then stolen the loose concertina that night and staked it down where he wanted it."[80]

What kept reliefs running smoothly was efficient recce, early warning notice of reliefs, writing and issuing solid orders and careful movement of troops in and out of the line. For a company of an outgoing battalion relief looked like this:

> On the day of a relief, the afternoon was spent … clearing away all rubbish … Kit bags were packed and made ready to be strapped on … Section commanders made out lists of the trench stores such as bombs, ammunition, periscopes, fixed rifles and sandbags. Platoon Commanders carried out thorough inspections of their platoon frontages. The Company

76 TNA: WO 95/2056: British 19th Division General Staff War Diary, February 1918, 'Standing Orders for Trenches (Second Edition)'; Colonel H.H. Story, *History of the Cameronians (Scottish Rifles) 1910-1933* (Aylesbury: Hazell Watson & Viney Ltd., 1961), p. 196.

77 Feilding, *War Letters to a Wife*, p. 15, 22 May 1915. It would be late 1918 before the 24-hour system of reckoning time came into effect (LAC, 2nd Brigade War Diary, October 1918). Victor Wheeler, *The 50th Battalion in No Man's Land* (Calgary: Alberta Historical Resources Foundation, 1980), pp. 352-53, recalled that orders to switch to the 'Continental System of Time' reached the unit on 28 September. "It was rather awkward," he wrote, "for us signallers to get used to, but the Continental System would leave no margin for error."

78 Adams, *Nothing of Importance*, p. 29.

79 Terraine (ed.), *General Jack's Diary*, p. 169.

80 Simpson, *Hot Blood and Cold Steel*, p. 13.

> Commander prepared a report on the company sector, describing the condition of the wire, trenches, saps, dugouts, 'No Man's Land,' enemy activity and work to be done. About an hour before dark, the last details of sentries mounted the firesteps with packs on, ready to move off when relieved. The advance parties, of one officer and one NCO per platoon of the relieving unit, arrived to check and sign for stores, a process which took some time.[81]

For the unit going in the process started with a Warning Order from brigade saying what unit it would relieve and when. The CO then warned his company commanders, Quartermaster, Transport Officer and Medical Officer of the impending move and directed his Adjutant to prepare an Operation Order. Company commanders then paraded their company either:

> at dusk, or at a time decided by the CO, in heavy marching order. A parade state accounting for every man was turned in at this time. This is termed a 'marching out state.' A record is thus established of just who went into the line. A full day's ration was carried by each man; his ammunition had to be inspected, and the full amount checked. Each rifle was inspected, each gas helmet examined. Foot examination carried out, and water bottles filled. Platoons fell in a full half-hour before the time stated in the battalion orders, and were checked on all these points by their platoon officers. At the proper hour all companies were turned over after being pronounced 'correct' by company commanders. Without a sound the companies moved off at intervals … timed to reach the trenches they were to occupy at a fixed hour.

While this account does not say so directly, although it mentions a "marching out state," commanders warned all ranks that they were going into the line, a necessary caution because desertion was not uncommon at such times. For a charge of desertion to stick absence had to be proven, as did the fact that the man had been warned for the relief.[82]

Well before these activities a recce party of company Seconds-in-Command (2ICs) and several NCOs per company would have departed to reconnoitre the new trenches and to take over trench stores from the outgoing unit. Where a relief was thought to be especially difficult the company commanders might go forward instead, leaving the 2ICs to bring the companies forward. In either case, a thorough and careful recce was crucial for the incoming unit since a little something or other could easily be missed during a relief. Training at the various levels of schools in the BEF provided guidance for those doing such recce. One lecture entitled "Recce of a Trench Prior to taking Over" urged officers conducting such recce to arrange what had to be looked at in four categories: own trenches, enemy trenches, no man's land and administration.

81 Corrigall, *Twentieth Canadian Battalion*, p. 37.

82 Military Advisory Board, *Canada in the Great World War: An Authentic Account of the Military History of Canada from the Earliest Days to the Close of the War of the Nations.* Volume IV: *The Turn of the Tide* (Toronto: United Publishers of Canada Limited, 1920), pp. 174-75; *SS 412b Circular Memorandum on Courts-Martial for Use on Active Service* (GHQ, August 1918), pp. 13-14; Bruce Cane, *It Made You Think of Home: The Haunting Journal of Deward Barnes, Canadian Expeditionary Force: 1916-1919* (Toronto: The Dundurn Group, 2004), pp. 154-55. Private Harold Lodge, who paraded with the 19th Battalion after it was warned to relieve the 78th Battalion near Passchendaele, and then deserted was captured, convicted and shot on 13 March 1918. (LAC, RG 24, Volume 2358, HQ-1822, Volume 2, 'Some Notes Regarding the Award and Confirmation of Sentences of Death on Canadian Soldiers in the Great War, 1915-1918').

Necessities included a general description with references to maps noting any significant tactical points such as any portions of the trenches subject to enfilade fire, or particularly exposed to fire, plus any other dangerous points, names of trenches, details of CTs, location and route to battalion HQ, positions of flanking troops, saps, listening posts, sniper posts, wire and other obstacles, dugouts, trench mortar positions, machine-gun emplacements, traverses and firing steps in main trenches, type of trench revetting, trench drainage, method of patrolling and routes, arrangements for co-operation with artillery, work in progress, means of sounding the alarm and reactions to gas attack. A description of no man's land was also required, as were the distances to well-defined objects and enemy positions, features of tactical importance and gaps in the wire. Units that maintained a daily log book would also hand this over plus any plans for raids and other offensive action contemplated. Administration was equally important: location of water, ammunition dumps and trench stores, medical facilities, information as to supplies and transport, how cooking was done, how rubbish was disposed of, location of latrines and how wounded were evacuated.[83] Trench stores always posed difficulties. The newcomer had to have his wits about him since departing units routinely hid deficiencies. If he was wise he checked paperwork against sight of actual stores present. The ancient question "Who ever saw a Company Quartermaster Sergeant with a shortage?" had to be firmly in mind. Given all that had to be done, every member of the recce party knew that there was not a moment to lose! Other early arrivers were often the snipers who wanted direct contact with the snipers of the departing battalion [84]

The outgoing battalion was responsible to provide guides, but there were no guarantees that they would appear, or that they would get the newcomers to where they had to be. Major R.T. Rees divided guides into two classes: "those who don't know the way but say they do, and those who don't know the way and admit that they don't." Rowland Feilding, who took command of the 6th Connaught Rangers on 7 September 1916, described one experience with guides as the battalion moved into the line the next night: "We were met by a guide [who] soon began to show signs of uncertainty. I asked him if he had lost his bearings – a not uncommon thing – he admitted that he had." In the end, though, the 6th got to its destination.[85]

An officer of 2nd West Yorkshires reporting on guides during his battalion's move into the line on the Somme in November 1916, described the first leg of the move to a rendezvous where the unit would be met by guides to take it forward to where the companies would be met and then taken on to the trenches by guides from the outgoing companies. As it turned out, the guides were two hours late. These guides and the companies then moved off through a sea of mud: "Picture it at night. Burdened with heavy equipment, harassed by shell-fire, sliding and slithering in and out of shell-holes and old trenches … following blindly a guide who had only the haziest notion of his whereabouts." Still, battalion HQ was eventually reached and the

83 TNA: WO 95/2056: 19th British Division General Staff War Diary, February 1918, 'Standing Orders for Trenches (Second Edition)', Appendix I. The lecture notes were in ink on the inside cover of this present soldier-historian's copy of Needham's *The Solution to Tactical Problems* (see Bibliography). These notes by an unknown student were made at the School of Infantry, Calgary, Alberta, sometime in 1916.

84 Kevin Shannon, *The Lion and the Rose: The 4th Battalion of the King's Own Royal Lancaster Regiment 1914-1919* (Croydon: Fonthill, 2015), p. 62.

85 Rees, *A Schoolmaster at War*, p. 75; Feilding, *War Letters to a Wife*, p. 113.

outgoing company guides, who were waiting, took the relieving companies forward along lines of white tape that marked the way. At about 2100 the newcomers reached the support trench and an hour later the fire trenches: "the relief had taken nearly seven hours."[86]

As each company of newcomers reached the trenches the Officer Commanding (OC) greeted his counterpart at company HQ where the two officers, and perhaps the 2ICs who had led the recce, would discuss pertinent matters. Platoon commanders were similarly engaged with their opposite numbers. As each incoming section reached its position, sentries took their place on the firestep beside the ones being relieved, who would then pass on any information.[87] Each outgoing platoon commander then gathered his sections and began the march out. On passing company HQ he reported his platoon relieved. Once all four platoons had so reported the company commander advised battalion HQ that his company was relieved. As soon as all companies had reported the incoming CO signed for the trenches. His was now the responsibility. Relief complete.[88]

One of the first things the CO of the outgoing battalion might do after the relief was gather his officers and NCOs to review what had gone right during the tour in the trenches and what had gone wrong and why and what might have been done better. The lessons were incorporated into training for the period out of the line. Companies, meanwhile, were cleaning up, going for baths and getting some new items of uniform. As for the newly arrived battalion, one of the first things the CO did was tour his area of responsibility, thereby making a start in achieving a sense of confidence about the layout and the situation. Company and platoon commanders were similarly occupied for familiarity could mean the difference between holding and losing a trench or becoming an easy mark for enemy raiders. Familiarity also enabled officers to quickly and confidently answer questions posed by senior visitors who otherwise would look askance at those who seemed ill at ease or hesitant about their trenches.[89]

Such tours were never easy or fast in trenches in poor condition or sodden in mud. One Subaltern in early 1917 took over three hours to visit outposts along a 300 yard stretch of trench. A CO of a Highland battalion told his diary about the five hours it took him to visit his companies daily, the trenches in a terrible state of mud caused by incessant rain. Such visits posed a

86 Lt.-Colonel J.H. Boraston and Captain E.O. Bax, *The Eighth Division 1914-1918* (Uckfield, East Sussex: Naval and Military Press, n.d.), pp. 91-94.

87 Corrigall, *Twentieth Canadian Battalion,* p. 37.

88 LAC, RG9IIIC1, Volume 3839, Folder 36, File 1; Edmonds, *Haig's Command to the 1st July: Battle of the Somme,* p. 186; Colonel G.W.L. Nicholson, *Official History of the Canadian Army in the First World War: Canadian Expeditionary Force, 1914-1919* (Ottawa: Queen's Printer, 1962), p. 140. These references describe a classic relief, one that in the words of Arthur Currie "went wonderfully well [despite] many and varied complications." This relief occurred in April 1916 when the Canadian Corps relieved V Corps in the St. Eloi-Hooge sector, the first ever relief of one corps by another. The staff work to complete it (relief and movement orders, road allocation programmes and timetables for changes of command during the relief) make up a solid one-inch thick file. Before this relief the normal routine was to relieve at division and lower, but the arrival of the Canadian Corps, which was also a National Army whose government wanted it put into and taken out of the line as a corps, meant conducting corps reliefs in the BEF.

89 *Notes for Commanding Officers* (Aldershot: Gale and Polden, 1917), 'Some of the Things That Please an Infantry Brigadier by a Brigadier'. Number 31 stated the case: "A CO who knows his line end to end, not only as regards the actual trenches, but is also thoroughly acquainted with the actual ground in front of his sector."

dilemma for a CO. Obviously he wanted to see the positions and know the company situations for himself and keep close contact with his companies, but protracted absences from his HQ and communications worried him. This dilemma was even worse at brigade level: "How long it took the brigadier to come up … can only be conjectured, but the very fact that he would be absent from his headquarters for many hours should be some answer to those who demand to know why general officers did not put in more frequent appearances in the front line."[90]

No division commander wanted to turn over trenches in poor condition since "Bad trenches are the work of a division that cannot be relied upon … There is, perhaps, nothing more demoralizing … than taking over badly-constructed and badly-kept trenches."[91] Handover of good trenches demonstrated that close attention had been paid to three elements: routine and discipline, sanitation and good security. The last was vital since any penetration of one's trenches drew questions and possibly worse. Consequently, brigade and division commanders demanded good security. If the last was found wanting the CO responsible could expect a bad time. The next chapter describes how one highly competent and demanding brigade commander viewed his trenches and, in particular, how he viewed trench security.

90 Edwin Campion Vaughan, *Some Desperate Glory* (London: Papermac, 1985), pp. 41-42; Terraine (ed.), *General Jack's Diary*, p. 128; Sidney Rogerson, *Twelve Days* (London: Arthur Barker Ltd., 1933), p. 58.

91 Bewsher, *Fifty First Division*, pp. 265-66.

2

"Book of Wisdom"

> Knowledge comes, but wisdom lingers.
> Alfred, Lord Tennyson

Trench Standing Orders, as the last chapter defined them, offered guidance on most, if not all, matters pertaining to life in the trenches. Examples of such orders show that when on the defence the primary concern of unit and formation commanders, not surprisingly, was security of their lines against enemy attack and penetration.

In executing their responsibilities formation commanders were not merely cognizant of, but jealous of their personal reputations and that of their command. In the Canadian Corps this pride and the competitive spirit got out of hand for a time, so much so that GHQ became aware of mutually insulting remarks that had passed between 1st and 2nd Canadian Divisions. In a letter to the King in July 1916 Sir Douglas Haig described Lieutenant-General Julian Byng's greatest contribution to the Corps as his elimination of most of the "jealousy and friction" that existed between Canadian divisions in 1915 and for the first half of 1916. When it became clear that 1st Division was the perpetrator of the two most egregious cases of insult, Arthur Currie, then commanding 1st Division, in the light of "indisputable evidence" apologized for the conduct of his division and warned participants that any further incidents would be severely punished.[1]

Brigades and brigadiers were just as competitive, perhaps more so. The 1st Brigade of the 1st Division of the Canadian Corps had always exhibited qualities in and out of the line that made it "something worthy of notice," nor was it shy about letting others know that. One senior officer remarked that it could "be readily understood why the battalions of the brigade [and the brigade itself] possessed no particular genius for self-abasement."[2]

From time to time, and in some brigades frequently, even incessantly, brigadiers issued guidance in the form of memoranda supplementing or even supplanting Trench Standing Orders, this being inevitable as units and formations integrated new technology, weapons and

1 Jeffrey Williams, *Byng of Vimy: General and Governor General* (London: Leo Cooper, 1983), p. 130; LAC, RG9IIIC3, Volume 4024, Folder 4, File 9, 16 July 1916; Corrigall, *Twentieth Canadian Battalion*, p. 66; Radley, *Get Tough, Stay Tough*, p. 96.

2 Colonel W.W. Murray, *The History of the 2nd Canadian Infantry Battalion (East Ontario Regiment) Canadian Expeditionary Force* (Ottawa: Mortimer Ltd., 1947), p. 185.

equipment. One Canadian brigadier, especially industrious in letting his battalion commanders know how he wanted things done, had by war's end filled four thick volumes of guidance. These he entitled the "Book of Wisdom," appropriately so, for as a proverb says, "Experience is the father of wisdom."[3] It is true that every brigadier, if for no other reason than survival, worked hard at educating and guiding subordinates, but the sheer volume, clarity and perspicacity of the "Book of Wisdom", the contents of which were carefully kept together in special folders as a package and turned over in that state to government archives after the war, make it a treasure and one that is possibly unique. The brigadier (and compiler) was William Antrobus Griesbach, CB, CMG, DSO and Bar, GOC 1st Brigade as of February 1917. While his "Book of Wisdom" is the primary concern of this chapter the British experience is not ignored.

Much of the wisdom Griesbach offers relates to raids, a major concern in maintaining security of brigade trenches. As an earlier chapter pointed out, one learned a great deal about how to raid from being raided. As the Germans raided they also learned much about how to defeat raids. Of course, not every raid triumphed, nor did the defence always prevail. One learns much from imperfection and from failure. Both cried out for justification, which at the time often meant unpleasant inquiry and, for some, removal from command. This chapter shows both sides of the coin, so to speak, useful knowledge in keeping with the complex nature of the raiding that became a significant feature of trench warfare for varying periods of the war. Captain Lionel Crouch, 1st Oxford and Buckinghamshire Light Infantry, exhibiting the early mutual respect of fighting men for each other, believed initially that the Boche "fought fairly … They were a good crowd." As the war dragged on opinions became less charitable.[4]

Griesbach, the son of a member of the North West Mounted Police, was born in 1878 in what is now southern Saskatchewan. Following service as a Trooper with 2 CMR in the South African War, he became a successful lawyer and politician, being elected as an Alderman in Edmonton, Alberta and then at 28 becoming Edmonton's youngest mayor ever. In 1914 he took a squadron of the 19th Alberta Dragoons overseas, but returned to Canada before the first Christmas of the war to take command of the 49th Infantry Battalion. His conduct as a CO in June 1916 during the German attack at Mount Sorrel where 3nd Division's GOC, Major-General M.S. Mercer, was killed and a brigade commander was captured, so impressed Mercer's replacement, Louis Lipsett, and the GOC 7th Brigade, Archibald Macdonell, that both recommended Griesbach for promotion and command of a brigade. This came to pass in February 1917 when he went to 1st Brigade. There he would shine thanks to his personality and consistency: a stickler for detail and a strict, but fair disciplinarian, he was also a superb trainer and an officer respected by all ranks despite his rather forbidding demeanour.[5] His "Book of

3 LAC, MG 30E15 (Griesbach Papers), Volume 3, Files 16A and 16B, 'Book of Wisdom'.

4 *Duty and Service: Letters From the Front From Lionel William Crouch* (London: Printed for Private Circulation, 1917), p. 95. The Germans called such mutual respect between fighting soldiers *Frontkameradenschaft*.

5 Griesbach was rather a prominent figure in Radley, *We Lead, Others Follow*. It is fortunate that we have the 'Book of Wisdom' since Griesbach's *I Remember* (Toronto: The Ryerson Press, 1946), is thin and rather disappointing. Griesbach died in 1945. There is much on him as CO 49th Battalion in G.R. Stevens, *A City Goes to War* (Brampton: Charters Publishing Company, 1964). While commanding 1st Brigade Griesbach ran as a Conservative-Unionist in the 1917 General Election and was elected, but did not take his seat until after the war. He was appointed to the Senate in 1921.

Wisdom" reveals the professionalism of a very capable officer and a clear view of his firm leadership and solid training concepts.

When it came to security the "Book of Wisdom" aimed to make it as difficult as possible for the enemy to enter Canadian trenches. Brigade commanders knew that penetration of brigade lines would surely raise the eyebrows of higher commanders, especially if the enemy made off with prisoners. Such a black mark could haunt. A brigade or battalion surprised by an enemy raid, or ill-prepared to counter one, or just plain unlucky, could expect frowning displeasure of division and perhaps Corps or, God forbid, even Army. The higher the level of unhappiness the greater the probability of embarrassing inquiry or worse. Such might just result in departure from one's command. The fact that perfect security does not exist could all too quickly be forgotten.

Four days after taking command of 1st Brigade in February 1917 Griesbach saw and heard about the gloom that descended upon an offending brigade, in this case George Tuxford's 3rd Brigade. The BM of that brigade, Major Paul Villiers, has left us a good account of what had transpired. For 10 days starting on 14 February 3rd Brigade endured periodic heavy artillery bombardment. Then at 0530 on the 25th raiders charged in, took two prisoners from 14th Battalion and one from 15th Battalion and withdrew, untouched and unhindered as far as was known. Tuxford quickly issued orders for a retaliatory raid, but it would be 2 March before the actual raid, which netted 10 prisoners, killed 29 more (body count) and an unknown number blown up in dug-outs. As this raid brings out certain lessons highly relevant to the context of Chapter 12 it is discussed there.

What is significant here is the decision by Arthur Currie, then commanding 1st Division, to personally investigate the circumstances of the enemy raid. This would certainly have caught the attention of Tuxford and the other brigadiers, Griesbach and Lipsett. The fact that the raid had been expected, the warning sounded by repeated enemy artillery concentrations on the raid area, lessened the sting for Tuxford somewhat. It helped, too, that he had prior to the raid ordered sentry posts doubled and directed that duty officers visit all posts frequently to ensure the occupants knew what action to take in the event the enemy raid actually occurred. Overall, 3rd Brigade had reacted swiftly and well. Nevertheless, the enemy had taken prisoners, such "body snatching" being, as Currie realized, virtually impossible to prevent, especially given the wider than usual company frontages at the time.[6]

Obviously, a breach of trench security worried all concerned. Security, which then and now is a principle of war, aimed at protecting and retaining "vulnerable points or areas." Failure to do so meant loss or impairment of "freedom of action and flexibility." Experience convinced the author of these thoughts that as often as not the best way to attain good security was not defence, but attack "provided conditions are favourable." As for surprise, another long-standing principle of war, he related it to flexibility, stressing that the only defence against surprise is readiness at all times for the unexpected. Such conclusions are equally valid when it comes to raids.[7]

6 LAC, MG 30E236 (Villiers Papers), Volume 4, Folder 7, Volume 3, Diary, 13-25 February 1917; RG9IIIC3, Volume 3858, Folder 84, File 16, Currie to Canadian Corps 27 February and 1 March; Kim Beattie, *48th Highlanders of Canada 1891-1928* (Toronto: 48th Highlanders of Canada, 1932), p. 204; Fetherstonhaugh, *14th Battalion*, p. 135; LAC, 3rd Brigade War Diary, February 1917, Appendices, 'Operation Order 130' and 'Report on Raid'.

7 Major-General W.H.S. Macklin, *An Introduction to the Study of the Principles of War* (Ottawa: King's Printer, 1952), pp. 6, 13-14, 16-17. In 1932 *Field Service Regulations* listed the principles of war as

Despite Tuxford's explanation, and the congratulations from Corps on his brigade's reaction, Currie believed that greater effort had to be made to ensure being prepared for raids and that firmer control had to be demonstrated when raids did come in. During the remainder of the first half of 1916 enemy raids did not do as well. Of the raids on 24 and 26 April and 5-7 May (two raids) only one penetrated Canadian lines and then for less than an hour. Some casualties were suffered, of course. Louis Lipsett thought the toll might have been less if the defence had been more elastic with fewer men at the parapet and had more reliance been placed on concealed wire, enfilade machine-gun fire and ready counter-attack parties. However, 1st Division received congratulations for its reaction from Corps which also advised how "extremely pleased" GOC Second Army was with 1st Division's good work.[8]

Sometimes sound explanations could not be provided. In such cases the CO paid the price. A case in point was Lieutenant-Colonel G.A. Le Cain, CO 25th Canadian Battalion (2nd Division) from its formation in May 1915 until 16 October. Before moving to France in September the battalion had trained in the Folkestone area. During its stay there the divisional Provost Marshal described the 25th as a unit of "very unsavoury reputation" and one whose discipline stood at "very low ebb." In one instance the battalion featured in a riot in Folkestone that lasted for hours and required two cavalry regiments to break it up.[9] On arrival in France on 15 September the battalion did a tour in the trenches by companies under supervision and then went into reserve for six days before returning to the trenches, this time as a battalion on its own. Le Cain would have little time to settle in as CO.

About three weeks later (8 October) the enemy raided. Neither the raid nor Le Cain are mentioned in Captain Clement's account. However, Lieutenant R. Lewis is blunt about the event and Le Cain. The enemy raid failed, he wrote, thanks to the battalion's "front line officers" who had the situation well in hand, but "the Colonel was nowhere to be seen." Being a private soldier at the time Lewis did not know all the details, but enough for him to say "If we did not always have competent officers at the head of the battalion we certainly have them in our companies."[10] Others shared this assessment for on going into reserve afterward the then Corps commander, E.H. Alderson, gave the battalion "a pretty severe lecture [but] said he had every confidence in them." 5th Brigade's report on events would surely have incensed Alderson:

maintenance of the objective, offensive action, surprise, concentration, economy of force, security, mobility and co-operation. These are written in black ink on the inside cover of this present military historian's copy of the *Manual of Military Law,* emergency use presumably by a student at the time. Macklin served with the 19th Canadian Battalion during the Great War.

8 LAC, RG9IIIC1, Volume 3859, Folder 85, File 3; Volume 4011, Folder 15, File 11, Lipsett to 1st Division, 9 May 1916, reports of 1st Division, April and May 1916; RG9IIIC1, Volume 3842, Folder 42, File 8, Second Army to Canadian Corps, 2 May; 'Book of Wisdom', Volume I; Topp, *42nd Battalion,* pp. 16-19.

9 LAC, RG9IIID3, Volume 5050, Reels T-10942-10943, War Diary, 2nd Division Assistant Provost Marshal; Brian Douglas Tennyson (ed.), *Merry Hell: The Story of the 25th Battalion (Nova Scotia Regiment): Captain Robert N. Clements, MC* (Toronto: University of Toronto Press, 2013), p. 49. This account makes no mention of Le Cain during and after the riot. This in itself is telling.

10 Lieut. R. Lewis, *Over the Top With the 25th* (Halifax: H.H. Marshall Limited, 1918), pp. 11-12, 17, offers no information about what went on at battalion HQ. Nor does the battalion War Diary which simply describes the enemy raid.

> During the bombardment the 25th Battalion ... did not behave very well. C Company of this battalion was quite out of hand and Battalion communication with its companies was extremely bad and entirely unsatisfactory ... C Company was quite panicky ... men coming from the trenches towards Battalion Headquarters without rifles ... [given] the generally unsatisfactory way in which this Battalion behaved, the GOC has asked for a written explanation and report from the CO.[11]

Le Cain, who left the unit within days, was 53 (born 1862), a fact that might explain some of his short-comings as a CO.[12] Curiously, his replacement had also been born in 1862, but there ended any similarity, Edward Hilliam being well-known as a "thruster." After arriving at the unit on 26 October his first act was firing the battalion 2IC who he believed had been no help to LeCain during his time in command.[13]

Another example of removal from command is briefly described by Lord Moran who served as a Medical Officer with the Royal Welsh Fusiliers. This example shows how imaginative narratives about operations could sometimes be. It features comparison of how a German raid was officially reported, how the press reported it and then an account of what really happened. First Army on 5 January 1917 reported that the enemy "had attempted a raid," but it failed, the enemy leaving several dead behind. *The Times* the following day said the raiders had "succeeded in entering our trenches," but were quickly driven out. The real story was this: "the Boche stayed forty minutes in our trenches extracting fifty-one prisoners ... a corporal and two men stuck to a machine-gun otherwise there was little fight shown, and that subsequently the officer commanding this battalion was removed."[14]

Neither Lord Moran nor Montague, nor Captain F.C. Hitchcock, who provides a separate account, named the CO or the battalion, but we do learn from Hitchcock that the parent

11 LAC, War Diary, 5th Brigade, October 1915.

12 Brigadier-General J.E. Edmonds and Lieut.-Colonel R. Maxwell-Hyslop, *Military Operations France and Belgium 1918: Volume V. 26th September–11th November: The Advance to Victory* (London: Macmillan, 1947). p. 163. In 1917 a new policy directed that no one over the age of 35 would be given command of an infantry battalion.

13 Hilliam was born in England. In 1883 he enlisted in the 17th Lancers. Later he went to Canada where in 1893 he joined the North West Mounted Police. During the South African War he served as a Captain with 2 CMR and with the Cape Mounted Police. In 1914 he became the Adjutant of the 5th Canadian Infantry Battalion. In June 1917 Hilliam became GOC 10th Brigade in 4th Canadian Division, remaining as GOC until November 1917 when he was replaced because his relationship with his subordinates had "steadily deteriorated." (Geoffrey Jackson, '"What Was the Point?": Raiding in the Summer of 1917', *Canadian Military History*, 19 (Autumn 2010), p. 33). What may have precipitated his departure was his decision to centralize recce at brigade level, the result being extreme friction with his battalion commanders and general dissatisfaction within the brigade. See also, Radley, *Get Tough, Stay Tough,* p. 195. Hilliam then took command of 44th Brigade, 15th (Scottish) Division and finally in May 1918 102nd Brigade of 34th British Division. (Major A.F. Becke (comp.), *History of the Great War: Order of Battle of Divisions, Part 3A, New Army Divisions (9-26)* (London: HMSO, 1938), p. 54, and *Part 3B, New Army Divisions (30–41) and 63rd (R.N.) Division* (London: HMSO, 1945), p. 42. During his service with the British Amy he was promoted Major-General.

14 Lord Moran, *Anatomy of Courage*, pp. 72-73. C.E. Montague included this case in *Disenchantment* (London: Chatto and Windus, 1922), pp. 113-14.

brigade was the 17th of 24th British Division.[15] Primary sources identify the battalion as the 8th Buffs, Lieutenant-Colonel Lucas commanding. The battalion War Diary describes the enemy raid thus:

> At about 4.30 a.m. a large enemy raiding party entered our trenches at the junction of … two companies. The parties avoided our sentry groups and got into our support line, bombing dugouts and capturing prisoners … 42 missing. This disaster seems to be entirely due to the fact that the higher authority order us to send our NCOs to all corners of the earth. The result is that we have to live with inexperienced NCOs in charge of important posts and these failed to show the leadership so necessary in case of emergency.

The report of the divisional commander differs:

> The enemy … having dealt with three posts … who failed to give the alarm [moved] along the support line which contains deep dugouts … occupied at the time … Our casualties … killed two, wounded 6, missing 42, 8th Buffs; 2, 3rd Rifle Brigade; 7, 3rd Australian Tunnelling Company … caught in the dugouts through no warning having been received … I wish a Court of Inquiry to be assembled.[16]

Captain Hitchcock thought the "disaster" began when an enemy patrol "snaffled" the occupants of a brigade advanced post without rousing any alarm. This patrol then returned home and briefed the enemy commander who sent out a raiding party on the spot. When it arrived, via a sap, at the British front line it moved down the main trench quietly "mopping up" every sentry it found. Then, having barricaded the area, it emptied dug-outs employing a clever ruse which involved yelling "Gas!" in English down the stairways whereupon out rushed the rudely awakened occupants wearing respirators, the lot "snaffled" and hustled away under escort. So skilful was the whole enterprise that flanking companies heard nothing suspicious. Hitchcock called the circumstances of how the raid was discovered "unique." When divisional staff heard and then appraised the GOC of a claim on German radio of the capture of 50 prisoners the GOC immediately went forward to tour the divisional front. On encountering in 17th Brigade's sector the barricades mentioned above he hastened to the battalion HQ responsible for the sector where he enlightened a very surprised CO who thought all was normal. GOC and CO then toured the front line where they saw above the German parapet a message board reading

> SAY: What about those 50 rations?

Lieutenant-Colonel Lucas, "unwilling to blame the relevant company commander, the real culprit according to many battalion officers," accepted full responsibility and was removed.[17]

15 Hitchcock, *"Stand To"*, p. 230.

16 TNA: WO 95/2207: War Diary, 8th Buffs and WO 95/2190: War Diary 24th Division General Staff.

17 Hitchcock, *"Stand To,"* pp. 230-31; Mark Connelly, *Steady the Buffs!: A Regiment, A Region and the Great War* (Oxford: Oxford University Press, 2006), p. 133; TNA: WO 95/2207: War Diary, 8th Buffs, reported one officer and nine ORs killed, 39 ORs wounded and 28 missing.

How different to see no removal during a similar case seven months earlier. W.D. Croft recalled that early in May 1916 an intensive bombardment of his lines began: trench mortars, field artillery and machine-guns "as hard as the Boche could lay in for a solid hour." Then a brief silence followed by another intense bombardment, this time all on the support line. Then more silence. Presently, along came a company commander to say he had 10 enemy dead in his trenches. "So," said Croft, "so they had come after all, we just knew nothing about it." He does not mention any personnel missing so perhaps that spared him grief, or perhaps such penetration was viewed less seriously at that time, or perhaps this was the case in the division he was with.[18]

A month earlier (11 April) the Germans raided the 1st Royal Irish Rifles (25th Brigade, 8th British Division) near La Boisselle. According to the enemy report on the raid, the 29 prisoners they took cost them only one man slightly wounded. As for the 1st, the enemy report said it:

> made a most favourable impression as regards ... their mode of repelling the assault. But for the effect of gas shell it would not have been possible to clear the section of trench held by one entire company and the flank of the company on the left so thoroughly that not an Englishman remained alive in the trench.[19]

However, Peter Hodgkinson states that the CO, Lieutenant-Colonel R.A.C. Daunt, was "removed from command four days after his battalion was severely criticized for its response ... although he later resumed command." He does not say when Daunt resumed command, nor does he attribute the content of the sentence. According to *SS 462* the German raid commenced at 2000 on 11 April. Presumably the criticism of the battalion came the next day (12 April) and if Daunt was removed four days later then that would make 16 April removal day. But this does not fit with the battalion War Diary. It is not clear from the diary if Major Mayne, who signed the March War Diary as CO, remained in command during the period 1-11 April, or if Daunt returned during those 10 days from the Sick List he had been on since 26 February. Neither Anthony Saunders nor Boraston and Bax mention Daunt during the period. The latter says only "On the 11th April the Royal Irish were raided after a bombardment and lost a number of prisoners."[20]

The battalion War Diary, which offers more information, is unusual in format in that events are reported in a column "Summary of Events and Information" while all personnel matters such as casualties, movement of officers in and out and awards and decorations are recorded in a column "Remarks and References to Appendices." Extra care must be taken in reading this battalion's diary since it is easy to miss cryptic notes in the second column. What appears for the months February – December 1916 in regard to the CO of the battalion is this:

> 26 February. Daunt to Sick List. Major E.C. Mayne, Royal Irish Fusiliers assumes command.
>
> March. Mayne signs March War Diary as CO.

18 Croft, *Three Years With the 9th (Scottish) Division,* pp. 41-42.

19 *SS 462 German Raid on the British Trenches Near La Boisselle, 11th April, 1916* (GHQ, GS, August 1916), p. 15, para 20.

20 Hodgkinson, *British Infantry Battalion Commanders,* p.119; *SS 462;* TNA: WO 95/1730: War Diary, 1st Royal Irish; Saunders, *Raiding on the Western Front,* Chapter 4; Boraston and Bax, *Eighth Division,* p. 62.

11 April. Brief account (one paragraph) of enemy raid.
14 April. Major G.H. Sawyer, 2nd Royal Berkshires takes over command from Mayne. Sawyer signs April War Diary as CO.
15-16 April. No entries; dates are not shown.
17 April-31 December. No mention of Daunt returning.
Succession of several Majors as acting CO.[21]

Just how troublesome a successful enemy raid could be shows in the extensive paper trail surrounding an enemy raid on 23 December 1916 on 17th Royal Welsh Fusiliers of 115th Brigade (38th Division) during which the enemy took eight prisoners. GOC VIII Corps, Lieutenant-General Sir A. Hunter-Weston, signalled in his first report to Second Army on 23 December his displeasure with the battalion's reaction to the raid: "A searching inquiry into all details … has been instituted." Major-General G.J. Cuthbert, GOC 39th Division, had been tasked to conduct the inquiry. Between 23 December and 5 January 1917 reports, queries and directives, 19 in all, went up and down the chain of command. This voluminous correspondence cannot be offered here, but the Corps report to Army and its missives to the division on 5 January (see below) show why the enemy raid succeeded and who was at fault.[22] During the week 24-31 December 115th Brigade produced five reports on the raid: one to 39th Division on the 23rd, two more to that division the next day, one to VIII Corps (direct) as per Corps demand (copy to division) and one more to 39th Division on 31 December. During the same period 39th divisional staff contributed reports to VIII Corps on 23 December (two reports) and one each on 26, 27 and 31 December. Some of the brigade and division reports are heavily annotated with queries and comments initialled by the brigade commander, Brigadier-General C.J. Hickie, and some by GOC 39th Division. Second Army's response to VIII Corps on Christmas Day (especially the last sentence) no doubt sharply focussed Hunter-Weston's mind:

> The Army Commander has read this report and directs me to ask you to re-submit together with reports from the Brigade and Division Commanders with your own remarks and recommendations or steps you propose to take to prevent any chance of a recurrence. He considers that this narrative discloses an unsatisfactory state of affairs and want of system … G.H.Q. has been informed.

VIII Corps' response on 1 January included the required reports and brief remarks:

> The officer temporarily in command of the Royal Welsh Fusiliers displayed lack of judgement … lack of energy in finding out what was going on and carelessness and delay in reporting what had occurred. The Divisional General has spoken severely to this officer.[23]

21 TNA: WO 95/1730: War Diary, 1st Royal Irish.
22 All pertinent documents are in TNA: WO 95/2565: War Diary 39th Division General Staff.
23 TNA: WO 95/2565: War Diary 39th Division General Staff, Second Army G.738, 25 December 1916, to VIII Corps and VIII Corps to Second Army, 1 January 1917.

Steps taken to prevent recurrence included additional wiring, improved infantry-artillery communications and GOC 38th Division (Major-General C.G. Blackader) "at pains to ensure greater promptness and energy in future." This did not end the matter.

Blackader heard considerably more, including verbal comment between Second Army and Hunter-Weston that said: "arrangements by the brigadier were defective." Hunter-Weston conveyed his "dissatisfaction with the lack of system in the Brigade and with the faulty arrangements made and action taken by the Battalion Commander." He continued with what he considered the principal faults of Major Edwards, acting CO of the battalion, and C.J. Hickie, GOC 115th Brigade. First, Major Edwards:

> (1) Should have got into direct communication with the Artillery Commander at once. To allow the Artillery officer with him to send an indefinite message in code showed great lack of judgement.
> (2) Should have previously enquired and thoroughly understood what the Artillery action would be if SOS were sent by telephone or rocket. To determine that he would never send an SOS message because he thought it would cause our Artillery to shell our own trenches was reprehensible.
> (3) Should have known of the … enemy emplacement in the abutment of the Railway Bridge.
> (4) Is much to be blamed for giving as an excuse at the end of his report the statement that his men did not know the trenches and in stating earlier in his report that he was not sure of the direction of his Right and that there were no direction posts. He had been in support within a few hundred yards of the front and it was his business to see that his subordinates knew the trenches they were to occupy and that he himself had a thorough knowledge of his front before they, or he, came into the line. Similarly, direction posts and any other necessities should have been prepared and provided by him before he came up to the line.
> (5) Is also to be blamed that there was such inexcusable delay between the receipt of the message from the front line about 5 a.m. and despatch to Brigade Headquarters at 5-40 a.m. It was then sent by runner instead of being transmitted by Fullerphone.

As for the brigade commander, he was at fault in not having a system that would make the above mistakes impossible and for not supervising arrangements made by "an inexperienced and not very capable officer acting as battalion commander. If the brigadier was unwell he should have sent his BM." In addition, brigade message handling was inadequate. In conclusion, Hunter-Weston thought neither brigade nor battalion commander had displayed sufficient energy to determine what had occurred and then to remedy the faults.[24]

Change was inevitable. The 17th Battalion went into reserve on Boxing Day. The battalion War Diary for December is signed off by "Lieutenant-Colonel H.J. Taylor, Commanding." No mention is made of when Major Edwards left. Hickie left 115th Brigade in March after only six

24 TNA: WO 95/2560: War Diary, 115th Brigade, 5 January 1917. During the Somme it had become clear that the enemy was able to "tap" British field telephone lines. The solution was the Fullerphone which could transmit Morse and voice, the signal being DC as opposed to AC which made it difficult for the Germans to listen in. Chapter 5 considers the problem of interception.

months in command. Cuthbert was transferred to England in August 1917 to command 72nd Division on "Home Service".[25] Blackader remained with 38th Division until May 1918.

Returning now to the "Book of Wisdom" another purpose was to stipulate how Griesbach saw his trenches and how he wanted his battalion commanders to manage their share of the brigade front. Without saying so he also wanted to keep his brigade out of the kind of troubles experienced by 3rd Brigade. In the many hundreds of pages of the "Book of Wisdom," most of which relate to his time as GOC 1st Brigade, are copies of the numerous instructions and directives and homely, but solid guidance, on training, tactics and doctrine, trench security, raids and patrols (ours and theirs), morale and discipline, conduct of officers and NCOs, offensive spirit and much else, all very clear as to what to do and what not to do. To Griesbach good security was paramount. In such matters he spoke out without hesitation. But even as a battalion commander in May 1916, after two tours in the line, then Lieutenant-Colonel Griesbach, thinking that defensive tactics required improvement, sent a lengthy letter on the subject to the then GOC 3rd Division (Malcolm Mercer) suggesting that doctrine in regard to counter-attack in particular was less than satisfactory. He also expressed his personal concept, one that did not consider minor loss of ground important, a view not then in vogue since the current view demanded immediate counter-attack. The letter reflects the serious nature of a thinking soldier unafraid to challenge doctrine. The proximity of the letter to Mount Sorrel where Canadians lost ground and suffered the loss of a division commander and a brigade commander is interesting, but more coincidental than prescient. Louis Lipsett, at the time GOC 2nd Brigade, and Mercer's replacement, was another officer quick to suggest doctrinal change.

One of the earliest Griesbachgrams in the first volume of the "Book of Wisdom", written while he was still commanding a battalion, went to his company commanders in mid-February 1916. In the four pages of his "Principles Governing Action to be Taken Should the Enemy Raid Our Trenches In the Manner In Which Other Battalions Have Successfully Raided the German Trenches" he defined such situations and the solutions. Having described enemy raids as to their likely strength, composition, development and purpose, and assuming the enemy had achieved surprise, Griesbach set out the objectives of the defence: limit the area of the fight and then prevent enemy raiders returning to their lines. Achieving these demanded three actions: lay down immediate interlocking fire in front of where the fight was in progress, thereby preventing reinforcements reaching the intruders; move every available machine-gun to the flanks in order to commence enfilade fire; and move defenders to where they could best bring fire to bear, specifically the men should

> dodge around the nearest traverse, and when out of sight of the oncoming bombers climb up on the parados, on the traverses, on the top of dug-outs, or even on top of the parapet, and from these points of vantage open a steady and aimed fire upon every bomber and enemy showing himself … from such positions [they can] offer the stoutest resistance … bombers naturally throw bombs into trenches and are not trained to throw bombs up on top of higher objects. Enemy bombers and bayonet men in the dark will come cautiously around traverses … and it may not even dawn upon them that our men have taken up these points of vantage.

25 TNA: WO 95/2561: War Diary 17th Royal Welsh Fusiliers and WO 95/2560: War Diary 115th Brigade.

In fact, as Griesbach reminded readers, Canadian bombers were coming up on either flank and the enemy, who could only carry so many, were running short of bombs. Moreover, some defenders should be moving to seal off the enemy entry point, thereby preventing enemy withdrawal. How this point was to be identified Griesbach did not say. Ever the realist, he stressed that he could not set out precisely what reaction to a raid should entail; rather, he could only suggest ways and means and would rely on the vigour and judgment of the officers and men on the scene. Finally, company commanders had to teach these principles to platoon and section commanders so that everyone understood his concept.

Another noteworthy aspect of this early entry lies in its title, which included the word "Other," this suggesting not criticism, but rather the frustration of a CO eager to get at the enemy. A look at the 49th Battalion's raiding record between its arrival in France in October 1915 and February 1917 when Griesbach left the battalion on promotion explains his frustration. Until the first tour in the trenches in January 1916 his battalion had been employed at seemingly endless working and carrying parties, tasks that continued well into the spring of 1917. Such manual labour also burdened 42nd Battalion, also in 3rd Division. The negative impact on training deeply bothered both battalion commanders. In April the enemy raided the 49th twice, the last time making off with four prisoners. In another raid in May the enemy took no prisoners, but inflicted 55 casualties (11 killed). In June the 49th suffered severely at Mount Sorrel losing 13 officers killed and wounded, 45 ORs killed, 257 wounded and 69 missing. Given this cull July and August were quieter, the battalion mostly in reserve or in billets gathering itself, with brief tours in the lines where some patrolling was done. September and October involved preparing for and engaging in major operations, Regina Trench coming during the latter month. Not until January 1917 did the 49th make its first raid, one officer and 20 ORs entering enemy lines where several Germans were killed and eight captured at a cost of only two wounded. Rather fulsome congratulations reached the unit from corps, division and brigade for this relatively small and simple raid, but it was the unit's first. The raid's most notable circumstances were these: six of the prisoners were unarmed at the time of capture, Stokes mortar bombs proved to be great dug-out busters and the artillery provided excellent support preventing enemy interference by eliminating their machine-guns. The OC Raid (Officer Commanding), Lieutenant J.H.M. Emsley, received the MC for his leadership. While the other battalions in 7th Brigade had each conducted several raids in 1916 the 49th, due to circumstances beyond its control and heavy casualties, had made its mark not in raiding, but during the major actions starting in June 1916. 49th Battalion did not have the good fortunate to be elsewhere when the big enterprises and the heavy casualties occurred.[26]

The "Book of Wisdom" also contains several directives issued by G.B. Hughes who became GOC 1st Brigade in November 1915. One describes Hughes' essentials in building and maintaining good security: trench discipline, frequent and aggressive patrolling, pre-planned counter-measures against raiding and a work programme designed to constantly improve trenches. Another concerned the use of SOS signals and responsibility for terminating SOS artillery fire after any enemy initiative.[27]

26 LAC, War Diary 49th Battalion, October 1915-February 1917; 'Book of Wisdom', Volume I; Stevens, *A City Goes to War*, p. 37.

27 LAC, RG9IIIC3, Volume 4074, Folder 2, File 6, 1st Brigade to battalions, 26 October 1915; Volume 4023, Folder 1, File 10, BM 1st Brigade to battalions, 11 February 1916, 'Responsibility as Between

A strong feature of the "Book of Wisdom" was Griesbach's concern about general defence and enemy raids and patrols and their ejection should these enter brigade trenches. His focus on monitoring security shows in his frequent visits to the fire trenches after which battalions soon heard about any faults or transgressions he had observed. The more learned of his battalion commanders might well have thought "Why considerest thou the mote that is in thy brother's eye, but considerest not the beam that is in thine own eye?"[28] Griesbach did not want to find himself in the situation faced by a British brigadier who on taking over a brigade was "horrified to learn that [it] had been so regularly raided that it was said to be 'At home to the Germans Tuesdays and Fridays.'"[29]

The "Book of Wisdom" would have served any brigade commander well as a ready reference, just as it is that for any military historian of the Great War. As one of the most dedicated trainers in the Canadian Corps Griesbach constantly stressed that even in the trenches opportunities to train existed, even if it was only informal 20-minute lectures on such subjects as impact of terrain, judging distances, sentry duties, communications, first aid, weapons, how to act if taken prisoner, enemy ruses, offensive spirit, wiring, gas alarms and drills, patrols and raids.[30] Regarding the last he suggested topics such as factors in selecting positions to be raided, dealing with enemy wire, preparations for raids, their impact on the enemy, accounts of successful raids and the good reputation of Canadian raiders. Another instruction concerned the training of officers, especially platoon commanders. Given the increased responsibilities devolving upon these young officers, battalion commanders had to pay close attention to their training and conduct and hold them responsible for all matters concerning their platoons: "I desire particular attention to the training and military education of junior officers … as far as possible … the platoon should now be the unit for duties, enterprises … so that the platoon be kept together as much as possible." In addition, he ordered that a half-dozen or so men from each platoon be instructed in the use of explosives and Stokes mortar bombs to destroy dug-outs during raids. While raids were led mostly by platoon commanders all officers had to devote "serious consideration" to raiding and to building offensive spirit. Yet another directive of direct relevance to raids concerned the chain of command within infantry sections and within raiding parties: "Thus, 'Section Commander, Prove.' 'As you

Infantry and Artillery Commanders'. During a recent operation it had been determined that a "high" rate of fire had been maintained for 90 minutes. An inquiry concluded that responsibility for terminating the fire lay with the infantry officer who had made the SOS signal. The 18-pounder field gun could fire up to 20 rounds per minute, but such rapid firing (and prolonged firing) quickly wore the barrel out. From January 1917 onward the 18-pounder was normally restricted to not more four rounds per minute. LAC, RG9IIIC1, Volume 3843, Folder 46, File 5, 22 March 1917, First Army, Artillery Instructions No. 3, set rates of fire per field gun per minute as follows: 18-pounder, Intense, four rounds per minute; Rapid, three per minute; Normal, two per minute; and Slow, one per minute. 4.5-inch howitzer rates were half the 18-pounder rates. The 60-pounder rates were rapid, one round per minute, normal, half that and slow half the normal rate.

28 Matthew 7:2-3. GOC 1st Canadian Division, Major-General Sir Archibald Macdonell, who replaced Sir Arthur Currie after Vimy, had as a maxim an updated version that urged commanders to pluck the beam out of their own eye before trying to remove a mote from a subordinate's eye (LAC, RG9IIIC3, Volume 4031, Folder 26, File 7, 'General Instructions Regarding Training').

29 Dunn, *The War the Infantry Knew*, p. 203.

30 LAC, RG9IIIC3, Volume 4031, Folder 26, File 7, 1st Brigade to battalions, 3 March 1917; Volume 4079, Folder 8, File 6, 'Book of Wisdom', Volume I.

were.' 'Second-in-Command, Prove.' 'As you were.' 'Next Senior Soldier, Prove.' 'As you were.' And so on."[31]

Griesbach's dedication to training also extended to the brigade exercises he prepared and conducted in preparation for the August 1918 offensive. Participants were closely observed and just as thoroughly criticized for shortcomings such as unclear and overly-long operation orders, over-direction by battalion commanders and inadequate knowledge of tactical doctrine. The last word on Griesbach the tactician should go to the officer who wrote his performance reports: according to Major-General Macdonell, GOC 1st Canadian Division, Griesbach was the "quickest officer that I ever had anything to do with to grasp the advantage or disadvantage of a given situation."[32] Had the war continued into 1919 Griesbach would probably have received command of a division.

Volume II of the "Book of Wisdom" also contains instructions he wrote during the period October 1916-January 1917 when for varying periods he was acting GOC 7th Brigade in 3rd Division. Here, too, we see his practice of not just setting a priority or task, but also prescribing a method by which to measure progress (or not). In October, for example, he issued the first of several instructions on wiring that he would write during the war. Having realized that a "great deal" of wiring would be necessary if the brigade was to be "reasonably safe against raids" he ordered battalions to submit daily by 12 noon a written report as to how much wiring had been done in the previous 24 hours. A "Nil" report required written explanation.[33]

In instances where error or poor decision-making handed success to enemy raiders Griesbach demanded immediate remedial action to prevent further error. In December 1916 enemy raiders got through the wire without being observed and by means of a ruse gathered in two prisoners. As they withdrew to what had been their entry point two sentries, thinking them friendly troops, did not open fire, an instance of indecision and confusion that Griesbach thought explained the loss of the two men. In his view, the only way to prevent more cases of this was for sentries "to fire at any sound or movement, this in practise meaning that any officer or man who left the line had to suffer the consequences. As an example, he referred to a man out checking wire who had neglected to inform sentries of his movement and was subsequently shot dead by a sentry. The sentry was "commended for his promptitude." Better this, thought Griesbach, than error that helped the enemy enter brigade trenches. As for sentries who did not fire, in a letter to their CO (49th Battalion) Griesbach expressed how "extremely dissatisfied" he was: "I think they should be brought to Court-Martial. Be good enough to have them at your Headquarters at 2:30 p.m. tomorrow [16 December] for examination by me." In the end, he warned that sentries who failed to fire would be punished for such "improprieties" as would those who had posted and instructed them."[34]

One last example of Griesbach's style as acting GOC 7th Brigade concerned a raid made by one of the battalions on 23 January 1917. At 0730 two officers and 22 ORs of The Royal Canadian Regiment (RCR) entered enemy trenches, took five prisoners, inflicted an estimated 30 casualties and destroyed several dug-outs during a 10 minute stay in enemy trenches, then

31 *Ibid.*, 18 February 1917; Vol, II, 29 January, 20 February and 28 May 1917.
32 LAC, MG 30E15 (Griesbach Papers), Volume 5, File 34B; RG9IIIC3, Volume 4016, Folder 31, File, 1st Division report, Section VI, Lessons and Observations.
33 LAC, 'Book of Wisdom', Volume II, acting GOC 7th Brigade to battalions, 29 October 1916.
34 *Ibid.*, 14 and 15 December 1916.

returned home having suffered only two men wounded. The OC Raid, Lieutenant F.J. Gray, received the MC for his efforts. Ever quick to point out lessons and pass them on, Griesbach stressed that the enemy "had very low morale and are all together miserable specimens." The raiders, he wrote, should lecture their company on "How they did the trick" and should they choose, "a certain amount of bragging will do no harm." But ever prudent he also warned that the enemy, having been given a good smacking, might retaliate with "storm troops." Overall, he believed the raid had afforded "splendid opportunities to keen officers and men to show their metal [sic] in schemes ... to bother, annoy ... the enemy."[35]

On 16 February 1917, two days after assuming command of 1st Brigade, clearly wanting to be seen to have taken command, and having made what he called "casual" inspections, the new brigadier filled three foolscap pages with matters requiring correction, 11 points in all, each relevant to the maintenance of good security and the ability to counter enemy raids. Griesbach's idea of "casual" covered even the fact that Private R. McConnel, B Company, 3rd Battalion, had presented a rifle so dirty it was corroded with rust, this an urgent matter for the man's platoon commander. It is often the case that a senior visitor will hit upon the soldier with a dirty rifle, or without all his kit, or in the act of violating some order or lacking a clear picture of what his duties are. Any man who has ever been a platoon commander can recall that sinking feeling when trying to explain the unexplainable to someone who sees the matter as unforgivable and is not famous for his toleration of such shortcomings. Such awkward situations will remind former or present Subalterns of a salient fact: "Inconveniences will arise which will tax the mind of the Platoon Commander."[36] Regarding bombs and bombing posts Griesbach became incensed when he found many bombs scattered about in the dirt and in very poor condition. To him, this indicated that some officers were not taking hold, nor was it acceptable that so few officers were about: "there should be an officer on duty ... on every company front at all hours." Some officers he had met were unarmed, as were many ORs, quite unacceptably so, since in the event of a raid disaster could ensue. Surprise, after all, was instrumental in the success of a raid.[37] The more astute may have taken to heart the proverb that says "Coming events cast their shadow before."

A firm believer in the follow-up action known as "Check!" four days later Griesbach was again out and about, the aftermath featuring another pointed directive to battalion commanders, although this one contained only two criticisms amongst a few exhortations. On this tour he had again encountered men moving about without their rifles, in violation (or perhaps ignorance) of his maxim that "the rifle follows the man and with bayonet fixed." Failure to comply stemmed mostly from the desire to avoid uncomfortable and wearisome loads in narrow trenches. A year later the minutes of one division commander's conference highlighted the intractability of the problem: "a good many men in the habit of going about the trenches without rifle or equipment." And a year earlier (mid-1915) Arthur Currie, then GOC 2nd Brigade, on visiting units had found no officer

35 *Ibid.*, 29 January 1917; War Diaries 7th Brigade and RCR, January 1917; David K. Riddle and Donald G. Mitchell, (comps.), *The Military Cross Awarded to Members of the Canadian Expeditionary Force 1915-1921* (Winnipeg: Kirkby-Marlton Press, 1991), p. 126.

36 LAC, MG 30E100 (Currie Papers), Volume 35, Folder 'Lectures of 47th Canadian Infantry Battalion'. This document bears the mark of Griesbach's list above of subjects for brief lectures in the trenches. Nine of its 38 pages concern raids and patrols, the whole broken into sections which could be presented in 10-20 minutes; for example, rehearsing raids, artillery support for raids and types of patrols.

37 LAC, 'Book of Wisdom', Volume I.

on duty in one of 5th Battalion's trenches, most men with bayonets not fixed (the excuse offered was that offenders thought only sentries had to have bayonets fixed) and very few men wearing web equipment. The problem remained perennial and persistent throughout the war.[38]

Less stringent regulations governed troops in support trenches so long as quick response to Stand To in an emergency could be made. Lieutenant C.S. Ashford, 6th South Staffordshires, described the routine thus:

> The men were permitted to remove their equipment during the day, for the sake of greater comfort. This … meant delay in standing to as the equipments were piled one on top of another in corners, and required much separating and untangling before they could be got into. I therefore had pegs driven into the sandbags at a convenient height, and each man had orders to hang up his equipment up in such a way that he could slip his arms into it at a moment's notice. I then posted a sentry to warn me directly anything in the nature of a 'brass hat' came in sight. As soon as the alarm was given the men were to sit about, casually, in the immediate vicinity of their own kits, and, at the whistle, they had only to slip their arms into the braces and take up their positions on the firestep. I rehearsed this … until all went smoothly.

Came the brigadier's rounds and all went well, the platoon commander waiting for the anticipated question:

> 'How long does it take you to stand to?', he asked.
> 'Not long, sir.'
> 'Give the alarm, and let me see.'

On the whistle blast the men sprang to their kit and almost before the sound had died away all were at their posts. Not a hitch! The brigadier made no comment: "Did he suspect it was not an altogether spontaneous performance? I had my doubts."[39]

Griesbach's other criticism concerned "gas sentries" whose ignorance about gas and uncertainly about their duties adversely affected their ability to warn of gas attack. Moreover, he often found these sentries poorly posted, quite unable to see the ground to their front and any bodies of enemy that might be approaching, be they attackers or raiders. In raising such faults with the officers of the unit he was touring, the conversation sometimes turned to the making of raids. Here he occasionally heard opinions quite hostile to raiding to which he answered "Many good arguments will be advanced against [raids] but … preliminary investigations [about where to raid] had to continue." When it came to attitudes, Griesbach strove to encourage an offensive spirit. If enemy snipers were active then Canadian snipers had to take them out. Enemy shelling had to receive retaliation on the basis of 20 to one. Raids had to be paid back double. Griesbach's customary vocabulary featured words like thrust, push, strike, bully and dominate. Get on with the war! When he heard or heard of complaints about artillery provoking retaliation he

38 *Ibid.*, 1st Brigade to battalions, 20 February 1917; MG 30E75 (Urquhart Papers), Volume 2, File 3, Currie to CO 5th Battalion, 16 August 1915. Currie had visited the trench unannounced at 0500.

39 Committee of Officers, *Sixth South Staffordshire Regiment*, pp. 37-38.

responded that the artillery had agreed to pound the enemy with field guns, howitzers and trench mortars and the infantry battalions would simply have to put up with enemy retaliation.[40]

He also promised that Stokes mortars would engage. Infantry dislike of these stemmed from the fact that their use drew enemy fire; to paraphrase Shakespeare, the infantry knew that something wicked would soon come their way. The historian of 44th Canadian Battalion called the Stokes the most deadly of light mortars, but also described how their use was "hampered by the prejudice of many infantry officers" who noted how it provoked almost instant retaliation. Such early opinions were not restricted to Canadians:

> if Sir Wilfred Stokes … had known what a volcano of unpopularity he would call down … upon the heads of those unfortunates who were … to manipulate his weapon, he would have confined his inventive genius to something which … irritated them less, and, consequently, aroused … less anger in the shape of high explosive thrown back at the imagined location of this flatulent weapon.

One British officer, appointed Trench Mortar Officer in the summer of 1915, and thereafter dubbed the "Rajah of Bomb," recalled that before doing a shoot from the trenches of a London Scottish battalion he was told by their officer that if he went ahead with the shoot he "would write to the paper about it." This aroused the brigade commander who remarked that the complainant suffered "under the erroneous impression that this is a health resort and that he is not a soldier, both of which impressions will have to be removed." Stokes Guns, as they were often called, provided incentive for the poetically inclined. An anonymous poet, writing in 7th Canadian Battalion's trench journal, *The Listening Post,* summed up the infantry view of the Stokes thus:

> Who is it when the 'Stand To' is o'er
> Throws bombs at Fritz till he gets sore
> And throws at us a score or more
> The Trench Mortars.

Ivor Gurney, a more polished poet, voiced similar thoughts in "The Stokes Gunners," who, he said, would scourge the enemy with a hundred bombs, then scram, leaving the infantry "to pay the piper – Cursing Stokes to Hell." Notwithstanding, Griesbach, as was his wont, issued clear direction:

> In the matter of the location of Stokes guns it is always desirable that the Stokes Gun Commander will not put his Stokes Guns in such positions as will draw fire upon the infantry, such as near a company headquarters and communications trenches. On the other hand, the Stokes Gun Commander should be given a free hand in … the location of his guns, the infantry merely indicating the target.[41]

40 LAC, RG9IIIC3, Volume 4007, Folder 4, File 4, 5 February 1918.

41 E.S. Russenholt, *Six Thousand Canadian Men: Being the History of the 44th Battalion Canadian Infantry 1914-1919* (Winnipeg: The Forty-Fourth Battalion Association, 1932), p. 32; Hutchison, *Thirty-Third Division 1915-1919,* p. 6; Randall Nicol, *Till the Trumpet Sounds Again: The Scots Guards 1914-1919. In Their Own Words: Volume 1. 'Great Shadows' August 1914-July 1916* (Solihull: Helion

On 25 February Griesbach warned his battalions that a neighbouring battalion (the 3rd) had been raided three times since the 20th and three men had been carried off by the Germans. Since 1st Brigade could well be next increased vigilance was necessary, including more frequent visits by officers to sentry posts and the manning of Listening Posts by "selected" men. Where four men could be spared two should be at each post with two others being 20 yards away, the split making it difficult for raiders to take out the post. Sergeant Alexander McClintock described how a wire ran from such listening Posts to the main trench, the number of pulls on the wire indicating various things: one pull, all OK; two pulls, I'm coming in; three, enemy in sight; and four, sound gas alarm.[42]

Prior to, during and for a brief time after Vimy in April 1917 German raids were less frequent, but in late spring they picked up the pace. Several documents in the "Book of Wisdom" relate to measures he instituted in 1st Brigade to check the Germans. While not all raids could be defeated, he aimed to keep raiders out to the maximum extent possible and to lessen the damage inflicted by any that did enter brigade trenches. In a memorandum to battalions on 18 July some anger and frustration is apparent abut a daylight enemy raid that netted them a prisoner, this loss due to "neglect of duty." Consequently, he reiterated certain principles that had to be rigidly observed in regard to sentries, in keeping rifles close at hand and in meeting officer responsibilities. All ranks had to appreciate the harm neglect could cause. First, he ordered the term "gas sentries" abolished since "a sentry is either a sentry or he is not." Despite his repeated cautions these "gas-sentries" were still poorly placed. If they were to be effective they had to be where their sweep of vision crossed that of a neighbouring sentry, thereby ensuring interlocking arcs of observation across the front. At night, whether in the fire trench or in outposts, sentries in pairs had to be posted, the men separated by 20 yards. Another old problem again surfaced in this directive: men persisted in wandering about without weapons at hand or within their reach; three unarmed men had recently been taken off as prisoners, and in one especially egregious case the enemy cut off eight men from their rifles that stood in a tidy row against the parapet, leaving only run or surrender. As he again emphasized battalion commanders were responsible for all that occurred in their units and they must hold company and platoon commanders responsible for their sub-units. He warned that any further loss of prisoners during enemy penetrations would result in formal inquiry with a view to disciplinary action. Unit commanders were to "forward by the 22nd [July] a certificate … that the memorandum [of 18 July] has been read to every officer and NCO." Griesbach had sometimes found such "certificates" a useful means of ensuring that his instructions reached the coal-face. Another "certificate" earlier in 1917 related to relief in the line, which was a stressful time for two reasons. First, a raid that came in while a relief was underway could cause additional casualties or worse. Second, he did not want to have to address complaints by incoming formations about the poor state of trenches on taking them over. No GOC enjoyed adverse comment circulating about his formation or trenches. Therefore he demanded that relief procedures be detailed and precise. Before one handover Griesbach was so anxious that it be satisfactory in all respects that he ordered battalions to obtain a certificate

and Company Limited, 2016), pp. 371, 373; *The Listening Post,* July 1916; Ivor Gurney, 'The Stokes Mortars', in Tim Kendall (ed.), *Poetry of the First World War: An Anthology* (Oxford: University Press, 2013), p. 127; LAC. 'Book of Wisdom', Volume I, 1st Brigade to battalions, 20 February 1917.

42 *Ibid.*, 25 February; Alexander McClintock, *Best O'Luck* (Toronto: McClelland, Goodchild & Stewart, 1917), p. 49. McClintock served with the 14th Battalion.

stating "all clean and satisfactory" from the incoming unit. That he thought this necessary highlights another source of stress that added to the burden of command.[43]

He followed up on return to his headquarters (HQ) with a memorandum to COs that should Germans enter brigade trenches and get away with prisoners he would "consider the Company Commander and the Platoon Commander fit subjects for Court Martial should it appear that precautions, whether set out in my Memorandum [of 18 July] or otherwise, had not been taken." At end month Griesbach cautioned battalions again about the German tactic that showered a point they intended to raid with trench mortar fire and rifle grenades and as the defenders sought cover the raiders rushed the trench. While enfilade fire from both flanks immediately on identifying a concentration of fire could defeat this, early recognition and immediate fire, as he had stressed several times, was the key to defeating the raid.[44]

In August and September Griesbach continued to see bad habits at work even in general trench maintenance. When he discovered on visiting a company of 4th Battalion that wire had been cut in the area of a sentry post he also learned that this post had not been checked by an officer for several hours. In 1st Battalion he found one sentry comfortably settled in a dug-out entrance where he could see nothing. Even more disturbing was a sentry sitting on the firestep reading a book! Griesbach estimated that of the 50 or so sentries on duty by day in the brigade only a dozen or so were doing what they ought. Such neglect could not be tolerated. He also found while speaking to a group of Subalterns that none of them had any idea of who was senior, a failing that could hinder reaction to an emergency. As for battalion commanders, he expressed to them his dissatisfaction with patrolling which he believed lacked boldness, determination and frequency. About all this one could only say that it had been a long war and no end in sight, which was so, but neither excuse was reason and general tightening commenced.[45]

December 1917 featured numerous Griesbachgrams. His first of that month explains why: the enemy had "adopted on this front a vigorous policy of patrolling and raiding" preparatory, it seemed, to some intended offensive action or to an attempt to fix the Canadian Corps in place. Second, he wanted no repeat in 1st Brigade's sector of the enemy raids on 2nd Division between 29 November and 1 December during which the enemy took several prisoners. Consequently, he warned units of enemy "strategems" that had brought them such successes. One had featured putting down mortar fire at either end of a length of a trench, whose occupants, seeking to avoid the fire, had been "shepherded … to the point selected by the enemy for his raid." Another employed a ruse. One of a small party of raiders that had gotten into a disused trench said authoritatively in English to some men a short distance away "There is a wounded man here, a couple of you men come over at once, never mind your rifles". In the main, however, it was not ruses, but the following that explained enemy successes:

43 LAC, 'Book of Wisdom', Volume I, 2 March 1917; Volume II, 18 July 1917, Volume III, 17 February 1918. During the first half of 1918 Griesbach continued to see improper placing of sentries and men without weapons. In one instance after finding a row of rifles in a rack at the door of a dug-out he entered to find the owners all sound asleep in the dugout. Their officers heard about it immediately and forcefully.

44 *Ibid.*, Volume II, 30 July 1917.

45 *Ibid.*, RG9IIIC3, Volume 4024, Folder 3, File 4.

> In 99 cases out of 100 the success of the enemy in a raid is due to negligence or neglect of duty on the part of officers and NCOs. In such cases there will be a searching inquiry and I will insist on the severest punishment upon the officer or NCO upon whom responsibility can be fixed. Only by vigorous and constant inspection, instruction and visiting can an officer or NCO clear himself of the charge of negligence.[46]

During this period of intensified enemy activity one brigade directive on 4 December was particularly revealing of anxiety about enemy raiding. This shows not just in the directive, but in the reaction of one CO, Lieutenant-Colonel J.B. Rogers, 3rd Battalion. Where previously Griesbach might have said something like "see my earlier memorandum" his December directive referred readers to a document he identified precisely by file number and date, his intent being to ensure there could be no mistaking the document he wanted COs to read again. How Rogers handled the instruction is telling of his state of mind. The copy in an appendix to the battalion War Diary differs from the copy in the "Book of Wisdom," in that the directive was re-typed at battalion HQ word for word, this obvious in the larger type, different margins and different number of paragraphs per page. This gave Rogers space to insert after each reference Griesbach had made the 3rd Battalion file number; for example, following Griesbach's notation "see my memorandum 872-8 of the 18th July" Rogers inserted the battalion file number "V.R. 581." On the last page he added the following: "I wish Company Commanders to keep this letter before them for the next two weeks and discuss it with their officers and NCOs and they in turn to discuss it with their men, I wish particular attention paid to para 4 section (b), also our V.R. 518 of July last."[47] Rogers' careful and prudent handling reflects his vivid recollection of Griesbach's angry reaction to two earlier German visits to 3rd Battalion's trenches.

Two weeks later during 3rd Battalion's last night in the line (18 December) the Germans raided, an event, said the battalion War Diary, "most unfortunate, happening on a relief night." The relieving unit, the 38th Battalion less one company, arrived at the railhead at 1700 where guides met the newcomers and guided them into battalion lines. However, the missing company did not arrive at the railhead until 2300. Consequently, the relief was not reported complete until after 0200 on 19 December. That morning Rogers received an order to conduct an inquiry "to enable higher authority to fix responsibility for the loss to the enemy of two men of C Company and a Lewis gun and the death of another man and wounds to two others." All leave for the battalion stopped "pending receipt and consideration" of the findings. The Inquiry asked numerous questions of the officers of C Company including details of company deployment, patrols, listening posts and wire obstacles, the conduct and reaction of all personnel in the immediate area of the post that was raided and to what extent the battalion had planned and trained to meet enemy raids and patrols.

Rogers' findings and Griesbach's comments show that battalion patrols had not discovered the gap of a few yards between the two posts the enemy had raided; at least this was likely, but as Griesbach said, those who knew for sure were dead, wounded or captured. Immediately after the raid "gooseberry coils" filled the gap as a temporary fix until a proper belt of wire

46 LAC, 'Book of Wisdom', Volume II.

47 *Ibid.*, RG9IIIC3, Volume 4017, Folder 35, File 18. Para 4 (b) concerned vigilance of sentries and posts. This paragraph also included Rogers' wishes.

could be installed.[48] The Inquiry also established that while Rogers' "Trench Orders" contained detailed instructions regarding the responsibilities of duty personnel, action to take in the event of raids and counter-attack plans to eject any enemy that had penetrated the line, many men in C Company had not been aware of them, or of the order for special vigilance that very night. The company commander, Captain J.K. Crawford, was censured, although it is evident that both Rogers and Griesbach sympathized with him, his record at Passchendaele, where he had been recommended for a DSO, being exemplary. He had, however, now been "unfortunate," having been let down by his Company Sergeant-Major (CSM) who had neglected to pass on orders including that which would have kept the company day garrison in the line until the relief was complete. The CSM was replaced. Two other men who had deserted their post were remanded for court-martial. Griesbach concluded his review with this: "since it is not the first time that the enemy have entered the trenches of the 3rd Battalion in the present year, I think it proper to observe that the 3rd Battalion has brought discredit on the brigade." Griesbach then issued instructions specifically pertaining to the necessity of better patrolling of battalion lines:

> in taking over a line of trenches a ground recce will be carried out by battalions … and a report will be … submitted … discussing the ground, wire, saps and trenches running between the enemy position and our position, ruined buildings, craters and shell-holes, dead ground, etc.
>
> This report will be based upon observation and patrol reports with a view to determining as far as is possible what portions of the line are reasonably secure against enemy raids and what portions of the line are dangerous.[49]

Returning now to earlier in December a lengthy directive from Griesbach reached battalions on the 7th. Much of it pertained to housekeeping, but three areas related to security. One concerned improving wiring about which Griesbach did not believe that "any earnest or serious attempt [had been] made." What he thought should be done was this: "Patrols disclose the fact that the enemy is not close to our front. If the enemy posts are close … they ought to be raided. If not … then wiring should be done. I consider the matter of wiring to be very urgent." Patrolling had to be constant, aggressive and well-organized. Second, when shortage of men made the line a mere series of posts additional security measures had to be implemented. Where posts were considerably separated then trench patrols of two or three men must rove between them to prevent any enemy lodgement in an unmanned area, or, at the very least, to warn of this. Also, an officer with his runner had to constantly move between posts over the whole of the company front. Such a system had worked quite well, he wrote, in many of the British battalions not on the Somme at a time when all reinforcements went to Somme battalions, meaning that elsewhere the front was often lightly held. However, in some instances enterprising Germans,

48 LAC, 46th Battalion War Diary, 20 December 1916; Fraser and Gibbons, *Soldier and Sailor Words and Phrases*, p. 106: "Gooseberry. Name for a wire entanglement device used for stopping gaps."

49 LAC, RGIIIC3, Volume 4017, Folder 35, File 18, 'Court of Inquiry on Hostile Raid on 3rd Battalion, 18 December 1917'; MG30E318 (3rd Battalion), Volume 9, File 63, War Diary, 18 December 1917; Volume 21, Folder 152. 'Convening Order for Court of Inquiry', 19 December, proceedings, 26 December; Goodspeed, *Battle Royal*, pp. 210-11; 'Book of Wisdom', 27 December 1917.

having entered a trench unobserved, had targetted and taken prisoners from the roving patrols.[50] Finally, Griesbach was dissatisfied with junior officers who he thought were not taking hold:

> They .. do not check the men. They allow men to stand in crowds. They allow men to be separated from their arms. They overlook the fact that some bayonets are fixed and others are not. Company commanders and senior officers must frequently ... check junior officers.[51]

On 27 December, in his penultimate instruction to battalions for 1917, Griesbach described to his battalion commanders the lessons all should absorb about the enemy raid on 18 December. First, Lewis guns had to have interlocking arcs of fire across the front. Second, while good wire and good patrolling went a long way when it came to security these could not supplant alert sentries and pre-arranged plans to deal with the unexpected. Third, he added a requirement for an additional report – "Trench and Wire Return" – that would have to be submitted. Of this proposal it can be said that Griesbach was mortal man and like all the rest he could err.

Before looking at this new Return a brief survey of the "Reports and Returns" that had to be submitted up the chain of command is illuminating. One British officer remarked that over time "Returns" developed to a formidable extent. In his unit a "Trench Log Book" had to record everything "that had happened, was happening and would happen," plus compilations of lists of trench stores received or handed over and the following reports (some report times not shown): Morning Situation Report (0330), Wind Report (0330), Daily Summary (for preceding 24 hours), Patrol Report (0930), Wire Report (0930), Artillery Test Report, Strength Report, Distribution of Rifles and Lewis Guns Report, Afternoon Situation Report, Afternoon Wind Report, Casualty Report and Certificate as to Frostbite Treatment.[52] Soon the list included an Intelligence Report, Patrol Reports and Weekly Returns for small arms ammunition expenditures and numerous other matters depending on the situation. This "Paper War" had many company commanders thinking that most of their time seemed to be occupied writing reports about things that they had not had time to observe. One company commander recalled how "the deluge of paper had increased proportionally with the deluge of shells. It took me, and I write fast and am a good liar, from 4 a.m. to 8 a.m.to compile or edit all the reports required daily ... By breakfast time the telephone started, and that daily deluge of signals began."[53]

The CO of 9th KRRC (14th British Division) sometimes thought that "Unless a man is very good the higher he gets the less he thinks."[54] Griesbach should not be charged with this since he was an officer who never stopped thinking, but as time passed he, like all higher commanders, did forget some aspects of life at the coal-face. Like all men he could not claim infallibility,

50 LAC, 'Book of Wisdom', Volume II; Crookenden, *Cheshire Regiment,* p. 99.
51 LAC, RG9IIIC3, Volume 4007, Folder 4, File 4, 5 February. A conference of division commanders at Canadian Corps HQ in early 1918 noted that "a good many men are in the habit of going about the trenches without rifle or equipment."
52 Committee of Officers, *Sixth South Staffordshire Regiment,* pp. 167-68.
53 LAC, MG30E60 (Matthews Papers), Volume 3, Folder 12; Christopher Page, *Command in the Royal Naval Division: A Military Biography of Brigadier General A.M. Asquith DSO* (Staplehurst: Spellmount, 1999), p. 82; Jerrold, *Georgian Adventure,* p. 166.
54 Maxwell, *Villiers-Stuart Goes to War,* p. 73.

and despite his competence and the usually sharp logic on display in his "Book of Wisdom," on occasion he came up with an idea that was not worth the candle.

As 1917 was about to become 1918 Griesbach issued notice that he proposed to introduce a "Trench and Wire Return." That it took him two full foolscap pages to describe it and how to complete it should have been a warning. Its purpose as he saw it was to better define the priority of work and make all levels of command more familiar with front line wire and obstacles and with enemy raid possibilities. His idea stipulated that on taking over a section of the front each battalion would divide the ground into a number of sections to match company frontages from right to left: for example, "Right battalion, No. 1 Section." Companies would report daily, text and sketches as necessary, on the trenches, ground, wire (friendly and hostile) and CTs, concluding with a summary of work to be done, wire and obstacles and an assessment of the likelihood of enemy raids. Battalions would compile these reports and forward a consolidated return to brigade HQ where brigade staff would maintain a map of the brigade front, adding information to it daily. One can imagine the enthusiasm of the recipients, company and battalion commanders and brigade staff, shuddering as they churned though this proposal in which the author had admitted that the initial report "will be lengthy and most difficult," but subsequent ones supposedly less so. This proposed "Return" disappeared. Everyone, it seems, had realized that the whole complicated idea would have been the bane of unit commanders already heavily burdened and struggling with paper.[55]

Assessment of the raid possibilities mentioned in the proposed return had of necessity to include no man's land, an area that varied greatly in depth, sometimes merely a few yards, or often 100-200 yards and sometimes extending a thousand or so yards. Anthony French, an officer of 15th London Regiment, described the extremes as either close enough to hear the enemy talking or half a mile of dead ground away. Sixth South Staffords at one point had a listening post so close to the enemy that even whispering was risky. A soldier in that post when asked replied that all he had ever heard was what "might be bacon frizzlin' on the brazier." [56] Commanders at all levels defined a good battalion as a battalion that dominated no man's land. Those COs who could, in truth, call it "Now My Land" demonstrated not only solid (and expected) offensive spirit, but "moral ascendency" over the enemy. Lieutenant-Colonel W.D. Croft said his Royal Scots battalion so owned no man's land that the enemy made no real effort to dispute ownership.[57] Conversely, battalions that did not rule became harried battalions, threatened on the one side by the enemy and on the other pushed and prodded by higher commanders. When it came to no man's land, the essence of good security was dominate by fire during the day and by incessant patrolling during the night: "There is no doubt that [this] gave more protection than … any number of sentry posts."[58]

Overall, the whole of the "Book of Wisdom" could be said to be Griesbach's personal vision and a combination of "Some of the Things That Please an Infantry Brigadier" and *SS 408 Some*

55 LAC, 'Book of Wisdom', Volume II, 30 December 1917.

56 Anthony French, *Gone for a Soldier* (Kineton: The Roundwood Press, 1972), p. 50; Committee of Officers, *Sixth South Staffordshire Regiment,* pp. 123-24.

57 Croft, *Three Years With the Ninth (Scottish) Division,* p. 42.

58 Crookenden, *Cheshire Regiment,* p. 99.

of the Many Questions …"[59] The latter spawned numerous "Questions" publications at Army and Corps levels and at Officer Schools. The Canadian Corps published at least three such items: "Some Questions a Platoon Commander Might Ask Himself in the Line," "Some Questions a Platoon Commander Should Ask Himself Before an Attack," and "Some Questions a Platoon Commander Should Ask Himself When the Objective Has Been Gained." Pity the poor platoon commander who was expected to have all the answers to all the questions! As one platoon commander during the Second World War said, "I doubt that at any time since the war have I carried the burden of responsibility that I bore as a Subaltern in battle." This applies fully to the Great War Subaltern.[60]

Griesbach also turned questions into expectations. Early in 1918 he warned battalion commanders and brigade staff that on going into rest they were to lecture as follows:

> Lieut.-Colonel A.W. Sparling, D.S.O, CO 1st Battalion,
> "What I Expect of Platoon Commanders in the Line."
>
> Lieut.-Colonel L.T. McLaughlin, D.S.O, CO 2nd Battalion,
> "What I Expect of Company Commanders in the Line."
>
> Lieut.-Colonel J.B. Rogers, D.S.O, M.C., CO 3rd Battalion,
> "What I Expect of Company Commanders When Battalions Are at Rest."
>
> Lieut.-Colonel L.H. Nelles, M.C., CO 4th Battalion,
> "What I Expect of Platoon Commanders While Battalions Are at Rest."
>
> BM, "What the Brigade Expects of Battalions in the Line."
>
> Staff Captain (Intelligence), "What the Brigade Expects of Battalions in the Line by Way of Reports and Intelligence."
>
> GOC, topic to be selected.

Griesbach further directed that company commanders would join platoon commanders in the tuition since on one of his many visits to battalion trenches he had been "much impressed with the constantly falling standard of company commanders [they] in particular … on the down grade." He added that all who attended the lectures by the four COs had to submit to their CO a written "precis" of the lectures they attended.[61]

59 'Some of the Things That Please an Infantry Brigadier' in *Notes for Commanding Officers* (Aldershot: Gale and Polden, 1917), pp. 372-76; *SS 408 Some of the Many Questions a Platoon Commander Should Ask Himself on Taking Over a Trench, and at Intervals Afterward* (N.p.: Stationary Services Press, April 1916 and January1917.

60 Sidney Jary, *18 Platoon* (Carshalton Beeches, Surrey: Sidney Jary Limited, 1987), p. 123.

61 LAC, 'Book of Wisdom', Volume III, 17 and 19 February 1918.

In summary, the "Book of Wisdom" is a fascinating repository of knowledge. It may seem in reading it that 1st Brigade held the all-time record of sins committed in housekeeping, trench discipline and security, but it was not unlike any other brigade in the BEF. Soldiers will be soldiers, exasperating and difficult at times, but the brigade had a very good reputation as did its GOC. By their very nature housekeeping and security duties are tedious drudgery usually without perceptible reward. This being so their state can never be assumed and inevitably one or more aspects may fail to meet expectation and requirement, perfection never possible. What keeps the machine running and officers and men up to the mark was constant, close checking to see that trench orders were obeyed; in short, seeing that trench discipline was maintained. Trench warfare was not only a highly untidy business, but an extremely wearing type of warfare. By 1917 it had been a long war. Griesbach knew that perfection was a chimera and that mistakes would be made. Arthur Currie agreed and added that "body-snatching stunts" – raids – were impossible to prevent, especially when unit and sub-unit frontages were very wide.[62]

While the historian of the Ninth (Scottish) Division rightly called counter-attack the "soul of defence" the eyes and ears of defence were patrols and raids and that is fundamental. Consequently, offensive spirit became dogma and *de rigueur.* The question that especially annoyed platoon commanders because of its constant repetition was this: "AM I AS OFFENSIVE AS I MIGHT BE?"[63] No doubt they thought that those in the rear could better afford to be offensive since they were unlikely to experience the "cataclysmic upheaval" of active aggressiveness, patrols, raids and attacks and the dread of the enemy's turn at such pursuits.[64] The next chapter begins the examination of the ways and means of the endeavours known as raids at which the BEF became so adept.

62 LAC, RG9IIIC1, Volume 3858, Folder 84, File 16, Currie to Canadian Corps 27 February and 1 March 1917.
63 Ewing, *Ninth (Scottish) Division,* p. 48; *SS 408 Some of the Many Questions ….*
64 Griffith, *Up to Mametz,* pp. 71-72.

3

The Name of the Game

Things 'ave transpired which made me learn
The size and meanin' of the game.
Rudyard Kipling, "The Return"

It would, indeed, be an unusual reader of military history who has not before encountered the words "raid" and "patrol," both as nouns and verbs. Most readers would not have long pondered their precise definition, but for the purposes of this book these words and others relevant to the story, such as "success" and "failure," require closer scrutiny. Definitions are always troublesome. It is a fact that military history abounds with words and terms not in the civilian lexicon and some of those that are familiar take on peculiar meaning once they are in uniform. The British Official History warns that fresh vocabulary came with the BEF: "breach" became a "gap," "retrenchment" became "switch," "mining" became "tunnelling," "Chinese" attacks took the place of "false" or "minor" attacks. Sometimes new words were misleading.[1] As David Fischer said, "some people do extraordinary things with their terms, and a good deal of confusion can result if definitions are not explicitly and consistently used."[2]

During the research for this present study it soon became evident that neither of Fischer's adverbs featured strongly in BEF usage of the words raid and patrol. Any number of sources seemed to pay little attention to definitions, a fact that made very careful reading essential in order to quantify minor enterprises and realistically assess their importance and impact. One regimental history conflates patrols, attacks and raids, seeing the last as merely varying in degree from mere exploring by a patrol in enemy trenches to much larger and more elaborate operations up to and including seeking to rectify the line or obliterate a salient and hold the ground. One example in an XI Corps report in July 1916 includes a patrol (type unspecified) raiding an enemy post and another describing two fighting patrols raiding enemy trenches. Conversely, it was not unusual to see in War Diaries something along these lines: "no active operations, but

1 Brigadier-General J.E. Edmonds and Captain G.C. Wynne, *Military Operations France and Belgium, 1915: Winter 1914-15: Battle of Neuve Chapelle: Battle of Ypres* (London: Macmillan, 1927), pp. 152-53.
2 David Hackett Fischer, *Historians' Fallacies: Toward a Logic of Historical Thought* (New York: Harper Torchbooks, 1970), pp. 264-65, 280.

considerable patrolling."[3] For the military historian of the Great War how helpful it would have been had "explicitly" and "consistently" prevailed! However, planners and participants in such risky endeavours as raids defined not for eternity or even for a century, but of necessity for their pressing purpose and immediate utility.

Coming up with definitions can be trying. Kipling, always so helpful, points the way, his first honest serving-man asks "what," a query that doubles here and asks what is a raid? what is a patrol? These queries are not as straightforward as they appear. The contemporary answers exhibit nuance, ambiguity, inconsistency and even contradiction reminiscent of Lewis Carroll's White Knight who so bewildered Alice "about the name of the song, as opposed to what the name was called, and what the song really was." Answering the double "what" just mentioned is the subject and the purpose, or aim, if you prefer, of this chapter.

Whatever the definitions decided upon – and such phrasing is not to suggest a cursory review, or an intent to denigrate or diminish their importance – reality for the officers and men of the BEF is how nocturnal adventures such as raids and patrols became murderous business. Certainly, as the *Oxford Concise Dictionary* advises, an enterprise (even a minor one) is an "undertaking esp. bold or difficult," one demanding courage, skill and readiness to engage. Readers have noticed, no doubt, the sequence of the two queries above: raids, then patrols. This sequencing reveals their relative importance in the sense of size, committed resources and impact, but in analysing them the order has been reversed for the simple reason that recce – patrolling – generally (and preferably) goes before a raid. In fact, when it came to raids one highly decorated Canadian BM called recce "the secret of success."[4]

Much of the terminology that features in this book originated well before 1914, some a legacy of the South African War. *Combined Training (Provisional.)*, a small pocket-sized maroon coloured manual issued in May 1902 under the signature of Field Marshal Roberts, C-in-C of the British Army, defined "certain principles" of command of troops in war. Roberts reiterated that the manual was "authoritative on every subject with which it deals." In a section on intelligence and recce it presented guidance on attack and defence prefaced with a reminder that "Time spent on recce is seldom wasted." It then listed the contemporary means of recce: personal observation, staff officers, patrols and scouts and balloons. Substantial content followed on the rules of recce, on "officer patrols," "strong patrols," "personal recce," and "recce in force." Most of these categories appear in the manual in use at the outbreak of war in 1914. It is noteworthy that in *Combined Training. (Provisional.)* the word "raid" appears only once.[5] All in all the manual offers knowledge and experience that would prove useful in the Great War.

Successor manuals, the ones that accompanied Empire troops to war, included *Field Service Regulations Part I. Operations. 1909 (FSR)* and *Infantry Training (4-Company Organization.) 1914*. Their contents including the sections relating to the general conduct of defence and attack

3 F. Loraine Petre, Wilfred Ewart and Major-General Sir Cecil Lowther, *The Scots Guards in the Great War 1914-1918* (London: John Murray, 1925), p. 58; Michael Senior, *Haking: A Dutiful Soldier: Lt. General Sir Richard Haking, XI Corps Commander 1915-1918 – A Study in Corps Command* (Barnsley: Pen & Sword Books Ltd., 2012), p. 277.

4 LAC, 6th Brigade War Diary, July 1918, 'Lecture on Raiding' to VI Corps School by Major The Hon. F.E. Grosvenor, DSO, MC, BM 6th Brigade. Grosvenor was commissioned Lieutenant in the 29th (Vancouver) Battalion in November 1914.

5 *Combined Training (Provisional.)*, Preface and Section 10.

are clearly revised versions of the 1902 manual. While neither included sections headed "Raids" or "Fighting Patrols," *FSR* did offer a large section on night assaults and *Infantry Training* defined a patrol as a "body of men sent out to reconnoitre or to guard against surprise."[6]

Both manuals in describing recce and intelligence considered the latter vital. As for the former, it had to be methodical and carefully planned if it was to supply the information that was required. What the manuals had to say about both echoes in an analysis by the historian of the Guards Division, Lieutenant-Colonel C. Headlam:

> It was during the winter months of 1915-1916, too, that the immense importance of accurate intelligence ... began really to be understood and appreciated ... close observation of the enemy's movements in, and in rear of his frontline trenches; the careful location of his guns, trench mortars and machine-guns; a day to day report as to the state of his wire and the condition of his defences; the identification of his units in the line were all items of information, the collection of which was of the utmost importance.

Headlam then related this to war as it had proved to be:

> In trench warfare, as in any other kind of warfare, there is only one road to success in attack or defence – and that is to keep in touch with the enemy. This can only be done if an accurate and never-ceasing watch is kept upon him by the troops who are actually facing him.[7]

The first extract bears careful reading for its clarity on intelligence as opposed to information and recce. Even today these terms seem to cause some confusion. To give just one example, a recent journal article (2010) reveals that the author does not understand that recce collects information, not intelligence. Information only becomes intelligence after it is weighed against information provided by all other available sources and an all-source assessment is made. Only then can information be said to be intelligence! There is no such thing, in the words of the author of the article, as "raiding and scouting intelligence." Raids "acquired" information, not intelligence! The article is permeated with misapprehension of this fundamental fact. The "ancients" knew this; viz. *Combined Training. (Provisional.),* 1902: "Recce is the military term for obtaining information." If, as the author of the article claims, "the extensive raiding and patrolling in Lens contributed to the selection of the wrong route" that is not an "intelligence failure," but a failure of the raiders; in short, a failure of recce and raid execution. When it comes to collection of information it is also a fact that raiding parties spent only a very short time in enemy trenches, usually less than 30 minutes and often only 10 minutes. The focus was more to get an information vendor (a prisoner) rather than information. A raiding party might have time to look about closely enough to render a fairly good description of enemy trenches, but not much more. References to enemy trenches being very much like BEF trenches abound. Of all the raids examined in this study very few had their purpose stated as "to gain information." Almost always their purposes were take prisoners, harass, destroy and kill. When it comes to

6 *Field Service Regulations Part I. Operations. 1909* (London: HMSO, 1909); reprint ed., 1912; *Infantry Training (4-Company Organization.) 1914* (London: HMSO, 1914).
7 Headlam, *Guards Division,* pp. 105-106.

definitions of intelligence, as opposed to information and recce, a useful adage to bear in mind is that "Kittens born in a cookie jar are still kittens, not cookies"! [8]

As for patrols which seek to gather information, *Combined Training* also stressed that a patrol must be given not only clear and specific tasks, but equally clear direction as to the specific points upon which information was required. This still applied in 1914 (and does today). Moreover, every member of a patrol had to be aware of these directions. During the Great War patrols often lacked precise direction, some examples actually expressed in patrol orders are these: "pick up such information as may be stumbled upon," or "do a general recce," or "discover if anything was doing or what the enemy is doing." At times patrols were asked to function as patrol and raid; for example, in June 1915 Second Lieutenant H.E. Cooper, Royal Warwickshire Regiment, led an officer's patrol of seven men out to a German listening post there to "wait for their patrol and scupper it; also discover what work was being done in their trenches." This was quite in violation of the tenet, based on experience, that no patrol should be asked to fight and reconnoitre. In the event, no enemy patrol appeared, probably much to the relief of Cooper and his small party, it being likely that all had doubts about the dual task since achieving the "scupper" could warn the enemy and entry to his trenches could then get very violent in short order.[9]

Since the enemy worked to similar concepts nights along the Western Front frequently meant "feverish activity" in the trenches and in no man's land: men erecting and improving their defences with wire and other obstacles, men in transit to raid or returning from one, men setting up an ambush or falling into one, men going out on patrol or heading home from one and men engaged in fire fights, patrol on patrol, raid on raid. Officers and ORs quickly realized that some aspects of trench warfare like patrols and raids "not only provided the greatest excitement but ... tested to the highest possible degree the bravery and nerve of the troops taking part." One British officer found that patrols were never boring. Yet another thought them "the most dangerous thing in war."[10] On occasion a patrol might be so extraordinary that it strikes one as reminiscent of the exploits of Richard Hannay, one of John Buchan's best-known characters. The history of 5th British Division describes a daring patrol in January 1916 that earned a junior officer the DSO. Lieutenant Eaton of a Royal Engineer (RE) Tunnelling Company in order to determine if the enemy had commenced mining operations had to cross a river, pass through a village and then through a heavily wooded area. In all, he spent six hours behind enemy lines before he returned with the location of an artillery battery, the state of German wire and trenches and confirmation that no mining had begun. During this period he had to overcome a German sentry and then took the opportunity to bomb two officers in a small dugout.[11] The word "dangerous," then, seems appropriate and is one reason to look closely at patrolling. Another is because recce patrols usually preceded raids and other types of patrols were related

8 *Combined Training. (Provisional.)*, Section 55; Geoffrey Jackson, '"What was the point?" Raiding in the Summer of 1917', *Canadian Military History*, 19 (Autumn 2010), pp. 31-40. See also Chapter 8 on the confusion.

9 Lieut.-Colonel M.M. Haldane, *History of the Fourth Battalion The Seaforth Highlanders* (Uckfield, East Sussex: Naval and Military Press, n.d.), pp. 266, 268; Thomas, *A Life Apart*, p. 63; Malcolm Brown, *The Imperial War Museum Book of the Western Front* (London: Pan Books, 2001), pp. 107-109.

10 Grey, *2nd City of London Regiment*, p. 25; Edward Wyrall, *The Nineteenth Division 1914-1918* (Uckfield, East Sussex: Naval and Military Press, n.d.), p. 19; Brown, *The Imperial War Museum Book of the Western Front*, p. 107; Hussey, *5th Division*, pp. 92-94.

11 Hussey, *Fifth Division*, pp. 92-94.

and useful to raiding parties. Consequently, their whys and wherefores were essential knowledge. While "aeroplane reports, secret service reports and [prisoner] interrogations" might point to troop concentrations and the intended point of attack, what confirmed such information was very often a patrol: men on the ground and in touch with the enemy. In one instance a British division saw from air photographs that a forward switch line that was not usually occupied appeared in use. If so, it would suggest a concentration for an early advance. A patrol subsequently confirmed occupation, enemy reaction to the patrol being strong and protracted. A less straight-forward task faced Captain Geoffrey Dugdale, 6th King's Shropshire Light Infantry, in March 1917 when he took out a strong patrol "to make quite sure if the enemy is still there. Don't lose any men, as it is not intended to be a fighting patrol." On reaching his objective he no doubt realized the ambiguity of his orders: the only way to "make sure" was to enter the trenches and that more often than not meant fighting. In this instance he found the enemy front and support trenches deserted.[12]

Whatever the type of patrol, participants performed certain "stimulating" preliminaries that focussed one's mind wonderfully:

> First you emptied your pockets of everything that might disclose your identity. For the same reason you removed all regimental badges. You saw to it that you were not carrying anything that might reflect a light. Your bayonet would be dulled, usually by having a sock drawn over it. Finally you blackened your face with burnt cork. Having then washed yourself out, so to speak, you were ready to move off … Scrambling over the parapet always gave one a kick. You were never quite sure that you wouldn't be greeted with machine-gun fire. Taking your bearings you made for the gap in the wire … But once you were through, there was no standing up. You moved off at the 'slither.' And then the fun – if you can call it that – began.[13]

Before examining the types of patrols a summation of the essential differences between a raid and a patrol is necessary. Most patrols sought information, the ideal being that the enemy should remain unaware that a patrol against him had even occurred. A raid, on the other hand, usually intended punishment: seek and destroy and get prisoners. Stealth, silent creeping, being the essence of recce patrols these did not receive the fire support given a raid. But a raid could feature stealth or fire support. If the latter, then the raiders might have the support of artillery, field and heavy, trench mortars, machine-guns and gas. Such support could be very extensive. Major R.T. Rees, 4th Loyal North Lancashire Regiment (55th British Division), for example, described a projected raid in mid-1917 that was to be supported by 300 guns. Rees requested permission to forego this support. This request may seem highly unusual but certain circumstances led to it. These are discussed in Chapter 5.[14]

12 Haldane, *Fourth Battalion The Seaforth Highlanders,* pp. 266, 268; Captain Geoffrey Dugdale, *"Langemarck" and "Cambrai": A War Narrative 1914-1918* (Uckfield, East Sussex: Naval and Military Press, n.d.), p. 45.

13 Thomas, *A Life Apart,* p. 63. Thomas served as a platoon and then a company commander on the Western Front.

14 Rees, *A Schoolmaster at War,* p. 60.

A raid by design and by intent went from home trench across no man's land and into the enemy trenches where it executed its assigned tasks. Patrols, recce or otherwise, also operated in no man's land, but were usually restricted to that real estate. A patrol tasked only to observe sought to get as close to the enemy wire as possible. If it hit upon a gap it might even try to get between the wire and the enemy trench, there to take up a good position from which to observe. Such a patrol listened and learned and once home again passed on details of enemy routine, strength and dispositions to a raiding party if one had been ordered. This is not to say that a recce patrol would pass up an opportunity to snatch a prisoner, but that was not its usual purpose. *SS 107 Notes on Minor Enterprises* stipulated that any objectives selected for raids required frequent observation beforehand and close and continuous observation from dusk on the night of the raid until the time it actually launched. In fact, selection and recce of an objective presupposed that superiority had been established over no man's land.[15] A patrol out in no man's land for aggressive purposes might be looking to ambush returning enemy patrols, or it might settle down to await, say, a working party to come out, this presenting a chance to wreck it, maybe even get a prisoner. A recce patrol might even be tasked specifically to enter enemy trenches, but this was not a frequent task.

Patrols and raids did not always succeed, of course. The trek into or across no man's land and back posed any number of pitfalls, not least of which was navigation. Poor quality maps and obliteration of landmarks made things more difficult. Navigation often posed less of a problem for raiders since patrols, had they been so tasked, might previously have found the best routes for raiders in and out and could update such information. Often white tape or other means marked routes. In many cases no man's land was so narrow that observation became more critical than navigation; in the serious business of patrolling knowing the ground was the key and, consequently, recce patrols were sometimes tasked simply to make "a systematic survey of the ground in front of us."[16] Chapter 5 reveals how very common navigational errors were and their negative impact. Other reasons why raids failed are examined in Chapter 5.

While the standard of training in the BEF generally and steadily improved during the war navigation was an exception and skills generally declined. Reading a map and reading the ground are two very different skills. One Canadian CO when asked his opinion about the poor standard responded that "many officers on arrival … knew nothing about map reading or [had] a smattering that … in many cases proved worse than useless." Navigational error usually resulted in delay that negatively affected patrols and raids "even to the point of failure and/or additional casualties." Patrolling demanded close attention to the basics such as counting of paces, use of compass and thorough map study. Shortcomings in these areas went beyond junior officers, a fact recognized in *Notes for Commanding Officers* by the inclusion of sections on compass work, resections and finding true bearings.[17]

15 *SS 107 Notes on Minor Enterprises* (GHQ: March 1916).

16 Charles Lyon Foster and William Smith Duthie (eds.), *Letters From the Front: Being a Record of the Part Played by Officers of the Bank in the Great War. Volume I* (Toronto: Canadian Bank of Commerce, 1920), pp. 100-102, 252. Very few of the letter writers are identified as to their units and in most cases the letters are not helpful in that regard. Nevertheless, these personal accounts are in the main informative and very useful.

17 LAC, RG9IIIC3, Volume 4032, Folder 28, File 1, Canadian Corps 'Notes on Training', November 1917; Volume 4051, Folder 19, File 8, CO 10th Battalion to 2nd Brigade, 15 November 1916; *Notes*

Some lighter moments can be found in accounts of patrolling and navigation; for example, when in May 1917 Lieutenant Charles Power and one of his men got too close to a German outpost, which they had been unaware of, instead of receiving lead they heard a voice say in perfect English "Hello, there. Come and have some breakfast." They declined and made off in great haste. Likewise, a British patrol encountered a charitable reception when on reaching German wire during a recce patrol they heard, in good English, "It you don't go away, we shall really have to shoot you." Advice tendered, advice taken![18]

While a patrol might fail, drawing little comment beyond disappointment and cursing, a string of failures could result in some mockery, a case in point being an entry in *The Swell,* a short-lived (two issues only) British trench journal, which suggested that little was to be gained from such adventures anyway:

> I went myself patrolling No Man's Land,
> To learn of Fritz's movements at first hand,
> But all the knowledge that I gleaned was how
> The bottom of a big shell hole was planned.

Repeated failure tended to irritate one's superiors; Major R.T. Rees, for example, recalled that his reception of a patrol that had failed to achieve its task was "lacking in cordiality." Failure often meant making another attempt, perhaps several, if in the CO's opinion there was a pressing need. While "the conduct of a patrol was left entirely to the officer in charge" repeated failure would see a tightening of the reins.

In both editions of *Notes for Commanding Officers* there appeared "Some of the Things That Please an Infantry Brigadier by a Brigadier." Number 31 of 36 applauded units that knew their trenches and the ground in front of them well. Both editions also included "Scheme for Training Patrols" which began with a list of "good" results from training: the enemy are killed or captured, minimum casualties are suffered, morale rises, no man's land becomes ours and good information is obtained and the enemy is deprived of it. In further evidence that recce patrols required additional guidance was "Notes on Recce" in the 1918 edition, which reiterated that a recce patrol must be given a simple question to answer. These notes also included the acronym "To Ride," which outlined what a patrol had to know before it went out:

> Time to be away.
> Other troops and what is known of them.
> Reports and where to send.

for Commanding Officers, 1918 edition, pp. 324-33. This manual was issued to new and potential battalion commanders attending the Commanding Officers Course at the Senior Officers School, Aldershot. The importance of this manual is evident in that it was issued by name to each student, rather than just the usual "here's the pile, grab one." Adams, *Nothing of Importance,* p. 55; *WO 2313 Notes on Map Reading* (London: HMSO, 1915) was widely issued. Also useful was *The Complete Guide to Military Map Reading* (Aldershot: Gale & Polden Ltd., 1911), an unofficial and excellent supplement focussing as it did on numerous exercises. Navigation and the training involved is discussed at length in Radley, *We Lead Others Follow.*

18 LAC, RG9IIIC3, Volume 4053, Folder 24, File 16, First Army, 9 May 1917; Brown, *Imperial War Museum Book of the Western Front,* p. 109.

Information on the points required.
Direction and distance to go.
Enemy and what is known of him.[19]

A Canadian patrol, Lieutenant D.H. Miller and two men, that went out on Thursday, 23 March 1916, saw considerably more. Miller's patrol entered the German trenches, either inadvertently, having lost its way, or under duress having been ambushed, and then saw something of Germany enroute to a prisoner of war camp. As Miller's company commander, not named in the account, said, the patrol "did not turn up ... nothing further seen or heard" until some weeks later when Miller's mother received a letter from her son. In a subsequent letter to Mrs. Miller the company commander made some interesting remarks about the patrol. First, he called it a "crawling" patrol, this being apparently a routine company task every night. Miller had been tasked to check a specific area where the enemy appeared to be extending his trench. Second, the patrol being an officer's patrol, Miller has been left to decide patrol routes, this not a prerogative an NCO in charge of a patrol had. What experience Miller had is not revealed, but he had left word that he was going "straight out ... and ... straight back by the way he had gone out, without going either to left or right." Here were the seeds of disaster, the decision probably made because after a similar patrol the previous night (22 March) Miller had "confessed to having been a little uncertain of his bearings." Whether or not he took his company commander's advice about carrying a compass during his second outing is not known. Third, bad weather may have played a significant role. An hour after the patrol departed at 0230 it found itself in the mist of a heavy snow storm "which made it impossible to see more than a few yards." By 0400 conditions were such that the company commander decided against hazarding a search party. In short, Miller and his men were put in the bag because of probable navigational error or ambush thanks to his bad decision about the route home.[20]

Recce patrols were usually just a few men, most often just an officer, sometimes an NCO, and two or three men, occasionally 10-20 men under a Subaltern if there were multiple tasks, but again sometimes just an NCO, there being only four Subalterns in a rifle company. The other two company officers were the OC, a Captain initially and later a Major, and the company 2IC, for a total of six which was almost as many as the eight or nine officers in a German battalion. BEF battalions had 25 or more officers usually present, some doing tasks that NCOs did in German battalions; one Bavarian prisoner expressed astonishment on learning that BEF officers routinely led patrols.[21]

SS 195 Scouting and Patrolling is one of the most curious manuals in the SS series, which by the end of 1917 totalled about 550 publications, 90 percent of them dealing with tactics, lessons and training. First, *SS 195* was not published until December 1917, three years after patrols had become normal infantry tasks. Second, only two of the 56 pages of the manual concern patrols. According to it, a patrol's principle task was "to secure complete mastery" of no man's land. It then listed three types of patrols: to gain information, to kill, capture and harass and to protect. Finally, it offered a half-dozen basic hints to members of patrols such as know your duties, study

19 Foster and Duthie, *Letters From the Front,* Volume I, pp. 100-102, 252; Rees, *A Schoolmaster at War,* p. 86; Haldane, *Fourth Battalion The Seaforth Highlanders,* p. 266; *Notes for Commanding Officers,* 1917 edition, pp. 23-28; 1918 edition, pp. 62-65, 211-13.

20 Foster and Duthie, *Letters From the Front,* Volume I, pp. 100-102, 252.

21 Radley, *Get Tough, Stay Tough,* pp. 108-109.

the ground and return by a different route. The manual concluded by saying that the principles laid down in *Infantry Training* "hold good," this presumably the grounds for excusing the lack of more substantial content and the delay in publication.[22]

Left unsaid was the fact that units, formations and the Corps and Army Schools had long since distilled experience into training and doctrine for patrols. One example of the patrol training at schools was a lecture presented at the School of Infantry, Calgary, Alberta. Of its 12 main points three concern the purpose and chief characteristic of recce patrols; in a word, stealth, such a patrol not to fight, but to watch, avoid being detected and take precautions against surprise. Three other points concerned reaction if detected: one man to go back to report, the rest of the patrol to disperse and then meet at a pre-arranged location and then the decision the patrol commander had to take, either to continue or to abort the patrol. The remaining content concerned patrol techniques such as use of different in and out routes.[23]

Training documents such as lecture notes on patrols that originated in 47th Canadian Battalion (4th Division) described the duty of "reconnoitring" patrols as learning no man's land so thoroughly that every advantage would be to the battalion. That this was not always recognized is evident in Cyril Falls' account of 36th (Ulster) Division: "The Higher Command often called for raids immediately troops had taken over a line, before they had learnt their way about in No Man's Land by dint of patrolling." The desired knowledge included realizing the relationship of the battalion line to the enemy line at every point, knowing the state of his wire and being able to immediately recognize what was new. As well, enemy habits and movements in no man's land required constant monitoring so any attempts to advance his wire and saps would be wrecked and he would be forced to stay within his wire.[24]

Unlike raids, which were occasional and no two quite alike, patrols became a standing and constant feature of trench warfare. As Lieutenant-Colonel Whitton, historian of the 40th British Division, pointed out, "The first thing a good battalion did on entering the line was to obtain superiority by night in No Man's Land." This echoes *SS 195* in its depiction of securing "complete mastery" of that real estate. The final questions for self-examination in *SS 408 Some of the Many Questions* reiterated this: "Am I as offensive as I might be with organized sniping, rifle grenades and patrols? Am I doing my best to make No Man's Land our land?" One British CO made patrolling a nightly event, which in time gave his battalion such firm title to no man's

22 *SS 195 Scouting and Patrolling* (GHQ: December 1917), pp. 18-20; *Infantry Training (4-Company Organization,) 1914,* Section 111. The latter's guidance on patrols was more informative than what was in *SS 195* as to the purpose, instructions, conduct and characteristics of recce patrols.

23 Notes of this lecture are in manuscript on the inside covers of *The Solution to Tactical Problems* (London: Hugh Rees Ltd., 1916) by Lieutenant-Colonel J. Layland Needham, psc. The abbreviation stands for passed staff college. Some without that qualification, and striking back at the supposed arrogance of staff officers, said it really stood for Practically Senior to Christ. Needham's book was one of the many unofficial, but generally helpful primers on various subjects written by serving or former officers that began appearing soon after the outbreak of war. These found a ready market in the large number of newly commissioned officers. The book went into a tenth edition in September 1915. The 1916 "Tenth Edition, Revised" included only a few minor modifications. In his preface Needham remarked that the book was "in line" with official manuals including amendments to these. Its guidance on the writing of operational instructions and preparation for battle in general feature in Chapter 6.

24 LAC, MG 30E100 (Currie Papers), Volume 35, Lecture 47th Battalion, p. 34; Falls, *History of 36th (Ulster) Division,* p. 71.

land that the enemy never made any real effort to claim it. As an example, he related the course of a silent raid in November 1916. Two officers out cutting enemy wire, while a raiding party waited some distance back, on looking up from their task spotted two sentries not five yards away watching them. Pretending not to notice them, the two officers finished their cutting and then joined the waiting raiders at which point it was decided to abort since a trap may have been set. As the party headed home it found itself "shepherded there by the kindly creatures who fired Very lights for their guidance but had never fired a shot." This is surely "complete mastery."[25]

SS 195 listed the second type of patrol as "patrols for protection of working parties." 47th Canadian Battalion's lecture notes broke the "protection" into defensive, listening and contact patrols, all of which it considered protective. 50th Canadian Battalion's War Diary spoke of "protective" patrols that were employed as a means "to change our policy and perhaps entice the enemy into sending out a patrol and giving us a chance to secure identifications." This battalion defined the purposes of defensive patrols as "take care of our own lines … ensure no enemy patrol is gaining any information … give ample warning of approaching danger." Appropo of that was another question from *SS 408:* "What points in front particularly require patrolling at night?"[26]

"Company Patrols," a sub-type within the defensive category, were mounted to cover the positioning of Listening Posts. Their aim was to prevent the enemy slipping into a post first and then waiting to attack the newcomers just as they arrived to man the post, or before they could get settled in. Listening Posts were established simply to watch, listen and give warning. The enemy, too, had used these for some time. In February 1916 units of 5th Canadian Brigade had discovered enemy Listening Posts at 15-yard intervals along his front as a precaution against stealth raids. But Listening Posts could not entirely guarantee security as 19th Canadian Battalion learned in November 1917. An investigation into how the enemy had got away with a prisoner determined that after gapping the wire between two posts the enemy had snatched a sentry. Suggested preventive measures included wiring the posts in and increasing the number of patrols and raids.[27] Another task of Company Patrols was patrolling the company front nightly. In late 1916 137th Brigade of 46th British Division held its 2.5 mile front with two battalions. Distances between listening posts were as much as 200 yards and, consequently, the two battalions patrolled frequently between the posts at night to prevent or at least lessen the risk of enemy incursion. Such patrols could be very risky as 31st Canadian Battalion discovered. During one night in early December 1917 a patrol of one officer and ten men from one company set out to patrol the front. The patrol disappeared. A search the next night found no trace and it was thought an ambush had snaffled the lot. In January 2nd Canadian Brigade continued to employ such patrols where the wire was thin and the posts were isolated: "Battalions will see that such portions of their front that are covered by isolated posts are protected by a strong patrol in front … This patrol must be out constantly from dusk to daylight. This will have priority over all work."[28]

25 Lieut.-Colonel F.E. Whitton, *History of the 40th Division* (Uckfield, East Sussex: Naval and Military Press, n.d.), p. 34; *SS 408 Some of the Many Questions a Platoon Commander Should Ask Himself on Taking Over a Trench and at Frequent Intervals Afterward;* Croft, *Three Years With the Ninth (Scottish) Division,* pp. 76-77.

26 *SS 195,* p. 19; LAC, MG30E100 (Currie Papers), Volume 35, pp. 34-35; *SS 408.*

27 LAC, War Diaries, 5th and 4th Canadian Brigades; RG9IIIC1, Volume 3858, Folder 84, File 16, report by GOC 4th Brigade.

28 *Ibid.,* Charles Beresford, *The Christian Soldier: The Life of Lt. Col. The Rev. Bernard William Vann, VC, MC and Bar, Croix de Guerre avec palme* (Solihull: Helion & Company Limited, 2017), p. 193; LAC,

In March 1916 the 9th East Surrey Regiment relieved a battalion of 3rd Canadian Division near St. Elci. The Canadians, who had held the area for six months, had had a very quiet time, their opponents being Saxons "who were only too anxious to live and let live." Unfortunately for the 9th their arrival coincided with Prussians relieving the Saxons, Things quickly hotted up! Part of the East Surreys' defensive measures followed the Canadian pattern of "patrols out all night in front of our own wire." These not only patrolled the front but acted as listening posts.[29]

"Contact Patrols," another sub-type, were made to maintain touch with troops left and right in cases where a gap existed between units. Since these patrols were moving they could not entirely prevent enemy penetration despite frequent contact. While they were as vulnerable to ambush as the "Company Patrols" these patrols had, nevertheless, to continue.[30]

Finally, there were the fighting patrols which went out to kill, capture and harass. The "rules" said these should be preceded by a recce patrol, but in the early days (and sometimes even later) this did not always occur, a fact evident in Lieutenant James Lovett's account of a Christmas 1915 encounter – "a fairly large party … to stir up our good friends." At an old hedge, very dense and wire festooned, suddenly "the Germans challenged … and in a twinkling the whole hedge started firing … a machine-gun opened up on us, and we had to get back into a nearby ditch and from there into the trench. I was very glad to get the party back safely."[31]

47th Canadian Battalion lecture notes do not use the term fighting patrol, preferring instead "Battle Patrol." These entered no man's land to engage the enemy or for any purpose "the accomplishment of which necessitates a fight." 50th Canadian Battalion also spoke of Battle Patrols, but in a War Diary entry described one such patrol going out to raid, the entry rather vague as to whether or not this involved holding the trenches entered. However, the lecture notes do make it clear that raids *enter* enemy trenches. Ashworth compares the Operation Order for the large-scale Canadian raid of November 1915 with those of the "early [1915] rudimentary attacks" and concludes that by the end of that year "the raid was clearly distinguished from other forms of minor assault, such as the fighting patrol." However, this was not as definitive as it sounds since fighting patrols did from time to time enter enemy trenches as did other types of patrols. In his biography of Richard Haking, Mike Senior says raids "generally aimed" at entering enemy trenches while patrols "generally aimed" at gathering information in no man's land, but could be given more aggressive tasks including entering enemy trenches.[32] On the second day of 1918 a battalion of 2nd Canadian Brigade noticed around noon that the enemy had removed some of his wire. Suspecting a raid the CO strengthened his posts, advised the neighbours and at 1745 sent out a fighting patrol of two officers and 25 ORs to "investigate the enemy wire, enter the

War Diary, 31st Canadian Battalion; RG9IIIC3, Volume 4067, Folder 5, File 7A, 2nd Brigade to battalions, 26 January.

29 Colonel H.W. Pearse and Brigadier-General H.S. Sloman, *History of the East Surrey Regiment 1914–1917*. Volume II (London: The Medici Society, 1923), p. 177.

30 Spencer (ed.), *Stanley Spencer's Great War Diary: 1915-1918*, p. 127. Spencer enlisted in 1915, was commissioned in 1917 and won the MC in August 1918.

31 *Letters From the Front*, Volume I, p. 78.

32 LAC, MG30E100 (Currie Papers), Volume 35, 47th Battalion lecture notes; Tony Ashworth, *Trench Warfare 1914-1918: The Live and Let Live System* (New York: Holmes and Meier Publishers Inc., 1980), p. 73; Mike Senior, 'Raids and Patrols: What's the Difference?' *Stand To!*, 89 (August/September 2010), pp. 9-11, includes a table listing the various terms for raids and patrols and examples of each. This table is also in Senior, *Haking*.

hostile trenches and obtain prisoners." On entry this patrol became engaged in a spirited fight, the trench being held in considerable number, quite likely by the members of a raiding party. First Army thought the action by the battalion highly commendable, aggressive and an excellent precaution against surprise.[33]

In April Sir Arthur Currie, in an instruction to division commanders on Battle Patrols, defined their purpose and drew a distinction between such patrols and raids:

> Much can be done by strong Battle Patrols and small raids. These Battle Patrols, which should never be less than a complete platoon … must aim at penetrating well into the enemy's forward system and fighting him there; their main objective being to cause him casualties … There is not sufficient time to allow of raids, carefully prepared and practised and carried out with artillery and machine-gun support, but advantage should be taken of any indications of weak points … to penetrate their lines immediately.[34]

Those who planned and carried out a Battle (Fighting) Patrol, or any patrol, or a raid, were perforce less concerned about terminology than they were about achieving their tasks and this with the lowest possible number of casualties. Occasionally an astute officer, who had done his homework, could turn definition to best advantage and in the turning camouflage deliberate sin. A case in point involved a former schoolmaster, Major R.T. Rees, a company commander in 4th Loyal North Lancashire Regiment. He determined during Passchendaele that at times an order had to be "liberally interpreted." At one point his battalion had reached some high ground which afforded good observation. To protect this position an advanced post in platoon strength was established some 150-200 yards forward. Given the nearby woods, and the absence of good trenches, it seemed obvious that the enemy might soon raid. When Rees spotted an enemy post within the wood he decided to seize its occupants that very night. He thought to lead the "patrol," but knowing that doing so would result in court martial – orders in his division prohibited Captains and above from taking part in patrols – he assigned the task to one of his Subalterns. The patrol failed when a patrol member prematurely opened fire thereby warning the enemy who immediately withdrew.

That night Rees decided that as the need for information had become more pressing he and an NCO would patrol, using the woods for cover, and find a good spot from which to observe. On return that evening, as he pondered how to report what he had seen without revealing his disobedience, Rees hit upon the solution:

> I suddenly remembered that in *Field Service Regulations* it is laid down that officers shall make a personal reconnaissance before action. What a blessed word! I promptly reported that in accordance with F.S.R. (para so-and-so), I had … made a personal reconnaissance … the results of which I begged to report. This report, moreover, was published in the Army Intelligence Summary. What if I had called it a 'patrol?' Truly there is much virtue in a name.[35]

33 LAC, RG9IIIC3, Volume 4067, Folder 5, File 7A, First Army to Canadian Corps, 10 January 1917 and 1st Canadian Division to 2nd Brigade.

34 *Ibid.*, Volume 4077, Folder 3, File 12, 15 April 1918.

35 Rees, *A Schoolmaster at War*, pp. 86-87. At war's end Rees became once again a schoolmaster.

Rees's "cover," the term "personal recce," mentioned early in this chapter, derived from *Combined Training which* stipulated that recce "shall be effected whenever possible by personal observation on the part of a commander," and from *FSR* which warned that a "commander should never commit this troops … until he has made a personal survey." Rees' recollection of these regulations while not quite accurate, did put him on safe ground.[36] Other officers, equally aware of what *FSR* had to say also used it to advantage; for example, Lieutenant-Colonel Harris, in early 1917 CO 1st Royal Berkshire Regiment, having made a "personal recce" of enemy wire, placed a raiding party in position to assault.[37]

Combined Training, which is essentially about open warfare, also instructed on "reconnaissance in force." While this does not appear in the 1914 manuals, *Infantry Training* and *FSR,* the term remained in use well into the war. In March 1917 the 11th Royal Scots made, as ordered, a "recce in force," an operation described by the battalion commander thus:

> A reconnaissance in force is not like a raid in which one skips nimbly over to the hostile trenches, bags a few prisoners and is back again before the enemy has time to sit up and take notice. No, we were asked not only to go over and stir up hornet's nest, but to count the hornets as they buzzed around. It meant not only breaking his front line, but testing the second line in order to see what reserves he had in hand – in short, to make him show his hand.

This was not new since as early as 25 September 1914 1st Royal Warwickshire regiment (4th British Division) received orders to make such a recce, to take prisoners and do so that very night. The battalion War Diary expresses how the CO objected to this because no daylight recce had been made. This task also violated the principle that recce should precede offensive action. As it turned out, the "recce in force" found the objective unoccupied. It is difficult to see, given the Royal Scots description of events, any difference between this "recce in force" and a raid, except perhaps in the time spent in this instance in enemy trenches and in the short time between order and execution.[38]

Turning now to raids, the central subject of this book, it is human nature that when one asks the question "what," the question of "who" immediately surfaces. Who made the first raid of the Great War on the Western Front is rather more complex than it seems because of the inconsistency of definitions of raid. Being first is a very human ambition and boast in every endeavour, especially in war, where the cachet "first" had much to do with reputation, both individual and corporate. Regiments have no particular genius for modesty. Being first feeds the sense of being best, part of an ethos whereby a regiment or division that does not think itself best might end up not being considered any good at all.

According to the British Official History the first operation "in the nature of a raid" must be credited to a platoon of 1st Coldstream Guards under Second Lieutenant M. Beckworth-Smith on 4 October 1914. This endeavour aimed to fill in a sap the Germans had run out from their

36 *Combined Training,* Section 35; *FSR,* Section 93.
37 Edward Wyrall, *The History of the Second Division. Volume II. 1914–1918* (Uckfield, East Sussex: Naval and Military Press, n.d.), p. 362.
38 *Combined Training,* Sections 10 and 58; Croft, *Three Years With the Ninth (Scottish) Division,* pp. 104-105; TNA: WO 95/1484: 1st Royal Warwick Regiment, September 1914.

front line. Across the 100-yard wide no man's land and into the German trench, through it and into another, Beckworth-Smith took his platoon, killing 17 Germans in all, but heavy fire made it impossible to fill in the sap. Nevertheless, and rightly so, Beckworth-Smith received the MC for his leadership. A month later (night 9/10 November) Major G.H. Taylor led 100 men, 50 from each of two battalions of the Garhwal Rifles, against a trench that enfiladed the Indian trench, the purpose being to render the German trench "unfit to the enemy." However, the trench proved too deep and too well-constructed to achieve that. A second attempt, presumably incorporating better means of ensuring serious damage, also failed. Taylor was killed. The British Official History concluded that Taylor's effort "closely approached the nature of a raid."[39]

Boraston and Bax distinguish 8th British Division's first raid differently. The 8th, a Regular Division, reached the BEF on Friday, 6 November 1914. Eight days later Lieutenant E.H. Impey, 2nd Lincolnshire Regiment, and eight ORs embarked on what the divisional history calls the "first embryonic" raid. The ground being snow-covered the party donned scrounged white sheets and women's nightgowns and so camouflaged approached the objective, a trench junction from which the Germans were enfilading an elbow in the British line. Once there the raiders brought effective fire to bear upon the enemy who presented easy targets in their dark uniforms, killing an unknown number, before withdrawing without loss. Thirteen days later (27 November) an officer and nine ORs of another battalion, together with several sappers, crossed to the German lines where they blew up a farm building housing a sniper's nest. "The idea of a raid," said the divisional history, "was beginning to take more definite shape."[40]

Another British Regular Division, Major-General Thompson Capper's 7th Division, had not been idle either, Capper never an officer to let troops become inactive or become adherents to a philosophy that said "live and let live." On the night of 24/25 November two officers and 15 ORs of the Royal Welsh Fusiliers and a few sappers rushed and demolished farm buildings from which snipers were harassing British trenches. The raiders suffered no losses. The division's historian, however, did not see this as a raid since he later credited an officer and nine ORs of the Scots Guards with carrying out the division's first raid.[41]

The somewhat amateurish nature of this endeavour on 27 November is obvious in a letter the OC Raid, Lieutenant Sir Edward Hulse, sent to his mother two days later. The raid's purpose was to confirm how the enemy was holding his trenches. It is not clear from the instructions issued to him that the raiders were to actually enter the enemy trench. In his letter he related that the enemy had been very quiet, especially at night, for several days. It was also thought that by day only snipers and work parties were holding the enemy trench, everyone, except a few sentries, moving rearward at night. The CO, on seeing the raiders off, instructed them to "get right up to the wire, peep over if not spotted … fire two rounds rapid … kill all we can,

39 Lieutenant-Colonel Sir John Ross of Bladenburg, *The Coldstream Guards 1914-1918* (London: Oxford University Press, 1928), p. 151; Edmonds, *August-October 1914,* pp. 452-53; Charles Messenger, 'Trench Raiding', *History of the First World War,* Volume 5, 1971, pp. 1846-47; *Trench Fighting 1914-18* (New York: Ballantine, 1972), p. 37; Edmonds and Wynne, *Winter 1914-15: Battle of Neuve Chapelle: Battle of Ypres* (London: Macmillan, 1927), p. 32.

40 Boraston and Bax, *Eighth Division,* p. 8.

41 Atkinson, *Seventh Division,* p. 117; Keith R. Simpson, 'Capper and the Offensive Spirit', *RUSI Journal,* June 1973, p. 55. Capper was killed in action in September 1915. TNA: WO 95/1657: War Diary, Scots Guards, 27 November 1914, Appendix 58; Peter Barton, *The Lost Legions of Fromelles* (London: Constable, 2014), pp. 28-31.

and then each man for himself." For his part, Hulse told his men that when he fired his rifle the whole party was to run forward, do maximum damage and then make off. In the event, an alert sentry challenged the raiders who then doubled forward, fired two rounds each (one man threw a bomb into the trench) and then all "ran like hares." Immediately an enemy machine-gun, which "we knew nothing about," opened fire. It is also unclear what recce was done before the raid and what information Hulse received. Halfway across no man's land he realized that the enemy trench was strongly held, "an unpleasant conclusion … when we were supposed to be raiding a lightly held trench." Summing up the affair he wrote "The great thing was that we found the enemy had brought up machine-guns, tripled their numbers … and were very much awake … all of which was very different from reports from our scouts. The CO frankly told me that [he] did not expect many to get back."[42]

Boraston and Bax, who described 8th Division's "embryonic" raid (see above), also wrote an account of a raid they dubbed the first "genuine" raid on the Western Front. "Genuine" was accurate, they thought, since Lieutenant F.C. Roberts, 1st Worcestershire Regiment, and his men actually entered enemy trenches, something the "embryonic" raid had not. Everard Wyrall, the author of a history of 50th British Division, agreed and to "genuine" added "the first recorded raid" by British troops. The British Official Historian shared Wyrall's view. Charles Messenger considered Roberts' effort the "first really successful" raid. Captain H.Fitzm. Stacke, historian of the Worcestershire Regiment, initially credited Roberts with the first trench raid of the war, but a page later declared his assertion "doubtful" in view of the raid by the Indian Corps in late 1914. However, he went on to say that Roberts' raid was "certainly the first to be widely known," a claim lacking confirmation. When the Worcestershires took over the trenches the German lines were about 200 yards distant. On the night 2/3 January recce patrols encountered German parties forward of their line and came under fire from these parties which were thought to be enemy patrols. On the morning of 3 January the right company of the Worcestershires observed a new trench a mere 40 yards away. It was then realized that the enemy parties of the night before had been covering the working parties while they dug the trench. Clearly, the enemy could not be permitted to man the new trench since it gave them a good jumping-off position for an assault. Consequently, at 2045 that night, 3 January 1915, Roberts and 25 ORs entered the new enemy trench, killed an estimated 30 Germans and then withdrew having lost two men killed. This raid, which lasted "not more than four minutes," had achieved total surprise. Roberts was awarded the DSO.[43]

A month later 1st Canadian Division joined the ten British Regular Divisions that then formed the BEF. Following a period under instruction in the trenches, a minor role at Neuve Chapelle and a short stay in reserve, the division moved to the Ypres Salient where it underwent

42 TNA: WO 95/1657: War Diary, Scots Guards, 27 November 1914; Nicol, *Till the Trumpet Sounds Again,* Volume 1, pp. 232-34.

43 Boraston and Bax, *Eighth Division,* pp. 8, 13-14; Wyrall, *Fiftieth Division,* p. 129. This was Wyrall's first book; in all he wrote 21, a remarkable series of regimental and divisional histories. Edmonds and Wynne, *Winter 1914-15: Battle of Neuve Chapelle: Battle of Ypres,* p. 32; Messenger, *Trench Fighting,* p. 38. Roberts later won the MC and the Victoria Cross (VC). For the introduction of the MC and the criteria for award of it and the DSO see Radley, *Get Tough, Stay Tough,* p. 262; Captain H. FitzM. Stacke, *The Worcestershire Regiment in the Great War*, Volume 1 (Uckfield, East Sussex: Naval and Military Press, n.d.), pp. 56-57.

a severe trial, suffering very heavy casualties, 208 officers and 5,829 ORs.[44] Within a month of that the 1st fought at Festubert, followed by Givenchy within another month. It was well into July before the division could assess the events of a harrowing half-year and identify and absorb the lessons of that period. Study of 1st Division's gradual progress along a complex and difficult learning curve reveals the division's ability to implement solutions to difficulties along the way. During the early months at war raids had not featured in the Canadian agenda; as Guy Chapman, a Subaltern in 37th British Division wrote, "These days were before the Canadians had set the costly and depressing fashion of raiding." 17th British Division's historian, who noted that until late December 1915 raids "except among the Canadians … were rare adventures" went on to describe raids by the 17th as "marking the beginning of raiding in its elementary state of development." 2nd Canadian Division, even before it reached France in September 1915, was thinking about raiding, although that word was not mentioned in a training directive in June 1915 on teaching techniques for "bombing along trenches" by small parties in which every man is "told off to his task."[45]

It would be mid-November, in fact, before the Canadian Corps made its mark when it came to raiding, a game that Sir Douglas Haig, C-in-C of the BEF as of 19 December, characterized as "Winter Sports," although he saw these extending into spring 1916.[46] On the night of 16/17 November, one "dull and warmer, some mist," two officers and 160 ORs of Louis Lipsett's 2nd Canadian Brigade launched the first large-scale raid by the BEF. Well-planned and rehearsed, this raid was so successful it established a reputation for Canadians as the raiding experts. Word got around for prior to their first raid in June 1916 the Australians, who had sought advice from 1st Canadian Division on raiding, were given temporarily two officers to assist them. The New Zealand Division before its first raid also requested assistance and received a substantial package of training notes on patrolling and raid tactics compiled by 1st Division.[47] As this Canadian raid set the pattern, and because it is so thoroughly documented in Canadian and British sources, primary and secondary, it features in Chapter 8. After it, large-scale raids became quite common, some approaching and even exceeding battalion strength.

James Dunn, Medical Officer with the 2nd Royal Welsh Fusiliers, saw, as others did, this raid as a game-changer:

> A new notion of a raid has been practised by the Canadians. It is the mode. Every self-respecting battalion will want to raid, the others will be ordered. The immemorial notion of a raid is to enter the enemy's lines by stealth or surprise, to kill or capture, plunder and destroy, and get away with no fighting or little. The new notion is a battle in miniature with all the preliminaries and accompaniments magnified.[48]

44 George Cassar, *Beyond Courage: The Canadians at the Second Battle of Ypres* (Ottawa: Oberon, 1985), p. 192.
45 Chapman, *Passionate Prodigality,* p. 69. In August 1915 Chapman had been a month with 13th Royal Fusiliers. Atteridge, *17th (*Northern*) Division,* p. 69; LAC, War Diary, 19th Canadian Battalion, June 1915, Appendix 13.
46 Duff Cooper, *Haig.* Volume I (Toronto: Macmillan, 1935), p. 298.
47 Pugsley, 'Learning from the Canadian Corps on the Western Front', p. 7.
48 LAC, 5th Canadian Battalion War Diary, 16 November 1915; Dunn, *The War the Infantry Knew,* p. 192.

Dunn, DSO, MC and Bar, DCM (Distinguished Conduct Medal) was a remarkable officer. He had been with the battalion since 1915. On 26 September 1917 in the midst of a very bad situation Dunn first manned a machine-gun and then for several hours found himself in command of the battalion. In his "A Footnote on the War" Siegfried Sassoon, who served with Dunn, said of Doctor Dunn:

> We'd got a Doctor with a DSO
> And much unmedalled merit. In the line
> Or out of it, he'd taught the troops to know
> That shells, bombs, bullets, gas, or even a mine
> … things he took
> For granted, and dismissed with one shrewd look.[49]

It is no surprise that Louis Lipsett's brigade was the game-changer. Lipsett, a British Regular (Royal Irish Regiment), was a graduate of Sandhurst and the Staff College. Following service in western Canada as a General Staff Officer he became CO 8th Battalion. At Second Ypres he had greatly distinguished himself so demonstrating his sterling abilities that he was beyond doubt the outstanding battalion commander in 1st Division. As a brigade commander, he continued to excel, and at age 42 became the youngest of the Canadian division commanders. It would not be unreasonable to say that he was the best of these. Some thought him a very hard master, but the consensus considered him a splendid trainer and leader who strove to inculcate self-confidence and the offensive spirit in subordinates, especially in his officers. While a serious no nonsense officer, Lipsett was blessed with the saving grace of charm and humour. Lieutenant Clifford Wells, who joined the 8th Battalion in July 1916 (Lipsett was then GOC 3rd Division) had this to say of Lipsett: "the best known, best liked and one of the most efficient officers … the 8th believe he is in a class by himself … his influence is still felt in the battalion and his name … a tradition of all that a CO ought to be."[50]

At Sandhurst Lipsett's classmate and chum had been Winston Churchill who in January 1916 took command of the 6th Royal Scots Fusiliers, Ninth (Scottish) Division. A few days after assuming command Churchill visited Lipsett's brigade. Churchill's biographer. Martin Gilbert, credits Lipsett with inventing the raid, which was not so, but certainly Lipsett was an aggressive commander who never ceased his earnest search for ways to harass and kill the enemy. Churchill was greatly impressed with Lipsett's demonstration of how a raid should work: "He made a realistic attack with his bombs on a section of our reserve trenches. The splinters flew all over the place … The Canadians grinned from ear to ear to see me. Wonderful fellows: like leopards."

Ever the politician, Churchill expressed his thanks in a speech, a "really good one," he told his wife. The visit appears in 5th Battalion's War Diary for 14 January: "Carried out practice attack … before Lt. Col. W. Churchill." Churchill again dined with Lipsett, an occasion after which

49 Siegfried Sassoon, *The War Poems* (London: Faber and Faber, 1983), p. 147.

50 For more on Lipsett see Kenneth Radley, 'Inescapable Realities: Canadian Command, Spring 1915', in Spencer Jones (ed.), *Courage Without Glory: The British Army on the Western Front 1915* (Solihull: Helion Publishing, 2015); O.C.S. Wallace (ed.), *From Montreal to Vimy Ridge and Beyond: The Correspondence of Lieut. Clifford Almon Wallace, B.A. of the 8th Battalion, Canadians, B.E.F., November 1915–April 1917* (Toronto: McClelland, Goodchild and Stewart, 1917), p. 168.

he wrote Lipsett "has gone out of his way to be helpful ... even coming out with me on a prowl in No-Man's-Land to see if there were any possibilities to bringing off an enterprise against the German trenches." Kindred spirits.[51]

Given Lipsett's record and his reputation it is uncommon to find a quite contrary opinion of him. One appears in a letter written two decades after the November 1915 raid by an officer who had been a Staff Captain at brigade HQ at that time. The writer related how he and a soldier of 5th Battalion had made a daylight recce the day before the raid to determine the state of enemy wire, after which they returned "penetrating our own trenches in broad daylight without detection." On reaching brigade HQ he told Lipsett and Major-General Arthur Currie that a night raid on the enemy was possible. Currie, supposedly, "was skeptical, but Lipsett was absolutely scathing ... Lipsett ridiculed the idea throughout, until after its successful carrying out, and it was only the fact that Currie viewed it with favour, that prevented his active opposition." This account does not square with what we know of Lipsett and of this particular raid; moreover, the account is contradictory within itself. Lipsett by all accounts was keen on raiding. Almost immediately after taking command of 3rd Division he spoke to officers of 52nd Battalion telling them of the special stress he placed on surprise raids. The Staff Captain's account cannot be verified. It was 5th Battalion's lines that he claimed to have penetrated without detection. Currie, supposedly, was "perturbed" about this breach of security and closely interrogated the Staff Captain about it. It is not clear if or when such an interrogation occurred.[52]

While generals could be "perturbed" more junior officers had to live with how raids disturbed the "even tenor" of trench warfare. Writing of the raiding "season" in the autumn of 1916 the author of *Thirty-Fourth Division* dubbed raids "little episodes ... little fights ... little affairs," such adjectives categorizing a series of 22 minor operations by his division between mid-September 1916 and mid-February 1917. Context says he is not being dismissive since he writes of the very gallant deeds done and how successful raids were a "triumph of care in organization and great gallantry in execution." Certainly, he does raise the question of the value of raids, a subject warranting close attention, as do the mixed opinions about this aspect, as well as his dismay at how much the series had cost in casualties. A "stunt" could be good, bad or indifferent, of course. James Dunn described one "thoroughly bad show ... futile in its aim ... organization was bad ... men were in doubt or ignorance ... therefore very windy ... bad weather ... indifferent morale." All this is in striking contrast to a raid a few days later, one successful in all aspects, prisoners taken, morale improved, congratulations arriving, commendations, too.[53] Some euphemisms for raids feature sarcasm. Siegfried Sassoon, referring in late 1916 to a fine raid pulled off earlier by "some Canadian toughs blamed them for making such entertainments popular with the staff." Edmund Blunden, Royal Sussex Regiment, more directly called raids "suicide" operations and "speaking for myself and for some of those I knew best, we hated these

51 Martin Gilbert, *The Challenge of War: Winston S. Churchill, 1914-1916* (London: William Heinemann Ltd., 1971; reprint, London: Mandarin, 1990), pp. 636-37, 745-46; LAC, 5th Battalion War Diary, 14 January 1916.

52 LAC, RG 24, Volume 1829, GAQ 7-38, 20 August 1936, Lt. Col. Ross Napier to Colonel A.F. Duguid; 52nd Battalion War Diary, 28 June 1916.

53 Shakespear, *Thirty-Fourth Division*, pp. 80-83; Dunn, *The War the Infantry Knew*, pp. 486-93, 497-502. The good and the bad raids occurred in June 1918.

raids." Blunden thought "raid" the one word in the whole vocabulary of the war as the one that "caused a sinking feeling in the stomach of ordinary mortals."[54]

"War Party" was a term peculiar to some Canadian units after the successful model raid on La Petite Douve farm in November 1915. Some Canadians considered participation in a War Party a mark of honour. At least two sources credit the Canadian Corps with initiating raids that aimed specifically at taking prisoners. Stephen Graham, the author of *A Private in the Guards,* was told this kind of "snatch" raid was a Canadian innovation. Such raids were also called "cutting-out" raids by some units and "winkle" raids by other units, a term possibly of German origin, although Cyril Falls thought otherwise: "The German methods of defence with outposts far in front … not always strongly defended and sometimes held at night only offered considerable opportunity for those silent little raids … which the Canadians had perfected and knew by the expressive term "winkling."[55] The historian of the 12th British Division, neutral regarding the origin of the term, in describing a German raid on his division in February 1917 related how one man of six in a sap went missing, having been what was "commonly called 'winkled.'" Whatever its origin, the term entered BEF vocabulary and beyond and was still in use decades later.[56] Another source defined winkling as "to force or bluff a small number of Germans during a raid or an attack to come up out of a dugout."[57]

It might seem that raids and local attacks were more or less the same sort of enterprise, a view held by Lieutenant-Colonel J.L. Jack, CO 2nd West Yorkshire Regiment, in September 1916 when he said a raid was "like any other small attack." But this was only partially so. A closer look says they are really two different things. John Terraine, who edited Jack's very informative diary, took pains to show that Jack's summation was rather misleading in view of the essential difference between a raid and an attack: "The first was designed to enter enemy trenches, which was done constantly by all armies; the second was meant to hold them, and advance further." The phrase "with a view to holding ground" in Sir John French's policy memorandum in 1915 applied to attack. A raid also "gains," but only attack "holds" ground. Lieutenant-Colonel H.R. Sandilands, the last wartime GSO1 (General Staff Officer 1st Grade) of the 23rd British Division, in describing that division's first raid in January 1916, used the term raid "in the sense of an operation undertaken with the object of entering but not holding the enemy's trenches, and distinct from the action of fighting patrols against hostile parties in No Man's Land." (see earlier in this chapter 47th Battalion's "battle" (fighting) patrols). Sandiland defined a raid as a

54 Siegfried Sassoon, *Memoirs of an Infantry Officer* (London: Faber and Faber, 1965), p. 20; Blunden, *Undertones of War,* pp. 44, 162-63. Attitudes toward raids are discussed more fully in Chapter 7.

55 Worthington, *Amid the Guns Below,* p. 40; Dunn, *The War the Infantry Knew,* p. 492; Graham, *A Private in the Guards,* p. 263; Ellis, *Eye-Deep in Hell,* p. 76; Falls, *36th (Ulster) Division,* p. 131. Haig used the term "cutting-out" in his despatch of 19 May 1916 (Boraston and Bax, *Haig's Despatches,* p. 4).

56 Scott, ed., *History of the 12th (Eastern) Division,* p. 94. A sap was a short trench that protruded from the main trench. At its end two or three men would watch and listen. See "to winkle" in John Brophy and Eric Partridge, *The Long Trail: What the British Soldier Sang and Said in the Great War of 1914–18* (London: Andre Deutsch, 1965), p. 205. Field-Marshal Sir William Slim, *Defeat Into Victory* (London: Cassell And Company Ltd., 1956), p. 331. Slim, who served in Mesopotamia during the Great War, was familiar with winkling. He used the term in his account of the Burma Campaign during the Second World War.

57 Topp, *42nd Battalion,* pp. 102-103; LAC, 42nd Canadian Battalion War Diary, January 1917.

"minor operation, carefully planned and rehearsed, designed to enter the enemy's trenches by surprise, to destroy his garrison and defence, secure prisoners and withdraw." The War Diary of the 18th Canadian Battalion described a "minor operation" as involving holding any position taken while a "minor enterprise" – a raid – did not. The last British GOC of the Canadian Corps, Sir Julian Byng, shared this view: a raid and a minor operation were two different endeavours. Suffice it to say that surprise was never guaranteed and could, in fact, be prejudiced by one's own side. Lieutenant-Colonel G.S. Hutchison, who commanded a machine-gun company and then 33rd Battalion, Machine-Gun Corps, referring to a raid by the 2nd Argyll and Sutherland Highlanders, muddies the waters somewhat when he tells us that "Technically, there were two types of raid: first, the 'raid and stay'; second, the 'raid and away.'" The latter was better known as the "smack and back." The example he offers shows that the 2nd Argylls held what it had seized; by definition, then, an attack, not a raid.[58]

The distinction between raid and attack was important then, and for purposes of this present study it is important now, since this study is limited to raids. If a unit report or other associated documents called an endeavour an attack and the Operation Order expressed the intent as seize and hold then it is not included here. Where ambiguity existed, the context usually provided clarification. In short, interpretation and assessment determined whether or not a particular endeavour met the definition of raid. When it did not, it was not included. This applied to even the earliest of such endeavours.

Writing of the period between Haig's appointment as C-in-C (December 1915) and the Somme the British Official History described the essence of a raid thus:

> That the raiders should enter the enemy's trenches, kill as many as possible and return before counter-measures can be taken. Special tasks may be added, such as obtaining prisoners for 'identification,' damaging mine shafts, destroying a length of trench or post which is giving particular trouble, but cannot be permanently held if captured. The number of men employed was usually 10 to 200. The instructions for a raid regarded as a model are given in Appendix 6.

But this proved subject to local interpretation. When in June 1915 two battalions of 39th British Division, in trying to reduce a German salient south of Neuve Chapelle, attacked and took the salient, but were forced out after two hours, the Corps Commander proclaimed success because, after all, it had only been a raid![59]

In March 1916 GHQ issued *SS 107 Notes on Minor Enterprises,* a manual that focussed on the planning, preparation and conduct of a raid. In a section entitled "General Principles" it introduced these as suggestions, not rules. It identified surprise as the most important factor in raiding, but stressed that success also depended on careful selection and recce of the objective.

58 Terraine (ed.), *General Jack's Diary,* p. 166; Sandilands, *23rd Division,* pp. 39, 41; LAC, War Diary, 18th Battalion, September 1918; Hutchison, *Thirty-Third Division,* p. 8; LAC, Canadian Corps General Staff War Diary, Notes by Commander Canadian Corps on Raid by 3rd Canadian Division, 20 December 1916. These notes are also in TNA: WO 95/2540: 38th (Welsh) Division General Staff War Diary. Byng's notes were widely distributed within the BEF.

59 Edmonds, *Haig's Command to 1st July,* p. 156; Miles, *2nd July to the End of the Battles of the Somme,* p. 544. Appendix 6 was the Operation Order for the Canadian raid in November 1915.

These could only be carried out if patrols had established dominance of no man's land. Another essential, planning, required at least one week if it was to be thorough. The manual did not recommend assault by separate parties at different points during a raid. It also warned that if a raid encountered a ready and prepared enemy it should be aborted. In application, some of these principles were violated or ignored and not always for good reason. One last "General Principle" is of most interest here because of how it distinguishes raids from patrols:

> The number of men ... varies according to the nature and extent of the objective. The German trenches have been entered by patrols of from 2 to 8 men, and for the purpose of securing an identification or obtaining information on some definite point a small patrol may be sufficient. Raids on the enemy's trenches have been made by parties varying from 30 to 300.

Another section in *SS 107* describes the purposes of raids. Having set out the composition of a raiding party – bayonet men and grenadiers (bombers) to clear the trench, men to clear dugouts, rifle grenadiers, Lewis gunners and sometimes RE demolition teams – the manual then listed the various purposes of raids: find gas cylinders and mine shafts, destroy weapons and equipment, take prisoners and even gather "loot." 25th Canadian Battalion, raiding on Christmas Eve 1916, did very well when it came to the last. During this surprise raid on enemy trenches the raiders wrecked a section of trench, took prisoners and looted numerous Christmas parcels meant for the occupants. The 25th paid a price, spending long periods on Christmas Day dodging shells fired in retaliation.[60]

SS 101 Notes for Infantry Officers on Trench Warfare, published the same month as *SS 107,* had this to say about raids:

> Minor local enterprises ... furnish the best means of maintaining the efficiency of the troops ... Constant activity in harassing the enemy may lead to reprisals ... but if persevered in, always result in ultimate mastery, it gives the troops a healthy interest and wholesome topics of conversation, and it achieves the double purpose of raising the moral [sic]of our own troops, whilst lowering that of the enemy.[61]

As this study will show the reality was not quite so rosy.

Notes for Commanding Officers (1917 edition) contained nothing on raids, but the 1918 edition included a short chapter entitled "Notes on Raids." By way of introduction the chapter noted that raids could not be standardized since originality and surprise were instrumental in success. It then listed the types of raids: to secure identifications, to ascertain damage done by bombardment, to inflict loss and damage, to lower enemy morale and to raise BEF morale. Success demanded adherence to the principles of raiding: simplicity, punctuality and determination. Another section entitled "Orders for Raids" discussed the content of orders and who prepared them, be it battalion or brigade. One section ("Preparations") stressed recce, rehearsals and the importance of securing prisoners. Perhaps the most important part of the notes concerned the organization

60 *SS* 107; Tennyson (ed.), *Merry Hell: The Story of the 25th Battalion,* p. 60.
61 *SS 101 Notes for Infantry Officers on Trench Warfare* (London: War Office, March 1916), p. 8.

of raiding parties, stressing that raids "must be carried out by complete tactical units" and within these raiding parties, if enemy counter-attack seemed likely, "blocks" consisting of a minimum of two riflemen, two Lewis guns and two rifle bombers had to be formed and trained to block trenches. Finally, since by this time the negative impact on surprise of artillery cutting wire was well known, the 1918 edition recommended "best method is to concentrate on cutting wire all the time with Stokes and trench mortars, so that there are always some gaps ready made."[62]

Two types of bombs served platoons, one being rifle grenades and the other being hand grenades (bombs). These became ever more important, especially hand grenades and those who threw them. The latter became "specialists," their exalted status evident in the flaming red grenade badge on the right upper sleeve.[63] Bombing officers became stars, the confidants of commanders and staff officers. Hugh Urquhart, historian of the 16th Canadian Battalion, called bombers "stormy petrels [whose] selection … for special duty brought strife, and [whose] entrance into the battalion interior economy caused more trouble." As more and more men became trained on bombs, the rifle became neglected. In October 1915 the Brigadier-General General Staff (BGGS) of the Canadian Corps, C.H. Harington, emphasized in a "lessons learned" instruction that as many men as possible had to be trained on bombs because all platoons had to be ready to carry out bombing attacks and to participate in raids. As Lieutenant Duncan Macintyre, 28th Battalion, put it, "We all have to learn to be bombers." With grenades came changes "tactical, organic and domestic." Even titles were affected:

> During 1915 each battalion formed a Grenadier Platoon – the legitimate successor of the Grenadier Company which headed each battalion of the Line in the far-off days of pipeclay and scarlet. Presently, however, the Grenadier Guards objected to the use by other regiments of the term "grenadiers" and in spite of opposition from those who valued tradition, the old designation disappeared, and the "grenadiers" of Line battalions were re-christened "bombers." The specialist platoon was abolished and all ranks were trained in "bombing" until at last the bomb became almost the principal weapon of the foot soldier.[64]

Manuals and various instructions reflected these developments. In October 1915 GHQ issued *CDS 74 The Training and Employment of Grenadiers,* this later replaced by *SS 127 The Training*

62 *Notes for Commanding Officers* (1918), Chapter IX. While this chapter does not cite references these points on "tactical units" relate specifically to GHQ O.B./1919, 2 February 1917 and *SS 144 The Normal Formation for the Attack* (GHQ, February 1917), p.1.These two were reprinted in *WO 3995* (General Staff, April 1917) which stated "The PLATOON is to be regarded as the unit in the assault." *SS 143 Instructions for the Training of Platoons for Offensive Action, 1917* (General Staff, February 1917) includes the same statement. To remind, at the time battalions, companies, platoons and sections were all referred to as units. Today all below battalion are called sub-units.

63 The red bomber badge is illustrated on page 127 of Peter Doyle, *Tommy's War: British Military Memorbilia 1914-1918* (Ramsbury: The Crowood Press Ltd., 2008).

64 Urquhart, *16th Battalion,* pp. 101, 104-105, 118; LAC, RG9IIIC1, Volume 3859, Folder 85, File 4, BGGS to divisions; Ian Hay [Major-General John Hay Beith] *The First Hundred Thousand: Being the Unofficial Chronicle of a Unit of "K(I)"* (Toronto: William Briggs, 1916), pp. 232-33: Stacke, *The Worcestershire Regiment,* p. 116; LAC, MG 30E241 (Macintyre Papers), Diary, 11 January 1916. The senior staff officer in a corps was the BGGS. A GHQ Routine Order in April 1916 officially made bombers of the grenadiers.

and Employment of Bombers. But in February 1917 another manual made it clear that the cult of the bomb had had its day. *WO 3995* was amended to read "the rifle and the bayonet is the first and the hand grenade the second weapon of every soldier and that all men in Rifle Sections must be trained either in the Lewis Gun or the Rifle Grenade."

During the first half of 1917 the comeback of the rifle became evident in the bullet and bayonet courses run at Army, Corps and Division Schools. Many new ranges were also built, these essential to improving small arms proficiency. Consequently, men became less dependent on artillery and on bombs; for example, men on reaching an objective now settled down to shooting, deadly rifle fire putting paid to counter-attacks. By early 1918 this was routine, the lesson re-affirmed, said the War Diary of the 87th Canadian Battalion, that bomb was inferior to rifle and bayonet. Siegfried Sassoon summed up the change thus:

> To these I turn, in these I trust –
> Brother Lead and Sister Steel.[65]

Raids often involved artillery and/or Stokes and trench mortars and at times various other support arms such as elements of engineer field companies, tunnelling companies and gas specialists. But a raid could instead ignore all of these and opt for stealth or silence, or as designated by some, a "surprise" raid, this perhaps more hope than designation. A raid could also be a cutting-out or winkle affair as described earlier. "Bombing" raids were another variant, as were "dummy" raids whose purpose was deception designed to deceive, turn attention from a real raid and cause the enemy to react needlessly and wastefully. Lieutenant-Colonel Shakespear describes these: "Besides real raids we also troubled the Boche with dummy raids, generally in another part of the line just before … real attack. A dummy raid might consist only of bombardment, or firing of Bangalore torpedoes coupled with the exhibition of dummy figures in No Man's Land." One dummy raid executed by 10th Canadian Battalion in March 1916 to assist a British attack on The Bluff, a low, forested mound on the north bank of the Ypres-Comines Canal, featured smoke bombs, rifle grenades, artillery and machine-gun fire on selected points, pouring petrol into the Douve River and setting it alight and an explosives-laden raft set loose to float down the river guided by an officer who as soon as he saw the German wire lit the fuse and got out of the way. The subsequent explosion was loud and bright. This diversion, which helped make the British attack a success, is more fully described in Chapter 9.

65 *CDS 74 The Training and Employment of Grenadiers* (GHQ, October 1915); Charles Messenger, *Call to Arms: The British Army 1914-1918* (London: Weidenfeld & Nicolson, 2005), p. 192; *SS 182 Instructions on Bombing Training and Employment of Bombers* (London: Harrison and Sons, November 1917); Ponsonby, *The Grenadier Guards*. Volume 1. Curiously, the matter of titles, bombers or grenadiers, is not mentioned by Ponsonby in his three volume account. *WO 3995*, amendment to Section 7; LAC, 87th Battalion War Diary, 10 April 1918. Sassoon wrote the poem after attending a lecture on bayonet fighting by Colonel Ronnie Campbell during which Campbell used the words brother and sister. See Roberts, *Siegfried Sassoon*, pp. 82-83. Campbell and his bayonet fighting "Circus" toured the BEF before the Somme lecturing and staging dramatic exercises emphasizing the "Spirit of the Bayonet." Campbell, who served with the Canadian Contingent during the South African War, died in 1963. See also Radley, *We Lead Others Follow*, p. 283 and note 20.

In August 19th Canadian Battalion staged a less dramatic, but quite successful dummy raid that had as its object "the drawing of Germans into their frontline [thereby] getting targets for our artillery." This quite imaginative enterprise, thanks to its novelty, fooled the enemy:

> Strong wires were attached to enemy wire at two points. From 2.45 am – 3.45 am rifle fire ceased on battalion front and only an occasional flare. Then 3 white flares were used ... and at same time enemy wire shaken by means of wire. 3 rifle grenades were fired at points in wire. Short words of command were given by an officer in our trenches. Artillery then fired on enemy front line, supports, communication trenches and selected points for 1 min. And trench mortars on front line. At 4 am German entanglements were again shaken and artillery fired again. The result was that enemy bombed his own wire along the entire front (about 600 yards) and started shelling ... the first rounds falling in his own lines ... then in No Man's Land. Subsequently 12 more shells fell into [his] lines.

While there was no way to accurately confirm enemy casualties, it is likely some resulted from Canadian fire and from German artillery fire, which may not have been so much deliberate fire on his own trenches, thinking Canadians there, but "drop shorts" which always angered infantry that suffered under them. One German artillery regiment, the 49th Field (not involved in this instance) fired short so persistently that it became known as the 48 and a Half Regiment!

That same month 9th Scottish Rifles (Ninth (Scottish) Division) staged a similar deception. After placing Bangalore torpedoes in the enemy wire dummies were then fixed in No Man's Land. These were worked by wires from the battalion lines so as to give the appearance of advancing troops. At the same time rifle and machine-gun fire, trench mortars and artillery hit the enemy line. It was thought that these activities caused the enemy to man his front, thereby presenting lucrative targets for artillery.[66]

A more elaborate type of deception, the "Chinese Attack," employed many of the same devices dummy raids did, all trying to convince the enemy that a major attack was beginning. Smoke screens were sometimes used to conceal the battalion front and help persuade that a major attack was underway. Again, how effective such measures were is debatable.[67]

Bombing raids and bombing attacks differed in the same way that raids and attacks did. A bombing raid, as Private E.W. Russell, 5th Canadian Battalion, experienced it can be summed up this way: follow the bombardment into the enemy trenches, kill as many as possible, snatch prisoners and get out quick. Another Canadian battalion, the 58th of 3rd Division, conducted a bombing attack during operations against Zollern Graben in the Courcelette sector on 20 September 1916. At 0500 the battalion launched what was hoped to be a surprise bombing

66 Shakespear, *Thirty-Fourth Division,* p. 81; Daniel G. Dancocks, *Gallant Canadians: The Story of the Tenth Canadian Infantry Battalion 1914-1919* (Calgary: The Calgary Highlanders Regimental Funds Association, 1990), pp. 73-74; LAC, 19th Battalion War Diary, August 1916; Ewing, *Ninth (Scottish) Division,* p. 78. A Bangalore was a tube filled with explosives and fired by a fuse. It effectively cleared a gap in wire. It was also prone to failure. Later chapters provide further detail and examples of the use of this device.

67 Fraser and Gibbon, *Soldier and Sailor Words and Phrases,* p. 54; Moorhouse, *Forged by Fire,* p. 76; Chris McCarthy, 'Queen of the Battlefield: The Development of Command, Organization and Tactics in the British Infantry Battalion During the Great War', in Gary Sheffield and Dan Todman (eds.), *Command and Control on the Western Front* (Staplehurst: Spellmount, 2004), p. 178.

attack up Zollern Graben in concert with the 43rd Battalion. About 75 metres or so up the trench the raiders found it blocked and from behind it the enemy poured heavy fire upon them. Then in came a counter-attack by a newly arrived regiment which pushed the Canadians back until by the end of the morning they retained only a small, precarious toehold. Sustained fighting has gone on for almost seven hours. Russell and his mates of 5th Battalion, on the other hand, had gone in, inflicted as much punishment as possible and got out, their bombing raid over in minutes.[68]

Stealth or silent raids by definition involved "no preliminary bombardment as this was to be a surprise raid." 47th Canadian Battalion's "Lecture Notes" described "two distinctive types of raids … STEALTH [and] ORDINARY." The former, as the notes had it, usually consisted of a bombing section of one officer and eight ORs seeking to enter enemy trenches unobserved and winkle a prisoner. No artillery, no "strafe." The latter involved 50-1,000 raiders plus artillery support, field and sometimes heavy as well. If a STEALTH raid

> the Bombing Section as laid down in *SS 143 Instructions for the Training of Platoons for Offensive Action* lends itself towards this as well as for the larger type of raid. Each Section must be a complete organization in itself so it can move about quickly. It must be capable of bombing down a trench, making a frontal attack or blocking a trench. In the New Platoon Organization you are not only able to manoeuvre each section independently, but you have men who have been together for some time.[69]

20th British Brigade (7th Division) in "Some Notes on Raids," which went to battalions on 26 July 1917, elaborated somewhat:

> Stealth Raids are those undertaken by a group of scouts or determined men. All details may generally be left to the leader, as no outside assistance is required. The object is usually to capture a post, sentry, machine-gun or to obtain an identification by stealth. Force Raids are those in which the raiders do the enemy as much Harm as possible in a short … time and then retire.[70]

The historian of the 42nd (East Lancashire) Division recounted a daylight stealth raid in June 1916 by an NCO and two men of the 10th Manchester Regiment. The three captured four Germans and a light mortar which the prisoners carried back to battalion lines. The Corps Commander personally congratulated the NCO and with his words came 14 days special leave for the trio.[71]

68 Imperial War Museum, 76/170/1, Pte. E.W. Russell, 'A Private Soldier's Views on the Great War 1914-1918', p. 25; Kevin R. Shackleton, *Second to None: The Fighting 58th Battalion of the Canadian Expeditionary Force* (Toronto: The Dundurn Group, 2005), pp. 82-84; Nicholson, *Canadian Expeditionary Force,* pp. 172-73 and sketch 27.

69 LAC, MG 30E100 (Currie Papers), Volume 35, 'Lectures 47th Battalion', pp. 30-33; Brophy and Partridge, *The Long Trail,* p. 186, define a stealth raid as "small scale, short and sharp," no artillery. They make the point that stealth raids were often successful because the enemy was taken off guard.

70 TNA: WO 95/1654, War Diary, 20th Brigade, July 1917.

71 Gibbon, *42nd (East Lancashire) Division,* pp. 94-95.

A one man, or in this case, a one officer raid, occurred in another area in July 1916. While a very small raid, this venture by Captain Siegfried Sassoon, MC was by definition a raid. He left battalion trenches, crossed no man's land, entered enemy trenches and after a time returned. This exploit and others during which he demonstrated great courage earned him the sobriquet "Mad Jack" and almost iconic status in his battalion of the Royal Welsh Fusiliers. With the facts about this one-officer coup came some myth. All his biographers, Robert Graves, John Stuart Roberts, Rupert Hart-Davis, Max Egremont and, most recently, Jean Moorhouse, agree with the basic facts. Neither Graves nor Hart-Davis produced biographies as such, but *Goodbye to All That* and Hart-Davis' editing of Sassoon's diaries suffice to warrant their inclusion in the list.

Graves was first to relate what was supposedly the inside story of Sassoon's daylight stunt near Mametz Wood when he went across and scared the occupants away:

> A pointless feat, since instead of signalling for reinforcements, he sat down in the German trench and began reading a book of poems which he had brought with him. When he finally went back he did not even report. Colonel Stockwell, then in command, raged at him. The attack on Mametz Wood had been delayed two hours because British patrols were still reported to be out. 'British patrols' were Siegfried and his book of poems. 'I'd have got you a D.S.O., if you'd only shown more sense,' stormed Stockwell.

Roberts echoes Graves. Sassoon's diary entry for 6 July reported the event thus: "I went across from our bombing post ... When I got there [the enemy trench] I chucked four Mills bombs ... to my surprise ... fifty or sixty (I counted eighty-five packs left on the firestep) ran away like hell." Neither Roberts nor the diary mention Sassoon failing to report to his CO. In an editorial note Hart-Davis says only that while a decoration was recommended it was not awarded. Nor does Egremont mention a burst of poetry reading, a story Wilson describes as "almost certainly apocryphal."[72]

Stealth did not always spell success. Anthony Eden, in July 1916 a Subaltern with the KRRC, described a stealth raid of six ORs he led as "no artillery preparation, the essence being secrecy and surprise on a night with little moon." Enroute to the enemy wire some 800 yards distant Eden positioned three of his men where they could support the entry party and cover its withdrawal. With the other three men he moved forward to the enemy wire where two of his men began cutting gaps. Once cut, Eden and one man would move through the gap, enter the trench and kill or capture the first man they encountered. Initially all went well, but just as the final strands of wire were being cut the enemy trench erupted in rifle and machine-gun fire guided by flares above. Surprise gone, the raiders withdrew.[73]

In October 1916 1st Canadian Division moved into the Souchez Valley area north of the Somme. For a few weeks relative quiet prevailed, the enemy seemingly averse to causing trouble;

72 Graves, *Goodbye to All That* (Harmondsworth, Middlesex: Penguin Books Ltd., 1960), p. 174; Roberts, *Siegfried Sassoon*, p. 123; Hart-Davis (ed.), *Siegfried Sassoon Diaries,* p. 89; Max Egremont, *Siegfried Sassoon: A Life* (New York: Farrar, Strauss and Giroux, 2005), pp. 103-104; Jean Moorcraft Wilson, *Siegfried Sassoon: Soldier, Poet, Lover, Friend* (New York: Overlook Books, 2014), p. 166. Sassoon had received the MC for his part in a raid in May.

73 Anthony Eden, *Another World: 1897-1917* (London: Allen Lane, 1976), pp. 88-91. At the time of the raid, Eden's first, he was not quite 19. At 20 he would become the youngest BM in the BEF.

3rd Battalion, for example, in 19 days in the trenches during November suffered just 23 casualties, of which only two were fatal. Spells out of the line allowed the unit to make good the heavy losses suffered earlier at Regina Trench. On 23 November Major J.B. Rogers on promotion took command of the 3rd, an appointment he would hold for the rest of the war. The battalion War Diary noted that on the last day of the month preparations began for what would be the unit's first relatively large-scale stealth raid. The subsequent report by 1st Brigade on this raid included the fact that earlier in November the 3rd Battalion had volunteered to do it, which for the battalion would become the principal event in December 1916. The raid's objective, the "Pimple," as revealed by air photographs and intelligence summaries, was an area the enemy kept in excellent condition. The raid had three purposes: survey enemy defences, including any sign of preparations for use of gas and locate any mine shafts, take prisoners and destroy as much as possible. The five officers and 90 ORs of the raiding party trained hard for the event, practising with dummy bombs and then with live ones. Zero, initially set for 0400 Saturday 9 December, had to be postponed for 45 minutes, the moon being far too bright. Guided by scouts who had earlier reconnoitred the ground at Zero the raiders crossed no man's land in three parties to positions 20 or so yards short of the enemy wire. In the charge that followed the right and left parties crossed the wire using duckboards (sometimes referred to as bathmats), but when the centre party could not surmount a very deep and heavy wire barrier the party spread out and began bombing the enemy trench. The right and the left parties soon cleared the trench to their front and seized a machine-gun. Eight minutes after entering the trench all the raiders withdrew under cover of artillery and trench mortar fire. Two enemy officers and 20 ORs were believed to have been killed and perhaps as many as 100 more in the bombing of a dozen dug-outs. Such estimates could not be verified and usually proved overly optimistic. Casualties amounted to two officers and 29 ORs wounded and two killed. While no prisoners were taken, and on that basis the raid had failed, higher commanders still saw it as a commendable effort. Major-General Arthur Currie, then GOC 1st Division, wrote personally to Rogers. The OC Raid, Major H.S. Cooper, received a Bar to his MC.[74]

Rowland Feilding, in February 1917 CO of the 6th Connaught Rangers (16th (Irish) Division), also experienced an unsuccessful stealth raid. What was most striking about it was the German reaction and afterward his meeting with GOC Second Army (Herbert Plumer). In a letter to his wife Feilding had told her of the "rather desperate enterprise" scheduled for the next day, the idea being to raid the enemy at three points in daylight in a fog, or failing that, under cover of smoke without any preliminary bombardment. These "arrangements" did not please him. First, the trench mortar officer he trusted had been sent on course leaving wire cutting to medium mortars that he was less sure of. Second, the original leaders of two of his assault parties were absent, one wounded and one on course. Finally, brigade had denied his request for an intense one-minute Stokes "stonk" at Zero (0330) since the GOC thought this would alarm the enemy. Nevertheless, at Zero, then, over the top went the three assault parties,

74 LAC, War Diary, 3rd Battalion, December 1916, battalion Operation Order and 1st Brigade report; Goodspeed, *Battle Royal,* pp. 168-70. Over 60 of the raiders were newly-joined reinforcements not previously in action, a fact that speaks well of their training and of the raid's leadership. Fraser and Gibbons, *Soldier and Sailor Words and Phrases,* define bathmats as "wooden battens that were laid over the bottom of the mud of trenches (see Duckboards)." and Duckboards: "the slatted, timber paths or walks laid down in trenches."

in a mad dash across no man's land, in all nine officers and 190 ORs, no preliminary artillery support. The centre party found enemy wire uncut. Its OC was killed and his 2IC wounded. The right party also lost its OC and 2IC and having eventually seen the centre party withdrawing it, too, fell back. The left party, now alone, recognizing failure, likewise withdrew. None of the three parties entered enemy trenches. Later after two hours of fierce fighting the enemy allowed a cease-fire so the wounded could be collected, an "extraordinary state of affairs," and a highly irregular but much appreciated one. Of the nine officers only three remained; in addition, the battalion lost one company commander seriously wounded during the preparatory stage of the raid. Feilding's worst fears about wire-cutting had come to pass. "The toll," said Feilding, "was to be expected from a raid when it is unsuccessful."

When on 3 March Second Army summoned the battalion commanders of the 16th Division to meet Plumer, one by one, this was not remarked upon since Plumer habitually made it a point to meet battalion commanders. In conversation with Feilding the raid came up, not surprisingly, Plumer expressing the view that there should have been an artillery bombardment to which the brigade commander who was also present responded that the trenches were too close together for that. Plumer then added that trench mortars should have participated as Feilding had requested. Feilding told his wife that he felt he "could see General Pereira (the brigadier) telling him [Plumer] this and explaining that it was he who refused it; blaming himself ... for the failure ... I repeat this that you may know ... why every officer and soldier ... swears by him."[75]

Another Canadian stealth raid, the 10th Battalion's first raid of the war, proved a frustrating and anxious business there being for various reasons a month between conception and execution. This raid, which is examined in detail in Chapter 9, finally got underway on the night of 5 February. At 1830 the OC Raid, Lieutenant Stanley Kent, set out with his wire-cutting party and a covering party under an NCO. Kent placed the latter in a lying-up area in no man's land and then took the wire-cutters forward to their chore. Once cutting began he returned to where he had left the covering party to put it in a position to cover the assault. But there was no sign of it. An hour later the NCO in charge of the party appeared saying he had had to move the party because of German patrols. Kent then returned to the wire-cutters. Unbeknown to him the NCO, who had seemed very nervous from the start, then abandoned the party and returned to battalion trenches with a story that all had been captured. However, after some delay all was straightened out, the wire-cutting almost done, and the Assault Party had joined Kent at the enemy wire. Then at about 0400 a German party 20 or so strong stumbled into the Canadians and fighting began. With no other option Kent ordered withdrawal.[76]

Whatever such high risk ventures were called, or how they were defined or categorized – stealth or ordinary, day or night, large or small – raids more often than not resulted in bloody, savage combat at a very personal level – face to face, hand to hand – usually in the dark after a trying trek across no man's land and then a leap into an unknown trench. Hard times, hard men! For real tension and anxiety not much in trench warfare topped that. Such endeavours also added to the heavy burden of command. The officer leading a raid (and most patrols), usually a

75 Feilding, *War Letters to a Wife*, pp. 151-57. Feilding, an officer of the Coldstream Guards, took command of the 6th Connaughts in September 1916.

76 Dancocks, *Gallant Canadians*, pp. 59, 63, 70-73, 76-77, 117. The CO, Lieutenant-Colonel J.G. Rattray, considered Kent one of his best Subalterns. LAC, 10th Battalion War Diary, February 1917.

Subaltern, a young man (almost always), nineteen or younger was not remarkable, had to be, in the words of one Subaltern, "alive to the task in front ... there must be no mistake about my own behaviour – a steady going forward ... My wits must be alert, for lives depend to great extent on my leadership. I must be sure to appear calm and cheerful."[77] During a raid a Subaltern was engaged not just in a raid, but also in a test of his spirit, ability and skill. Middle-ranking officers, marked by their greater experience, led far fewer raids, their superiors reluctant to expend them since they were the very officers who would soon have to lead battalions. Patrols, regardless of type, could also end in vicious, deadly fights, albeit usually on a smaller scale. Here, too, skill was at a premium.

It would be very difficult, even impossible, to state definitely how often any particular officer was so challenged and tested, nor can the number of raids made by British and Canadian officers and men be stated precisely. For one thing, what constituted a raid, as opposed to an attack, is a matter of interpretation. Terminology has had great impact on the tally and the audit. A concomitant circumstance is the ambiguity so often evident in reports on raids, this presenting dilemmas as to how to designate an endeavour. Perspective also drove reportage, higher levels of command did not always report what subordinate commands did. Moreover, it is not always clear as to whether or not figures for BEF raids include Dominion raids. Different methods of accounting have also led to duplication and inconsistency. It seems, for example, that the British Official History figures for raids for the period December 1915 to May 1916 include only raids sized "from 10-200 men."[78] On the other hand, the BGGS of the Canadian Corps, P. deB. Radcliffe, reporting on Canadian raids 1 November 1916 to 1 April 1917, included 69 raids "varying in size from the stealth raid by a few ... to a regular operation by two battalions, or even more." He included, it seems, any and all raids.[79] Unfortunately, sources do not always state their method of compilation.

Notwithstanding, a man must hang his coat somewhere. Ashworth provides a peg when he tells us that between December 1915, when Haig became C-in-C, and March 1918 the BEF launched just over 800 raids. Presumably this figure included British and non-British raids:

19 December 1915 – June 1916	106
July – December 1916	310
April – December 1917	270
December 1917 – March 1918	125[80]

The figures, whether accurate or not, are useful. If we include the seven Canadian raids October-December 1915, the 15 made in the period October-December 1916, and add a reasonable number of British raids for October-December 1915 and January-March 1917 we are looking at something in the order of 850-900 raids. There were, of course, raids after March in 1918 but as these are outside Ashworth's limitation we will leave it at that saying only that there were fewer between March 1918 and the Armistice. Based on Canadian Corps HQ Weekly Operation Summaries and on War Diaries, Canadian figures for raids look like this: 1915, 7; 1916, 25;

77 Peter Hart, *The Somme* (London: Weidenfeld & Nicolson, 2005), pp. 110-11.
78 Edmonds, *Haig's Command to the 1st July*, p. 242.
79 LAC, RG9IIIC1, Volume 3846, Folder 51, File 7, 'Notes on the Vimy Ridge Operation'.
80 Ashworth, *Live and Let Live*, p. 185.

1917,105; and 1918, 33. These figures, which total 170, cannot be graded definitive, but they are not unreasonable. Given that the Canadian Corps was one Corps (four divisions) and an active one, 20% of the 850-900 mark seems a fair slice. Considering the Canadian raiding record such a percentage is not by any means unreasoned or wild.[81]

Clearly, raids and patrols were a major consumer of time, effort, men and resources in their planning, preparation and execution. It is equally clear that much courage was expended (and recognized) during and after raids. The Riddle and Mitchell compilation for award of the MC in the CEF shows that just over 250 were awarded for raids and patrols. This figure includes awards where the citation includes the word raid or patrol. As for DSOs, the compilation for this award shows that 22 were awarded for raids and patrols. Again, the award was counted only when the key words appeared in the citations. Citations for the VC that include the word raid total 20. However, in about as many more the citation is such that the award may have been made for conduct during a raid. Raids and patrols often created situations where individual combat resulted and courage came to the fore. This partly explains the award of 633 VCs during the Great War, as opposed to the 182 awarded during the Second World War.[82]

Kipling's second honest serving-man is "why," a fundamental word in this present book. There are numerous answers, of course, some intuitive, some unstated, some more controversial than others and some less convincing than others. At the time, what one thought of a particular reason for raiding, or group of reasons, or the very concept of raiding, had much to do with the perception inherent in rank and command responsibility and the extent of one's participation. As losses mounted, the question of value arose and attitudes and opinions hardened. Failures, which were inevitable, also played a role in these changes. "Why" raid is the subject of the next chapter.

81 Edmonds, *Haig's Command to the 1st July*, pp. 242-43, 310; Senior, *Haking*, pp. 286-87; LAC, Canadian Corps General Staff War Diary.

82 Daniel Harvey, *Monuments to Courage: Victoria Cross Headstones and Memorials. Volume One 1854-1916 Volume Two 1917-1982* (Bahrain: Published on behalf of the Author by Kevin and Kay Patience, 1999).

4

The Reasons Why (1)

There is occasions and causes why and wherefore in all things.

Henry V

The title of this chapter may bring to mind a charge over a century ago by 600 officers and men of the Light Brigade, their gallantry immortalized by a famous poet and later reiterated in Cecil Woodham-Smith's classic account. Much changed in the British Army between that charge and 1914. For one thing, it became important and necessary that men knew why they were to do this or that, and, consequently, they sometimes did make reply and did reason why, but in the end the course of the soldier was to do and often to die, sometimes like the men of earlier times, in the jaws of Death and the mouth of Hell.

As the title suggests this chapter concerns reasons to raid. Perspectives on that question and raiding in general depended upon one's place in the great scheme of things. As Ole Luk-Oie pointed out well before 1914 there are usually three accounts of any battle (or raid), the first in his story being that of a group of soldiers who have a sort of resigned fury because they know fighting, the second being that of staff officers methodically recording progress and the third being that of the General, who after issuing his orders, can have no further influence until reports come in. Charles Carrington, a veteran of both world wars recalled how Ole Luk-Oie's story drove considerable discussion when he was a young officer.[1] Perspective also drove definitions of success and failure. Consequently, these were often inconstant, shifting to meet circumstances. This chapter, in short, describes and analyses why raids were made.

To begin, the policy regarding raids requires explanation since it drove raiding. In February 1915, when the then C-in-C, Sir John French, concluded that "the enemy was showing too much initiative" he issued a "GHQ Memorandum" that "gave official authority to what were known in the British Army as raids." This instruction, being genesis, bears repeating, not just because it marks a beginning, but because it defines, in part, the nature, purposes, criteria

1 Major-General Sir Ernest Swinton, R.E. [Ole Luk-Oie], 'The Point of View', in *The Green Curve* (London: William Blackwood & Sons, 1909), pp. 251-276; Charles Carrington, *Soldier From the Wars Returning* (London: Hutchinson, 1964), p. 23. Swinton's timeless *The Defence of Duffer's Drift* (Oxford: George Ronald, 1949) also drove discussion. Of this small book, first published in 1904, Field Marshal Wavell recalled in the Foreword how appropriate its lessons were on siting trenches and on common sense principles of defence.

for selecting objectives, importance of proper planning and the value of raids as seen by the highest commander and his staff. French also directed that the BEF would conduct its defence in accordance with the prevailing pattern that applied when an Army went over to that phase of war. He knew that for a time the BEF would be settling down to trench warfare including establishing trench routines, ensuring co-ordination with flanking troops, preparing defences to defeat any enemy attack and enacting measures against surprise. While French did not use the word, his memorandum also concerns the attrition to which "minor enterprises" had to contribute.

Once firm on the ground, and with French's policy in mind, Army commanders and their subordinates began the task of dominating no man's land as a precursor to offensive operations, minor or otherwise. They had also to amplify and refine for their commands the C-in-C's direction, a process that would be a work in progress for many months, this another reason why French's "GHQ Memorandum Ordering Raids" warrants careful reading. Its most significant paragraphs pertaining to raids are these:

> 2. We are for the moment acting on the defensive … but this should not preclude the planning and making of local attacks on a comparatively small scale … Such enterprises are highly valuable … since they improve moral, while they have a corresponding detrimental effect on the moral of the enemy's troops.
>
> 4. These minor operations … should not be of an aimless character but should be based on a specific object, have a reasonable chance of success, and be commensurate with the losses likely to be entailed. They should be methodically initiated … must invariably be well thought out … and careful preliminary arrangements made.

In the absence of a subject heading in the memorandum the British Official Historian later inserted a central heading. It is the only place in the memorandum where the word "raids" appears. Nor does the memorandum mention one purpose of raids that became of such great importance that it became their *raison d'etre*. The Official Historian identifies it in his introduction to the memorandum: "capture prisoners for identification purposes … to determine what units were on a particular front." While it is not stated in such terms, it would have been clear that the C-in-C expected "troops to be kept up to the mark, tails-up with high morale and offensive spirit," but he then included paragraph 4 above by way of balance. Despite the memorandum, occasions inevitably arose where the desirable characteristics in that paragraph were notable only for their absence, all having "gang aft agley." The purpose stated in paragraph 2 of French's memorandum, damage to enemy moral (sic) would prove a highly debatable and contentious one, any conclusions about enemy morale depending very much upon the place of the auditor: for example, after the Somme one battalion CO rejected intelligence claims that German morale had declined.[2] In time, "raid," a common term in the Army, would also be tagged "stunt" or "show" to denote any special or elaborate operation, demonstration, action or raid. An officer of the 8th Canadian Battalion thought the best way to get into the "game" was

2 Edmonds and Wynne, *Winter 1914-15: Battle of Neuve Chapelle: Battle of Ypres*, pp. 31-34; Dunn, *The War the Infantry Knew*, p. 298; Terraine (ed.), *General Jack's Diary*, p. 191.

"to go through a show … the first thing and learn the worst there is to experience. Anyway, that is what happed to me, and I am none the worse for it, and can look forward to ordinary peaceful trench warfare with perfect equanimity."[3]

In October French reiterated his policy for the coming winter. So long as major operations could not be undertaken it remained, he wrote, "to wear out and exhaust the enemy's troops, to foster and enhance the offensive spirit of out own troops, and to encourage them to feel superior to the enemy in every respect." Pressure, he added, had to be relentless in the form of constant harassment by minor enterprises. This recipe would be repeatedly stressed at every level of command. General Haig, then GOC First Army, issued in November "Instructions for Divisional Training" in which he further refined policy: "Small offensive operations, carefully planned, should be carried out with determination … Patrolling should be active … no commander should be content unless he has absolutely the upper hand of the hostile troops in front of him."[4]

That same week the GOC Canadian Corps, Lieutenant-General E.A.H. Alderson, announced at a Corps Commander's Conference his policy for the winter months: constant harassment of the enemy by local attacks, demonstrations, mining and employment of artillery to best advantage. GOC 1st Division, then Arthur Currie, in an instruction the next day (4 November) reminded subordinates of the necessity to maintain ascendency over the enemy by means of bold patrolling and enterprises "to force the conviction on the enemy that 1st Canadian Division was his superior." What Currie preached his battalion commanders practised. Lieutenant-Colonel George Tuxford, CO 5th Battalion, for example, did so repeatedly, so much so that he could come to claim in all honesty "our ascendency became so pronounced that we called it [no man's land] CANADA, where no Hun should be allowed.[5] Richard Haking, in September 1915 GOC XI Corps, had found French's and Haig's policies completely in line with his own and much to his liking. To him it was clear that "If we do not raid the Germans they will raid us." In his *Company Training*, first published in early 1913, he had extolled the offensive spirit: "the only weapon which can possibly lead us to success is the spirit of the offensive [which] will carry the army against the enemy in vigorous attacks, on every possible occasion and without any hesitation." This he elaborated upon in his "Winter Campaign of 1915-1916" (4 November 1915):

> Every effort should be made … to foster and increase the [offensive] spirit throughout the winter months … by constantly harassing the enemy, compelling him to keep his reserves on the move … we can constantly improve the moral of our own troops and wear out and depress the enemy … the offensive spirit of our own troops must be carefully encouraged … and the natural desire of the troops to have a quiet time in the trenches must be discouraged in every way.[6]

3 Edmonds and Wynne, *Winter 1914-15: Battle of Neuve Chapelle: Battle of Ypres,* p. 31; Fraser and Gibbons *Soldier and Sailor Words and Phrases,* pp. 257, 273; Wallace, *From Montreal to Vimy Ridge,* p. 214.

4 Senior, *Haking,* pp. 78-79. Haig became C-in-C at noon on 19 December 1915.

5 LAC, RG9IIIC3, Volume 4007, Folder 4, File 4, 'Conference of Corps Commander', G952, 3 November 1915; G191, 4 November 1915, 'Principles of Defence, 1st Division'; Saskatchewan Provincial Archives, R2.247, 'The Great War As I Saw It', Memoirs of Brigadier-General George Tuxford.

6 Senior, *Haking,* p. 160; Haking, *Company Training,* pp. 103-104; TNA: WO 95/1190: Guards Division General Staff, November 1915, Appendix 118, 'Winter Campaign of 1915-1916', 4 November, paras 1 and 3. The word raid does not appear in this document.

When this reached the Guards Division, then in Haking's XI Corps, the Guards, being Guards, took umbrage at the last part of this and at the suggestion in a subsequent paragraph about a "hibernating habit." The Guards Division, wrote the divisional historian, did not require such a caution since its officers and men were apt

> to consider that the higher authorities exaggerate the morale value of an aggressive policy … and to resent being continually called upon to carry out raids for apparently no other purpose than to satisfy the insatiable curiosity of the Intelligence Branch of the General Staff. But, nevertheless, they possessed the true spirit of the offensive [and] were never satisfied until they had established a moral ascendency.

Lord Cavan, GOC Guards Division, responded by ordering artillery to cut enemy wire at various points and keep it permanently open and battalions would raid selected points at night in not more than two-company strength, assaults to be preceded by artillery bombardment, the purposes being to kill and capture defenders, destroy machine-guns and mortars, blow up defences and dugouts and return to own lines with the least possible delay. Cavan believed that this policy offered certain advantages. First, given the number of gaps cut in their wire the enemy would not know which points would be raided. Second, the spirit of own troops would rise and the "boredom and possible slackness occasioned by ordinary trench warfare" would be banished. This statement reflects the underlying worry of senior commanders that trench warfare had a negative effect on fighting spirit, initiative and determination. Finally, the strain of expecting attack at night in any one of numerous places would affect enemy morale adversely. The results pleased not only Haking, but his superior, Sir Henry Rawlinson, who in January 1916 congratulated the Guards for their six raids during a four-week period.[7]

As time passed, when it came to raids it did not take long for great expectations to surface and grow. The prevailing view tied a division's fighting efficiency and its general condition to the state of its trenches (see Griesbach's concerns in Chapter 2) and to what a division was doing forward of its trenches. Obviously, this applied equally to brigades and battalions. The historian of the 17th (Northern) Division (XIV Corps), in writing about attitudes toward raids, said that in December 1915 they were" rare adventures, except among the Canadians" but it was not long before a division that did not report a number of raids each month was regarded as idle and lacking in spirit. Within less than a year V Corps issued instructions that each of its divisions must raid "at least" twice weekly.[8]

Cyril Falls, writing of the period from the Somme to Messines (July 1916-June 1917), dubbed the Second Army (Plumer) the "Cinderella" of the BEF since it held a long line lightly and with few reserves while most of the ammunition and material of war passed on to the Somme where the British were "creeping forward in desperate fighting." Second Army's role was three-fold: "harass by all means … the troops that faced [it], prevent divisions that were sent down to the Somme from going as fresh troops and prevent those others that had been withdrawn from the

7 Headlam, *Guards Division,* Volume 1, pp. 107-109; TNA: WO 95/1190: War Diary, Guards Division, November 1915, Appendix 148, 'Suggestions as to Winter Campaign 1915-1916', paras 4-6, 19 November. Three of the four pages of this Appendix refer to raids and how to conduct them. *SS 101 Notes for Infantry Officers on Trench Warfare,* paragraph 4.

8 Atteridge, *17th (Northern) Division,* p. 69; Hussey, *Fifth Division,* p. 142.

hell-broth of the Somme from recovering too quickly and easily from its effects." In short, Falls saw raiding as useful in three realms: tactical, strategic and psychological.[9]

But this had not been so prior to the commencement of preparations for the Somme when Haig thought raids merely the tactic of an active course of trench warfare. However, his dairy entry for 14 January 1916 reveals a broader concept wherein raids would be a precursor to a "wearing-out fight similar to [raids] but on a larger scale at many points along the whole front … to draw in the enemy's reserves." Decisive attacks aimed at breakthrough could then follow. In essence, tactics had been tied to strategy. *SS 101 Notes for Infantry Officers on Trench Warfare,* issued in March 1916, reflecting this new strategic role, reiterates the tactical and psychological roles expressed in French's "GHQ Memorandum" of February 1915: "The objects … are to harass and inflict loss … by good organization of the defence and minor offensive enterprises to compel the enemy to keep as large or a larger garrison than ourselves and to increase his rate of wastage compared to our own." Restated, this was Falls' premise above. The number of casualties suffered, as opposed to the number inflicted in any particular raid, soon became a determinant in defining and assigning "success" or "failure." Moreover, this featured strongly in any debate about cost versus value of raids. "Wastage percent per month" was based in 1917 on a figure of 10 percent for infantry.[10]

Such an additional role raised questions about control. By 1916 GHQ had demanded minor enterprises and formations had complied, Army down to brigade ordering them for various purposes, or they were initiated by battalions for local purposes. In cases where the raids proposed by COs could affect other units, or they required outside support and resources, or they might influence brigade or division plans, then they required clearance at brigade and/or division. *SS 107 Notes on Minor Enterprises,* also issued in March 1916 by GHQ, included a suggestion that "The preparation and working out of the details of a minor operation should be left as much as possible to the unit engaged upon the enterprise. But the Brigade or Division Staff must check the scheme when it has been prepared." Here *SS 107* is astride the fine line between command and control, the latter being part of the former, but there being an essential difference, one that in a later war would be so well drawn by a division commander: "Command is often not what you do, but the way you do it." He went on to say how his corps commander failed to realize the difference: "All he had to do was tell me what he wanted done. But not how to do it." These thoughts apply equally well to the Great War.[11]

"Check" is a nuanced word. *SS 107* having provided checkers with considerable scope checking soon became detailed checking; for example, one experienced Canadian officer and raider thought wearing steel helmets on a raid absurd: "They are heavy and awkward and serve as a warning gong when coming against barbed wire or any obstacles. However, these facts did not impress the 'higher ups' for permission [to wear soft headgear] was refused." As checking became

9 Falls, *36th (Ulster) Division,* pp. 68, 71.

10 *SS 101 Notes for Infantry Officers on Trench Warfare,"* pp. 48-49; LAC, MG 30E100 (Currie Papers), Volume 43, 'Canadian Corps Reinforcement Camp'.

11 *SS 107 Notes on Minor Enterprises,* para 2; Major-General Chris Vokes, *Vokes: My Story* (Ottawa, Gallery Books, 1985), p. 184; Dan Todman and Gary Shieffield, 'Command and Control in the British Army on the Western Front', in Gary Sheffield and Dan Todman (eds.), *Command and Control on the Western Front: The British Army's Experience 1914-1918* (Staplehurst: Spellmount, 2004), p.1 cites Martin van Creveld's definitions which are similar to Volks': command is what a commander does and control is how he does it.

increasingly detailed the incidence of less than sound "suggestions" mounted. Complaints about bad Operation Orders were legion. One prominent example – more are offered in later chapters – reached 2nd Royal Welsh Fusiliers in early 1917. This document, in the eyes of those ordered to execute it, represented order, counter-order, disorder: contradictions, ambiguities, erroneous timings and map references, the whole extremely bad. The amended version, despite dozens of amendments, was little better. Captain James Dunn summed matters up: "no release from the caprice of the absent tactician who from far-away disposes of us: someone playing fantastic tricks with reality."

However, it must also be said that the checking that commenced did mark the implementation of a systematic policy for raiding in the exertion of control, codification, education, audit and the learning of lessons that would ease to some degree the learning curve that all had to travel along. This curve became more widely obvious as raids became larger, required more time for training and preparation, evolved into all-arms affairs (infantry, artillery (Field and Heavy), Stokes and trench mortars, machine-guns and RE support of various types), introduced new skills such as bombing and handling explosives, brought air resources into play (air photography and overflights) and resulted in other innovations. Given all this, it is just not reasonable to think that there was not a learning curve. Timothy Bowman points out that raiding also reinforced division control because any proposal to raid that required resources outside division control needed that level of command to procure the "extras." In so doing division thought this conferred checking rights. Quid pro quo! Before long, divisions were requiring "proposals" for raids, this imposing control right from the very conception of a raid. As time passed, higher command involvement in the planning of raids increased substantially.[12]

Patrolling also received increasing emphasis, it having long been recognized how crucial recce was to both defence and offence. Various publications in the SS series stressed "night-work," a category that included patrolling, "the close recce of the enemy's front line … obstacles … ground to be crossed by an assault." The very first paragraph of *SS 107* detailed what it saw as the first principle: "Success in minor operations against the enemy's trenches depends mainly on recce of the objective." In turn, recce depended upon establishing superiority in patrol work between the lines. Consequently, divisions came to recognize the importance of training junior officers in patrol work and getting them accustomed to moving about in no man's land. *SS 135 Instructions for the Training of Divisions for Offensive Action* put this more directly some months later saying that before any assault patrols had to obtain complete command of no man's land. One of Sir Arthur Currie's first acts upon assuming command of the Canadian Corps in June 1917 was to issue instructions on patrols and raids. Archibald Macdonell's instructions on these when he replaced Currie as GOC 1st Division in July 1917 warned that

> The Corps Commander wishes the most active and pushful patrolling … He requires us to obtain complete mastery of No Man's Land. We must absolutely dominate it … The patrolling … if properly pushed should obtain the necessary information, upon which successful raids might be launched. [He] also wishes raids freely carried out … but this must not be

12 Kultus Nanich [Murray], 'Raids', p. 339; Dunn, *The War the Infantry Knew*, p. 298; Timothy Bowman, *The Irish Regiments in the Great War: Discipline and Morale* (Manchester: Manchester University Press, 2005), pp. 29-30.

> misinterpreted into an order to make indiscriminate raids entailing loss of men without corresponding advantage. Each raid must be carefully worked out on its merits, have a very definite object and a very reasonable chance of success.[13]

Apropos of this, Colonel H.S. Cooper recalled Currie's concern during his time as GOC 1st Division for his men when it came to raiding:

> My first contact with him was when I was training a crowd for a raid. He'd got the information from prisoners … so the raid was going to be called off. Well, we were keyed up for the thing. At any rate when Currie wanted to see me I got into his office and he told me that it was going to be called off … we coaxed him not to call it off but he said I'm not sacrificing one man when I don't have to. I never forgot that.[14]

In fact, Currie cancelled several raids in early 1917 prior to Vimy because other sources had provided the information he sought. On the other hand, where another source did not exist, and where a pressing need for information existed, he did not hesitate to demand a raid and could be ruthless should occasion arise, or when he thought a battalion commander had not demonstrated sufficient acumen and determination. His brigadiers were not spared either, this evident in the following missive which without saying so suggests that the recipient (GOC 1st Brigade, William Griesbach) get a grip on one of his battalion commanders:

> My orders regarding the capture of a German prisoner are evidently not clearly understood. I want a prisoner, not for curiosity's sake, nor to see what he looks like. I want to get information that will be of some use … so naturally I want the prisoner before Zero Day. The plan submitted by the 2nd Battalion was puerile. In the first place because it involved the employment of nothing but scouts, and for a Battalion Commander to send in, as a raiding party, the scouts … shows that at least he has no expectation of the open warfare season

13 *SS 101,* pp. 8-9; *SS 107,* para 1; TNA: WO 95/1294: 2nd Division General Staff, 24 January 1917; *SS 135 Instructions for the Training of Divisions for Offensive Action,* p. 52; LAC, RG9IIIC3, Volume 4017, Folder 35, File 18, 1st Division to 1st Brigade, G.5-17, 7 December 1917. Macdonell, age 53 when he became GOC 1st Division, had an interesting career. After graduating from the Royal Military College, Kingston, he continued military service until 1889 when he transferred to the North West Mounted Police as an Inspector and was posted to the Northwest Territories. In 1899 he joined 2CMR for service in the South African War where he was awarded the DSO. On return to the North West Mounted Police he was promoted to Superintendent. In 1907 he joined a cavalry unit that became Lord Strathcona's Horse (Royal Canadians), becoming CO in 1912. He took that regiment to France in May 1915. On promotion six months later he took command of a brigade. As an officer he received mixed reviews. To some he was "Daddy", to others "Batty Mac." Certainly, he was unconventional, a man of "vivid behaviour … and terse exposition [that made him] a personality about whom the rear rank wove many far-fetched stories." (Stevens, *A City Goes to War,* p. 91). Tough and colourful, he was a good brigade commander and was chosen by Currie to command 1st Division. Currie was not disappointed. In March 1916 Macdonell had been wounded while out looking at wire in broad daylight: "He was shot at two or three times and would have been killed but for the fact that the German sniper was so excited shooting at a General that he could not aim straight.' (LAC, MG 30E241(Macintyre Papers), Diary, 8 March 1916.)

14 LAC, RG 41, CBC Interviews, Colonel H.S. Cooper.

> commencing. In the second place, for a raid to succeed, there must be sufficient weight to it. Also the chances of success are increased when the men dash in under a barrage. At the present time, you cannot steal into the German trenches. This is not a game of hide and seek we are playing. I want you to tell your Battalion Commanders that, if they are not successful tonight, you will order raids at three hour intervals until they are successful. Tell them I want results and I want them now.

This memorandum is in at least two archival files. One copy includes the minor pen corrections made by Currie, while another in Griesbach's "Book of Wisdom," was clearly re-typed at brigade and has at the bottom Griesbach's comments to two COs: "The plan of the 1st Battalion is approved … The 2nd Battalion claim … that the wire is too strong. I would urge the 2nd Battalion to reconnoitre … to find a break... through which it can make an attempt similar to the 1st Battalion … There is a possibility that these battalions will be kept in the line until a prisoner is captured."

The War Diaries of the two battalions and that of 1st Division General Staff describe how on the night of 4 April a patrol of 2nd Battalion entered an enemy trench, no enemy in sight, but an hour later the patrol engaged and dispersed a party of seven Germans, killing in the process one officer. The body, when taken back to battalion lines, showed him to be an officer of 3rd Bavarian Reserve Regiment. A raid by 1st Battalion early the next morning also secured identifications. Currie had his information.

Griesbach has addressed his COs in similar vein on 20 February in a three-page instruction on raids and attitudes, the heart of which was this:

> RAIDS. I trust that the matter of raids is receiving the serious consideration of all officers. There must be bold and skillful patrol work … many good arguments will be advanced against raids but I should like the preliminary investigation pushed on.
>
> ATTITUDE. We must have more thrusting, pushing and striking to greater extent than is now being done in other divisions. There are, doubtless, good reasons against this course. Please do not advance them.

He may well have regretted he had not been as precise and direct as he might have been in his earlier instruction.[15]

In the Canadian Corps raids and patrols remained a prominent topic on the agenda of Corps Commander Conferences throughout 1917 and 1918, such matters either raised by division or initiated by Corps HQ. The same is true of British Corps. First Army, for example, in an instruction to its formations "drew attention to the importance of maintaining our policy of raids [and stressed] the value of thorough preparations and determined execution of raids." In February 1918 Sir Arthur Currie ordered that raids must continue but warned that

15 LAC, MG 30E15 (Griesbach Papers), 'Book of Wisdom', Vols. 2 and 3; RG9IIIC3, Volume 4012, Folder 19, File 4; Murray, *2nd Canadian Battalion,* p. 159, states that from 3-5 April the battalion made eight forays into enemy trenches: seven involved one officer and between two and 20 ORs and the last consisted of just two officers. All sought identifications.

> A raid must be a success or it had better not be attempted ... Having once decided to undertake a raid ... the commander must be absolutely determined that it should succeed and employ every possible means to insure that it does. A formal investigation should be held in every case of failure, because a failure is a prima facie case for blame and the burden of proof lies with the unit to clear itself. A similar investigation should always be held whenever the German succeeds in getting into our trenches.

As for patrols, Currie reiterated their purposes, offensive and defensive, and expressed his concern about the standard of patrolling: "Our patrolling has not been satisfactory lately and several incidents have shown a want of knowledge of the elementary rules due to the number of new and inexperienced officers and NCOs now in the Corps. Platoon Commanders should instruct their men on the subject." Three weeks later he expressed concern about how the inexperience of platoon commanders, and the necessity of close supervision of platoon training, distracted senior officers, an opinion shared by division commanders, one of whom (Macdonell) considered the competence of platoon commanders his most challenging problem. Griesbach, GOC 1st Brigade, shared this opinion as did many other brigade commanders. Over that winter company training received renewed emphasis. By spring much improved individual skills allowed units to conduct sub-unit and unit exercises before engaging in a series of sophisticated brigade exercises. All in all, by summer Currie thought his divisions fully ready for the operations that would end the war.[16]

In reiterating Corps policy during a Corps Commander Conference in February 1918 Currie stressed what he saw as the primary purposes or reasons for raiding: encouraging fighting spirit, lowering enemy morale and gaining information by taking prisoners. The first two are examined later in this chapter. As for the third, Currie left unsaid the simple fact that commanders always have a need and desire to know what is over the hill, or in the case of raiding what and who are on the far side of no man's land and what are they doing or intending, although raiding alone could not answer for intention. That same month William Griesbach, keeper of the "Book of Wisdom," issued direction on patrols and the relationship between these and raiding: if patrols could satisfy the increasing need for prisoners then raids would not be necessary for that purpose. But to do so patrols would have to more vigorously strive to obtain identifications by remaining out after patrol actions and search enemy dead and wounded and gather their arms and equipment. Later in 1918 Lieutenant-Colonel J.L.R. Parsons, Currie's GSO2 Intelligence (General Staff Officer 2nd Grade) looking at raids from the intelligence point of view, listed the purposes of raiding as: securing prisoners, documents and equipment for identification purposes; ascertaining enemy strength and deployment in his front line; determining if gas apparatus or mine shafts were present in enemy lines; inflicting losses upon the enemy and inducing him to move support troops forward so they offered targets; inducing him to disclose mortar and machine-gun positions; and decreasing enemy morale. What to look for when it came to documents and where the German soldier

16 LAC, RG9IIIC3, Volume 4007, Folder 4, File 10, Record of Corps Commander Conferences November 1915 – February 1918; Macdonell to brigades, 27 July; Volume 4032, Folder 28, File 1, Notes on Training; Volume 4077, Folder 3, File 6, 1st Division to brigades, 24 February 1918.

carried them had been described in late 1915 in an SS publication.[17] A good summation of the value of identifications is this:

> It is by discovering the whereabouts and movements of one enemy unit after another that the enemy's order of battle is eventually deduced. Every detail aids the whole; but one or two missing details may render valueless a mass of information. It is to obtain the essential detail, or the essential confirmation of a conclusive detail, that the raid is undertaken. It is important to emphasize this aid to our own Intelligence so that the true value of a successful raid may be seen.[18]

Parsons had been appointed GSO2 (Intelligence) in October 1916, replacing Colonel C.H. Mitchell who had been a year in that appointment and before that GSO3 with 1st Division. Mitchell, the father of the Canadian Corps intelligence organization, had built the system based on his experience with 1st Division and with the considerable help given him by his British counterparts, there being no Canadian precedent to guide him. In September 1916 GOC Second Army, General Herbert Plumer, an officer who "chose his Staff admirably" and possessed the "remarkable gift" of knowing who to chose, asked Mitchell to head Second Army's Intelligence Branch. When Plumer went to Italy he took Mitchell with him, not willing to lose Mitchell's undoubted expertise and knowledge.[19]

Raids also served more than local purposes. Cyril Falls described above how the Armies not engaged (First, Second and Third) on the Somme were called upon for strategic purposes such as preventing, as much as possible, German reinforcements reaching the Somme. To do this units of the three Armies had to raid frequently. Attrition goes both ways, of course. Divisions holding the "quiet" fronts had to take a turn on the Somme, it not being long, the British Official History reminds, before every division, with only two exceptions, had a "go" in the "big show." Inevitably, divisions rotating into an oasis of quiet arrived depleted with the holes only partially filled and then mostly by "ill-trained" and inexperienced drafts. Nevertheless, these had perforce to raid almost immediately, often with little or no opportunity to become familiar with their new "digs" and what lay in front of them. The impact was severe, many units being left "to deplore the loss of the very cream of their officers, NCOs and men in raids. And the cold-blooded courage demanded … took heavy toll of the nervous energy of even the biggest thruster."[20] Sir Arthur Currie, GOC the Canadian Corps, stressed another aspect of this purpose, this being to draw upon the Armies not on the Somme as many enemy divisions

17 LAC, RG9IIIC3, Volume 4007, Folder 4, File 10, 'Record of Corps Commander Conferences, November 1915-February 1918'; MG30E15 (Griesbach Papers), Volume 3, File 16A, 'Book of Wisdom', 24 February 1918; MG 30E61 (Mitchell Papers), Volume 16, Western Front Orders and Instructions 1916-1918, 20 August 1918, 'Trench Raids. Based Upon Raids Done By Canadian Corps'; *SS 381 Collection of Information Regarding the Enemy* (GHQ 'I', October 1915).

18 Committee of Officers, *Sixth South Staffordshire Regiment,* pp. 154-55.

19 C.R.M.F. Crutwell, *A History of the Great War 1914-1918* (Oxford at the Clarendon Press, 1964), pp. 157, 437; Major S.R. Elliot, *Scarlet to Green: A History of Intelligence in the Canadian Army 1903-1963* (Toronto: Canadian Intelligence and Security Association, 1981), Chapter 2.

20 Miles, *2nd July to the End of the Battles of the Somme,* p. 543; Falls, *36th (Ulster) Division,* p. 71; Boraston and Bax, *Eighth Division,* p. 81.

as possible which might otherwise go to the Somme and also force him to relieve or reinforce divisions opposite. But this demanded "continual aggression ... by raids, artillery fire and gas."[21]

Another purpose of raids was to divert the enemy. In mid-1916, for example, Second Army ordered the Canadian Corps to conduct 10 raids to divert the enemy's attention from an attack by Fourth Army at Flers-Courcelette. Earlier in 1916 (February) Sir Richard Haking, GOC XI Corps, had stressed at a conference that all divisions had to carry out minor enterprises and how valuable diversions could be: "if activity is confined to one locality the enemy's reserves are drawn to it and small enterprises become difficult or impossible. If, on the other hand, the enemy is prevented from concentrating his reserve the arrangement of further raids is facilitated." GOC First Army (Sir C.C. Monro), Haking's superior, much appreciated Haking's attitude and efforts that so supported his own views about raids and ruses and how Haking had taken all means to encourage offensive spirit and initiative.[22]

Another example of a diversion involved a joint effort. On 1 June 1916 3rd Canadian Division held the most easterly projection of the Ypres Salient. Within the division's real estate lay the only part of Ypres Ridge still in British hands, a vantage point that provided good observation over the enemy line from Mount Sorrel north to Hill 62. At that point a broad spur, known as Observatory Ridge, thrust westward for almost a thousand yards. If the enemy took Hill 62 he could then move westward along the spur which would secure him a commanding position in rear of 8th Brigade's lines. This could well force withdrawal from the salient.

The enemy attack, when it came early on 2 June, began with hurricane fire for over four hours on the 7th and 8th Canadian Brigades, 4CMR of the latter suffering 89 percent casualties. 3rd Division's casualties also included the division commander, Major-General M.S. Mercer, killed on forward recce, and the GOC 8th Brigade who was wounded and captured. Overall, the enemy achieved gains of 600-700 yards including a dangerous penetration along Observatory Ridge. A corps counter-attack that began early on 3 June did not entirely succeed, although it did close a large gap that had opened both sides of the ridge. Bad weather delayed a subsequent counter-attack until the 13th. The day before 300 guns pounded German positions for 10 hours followed in the evening by an intense barrage 30 minutes long and then intense fire for 45 minutes before Zero at 0130. This fierce fire proved decisive, the counter-attack, "the first Canadian deliberately planned attack in any force" had considerable success, "Mont Sorrel and Hill 62 and about half the original Canadian lines north of the ridge being recovered." Canadian losses for 2-14 June came to about 8,000.[23]

This second counter-attack involved the assistance of 20th British Division. On 12 June XIV Corps ordered the 20th to discharge gas and smoke along its front and then send out patrols, following these up with raiding parties at four selected points, Zero to be 0130, 13 June. 61st Brigade opted to go directly to raids, ordering the 1st Somerset Light Infantry to found two raiding parties. One raid had immediately to be cancelled, the ground being too boggy to permit movement. The other party consisted of Lieutenant John Peard and 20 ORs. The plan called for a brief bombardment of the enemy trenches and wire and then a gas discharge, followed by the raiders just as soon as the gas passed over. Peard designated two of his men as wire-cutters and

21 LAC, RG9IIIC3, Volume 4077, Folder 3, File 12.
22 Monro and Haking are quoted in Senior, *Haking*, pp. 81-82.
23 Nicholson, *Canadian Expeditionary Force*, p. 149; Edmonds, *Haig's Command to the 1st July*, p. 241.

two others to lay guide tapes to the enemy trench. Gas helmets were ordered to be worn and Peard had a horn to signal withdrawal. No preliminary recce was made, Peard's only opportunity to look at the ground being by trench periscope during the afternoon of 12 June.

Soon after leaving the battalion trench Peard ordered the gas helmets removed, it obvious that raiders "muffled" in a helmet stood very little chance of navigating their way across no man's land. Enemy wire was found "practically intact," the trench mortars not having done the job, which meant his wire-cutters were soon hard at work. Unfortunately, the tape layers and the main body of raiders did not appear, the tape having become tangled in the British wire, and the main body having opted to stay with the tape layers. As a result, contact between the two groups was lost. Peard was then wounded. With the enemy now firing madly and surprise gone, he signalled withdrawal and began crawling toward home. The raid cost three men killed and in addition to Peard, ten others were wounded. Peard summed things up: "More than half of the party had become casualties, without apparently having accomplished anything. I heard afterwards that the [Canadian] counter-attack was completely successful."

A separate party founded by 11th King's Royal Rifle Corps (KRRC) did enter enemy trenches which at the entry point appeared to have been practically obliterated by the preliminary bombardment. This party defeated an enemy counter-attack and then returned to own lines having suffered only five men slightly wounded. A third party reached the German wire, but being only a "small patrol" did not enter the German trench.[24]

In July Canadian operations again featured diversionary measures, in this case by 20th British Division and 3rd Canadian Division in support of a minor attack by 1st Canadian Division that aimed at re-establishing a part of the original Canadian line at Mount Sorrel by seizing the new German front and support line trenches. Both the 20th and the 3rd Divisions were to bombard the trenches opposite their front. The latter would also to send out four "strong offensive patrols" each under a Subaltern. This task went to 9th Canadian Brigade, specifically 52nd and 58th Battalions, which mounted two patrols each. The average strength was 29 ORs. One of the 52nd Battalion patrols, Lieutenant Fryer commanding, found its objective unoccupied. Before leaving the start point this patrol had four killed and seven wounded by enemy artillery. The other patrol, led by Lieutenant William Dougall, also found its objective empty, but did capture two occupants of an outpost and delivered them to Battalion HQ. One of the 58th Battalion patrols found its objective empty, but the other patrol found the enemy trench strongly held with a party out front improving the trench. The leader of the latter, Lieutenant N.C. Pearse, was wounded by shrapnel during the patrol's return. In his report to Second Army the GOC Canadian Corps thought the failure of 1st Division's minor attack due to insufficient fire support and expressed his hope that it had helped cause the enemy "to retain troops that might otherwise have been withdrawn for other operations." "Hope" was often the keyword given the extreme difficulty, if not impossibility in determining what, if any, re-deployment the enemy had done (see also Lieutenant Peard's plaintive and erroneous summation above). The postwar "Lessons" report concluded that while diversions/deceptions achieved some success on the Somme, before that they had not achieved advantages commensurate with the cost.[25]

24 LAC, Canadian Corps General Staff War Diary,13 June 1916; Captain V.E. Inglefield, *The History of the Twentieth (Light) Division,* (Uckfield, East Sussex: Naval and Military Press, n.d.), pp. 53-54; Moorhouse, *Forged by Fire,* pp. 51-54.

25 LAC, Canadian Corps General Staff War Diary, 9 July 1916; 52nd and 58th Battalion War Diaries, 9 July; RG9IIIC3, Volume 3842, Folder 43, File 2, 3rd Division 'Report of Minor Operations' carried out

"Notes on Raids" in *Notes for Commanding Officers* (1918 edition) described three "sorts of raids": to secure identifications, to ascertain damage done by bombardment and to inflict loss and damage and lower enemy morale. It then added "All above three can be combined." A fourth "sort" sought to raise British morale, but the "Notes" hint at just how uncertain such claims could be; the guidance offered on raising morale said that if raids are to do that they should "invariably be of simplest character and as fool-proof as possible." Fighting spirit and raising morale are so interwoven that these are best discussed together when it comes to reasons for raiding.[26]

The impact of raids on morale and fighting spirit on both sides and assessment and conclusions depended upon one's appointment and involvement, either as planner or initiator or participant. Senior commanders preached incessantly of the virtues of offensive spirit and achieving it through training and then maintaining it. In July 1916 the GOC 46th (North Midland) Division, for example, insisted upon raiding "to the utmost as being the type of warfare best calculated to improve the offensive spirit of the men. "Raids", wrote the division historian, "improved the fighting capacity of the Division [in making] it as hard as nails." SS *101 Notes for Infantry Officers on Trench Warfare* reflected the official and common concern about trench warfare and its pernicious effects:

> There is an insidious tendency to lapse into a passive and lethargic attitude, against which officers and all ranks have to be on guard and the fostering of the offensive spirit ... calls for incessant attention. Minor local enterprises and constant occupation ... furnish the best means of maintaining the efficiency of the troops ... constant activity in harassing the enemy may lead to reprisals ... but if persevered in always results in ultimate mastery ... and it achieves the double purpose of raising the morale of our own troops while lowering that of the enemy.

Concern about lethargy was not a modern preoccupation. The Romans, too, believed that idleness led to poor discipline and morale. Captain F.C. Hitchcock, 2nd Leinsters, summed up such concerns by describing the purpose of raiding as sharpening everyone's wits after months of stagnant trench warfare. An officer of The Buffs thought that while raids did not greatly influence the winning of the war they did foster martial spirit, there being "something about perfectly passive defence which makes for despondency and depression but a raid ... evokes a spirit of enterprise ... and shows the enemy that the spirit of those opposite them is quite undismayed." Likewise, *SS 408* asked many questions about one's state of offensiveness starting with "Am I As Offensive As I Might Be?"[27] Harassing the enemy by any and all means became the mantra, raids being "invaluable in keeping all ranks braced up to the highest pitch."

in support of 1st Division, 8 July. Lieutenant Dougall was awarded the MC. *Report of the Committee on the Lessons of the Great War* (Uckfield, East Sussex: Naval and Military Press, n.d.), p. 23, which refers to Edmonds, *Haig's Command to the 1st July*, p. 310, "There has been much discussion as to the value of these raids, which cost many lives ... but there remains the definite fact that the German Supreme Command, if not deceived, was left in doubt as to the Allied intentions." This volume of the Official History also directs the reader to the note on pp. 316-19, 'German Intelligence as Regards the Somme Offensive'.

26 *Notes for Commanding Officers* (1918 edition), Chapter 9.

27 Major R E. Priestley, *Breaking the Hindenburg Line: The Story of the 46th (North Midland) Division* (London: T. Fisher Unwin Ltd., 1919), p. 20; *SS 101*, para 4; Hitchcock, *"Stand To,"* p. 229; Colonel

The GOC XI Corps (Haking) being very much a thruster became well known for his policy of "cumulative aggression." Never reluctant to express his views about offensive spirit, or the lack thereof, in his view 39th Division had not "shown much" until 30 June 1916 when two battalions of 116th Brigade assaulted an enemy salient near Fromelles, a diversionary operation that he thought "greatly improved the fighting value" of the division. This operation, which cost the 12th and 13th Royal Sussex Regiment, 1,128 casualties, about 60 percent of the raiding force, came to be known as "The Day Sussex Died." In August Haking expressed his conviction that by continuing to wear down the enemy it also lowered his morale while that of his troops rose, and it was the duty of commanders to prove to officers and men that "by their own action … they can get into the German trenches whenever they are called upon to do so. This can only be done by raids." Battalion commanders echoed this sentiment; for example, Lieutenant-Colonel J.L. Jack, in 1917 CO of 2nd West Yorkshires, believed that "We must worry the enemy to death and maintain by every means our fine fighting spirit so that all ranks may continue to realise that they are individually more than a match for the Germans." The historian of the East Surrey Regiment thought a raid highly beneficial for "recently joined young soldiers [who] had an opportunity of proving their superiority to the enemy."[28] Summing up, what was afoot was convincing men they were better than the enemy.

Haking's contentions about the ups and downs of morale were not universally shared. Lieutenant-Colonel Jack, for example, also realized that while successful raids raised morale, costly failures lowered it temporarily, perhaps considerably." Cyril Falls wrote that raids to obtain identifications and to keep the enemy "on the stretch" were justifiable but those with the object of raising the moral[e] of the troops were not, because they did not succeed in that object. 'No doubt,' wrote one of the Brigadiers of the 36th Division who was responsible for many raids, 'no doubt a successful raid had a good effect in a unit, but not always among the raiding party.

It is noteworthy that in his lecture on trench raids to the Canadian Corps Officers School, Colonel Mitchell, GSO2 (Intelligence), listed lowering enemy morale as one of the objects of raiding, but he made no mention of maintaining or building morale of own troops, an omission that could be said to tally with a modern historian's assessment: "There seems to be little evidence … that trench raids did anything to raise morale." Nor did Jack share the Intelligence Staff assessment that enemy morale had plunged. Such contentions were one reason why battalions distrusted Intelligence Summaries, be their origin division, corps or higher, and routinely referred to them as "Daily Lies." Some thought truth abided in the accusation that too often the summaries were nothing but extracts from the Daily Mail of two days past. It is always easier, of course, to assess capabilities than intentions. While the following example is exaggerated, it does show the effects of this limitation:

R.S.H. Moody, *Historical Records of The Buffs East Kent Regiment 1914-1919* (London: The Medici Society Limited, 1922), p. 157.

28 *SS 408;* Wyrall, *Fiftieth Division,* p. 109; James Roberts, 'Making the Butterflies Kill," *Stand To!* 68 (September 2003), p. 38; Barton, *Fromelles,* pp. 175-76; Senior, *Haking,* pp. 104, 256, 279. Haking had told his superior (Monro) in April that he was recommending the immediate removal of all three brigade commanders in 39th Division and only then would the brigades be "reliable." Terraine (ed.), *General Jack's Diary,* p. 218; Pearse and Sloman, *East Surrey Regiment,* pp. 135-36.

> The enemy might attack, or he might elect to remain on the defensive, or he might do both, either tomorrow morning at 5:30, 12 noon or at any hour of the day or night within the next two years. If there was an attack, it might confidently be expected from the North or from the South, while there was undoubtedly signs of a very good possibility of a drive from the East … while it is impossible at the present time to arrive at any conclusion with any degree of inexactitude I must say that … the general opinions … seem to indicate that … broadly speaking …[29]

Any assessment can be wrong, of course, since indications of enemy intentions can be misinterpreted or completely missed. Such "intelligence failures" are sure to raise eyebrows and tempers since staffs and commanders hate surprises.

The authors of the postwar *Lessons* report had this to say about raids and morale: "If the primary object … was to improve morale … it may be at once admitted that, as conducted, they completely failed in their purpose … as a morale raiser they may be definitely ruled out.[30]

Part of being better soldiers, in the eyes of unit and formation commanders, was dominating no man's land; indeed, this was not only advantageous, but necessary. Domination could sometimes be more desirable, supposed and debatable than factual. One very interesting case concerns the immediate aftermath of the disaster at Fromelles in mid-1916. Here it is necessary to step once outside the British and Canadian experience for the reason that the best example of what proved an erroneous assessment is Australian. The historian of the 5th Australian Division, Captain A.D. Ellis, relating how it was assumed that the reason Australian patrols could move at will in no man's land was because of Australian domination of no man's land, concluded by saying that that ground had become "our" land. In fact, as postwar German records reveal, the commander of the opposing 6th Bavarian Reserve Regiment was setting traps. The ironic thing is that the idea arose in his mind after an Australian prisoner volunteered the information that British and Australian practice was to collect every night identification tags from their dead in no man's land. On 12 August the German commander issued the following orders:

> It is best not to prevent such efforts … rather we should use them as an opportunity to take as many prisoners as possible on the entire divisional front … For this same purpose Stormtroops will be deployed from today until 18 August to assist [in hunting] Australian and English troops in No Man's Land.[31]

As of December 1916 each German Army had on strength a *sturm* battalion of five companies. Ernst Junger, who commanded such a company, related his experience in *The Storm of Steel* and *Copse 125,* both books well worth reading.

29 Terraine (ed.), *General Jack's Diary,* pp. 166. 191; Falls, *36th (Ulster) Division,* p. 71; LAC, MG30E61 (Mitchell papers), Volume 16, Western Front Orders and Instructions 1916-1918, "Trench Raids. Based upon Raids Done by the Canadian Corps," 20 August 1916. A typical Intelligence Summary was two or three pages in length, the general format being operations (both sides), enemy artillery and activity and identification of enemy troops and prisoners. Murray, *2nd Canadian Battalion, p. 235;* Lieutenant-Colonel The Hon. Ralph. Hamilton, *The War Diary of the Master of Belhaven* (London: John Murray, 1924; reprint, Barnsley: Wharncliffe Publishing Limited, 1990), p. 171; Captain W.P. Lipscomb, *Staff Tales* (London: Constable, 1920), pp. 27-28.

30 *Report of the Committee on the Lessons of the Great War,* p. 23 (Lesson 18).

31 Barton, *Fromelles,* quoting Captain Ellis, pp. 282-83.

While not a frequent occurrence, raid meeting raid in no man's land, or one side's raid being stymied by an enemy raiding party, or by parties forward of their wire for some other reason, were not unheard of. In May 1916 raiders of the 15th Cheshires (35th British Division) enroute to their objective met in no man's land a covering party protecting a working party and a terrific bomb fight ensued. Another enemy party then arrived and entered the fray, and while all were driven back, the delay had wrecked infantry-artillery co-ordination (the barrage had ceased) and with all bombs expended the Cheshires only option was withdrawal. In late 1916 another battalion of the 35th was all set to raid, Zero at 0300 on 26 November. But at midnight, the CO thinned his front line garrison thinking to minimize casualties during the enemy artillery retaliation that would probably occur at the end of the raid. Sometime around 0230 – events were very confused – enemy raiders came in, wounded two officers and several ORs, took one captive and departed. Nevertheless, the raiding party went out at 0300 despite the likelihood that the enemy would be alert. And so it proved, nothing of value being achieved. 16th Canadian Battalion (1st Division) also had to abort a raid after an encounter with a strong enemy fighting patrol immediately after entering the sap leading to the raiders' forming-up place. The enemy drove in the rear party of the battalion's raiding force, this isolating for a time the leading party and the OC Raid. Getting all put right took so much time that the OC Raid wisely ordered return to battalion trenches. Raiders of the 4th Loyal North Lancashire Regiment had a very similar experience two weeks later. When three enemy parties were encountered forward of their wire, a "sanguinary" struggle erupted. Again, withdrawal was the only course: "There was no doubt that the raid coincided with one arranged by our opponents." The enemy had at times also to abort. In the spring of 1918 a German raid against 37th Brigade of 12th British Division ran full tilt into a British working party forward of British wire. The enemy then withdrew. The following morning a patrol searching the area where contact had been made captured what it supposed was one of the German raiders. But he turned out to be just an unlucky man, an escapee from a prisoner of war cage well to the rear, who would have gotten home "but for the incessant raiding." In another case in April raiders in platoon strength from 2CMR (3rd Canadian Division) on entering the objective trench encountered fierce resistance which ended with no German survivors. However, on searching the 17 bodies and not finding any of the usual identification such as papers and discs it was thought that the dead could have been a raiding party. The grouping of the dead in the trench and their equipment also suggested this.[32]

Yet another much-heralded reason to raid was to educate officers and men and units, the value here expressed in terms of practise, validation and lessons learned, all stemming from experience. Raids, it was generally agreed, were an effective way to train new drafts, get them accustomed to leaving their trenches and to feel at ease in no man's land; encourage the offensive spirit; and assist in the training of officers. The last became increasingly important as experience demonstrated the principle that raids, if they were to be successful, had to be carried out

32 Davson, *35th Division*, pp. 20, 76-78; TNA: WO 95/2487: 15th Cheshire Regiment and WO 95/2468: 35th Division General Staff; LAC, War Diary 16th Canadian Battalion, July 1917; The Rev. J.O. Coop, *The Story of the 55th (West Lancashire) Division* (Uckfield, East Sussex: Naval and Military Press, n.d.), pp. 191-92; Scott, *12th (Eastern) Division*, p. 166; LAC, War Diary 2 CMR, report on raid by D Company on night 27/28 April 1918; Lt. Col. G. Chalmers Johnston, *The 2nd Canadian Mounted Rifles (British Columbia Horse) in France and Flanders 1914-1919* (Ottawa: CEF Books, 2003), p. 63.

by "complete tactical units." This usually meant a platoon.[33] Eventually the centrality of the infantry platoon and its young commander was recognized, the platoon being variously dubbed as the basic tactical unit, the unit of assault or the critical element. Such distinctions made the platoon and its commander the focus of training and training manuals, the latter also the key in operations, including raids, since many of these, in fact most, were led by a Subaltern, or in the case of larger raids in company strength or more, Subalterns would command elements of the raiding force. The following, although speaking of attacking, applied to raiding:

> a Subaltern with a platoon attacking a strong point is not an unimportant young man about to get killed, but a god with the powers of life and death, with the duty of creative activity, a whole army at his command and the whole military experience of the world at his disposal, to apply or misapply, at the peril of his immortal soul – a field-marshal's baton no longer in his pocket, but in his hand.

Death's Men describes raids as "a very valuable means of training and producing a school of daring and thoroughly competent leaders," although, in the author's eyes, the short duration of raids did limit the experience gained. The historian of the 34th British Division saw raids as a way to develop the initiative and resourcefulness of officers. Raids also provided a means of familiarising units with assault tactics, thereby contributing to tactical education, development of doctrine and organizational improvements.[34]

The hope was always, when it came to officers, men and units of green troops, that the cost of education and experience, for which there was no substitute, would be low. Lieutenant R.B.T. Kelly, who was the Forward Observation Officer (FOO) for a raid by the 9th Scottish Rifles (27th Brigade, 9th (Scottish) Division), recalled another aspect of education, one peculiar to military endeavour: "The battalion had suffered heavy casualties in the Somme fighting … and had newly received from home considerable drafts of young soldiers and the Colonel … felt that if these … could partake in a successful raid they would be fully "blooded" in one short encounter." Kelly noted that of the 300 men on the raid only 30 or so had more than four weeks experience of war. As it turned out, the raid was a huge success, 46 prisoners taken at a cost of one killed and 13 wounded, all in all a tribute to training and leadership. Captain F.C. Hitchcock, 2nd Leinsters, also believed "blooding" was one of the purposes of raiding. Many officers agreed, seeing raiding as a way to accustom men and units to battle starting with a small engagement rather than with a "big show" where failure or severe loss could seriously damage the process of acclimatization.[35]

Beyond giving new men experience and confidence, while making a contribution to tactical education and improved doctrine and organization, raids (and patrols) also tested new officers,

33 LAC, RG9IIIC3, Volume 4007, Folder 4, File 4; *Notes for Commanding Officers* (1918 edition), p. 214.

34 Radley, *We Lead Others Follow*, pp. 284, 292, 353, discusses the organizational and doctrinal development of the platoon. Jerrold, *Georgian Adventure*, p. 184; Denis Winter, *Death's Men: Soldiers of the Great War* (Harmondsworth: Penguin, 1985), p. 92; Paddy Griffith, *British Fighting Methods in the Great War* (London: Frank Cass, 1996), p. 532; Shakespear, *Thirty-Fourth Division*, p. 137.

35 Albert J. Fyfe, *Understanding the First World War: Illusions and Realities* (New York: Peter Lang, 1988), p. 171; Kelly, *A Subaltern's Odyssey*, p. 136; Hitchcock, *"Stand To,"* p. 227.

NCOs and units, tests that allowed COs to assess the standard of training, aggressive spirit and quality of the newcomers.

An interesting test, and one offering lessons as well, was the raid by a platoon of 15th Royal Welsh Fusiliers, 38th (Welsh) Division, a New Army Division, in June 1917. The battalion commander, Major J. Edwards, stated the purpose as "to test the esprit de corps of a platoon." The selected platoon, 13 Platoon of D Company under Second Lieutenant William Griffith, was tested "under the direction" of OC D Company, Captain H.V. Williams. The objective of the raid was a dug-out in the enemy command trench. The plan called for part of the platoon under Griffith to advance straight to the dug-out while the remainder, organized in two blocking and clearing parties and two flanking parties, were placed by an NCO. At the dug-out Griffith and his senior NCO were both so seriously wounded that they had to be carried. Command devolved to a junior NCO. Afterward Edwards thought the platoon had demonstrated strong esprit. The brigade commander rightly believed it had been a mistake for both Griffith and the senior NCO to have become involved in the fight at the dug-out, but he did not elaborate. The real problem seemed to be the organization for the raid. Griffith had not placed himself where he could direct and command his platoon. The junior NCO who had to control the withdrawal did so effectively. Presumably Edwards based his conclusion on the conduct of the withdrawal. Neither he nor the brigade commander commented on the organization of the raiders, at least not in their reports.[36]

Large scale testing was not uncommon given the initial distrust of New Army and Territorial Divisions. Sometimes Regulars, were also tested, one example being recalled by Captain James Dunn:

> The Battalion was warned for a big raid on returning to the line. There is no doubt it was intended as a test, from Division's point of view, of this Regular Battalion that had been transferred to what was an entirely New Army Division. We were a Regular Battalion in name only … in D Company … only six were Regular Soldiers, they were nearly all NCOs.

Dunn went on to say that the brigade commander "had not the courage" to say the raid was unnecessary.[37]

Another reason to raid was retaliation, or call it retribution, or as Kipling said, "the vengeance we must take."[38] In any case, according to one divisional history "it was a recognized thing that the enemy was paid doubly for what he gave."[39] 18th British Division under Ivor Maxse practised an eye for an eye and then some. In September 1915, tired of persistent enemy sniping, Maxse had an 18-pounder brought forward and emplaced. Well-camouflaged, it remained unseen until 0545, 13 September, when the gun crew commenced six minutes rapid direct fire on the sniper post. For some time afterward the division was untroubled by sniping, but this was not so of enemy raids, one inflicting 46 casualties in April 1916. Maxse, thinking it good for morale and seeking an outlet for the men's combative spirit, ordered retaliation. The subsequent platoon-

36 TNA: WO 95/2553: 15th Royal Welsh Fusiliers, June 1917, Appendix 23B, narrative of raid.

37 Dunn, *The War the Infantry Knew*, p. 486.

38 Rudyard Kipling, 'The Man Who Was', in *The Cambridge Edition of the Poems of Rudyard Kipling* Volume II: Collected Poems II. Thomas Pinney (ed.) (Cambridge University Press, 2013), p. 880.

39 Wyrall, *Fiftieth Division*, p. 109.

sized raid provided 30 minutes of hand to hand fighting in the enemy trench, leaving the raiders from the 7th Bedfords to think "highly of themselves." During the raid over 350 Mills bombs (grenades) were used, this and the hand-to-hand causing significant enemy casualties. "There can be no doubt, said the divisional historian "that the desire to worst the Boche was exceedingly keen." Some demonstrations of spirit were absurd, however. Sergeant Edwards of the East Surreys, for example, proposed to reconnoitre some ground about which little was known due to close enemy observation and fire: being a very fine runner Edwards offered to sprint around the area in shorts and track shoes and be back in seconds thereby leaving the enemy no time to hit him. This unique proposal was deemed too risky. Another proposal came from Lieutenant Vint, a Canadian rancher serving with a British artillery battery. In one part of the enemy trench was a small tunnel which the enemy used for moving to a sap. Vint proposed to go forward and lasso a German emerging from the tunnel. The CO of the battalion opposite the tunnel listened to this astonishing plan, but wisely rejected it. Vint, said a friend, "will always be remembered for this and for his unorthodox fire orders, one example being 'Cock her up, Bill, and loose her off again.'"

By all accounts Maxse's 18th Division was a very fine formation, one reason for its high reputation being that it had only two GOCs during the whole of the war: "Happy is the division [so blessed]. Such a division is almost certain to be accustomed to success … and to have developed qualities and characteristics upon which the Higher Command can calculate." As for the divisional history by Captain Nichols, if not the best it is certainly one of the best of the whole group of published British division histories. Cyril Falls awarded it two stars, which by his marking guide meant "very good." And so it is.[40]

On 22 June 1916 a unit in 33rd British Division, the 2nd Royal Welsh Fusiliers, had an experience that engendered a "general wish" to strike back and hard. OC B Company, Captain H. Blair, in his report related how he had "just stepped off the firestep … when he felt his feet lifted … and the trench walls seemed to move upward. There was a terrific blast of air." Blair, fortunately, was only partially buried and managed to dig himself out, but of his company only 40 men were left. The mine explosion was followed by heavy bombardment and a raid in a strength of about 150 men, some of whom penetrated the line where B Company had been. Men on the shoulders of the new crater managed to seal the gap. The CO very soon proposed a raid which was quickly approved. When it occurred two weeks later (5/6 July) it involved 200 men and strong fire support by 18-pounders, 4.5 and 6-inch howitzers, plus Stokes mortars, all together more artillery support than the battalion was ever given before or after. While the bombardment "let the enemy know what was afoot," and he retaliated with artillery, the raid was very successful, many dug-outs destroyed and many weapons and 43 men being captured. While one officer and six ORs were killed, plus one and 40 wounded, this raid "amptly set off their [2nd Battalion] misfortune."[41]

The enemy also saw the virtues of retaliation, a case in point being their reaction to a raid by 6th West Yorkshires (62nd British Division) on the night of 11 September 1917. Prior to

40 Nichols, *18th Division*, pp. 5, 20-21, 26-29; Falls, *War Books*, p. xx; John Baynes, *Far From a Donkey: The Life of General Sir Ivor Maxse* (London: Brassey's, 1995), p. 136. Maxse was GOC from October 1914 to January 1917. He was then promoted to command XVIII Corps. Widely considered to be one of the best trainers in the BEF eventually he became Inspector-General of Training in the BEF.

41 Dunn, *The War the Infantry Knew*, pp. 209, 212-18, 221; Hutchison, *Thirty-Third Division*, p. 9.

the raid while the raiders were training for it behind the lines the officers who were to lead it went out each night with recce patrols to see the ground and the extent of damage to the enemy wire. One of these officers was killed during one of these patrols. Another CO, J.L. Jack of 2nd West Yorkshires (8th British Division), also allowed raid leaders to go into no man's land, but restricted them to only one or two patrols beforehand, his concern being that "Much intense employment ruins the nerve."

Occasionally even COs might became actively involved; for example, two nights before a raid by 1st Royal Berkshire Regiment (2nd British Division) on an enemy salient, the CO, Lieutenant-Colonel Harris, DSO, made a personal recce of the enemy wire and then subsequently placed the raiding party in position on the night of the raid. In another instance, some officers of the 6th Royal West Kent Regiment thought their CO, Lieutenant-Colonel William Dawson DSO, sometimes more

> foolhardy than he should have been. A Colonel has no business to go out on patrol ... But before a raid it was Dawson's habit 'to have a look round', which meant that he would creep out in front preferably alone, slithering along on his belly, to see, for example, that the barbed wire had been properly smashed by the gunners so that his men should be able to get through. If by chance [they] had not done their job, they would hear about it from him – at first hand. Rarely can a CO have been so reckless and foolhardy – or have commanded such devotion from his men.

In the trenches while courage was admired, old soldiers like John Lucy wished that officers would take better care of themselves since when they were lost their responsibilities fell too soon on their juniors. This was especially true of COs since their loss was so damaging and demoralizing.[42]

But to return to the West Yorkshires' raid at 2000 on the 11th the raiders moved into no man's land and took up a position where they could wait for Zero without being detected. At 2300 the artillery and trench mortar support commenced, the noise and effects enabling the raiders to move forward to within 50 yards of the enemy trenches. Three minutes after Zero the raiders charged and entered the trench where several Germans were killed and a number of dug-outs were blown up. A second wave then swept through to the support trench where more punishment was inflicted. On the withdrawal four enemy prisoners accompanied the raiders home. Only three men were wounded. The OC Raid, Second Lieutenant J.R. Allett, won the MC for the night's good work.

On the 12th all was quiet, the enemy artillery fire "feeble,' but at 0400 the next day a hurricane of fire fell on the 6th West Yorkshires, this lasting for over an hour. As the fire lifted, about 100 Germans rushed forward entering the trenches between the left and right forward companies. This party was soon ejected as was another further along the line. Four Germans were killed and two captured. The defenders lost one officer and 10 ORs killed, plus 30 wounded. The

42 Everard Wyrall, *The Story of the 62nd (West Riding) Division 1914-1919*. Volume One (Uckfield, East Sussex: Naval and Military Press, n.d.), pp. 64-67; Terraine (ed.), *General Jack's Diary*, p. 199; Wyrall, *Second Division*, Volume II, p. 362; Thomas, *A Life Apart*, p. 58; John F. Lucy, *There's a Devil in the Drum* (London: Faber and Faber Limited, 1938), p. 189.

Corps Commander expressed his admiration for the Yorkshires' raid and for their stout defence of Battalion lines a day later.[43]

In late March 1917, as the Canadian Corps was preparing for Vimy Ridge, the Germans raided 8th Brigade's lines, capturing two men and killing three manning an outpost of 2CMR. The raid involved only a few Germans, but it was "very serious and annoying [since] one could never tell how much information the Germans could get out of the men by either direct or indirect methods." German documents captured later revealed that the two men had not given anything away, instead giving their captors "a mass of lies." 2CMR, to wipe out the affront and to obtain identifications, raided the enemy on 31 March, killing a large number of enemy. No prisoners were taken, but identifications were secured. 2CMR then carried on preparing their jumping off trenches for the offensive set for 9 April.[44]

About a month earlier (25 February) the Germans had raided an outpost of 3rd Canadian Brigade (1st Division), taking two prisoners from 14th Battalion and then one from 15th Battalion. The then BM, Major P.F. Villiers, included in his diary a fulsome account of the raid, its immediate impact and the retaliatory raid on 2 March, the whole adding a good deal to the cryptic War Diary entry.

Within hours of the enemy raid, and the disgrace of losing prisoners to the enemy, the GOC 1st Division, Arthur Currie, and the GOC of the Canadian Corps, Julian Byng, arrived to see George Tuxford, GOC 3rd Brigade, for whom it would surely have been an awkward visit, Currie and Byng "both walking as if they had a horrid smell under their noses. They were frigidly polite and hoped that we were going to counter raid." Villiers, who thought the raid the first one that had ever penetrated brigade lines, wrote that the loss infuriated the whole brigade, especially the two battalions. Indeed, the 3rd was desperate to raid at once. That very night patrols went out to examine the wire at the chosen objective. However, the raid had to be postponed because of 4th Division's upcoming large-scale raid that would require all heavy artillery. Tuxford and his brigade had to wait, left for a time "wearing a bullseye scored against us … and so far [no] opportunity to get our own back … the temper of the two battalions did not improve."

On the 28th the brigade learned that the raid could go ahead on Thursday, 1 March, but at this point both battalion commanders requested changes to the artillery fire plan, whereupon Villiers went post-haste to finalize the plan with the heavy artillery. On arrival at Corps HQ he found the gunners most obliging, readily incorporating the desired changes and topping him up with a very fine port while he waited: "right good support," he recalled. At this time the SOS

43 Wyrall, *62nd Division,* pp. 64-67; Major A.F. Becke, 'The Coming of the Creeping Barrage', *Journal of the Royal Artillery,* 58 (January 1932), p. 22, states that First Army Operation Order 85, issued for the Battle of Loos (25 September-13 October 1915) made "possibly the first use of the term "Zero," Zero Hour. Lieutenant-Colonel C.N.F. Broad, 'The Development of Artillery Tactics,1914-1918), *Journal of the Royal Artillery,* 49 (1922-1923), p. 80, defined Zero as "the hour at which the artillery barrage opens." Captain Stair Gillon, *The Story of the 29th Division: A Record of Gallant Deeds* (London: Thomas Nelson & Sons Ltd., 1925), p. 101, says he was told that Zero was only an "approximation." "Watch the barrage," was the rule. Today Zero, now known as H Hour, is the time at which the infantry crosses the Start Line.

44 Johnston, *The 2nd Canadian Mounted Rifles,* p. 43. This book was Johnston's personal diary. 2CMR War Diary for 22 March notes that the enemy raid was a surprise because there was no preparatory bombardment.

signal also changed, it being thought that the enemy had discovered its colour and would try to imitate it during the raid to confuse or wreck artillery support. The coloured SOS and other signals fired by own troops and enemy troops changed frequently to prevent the enemy determining the colours in use and copying them. Some signals became very complicated. German light signals were often quite a show, sometimes red, orange and green rockets, also rockets which burst into "showers of gold and silver stars." The last were often referred to as golden rain.[45]

3rd Brigade decided that the raid, designed to retaliate, inflict loss and take prisoners (the identity of the opposing infantry was unknown) would be made by two companies, one each from the 14th and 15th battalions, Zero to be at 0200, 2 March. Fire support included 16 field guns, Stokes and trench mortars and Heavy Artillery (9.2, 6 and 4.5-inch howitzers). Prior to Zero scouts reported no man's land clear of enemy.

14th Battalion's raiders, 77 in all, were split into three parties: No. One, 25 men under Lieutenant D.M. McRae; No. Two, 24 men under Lieutenant H.N. Pitcher; and No. Three, 16 men under Lieutenant T.G. Bingley. No. One was divided into two groups. McRae described the supporting barrage as so excellent that it enabled the whole party to move up to within 40 yards of the enemy trench and then when it lifted the party moved forward to the trench. On reaching the parapet one group worked its way along it bombing as it went while the other group entered the trench where a stiff fight ensued. This group took several prisoners and bombed several dug-outs. Pitcher's party worked in three groups. One quickly entered the enemy trench and moved to a nearby junction with a CT. Of the six enemy encountered, two were killed and two captured. Picher's other two groups worked along the parapet putting to flight an enemy section. No. Three Party (Bingley), tasked to place a block at the junction just mentioned, entered the main trench immediately behind Pitcher's party. No enemy was encountered. Overall, the enemy reacted slowly and not in any strength. Two of the three parties reported afterward that the signal for withdrawal, horns and bugles, were not heard. Clearly, signalling would have to be looked at. 14th Battalion suffered one officer and nine ORs wounded and one killed.

The 75 raiders of 15th Battalion operated in two parties, the OCs being Lieutenants S.J. Reeves and M.P. Neilly. Part of Reeves' responsibility was marking the boundary between the two battalions with a white tape as a precaution against confusion. His party encountered masses of wire that had been cut, but still presented an obstacle. Despite this, and enemy fire, it got into the trench and worked down it, bombing a dug-out and then blowing it up. On encountering resistance at a traverse the party held the trench until the signal to retire was heard. Neilly reported that his party had been 100 yards away form the enemy trench when the barrage lifted. He then rushed the trench, but the party was caught by machine-gun fire and met stubborn resistance in the trench. Stokes bombs destroyed five dug-outs. Battalion casualties totalled 21: two officers and 16 ORs wounded, two ORs killed and one missing. Both officers received the MC for the raid.

Tuxford attributed the 15th Battalion's proportionally higher casualties to this: "the men were not as close up to the barrage … the enemy had time to re-man their machine-guns" and

45 R.C. Fetherstonhaugh, *The Royal Canadian Regiment 1883 – 1933* (Montreal: Gazette Publishing Company, 1936), p. 289; Thomas, *A Life Apart,* p. 89.

the raiders had experienced "undoubtedly much stiffer fighting" than the 14th Battalion had. Both battalions had been instructed to take particular note of the number of enemy dead. 15th Battalion reported 28 while the 14th reported nine. How many were in the dug-outs could not be known. Ten prisoners were taken. Villiers noted that 3rd Brigade received "a very nice telegram from the GOC, and had the satisfaction of knowing that they had got their own back."[46]

Finally, there arose a set of reasons for raiding somewhat perverse and in part even perverted. Some involved certain personal characteristics that establish attitudes, which are the subject of a later chapter, but as they are reasons why raids were conducted, they are considered in part here. How many raids were ordered because of these characteristics and attitudes we cannot say, but sufficient evidence exists to state that they were a motive in many instances.

Earlier in this book it was said that the battalion (or brigade or division) that does not think itself best is not worth a damn. This is fundamental for the simple reason that "we" are far better than that other "mob" over there. The driver is often rivalry and competition, these engendering in the corporate and individual senses ambition and the desire for reward or to build or enhance reputation. Lieutenant R. Lewis, describing his service with the 25th Canadian Battalion, recalled that during 1916 intense rivalry arose between the 25th and one of the other battalions in 5th Canadian Brigade, but "thanks to our CO we never took second place." In June the battalion "got word that a battalion on our right was going to pull off a raid. Our Colonel immediately ordered Lieut. Wise ... to raid." This hastily mounted effort succeeded in entering enemy trenches where several Germans were killed, but at the cost of several wounded including Wise. The "other" battalion had to postpone its raid. A few days later, the 25th busy preparing another raid, had to postpone it because the "other" battalion was first off the mark and brigade ordered the 25th to stand down.[47] Competition, while healthy and, indeed, inevitable, grows as time passes, as does the aggressive spirit, and these can become divisive. Victor Odlum, GOC 11th Canadian Brigade in January 1917, had strongly expressed his desire that the attitude of the brigade "become more aggressive." This was not uncommon. Archibald Macdonell, the last GOC of 1st Canadian Division, told his brigadiers "We lead others follow. The best is none too good for this Division and nothing but the best will do. Get your backs into it." One of Macdonell's brigadiers, William Griesbach, stressed time and again the offensive spirit.[48] One of the dangers with spiraling competitiveness is evident in the adage that says "If you want it bad you will get it bad." In practice, this

46 LAC, MG30E236 (Villiers Papers), Volume 4, Folder 7, Diary, Volume 3. Paul Villiers, a British officer, was highly respected. Following service with 15th Battalion he was appointed Staff Captain at 3rd Brigade, then BM (July 1915-January 1918), GSO3 at 1st Division and finally GSO2 with 29th British Division. Had the war continued it is likely that he would have been appointed GSO1 of a division, British or Canadian. His was very much the preferred profile of increasingly senior appointments up the staff levels. LAC, 3rd Brigade War Diary, February 1917, Operation Order 130, 27 February, 3rd Brigade report on the raid, 4 March, and the reports of both battalions; Beattie, *48th Highlanders of Canada*, pp. 205-208; Fetherstonhaugh, *14th Battalion*, pp. 135-39.

47 Lewis, *Over the Top With the 25th*, pp. 12, 17, 24. Wise was awarded the MC for the raid. The CO at the time was Edward Hilliam, described by Lewis as a "fire-eater," wanting to be at the enemy all the time, and as a "bulldog," very strong on discipline. Hilliam had been wounded at Second Ypres, but recovered quickly and took command in October 1915.

48 LAC, MG30E300 (Odlum Papers), Volume 24, 'Trench Discipline', 6 January 1917; MG30E318 (3rd Battalion), Folder 188, Macdonell to brigades.

can mean poor battle procedure, poor planning in general, rushed and inadequate preparation, absence of proper recce, inadequate fire support and several other evils that spell failure. Captain F.C. Hitchcock considered rivalry "excellent, but when overdone … most dangerous. The rivalry that existed in 1916 and 1917 over raiding operations had, indeed, been carried to an extreme limit."[49]

Competition usually involved reward in one form or another. Some COs offered money for capturing a prisoner during a raid or patrol, £10 often being the going rate. One other aspect of monetary award is relevant. When in March 1917 the then BGGS of the Canadian Corps, P. deB. Radcliffe, reacting to a memorandum about "want of consideration" for infantry working parties (and a suggestion as to one remedy) said "I do not think the payment of working parties … feasible. If you pay men extra to dig a trench, how much will you pay them to take one?"[50]

Richard Haking, GOC XI Corps, originated another type of award, possibly a unique one. At a Corps Commander Conference in January 1917 he announced the results of his "Raids Competition." Having personally reviewed 30 proposals for raids sent in by battalions, all displaying sound knowledge and many featuring what he considered the essentials for success, he awarded first prize to Captain White of 5th London Regiment (169th Brigade). Runners-up were Major Higgins (13th London Regiment) and Captain Douglas (2nd King's Own Scottish Borderers). The War Diary of 168th Brigade, the parent brigade of the 13th London, shows that Higgins' proposal was executed on 17 February, Zero at 0715. The raiders, four officers and 142 ORs, penetrated enemy trenches as far as the support line, which was found empty and derelict, took five prisoners and killed 40 Germans in their front line. The cost was one officer and four ORs killed and 33 wounded, almost all the wounds due to enemy artillery fire as the raiders withdrew across no man's land. The raid report attributed success to a simple plan that contained "no complicated orders which depend on a number of prearranged things happening." White's proposal was carried out on 17 February, Zero at 1000. His raiders, four officers and 115 ORs, did almost as well as Higgins had done.

At division level, too, competitions were not uncommon; for example, in the tense period before the German offensive in the spring of 1918 General Gough, GOC Fifth Army, at a conference on 5 February warned that the main attack would strike Fifth and Third Armies. Amongst other things he emphasized the necessity for defence in depth, great alertness and frequent raids. The British Official History, commenting on the last, noted the rules for a competition: "During the period of waiting some divisions instituted a monthly cup for competition between battalions, marks being given as follows: identifications from killed, 1 point; prisoner or deserter, 2 points; machine-gun or trench mortar, 3 points."[51]

49 Hitchcock, *"Stand To,"* p. 230.

50 Terraine (ed.), *General Jack's Diary,* p. 174; LAC, RG9IIIC1, Volume 3839, Folder 34, File 1, 12 March 1917. Radcliffe, widely regarded as an "outstanding planner" and the "ablest tactician" in the Army, was one of the splendid British officers who served with the Canadian Corps. He came from II Corps where he had been BGGS, having previously been a GSO1 at Third Army. In 1918 he became Director of Military Operations at the War Office.

51 TNA: WO 95/2957: 169th Brigade and WO 95/2955: 13th London Regiment. The published histories contain nothing on the two raids. Brigadier-General J.E. Edmonds, *Military Operations France and Belgium, 1918: The German March Offensive and Its Preliminaries* (London: Macmillan, 1935), p. 97.

Postwar, *Lessons of the Great War* flatly stated that raids "have no place … when carried out merely as a sort of competition … with no specific military object, and when needlessly ordered they impair the confidence of the troops in their leaders and lower their morale."[52]

References to ambition and reputation voiced by regimental officers and men mostly reflect views about particular brigadiers. Far fewer references are made to division commanders, not surprisingly given that one's shirt is closer than one's tunic. But this also indicates recognition of the fact that raids made a name for brigadiers and brigades that battalions paid for. Also, brigadiers were usually more involved than division commanders. In *Journey's End,* R.C. Sherriff's famous play, we read of a company commander in despair about the loss of his 2IC and a Subaltern and six men for nothing more than a feather in the brigadier's cap. In an actual instance just before a raid on 3 June 1916 by the 22nd Manchester Regiment (7th British Division) one of the company commanders, Captain Charles May, expressed the frustration within the battalion: "We are a trifle sick about it, the Brigade having more or less taken it out of the COs hands … But I suppose it is one of the things we have to put up with for having a young and ambitious Brigadier who wants to run everything himself." In the event, the stunt cost half the raiding party, two officers killed, one wounded and one missing, plus 30 ORs wounded and six missing: "a heavy price [that] cast a shadow over us all." Possibly the most damning remark about brigadiers and raids was related to D.W.J. Cuddeford, an officer of the Scots Guards, before the April 1917 offensive: "The lives of infantrymen were cheap … I was told by an officer attached to a HQ Staff of two brigadiers who … made a bet … as to whose brigade would capture the most prisoners in a trench raid competition." None of this can be corroborated, of course.[53]

Later that month (26/27 June) the 8th Royal Warwickshire Regiment (182nd British Brigade, 61st Division) raided trenches north of Neuve Chapelle. According to the raid report up to the morning of the 26th only one gap had been made in enemy wire. Consequently, artillery wire-cutting continued until dusk, "this somewhat advertising our intention." At three minutes past midnight the first raiding party, two officers and 30 men, in the face of machine-gun fire reached the parapet and entered enemy trenches. During this movement it lost touch with the second party which did not enter the trench. In all, the battalion lost one officer and two ORs killed, 20 ORs wounded, and Captain G.C. Field, Lieutenant E.C. Hooton and 14 ORs captured. Field later spoke bitterly of the raid and how "The idea for it came from the Brigade commander, who evidently wanted it to get him noticed." He went on to call the raid "pointless from the outset."[54]

An especially arresting instance of a raid supposedly having much to do with building reputation, which always drew anger and resentment by participants, was to be conducted by 25th Canadian Battalion (2nd Division) in July 1917. Its purpose was to secure identifications. According to Captain Robert Clement MC, who served with the battalion from mobilization

52 *Report of the Committee on The Lessons of the Great War,* p. 23.

53 R.C. Sherriff, *Journey's End: A Play in Three Acts* (London: Victor Gollancz Ltd., 1929), Act 3, Scene 1, p. 107; Brown, *The Imperial War Museum Book of the Western Front,* pp. 111-12; Atkinson, *Seventh Division,* p. 251; Cuddeford, *And All For What?* p. 124; Harrison, ed., *To Fight Alongside Friends,* p. 187.

54 TNA: WO 95/3054: 182nd Brigade, 61st Division, 'Report of Raid by 8th Warwicks on Night 26/27 June 1916'; Barton, *Fromelles,* p. 114.

to demobilization, as the 25th was preparing to return to the line it became aware that "Big Brass" wanted a strong raid. General resentment surfaced about "the idea of acting as sacrificial pigeons to satisfy the aspirations of one in particular of their seniors securing a DSO for himself at their peril." Raid plans continued as the 25th returned to the trenches, this allowing Clement and others he does not identify to make an immediate and careful study of the objective. A first recce determined that by day the Germans stuck to their dug-outs with only a few sentries on duty. It also found a deep ditch full of tall grass that led directly into the enemy lines. A second recce convinced two Subalterns that a snatch raid could be done, and they organized a "hurry-up" raid which set out with a covering party with a Lewis gun and a second party consisting of themselves and three men to creep forward to the enemy trench. They entered the trench unseen, no sentries present, and winkled several Germans out of a cellar without alerting anyone. The whole affair lasted 20 minutes, not a shot fired, two prisoners and the whole party safe at home, thanks to inexplicable enemy carelessness and failure to appreciate ground. Daring and luck, the latter for once a lady, had prevailed! Clement summed it all up:

> The capture of the two prisoners eliminated the official reasons which had been pressed to justify … the big raid. Before the promoters could get going again the 25th's tour of trench duty ran out … the expectant promoter of the original idea did not get his DSO but he saw to it that neither of the officers or any members of their little party received official recognition.[55]

Regardless of what officers and men thought of the validity of the reasons to raid, they were "it." Railing against raids was usually futile; one might just as well have condemned the sun for coming up. Not all raids triumphed, of course. The next chapter examines a second set of reasons why, specifically the reasons why a raid might fail.

55 Tennyson (ed.), *Merry Hell,* pp. 176-77. Clement does not name the individual pursuing a DSO. Neither the 5th Brigade nor the 2nd Division War Diaries mention any proposed raid to be executed by the 25th Battalion at the time.

5

The Reasons Why (2)

> It is possible to fail in many ways … to miss the mark easy, to hit it difficult.
>
> Aristotle

Not every flower blooms. Nature and man dictate that. This applies equally well to raids and patrols. Throughout the war various levels of command annually issued compilations entitled "Lessons Learned During the Year's Fighting" and similar documents. The Canadian edition for 1917, for example, is very fulsome, running to 39 foolscap pages, with considerable emphasis on a few topics including patrolling and raiding. In addition, numerous "Lessons" instructions and other guidance circulated frequently, almost constantly. Most of these filtered downward to units. While the whole of their content could be helpful, they highlighted an inevitable aspect of the education of commanders: "special value is to be gained by studying causes of failure." Indeed, as Brigadier-General Collyer stressed (see the Introduction) wisdom comes more from failure than from success.[1]

The aim of this chapter is to identify, examine and illustrate the many reasons why raids failed. In assessing failure one can usually see the course or decision that had it been taken would have meant success. Less frequently, fortunately, everything in a raid went wrong. Failure, despite the tragic losses, did offer some practical benefit, a nudge for corporate and individual progression along the learning curve. Officers and men had much to learn about trench warfare in general and raiding whether they were Regulars, Territorials or men of the New Army or the Dominions. Few Regulars were with the Canadian Army in 1914.[2]

Making definitive statements about the outcome of any raid could be difficult for those who had to report upon it. For one thing, the purist may carp upon seeing summations such as

1 LAC, RG9IIIC1, Volume 3859, Folder 85, File 8, Canadian Corps to Second Army, 20 November 1917; File 2, Canadian Corps G.116/3-23 and divisional replies; RG9IIIC3, Volume 4026, Folder 11, File 3, Canadian Corps to divisions, 3 November 1917; Collyer, *The Campaign in German South West Africa 1914-1915*, Preface.

2 Nicholson, *Canadian Expeditionary Force*, pp. 6-7. The Canadian Army in 1914 stood at 3,110 officers and men organized in one infantry regiment, one artillery regiment, two cavalry regiments and the cadets of the Royal Military College, Kingston. That same year the Canadian stock of Staff College graduates was nine plus three not graduated (LAC, Militia Reports, 1906-14). The "sunny ways" of a muddled government had ensured an empty larder.

"total failure" or "complete success," for after all, failure is failure and success is success. Raids could also be "unqualified success" or "disastrous failure," or they could be "partial" success or failure. Failure being a red-flag word that one's superiors did not like to see, euphuism soon found employment: how much better to speak of "non-success" (a brigade HQ to British 5th Division HQ November 1916) or "We didn't succeed." (10th Canadian Battalion to GOC 2nd Brigade February 1916). While the extremes of success and failure stood out, between the two the spectrum was equivocal because of perspective and degree of involvement, sometimes reflecting wish rather than reality. Nor was there unanimity about the criteria for success and a preference for that grievous military sin – "Situating the Appreciation" – sometimes surfaced. Composing a report on a failure presented the writer with what Rosalind exclaimed in *As You Like It*, "Oh, how full of briers is this working-day world." A classic case featured the acting brigade commander of 99th British Brigade (2nd Division) who explained that the raid was robbed of "complete success" by enemy wire, but it was "partially successful" and the "partial failure" was due to enemy alertness because of an "extremely successful" raid by another of his battalions. But the KRRC raid was "not successful" because the enemy was waiting for it.[3]

It seems clear enough that a raid that did not achieve its assigned task failed. But beyond that lay the "complete failure" – total crushing failure – related in Henry Dundas' succinct summation of a raid: "The other night [in October 1915] a raiding party went over and not one of them came back." At the other end of the spectrum D.V. Kelly summarized a raid by a unit of 110th British Brigade as an "admirable … success … the result of a careful study of the local conditions, adequate preparation and the application of elementary psychology … surprise and deception were fully exploited and miners, engineers, infantry and intelligence work were all used in co-operation."[4]

One commonly held determinant when it came to awarding the accolade "success" features in the history of 34th British Division which carried out 22 minor operations between September 1916 and February 1917: "of these … 13 may be classed as successes; that is, we got into the Boche line and did more or less damage. In the remaining nine … the party failed to get into the Boche front line." This distinction echoes the British Official History, which defined the "essence of a raid" as entering the enemy trenches, a standard by which 47 of 63 BEF raids of from ten to 200 men between December 1915 and May 1916, were classified as successful.[5] J.L. Jack, in 1915 a company commander with the 1st Cameronians, wrote about another criterion of success. He had read reports that "allege that the raid by the 17th Highland Light Infantry … was most successful, from which I suppose that some prisoners were taken and casualties inflicted." The capture of prisoners, where this was one of the tasks assigned by the Operation Order for the raid, came to be a highly visible and measurable mark of success. Loss versus gain also coloured "success." Given the circumstances, estimates or assumptions led to gradations of "success." Cyril Falls, for example, relating the result of a raid by 109th British Brigade, recognized lesser success: "Though the enemy's casualties were estimated at 30, and a prisoner was

3 TNA: WO 95/1371: 1st KRRC, 99th Brigade, 2nd Division, raid report on 25/26 September 1916.
4 Dundas (ed.), *Henry Dundas Scots Guards; A Memoir*, p. 72; Kelly, *39 Months With the "Tigers,"* pp. 55-56. Kelly served with the Leicestershires in 37th Division.
5 Shakespear, *Thirty-Fourth Division*, p. 80; Edmonds, *Haig's Command to the 1st July*, pp. 156, 242. Of 33 German raids during the same period 20 succeeded, a 60 percent success rate. The BEF success rate was 74 percent.

taken, the raid hardly ranked as a success since our casualties were 17." On the other hand, a venture by 107th British Brigade shouted success: of ten enemy encountered two were captured, eight killed. No casualties were suffered.[6]

Another "complete" success attended a raid by three officers and 60 ORs of 1st Border Regiment (29th British Division) near Wieltje in the Ypres Salient on 30 September/1 October 1916. This raid aimed to take prisoners and/or secure identifications. It could well have been counted perfect were it not for the failure of Bangalore torpedoes to cut the wire (see later in this chapter on these explosive devices). But even here the sharp eye of the OC Raid and some luck intervened when he spotted an existing gap in the wire that allowed the raid to proceed and prosper. Looking at the diagram of the raid (see MSD 1) it shows ground favourable to the raiders and how it enabled simplicity of plan and organization of the raiders. Starting at the top lay the objective, about 100 yards wide and 300 yards from the British lines, and bounded on either side by a CT. Some 70 yards short of the enemy trench ran a line of willows, a perfect place to pause before launching the final assault. It was so close to the enemy trenches that when the preliminary bombardment ended the raiders reached the objective trench before the Germans could stand to. Halfway between the lines stood a second line of trees that provided cover for the raiders as they moved forward. All members of the raiding party were familiar with the ground as all had participated in patrols of the area. The whole party would enter the enemy trench at the centre point of the objective and then move toward the junctions with the CTs.

The raid went like clockwork. Eight prisoners were taken, several more Germans killed and only one man was slightly wounded in the hand, this wound inflicted by friendly artillery during the 15-minute preliminary bombardment. The Operation Order for the raid, an example of good operational writing, reflected the very close co-ordination of the infantry and the supporting artillery. The order's simplicity, the thorough briefings of all ranks and the rehearsals of the raid ensured that every man knew his task and that of his comrades.

Damp probably caused the failure of the Bangalore, the cover of the fuse being lost during the move across no man's land. The diagram shows only one "Bell Man" but the Operation Order actually included two. This raid is the only instance found of bells being used as the signal to withdraw. The raid report makes no mention of any difficulty hearing the bells, nor of any difficulty during the withdrawal.[7]

2nd Irish Guards had a particularly expensive venture on the night of 3 July 1917 near Ypres. While the raiders, 40 from the battalion and a detachment of engineers, took two prisoners and did some damage, casualties were "unfortunately somewhat numerous," more than half, including the OC Raid, most caused by intense enemy artillery fire during the withdrawal. Strictly speaking, prisoners meant "success," but given Falls' example above "hardly" success. Perhaps the last word on the numbers game should belong to the 1924 edition of *FSR*, which incorporated many of the lessons of the war: "It is the first principle of a raid that it should result in greater losses to the enemy than to the troops which carry it out."[8]

6 Terraine (ed.), *General Jack's Diary*, p. 134; Falls, *36th (Ulster) Division*, p. 249; TNA: WO 95/2502: 107th Brigade.

7 TNA: WO95/2305: 1st Border Regiment (29th Division), report on raid 30 September 1916.

8 TNA: WO 95/1220: 2nd Irish Guards, July 1917, report on raid 2/3 July; *Field Service Regulations*. Volume II. *Operations* (London: HMSO, 1924), p. 241; Headlam, *Guards Division* Volume One,

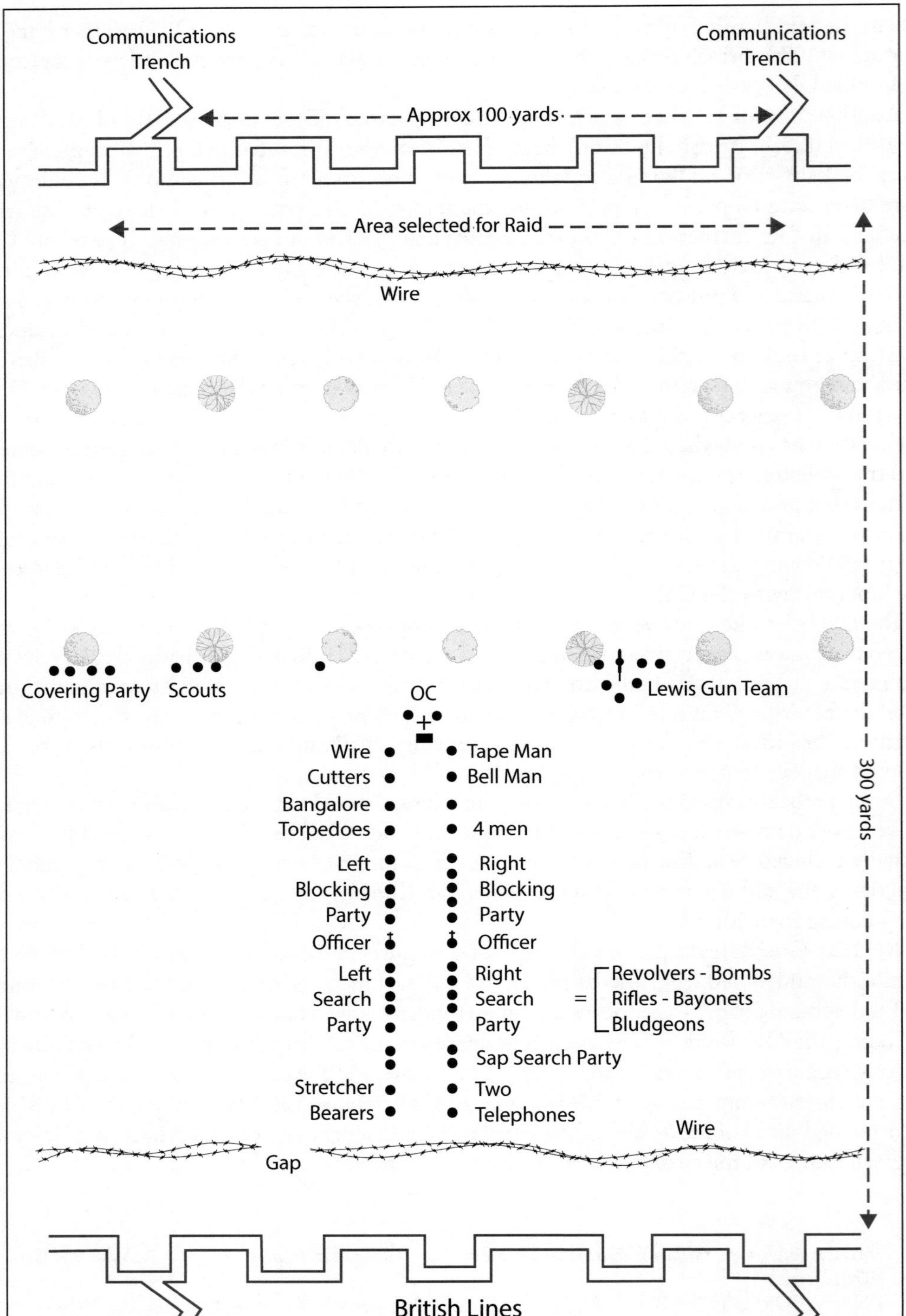

1 Typical Small-Scale Raid Scenario, 30 September 1916, Wieltje, Ypres Salient, 1st Border Regiment.

In getting at the enemy raiders faced any number of challenges. These demanded close attention lest challenges become reasons for failure. For one thing, the distance trench to trench posed time and space difficulties, the distance varying between 50 yards or even less and 1,000 yards or more. In each case one had always to consider approaches (cover or lack of it), dead ground, obstacles (not least of which was wire), positions available for covering parties and good positions for observation. The state of the ground warranted equally close study. Ground extensively cut-up by artillery and trench mortars could slow movement and/or channel it and create bunching-up (and lucrative targets). A raid by 51st (Highland) Division in November 1916 encountered ground so cut-up that it caused failure, the raiders finding it "a physical impossibility to keep up with a very slow-moving barrage. Not an officer or man could move a yard at the double." Constant rain, the ground sodden, oozing mud as thick as porridge, caused postponement of this raid seven times.[9]

Snow could have negative impact, too. In February 1916, 2nd Canadian Battalion, seeking identification of the enemy opposite, launched a 40-man raid under Captain George Richardson. Raid night, 3 February, featured bright moonlight and light snow on the ground: "objects in No Man's Land could be detected at a great distance. These facts were not lost on the men, who felt it was suicidal to persevere with the operations. They hoped that orders would be issued cancelling it." But the raid commenced. While the main body waited in the trenches, two small parties of three men each carrying explosives reached the German wire. At this point Richardson, concerned about the brightness caused by the snow and moonlight and about an enemy, who appeared to be fully alert and manning the parapet in strength, returned to battalion HQ where he briefed the CO who cancelled the raid. Eventually white smocks were issued to raiders when snow prevailed. Such camouflage did not always solve the problem as the Germans learned in February 1917 when their white smocks could not protect them against their own carelessness. A few days later British raiders similarly attired, but better disciplined, executed a successful winter night raid securing several prisoners.[10]

Moonlight remained a more persistent hindrance. In December 1916, for example, raiders of 6th Queens (Royal West Surrey Regiment) commenced a raid under a cloudy sky, but when the moon came out brightly at about 2100 they were discovered and received heavy fire. The party withdrew, thinking to wait until the moon had gone down, but during the return to their own trenches they lost the OC Raid and six men to mortar fire, this causing cancellation. That same month 3rd Canadian Battalion founded a raid by five officers and 90 ORs under Major H.S. Cooper. On 8 December, the night before the raid, the party moved forward to the departure trench, Zero having been set for 0400. But bright moonlight meant postponement for 45 minutes. Once underway all three parties reached the enemy wire undetected, two of them entering the trenches where two German officers and 20 ORs were killed and several dug-outs were blown up. Despite the loss of three officers wounded, five ORs killed and 29 wounded, this raid was considered a success, congratulations being received from both Corps and Army. According to the battalion historian, the raid did much for fighting spirit, 70 percent of the men being newcomers who had not been in action

p. 127.

9 Bewsher, *Fifty-First (Highland) Division*, pp. 104-105.

10 Murray, *2nd Battalion*, pp. 78-79; Donald A. MacKenzie, 'Bogie Raids on Winter Nights', in *From All the Fronts* (Glasgow: Blackie and Son Limited,1917), pp. 103-110.

before.[11] A raid by 4th Canadian Battalion, and its unusual denouement, which will be related in Chapter 7, marked an instance where bright moonlight wrecked a raid. Similarly, in March 1917 raiders of the 10th Northumberland Fusiliers (23rd British Division) were spotted and beaten off, the party leaving two of their dead near a forward sap. For the remainder of the night and throughout the next day the area was kept under fire to prevent the enemy recovering the bodies and possibly obtaining identification, as one was that of an officer. However, that evening the Germans reached one of the corpses, tied a rope to it and dragged it into their trench where a search revealed the dead man to be the Adjutant of the 10th, a valuable recovery since it helped the Germans confirm in March 1917 that the British had replaced the French in the Vimy sector.[12]

Stuart Cloete, who first served with the King's Own Yorkshire Light Infantry and then with the Coldstream Guards, believed, as did many officers, that while men were "very alert in moonlight and impossible to approach" a raid at midday could sometimes be carried out as the Canadians and the Australians had demonstrated. Colonel H.H. Story, historian of the Cameronians (Scottish Rifles) agreed, noting that while night raiding initially offered a chance of achieving surprise, the odds declined after each raid and "the idea of making a short, sharp raid in full daylight when the enemy might be expected to be less alert was conceived and put into practice." By the summer of 1917 many units were doing so. James Neville, Oxfordshire and Buckinghamshire Light Infantry, having been told about such daylight jaunts to "snaffle a Boche," was itching to do likewise and worked hard on such a scheme, which due to a move elsewhere he could not implement. Lieutenant-Colonel W.D. Croft, CO of 11th Royal Scots, and afterward GOC 27th British Brigade, on returning to his battalion in late 1916 from the Divisional Tactics School where he had been Chief Instructor, found the raiding season in full swing. He recalled one raid in February 1917 which took place at noon when the enemy was asleep or feeding that took 42 prisoners, two machine-guns and a light mortar at a cost of two killed, 15 wounded and one missing. His rules for when to raid were these: never at dawn when the enemy is alert, it being criminal folly to do so unless unavoidable; go instead after morning stand down when it becomes broad daylight and sentries are not alert and soldiers think of food and sleep; and it not being the usual plan to attack at midday this could surprise, mystify and mislead, but he warned against over-playing this card.[13]

Time was critical in another sense, this being the time available for planning and preparation of a raid. A crucial aspect of this was training. Anyone who has ever watched a Trooping of the Colour knows that behind the absolute precision and perfection of every movement lies intense and repetitive drill, including rehearsals which serve as a check and an audit. The same applies to raids. *SS 107 Notes on Minor Enterprises,* having stated that at least a week was necessary

11 Scott, *12th (Eastern) Division,* pp. 87-88; Goodspeed, *Battle Royal,* pp. 168-69. Cooper received the MC.

12 Sheldon, *German Army on Vimy Ridge,* p. 146.

13 Cloete, *A Victorian Son,* p. 201; Story, *Cameronians,* p. 141; Lt. Col. Sir James Neville, *War Letters of a Light Infantryman* (London: Sifton, Praed & Co., 1930), p. 58; Ewing, *Ninth (Scottish) Division,* pp. 174-76, 178-79. What was being taught at the Tactical Schools was this: "Hitherto, officers had been guided only by the general principles in *Field Service Regulations,* but the pamphlets provided illustrations showing the application of these principles to actual problems. The more junior the commander, the more desirable it was to make things clear to him by concrete means, and in this respect *SS 143* was invaluable." Croft, *Three Years With the Ninth (Scottish) Division,* pp. 100-102.

for proper preparation of a raid, dedicated one of its seven pages to training. Raid members practised grenade throwing, dug-out destruction, rifle shooting, attended briefings on the raid and rehearsed the entire raid several times. These rehearsals also included an advance to the practice trenches over the same distance as that to the enemy trenches as a check on timing and movement, then entry to the enemy trench and subsequent action in that trench. Depending on the size and scope of the raid observers could include brigade, division and even higher commanders. Rehearsals when possible were done at the same hour as the raid would occur and under the same conditions. 19th British Division, in its "Some Notes on Raids," issued in February 1918, considered it of the greatest importance that raiding parties practice by night as well as by day for at least two or three days and preferably a week until every man knew exactly his part in the raid.[14]

Practice trenches, if old trenches did not exist or did not resemble the trenches to be raided, might be dug to normal trench depth time permitting, but more often than not they were dug only a foot or so deep, or they might simply be spit-locked, or even just taped. Sometimes a small-scale model, 1/100th or so, might also be available to explain the raid to the raiders. Sergeant Alexander McClintock, 87th Canadian Battalion (4th Division) recalled the battalion's first big raid made 15 days after the battalion first experienced the trenches in August 1916. Taken to an area 20 miles to the rear, the 60 officers and men had the luxury of a full week's training. On the first day, while sappers created a duplicate of the trenches to be raided, the raiders received detailed briefings and worked at other preparations. Then the next morning rehearsals commenced and went on day and night.[15]

A week, the ideal, or just two or three days, could not always be granted. Lieutenant-Colonel Frank Maxwell, in June 1916 CO 12th Middlesex, spent 29 June

> hard at it till 4 p.m. without stirring from my dugout, working out a raid I have to make tonight. Very short notice, and over absolutely strange ground … one day scarcely gives me a chance of working out a good show for them and I am wondering whether what I have evolved will be productive of anything. With a little luck it may.

The four officers and 100 ORs had orders to "mob the Germans … and scupper all they could." This the raiders did, killing over 20 Germans at a cost of only one man wounded. The enemy trenches, found to be severely damaged, were nevertheless being held in strength. Given the short time for preparation the 12th did very well indeed.[16]

One of the worst cases of a unit not receiving adequate time to plan and prepare a raid occurred in July in 35th British Division. At 1700 on 21 July the 18th Lancashire Fusiliers received orders to make a strong raid that night with a view to demolishing enemy wire so that attacking troops could pass through. This wire had not been visible to any observation. In order to accomplish this unusual purpose, the raiding party would have to enter the enemy trench:

14 TNA: WO 95/2056: 19th Division General Staff, 15 February 1918.
15 Spit-locked was a term used to denote digging only to the extent of removing a narrow band of turf or surface soil. McClintock, *Best O'Luck*, pp. 63-64, comprehensively describes preparations for a raid. His account is one of the best for this aspect.
16 TNA: WO 95/2044: 12th Middlesex, June 1917; Mrs. Charlotte Maxwell (ed.), *Frank Maxwell Brig. General, V.C., C.S.I., D.S. O.: A Memoir and Some Letters* (London: John Murray, 1921), p. 145.

> As time was short the 18th … were ordered to prepare … and were relieved in the line by the 17th Lancashires. By the time this was done and the company commanders had received their orders it was 9 p.m. The raid took place … at 1:30 a.m. The left column was unable to reach the enemy trench. The right column reached its objective but was forced to retire. In his report the brigade commander was of the opinion that the time allowed was too short to permit of proper organization.[17]

Such situations were not limited to 1916. In July 1917, 2nd Grenadier Guards, which had returned to the line early on 2 July, received at 2330 orders from brigade to conduct two raids immediately to obtain identifications and accurately locate the enemy trench. The raiders, two parties of one platoon each, set out, no training, no recce and scant time to prepare much of anything. One party could not find the enemy trench, just shell holes. When fired on and bombed, the party scattered: "Beyond this … little is known. This being so a search for the missing was not made. Of the other party, what transpired was "even more obscure." While it found a trench it was blocked. There the OC of the party lost sight of most of his party, orders obviously not having been understood. This party was thought to have lost direction. Two officers were missing as well as a number of ORs. Nothing whatsoever was achieved.

During the night of 26 August the 6th South Staffordshires (46th British Division) were ordered to raid, Zero to be at dusk the next day. The OC Raid worked very hard so that he could issue his orders at daylight on the 27th, but then had the benefit of extra time, the raid being postponed 24 hours because of weather. In this instance, the raid had been known about since 15 August when the battalion was out of the line so training time had been more than adequate. Moreover, the designated OC Raid knew the ground well. The postponement was also fortuitous in that it gave time for more than one briefing of the raiding parties. The raid, as it turned out, did not get beyond its first objective, but did take five prisoners. Days later another unit received orders at 1300 for a raid at 2000. The OC Raid later described the time available as "most dangerously short." No enemy were encountered at the objective, nor could any damage be done because the sappers who were to accompany the raiders did not arrive before Zero.[18] In all these cases urgent requirements did arise and had to be met despite that fact that the pressing need was not always appreciated by those who had to do the job.

SS 107 Notes on Minor Enterprises for good reason called surprise "the most important factor" in raiding. But fire support, be it artillery and/or trench mortars was also critical. It was also stressed at the Canadian Corps Officers School that any raid of 20 or more men required fire support, a stipulation that was not peculiar to the Canadian Corps, and although the number of men set as the threshold varied, generally the larger the raid the more artillery became involved. A vital part of pre-raid preparation was infantry-artillery co-ordination. One example of inadequate or no co-ordination occurred in 5th British Division in November 1916 when a raid by 95th Brigade failed because artillery began firing an organized shoot on enemy trenches near the raid objective, this causing the enemy to man his trenches "along the whole of the divisional front." Frank Maxwell before the July raid by his 12th Middlesex (see earlier) expressed some uncertainty and distrust about co-ordination:

17 TNA: WO 95/2484: 18th Lancashires; Davson, *35th Division*, p. 37.
18 Ponsonby, *The Grenadier Guards*, Volume I, pp. 182-85; Committee of Officers, *Sixth South Staffordshire Regiment*, pp. 191-93; TNA: WO 95/1740: 9th Division General Staff.

> In these shows one has the run of a large group of guns, and you just tell them to fire here for so many minutes, 'lift' to there for so many more, etc … Much too often, however, something goes wrong, and guns and infantry get tangled up in their plans, with the result that our infantry run into the fire of the guns, and have to come back.[19]

In a post-war study of artillery tactics one senior gunner officer stressed four new factors that emerged during the war to which tactics had to be adapted. First, the 5.9-inch howitzer that equipped German field artillery outranged all BEF equipment except the 60-pounder. Second, the BEF's 18-pounder field gun proved far superior to the German 15-pounder. Third, night firing became normal shooting from which development harassing fire and defensive (SOS) fire also became normal. Finally, and "first in importance," as the gunner emphasized, was the use of wire on a large scale. Thick belts of wire, a new feature of defence, "had always to be cut before an attack." If it were not, then troops seeking to enter enemy trenches were channelled into any gaps designed as killing zones. When it came to raids, artillery provided preparatory bombardment, boxed-off objectives, provided covering fire to and from the objective and cut wire. Some of these activities, unfortunately, often "fairly clearly defined" an objective for all to see.[20] Whether a raid went by day or by night, a decision had to be made about employing preparatory fire support or not. This put those who planned and those who executed raids "between Scylla and Charybdis," which in plain English is simply to say between a rock and a hard place. It was a matter of fine judgement. In avoiding one evil, one could fall into a greater evil. While those who opted to forego preliminary bombardment, be it just offered and not mandated by superiors, could see that such fire might prove advantageous, they also realized the cost of loss of surprise. Experience also taught that proximity to the preliminary bombardment was a matter of fine judgement that could make a substantial difference. A raiding party of the 4th King's Own Royal Lancaster Regiment, for example, in June 1916 advanced so close behind the fire that the enemy had no time to man his parapet and into the trench the raiders leaped quite unobserved, taking six prisoners and suffering no losses. An artillery manual published in August 1915 had as guidance on how close infantry could be to artillery fire the following: at 3,000 yards half of all 18-pounder shells would fall within 10 yards of a target and at 5,000 yards half would fall within 25 yards. The figures were the same for 4.5-inch, 6-inch howitzers and 60-pounders. The figures were based on the "50 percent zone," this being the area in which 50 percent of rounds should fall at a given range. A diagram portrayed fall of shot at 3, 4 and 5,000 yards.[21]

A central factor in wire-cutting, designated by the gunner officer above as "first in importance," was what the artillery had available to do that job. In 1914 shrapnel and star shells were available to 18-pounders and the 4.5-inch howitzers. Before 1917 shell production concentrated on the less complicated shrapnel shell which left most wire-cutting to the 18-pounders. Shrapnel's reduced effectiveness at longer ranges meant not only increased expenditure of ammunition, but it also demanded good observation and extreme accuracy, both problematical at longer ranges. On detonation shrapnel spread over 300 steel balls all round, the radius depending on height

19 TNA: WO 95/1514: 95th Brigade, remarks by GOC on reasons for failure; Charlotte Maxwell, *Frank Maxwell*, p. 146.

20 Broad, 'The Development of Artillery Tactics', pp. 66-68.

21 Shannon, *The Lion and the Rose*, p. 130; *WO 33/723 Notes on Close Shooting by Guns and Howitzers, Registration of Targets and Calibration* (H & S, 8/15), p. 2 and diagram.

of burst. To cut wire shells had to burst at exactly the right height. *SS 98/5 Artillery Notes No. 5 – Wire-Cutting*, an eight-page manual issued in June 1916, reported "18-pounder shrapnel [as] the most effective projectile against wire [providing the shell] burst as close to the wire and as low down as possible." This demanded not only good observation, seldom available in battle, but a high degree of gunner skills. Skill, given the huge expansion of the BEF and the casualties, soon became degraded to the point that "it clearly became beyond the gunner's competence to guarantee to cut wire by shrapnel." At Mount Sorrel in June 1916 and later "the type of shell was in many instances unsuitable ... those who were there will recollect their disheartening task of endeavouring to cut wire with field gun shrapnel."[22]

Eventually, High Explosive (HE) became available, but not in steady and sufficient supply until Loos (September 1915). General Staff Notes for June 1916, summarizing the initial use of HE shells, which at that time had the No. 100 delay action fuse, reported that the combination had "practically no effect against wire" although a mix of shrapnel and HE, 10-15 percent of the latter, was "sometimes useful."[23] But this fuse not being instantaneous meant the shell partially buried itself before detonating, which did not cut the wire, but merely uprooted the pickets to which it was fixed and generally further tangled the entanglement. Nor could shrapnel destroy coils and the HE simply tossed them about. In October, in response to a Second Army request for comment on wire-cutting, the Canadian Corps offered several deductions based on 18-pounder experience:

> wire cannot be cut effectively at over 3,200 yards; that six rounds shrapnel per yard should be allowed for; that the small depth of wire, 30 yards at most, requires extreme accuracy, hence closely observed fire is essential; wire-cutting should be deliberate and not rushed.

When it was issued *SS 98/5 Artillery Notes No. 5 – Wire-Cutting* was a composite of all comments received from all the Armies of the BEF:

> wire cutting was effective from 1,800-2,400 yards; for belts 10 yards deep 5-6 rounds per yard were required; wire could be cut out to 3,200 yards with much larger expenditure of ammunition, but the 18-pounder at longer ranges was non-effective; trench mortars should participate in wire-cutting, especially the 2-inch medium mortar. [24]

Mortars are examined later in this chapter, but having mentioned the 2-inch it is appropriate to now briefly mention it in connection with wire-cutting. It, and its successor, the 6-inch mortar,

22 *SS 98/5 Artillery Notes No. 5 – Wire-Cutting* (GHQ: February and June 1916); LAC, RG9IIID3, Volume 4813, Canadian Corps General Staff War Diary, 9 July 1916; 2nd Brigade War Diary, June 1916; Brigadier-General A.G.L. McNaughton, 'The Development of Artillery in the Great War', *Canadian Defence Quarterly*, 6 (January 1929), p. 163.

23 Brigadier R.J. Lewendon, 'The Cutting of Barbed Wire Entanglements by Artillery Fire in World War 1', *Journal of the Royal Artillery*, 112 (September 1985), p. 115; *SS 98/5 Artillery Notes No. 5 – Wire-Cutting* (June 1916); Adkin, *The Western Front Companion*, p. 235.

24 LAC, RG9IIIC1, Volume 3859, Folder 86, File 9, correspondence 1st Division and Canadian Corps HQ, 18-20 October 1916; *SS 98/5* described the 2-inch with the Newton fuse as the best mortar for wire-cutting. One bomb per 10 yards of barbed wire and one per six square yards of loose wire was settled upon as the measure by which to estimate ammunition requirements for cutting.

were both introduced in 1917. Both proved effective against wire. The 52-pound bomb of the former could reach out to 550 yards, a range the 6-inch more than tripled.[25]

The No. 106 instantaneous fuse, introduced in early 1917, had its first serious use in April during the Battle of Arras. For the Canadian attack at Vimy, artillery support included 18-pounders (558), 4.5-inch howitzers (186) and medium trench mortars (120), of which 88 percent tackled enemy wire. The new fuse burst the shell immediately it touched wire or the ground, the whole of the charge being expended in the air against any wire. Another advantage of HE with this fuse was that the shell did not create craters. Nevertheless, there was no guarantee that wire had been sufficiently cut, especially at longer ranges (2,000 yards or more). This applied to the medium mortars as well. In September 1916, 23rd Manchesters (35th British Division) launched a raid on some enemy saps with the aim of securing identifications. Two nights prior to the raid 4.5-inch howitzers and medium mortars put down heavy fire on the saps and on the wire. This fire, according to patrols, did not destroy the latter. However, it was decided not to draw further attention to the objective. Instead, the raiders would try to cross the wire by means of mats. Before the raid began at 0230 on 16 September the raiders, two parties of 20 men each led by an officer and a covering party of 10, moved off into no man's land. At five minutes to Zero the guns put intense fire down on the enemy line and the raiders advanced to the wire only to find it thicker than anticipated. One party then withdrew, the other gaining entry to the sap which was unoccupied. Summarizing the raid, the division historian described enemy retaliation as feeble, thanks to the bombardment before Zero, and noted that had the wire been "properly cut the raid would have been a sure success."[26]

Wire also affected infantry-artillery co-operation. The major and constant concern was that the artillery definition of "sufficiently" or "properly" cut never quite matched the infantry definition. After a raid failed in June 1916 Captain Charles May, 22nd Manchesters, attributed this to "complete failure of our artillery to cut the German wire at the correct place." He did not elaborate.[27] To be fair, infantry patrols sometimes failed to correctly locate wire. As for the enemy, he had become more inventive with wire, setting out low trip wires, for example, and filling shell holes, ditches and the like with concertina. This could cause havoc if pre-raid recce did not discover such obstacles. Sometimes long grass could prevent damage to enemy wire being accurately determined, or could even prevent wire being seen in the first place.[28] Lieutenant-Colonel Graham Seton Hutchison, who served with the 33rd British Division from 1915 on, related how for one raid the FOO, "owing to ground mist, and after watching many hours with tired eyes thought that the shrapnel had … cut a path for the infantry through the enemy's wire. And it was not so!"[29] Such situations could cause some loss of mutual confidence. A raid that

25 Hudson, 'Trench Mortars in the Great War', p. 25.

26 Davson, *35th Division,* p. 63; Hitchcock, *Stand To!,* p. 238. Mats suitably placed could serve as a bridge across wire provided it was not too thick.

27 Harrison, ed., *To Fight Alongside Friends,* p. 197.

28 LAC, RG9IIID3, Volume 4824, 1st Division General Staff War Diary, June 1915, Appendices 7, 11, 14-15 and 1st Brigade report, Appendix 17. Long grass and weeds could hide low wire entanglements even from air photographs.

29 Hutchison, *Thirty-Third Division,* p. 8. Confusion reigns as to whether it is Hutchinson or Hutchison. Falls, *War Books* says Hutchinson. A.G.S. Enser, *A Subject Bibliography of the First World War: Books in English 1914-1978* (London: Gower, 1990) says Hutchison. Peter Warrington, *For Distinguished and Meritorious Service in Time of War: The Great War Recipients of the Military Cross 1914-1920: A Register*

encountered uncut wire and because of that became "more or less a fizzle," according to Private Will Bird of 42nd Canadian Battalion (Black Watch), was sure to cause hot arguments about wire and wire-cutting. Sometimes new belts of wire escaped detection until a raiding party stumbled into it, as did a party of 2nd West Yorkshires in September 1916. The raid had to be aborted, a "wash-out." An officer with 35th British Division, reflecting upon shrapnel's effect on wire, questioned why this seemed never to be "commensurate with the amount of ammunition expended."[30]

Patrols were the primary means available to raiders who wished to satisfy themselves of sufficient wire-cutting. Before a raid in October 1917 the CO of 6th Sherwood Foresters (46th British Division) noted in his diary that prior to Zero a total of 25 patrols had gone out to check on the state of enemy wire. Such patrolling became a general practice. However, even this provided no guarantee. A patrol might well find no obstacle the night before a raid or even a few hours before it, but raiders might arrive to find damage had been repaired, or wire had been thickened with concertina, or even that gaps had been filled with pegged-down knife-rests. When the enemy would set these out could not be predicted meaning that on occasion raiding parties would be the first to encounter them, as a unit of 51st (Highland) Division did during a raid in October 1916. A partial solution was to fill the interval between patrol and raid with artillery or machine-gun fire directed against working parties trying to repair or add to the wire. In one case, 20,000 shells were so used. Knife-rests opposite the 51st grew to such "formidable" numbers that they became a "serious proposition" and an objective in themselves.[31] Another means to destroy these and wire in general was Bangalore torpedoes. These are examined later in this chapter.

An elaboration of the wire-cutting controversy and a larger problem had appeared earlier in May in "Notes on Offensive Action During Normal Periods of Warfare":

> The question of artillery fire in connection with raids requires greater attention. Successful raids have been carried out by us as a sudden surprise without any artillery bombardment, but the Germans usually [prefer] an intense bombardment before the raid is made … The decision as to which method is to be adopted must rest with the local commander, but if a bombardment is carried out preliminary to a raid, it is not sufficient merely to cut the enemy's wire and knock his trenches about. A comprehensive plan combining artillery, trench mortars and machine-guns … must be brought to bear … such as to obliterate the garrison and prevent the enemy withdrawing troops or sending up reinforcements.[32]

Lieutenant-Colonel Joseph Hayes' history of his battalion (85th Canadians) illustrates how the enemy also lost surprise: "The enemy became so active with artillery and trench mortars that an

British and Empire (Uckfield, East Sussex: Naval and Military Press, n.d.) says Hutchison. And so it shall be here.

30 Will R. Bird, *Ghosts Have Warm Hands* (Toronto: Clark, Irwin & Company, 1968), pp. 84-85; Terraine (ed)., *General Jack's Diary,* p. 167; Davson, *35th Division,* p. 91.

31 Beresford, *The Christian Soldier,* p. 212; Bewsher, *Fifty First (51st (Highland) Division,* p. 107. Knife-rests were portable wire entanglements, at either end a timber or iron framework with numerous strands of barbed wire and/or concertina stretched between, hence knife-rest.

32 TNA: WO 95/2563: 39th British Division General Staff, May 1916, GHQ O.B./1665.

attack or raid was confidently expected." A.H. Atteridge in describing an enemy raid against the 17th British Division put the enemy failure down to his "faulty artillery methods which gave us adequate warning and enabled our artillery … to intervene effectively and interfere seriously with the raiding party during its advance." During that month (July 1916) 183rd British Brigade committed the same sin: reporting on a failed raid by one of its battalions, brigade HQ concluded that the enemy were "probably standing to because of [British] artillery fire." An officer with the raiders said simply that the Germans were "ready to receive them." Fortune smiled at the raiding party, it suffering only three casualties. 31st Canadian Battalion (3rd Division) had its first ever raid in mid-August 1916 wrecked by artillery bombardment, the game given away by "far too much attention" being paid to the objective. The enemy clearly anticipated a raid. With surprise gone, the party could not get past heavy machine-gun fire and the OC ordered withdrawal.

Similarly, when a raid by 2nd Irish Guards was "shot in" by artillery, this put the enemy on the alert and ready for the fray. Nevertheless, D.V. Kelly, observing preparations for a raid, realized that the sole chance of success lay in surprise, but knew Corps would insist on a big artillery fire plan. He also knew how the enemy would react:

> What commonly occurred was that the enemy finding his wire being ostentatiously shot to pieces, withdrew his posts to the flanks of the threatened trench: and when the forward troops (by means of an admirable system of light signals, much superior to our own) gave warning, down came a barrage of shells, trench mortar bombs, and enfilade machine-gun fire on the gaps in the wire and the jumping-off point.[33]

While raiding without preliminary bombardment could increase the chance of achieving surprise, doing so posed serious disadvantage. An example of man supposing and uncut wire disposing occurred in August 1916. HQ 11th British Division warned the 32nd Brigade that it must mount a raid, but it also advised that because the artillery was employed on a special operation no ammunition would be available for wire-cutting. However, attempting to make a virtue of necessity, division told brigade that "success is usually gained in these operations by surprise action unpreceded by artillery bombardment." The raid report, submitted on 17 August, ascribed failure to the raiders being "quite hung up by the barbed wire, which appeared to be impassable." Alexander Johnston, CO of the 10th Cheshires (25th British Division) in February 1917 also recalled the impact of uncut wire on a battalion raid:

> I saw the left party reach the enemy trench all right and the right party get to their wire [but] soon heard that [it] had failed to get in owing to the wire being uncut. Apparently it had been much knocked about by the artillery but not properly destroyed as reported erroneously by my patrols. Left party entered trench but owing to failure of right party … they got 'badly pinched' and suffered a lot of casualties from machine-gun fire from both flanks

33 Lt. Col. Joseph Hayes, *The Eighty-Fifth in France and Flanders* (Halifax: Royal Print & Litho Limited, 1920), p. 83; Atteridge, *17th (Northern) Division*, p. 240; TNA: WO 95/3058: 183rd Brigade, 48th Division, report on raid 4/5 July 1916; Stacke, *The Worcestershire Regiment*, Volume One, p. 161; Singer, *31st Battalion*, pp. 137-38; Headlam, *Guards Division*, Volume One, p. 127; Kelly, *39 Months With the "Tigers,"* pp. 40-41.

> … a disappointing show ruined by the failure of the right party to get in owing to the wire being uncut; rotten luck, as the patrols had said it was cut all right.[34]

By early 1916 the price to be paid for a preliminary bombardment often became a matter for sardonic comment. Wyn Griffith, a Subaltern with the Royal Welsh Fusiliers, describing a night raid in May 1916, spoke of artillery busy all day cutting the enemy wire "lest he [the enemy] should have any doubt where we proposed to attack him." As for the actual assault, "it was clear, wrote Griffith, "that the visit was not unexpected." The cost was two officers killed and "many friends we would never see again." No prisoners, such being the purpose of the raid, were taken, all in all, a dismal evening not worth the cost. Frank Maxwell, describing his 100-man raid in July 1916, remembered how he had "begged to be allowed to have my little jaunt without guns, so as to surprise Bosch, unwarned by artillery fire … but was disallowed." In another instance, Lord Moran, Medical Officer of 1st Royal Welsh Fusiliers, recalled this conversation with his CO during the winter of 1916/17:

> Doc, we've got to do a raid, the Corps wants us to send over a hundred and twenty men with eight stretcher bearers.
> At night?
> Yes, they are going to have a preliminary bombardment.
> Good God, to warn the Boche we're coming?
> It's damn silly I know, but we've got to do it. Doc.

At 2230 Moran listened to the outgoing fire, the "swishing sound of whizzbang stuff overhead, followed by the lower ripple of the heavies" and 10 minutes later the raiders, Moran and the stretcher bearers, the last to go, went over the top. As they reached the enemy wire he noted that the guns had effectively cut gaps and how after 40 minutes in the enemy trenches the raiders returned with three prisoners.[35]

Trepidation often surfaced when men knew of artillery involvement in the raid they had to do. Private Fraser of 31st Canadian Battalion, for example, was "badly disappointed" with the news that artillery would cut wire, seeing it as advertising the raid (in August 1916). The result he called "ignominious failure, the Germans being fully prepared with men out in front of their wire waiting for the raiders to appear." Of 30 raiders, 16 were wounded. Another account of this raid, whose purpose was taking prisoners, described it as well-planned and organized, but "unfortunately [the objective], which should not have been severely shelled, came in for too much attention by the artillery, with the result that the enemy … made arrangements for reception."[36]

34 TNA: WO 95/1806: 11th British Division General Staff, CRA report and 32nd Brigade report, restriction on artillery support; Edwin Astill, *The Great War Diaries of Brigadier General Alexander Johnston 1914-1917* (Barnsley: Pen & Sword, 2007), pp. 203-204. Casualties were 40 killed and 60 wounded. About 100 Germans were thought to have been killed. This raid is not mentioned in the divisional history. M. Kincaid-Smith, *The 25th Division in France and Flanders* (London: Harrison, 1920), admits in his preface that it is the "very briefest sketch' of the division. Crookenden, *Cheshire Regiment,* pp. 97-98, offers considerably more detail on this raid, for which see Chapter 7.

35 Griffith, *Up to Mametz,* pp. 111, 116, 118; Charlotte Maxwell, *Frank Maxwell,* p. 146; Lord Moran, *Anatomy of Courage,* pp. 142, 145, 147.

36 Roy (ed.), *Journal of Private Fraser,* pp. 185, 187; Singer, *31st Canadian Battalion,* pp. 123-24.

Eventually changes in fire procedure, specifically registration, came. In early 1917 "offset" registration was tried, the idea being to register on nearby targets and then correct as required on raid day, but even this gave the enemy some warning. Nor could accuracy be guaranteed. The GOC 118th British Brigade (39th Division) reporting on a raid by one of his battalions in May 1917, wrote how it had convinced him that "to trust to the efficacy of a hurricane bombardment to cut wire is a gamble with the odds in favour of the wire." His raiders entered the enemy trench only because of pure luck in finding the one place where the wire was thin. The raiders also reported gaps in the wire as very difficult to find, some having been filled with loose concertina. Frank Richards, for one, believed there was always an "element of luck" in a raid. This comment came after a raid that failed because of uncut wire.[37]

In August, 104th British Brigade (35th Division) had no such luck. In order to give no indication of a forthcoming raid by 17th Lancashire Fusiliers and 23rd Manchesters no preliminary wire-cutting was permitted, trust being put in the covering artillery barrage to enable raiders to cross the wire which had been reported as thin. This proved to be quite the opposite and delays in crossing meant the barrage had lifted before the raiders could reach the enemy trench. The raiders now faced a fully manned parapet. Casualties came to seven officers and 95 ORs wounded and 27 killed. In September, with the changes in enemy defensive tactics, the conundrum thickened: "If a wire-cutting bombardment is carried out he temporarily abandons the threatened posts. If there is not bombardment it is difficult to get through the wire."[38]

Before Passchendaele Major R.T. Rees, 4th Loyal North Lancashire Regiment, received an order to mount a company-sized raid to secure prisoners, a task considered of sufficient importance to warrant the support of 300 guns. These would put a box-barrage around the objective, which was the junction of the main trench and two CTs, and shoot the raiders onto the objective by means of a creeping barrage. Extensive rehearsals over several days preceded the raid, including taking the entire company into no man's land to get every man accustomed to his place on the jumping off line. On the morning of Zero Day Rees noticed "with great misgiving that some of our guns were registering on their targets for the evening, and with still more misgiving, that the enemy replied by registering apparently *on his own front line.*" From what he had seen Rees reached two conclusions: first, the enemy line was unoccupied and, second, that when their barrage began the enemy would fire on their front line and the raiders would have to walk through that. Consequently, he asked that the raid be made without artillery bombardment, but this was refused on the grounds that it was too late to alter arrangements. To Rees the situation portended a death trap. That evening just 30 minutes before Zero he was ordered not to lead it, the GOC adamant that he could not afford to lose a field officer. Instead, he had to appoint a Subaltern as OC Raid. The enemy did just as Rees had predicted, their fire causing many casualties, including the Subaltern (killed). No prisoners were taken.[39]

Any number of accounts of raids are also extant where COs were allowed to launch without preliminary bombardment. Anthony Eden, age 18, led his first raid, a small one, he and a half-dozen men, no preliminary artillery bombardment asked or offered, "the essence to be secrecy

37 TNA: WO 95/2588:118th Brigade, raid report; Frank Richards, *Old Soldiers Never Die* (London: Faber and Faber, 1933; reprint ed., Baston, England: H.J. Krijnen and D.E. Langley, 2004), p. 123.

38 Davson, *35th Division,* p. 143; TNA: WO 95/1379: 3rd British Division General Staff, IV Corps to Third Army, 1 September 1917.

39 Rees, *A Schoolmaster at War,* p. 63, italics in the original.

and surprise." Across the 100 yards of no man's land they went to the enemy wire which foiled two attempts to enter the enemy trench, their efforts at cutting being heard by the enemy. In January 1917 Captain F.C. Hitchcock, 2nd Leinsters, led a raiding party of five officers and 80 ORs, the raid's main feature being that it was the first of the unit's daylight raids, one with a "very important variation" – no preliminary bombardment, thereby keeping to "one of the greatest principles of warfare – surprise." During the whole of the first week of January the raiders trained in practice trenches, followed with bombing practice and recce tours by the officers and senior NCOs. The enemy was "greatly surprised" by the raid, Hitchcock recalling that on jumping into the trench he landed on top of a sentry who was reading a newspaper! The sentry and seven others were taken prisoner, a "great success" said Hitchcock despite the five dead and 18 wounded.[40]

Sometimes a CO could accept some and reject some fire support. In September 1917 6th Sherwood Foresters (46th British Division) was preparing a large raid in the Hill 70 sector near Loos. The CO, Lieutenant-Colonel Bernard Vann, expressed his concern about the preliminary artillery and machine-gun fire to his brigade commander who passed this on to divisional HQ: "we nearly always start our Machine Guns firing at the same time that the Infantry move forward, and the fact that both Artillery and Machine Guns open intense fire, proves more or less conclusively that we are about to raid, whereas an Artillery barrage alone does not necessarily imply this." The preliminaries were changed accordingly: no machine-guns.

Sometimes brigade HQs refused requests for artillery and mortar support, a case in point being a raid by Rowland Feilding's 6th Connaught Rangers (16th Division) in February 1917. The reasons for refusal were matters of judgement. This stealth raid might well have surprised the enemy, but whether or not that would have been so cannot be said. Uncut wire prevented entry to the enemy trench. Many casualties were suffered. Chapter 3 described this raid more fully.[41]

An unhelpful element of fire support was errant friendly fire. Captain James Neville recalled a raid by his battalion on 9 March 1918 during which 6-inch mortars manned by artillery personnel would cut wire. The first bomb sailed well over into the enemy support line, the second into the wire and the third into an enemy outpost. On requesting that the fire cease the gunners told Neville the last could not possibly have been theirs, this in Neville's opinion "the stock reply of gunners when accused of firing short." When the mortars fired again the first bomb went into the support line, the second into the battalion's wire and the third 150 yards behind the enemy trench. Neville's CO managed to get the firing checked, concluding that it was better to risk uncut wire. As it turned out, uncut wire prevented entry at the objective, which was full of men "apparently unprepared."[42]

Another raiding party, lying "doggo" in no man's land, waiting for enemy wire to be cut, suddenly received off line friendly mortar bombs that killed one officer and wounded another, plus eight ORs: "This … at the hands of our own people, through a vagary of the wind, appeared some sinister and malignant stroke, an outrage." In another case, surprise was lost when machine-guns in support fired early. The raid went ahead anyway, but came to an abrupt

40 Eden, *Another World*, p. 88; Hitchcock, *Stand To*, pp. 229-45 and Appendix.

41 Beresford, *The Christian Soldier*, p. 213; Feilding, *War Letters to a Wife*, pp. 151-57; LAC, War Diary, 46th Battalion, January 1918.

42 Neville, *War Letters*, pp. 91-92.

end when 18-pounders fired short into the raiding party. A particularly hard-hitting example of the moral and physical impact of friendly fire was experienced by 1st Canadian Battalion just four days before the Canadian attack at Vimy Ridge. In his report on three small raids made by his battalion the CO, Lieutenant-Colonel G.C. Hudson, complained that one party of the C Company raiders "could not enter the Hun line on account of the erratic shooting of our artillery." The other party, founded by D Company, could not enter the enemy trench because Canadian artillery was still firing on it. Eight of C Company's casualties were caused by this friendly fire. "Erratic shooting" also prevented D Company from linking up with C Company. Of the six men killed during the raid, four fell victim to friendly artillery fire, as did 11 of 15 wounded; in short, 75 percent of the casualties were due to friendly fire: "All ranks regret [this] especially as they feel that had our artillery barrage been laid down as arranged, our objective would have been gained easily." Brigade, he said, could expect soon a runner carrying an 18-pounder shell case picked up in the battalion line, it having been found during the raid, with the driving band not marked by the rifling of the gun. But "while regretting these casualties" he had impressed silence on his company commanders about the occurrence because the confidence of the infantry in the guns "must not be impaired." Moreover, he believed that given "the right guns and the right ammunition" the artillery would always do what the infantry expected.[43]

Such complaints were not uncommon during the last half of 1916 and well into 1917. In July 1916 the GOC 3rd Guards Brigade reporting on a raid stated that many British shells had fallen short but other than causing delay little damage was done. 1CMR of 3rd Canadian Division had a worse time in mid-September when friendly fire left the raiding party scattered and disorganized and all three officers wounded. The raid commander reported that most of the casualties were inflicted by Canadian artillery.[44] Two weeks later (30 September) a proposed attack by 2nd Canadian Brigade did not proceed, first because fighting strength of the assault brigade stood at only 1,134 and, second, because of the "shooting short," this causing bombardment of the objective in progress to be "interrupted in order to check the fall of the shell." By mid-October many guns were said to be too worn from continuous action over two months to provide accurate fire. In November the "cruel mischance" of inaccurate fire had driven British troops from an enemy trench into shell holes some distance away. The British Official History describes complaints about "shorts" as "frequent and sometimes justified: the principal reasons for this failing [being] worn guns, defective ammunition [see previous paragraph on the driving bands] and inaccurate locating of the infantry forward positions." But it must be said that enemy enfilade fire could and did sometimes seem to the infantry to be friendly artillery firing short. The enemy as perpetrator is a possibility in 2nd Brigade's case. It is not possible to be more definitive. "Shorts" would remain a problem for the rest of the war.[45]

Mortars, when they eventually reached the BEF, had to be carefully co-ordinated with other fire support. The Germans had enjoyed a monopoly in mortars until early 1915 when the first primitive tubes reached the BEF. One of these inventions on its arrival at 6th British Division drew this assessment:

43 Neville, *War Letters,* pp. 91-92; Chapman, *A Passionate Prodigality,* pp. 83-84; Winter, *Death's Men,* p. 95; LAC, War Diary, 1st Battalion, April 1917.

44 TNA: WO 95/1221: 3rd Guards Brigade; LAC, War Diary 8th Canadian Brigade.

45 LAC, RG9IIIC3, Volume 4012, Folder 19, File 4; Miles, *2nd July 1916 to the End of the Battles of the Somme,* pp. 195, 413, 457, 507.

> more dangerous to friend than foe; and great care had to be exercised in its use. This primitive weapon would only function twelve times; and the thirteenth bomb would explode it. Hence, before requesting an exhibition, an inspecting officer would never forget to ask 'How many bombs has it fired?' Although the bomb made a goodly noise, the mortar had a low coverage for hitting anything in particular.

Early models had various names such as trench howitzers, trench guns or bomb-throwers, the first, if not an accurate tag, made the point that the mortar, like a howitzer, fired a projectile way up high until it reached apogee when it plunged down at a very steep angle. Some of the contraptions faded quickly out of sight, the first truly effective type being the 2-inch mortar (later confirmed as the BEF's Medium Mortar) which arrived in early 1915. Its "fearsome looking" bomb was best described as a toffee apple because of its shape. This cast-iron sphere, stuffed with 42 pounds of ammonal, sat at the end of a two-foot stem or tail that had to be placed in the mortar tube to be fired. The fuse, a serious limitation initially, was the same as the one used on artillery shells. Bombs so fused on detonation created a crater the size of a small room, an obvious obstacle for infantry. When that fuse gave way to the "Newton 107," which detonated the bomb before it penetrated the ground, the explosive force proceeded outward into wire entanglements, the rule of thumb being that one bomb took out six square yards of wire. Experience, however, revealed that only about 10 percent of the force was effective. Nevertheless, wire-cutting and destruction of earth works became the role of the 2-inch (and later the 6-inch) medium mortar. Another new entry to the field in 1915 was the 9.45-inch heavy mortar whose role, given its size, was demolition, its 150-pound bombs becoming famous as "flying pigs."

By January 1916 the BEF inventory consisted of 200 heavy, 1,200 medium (2-inch and 6-inch) and 2,500 light mortars of various types. In December, according to the historian of 50th British Division, light and medium trench mortar batteries, each of four tubes formed, the light being manned by infanteers and the latter by gunners; in fact, at that time infanteers manned light and medium, the artillery the heavies. In April 1916 GHQ decreed that three categories of mortar would be on establishment: heavy, 9.45-inch; medium, 2-inch and 6-inch; and light, 3-inch. Two months later the artillery took charge of the mediums, leaving only light mortars to the infantry. Even so, many infanteers continued serving with medium batteries. Major N. Hudson, a gunner, thought infanteers keener than gunners about mortars: "To the infantryman [such duty] meant leaving behind battalion and routine, and taking over a new piece of mechanism. To the gunner it meant leaving behind his horse and taking over an old piece of drainpipe." At this time GHQ also authorized a Division Trench Mortar Officer. One appointee, Major R.T. Rees, describes his half-year as a DTMO, his duties and activities, in his *A Schoolmaster at War,* which provides one of the very few longer accounts by a trench mortar officer.[46]

Turning now to Mr. Wilfred Stokes the story of his "wonderful drain pipe," which was offered to and accepted by the British Government, is an amazing one. Stokes, a civil engineer who by

46 Grey, *2nd City of London Regiment,* pp. 34-35; Spencer, ed., *Stanley Spencer's Great War Diary,* p. 30; Wyrall, *Fiftieth Division,* p.108; Hudson, 'Trench Mortars in the Great War', pp. 18-20, 25; Peter Doyle and Chris Foster, *Remembering Tommy: The British Soldier in the First World War* (Stroud: Spellmount, 2013), pp. 136-37; Rees, *A Schoolmaster at War,* pp. 35-36.

his own admission knew virtually nothing about weapon design, had "educated" or transformed a drain pipe into a formidable weapon of trench warfare, indeed of warfare. Equally effective after some refinements in the Second World War, and even today in calibre 81mm, it is in wide use in many Armies. Stokes became Sir Wilfred and his "Stokes gun," as it was commonly known, became legend: "the outstanding weapon of the war." First tested in January 1915, and by year's end in use at training centres, the Stokes entered front line service in March 1916. In describing the Stokes' competitor, the West Spring Gun, Peter Scott explains why the Stokes and not the West entered general service: the latter could strike out only 240 yards, less than one-third of the eventual range of the Stokes, its bomb weighed far less than the 11-pound Stokes bomb and it could not match the Stokes' high rate of fire.[47]

By May 1916 most divisions had, or were about to have, three batteries of Stokes (one per brigade), each with eight tubes. Initially, the Stokes and mortars in general were "unwelcome" mainly because they drew retaliatory fire. Their alleged method of operating, as one infantry officer sarcastically pointed out, increased the dislike:

> There was the trench-mortar officer who was never to be found, but who left a sergeant with instructions not to fire without his orders; there was the trench-mortar officer who 'could not fire except by Brigade orders'; there was the trench-mortar officer who was 'afraid of giving his position away'; there was the trench-mortar officer 'who couldn't get any ammunition'; there was the trench-mortar officer who started firing on his own, without consulting the company commander, just when you had a big working party in the front trenches.

Soon, however, everyone realized how good the Stokes was at producing casualties and with the Newton 107 fuse how its "real value" lay in wire-cutting. 35th British Division, for example, experimenting with the Stokes as wire-cutter, found it "very effective." An Australian recalled how during a raid later in 1916 "a battery of Stokes fired rounds that went up and up in strings of ten and eleven, each [falling] in successive crashes [that] smashed the German wire into 'long thin knives which could cut off a head as cleanly as a sword, or shear through thickets of strong wire.'" In its report on a raid on 11 September 1917, 6th West Yorkshires (62nd Division) described the effectiveness of the Stokes on other tasks: "combined with the artillery and machine-guns [they] fired a very successful barrage, which absolutely prevented the enemy sending forward troops to the assistance of those being raided."[48]

47 Hutchison, *Thirty-Third Division,* p. 6; Anthony Saunders, *Weapons of the Trench War 1914-1918* (Stroud: Sutton Publishing, 1999), pp. 124-25; Peter T. Scott, 'Trench Weaponry: 3 The West Spring Gun', *Stand To!,* 5 (Summer 1982), p. 16; 'Mr. Stokes and His Educated Drainpipe', *The Great War, 1914-1918* 2 (May 1990), pp. 80-85, provides an excellent account of how the Stokes entered service. By way of comparison an 18-pounder in 1917 was set an intense rate of fire of four rounds per minute (LAC, RG9IIIC1, Volume 3843, Folder 46, File 5, Artillery Instruction No. 5, First Army, 22 March 1917). The Stokes at high rate managed five times that. Ewing, *Ninth (Scottish) Division,* p. 14, gives the West Spring Gun a range of 400 yards. He notes that the crew consisted of eight men and the weapon required an enormous emplacement.

48 Corrigall, *Twentieth Canadian Battalion,* p. 97; Adams, *Nothing of Importance,* p. 183; Davson, *35th Division,* p. 18; Aaron Pegram, "'The Bosches seem to have done pretty well what they intended to do." I ANZAC Corps and the German Raid on the Bridoux Salient, May 1916," *Stand To!,* 97 (May 2013), pp. 4-7. During this enemy raid on the Australian 20th Battalion the Australians had 23

A raid in September 1916 by the 8th Black Watch and 5th Cameronians, 9th (Scottish) Division, was intended, in addition to the usual purposes, "to test the efficacy of an intense Stokes bombardment on enemy trenches and personnel." The test featured 30 Stokes on a 300 yard front. The plan called for a hurricane bombardment at Zero (2300), the raiding parties advancing as close as possible to their objectives under cover of this fire. At Zero plus two the Stokes would lift onto the enemy support line and the riders would enter the enemy front line. The Black Watch did well advancing to within 40 yards of the enemy trench under cover of "punctual and accurate" Stokes fire. On entering the trench, the raiders found it so damaged by the Stokes that in places they could hardly follow it. "Bunches" of enemy dead were found at dug-out entrances as if they had rushed to enter them when the Stokes began firing. The Cameronians' raid did not go as smoothly. The Stokes opened two minutes early and some of the bombs were short of the enemy front line. The fire plan called for a lift to the support line, but instead it lifted to the front line, this making things very difficult for the raiders. In all, the Stokes were to fire 20 bombs per minute per tube for two minutes and then eight bombs per minute per tube for 30 minutes for a total of 8,400 bombs. Actual expenditure was 5,800. Enemy trenches were found severely damaged. GOC 26th Brigade in his report included four comments on the Stokes. First, while the infantry got to within 40 yards of the bombardment the concussion was so terrific he thought the infantry should not remain in such close proximity for more than one minute. Second, in the latter stages of a raid the barrage should not be less than 100 yards from the infantry. Third, he considered one mortar per 20 yards sufficient to produce an intensive barrage. Finally, he thought the shortcomings in support of the 5th Cameronians not the fault of the Stokes itself, but rather indicated inadequate registration and battery training.

The GOC IV Corps, to which 9th Division belonged, told First Army: "The raid is interesting as being the first raid we have tried which was chiefly dependent on the fire of the Stokes and it is very satisfactory to read that Gen. Furse [GOC 9th Division] considers that the Stokes was almost too powerful at the rate of fire employed."[49] Lieutenant-Colonel W.D. Croft, CO 11th Royal Scots in late 1916, commenting on the great success of the raid from "the killing point of view, and that is the only view in war," went on to write that the raid had caught a strong German working party in the front line and how these "luckless" men were "piled up against dugout entrances to which they had all rushed when the bombardment began – pretty beastly, no doubt, but war is not exactly a drawing-room pastime."[50] Clearly, the Stokes, to use an archaic term, did good execution.

As the Stokes batteries gained experience, the infantry better appreciated their capabilities, including their versatility. Batteries were allocated more often and took on additional tasks, one being the provision of smoke screens. This task the 3-inch Stokes could not do. But in late August 1915, after attending a demonstration of a French smoke bomb, General Haig, at that time GOC First Army, ordered smoke bombs "to be made and sent out at once … I wish to use them for the

killed, 72 wounded and 13 missing. Also missing were two Stokes guns that had not been withdrawn, in violation of GHQ orders, to support lines after use. Wyrall, *62nd (West Riding) Division,* Volume 1, p. 65.

49 TNA: WO 95/1736: 8th Black Watch, 5th Cameronians, 26th Brigade and 9th Division General Staff, and letter GOC IV Corps to First Army; Ewing, *Ninth (Scottish) Division,* p. 149.

50 Croft, *Three Years With the Ninth (Scottish) Division,* pp. 77-78.

purpose of covering the flanks of an attack [raid] from the enemy's machine-guns … enfilade fire." In fairly short order the first of the 4-inch Stokes had been tested and accepted and on 14 September tubes and bombs were enroute to First Army Trench Mortar School. For the 25 December offensive at Loos the 4-inchers provided smoke to mask the attacking infantry of 47th British Division from enemy artillery observers, their work being summarized as "very effective … especially on the right [where the smoke] made a good curtain … shrouding the advancing infantry."[51] Stokes proved just as accurate firing at specific targets. During the retreat in April 1918, a Stokes battery of 9th (Scottish) Division was lauded for its sterling work in helping repulse enemy attacks, the battery, it was said, never doing finer work than it did on 25 April. The fire plan for a raid by 2CMR on 27 April, to give just one other example, included five bombs rapid on a machine-gun emplacement at a specific grid reference and another Stokes to engage at another grid reference.[52]

The urge to intimidate, as always, drove activity. In one instance in the fall of 1916 the "Jocks" of 51st (Highland) Division indulged in the "most excessive" trench mortar work, in one shoot a Stokes battery hurled over 1,200 bombs into an enemy trench, this effort provoking very feeble retaliation. The "Jocks" now felt able "to really bully him and make his life a burden … he was unmercifully harassed day after day to the great delight of the troops."[53]

But German trench mortar performance and competence could not be slighted either. D.V. Kelly emphasized that while the Germans raided less frequently, when they did "it was an unpleasant experience. Their favourite method was to cut the necessary gaps in the wire, and simultaneously isolate and stupefy our posts by a very short but terrific and accurate trench mortar bombardment. The German trench mortars were remarkably effective, both as to handling and equipment." In July Lieutenant-Colonel Croft reported how every Stokes in the 9th (Scottish) Division had again concentrated on an enemy strong point "at the same time putting down a smoke screen" that was perfect. Prisoners were taken in this raid, but in testimony to German mortar excellence one raid report wrote about "the extraordinary event of several prisoners … finding no one to receive them in our lines running back to their lines," all of the reception party having been killed by mortar fire.[54]

But when it came to wire-cutting Stokes and other mortars could not provide a guarantee. In July 1916 a raiding party of 2nd Royal Welsh Fusiliers discovered that of the enemy wire "not a quarter of it had gone and [we] were soon entangled, [the raid] a washout, not a man getting in the enemy trench and we had many casualties." Likewise, 1st Sherwood Foresters, raiding in October, found that despite rapid fire on enemy wire throughout the day, "very little cut by trench mortar fire." One other concern about preliminary mortar fire was that just like artillery fire too much attention paid to an objective or task could warn the enemy. Trotter in R.C. Sherriff's play, for example, complained that "The trench mortars go and knock an 'ole in the Boche wire … and in the night the Boche … tied bits o' red rag on each side of the 'ole."[55]

51 Scott, 'Mr. Stokes and His Educated Drainpipe', pp. 91-93.

52 *Ibid.*, Ewing, *Ninth (Scottish) Division*, pp. 311, 315; LAC, War Diary, 2CMR, April 1918, diary entry and 'Preliminary Raid Order'.

53 Bewsher, *Fifty-First (Highland) Division*, p. 97.

54 Kelly, *39 Months With the "Tigers,"*, p. 41; Croft, *Three Years With the Ninth (Scottish) Division*, p. 236.

55 Richards, *Old Soldiers Never Die*, p. 123; Colonel H.C. Wylly, *The 1st and 2nd Battalions The Sherwood Foresters (Nottinghamshire and Derbyshire Regiment) In the Great War* (Aldershot: Gale & Polden Ltd., 1925), p. 37; Sherriff, *Journey's End*, p. 87.

Another means of cutting wire is defined in Fraser and Gibbons invaluable glossary:

> Bangalore Torpedo: A device for clearing a pathway through a barbed-wire entanglement. A tube of sheet-iron with conical wooden head, filled with high explosive, thrust in advance into the obstacle and exploded … Several tubes can be joined together. Bangalore, in Mysore, is the Headquarters and Depot of the Q.V.O. Madras Sappers and Miners. Introduced on the Western Front in 1915.

The joinable tubes, six, ten or twelve feet long in diameters of two, three and four inches, made of tin or sheet iron, were filled with ammonal or gun-cotton. The ignition device was either a primer in the trailing end, or a time fuse or a separate small igniter tube. Demonstrations of the Bangalore's utility conducted at the Technical School of 25th British Division in December 1915 favourably impressed observers, including some from 28th Canadian Battalion. The tests first targeted three-row wire entanglements about 12 feet wide, heavily wired and picketed and, second, two rows of timber knife-rests similarly wired and picketed. Observers considered these targets considerably stronger that those usually seen on the front line. Electrical firing proved satisfactory providing the leads were sound and the joints covered against wet ground. During these tests ammonal proved more effective than gun-cotton. Against the wire the Bangalore could gap it for two yards either side of the Bangalore and when used against knife-rests completely destroyed them. Canadian Corps HQ observers reported the results of the tests as "completely satisfactory." In March 1916 Lieutenant-Colonel V.F. Eberle, RE, and Lieutenant Geoffrey Walker, a Brigade Bombing Officer, both with 48th British Division, were one of several teams experimenting with the device. Eberle had insisted on Walker being present because, as Eberle said, it would be infantry who would use the devices, sappers not always available to accompany infantry on raids. Experiments with Bangalores continued in 1917 and 1918. In February 1918, 8th Canadian Brigade conducted tests with the aim of demonstrating that a Bangalore could be easily exploded by a bomb if the fuse failed. A Mills hand grenade or Stokes bomb tied to the Bangalore proved effective in detonating the device.[56] Of course, failures in detonating Bangalores occurred during raids. Such failures, or enemy detection of Bangalore firing parties, most often meant aborting the raid.

Whatever the length of the tubes, and regardless of who fired them, the heavy and awkward tubes could be very difficult to place under enemy wire. During a raid by elements of 38th British Division in May 1916, the OC Raid reported that placing the Bangalore took three hours. Obviously, such a length of time would affect selection of Zero hour. In July 1916 during a raid by 2nd City of London Regiment (56th British Division) the Germans detected the sappers placing the Bangalores (more than one lane had been decided upon), inadvertent noise probably alerting the enemy, and, consequently, the raid had to be aborted.[57] On occasion, failure resulted from an insufficient supply of tubes; for example, in November 1916 raiders from

56 Fraser and Gibbons, *Soldier and Sailor Words and Phrases*, p. 16; TNA: WO 95/2232: 25th Division General Staff and Royal Engineers, December 1915; LAC, War Diaries 28th Canadian Battalion and 8th Canadian Brigade; RG9IIIC3, Volume 4053, Folder 24, File 4, Corps to divisions 5 March 1916; Lieutenant-Colonel V.F. Eberle, *My Sapper Venture* (Bath: Pitman Publishing, 1973), pp. 76-78, 82.

57 TNA: WO 95/2960: 2nd Royal Fusiliers, raid report; Grey. *2nd City of London Regiment*, p. 125.

6th Gordon Highlanders (51st (Highland) Division) exploded four Bangalores under enemy knife-rests, traversed the resultant gap to a second set which were also destroyed, but then had to withdraw no more Bangalores being at hand to take out a third set of knife-rests.[58] The same had happened during a raid in June 1916 by 14th York and Lancaster Regiment (31st British Division). The wire known to be very thick, the Bangalore party, after experiments in the rear, put together 60 feet of tube. This monster detonated as expected during the raid, but on getting through the gap the raiders found 14 more feet of uncut wire. Hand-cutting went quickly and was not, as it proved, critical, for surprise had been lost because of the preliminary bombardment. Intense enemy retaliation by artillery and trench mortars wrecked the raid. Of the 50 men tasked to enter the enemy trench, only a dozen did so and they remained only very briefly. The raid was recorded as a success, despite the fact that no prisoners were taken, only two Germans were thought to have been casualties and no dug-outs had been destroyed.[59]

From the beginning Bangalore unreliability had worried those who had to use them, although experience and a decreasing failure rate helped build confidence. Nevertheless, Bangalores remained worrisome. Looking at a dozen instances of Bangalore failure between May and October 1916, six did not detonate (reason not stated), two did not detonate due to fuse failure, two others broke during carriage across no man's land and could not be repaired and two failed to cut through the whole depth of the wire. In one other case the Bangalore party, detected before they could fire the device, forced the raiders to withdraw. In only the last were sappers present. The report on one of these raids by 32nd British Division commented that "It was essential to have an officer with the Bangalore party … to ensure correct placing." In fact, while the presence of sappers whenever Bangalores were to be used was neither mandatory nor automatic, this became the preferred option of many planners and raid commanders. Surprise also played a role in deciding to use Bangalores. 7th Black Watch, 51st (Highland) Division, raiding in September 1916, reported perfect detonation and "unlike artillery bombardment the Bangalore gave no inkling of what was to happen." This opinion was not universal; Captain F.C. Hitchcock, 2nd Leinsters, thought the Bangalore should only be used as a last resort since "if used, the chief element … surprise, would be lost and the Boches put on their guard." [60]

Finally, when it came to wire-cutting there remained what Captain Hitchcock called "wire clippers." Hand-held cutters came in any number of types, those with long handles preferred as being most effective. An obvious problem for those doing the cutting was being seen or heard. Experience or lack thereof had much to do with this. Sometimes a Bangalore followed hand-cutting; for example, during a raid by 17th West Yorkshires, 35th British Division, on 9 November 1915 hand-cutting one night was improved by Bangalores the next night. The raiders had no difficulty entering the enemy trenches and returning home with insignia of the 89th Grenadier Regiment, thereby achieving the raid's purpose.[61]

58 TNA: WO 95/2559: 6th Gordon Highlanders.
59 Tim Lynch, 'Not Just a Name on a Wall: Finding George Galloway', *Stand To!*, 82 (April/May 2008), pp. 49-50, 53.
60 TNA: WO 95/2367: 32nd Division General Staff, report on raid by 22nd Manchesters; TNA: WO 95/2877: 51st Division General Staff, report on raid by 7th Black Watch; Major-General A.G. Wauchope, *A History of the Black Watch (Royal Highlanders) in the Great War, 1914-1918 Volume Two: Territorial Force* (London: The Medici Society Limited, 1926), p. 269; Hitchcock, *"Stand To,"* p. 188.
61 Doyle and Foster, *Remembering Tommy,* p. 107; Davson, *35th Division,* p.71.

Turning now to security concerns, by which is meant maintaining secrecy about operations, and denying the enemy any knowledge of such, including ensuring that raiders carried nothing that would give away anything to the enemy, proved a significant challenge.

Inability to always recover bodies of the dead, or their identity papers, created serious complications. In early 1916 *SS 107 Notes on Minor Enterprises* directed that raiders carry no identification at all in order "to prevent the enemy obtaining any useful information." This raised an obvious concern in the minds of raiders. In many units, British and Canadian, an early expedient had each man carry "a slip of paper in his right-hand breast pocket, bearing his name and regimental number." This worried those concerned with security since from the regimental number the soldier's original unit and his place of enlistment could be determined.[62] The fragility of paper worried everyone. The problem engendered considerable and widespread debate about how to maintain security while relieving individuals of anxiety. Initial direction, which caused hilarity followed by disgust, directed that raiders leave pay books and badges behind, but carry their identity discs which had stamped on them number, rank, name, battalion and regiment. One soldier remarked that "the Big Pot who had issued that order should have been immediately a Field Marshal."[63]

In May 1916 4th York and Lancaster Regiment implemented an interim internal measure as did other battalions. Each member of a raiding party received an identity number which was then entered on a nominal roll opposite names and service numbers. Only officers' names appeared on these rolls since officers did not have service numbers.[64]

The next step, the issue of "special" raid identity discs, appeared in the Quartermaster General Branch (QMG) War Diary at GHQ in October 1917: "The ordinary red No. 2 disc [is] to be used for this purpose and 4,000 to be issued to each division. The discs are to be stamped in duplicate with index letters and numbers ... Instructions regarding ... use and reporting casualties will be issued." In late October a QMG Circular went to Armies. Second Army passed it on to its constituent corps, at that time I, VIII, IX and X Imperial Corps, I and II ANZAC and the Canadian Corps, advising addressees that each division would receive 4,000 discs, these to be stamped by the recipient divisions sequentially numbered within an assigned number block. As for procedure, prior to a raid each raider would hand in his normal identity disc and would receive in lieu a raid identity disc. The normal disc then had the duplicate raiding disc securely attached to it. The nominal roll of the party was marked as described above. On return, a raider handed in his raiding disc and received his normal disc. If a man went missing on a raid, his normal disc and the duplicate raiding disc went to GHQ, the casualty then being reported in the usual manner. If a raider's corpse was recovered his raid disc went to GHQ to be matched with the man's normal disc and the duplicate raiding disc.[65]

62 Matthew Richardson, 'The Ypres Raid – 7 April 1917', *Stand To!*, 84 (September 1995), pp. 10-12; Edward H. Wigney, *Serial Numbers of the C.E.F.* (Nepean, Ontario: privately published, 1996), introductory page.

63 Richards, *Old Soldiers Never Die*, p. 125. These directions came before a raid Richards called a "great" success, 40 prisoners and a trench mortar captured. Of the 60 battalion casualties suffered most were from the two companies in the line rather than the two raiding companies. Enemy artillery had concentrated on the trenches.

64 Lynch, 'Not Just a Name on a Wall – Finding George Galloway', p. 49.

65 TNA: WO 95/1264: 1st Cameron Highlanders (1st British Division), Appendix, 'Raid Identity Disc', copy of instruction from Major-General G.A.W. Graham, Deputy Adjutant General, GHQ,

This system seems to have taken several months before it became general. In 4th British Division, for example, the Operation Order for a raid in November 1917 by 1st Royal Warwickshires directed that all identity discs or other means of identification "except special raiding discs" must not be carried by raiders. For a raid in January 1918 the Operation Order issued by 2CMR (3rd Canadian Division) contained the direction outlined in the preceding paragraph. [66] It is evident, however, that in early 1918 the system was still not in use in all divisions. 96th British Brigade (32nd Division) in its Operation Order 26 for a raid on 18/19 February included this instruction: "Each man is to be allotted a number which will be on card or paper. A list of numbers with names will be kept by the OC Operations and each man on return will hand in his card." Brigade established three "check in" stations each under an NCO for this purpose, one for each party of raiders. The division's report on this raid commented that it was found "very difficult to find out if all men were in after the raid," because of delays caused by enemy shelling, but the system had "worked well." For a raid a week later 2nd Manchesters (96th British Brigade) had in its Operation Order this instruction: "Each man will carry a card-board disc showing his party number, i.e., 'No. 1 of No. 3 Party.' A checking Party ... will be established ... and each man as he passes will hand his disc to the officer who will have a full [nominal] roll and check all who have passed." No mention was made by the division about the durability of card or paper. For a time, then, a transition was underway.[67]

The warning in a later war about loose lips sinking ships applied equally well to Great War raids. While preliminary bombardments were often the cause of loss of surprise, the enemy could and did gain prior knowledge of raids and other operations by other means. Lieutenant-Colonel J.L. Jack, whose 2nd West Yorkshires relieved the 2nd Rifle Brigade in September 1916, made a poor decision by that unit the feature item in his diary entry:

> The Rifle Brigade had just lost heavily in a full battalion raid ... the raid should have been cancelled because on the preceding night an R.B. patrol became missing, and it was fair to assume that the enemy had captured it and had possibly obtained some hint of the plan ... The Germans withdrew from their trenches beforehand, and on arriving in them the raiders were met by very severe shell fire while machine-guns swept No Man's Land, thus blocking the retirement. The operation was a failure, the casualties being 11 out of 22 officers together with a large proportion of Other Ranks.

In a similar instance the Welsh Guards were wiser. Ordered to raid in late December 1915, supported by a detachment of RE, the battalion abandoned the scheme when the night before the raid one sapper, out to check enemy wire, was captured. The next, and the last example,

3rd Echelon, to GOC Second Army, directive on raiding discs as per QMG Circular 4/110 (Q.A.3), 24 October 1917.

66 TNA: WO 95/1484: 1st Royal Warwickshires, Appendix I, Operation Order 83; LAC, War Diary, 2CMR, Operation Order 99, January 1918; Nigel Dorrington, 'Live and Let Die' – The British Army's Experience of Trench Raiding 1915-1918', *Journal of the Centre for First World War Studies* (University of Birmingham), refers to raiders carrying "dummy identity discs." Given the meaning of "dummy" (counterfeit object), the carriage of such discs would have had exactly the opposite effect of what the "special raiders' disc" was intended to do. This cannot be what Dorrington intended.

67 TNA: WO 95/2397: 2nd Manchesters, Operation Order 21; LAC, 2CMR, February 1918.

fictional, but likely based on fact, does lead nicely into another form of early warning to the enemy that had to be stamped out: "This god-damned Raid's been a funny story for the last fortnight and we've done everything except to send word over to the Fritzies to say when we're coming; and now its fixed up for next Thursday."[68]

The "word" mentioned referred to loose talk in the trenches that might have been overheard by German patrols and/or telephone conversations, which became the primary culprit when it came to breaches of security. Initially, it proved difficult to convince users that the enemy could listen in; for example, in June 1915 Lieutenant-Colonel Villiers-Stuart, CO 9th Rifle Brigade (42nd Brigade, 14th British Division) found that two of the other battalion commanders in the brigade did not believe that the enemy could monitor telephone conversation. The Germans soon proved that they could; after one raid it was realized that they had known exactly what the raid intended and had planned accordingly. Before another raid Villiers-Stuart prohibited use of telephones in his battalion. He later wrote "It was lucky that I stuck to my opinion and thereby saved a fiasco." Nevertheless, it took time for German capability to be generally realized. Starting in mid-1915 intelligence reports routinely referred to enemy interceptions, which is evidence that the whole of the BEF had not instantly become security conscious. In October, when the 2nd Grenadier Guards received orders to cut wire in preparation to attack two days later, the cutting had scarcely begun when the enemy shelled the very location where it was underway. Such almost uncanny accuracy presented conclusive proof of wire tapping. Along 12th British Division's front both sides sought to tap telephone line by placing "earth pins," the results not being very successful, the devices then not being sensitive enough. With new equipment valuable information would be obtained.[69]

Along came rules for use of telephones such as avoiding unit names, times of any movement or operations and activity of supporting arms, all of which helped, but the danger of breaches of security remained since users could not or did not always comply. "Fancy" names for units came into use in March 1916. Initially, these had some sort of system, but that gave way to unrelated names; for example "Nabob rang up Nurse and was erroneously put onto Oily." Then, says the published history of the 47th British Division:

> In 1918, the great co-ordinators at GHQ brought their minds to bear and every unit … had a separate and meaningless combination of four letters, a scheme which had the single good result of making one chary of using the telephone at all. Mercifully, at all times of real stress in Operations it was assumed that the Boche was too busy to listen to us, and it was possible to call things what they were without the fear of unintentional treachery or of a FGCM [Field General Court Martial].

Cyril Falls recalled how in 36th (Ulster) Division "extreme imprudence" in telephone use gave way to "comical extreme" caution:

> It was still possible to send telegraphic messages, using the 'fuller-phone,' an invention which greatly diminished the risk of tapping. And an instrument of torture, known as the

68 Terraine (ed.), *General Jack's Diary*, p. 163; Dudley Ward, *History of the Welsh Guards*, p. 59; Sassoon, *Memoirs of an Infantry Officer*, p. 17.

69 Maxwell, *Villiers-Stuart Goes to War*, p. 81; Ponsonby, *The Grenadier Guards*, p. 333; Scott, *12th (Eastern) Division*, p. 9.

> B.A.B. Code Book became part of the equipment of every officer. How many company commanders have sat ... translating a series of numerals into amazing gibberish, to discover that they had wasted half an hour by using last month's correction!

Throughout 1916 formation HQs up to and including GHQ issued instructions designed to prevent breaches. In February Second Army, in "Lessons Drawn From the Various Minor Operations," drew attention to telephone usage: "No conversation with regard to an enterprise of this kind [raids] must be held over the telephone or in the vicinity of the trenches." In early March a Commanding Officers Conference at First Army, warned attendees that when it came to use of telephones in the forward area "No restrictions on use could be too severe ... runners were the only course ... No telephones should be in front of support lines and severe disciplinary action is the only method of restricting improper use."

Various mechanical means designed to prevent tapping also came into use such as double cable metallic circuits and twisted cables. In April *SS 103 Orders Regarding the Sending of Messages Within 1500 Yards of the Firing Line* was issued. This instruction or "card" (it was a single page) stipulated procedure for the use of the "Buzzer" telegraph and telephones, specifying that the former was liable to interception if used within 1,500 yards of the front trench, the latter within 600 yards. Written messages to be sent by Buzzer required authorization by an officer. New equipment included the Fullerphone, a portable DC-line Morse telegraph whose transmissions were virtually proof against listening in. However, voice was only truly secure on Buzzer circuits. Consequently, the speaking part of the Fuller-phone was detached and carried by an officer for emergency use only. That spring some divisions, including 47th British Division, received only sufficient Fullerphones to serve brigades and battalions. It would be winter before sufficient numbers arrived to permit use between companies and battalions. It took even longer to equip all divisions.

Discipline was the nub in usage, of course, and the simple fact remained that an order issued is not necessarily obeyed to the letter and at all times. A costly instance of improper use of the telephone came to light during 25th Brigade's (8th British Division) brief occupation of the village of Ovillers-la-Boiselle. There a copy of a brigade order of 1 July was found. This order had been repeated over the telephone by the BM at the insistence of his GOC. Its interception cost the 2nd Berkshires and the 2nd Lincolnshire a total of 48 officers and 797 ORs: 53 percent casualties for the former and 62 percent for the latter. The Berkshires came out under the command of Second Lieutenant C. Mollet, the Battalion Adjutant. On a happier note, "It may be mentioned [as Cyril Falls did] that ... before the Somme ... the efficacy of the German [listening] apparatus was realized by the British. In one demonstration an officer of the 9th Irish Fusiliers used the telephone to set a trap. This he did by speaking loudly on a telephone at a company HQ that two officers and seven men would be at a clump of willows in no man's land at midnight. At 2130 out he went with 16 ORs and arranged his ambush near the willows. Before midnight he heard a party of 20 or so men moving toward the willows:

> Twenty-five yards off and coming, oh, so slowly ... moving down a little ditch. I level my revolver. I see the first distinctly now, ten yards off, – nine, eight, seven, six, five ... Bang, bang, bang, ring out the rifles! I let off five with my revolver. 'Come on, boys!' I'm up and out. I see a figure on his back. I leap at his throat. 'Kamerad. Kamerad!' he shouts.

The ambushers took four prisoners and killed several others: "that the telephone message had been overheard could never be exactly proved, but the probabilities seemed to be in that direction."[70]

Leutnant Ernst Junger, commenting in late 1916 on German intercept capability, remarked how "often" this occurred before British raids and other endeavours: "Intercepted English telephone message: The English give precise information of the gaps in our wire and are asking for steel helmets, possibly a codeword … be prepared." Across no man's land 1st Royal Irish Fusiliers, after discovering signals wire laid across no man's land, a sign of German interception attempts, resorted to sending reports by runner only. In the Guards Division during the late summer of 1916 divisional HQ issued several warnings regarding telephone and Buzzer use and operator chatter during unauthorized conversations within and outside the danger area specified in *SS 103*. By early 1917 technology provided another means to improve security, a listening device referred to only as "IT." This item, according to Brigadier-General A.H. Hussey of 5th British Division, "acted as a sort of spy on any illicit conversations, which were at once reported, in order to bring culprits to book." But "IT" could not be everywhere and perfection impossible when it came to operational security:

> The Boche was extraordinarily good at picking up our order of battle and other information … by means of their listening sets through which he overheard indiscreet and unofficial conversations between telephonists. Our sentries helped him a bit, though; for I well remember one night, when I was further away from the front line than the enemy, overhearing one of our sentries challenge and the answer quite clearly.[71]

Another reason why raids could fail was incompetence or inadequacy in some military skill. In March 1916 Field Marshal Haig, then in his fourth month as C-in-C of the BEF, remarked that he did not have "an Army in France, really, but a collection of divisions untrained for the field. The actual fighting force will be evolved from them."[72] This evolution came about because of a training system and policy, standards and verification, facilities, staff and curriculum. One part of the last, for obvious reasons, was map reading, navigation and direction keeping, crucial skills in a soldier's education, effectiveness and survivability. Right from the start navigation as a whole presented a tough challenge, maps being inaccurate, some with co-ordinate numbers reversed and some printed upside down with north at the bottom of the sheet. Moreover, it escaped many that reading a map and reading ground were two very different skills. The CO of 10th Canadian Battalion found that many officers new out from Britain or Canada

70 Maude, *47th (London) Division*, pp. 72-74; LAC, RG9IIIC3, Volume 4052, Folder 23, File 2, 9 February 1916, 'Lessons Drawn From the Various Minor Operations Carried Out By Second Army up to 9 February, 1916', para 11; *SS 103 Orders Regarding the Sending of Messages Within 1500 Yards of the Firing Line* (GHQ, February 1916, O.B./630); Adkin, *The Western Front Companion*, p. 320; Falls, *36th (Ulster) Division*, pp. 72-73; Boraston and Bax, *Eighth Division*, p. 77.

71 Junger, *The Storm of Steel*, p. 76; Brigadier-General A.R. Burrowes, *The 1st Battalion The Faugh-A-Ballagh in the Great War* (Uckfield, East Sussex: Naval and Military Press, n.d.), pp. 71, 76; TNA: WO 95/1007: Guards Division General Staff, G.D. 2037/G, 10 August 1916; LAC, RG9IIIC3, Volume 4046, Folder 4, File 2, Summary of Conference, 7 March; Hussey, *Fifth Division*, p. 141; Croft, *Three Years With the Ninth (Scottish) Division*, p. 39.

72 Quoted in Ashworth, *Live and Let Live*, p. 178.

knew nothing of maps, or they personified the adage that a little knowledge can be dangerous. Obliteration of most natural landmarks often made accurately locating positions problematic. In no man's land the ground changed frequently as shells produced new craters and the enemy prepared new trenches and saps. Consequently, methods such as resections had to be added to the curriculum. A further complication in late 1917 was the advent of more "open" warfare, "the greater distance between the lines and the changes in systems of defence [adding to] the range of our patrols [and raids]." Prior to 1915 when *WO 2313 Notes on Map Reading* was published, those seeking guidance had only the 1905 edition of Gale and Polden's *The Complete Guide to Military Map Reading*. In some aspects this unofficial manual was the better of the two.[73]

While training and maps improved during 1916 and 1917 it is debatable as to whether or not this can be said of map reading and navigation generally. *Notes for Commanding Officers* (1917 edition) included only a suggestion that map reading be included in training plans. Even in 1918 map reading errors occurred, these sometimes causing great embarrassment. Lieutenant Stanley Spencer, 10th West Yorkshires, during his time as Battalion Intelligence Officer recalled the general glee of his CO over a brigade error:

> On the very day I took over this appointment orders came through from Brigade giving the positions the Battalion was to occupy during the next tour in the line. In checking over these instructions … it appeared to me that we were ordered to occupy ground which was … in the possession of the enemy and behind his front line. I pointed this out to the CO but he did not agree and said he thought I was mistaken. I was convinced that I was right, so I asked him to look at the maps once more, finally proving to him that the Brigade instructions were wrong … The Brigade Staff were always very ready to point out sarcastically any mistakes made by the Battalion, so when the CO realized that the Brigade had made a slip he was delighted and spent a pleasant half hour composing an ironical request for instructions as to how we were to take over a position behind the enemy lines. Incidentally, my map reading abilities went up in his estimation.[74]

Embarrassment could become tragedy. Lieutenant-Colonel Hutchison, 33rd British Division, remembered one such event that cost many lives. A very young Subaltern with his platoon following a compass bearing forgot the existence of a true and a magnetic north and led his men too far to the left where they stumbled into uncut wire: "memory asserting itself [he[had made endeavour to correct his bearing … but had not only thrown himself in desperation … on the wire … but had … sacrificed his platoon to the chattering fire of enemy machine-guns."[75]

Direction keeping proved a major difficulty during night raids. Accounts of individuals and raiding parties getting lost are legion. Major C.H. Dudley Ward became convinced that in raiding "The most important point was direction – to strike through the darkness the exact

73 LAC, RG9IIIC3, Volume 4051, Folder 19, File 8, CO to brigade, 15 November 1916; *WO 2313 Notes on Map Reading* (London: Harrison and Sons, 1915). These notes consisted of 31 pages, but no practical exercises for the reader. Gale and Polden's guide (second edition, January 1915) consisted of 98 pages and numerous exercises designed to test comprehension. The guide, overall, is notable for its clarity and exercises.

74 Spencer (ed.) *Stanley Spencer's Great War Diary*, p. 116. Spencer provides a good account of his duties.

75 Hutchison, *Thirty-Third Division*, pp. 8-9.

spot selected, where the enemy wire had been cut … an error of a few yards would cause delay, which might prove fatal to the enterprise."[76] Even experienced officers and men lost direction at night. Eventually members of patrols and raids began to carry compasses and took care to know the bearing back to their battalion trenches. Stories abound of officer misdirection. VC winner Thomas Dinesen made possibly the best of the many OR comments on this shortcoming: "our kind and brave officers are no more capable of using a map than the average cow."[77] Repeated navigational errors resulted in a flow of adverse remarks. In March 1916 a raiding party of two officers and 30 ORs of the 10th Argyll and Sutherland Highlanders, 9th (Scottish) Division, having lost direction failed to find a gap that artillery had opened in enemy wire. The division's historian thought in this instance that navigation was more symptom than cause, which he put down to "inexperience and insufficient preparation for the raid." Whichever, it disappointed divisional HQ. Another officer was very lucky he did not pay with his life for becoming lost. Lieutenant Dennis Terry, 7th Queens (18th British Division), in the spring of 1916 on entering a sap he thought was British, and having answered a repeated challenge with "I'm Mr. Terry," suddenly realizing his error made a mad and successful run for it, bullets zipping about him, but luckily not in him. In another instance an officer and two men out on recce were "presumed [to have] lost their bearing, got into an enemy trench and were taken prisoner." Lieutenant Bernard Martin, North Staffordshire Regiment, also found movement in no man's land far more difficult than he had anticipated and he soon lost his way, could not find what he sought and often did not know whose front line he was moving toward. After an hour or so of this a flare suddenly shot up and he found himself only a few yards from the enemy trench and a sentry staring straight at him: "how I got back I don't know, I stood up and ran for it." It later dawned on him that he had, at last, after three months in the trenches, seen a living German.[78]

In May 1916 navigational error wrecked a raid by 16th Cheshires of 35th British Division. The raid report related how everything had gone like clockwork, but then, ruefully, the men lost direction when the OC Raid became separated from the main party. The raid was aborted.[79] In June a raiding party of 9th Black Watch (15th (Scottish) Division) lost direction, only two men actually entering enemy trenches. Confusion and delay because of the navigational error caused many if not all of the casualties. In August 5th Northumberland Fusiliers (50th British Division) set out to raid an enemy sap, but had to abort after losing direction. This raiding party was fortunate to suffer only light casualties.[80] Also in August, Captain C. Place, 8th East Surreys, in company with two ORs, having been in no man's land for some time, then headed for home, or so Place thought:

76 Ward (comp.), *Regimental Records of the Royal Welch Fusiliers (23rd Foot)*. Volume III. *1914-1918 France and Flanders* (London: Forster Groom & Co. Ltd., 1929), p. 314. The Royal Welsh Fusiliers became the Royal Welch Fusiliers after the war.

77 Thomas Dinesen, *Merry Hell: A Dane With the Canadians* (London: Jarrolds, 1929), p. 238. Dinesen was later commissioned.

78 Ewing, *Ninth (Scottish) Division,* p. 78; Nichols, *18th Division,* p. 30; LAC, War Diary, 46th Canadian Battalion, April 1916; Bernard Martin, *Poor Bloody Infantry: A Subaltern on the Western Front* (London: John Murray, 1987), pp. 70-71.

79 TNA: WO 95/2487: 16th Cheshires, report on raid on 25 May 1916.

80 Lieut.-Colonel J. Stewart, D.S.O. and John Buchan, *The Fifteenth (Scottish) Division 1914-1919* (Edinburgh: William Blackwood And Sons, 1926), p. 73; Wyrall, *Fiftieth Division,* p. 234.

> The party climbed over two belts of wire, and dropped into the trench. 'Go to Company Headquarters and say we're back,' [he] instructed one of his party. At that moment an unarmed man walked round the corner of the trench. He was a man with a beard. Place flattened himself and his men against the trench side. The man with the beard said 'Gute Nacht.' Place replied 'Gute Nacht.' The man with the beard … walked on, round another corner. Immediately Captain Place whispered 'Off like hell! We're in the Boche trenches.' But the Boche knew … the whole trench was now alive with shouts.

One of Place's party was killed, but he and the other man got out, through the wire and then reached safety.[81] Cyril Falls offers another example of loss of direction. Two officers out in no man's land became confused as to which way to go. Eventually they approached some wire. One of the pair put up his head and was promptly shot at and a second look also drew fire. The two then heard a voice say to a sentry "Jasus, what are ye shooting at?" This was a welcome voice; they had reached the lines of another battalion of their brigade. They were fortunate since it could be very dangerous to approach friendly trenches held by another battalion whose men were unaware of "friendlies" being out in no man's land.[82]

Even after compasses became more common they did not always ensure that users kept direction. Frank Maxwell, in mid-1916 CO 12th Middlesex in 18th British Division, related in a letter his concern about a raid the unit had to do in an area where the distance between the trenches (unstated) was so considerable it meant moving on a compass bearing "and the way may be easily lost. Then if they get there … ." Left unwritten was his equal concern about the withdrawal. We have also seen how failure to consider true and magnetic north ended in disaster. That errors in compass work remained a serious problem is evident in the 1918 edition of *Notes for Commanding Officers* which contains a complete section on compass work.[83]

Another aid to navigation was the family of directional markings to point the way. 58th Canadian Battalion, for example, reeled off a wire that raiders could follow to their jumping-off line in no man's land. Cloth tape also sufficed for this purpose, but probably less so a line of lime laid out on the ground. 2nd Worcestershires marked not only the route out, but the gaps in enemy wire as well. 1st Royal Berkshires (2nd British Division) employed a more sophisticated system in February 1917 during a raid on an enemy salient where it was thought prisoners could easily be snaffled. Prior to Zero (0300 on 5 February) the CO personally reconnoitred enemy wire and on return he then placed the raiders, two officers and 60 ORs in position:

> Three small wooden tripods covered with canvas (black on our side, white on the enemy's side) marking the flanks and centre of the party, had been placed beforehand in No Man's Land, about 30 yards outside our wire, and parallel to the enemy's trench. The men, dressed in white smocks with white helmet covers [fresh snow covered the ground] crawled out in

81 Nichols, *18th Division,* p. 19.
82 Falls, *36th (Ulster) Division,* p. 75.
83 Charlotte Maxwell, *Frank Maxwell,* p. 146, letter of 29 June 1916. No further mention is made of this raid in this source. British War Diary, 12th Middlesex, states that the raid commenced on 29 June at 2230, the aim being to determine the state of enemy trenches and in what strength they were held. The raiders penetrated as far as the support trenches. No prisoners were taken. Only one casualty was suffered. Hutchison, *Thirty-Third Division,* p. 8; *Notes for Commanding Officers,* pp. 324-35.

> pairs, and were on the alignment … 15 minutes before Zero. Three similar tripods had also been placed parallel to the three already mentioned, and 30 to 40 yards nearer the enemy's line. These gave the direction of advance, and proved effective.

So, too, was the raid. During 20 minutes in the enemy trench the raiders killed 14 Germans, including two officers, and captured 49 ORs. Friendly casualties were one officer and 11 ORs wounded and one killed. The OC Raid, Second Lieutenant Burgess, received the DSO.[84]

The enemy, it must be pointed out, was often no great navigator either. In August 1916 a patrol of 12th Canadian Brigade, after an encounter with an enemy party in no man's land, found while searching enemy dead identifications indicating that the enemy were well of course: "how they got so far north is rather a mystery … [possibly] the width of No Man's Land from 500 to 1,200 yards … caused the patrol to lose its bearings." Various markings were also used by the Germans. For both sides when such markings were discovered by the other side it could be disastrous. In March 1917 a patrol by a unit of 35th British Division on discovering enemy markers leading to a point where British wire had been cut, prepared an ambush, but no enemy appeared.[85]

Markers also greatly assisted returning raiders. When in August 1917 11th Royal Warwickshires raided at 0230 without the benefit of a moon, considerable time was spent marking the way. First, flanking tapes were laid some way out before the first wave went over and these were then carried on to the farthest limit reached by the raiding party. Within these tapes left and right the raiders had to remain in going out and in coming back. Red lights were also to be set out behind the centre of the outpost line to guide any stragglers. As insurance the tapes were placed on compass bearings checked by an experienced officer. After the raid, which was a success, several prisoners being taken, the precautions were judged as very useful, especially during the withdrawal. In July 1918 1st Royal Berkshires used searchlights to mark the way for withdrawing raiders. These remained on for 60 minutes, during which time they drew no enemy fire.[86]

Having entered enemy trenches or not, raiders had to withdraw and get home. Macbeth's complaint that "returning were as tedious as go o'er" often marked the withdrawal phase. The historian of 40th British Division considered it the "great difficulty" in any raid. Whatever the signal to scoot, visual, audio, pre-arranged or a combination, it was critical that all be aware of it and respond quickly. But in the heat of battle signals visual or audible could be missed. All members of a raiding party of the 11th Border Regiment (32nd British Division) in June 1916 heard the Klaxon Horn sounding withdrawal. All members of a raiding party of another unit in 40th Division heard the hammering on a shell-casing signalling time to leave. Conversely, a raiding party of 10th Royal Fusiliers (37th British Division) in June 1916 did not hear the

84 Shackleton, *Second to None,* p. 40; Roy, *Journal of Private Fraser,* p. 186; Stacke, *The Worcestershire Regiment,* p. 160; Wyrall, *Second Division,* Volume 2, pp. 362-63. In the butt of the rifle was a cleaning kit consisting of a small bottle of oil, a pull-through and one or more two inch by two inch off-white cloth patches. These were cut from long rolls, "rounds," as Fraser put it, of the cloth. The rounds were perfect for rolling off as guiding tapes.

85 LAC, War Diary, 12th Brigade, 4th Canadian Division, August 1916; Davson, *35th Division,* p. 89.

86 TNA: WO 95/2536: 11th Royal Warwickshires, report on raid 26/27 August; Wyrall, *Second Division,* Volume 2, p. 597.

horn signalling withdrawal because of other noise, but the OC Raid, who was keeping note of the time, used his whistle to signal withdrawal and all obeyed. Staying past the time set could be costly. Private Fraser, 31st Canadian Battalion, recalling a raid by 28th Battalion in June 1916 reported that in failing to keep to the timing the raiders suffered considerable loss of men during the withdrawal. Fraser does not say if this was because the signal was missed or because no signal was made. Sometimes the latter was the case. An NCO of 44th Canadian Battalion taken prisoner during the large raid by 4th Canadian Division on 13 February 1917 told his captors that he knew of no designated signal for withdrawal. Nor does such appear in the Operation Order for the raid. Light signals were also used. During a raid by 2CMR in January 1918 red flares were used and proved effective, the whole party starting back at sight of them. Such signals could be missed, of course, or could be confused with other coloured signals of both sides. That the withdrawal remained problematic throughout 1916 and early 1917 is evident in the record of decisions at a conference of COs at First Army School of Instruction in March 1917. Those attending agreed that the best signal for withdrawal was a pre-arranged time limit. The Army commander agreed, but this did not entirely solve the problem.[87]

Despite the various marking systems raiders could still go astray for reasons other than navigation or failing to withdraw on signal, for example, and could end up having to enter the trenches of neighbouring units or formations, either as a group or one by one over an extended period. In theory, neighbouring units as a matter of routine were notified of all raids and the associated timings, but seeking entry to trenches in another unit's patch remained a dangerous business. It was not unknown for men to be shot by sentries of their own or other units. Siegfried Sassoon, returning home from a patrol in January 1918, was wounded by an NCO of his company who took the patrol for German raiders. More fortunate was a party of one unit that entered the trenches of the neighbour, 4th King's Own Royal Lancaster Regiment, without incident.[88]

What made the risk even greater was a complication that raiders and units did not like. This was the practice that existed in 1916 and 1917 of a raiding party "coming up to the line … while [it] was held by some other battalion who knew little or nothing of the purpose of the operation." The inherent danger in this is obvious. In June 1916 the CO of 4/5 Black Watch carefully arranged for a platoon of another regiment (Cheshires), then holding the front line, to vacate in order that the raiding company of his battalion would man the area from which a raid by his unit would depart. Just as carefully he arranged the recall to the front line of the Cheshire platoon when all his raiders had been counted in. In late 1916 the CO of 2nd Leinsters, when faced with such a situation, arranged to have one of his companies, which had just left the trenches, return there for two days during which period the 2nd would raid: "it was only natural that we wanted the line to be held by Leinsters, and not by another regiment, while the raid was in progress."[89]

87 Whitton, *40th Division,* p. 77; Julian Sykes, 'A Trench Raid Near Arras, June 1916', *Gun Fire,* 6, p. 48; Roy (ed.), *Journal of Private Fraser,* p. 89; Sheldon, *German Army on Vimy Ridge,* p. 235; LAC, RG9IIIC3, Volume 4046, Folder 4, File 2, 'Summary of Subjects Discussed at COs Conference at First Army School of Instruction', 7 March 1917; 2CMR, War Diary, January 1918, Operation Order 99.

88 Egremont, *Sassoon,* p. 203; Shannon, *Lion and the Rose,* p. 126.

89 TNA: WO 95/2588: 118th Brigade, 39th Division, June 1916, orders and reports on raid 17 June by 4/5 Black Watch. This raid is further examined in Chapter 9. Jerrold, *Georgian Adventure,* p. 145; Hitchcock, *"Stand To,"* p. 185. The day before returning to the trenches on 2 October Hitchcock was

Brigadier-General J.L. Jack, who assumed command of 28th British Brigade (9th Division) in September 1918, included in his invaluable diary an excellent assessment of why attacks of any kind fail. It offers a useful introduction to the importance of planning in raids and to inadequate planning as a cause of failure:

> Failure may follow the best laid plans, carried out by the finest troops, because after all, one can only guess the enemy's strength and what he will do … and other factors. But the risks of failure, or even of unduly long casualty lists, are tremendously increased by unsound or incomplete plans; by troops not thoroughly knowing their role, or being insufficiently rested before action; by slack discipline, shortage of training and poor leading … For the many instant decisions required in action one has to rely on the courage and training of junior leaders.[90]

Anyone who has ever attended even one Officers' Study Group evening will surely recall the adage "The plan's the thing." The War Diary of 20th Canadian Battalion (2nd Division) makes this point in referring to the failure of a raid by the battalion on 27 April 1916, the writer of the entry saying, "This experience only confirms … that such enterprises cannot hope to be successful without a great deal of preparation." By one definition this raid failed since none of the raiding party got into the enemy trenches. The dead included the OC Raid. Several men were wounded and one went missing, presumed captured. Very early on the raid had to be aborted, the cause infantry/artillery "misunderstanding" of the fire plan. In June 21st Battalion of the same brigade (4th) had also to abort "owing to the artillery receiving orders conflicting with ours." Neither War Diary offers any explanation, but something was clearly amiss in infantry/artillery co-operation. Second, the pre-raid briefing was not all it should have been; for example, none of the men were aware of the signal for withdrawal.[91] The Operation Order for a raid at about the same time by 58th Canadian Battalion (3rd Division) had the same shortcoming plus other flaws. While all the raiders entered enemy trenches, a series of whistle blasts by the enemy soon afterward was taken as the signal to withdraw and the party immediately did so. This raid, it should be noted, had scant time for preparation and planning, the raid being executed on the same night as it was ordered. During a raid some days later by 7th Middlesex Regiment of 56th British Division (167th Brigade) the raiders withdrew prematurely on the firing of a rocket signal which they "believed to be the withdrawal signal." The brigade report thought rocket signals bad as they were "apt to be mistaken … thus causing confusion."[92]

A raid by 6th Royal Scots in September 1917 offers graphic evidence of what occurs or does not occur without proper briefing beforehand. For one thing, the primary purpose of the raid was to secure identifications. The brigade commander's report attributed failure to do so as

appointed acting Captain, having completed the 21-day period in command of a company on active service that was necessary for the acting rank.

90 Terraine (ed.), *General Jack's Diary,* pp. 267-68. Jack was a well-experienced battalion commander: 2nd West Yorkshires, August 1916 to July 1917 and 1st Cameronians September 1917 to September 1918.

91 LAC, War Diaries 20th and 21st Battalions; Corrigall, *Twentieth Canadian Battalion,* pp. 69-71; Shackleton, *Second to None,* pp. 120, 122.

92 LAC, 58th Canadian Battalion; TNA: WO 95/2950: 7th Middlesex.

"regrettable and should not have occurred. The feeling seemed to prevail that somebody else had identifications." Moreover, the ORs of the party seemed unaware of the requirement. This brigade was not alone in failing to search enemy dead for identifications. His greatest concern was how most ORs in the party "displayed some helplessness in adapting ... except where they were under the immediate control of officers. This necessitated the shouting of orders and directions by the officers, thereby arousing the enemy." However, he thought the experience had been useful since the battalion had little experience of operations and had "never really been blooded." As well, the men involved were not volunteers, but simply picked from the Reserve Company which happened to be readily available.[93]

Death or serious wounding of raid leaders often spelled failure. During a raid in February 1917 by 8th South Lancashires all four officers became casualties early on. This accounted for the failure, wrote the brigade commander. In another raid when all three officers were put out of action, only one of the three raiding parties entered the enemy trench and of that party only six men actually did. This raid achieved nothing. In neither of these cases do the raid reports say anything about the performance of the NCOs who assumed command.[94]

It is a simple fact that in any operation in any war leaders will make mistakes, may demonstrate lack of control of their men and will commit errors in judgement that can cause unnecessary casualties and partial or complete failure. It should be remembered that raids in most cases were led by very young officers, usually Subalterns, many with little or no experience, perhaps newly arrived and not having raided before. 29th British Division, when it arrived in France in March 1916 from Gallipoli where 1,100 officers had been lost, was a division of only cadres of untrained and inexperienced junior officers. While many were brave and resourceful, "they knew so little." Anxious as the 29th was to avenge an enemy raid on 6 April that cost it more officers and 100 ORs, it was soon realized that "the direction of a raid demands experience and luck." Neither element being present the raid failed despite "the ardour and zeal shown ... in practising for the hazardous enterprise or their determination."[95]

Neglect of detail, carelessness, poor planning and inadequate recce could doom a raid to failure. The brigade report on a failure by 20th Canadian Battalion, for example, blamed "inadequate recce" for most of the troubles of the raiding party. Errors in judgement that caused raids to fail partially or completely were not uncommon. Lieutenant-Colonel Graham Hutchison related one particularly tragic instance that occurred in 33rd British Division during the first half of 1916 (he does not precisely date the raid). This raid involved the blowing up of an enemy mineshaft. For safety reasons the occupants of the raiding battalion's front line were put in dug-outs while the raiding parties remained in the support line. The mine, when it went up, created devastation. Forward of the support line the debris filled even the CTs and otherwise so changed the terrain that the division's front line resembled no man's land. This so deceived the OC Raid that on moving forward to what had been the front line he thought he had already crossed no man's land:

93 TNA: WO 95/2392: 14th British Brigade, 32nd Division.
94 TNA: WO 95/2249: 25th British Division General Staff, 75th Brigade report on raid and report of VI Corps to Third Army.
95 Gillon, *29th Division*, pp.78-79.

> By the dim light, through mountains of debris, he could detect the mouths of dugouts, at the bottom of which he could see lights and hear the murmur of voices. He thought that these were German dugouts … He organized his party, attacked with bombs, and then himself entered a dugout, revolver in hand. He saw no enemy, but the torn and bleeding bodies of men of the Battalion which he knew had garrisoned our front line. An error of judgement.[96]

On 13 April 1916 during a raid on 54th Brigade of 18th British Division (Major-General Ivor Maxse) the Germans inflicted 46 casualties upon one of the battalions and took away two of its men. Maxse immediately ordered retaliation.[97] 54th Brigade promptly issued "Extracts from Instructions Regarding the Raids to be Carried Out … by 54th Infantry Brigade During the Night 26/27 April." A three-page, 15 paragraph order instructed two raiding parties, one each from 12th Middlesex and 7th Bedfordshires. Due to its considerable length it will not be further described except for one point, which defined one part of the first phase of the artillery fire plan as wire-cutting by a single gun at a specific point.[98] The plan produced by the CO of the 12th, Lieutenant-Colonel H.P. Osborne, was transformed into a concise (two pages), clear and finely-crafted Operation Order. Nichols makes no mention of the raid by the 12th Middlesex, but he writes a fulsome account of that by the 7th Bedfordshires. Why no mention is made of the 12th is evident in Osborne's report submitted on 27 April which began with this: "The raid should have taken place last night" and continues with the "reasons for its failure."

The plan called for the raiding party of the 12th under Second Lieutenant Chase to be at the jumping off position by 0130. When at 2310 a German party was observed at the battalion's wire Chase and his raiders became involved in searching the trenches on the premise that some raiders had already entered battalion trenches. During this the party took casualties that necessitated some re-organization. Delay ensued, it being such that the party did not get to the far side of the line of fire of the single gun doing wire-cutting before the preliminary bombardment began. Because it had been firmly impressed on Chase that his party had to be on the far side before fire opened, he decided not to continue with the raid. His order to withdraw was "altogether unlooked for by his party, and by the men on the parapet. The conclusion seems to have been jumped at … that only the presence of … Germans could have occasioned such an order and fire was opened from the parapet. In this fire seven men were hit." Chase then ordered his raiders to go to their dug-outs. On being informed of this around 0200, Lieutenant-Colonel Osborne ordered Chase to make the raid which he did at 0230, but the party failed to enter enemy trenches.

Osborne's report focussed on the "error in judgement" which was "wholly unforeseen." First, he remarked that he had appointed Chase OC Raid because he thought him the "most likely officer in the Battalion." Second, while Chase had committed "a very extraordinary error of judgement in deciding to abandon the enterprise … I know him to be a very gallant officer, and I know it was nothing more than an error of judgement." Osborne believed the raid failed because

96 LAC, War Diary, 20th Battalion, May 1916; Hutchison, *Thirty-Third Division,* pp. 8-9.
97 Nichols, *18th Division.* This New Army Division was trained and commanded by Maxse until January 1917 when he was promoted to command XVII Corps. The 18th was then commanded by Richard Lee until war's end.
98 TNA: WO 95/2043: 54th Brigade, 18th Division.

of that error and "no other cause." It is evident that Osborne sought to protect Chase to some degree, the error in his mind being a "one-off" that a relatively inexperienced officer could well make. This CO, as any good CO would do, also defended the reputation of his battalion. It is unclear from his report what transpired afterward, but whatever it was, he forthrightly thought it had gone too far and he had the moral courage to say so:

> All ranks … feel very keenly the Brigadier's stated displeasure at a personal interview this morning after the incident. If he [the Brigadier] is still dis-satisfied … I respectfully beg that this report be forwarded to higher authority [and be] officially enquired into. All ranks … feel keenly disappointed at the failure and also feel very keenly his displeasure which I venture to hope will be withdrawn.

Given the absence of any further information it is not possible to say whether this "hope" was realized or whether Brigadier-General T.H. Shoubridge took any further action.[99]

In another instance of questionable judgement by an officer, Corps came down hard on what it considered a bad decision made during a raid on the night of 4/5 August 1917 by 100 officers and men of 8th Sherwood Foresters of 46th British Division. Captain Simonet, OC Raid, commanded the right party and another officer the left party. Shortly after dusk two tape-laying parties began laying tape from the front line toward the gaps made in the enemy wire. At this time the right tape party received some fire. At Zero (2330), as the assault parties moved toward their objectives, Simonet's party was hit by artillery and trench mortar fire, this due to the enemy earlier sighting the tape-layers. In addition, an enemy party of 20 or so men tried to outflank Simonet's party. The left party, meanwhile, had entered the enemy frontline where bombing fights began. At 2340 after 30 minutes had passed (the division's Operation Order had stipulated that the raiders were to remain in the trenches for 60 minutes) Simonet, thinking the left party might be cut off by the enemy party, sounded the withdrawal signal.

The brigade commander attributed the partial failure to the loss of surprise, the game given away upon detection of the tape-layers. He believed that better results might have been achieved had Simonet moved to the support of the left party, but he was "not at all certain that that would have been possible." This statement appeared only in his manuscript draft report and not in his final submitted report. Division HQ forwarded it to Corps HQ, which did not find it satisfactory, the response stressing the GOC's view that Simonet had "exaggerated" the enemy flanking movement, its 20 men not a big threat to Simonet's 50 men, and he had ignored the fact that the box barrage around the objective would prevent any enemy from entering the box. In short, Simonet made a "weak" decision that prevented the raid achieving its full purpose. As for the loss of surprise, the laying out of tapes had been done without "sufficient care." In the end, it seems that no further action was taken by any level of command.[100]

At the end of August a raid by a battalion of 3rd British Division resulted in divisional HQ criticizing the OC Raid and the battalion commander about the preparation and execution of the raid and with that came an order to do the raid again and that very night. The second attempt launched at Zero (0230, 30 August). The first raiding party enroute to the objective discovered

99 TNA: WO 95/2044: 12th Middlesex, report of Lieutenant-Colonel H.P. Osborne, CO, to 54th Brigade.
100 TNA: WO 95/2693: 8th Sherwood Foresters, 139th Brigade, preliminary report.

a large enemy patrol, 60 or so men. The OC, Captain W.R. Busk, 4th Royal Fusiliers, decided to follow the enemy party with the intention of surrounding and destroying it. Having failed to catch up with the enemy, he proceeded again toward the objective. Some 150 yards short of it he again came upon the enemy party which was now trying to move round to his right flank. He again attempted to pursue, but then had to withdraw, it becoming too light to continue. The CO, Lieutenant-Colonel E.B. North, in his brief report to brigade on 30 August ascribed failure of the raid to insufficient darkness (why then did the raid not start much earlier?) and to Busk being distracted from his objective. This report went to division, the brigade commander adding that a fresh recce would be made that night and the OC Raid had been ordered to prepare to raid the same objective in the next few days. On receipt of this the divisional commander, C.J. Deverell, forwarded the report to IV Corps having summarized the affair as unsatisfactory:

> The whole raiding party should not have been diverted from its purpose and the action against the enemy patrol lacked vigour. The OC … failed from lack of experience and training, and will profit from the experience gained. I am of the opinion that the training and preparation for the raid by the OC … lacked thoroughness, and was primarily responsible for the slowness and lack of vigorous action displayed.

On 31 August IV Corps was advised that Captain Busk had raided the same objective, this time with vigour, the raid led "in a soldierly manner well backed up by all ranks of the party." In passing the report up to Third Army, the Corps commander added that Captain Busk energetically conducted the repeat performance.[101]

Lack of control was another shortcoming that could not be countenanced. A raid in November 1917 by three officers and 60 ORs of 4th Royal Berkshires drew considerable unfavourable comment from the brigade commander who concluded that in getting too involved in the fighting the "younger officers did not keep a tight enough hand on the men." In short, rather than directing operations they were fighting. The underlying problem, he thought, really stemmed from raid organization, the parties being too big for a night raid. But this comment does not square with the Operation Order for the raid which shows the largest party as only 14 strong. Corps noted only that the smaller the party the easier the control, which is true, of course, but smaller parties on entering trenches could find themselves easily overwhelmed.[102]

Finally, much earlier in this chapter the relationship between wire and recce was stressed. At this juncture, the point to reiterate is that failure of a raid due to missed wire usually drew ire! This, Second Lieutenant A.M. Brown and 25 ORs of 15th Highland Light Infantry (14th Brigade, 32nd British Division), learned in mid-1918. It is more accurate to say attempted raid for according to the War Diaries "they encountered an unknown belt of wire so could not proceed as they would be late for the artillery barrage lifting." The brigade report (only one page in manuscript in the War Diary of 14th Brigade) of the battalion being hung up "in unlocated" wire drew this response from the GSO1:

101 TNA: WO 95/1379: 3rd Division General Staff.

102 TNA: WO 95/3065: 61st Division General Staff, brigade and battalion reports, Memorandum XVII Corps to Third Army.

> I am directed to inform you that the Divisional Commander considers that the explanation offered as to the failure of the Officer in charge of the raid to carry it out, indicates faulty previous recce. The Divisional commander wishes to be informed of the name of the officer in charge and of the names of any other officers concerned in the failure … He further wishes for a detailed report as to the circumstances which led to the raid not being carried out.

One can imagine the utter gloom that burdened Brown. No detailed report, or any report at all, is in the War Diaries of the division, brigade or battalion. Perhaps this was a case of enough said! Or perhaps it was recognized that while the raid had failed, no casualties had been suffered.[103]

On occasion, a raid might fail because whatever can go wrong did. In short, fiasco! A raid in November 1916 by two parties of the 12th Royal Fusiliers, 24th British Division, suffered this fate. First, the Bangalore that was to gap wire for the left party was not placed because the correct position for it could not be found. Second, the left party lost direction and on trying to find their proper position ended up in front of the Bangalore party, who thinking them enemy, opened fire, thereby bringing on a bombing fight. No casualties occurred during this friendly on friendly. Owing to all this, the left party returned to battalion trenches. The right party, their Bangalore correctly placed, then found thick new wire that had not been cut. As they tried to get through it the enemy, now clearly on the alert, opened heavy fire. During the firefight one of the supporting Stokes dropped several bombs on the right party, scattering the men and causing several casualties. Under these circumstances, this party also withdrew, but under an NCO, the officer having been killed by the errant Stokes bombs.[104] All this comes nowhere close to " the forty million reasons for failure" in Kipling's "The Lesson," but such a litany of woe wore hard on everyone. However, the key had to be learn the lessons![105] Often failure meant having another crack at it soon in circumstances perhaps less propitious for success. While all participants in a raid that failed might be looked at askance, the focus of discontent was usually the officer who had led the raid, or who had planned it or both. The questions arise, then, regarding who planned raids and how did they go about it. These questions and the answers are the subject of the next chapter.

103 TNA: WO 95/2393: 3rd Division General Staff; TNA: WO 95/1379: 14th Brigade; and TNA: WO 95/2393: 15th Highland Light Infantry.

104 TNA: WO 95/2208: 24th Division General Staff.

105 Rudyard Kipling, 'The Lesson', in Thomas Pinney (ed.), *The Cambridge Edition of the Poems of Rudyard Kipling Volume I Collected Poems I* (Cambridge: Cambridge University Press, 2013), p. 550.

6

The Plan's the Thing

> 'He's a cheery old card,' grunted Harry to Jack …
> But he did for both by his plan of attack.
> Siegfried Sassoon

This did not apply to every attack, nor was it true of every raid, but, certainly, a bad plan for either greatly reduced the chances of success. As this present study has already shown, raids were sometimes launched for bad reasons, and sometimes neither preparation nor plan were what they should have been. Such failings "did for" many men. A bad plan, while it did not always spell failure, did increase the level of anxiety, damaged credibility of planner and commanders and caused needless casualties. Worth noting, since most raids were night enterprises, is what Field Marshal Wavell, who served with the Black Watch during the Great War, had to say about night operations: they must not be "enterprised nor taken in hand, unadvisedly, lightly or wantonly … but reverently, discreetly, advisedly, soberly."[1] A current British Army adage puts this less grandly, but in more memorable fashion: "Proper Planning and Preparation Prevents Piss Poor Performance." Such comment applies to any operation.

The aim of this chapter is threefold. First, it examines the general and consistent principles that governed raiding and the elements involved in planning a raid, and, second, it details who planned raids and how they crafted plans. Finally, it examines the essentials of Military Writing and Staff Duties associated with raids and the fundamentals of planning from concept through Appreciation to plan and translation into Operation Order and/or Instruction and Preliminary and Supplementary Instructions.

The plan being the thing we can start by realizing that the meaning and characteristics of plans and planning at the time differ little from today's concepts. A plan, according to the *Concise Oxford Dictionary,* is a scheme of intended proceedings, a way of proceeding, as in a campaign. It is curious, given the fact that everything in the Army, even the routine and repeatedly performed operation of relief in the line, was carefully planned, monitored and validated, but there is not an abundance of studies on planning itself during the Great War. Contemporary manuals said little about planning and nothing about how an Appreciation (the capital letter

1 Field Marshal Earl Wavell, *Soldiers and Soldiering or Epithets of War* (London: Jonathan Cape, 1953), p. 159.

is deliberate and warranted given the importance of this document) ended in plan and how plan became order. Perhaps this is because planning is neither simple nor easy, aspects that in themselves perhaps discourage more study. While plans for major and minor operations differ they are alike in that both will encounter the enemy who has plans of his own and the ability and means to deny and defeat. It is uncertainty and the other frictions of war that so complicate planning. Those who planned the early raids were likely to lead them and this being so, the penalty for poor planning was often paid directly and immediately: on your head be it! But failure was not always due to just a poor plan.

At first sight, it may seem absurd to speak in the same breath about the Principles of War and minor enterprises such as raids, but the principles apply just as much, the difference being in scale. In the collection of this present historian is a copy of the *Manual of Military Law* (1917 reprint) whose inner covers were used by a Subaltern lacking paper to write down the Principles of War presented in a lecture at a training school: "maintenance of the objective, offensive action, surprise, concentration of force, economy of force, security, mobility and co-operation." These were unchanged until 1935 when "Object or Aim" replaced the first. After the Second World War economy of force and co-operation were dropped, maintenance of morale and administration were added and mobility became flexibility. Other changes have followed. While we can accept the *Concise Oxford Dictionary* definition of principle as "fundamental truth as basis of reasoning" or as "general law as a guide to action" one senior officer, a veteran of the Great War, rightly pointed out that offensive action seems method rather than principle and flexibility may simply be a characteristic rather than a principle. No list can please all, but whatever the range of opinion there is obvious similarity. This also applies to the principles or essentials involved in raiding, this being evident in the manuals and in the words of participants during and after the war.[2]

SS 107 Notes on Minor Enterprises, the manual on raiding, presented in March 1916 what GHQ called "General Principles" or essentials upon which success depended. These could not always be adhered to. Of a list of 10, some are really more method than principle, but let us accept them as principle, as did officers of the time. They, no doubt, and us, preferably, do not wish to engage in academic argument as to whether or not this or that is principle or method. Given the nature and circumstances of raiding, the manual calls the factor of surprise the "most important in raiding." Secrecy, which equates to security, also makes the list of 10. Three other essentials on the *SS 107* list – thorough planning, ample time to prepare and pre-established dominance of no man's land – were joined by two cautions: do not persevere if the enemy is alert and prepared and do not separate parties and attack at different points. These cautions clearly relate to two of the Principles of War listed above. The word "objective" appears three times in *SS 107* which describes success as dependant on careful selection and recce of the objective, which must be limited and definite, its nature and extent determining the size of the raiding force.

Some raiding parties included specialists and were organized and equipped for specific objectives beyond the usual kill, capture and destroy. A case in point was a raid by the 9th Highland Light Infantry on 27/28 June 1916. Because the objective included two suspected mineshafts,

2 Macklin, *An Introduction to the Study of the Principles of War*, pp. 6-7; Kultus Nanich [Colonel W.W. Murray], 'Raids'.

elements of 212th Field Company RE and 251st Tunnelling Company RE joined the four officers and 146 ORs of the 9th. In addition to engineer explosives, the raiders carried over 600 bombs and numerous electric torches. The men of the tunnelling company destroyed the mine-shaft galleries while the field engineers using specially prepared charges completely blocked trenches that enemy reinforcements might use to enter the objective area. The sappers also monitored bombing of dug-outs in order to prevent indiscriminate bombing, a precaution that resulted in more prisoners, 61 according to the history of the division (33rd British Division), but 47 according to the battalion War Diary. The battalion suffered only three casualties during the raid. In an effort to mislead the enemy, a successful one as it proved, several identical artillery bombardments along the line and including the objective area were fired during the three nights before the raid, and a single bombardment of the objective area early on the morning of Zero day with the hope that a repair party would be repairing the line there at the time of the assault. This is exactly what transpired. All in all, this highly successful raid was very well planned and executed. Captain A.C. Frame, OC Raid, received the DSO for the night's work.[3]

In August Canadian Corps Intelligence Staff, lecturing on raiding at the Corps Officers School, focussed on "General Principles," methodology of preparation, equipment, artillery/infantry co-operation and the assault phase of a raid, concluding with an assessment of Canadian raids between 30 June and 18 August as to the "Features Contributing to Success or Failure" and raid results. Of the 13 raids during the period two failed, in one case because of uncut wire, and in the other because of enemy "readiness." It is striking how frequently the words surprise and boldness appear as reasons for success of the other 11. In one case, recce each night for a full week and a well-designed plan accounted for success. The lecture also offered seven essentials for success, the first being the attainment by patrols of dominance of no man's land. Patrolling also built confidence, accustomed men to enemy habits and familiarized them with the ground. Second, surprise required originality, boldness and imagination on the part of planners and raiders. Third, an incentive to this, as a matter of principle, was to leave units "as much as possible to work out details and the more latitude given the better." Fourth, secrecy while an obvious and critical requirement, had been violated repeatedly. Another general principle in the Canadian Corps at that time stipulated that raids consisting of 20 or more men should, as a rule, be supported by artillery and trench mortars. Sixth, success depended on preparation, training and attention to detail. For big raids, 50 or more men, Corps HQ recommended that a week be allowed for preparation. Finally, as *SS 107* stated, an objective had to be limited and definite, its size matching the purposes of the raid and the force to be used. Contrary to what *SS 107* had not recommended – "attacks by separate parties at different points" – the lecture concluded that "Two objectives simultaneously attacked, while difficult in co-operation, have a great moral effect … and are an advantage if far enough apart to be independent." The lecturer admitted that failure or delay in one could adversely affect the other, but he considered that careful training made the risk negligible. As an example, he referred to the Spanbroekmolen raid in January 1916 where two raids had gone in 900 yards apart. The key had been "particular training" to ensure success.[4]

3 Hutchison, *Thirty-Third Division*, pp. 9-10; TNA: WO 95/2405: 100th Brigade, report on raid.
4 LAC, MG30E61 (Mitchell Papers), Volume 16, Western Front Orders and Instructions 1916-1918, 'Trench Raids Based Upon Raids Done by Canadian Corps (A Lecture to the Corps Officers'

In February 1918 *Notes for Commanding Officers* listed five principles that when followed would spell success: simplicity, punctuality, determination, fire support and execution by complete tactical units. The BM of 168th Brigade, 56th British Division, attributed success of a raid on 18 February 1917 to the scheme's simplicity: "no complicated Operation Order which [depended] on a number of prearranged things happening." He thought, though, that once the objective was cleared of enemy the OC Raid rather that giving the withdrawal signal "should have considered action [to] take to further success by co-operating elsewhere." Had he done so the prisoner haul would have been larger. In other words, more initiative should have been shown.[5] These five principles were not new to raiders and planners. The last had also been enunciated in February 1917: "The platoon should constitute a unit for fighting and training, and should consist of a combination of all the weapons with which the infantry is now armed." A week later GHQ pronounced that contrary to *Infantry Training (4-Company Organization.) 1914* it had become necessary to lay down a "normal formation" for the attack, a step the 1914 manual had considered not only impossible, but undesirable. By April *SS 143, SS 135* and *WO 3995 The Normal Formation for the Attack* had made the platoon the "unit of assault." A "normal formation" was also widely implemented in the BEF for trench raiding. Composition of these trench raid "units" varied depending on local circumstances. Two variants are discussed and illustrated in Chapter 8.

In the experience of Colonel W.W. Murray, 2nd Canadian Battalion, only three principles were "inherently essential" in raiding. Surprise was indispensable since a raid involved attack by an inferior force upon an entrenched and presumably a superior force. Without surprise a prepared enemy would prevail. The second essential, information, occurred before surprise. Recce gave the raiders a reasonable knowledge of the ground and some idea of enemy strength and dispositions. *FSR* had stressed in 1914 the importance of recce and cautioned that units should not be committed until a personal survey of the ground could be made. Clearly, experience had shown that commanders could seldom personally reconnoitre, but the overall thrust said thorough recce spelled success. Third, and finally, having accumulated knowledge and effected surprise, speed and force in a rush would overwhelm the enemy and create confusion; in other words, "utmost audacity, cast caution to the winds, and leave the result to fortune." In illustration of these essentials in action Murray described the raid by 14th and 16th Canadian Battalions near Gavrelle on 27/28 April 1918, a raid also commented upon at some length by the historians of both battalions. Hugh Urquhart, a former officer of the 16th and then CO of another battalion, called Gavrelle the most successful raid by the battalion in the battalion's history: "certainly if thorough planning … makes for success, it deserved to be so." Equally thorough recce commenced during each of the three nights before the raid, participants including the nine officers who would lead the raid, the issue to all section leaders of a sketch map of the objective, and the day before the raid all NCOs and one-third of the men were taken to the assembly area where they had the objectives pointed out to them. Thoroughness certainly paid off since during the two nights before Zero day recce discovered the enemy hard at work digging

School)', 20 August 1916; Broad, 'The Development of Artillery Tactics, 1914-1918', *Journal of the Royal Artillery*, 49 (October 1922), pp. 66-67; *SS 107 Notes on Minor Enterprises.*

5 *Notes for Commanding Officers* (1918), Chapter IX, Part IV; Spartacus, 'Simplicity,' p. 48; TNA: WO 95/2951: 168th Brigade, raid report, 18 February 1917. Spartacus warns that the opposite of simple is complex, that of easy is difficult.

a new outpost line. Consequently, the original objectives, the enemy front and support lines, were instead the newly dug ljne and the front line. At zero both were easily entered, wire being insignificant, and 28 prisoners, including one officer, were put in the bag. Of the nine officers and 142 ORs who participated, one officer and four ORs were killed and two officers and 15 ORs wounded. So efficiently was the raid done, wrote Urquhart, that "the enemy did not even send up an SOS." Captain J.A. Scroggie, OC Raid, received a Bar to his MC and three other MCs were awarded.[6]

The 14th Battalion's officers and men did equally well, the raiding parties once in the enemy trenches worked outwards in two directions, systematically clearing out defenders as they went. The CO of the 14th, Lieutenant-Colonel Dick Worrall, reported that each of the officers on the raid killed at least one man. Lieutenant G.B. McKean (see Plate) received special mention. When he and his party encountered a strongly defended block they were rebuffed several times. Time passing by very quickly, McKean

> set the example by making a flying dive over the block, landing head on and striking the stomach of a Hun. The Hun was considerably startled – Lieutenant McKean's revolver was in his hand ready for use as he dived – exit Hun. The rest of the group then tumbled over … Too much credit cannot be said of the excellent leadership and personal courage of Lieut. McKean.

During the raid the 14th took 26 prisoners at a cost of two men killed and 11 wounded. Three MCs were awarded. McKean won the VC. Fetherstonhaugh, the historian of the 14th, provides a fine detailed account of the raid including in one paragraph this graphic summation of what raiding really entailed:

> Something in the secrecy of the occasion, in the tense quality of the silence, and in the diablerie of the black-faced figures who, with black bayonets fixed, moved in obedience to low-spoken commands, stirred the imagination of observers, who found themselves shivering with excitement, and with a strange sensation, nameless, yet akin to fear. Something ghastly was to happen; men alive at the moment would not see dawn; some would die in dugouts far below the ground; there would be shouts, cries, groans; the crack of rifles, the blinding flash of high explosive; the courage, the ferocity, the savagery, the fierce joy, the madness, of those hours when humans exterminate their kind.[7]

Earlier it was noted that some sources distinguished method from principle, the former being, so to speak, of a lower order than the latter. Having defined the objective the planners then turned to determining the method to be employed in attaining it. Here it was necessary to identify any factors or considerations that affected attainment, a factor being simply a circumstance that could contribute to or influence the result. The plan had to draw from each factor any

6 Murray [Kultus Nanich], 'Raids'. pp. 336-40; Urquhart. *16th Battalion,* pp. 258-60; LAC, 16th Battalion, War Diary, April 1918, Appendix, Operation Order 17 and report by CO.

7 LAC, 14th Battalion War Diary; Arthur Bishop, *Our Bravest and Our Best: The Stories of Canada's Victoria Cross Winners* (Toronto: McGraw-Hill Ryerson, 1995), pp. 86-87; Fetherstonhaugh, *14th Battalion,* pp. 203-209.

deductions bearing upon attainment of the objective. Here the key was the question "So what?" The good planner kept asking it until he could no longer come up with an answer, at which point he could be satisfied that he had derived every possible deduction.[8]

Having now mentioned the word "objective" several times, and while it is a simple enough word, when placed near "object" confusion seems to spring up just as it did during those long-ago days on the Western Front. However, the dictionary meanings of the two words seem clear enough: object, "thing aimed at, end purpose;" objective, "point aimed at." Major W.K.M. Leader, MC, the author of a post-war study of Military Writing, described object as the "ultimate aim" and objective as "the means toward attainment of that aim." There is also a topographical aspect inherent in the word "point." *SS 107 Notes on Minor Enterprises,* in showing that objective was physical location, described the relevant aspects of objective in the specific sequence described earlier in this chapter: successful raids were the result of careful selection and recce of the objective, of ensuring that an objective was definite and limited and that its nature and extent determined the size of the raiding force. Other questions then came up: what is the best approach to the objective, is there a covered approach; is the proposed objective so located that the enemy can neither support it or reinforce it; and does the objective sit, perhaps, between two posts or along a tactical boundary. Solid answers denote solid recce. An instruction to battalion commanders in late 1917 from William Griesbach (GOC 1st Canadian Brigade) sets out his sequence:

> In my opinion the first step ... is to decide upon the magnitude of the raid. The second step is to secure a leader who will take full charge ... keeping his Commanding Officer informed of his plans. The third step is to decide upon the place where the raid shall be made. A keen, energetic officer who has not yet secured distinction is sometimes preferable for this work.

For now suffice it to say that this sequence is the opposite of the sequence in *SS 107,* which begins with the selection of the objective. This sequence is compared against other versions later in this chapter.[9]

Ground was usually the decisive consideration in the selection of an objective and in getting at that objective. Here recce was fundamental; for example, in November 1917 two German raiding parties, 60 men in all, broke in between two posts of the 6th King's Shropshire Light Infantry and made off with a prisoner. And in February 1918 German raiders chose their objective with care "between two posts." Their choice would have left them undetected had not the

8 Russenholt, *Six Thousand Canadian Men,* p. 47; Major O.G. Body, *Notes on Appreciations, Instructions, Operation Orders and Message Writing* (London: Hugh Rees Ltd., 1930), p. 1.

9 *SS 107 Notes on Minor Enterprises,* 'General Principles' March 1916; Major W.K.M. Leader, *An Elementary Study of Appreciations, Orders and Messages* (London: Sifton, Praed & Co. Ltd., 1936), p. 4. Leader, a Canadian, won the MC while with the Duke of Cornwall's Light Infantry. He remained in the British Army after the war. Before the war he had been an employee of the Canadian Bank of Commerce in Toronto. LAC, MG30E 61 (Mitchell Papers), Volume 16. In a lecture in August 1916 at the Canadian Corps Officer's School a guide to determining the force required said the proportion of men to a front attacked or raided should be about 25 men to 40-50 yards, or roughly one man every two yards of front. LAC, RG9IIIC3, Volume 4017, Folder 35, File 18, Griesbach to battalions, 4 December 1917.

Welsh Guards company commander on his rounds happened to be passing their entry point precisely at the time they were about to enter the trench. On looking over the parapet, he heard movement and blazed away with his revolver at the sound. At the time, an enemy raid had "every chance of success" since the battalion was holding 2,000 yards of front with only three companies.[10] Recce and the taking of prisoners could also identify another prime location at which to raid, specifically along a boundary, be it inter-company, battalion, brigade or division. The problem with boundaries is that without close co-ordination they may become orphan territory, each commander thinking the neighbour has it in hand. A case in point occurred near Hill 60 in July 1916 when raiders entered Canadian trenches at the boundary between two battalions of 3rd Brigade. No men of the 16th Battalion being in position to stop the raiders the 13th remained unaware of the intrusion until it was attacked. What brought this about was the decision by the OC of the listening posts of the right company of the 16th Battalion to withdraw the men manning the posts into a sap where they could avoid enemy mortar fire, which was exactly what the enemy had counted on. The OC of the posts of the left company of the 13th Battalion also withdrew most of his men. This left the gate open. Canadian casualties included one officer and 10 ORs killed, 29 ORs wounded and one missing, presumed captured. Arthur Currie, then GOC 1st Canadian Division, was furious, telling the brigade commander, George Tuxford:

> In withdrawing all his posts [the officer of the 16th] showed a lack of tactical knowledge … Had he paid sufficient attention to the lessons of Trench Warfare … he would have expected a raid or at least made arrangements to deal with a raid … The whole affair is a serious reflection on the training and discipline of this Battalion … and a lack of appreciation of the responsibility of officers, which I will not tolerate.

Unappeased with Tuxford's explanation, Currie ordered all concerned to be at his HQ two days hence. No doubt strong language ensued, Currie well known for blunt, forceful and colourful language. He may well have reminded all present of the wisdom that says: "Do your duty and you have nothing to fear; just be damned sure you know what your duty is." Currie knew, however, that mistakes were inevitable. Still, the word got around and a good bet would be to say that brigade commanders, certainly in 1st Division, placed increased emphasis on being prepared.[11] Trench junctions, such as where CTs joined main trenches, presented other good targets. The narrow CTs, which were not designed to fight from, could be easily blocked to prevent or delay enemy reinforcements coming forward to counter-attack. If a raid coincided with a relief in the line, as Chapter 2 related, then so much the better for the raiders.

But to return to object and objective Major H.G. Eady, writing a decade before Major Leader, having concluded that the difference between the two was "not always clearly understood," demonstrated the difference with the story of the "proverbial chicken [whose] object is to cross the road; its objective [being] the other side." Put another way, to him the object (or purpose)

10 Dudley Ward, *Welsh Guards,* p. 197; TNA: WO 95/2097: 20th Division General Staff.

11 LAC, RG9IIIC1, Volume 3842, Folder 43, File 6, Currie to 3rd Brigade and to Canadian Corps, 19 July 1916; 3rd Brigade War Diary, July 1916. The CO of the 16th at the time was Lieutenant-Colonel J.E. Leckie, whose ideas about leadership did not please Currie; see MG30E100 (Currie Papers), Volume 15, Folder 43, and RG9IIIC3, Volume 4074, Folder 2, File 6, 26 October 1916 for the reaction of the brigadiers.

is that which must be attained, while objective is the method of attaining the object.[12] A few examples from war-time orders and reports illustrate the varying degree of familiarity with proper usage of these two words. In June 1916 10th Royal Fusiliers (37th British Division) reporting on a raid on the 5th, stated the object of the raid as "to make a raid," this hardly an object in that it does not say what had to be attained. Not until page three of the report would the recipient have known the specific object or purpose of the raid which was to identify the enemy opposite the 10th. The raid report by the OC Raid, Second Lieutenant P.M. Rees, is otherwise clear and comprehensive, skillfully written by an obviously well-educated Subaltern. Under the heading "Selection of Point of Entry" Rees indicated precisely why the objective had been chosen. First, the distance to it was the shortest in that part of the line. Second, it could not be adequately defended by the enemy. Third, it had not been previously raided, a fact that might enable surprise. Of the two raiding parties that entered the enemy trench only one encountered enemy. These, it was thought, were all killed, but because the party, led by an NCO, did not search the dead, no identifications were secured. Nothing had been said in the briefing of this party about securing identifications. According to the plan only the other party, which encountered no enemy, received instructions to collect "papers, badges" for identification purposes. One can surmise that had an officer rather than an NCO led the party then the enemy dead would have been searched. Despite failure to achieve the object, the CO of the 10th Battalion was "pleased" since the raid had "been carefully prepared." Rees received the MC.[13]

Earlier that year 2nd Leinsters' plan for a raid listed objectives for each of the two parties in the raiding force, but nowhere is there a statement of the object of the raid. While it can be surmised from the report this does not suffice. We only learn what the object was from a postwar account by the OC Raid. This very basic flaw did mar a good number of orders initially, but generally thereafter most Operation Orders did present the object and objectives clearly. Lieutenant-Colonel J.C.R. King, CO 13th London Regiment, for example, carefully defined a three-part object – take prisoners, secure identifications and destroy machine-gun emplacements – and stated four precise objectives that clearly enunciate how the raiders were to attain the objects of the raid. Likewise, Lieutenant-Colonel R.M. Husey, CO 1st London Rifle Brigade, in an Operation Order for a raid in February 1917, sets out objects and objectives clearly, but, unfortunately, his order also includes numerous conditionals such as "if possible," which brings to mind Corinthians: "If the trumpet give an uncertain sound, who will prepare himself to the battle?" In contrast, that same month 1st Royal Berkshires displayed great care in an Operation Order as to the object of a raid; no conditionals, just an imperative statement of what had to be achieved.[14]

Ambiguity is often apparent in the Military Writing of the time, quite contrary to the essentials of this particular discipline, which are clarity, accuracy and brevity in the crafting of written staff work pertaining to deployments and operations. That clear, accurate and brief orders could

12 Major H.G. Eady, MC, 'On Writing Appreciations', *RUSI Journal,* 484 (November 1926), p. 684.

13 The 10th, which was raised in the City of London, became known as the "Stockbrokers." The battalion arrived in France in July 1915 and made its first raid in June 1916 (see also TNA: WO 95/2532) and Julian Sykes, 'A Trench Raid Near Arras. June 1916'. *Gun Fire,* 6, pp. 42-50.

14 Hitchcock, *"Stand To,"* pp. 232-35; TNA: WO 95/2955: 13th London Regiment, Operation Order 44, 14 February; TNA: WO 95/2961: 1st London Rifle Brigade, Operation Order, 16 February; Wyrall, *Second Division,* Volume II, pp. 361-62.

not be achieved at once should not surprise given the necessity to raise and field many divisions consisting of non-Regular troops: New Army, Territorials and Dominion. Military Writing was part and parcel of what is now loosely described as Staff Duties. This discipline, for that is what it is (and was), employs a methodology, language and procedure that strives for standardized format, conventions and composition. Good written orders do not contain conditionals such as "if possible, it is believed, it is hoped, perhaps, possibly, if practical, if thought feasible" and other examples from actual orders and instructions. A gem in one order declared: "It will perhaps be possible." A striking surfeit of such perverse and dangerous language occurs in the Operation Order of 10th Canadian Brigade for its attack on Regina Trench on the Somme on 23 October 1916. A number of the conditionals just listed appear in that order. True, by definition this was not a raid, but this brigade order could serve well as a warning to the unwary. Even worse, as E.S. Russenholt emphasized, lay in how the order "contrary to recognized principles of tactical procedure [contained] a series of alternative proposals – instead of communicating a single, definite plan." Failure to state the object clearly made the Appreciation "involved, and [left] the decision [the plan] shrouded in doubt." It should be remembered that 4th Canadian Division's three brigades (10th, 11th and 12th) did not reach France until August and only arrived at the front on 10 October.[15]

These fundamentals of Military Writing had to be absorbed rapidly. In a battalion ordered to raid the OC Raid and his officers were obviously intimately involved in planning, but so, too, the CO for he had responsibility for everything that happened in his battalion. While he had no staff officers his Adjutant functioned as such and as disciplinarian and as anything else the CO decided upon. Before long Adjutants would have much more than just a passing interest in raids. Brigade commanders, on the other hand, had proper Staff Officers in the persons of the BM and his Staff Captain assistant. In Canadian brigades the BM had two Staff Captains to assist him. Whether they were with British or Canadian brigades these officers became closely involved to the extent demanded by their GOC and by the need to co-ordinate operations including raids. In British divisions the officers responsible for operations included the General Staff Officer Grade 1 (GSO1) assisted by a GSO2 and a GSO3 (General Staff Officer 3rd Grade). In Canadian divisions the GSO1 had two of each to assist him. While divisional staff were generally and initially less involved than brigade staff they were attentive, nevertheless, to raiding to the extent their commanders were. Corps staff, too, were in the loop since some raids required support that only corps or above could provide. The interest aroused by rendering such assistance could perk up dramatically should the results of a raid be disappointing or downright disastrous.

A crucial step in planning, and the focus of Major Leader's book, was the "Appreciation," a document, or time not permitting, a train of thought whereby a plan resulted and had then to be translated into orders. In his very useful article Major H.G. Eady defined an Appreciation as "a logical process of thought by which one arrives at a definite decision after considering the various factors which could possibly affect that decision." Today's version, shorter but not strikingly different, calls an Appreciation "an orderly sequence of reasoning leading logically to the best solution to a problem." More simply, Leader just said an Appreciation was "taking stock of

15 Russenholt, *Six Thousand Canadian Men*, p. 47; Body, *Notes on Appreciations*, pp. 1-2; Nicholson, *Canadian Expeditionary Force*, pp. 134, 187. It had become the norm that the object be in a separate paragraph to highlight it and assist in clarity.

the situation and deciding what to do." This everyone does in their daily lives; no mystery about it.[16] Whichever definition one likes best, the most critical part of an Appreciation is the statement of the object or aim for if it is not carefully defined then the writer will almost certainly go off on a tangent. It must be a clear statement of the problem to be solved, the question to which the plan will provide the answer. If the object is mis-stated then "the whole of the Appreciation is worthless." Whether or not 10th Canadian Brigade prepared an Appreciation for its attack on Regina Trench cannot be definitely stated, but one must assume so. If one was, it is not in the relevant War Diaries, nor is one mentioned. Given the conditionals in the Operation Order, and the absence of a "single, definite plan," one must conclude that if an Appreciation was done, it, too, lacked a clear statement of the object.[17]

An Appreciation could be a fairly lengthy and "formal" document, but it could also be a brief consideration of just aim and ground: what must be done, where, when and how. During the early days of raiding in the Great War a written Appreciation was rare indeed, but this is not to say that those who planned the early raids did not think hard about the task at hand. The plan that stemmed from the Appreciation was what the writer saw as the best solution to the problem posed by his superiors. Appreciations came to be expected; for example, in mid-1917 GOC 1st Canadian Brigade (William Griesbach) demanded from his COs "by the morning of the 9th instant [9 February] a memo on raids, giving ideas as to size … and point of attack with appreciation of the situation."[18] Woe betide he who responded with the cardinal military sin known as "Situating the Appreciation," the commission of which entailed making a plan and then twisting the facts to make them seem reasonable; in short, mustering argument to fit a pre-conceived notion. It is not uncommon to find examples of so "situating" in academic dissertations, one memorable case being this statement of intent "Napoleon was a good tactician." Commencing with a conclusion, which is pre-conceived notion, is not a signal one should send; better surely to ask "Was Napoleon a good tactician?" This formulation makes it clear that courses open must be considered and compared. The sixth of the "good rules" of Charles I – "make no comparisons" – was not sound advice, neither for Appreciations nor for raids. Perhaps he later reflected ruefully upon his rule six.

These considerations came into play during what became known as battle planning or battle procedure, which might be described as all of the activities necessary in planning, preparing and delivering orders and the readying of men and material for operations. Early notice to subordinate commanders of impending operations became essential so they would have time for their battle planning. Early notice also enabled concurrent activity that made the best use of time. Detailed plans, sometimes with good reason, have often been sneered at; for example, Lord Eythin, a Royalist advisor during the English Civil War, pointed out to Prince Rupert before Marston Moor, "By God, Sir, it is very fine in the paper, but there is no such thing in the field." Less eloquently, Will Bird, Private, 42nd Canadian Battalion, thought that a raid should never

16 Eady, 'On Writing Appreciations', p. 684; *Canadian Army Manual of Training, CAMT 1-36. Staff Procedures Volume 3 Staff Duties in the Field* (Ottawa: Army Headquarters, 1963), p. 511; Leader, *An Elementary Study*, p. 2. A fairly recent development was the replacement of "Appreciation" by "Estimate." Readers can ponder the nuances of such a change for themselves.

17 *Ibid.*, p. 4; Body, *Notes on Appreciations*, pp. 4-5;

18 LAC, 47th Canadian Battalion War Diary, 16 September 1916; MG30E15 (Griesbach Papers), Volume 3, File 16A, 'Book of Wisdom', Griesbach to battalion commanders, 7 February 1917.

be planned on paper, and while some might "look good on paper, all did not go as expected," not an unreasonable remark in itself, and a point worth making, although Moltke made it first and made it better: "No plan survives contact with the enemy." Quite so. One must be careful with Bird, however, since his hostility toward and contempt for all officers colours his writing and, second, a good many comments on plans, including his, are those of ORs who were not called upon to plan raids. Also, Napoleon wrote that "Nothing succeeds in war except in consequence of a well-prepared plan." Equally quite so, raiding no exception. But certainly early written orders for raids did not fill much space: in one instance on the Somme the Operation Order for a raid consisted of three pages (one side only) of a Field Notebook.[19]

As raids became larger and more complex plans grew apace. In late 1916 an Operation Order for a raid by 47th Canadian Battalion filled 23 Field Notebook pages. By early 1917 James Dunn, Medical Officer of 2nd Royal Welsh Fusiliers, commenting on a brigade Operation Order for a raid, sarcastically described it as a "masterpiece" containing "dozens of manuscript changes," including many inaccurate map co-ordinates, this creating a chill in those who were to execute the order. Orders with flaws such as this were an easy way to lose the confidence of subordinates. Meticulous attention to detail, and double checking, were prerequisites of a good order. The Operation Order given to the 2nd was followed by an amended version, little or no better, leaving the recipients thinking "There are times when foolscap is fitting, and ironic mirth is a safety valve." Dunn also dubbed the Operation Order by the other participating battalion a "curiosity." In the event, the raid was cancelled, ending "a three week's run of this farce."[20]

He who makes a plan must ask himself before he issues it "Is this plan in sufficient detail for the recipient to be able to write orders from it?" At a bare minimum a statement of what must be done is necessary and so, too, are the most important aspects of how the plan is to be executed. "Necessary" is the key. A battalion commander, for example, would not have been justified, nor would he now, in simply stating in an attack plan "two companies up" and leave his Adjutant the responsibility of deciding which two companies. Therefore, inevitably, the plan must include a certain amount of detail. Consequently, the real question the planner must ask himself is this: "Does this plan contain all the information necessary to enable orders to be written by the recipient without further reference to me?" Serious faults in a plan are not being definite enough and including too much detail, the latter requiring the walking of a fine line.

From an Appreciation came plan which was then translated into orders. Each order as received had to be translated into an order for the next lower level of command. The process of translation, while it has been refined and some terminology differs, has remained much the same, meaning that the modern reader can readily comprehend the process as it was. On 2 January 1917 Field Marshal Sir Douglas Haig could say to General Sir Henry Horne, GOC First Army, "Horne, take Vimy Ridge." His plan was barely two pages long. Horne, turning to the GOC the Canadian Corps (one of three Corps in First Army), said "Byng, take Vimy

19 Brigadier Peter Young, *Marston Moor 1644: The Campaign and the Battle* (Kineton: The Roundwood Press, 1970), p. 93; Wavell, *Soldiers and Soldiering*, p. 141; Bird, *Ghosts Have Warm Hands*), p. 95. A Field Notebook's pages measured 4.5 by 6.5 inches. The modern Canadian Army version, the Field Message Book, is virtually identical to the Great War version.

20 Dunn, *The War the Infantry Knew*, pp. 297-99.

Ridge." Horne's plan also fills less that two pages. His order is even shorter.[21] From there down plans get longer, being that the lower the level of command the more detailed the plan becomes. At the top the explanation is an open hand sweeping over a large-scale map. As the command level lowers open hand becomes pointed finger on a smaller-scale map. At the bottom of the chain, though, the order is simple: the platoon commander blows his whistle and leads his men over the top. But no whistles when a raid began. It was in the middle levels of command where numerous complications arose.

Early in the war he who wrote orders and sought guidance had only *FSR* at hand. It stipulated that all operations required an Operation Order consisting of a statement of the general situation of the enemy and own troops (Information), the Intention of the commander, the method to be employed, administration and communications. This manual's relevant sections (9 and 12) did not even mention Appreciation and plan. An Operation Order could be verbal or written, but if it were the former the order had to be confirmed in writing "whenever practicable" since verbal orders could be incorrectly delivered or misunderstood. *FSR* also stressed that orders had to be issued early enough to allow subordinates time to frame and deliver their orders. At lower levels it was not uncommon for time to collapse leaving lower commanders scant time for these vital activities. Section 9 offered only conventions or mechanics of writing orders, such as use of capitals, timings and map references; in short, minor military conventions. Section 12 spoke only of the necessity of Operation Orders and in general terms of their content. As late as 1917 *Notes for Commanding Officers* offered little more on writing orders, its focus being report writing. Nor did the 1917 edition contain anything on raiding. The 1918 edition did include a useful check list for raiding. An officer writing orders who had any appreciable experience had his knowledge and experience to rely upon, while the newly arrived had to trust to common sense and the advice of others while learning on the job. No written guidance on plans and preparing them was to be found in the manuals, but some guidance on orders became available in the "lessons" documents that proliferated as time wore on.

Realizing the gap in knowledge formation commanders had to state what they expected to see in Appreciations, plans and orders submitted by subordinates. To give just one example, William Griesbach, GOC 1st Canadian Brigade, issued clear instructions, his primary points being two-fold. First, he wanted orders as "clear and short as possible … they should be merely the quick march." This proved difficult to maintain since "paper" lengthened as the war did, no matter how often or how loudly the demand for brevity. Second, he desired a standardized orders format and expressed his hope

> That Brigade Orders for operations will always be in the same form and standard and that orders of Battalions will vary in form as little as possible so that the form … will become impressed upon the minds of all ranks. If this observation is complied with, then … officers

21 Captain Cyril Falls, *Military Operations France and Belgium, 1917: The German Retreat to the Hindenburg Line and the Battle of Arras* (London: Macmillan, 1940), pp. 10-12 and Appendix 6; Captain Cyril Falls, *Military Operations France and Belgium, 1917: The German Retreat to the Hindenburg Line and the Battles of Arras: Appendices* (London: Macmillan, 1940), Appendices 10-12, 27: Haig's plan for Army commanders was in the form of GHQ Letter 2 January 1917; Appendix 11, pp. 23-25, Plan of Operations First Army; Appendix 27, pp. 92-93, First Army Order No. 101, 26 March. Appendix 12, pp, 26-42, is the Canadian Corps Scheme of Operations.

> writing orders under difficulties will instinctively conform to the form and recipients … will know to look for the information … which affects them.

A bonus of standardization was how it reduced the likelihood that anything would be missed. Griesbach also stressed that when it came to the method section of an Operation Order while the paragraphs within it would vary according to circumstances, they should be set out in order of importance so that the "chief essentials are brought to mind first."[22]

Major O.G. Body in his *Notes* thought the most serious fault when crafting a plan was "wandering off into details" for this often ended in so elaborating the plan that it developed into the method paragraph of an Operation Order. Body's useful book lists several other faults, several directly relevant to raids: first, failure to realize that the order should include only as much detail as is necessary for all recipients to know; second, improper organization of command and unclear functions of the raiding parties; third, unclear intention; fourth, inadequate attention to fire planning; and, finally, over-elaborate orders.[23] The best example of the last was an order received on 30 January 1917 by a battalion of 117th Brigade of 39th British Division:

> Your Battalion is detailed to carry out a raid, strength three companies with Lewis guns, approx. 350 officers and men on the shaded area on the attached map. Please send in, in the form of an instruction, by 12 noon, February 1st, your detailed proposals as regards the following points, adding any further that occur to you. The duration of the stay in enemy trenches will be not more than 45 minutes.

The devil was in the "following points" which list every conceivable aspect of a plan for a raid and then some; for example, the CO had to include in his proposal such details as how men detailed to carry wire-cutters would carry them. Brigade's list is so long it is impossible to see what more the CO could possibly have included.[24]

A plan for a raid did not state the time for Zero, simply leaving a blank or inserting "To be Advised," thereby leaving he who had to execute the plan to come up with the time once he had done the necessary preliminaries such as recce. From the plan came the Operation Order which at that time included the sections mentioned above: Information, Intention, Method, Administration and Communications. Experience led to the plan also adhering to this sequence. Eventually, Operation Instructions were also frequently issued. These late-comers, which did not appear until early 1918, are left to later in this chapter.

Part of good planning and preparation for a raid included providing adequate rest for raiders, *SS 107* recommending that for a week before a raid the participants should be quartered together in a billet to the rear, this in Alexander McClintock's experience usually being a barn, about which he made no complaint. A week was ideal, of course, but such could not always be guaranteed. One "perk" was the "customary extra" rum before the raid. While a few men, concerned

22 LAC, MG30E15 (Griesbach Papers) 'Book of Wisdom', Volume III.

23 Body, *Notes on Appreciations,* pp. 9, 41-56; Needham, *The Solution to Tactical Problems,* p. 158, stressed that in framing an order care had to be taken that it contained everything that a subordinate commander could not arrange for himself and nothing more.

24 TNA: WO 95/2586: 117th Brigade and 39th Division General Staff.

about impairing their alertness, refused it, most took it, their dictum being take what is offered when it is offered; as McClintock put it "there were no prohibitionists in our set."[25]

Final preparations for a raid in the period immediately before Zero were simple, routine common sense, but this is not to say they were unimportant. Men had to be checked to ensure they carried no identification other than the raid identity discs which eventually came into service. Means to permit recognition of each other such as a white armband were added to uniforms, and all received the password to be used once out in no man's land. Blackened faces, beyond being camouflage, also provided a recognition feature: said Private Stephen Graham of the Guards, "if you see a white man you know at once he's not on your side.[26] Equipment of each man had also to be checked to ensure their gear did not "jangle. One "jangler" that, for a time, burdened raiders was the steel helmet, but eventually experience of how it inhibited hearing, and was a proven or potential noisemaker, saw it mostly given up in favour of soft caps such as Balaclavas.[27] What a man had to carry on a raid grew to be quite a load, be he German, British or Canadian. *Leutnant* Ernst Junger, dressed to kill for a raid in 1917, described his "readies" thus:

> I was in full array; two sandbags in front of my chest, each with four stick bombs, the left one having instantaneous, the right hand with time fuses; in the right hand pocket of my tunic I had an 08 revolver on a long cord; in my right trouser pocket a small Mauser pistol; in my left tunic pocket five egg bombs; in the left trouser pocket a phosphorescent compass and a policeman's whistle; in my belt spring hooks for pulling out the bomb pins, a dagger, and wire-cutters. There was a pocket book in my breast pocket and my home address, and in the pocket of the back of my tunic a flat flask of cherry-brandy.[28]

Change the names of the weapons and the uniform details, put Mills bombs in the sandbags or in a haversack and, more or less, you have the raiding kit of a Canadian or British officer. In one hand he might have a pistol or revolver, the other kept free to carry a well-sharpened bayonet or trench knife, a cosh or knobkerry or club of some description, or for some a cut-down Lee-Enfield with bayonet (in February 1917 2CMR described this expedient "exceptionally good for trench fighting," as had 50th British Division earlier). The revolver, the Mark VI Webley, a powerful calibre .455, could bring down and keep down any opponent. It had so proven itself in the trenches that it was also routinely issued to ORs going on raids. Many other pistols also saw active service since officers could buy and use any pistol they wished. Few chose small calibre ones since they lacked the Webley's stopping power. Robert Graves recalled another expedient in use in his battalion of the Royal Welsh Fusiliers in July 1916: "I noted that

25 *SS 107;* TNA: WO 95/2056: 19th British Division General Staff, Appendix 36, 'Some Notes on Raids', February 1918; Scott, *12th (Eastern) Division,* pp. 121-22; McClintock, *Best O'Luck,* pp. 63-64, 70-71; Wheeler, *50th Battalion,* p. 131.

26 Jon Cooksey and David Griffiths (eds.), *Harry's War: The Great War Diary of Harry Drinkwater* (St Ives: Ebury Press, 2013), p. 361; Moran, *Anatomy of Courage,* p. 145; Richards, *Old Soldiers Never Die,* p. 125; Graham, *A Private in the Guards,* p. 261.

27 Griffith, *Up to Mametz,* pp. 116-17; Paddy Griffith, *Battle Tactics of the Western Front: The British Army's Art of Attack 1916-18* (New Haven: Yale University Press, 1994), p. 61; Graham, *A Private in the Guards,* p. 261.

28 Junger, *Storm of Steel,* pp. 196-97.

for the first time since the 18th century the regiment had reverted to the pike … some of the raiders had tied butcher's knives secured with medical plaster to the ends of broomsticks. This pike, a lighter weapon than rifle and bayonet, was a useful addition to bombs and revolvers.[29]

Once all was ready it remained only to raid and then report. After every raid, successful or not, the preparation, planning, conduct and results were evaluated and lessons drawn. Each report usually concluded with what the OC Raid and his CO saw as the lessons of the raid: what had gone right and what had gone wrong and why. These reports, plus the Operation Order and other relevant documents, were routinely appended to the War Diary which existed not only for historical purposes, but for study by those tasked to plan and lead subsequent raids. Given the large number of raids 1915-1918, the cascade of Operation Orders and reports can seem after repeated examination like the steady dripping of a leaky tap, or so it must have seemed to those who wrote orders and reports on raids. Post-war, Lieutenant-Colonel A.A. Hanbury-Sparrow, who at age 25 commanded 2nd Royal Berkshire Regiment during the Third Battle of Ypres, recalled, somewhat dismissively, writing up his orders for the attack:

> The battalion's duties were so precisely defined that the task … required no more than a comprehensive knowledge of the stage to which tactics had developed. This you possessed, so as you wrote page after page of orders covering every conceivable detail, you were doing little more than assembling and winding up a clock.

A good many of the officers who wrote orders for a raid would have agreed with this summation, perhaps accepting to some degree Hanbury-Sparrow's conclusion that the

> Orders were eye-wash. Technically they were as good as they could be, but … they would have done almost equally well for an attack on any other part of the front. All that would have been needed would have been an alteration of a few names and map references … Within their narrow framework the orders, you knew, were technically perfect. You had no need to worry on that score.

Just as many would have disagreed. It would have been very hard, indeed, to convince Captain James Dunn of such technical "perfection" (see Dunn's disgust with poor orders earlier in this chapter). Hanbury-Sparrow does not say it, but it is clear from the War Diaries and their appended documents such as plans and orders that raid orders improved dramatically during the war. What worried him most was the part brigade and division played: in short, their "call" as to the object of a raid. This often concerned and disillusioned officers leading raids and their COs who recognized spurious reasons for raids when they saw them. *"Absit omen,"* wrote Hanbury-Sparrow. But there is always a gap between a plan and its execution.[30]

Throughout the war a stream of instructions and "lessons" documents originated at all levels battalion and up. Of these, some pertained only to a single raid, while others were summations

29 Johnston, *2nd Canadian Mounted Rifles,* p. 41; Wyrall, *50th Division,* p. 130; Graves, *Goodbye to All That,* p. 171.

30 Hanbury-Sparrow, *The Land-Locked Lake,* pp. 249-51, 262, *absit omen,* "May no ominous significance be attached to the words, may my fears not be justified." Fraser and Gibbons, *Soldier and Sailor Words and Phrases,* p. 90, "eyewash": humbug, sham, deceit, flattery, outward show.

of recent raids or of periods of varying length. One of the most interesting and influential lessons documents relating to raids was Second Army's "Lessons Drawn From the Various Minor Operations Carried Out by the Second Army Up to 9 February 1917," a document prepared for the Army Commander's Conference (Plumer) on 13 February. While each corps would have contributed comment, Second Army's Major General General Staff (MGGS), H.B. Williams, also wrote directly to Lieutenant-Colonel Victor Odlum asking for suggestions and amendments to the document by 12 February. Odlum's 7th Battalion had conducted the highly successful, indeed iconic Canadian raid, on Petite Douve Farm on 16/17 November 1915. Identical wording of part of the Second Army draft and Odlum's response shows that at least one of his comments had been incorporated verbatim. The final version (15 pages long) contains lessons covering every aspect of raiding through to the raiders' return to home trenches. It is thick with lessons, too many to discuss or list here; the section on pre-raid preparations alone lists 10 lessons and Preliminary Instructions a further 14. In all, 88 lessons make up the document, some having already been discussed herein, and some will be in later chapters.[31]

No two raids were identical. Lessons were sometimes peculiar to a particular raid because of topography or circumstance, or because the lessons were based on opinions not generally held. Commonalities were immediately apparent or soon evident in compilation of raid histories. "It seemed," said the historian of the Welsh Guards, "as though each time a successful raid was done the particular formation adopted for that raid became the standard for future practices." While this was virtually inevitable it posed danger. Re-evaluation had also to be immediate and vigorous. An important point about the growing importance of lessons, but the delay in recognizing them, is also made by the historian of 19th British Division when he says that not until 1917 did raiding get "studied more carefully."[32]

The stream of lessons documents applied to all operations, not just raids. Successful or not, all had their lessons, what went wrong and why and how to do better. In the aftermath of failure, or less gain than had been anticipated, the BEF sought to identify the lessons, and then responded with tactical, technological and organizational innovation, a continuing process that is evident in official publications of every sort, and in the curriculums of the network of training schools within the BEF at formation levels from brigade to Army and of the numerous specialist schools behind the BEF in France and at home. The BEF gained the ability to evaluate, validate and manage training and to respond to challenge. After all is said and done, this emerged from experience. One can conclude that a learning curve existed and was recognized as such. To doubt this is to ignore not only military probability and logic, but military common sense. A learning curve, after all, consists not just of the wildly dramatic or earth-shattering event, but also of the very basics; for example, anyone who has ever instructed young officers in minor tactics and began by simply showing them what an infantry platoon looks like deployed on the ground will recall their sudden look of comprehension of the command problem inherent in the large space a platoon occupies on the ground. Few outside the Army witness such small links in the chain that the curve runs along. The learning curve might be better described as the lessons curve that builds war-fighting skills. Swinton's classic

31 LAC, RG9IIIC1, Volume 3858, Folder 82, File 1 and RG9IIIC3, Volume 4052, Folder 23, File 2. Everything pertaining to the Second Army document is in these two volumes. On Canadian raids from February 1916-June 1917 Odlum's papers are very useful (MG30E300, Volume 24).

32 Wyrall, *Nineteenth Division,* p. 72.

The Defence of Duffer's Drift (1904) is about these skills. Of the 22 lessons learned by the book's Subaltern, 16 still applied during the Great War. The author of this present book on raiding has never met an Army officer, Canadian or British, who doubts the existence of the learning curve, nor is it logical in view of the abounding evidence to think that officers of the Great War would have doubted it.[33]

It bears reiterating that experience, the driver of lessons, also drove training and doctrine. Many of the lessons documents reflect doctrinal and technological change and specific aspects of raids that had proved especially challenging and difficult to master throughout. In June 1917 Canadian Corps HQ highlighted these aspects in "Some Notes for Raids":

> Rifle Grenades. It has been found that the rifle grenade and Lewis Gun are usually the best trench clearers. The Rifle. Men to be taught to shoot at retiring or advancing enemy and not to rely on hand grenades. Reconnaissance. It should be left to officers who are to carry out raid to decide … when wire is sufficiently cut. Navigation. Necessity in night raids for marking return route. Signal for Withdrawal. Safest method is to set time for withdrawal. Artillery registration. To be observed and checked by infantry officers.[34]

Several British and Canadian Divisions issued lessons documents entitled "Some Notes on Raids." While not all the lessons were universal, some were gems, an example being 7th British Division's conclusion that "rifle and bayonet are invariably … most effective."[35]

One officer who had repeatedly demonstrated a "genius" for raiding, soon in demand for command performances, so to speak, was Lieutenant-Colonel R.D. Davies, DSO and 2 Bars. At 0400 hours on 13 February 1917, 12 days after he took command of 44th Canadian Battalion, 70 of his officers and men executed a raid during which 30 enemy were killed and 17 captured at a cost of one man killed and several slightly wounded. Davies, who had considerable to do with the planning, had made a good start. A week later he turned over command to his 2IC because he had been appointed OC of a raiding force of 870 all ranks, 200 from each battalion in 10th Brigade (44th, 46th, 47th and 50th Battalions), plus detachments from 10th Field Engineer Company and 67th Pioneer Battalion, the sappers and pioneers adding 70 more men. Raid participants would also include an officer and several sappers from 176th Tunnelling Company RE. These would be escorted and protected by a party of 47th Battalion as they worked at

33 For the school system in the BEF and its policy, system, content and conduct see Radley, *We Lead Others Follow*. Major-General Sir Ernest Swinton, *The Defence of Duffer's Drift* (Oxford: George Ronald, 1949), Foreword.

34 Dudley Ward, *History of the Welsh Guards*. p. 61; LAC, RG9IIIC3, Volume 4028, Folder 17, File 2, Canadian Corps HQ, BGGS, 6 June 1917, 'Some Notes on Raids'; Bernard McEvoy and Captain A.H. Finlay, MC, *History of the 72nd Canadian Infantry Battalion Seaforth Highlanders of Canada* (Vancouver: Cowan & Brookhouse, 1920), p. 74. For a time, grenades virtually replaced the rifle. One report told of a soldier who followed a solitary German for a time at a distance of 300 yards trying to get close enough to throw a bomb, ignoring his rifle which would have done the job nicely! 2nd Canadian Brigade in its report on the Somme mentioned this sort of amnesia, remarking that bombs had often been used when the rifle would have done better. (LAC, RG9IIIC3, Volume 4051, Folder 19, File 8). Arthur Currie in his summary of the lessons of the Somme also referred to bomb-happiness (Volume 4051, 15 August 1916).

35 TNA: WO 95/1654: 20th British Brigade, 7th Division, July 1917, 'Some Notes on Raids'.

destroying three mineshafts.[36] The only diagram available of the raid area is very faint, in large part illegible and is not annotated, meaning it could add nothing to an account of the raid. Fortunately, the raid reports are clear and comprehensive.

In describing how he went about planning this large-scale raid Davies said he began with what he called a "rough outline" consisting of the decisions to be made as to command of the raid, its strength and it organization (number of parties) and its movement from assembly trenches to the objective. From this he prepared "Preliminary Orders" which included a general idea of the plan, the composition of the parties and orders for recce and training for the raid.

"Final Orders" which were prepared and issued at the appropriate time, defined the objective and additional tasks followed by artillery, trench mortar and machine-gun tasks. Then came what Davies called "Detail and Action of Parties," a section that dealt only with activities from the departure from own trenches to the commencement of the return. Separate sections of his order covered the periods prior to leaving own trenches and after withdrawal began. His orders concluded with administration and communications. These orders are a model of clarity."[37]

Jack Sheldon's *The German Army on Vimy Ridge* relates how an NCO of 44th Battalion captured before the raid told his captors that there were only 80 raiders from each battalion, total strength of the raiders being only 324. Given that all of the archival information including the Operation Orders and reports say 200 per battalion the NCO seems to have been out to deceive the enemy. Sheldon's note that the raiders "claimed" 52 prisoners including one officer agrees with 10th Brigade's report. Looking at Davies' preliminary report we see that 44th and 50th Battalions do not mention prisoners, 46th battalion reported "very few" and 47th Battalion mentions "a number of prisoners including 10 from one dugout." In his final report the picture is this: 44th, "some" prisoners; 46th, "several" prisoners; 47th, "a good number'; and 50th, no prisoners.[38] Davies noted that all raiding parties met with "most determined resistance" that reduced the taking of prisoners. It may seem, then, that the claim of 52 is on the high side, but the report of 11th Bavarian Regiment cited in Sheldon said 52 men were missing. Davies knew that 47 prisoners including one officer had "passed through" battalion lines enroute to 10th Brigade HQ. Canadian reports also referred to 160 German casualties which is very close to the German report of 44 killed and 110 wounded. Canadian losses were two officers and six ORs killed, five officers and 125 ORs wounded and 15 ORs missing, a total of 153. Sheldon's figures total 161. Based on his figures of 324 participants and 161 casualties that would mean a casualty rate of 50 percent. The Canadian figures of 870 participants and casualties of 153 indicate a 17 percent rate.[39]

36 LAC, War Diary, 10th Brigade, Davies' preliminary and final reports. Each battalion contributed a full company of 200 organized into four platoons in accordance with Davies' Operation Order. Lieutenant-Colonel W.N. Winsby, CO 47th Battalion, chose to contribute a composite company of 200 volunteers.

37 LAC, War Diaries, battalions of 10th Brigade; TNA: WO 95/1297: 2nd Division General Staff, July 1917, 'Detailed Sequence for Raid Preparation'. Davies used this in lectures he presented at several divisions, British and Canadian. Preliminary Orders served to get preparations underway immediately, but they could not always be done due to time constraints.

38 Sheldon, *German Army on Vimy Ridge*, pp. 233-34; LAC, War Diaries, 10th Brigade and the four battalions.

39 *Ibid.*, Sheldon, *German Army on Vimy Ridge*, p. 234.

Nor is there agreement about the depth of penetration of enemy lines. 44th Battalion reported this as about 700 yards, which is about the distance enemy front line to the final objective. Davies reported "significant" penetration: "in the case of prisoners taken within the farther limits of the area raided the distance was such … that very few prisoners taken were brought back." German reports cited in Sheldon admit only to penetration of forward positions. However, raiders coming on in three waves, each almost 300 strong, against two companies attenuated by artillery and mortar fire must have done better than just forward positions especially given that "no enemy machine-guns were heard or seen anywhere in the immediate raid area." Here, too, the captured Canadian NCO had something to say. He believed that only a few raiders got into the second objective; of course, he is referring only to his battalion, the 44th. As for the final objective, Davies' orders were that only the 44th and 50th Battalions were to "pass through the second objective and enter the third." His final report describes in detail the activities of the 44th and 50th at the second objective, including blowing up dug-outs there and beyond.

Assessments of the raid differ. Sheldon calls it not "particularly successful" because of the high number of casualties. Still, the raiders achieved all the stipulated purposes: they killed many Germans, took a good haul of prisoners, did some destruction and searched for, but did not locate, trench mortar emplacements that had been thought to be in the objective area. This last task had been specifically allotted in the brigade Operation Order. While the raid was costly, it continued the chain of Canadian successes. As always, determining the balance of profit proved as challenging as the raid itself.[40] Comments in Sheldon made by the captured Canadian NCO refer to a "lack of complete success" due to "insufficient preparation" for the raid, the raiders storming ahead 'blindly" with no clear idea of what they were to do. The NCO also mentioned that the enemy seemed ready for the raid because their artillery "came down like lightning." Clearly, the NCO is referring to his battalion, the 44th, which is the only one he could observe. If what he says about inadequate preparation is true, then the fault was with the officers of the 44th who took part in the raid and, specifically, it suggests that training and briefings of raid personnel of that battalion may not have been up to the mark. On the other hand, Russenholt describes 44th Battalion's preparation as thorough: "training on a large scale. The plan of the German trench … laid out in actual size … Each man repeatedly rehearsed in his part." It is hard to believe that Davies would not have briefed the entire force if for no other reason than to show himself and build their confidence, followed by detailed briefings of the parties and considerable discussion with all officers on the raid. Certainly, he would have conferred frequently with them and monitored progress. He had, after all, turned over command to his 2IC so he could focus entirely on the raid. It is possible that there were shortcomings when it came to briefings, but there is no evidence for this beyond 44th Battalion.[41]

Davies' reports are both dated 13 February. His two-page preliminary simply summarizes events and casualties, when the withdrawal occurred and enemy casualties and retaliation. His final report makes no mention of lessons which is not surprising since he would have had very little time to reflect on such. One of his comments in a section of his second report entitled "Special Notes" suggests there may have been some difficulties of control during the raid, particularly during the withdrawal, a phase that always proved very challenging. Sheldon says

40 Sheldon, *German Army on Vimy Ridge*, p. 234; LAC, War Diaries, 10th Brigade and battalions.
41 Sheldon, *German Army on Vimy Ridge*, p. 233-34; Russenholt, *Six Thousand Canadian Men*, p. 74.

there was "no designated signal "for the start of the withdrawal. However, Davies did describe arrangements for the "return" in his Operation Order: an officer of 50th Battalion was to signal withdrawal of the parties of 50th and 44th Battalions to a "rallying point" under cover of a screen that would stay in position until all parties had passed through the point. In case of this signal failing, then withdrawal was to commence at Zero plus 35. In his final report Davies described the withdrawal being in "fair" order and by Zero plus 70 these parties were at the rallying point. Davies also wrote that "It was found that with the large number and diverse character of parties used [that] touch was most difficult ... owing to smoke and darkness." Given this, he may have left the signal for withdrawal of 46th and 47th contingents to the OC of each company. While all the parties apparently got out without great difficulty, it is clear that when to withdraw, how to signal it and how to control it warranted as always close attention and firming up.[42]

It should also be noted that this raid on 13 February was Davies' initiation into the world of large-scale planning. Despite the flies in the ointment, and the casualties, this raid gave him a reputation as an excellent raid planner. As such, he became rather well known within the Canadian Corps and outside it, too. After the raid he received the first of his three DSOs. Subsequent raids by his 44th Battalion burnished his lustre.[43]

Afterward, Davies wrote his "Detailed Sequence for Raid Preparation" a two-page, 15-point primer on planning raids, a distillation of his experience in planning them and, no doubt, the wisdom of others with significant planning experience. This document was widely distributed throughout the Canadian Corps and beyond. On 27 July 2nd British Division distributed copies to its brigades: "The attached notes ... have been drawn up by an officer who has had great experience. This officer has recently carried out conspicuously successful raids ... and in consequence of a request ... will be only too glad to talk over raids with any brigadiers or Commanding Officers." Two brigades, the 5th and the 99th, then requested that Davies be invited to the division for additional discussion on raids. This the division arranged. The 15 points of his sequence fall into three parts, the first concerning initial battle planning: selection of objective, recce and a battalion conference followed by a brigade conference where a "rough" plan would be produced. Part 2 listed preliminary matters requiring immediate decision such as selection of OC Raid, strength and organization of the raiding force and positioning of the raiders. Part Three concerned "Final Orders." As Davies intended the document as a checklist he kept it short and did not include brigade commander responsibilities.[44]

Davies' sequence is select the objective, appoint the OC Raid and then determine size. This echoes *SS 107*. Earlier in this chapter William Griesbach's version of the sequence of planning was related. It is summarized here for reader convenience: decide on magnitude of raid, select OC Raid and select the objective. At first sight Griesbach's sequence seems upside down. For one thing, the size and conformation of an objective pretty much determined the size of

42 Sheldon, *German Army on Vimy Ridge*, pp. 234-35; LAC, War Diary, 10th Brigade, Davies' Operation Order and final report.

43 David K Riddle and Donald G. Mitchell (eds.), *The Distinguished Service Order Awarded to Members of the Canadian Expeditionary Force and Canadians in the Royal Naval Air Service, The Royal Flying Corps and Royal Air Force 1915-1920* (Winnipeg: Kirkby-Marlton Press, 1991). Davies received a Bar in February 1918 and another in October 1919.

44 Nothing on Davies' visits appears in Russenholt's account of 44th Battalion. TNA: WO 95/1297: 2nd British Division General Staff, 13 and 27 July 1917.

the force required. For another, the objective's location could influence selection of the OC Raid, perhaps because of his experience or familiarity with the ground, or lack thereof. But Griesbach's sequence is that of a brigade commander. Even at the lowest level of formation (brigade) the GOC had necessarily to think, not of men, but of numbers and resources, the question for him being what can be afforded. He wants to know "magnitude" first off because that directly bears on resources that he controls or can get from division. He has in his mind how much of his "readies" he wishes to commit to any one proposal to raid. He also knows if the proposal will fit with division's plans. If the proposal fit, then the CO who submitted it was left to select the OC Raid and the objective. Another sequence, which mirrors Davies' sequence, was the norm in 34th British Division and was later described by that division's historian:

> First, the spot to be attacked had to be selected. This was generally done by the Brigadier and the officer commanding the battalion which was to carry out the raid. Then a rough programme had to be drawn up by the Battalion Commander, and this had to be thrashed out with the Brigadier, the Commander of the Field Artillery group covering the front, and the trench mortar and machine-gun men. When a definite result had been arrived at, the Divisional Commander's views had to be taken.[45]

While sequence had much to do with the individual brigade commanders Ashworth points out how "From 1916 raids were increasingly directed by higher command." But not all higher commanders and not all the time; for example, 19th British Division in February 1918 left initial planning to battalion commanders, division seeing its role and that of brigade as only guidance and monitoring "to ensure that no available means are overlooked which might increase the chances of success or diminish the risk of failure … after Divisional HQ has approved of the main outline … further arrangement and details should be left as much as possible to the battalion commander." But a battalion scheme that asked for considerable external support could expect a proportionate degree of guidance and monitoring.[46]

In 1918 "lessons" and "notes" on raids continued to appear, not surprisingly, since new arrivals always needed a place to start. In February Lieutenant-Colonel H.F. Montgomery, DSO, Royal Marine Light Infantry, GSO1 19th British Division, prepared and issued "Some Notes on Raids," its 28 points filling six pages. The first half of his Notes, nine paragraphs on three pages, is more about how to plan a raid than about the lessons of raiding. Marginal headings serve to introduce the nine paragraphs relating to planning: value of raids, guidance of higher command (brigade and division), strength of raiding force, planning, artillery planning, air photo use, knowledge of no man's land, Zero hour and selection of the objective. It is the last that receives attention and emphasis here, just as it does in Montgomery's Notes. What he provides is a possibly unique list of the criteria or considerations that have to be weighed in every selection of objectives. Of the 10 criteria, five concern artillery. As the text of some of the 10 are lengthy, their essence has been summarized and translated into questions:

45 LAC, MG30E15 (Griesbach Papers), Volume 3, File 16A, 'Book of Wisdom', Volume II; Shakespear, *Thirty-Fourth Division,* p. 81.

46 Ashworth, *Live and Let Live,* p. 96; TNA: WO 95/2056: 19th Division General Staff.

> Can the artillery cut the whole of the wire beyond which the raid is intended to go? If the riders are to go beyond the first line it is not sufficient to cut wire at the first line only.
>
> Can the artillery destroy the objective in so far as destruction is essential to the plan?
>
> Can the artillery protect raiders with a barrage?
>
> Can the artillery provide counter-battery fire against enemy guns able to barrage no man's land?
>
> Is observation such that rehearsal, observation and registration can be achieved without arousing suspicion and retaliation? This applies also to trench mortars and machine-guns.
>
> Is the point of entry such that the risk of enemy enfilade fire, especially by machine-guns, is minimized? The face of a salient may sometimes be favourable for this reason.
>
> What is the "going" across no man's land? Covered approaches and distances require consideration.
>
> Is flank protection for raiders out and back possible?
>
> What facilities for communications exist? Is there a point suitable for visual signals?
>
> Can the course of the raid be observed from battalion lines? But this alone must not take the place of reconnaissance.

The last three pages of Montgomery's "Some Notes on Raids" concern lessons and are reserved to Chapter 15. His Notes as a whole can only be described as splendidly comprehensive. While they could have been better organized, perhaps as policy, pre-raid, raid and aftermath, his notes, together with Davies' sequence, would have been invaluable to any officer tasked to plan and/or lead a raid. They also clearly portray the complexity of raiding and the necessity that planning pay the closest attention to detail.[47]

Another division that had raiding on the mind during the first half of 1918 was 2nd Canadian Division, especially 6th Brigade. During a stay in the line for the first 10 days of June 29th Battalion experienced a very successful raid on 3 June, the eight officers and 175 ORs participating securing eight prisoners and two machine-guns at very low cost. The 6th Brigade then went into reserve for the week 10-16 June. Before returning to the line the BM and Staff Captain "I" conducted a special recce for a forthcoming raid on the village of Neuville Vitasse about four miles south of Arras. The BM, Major The Hon. F.E. Grosvenor, DSO and Bar, MC and Bar,

47 Wyrall, *Nineteenth Division*, p. 235. Montgomery, GSO1 from October 1917 to the end of the war, was described as a very capable officer, "full of ideas … practical … his views always sound and sensible."

became deeply involved in the arrangements for the 3 June raid and even more so for the raid that took place on 25 June.[48]

Early in this chapter Operation Instructions were first mentioned. At the outbreak of war the only reference to these in *FSR* (Section 10) stated that "In addition to [orders] special instructions may be required in the case of detached forces, instead of or in addition to Operation Orders." In the staffing of the raids on 3 and 25 June we see mention and issue possibly for the first time of Operation Instructions in addition to Operation Orders, this an indication of how sophisticated planning for raids had become and how the standard of Military Writing had greatly improved. Clearly, Major Grosvenor appreciated the difference between Orders and Instructions, the use of both and the method of controlling operations by the issue of Instructions. Post-war manuals and non-official publications focus on the circumstances where a commander might issue Operation Instructions and their uses and purposes, these being relevant to raids. Major Body in his *Notes on Appreciations* (1930) thought many officers no longer understood the difference.[49] Major Leader, also writing post-war, summarized their purposes:

> Whilst an Operation Instruction may on occasion be used to amplify the information in an Operation Order … one of the main objects of its use is to cover a situation where a subordinate commander must necessarily be allowed more than usual latitude and is called upon to act largely upon his own judgement [as] the case of a commander of a detachment who is being sent to carry out an operation at a distance; beyond stating his Object it may be impracticable or is inappropriate to give him very definite orders.

This is a clear statement of the actual use made of Operation Instructions during the war. A modern manual describes the greatest users of Operation Instructions as those in command of "swiftly moving" operations, an uncommon event during most of the Great War, but added that subordinate commanders could use them when given an independent mission, "such as a special raid." All postwar accounts have stressed that such instructions should follow the same sequence as orders, in both the object to be attained to be clearly stated.[50]

For the 3 June raid Major Grosvenor issued an Operation Order (two pages) and then a three-page Operation Instruction. The first contained only a definition of the raid's purpose, the objective, artillery support and timings. The second added the method of attack, communications and final timings. For the larger raid on 25 June he issued an Operation Order and two Operation Instructions. The first instruction set out the objective and method of attack, six pages being necessary because two battalions were involved, plus extensive support: field and heavy artillery, trench mortars and Stokes, machine-guns and a Special Company RE to project gas on targets in the vicinity of Neuville Vitasse to deceive the enemy and cause him to wear gas masks. Oil would also be projected in adjacent areas in hopes the enemy would mistake it for gas. The second instruction became necessary due to the inclusion of engineer demolition parties and additional medical support. The three documents epitomize good Military Writing.

48 Before the war Grosvenor emigrated to Canada where he become a successful contractor in Vancouver. He was commissioned Lieutenant, 29th Battalion, in November 1914. Post-war he became 4th Baron Ebury.

49 Body, *Notes on Appreciations,* p. 13.

50 Leader, *An Elementary Study of Appreciations,* p. 30; *CAMT 1-36 Staff Duties in the Field,* p. 537.

The actual raid for 6th Brigade marked the largest it had done up to that point. The GOC, A.H. Bell, summed it up nicely:

> The preparatory work was necessarily extensive; many recce patrols and it was essential that strong battle patrols be constantly in No Man's Land to keep down all hostile patrolling and thus preclude all possibility of our assembly being discovered on the night of the assault. Zero was fixed at 1:15 a.m. on the morning of the 25th ... at this time raiding party of 250 all ranks jumped off ... 27th Bn on the right, the 31st on the left. Both reached all objectives, completely overrunning the village and penetrating the enemy's defences to an average depth of 450 yds on a frontage of over 1,000 yds. At Zero plus 25 the raiding party retired, having carried out their task with conspicuous success. The enemy lost heavily in the severe fighting which took place and our captures were 1 officer and 21 ORs, 7 machine-guns and 1 trench mortar.

In a lecture on raiding he later presented at VI Corps School, Major Grosvenor used the raid as a vehicle to illustrate how good recce was the "secret of success" when it came to raiding.[51]

Those who planned and led minor enterprises had been instructed as early as February 1915 that raids were directly relevant to and highly valuable in the planning of major operations and in the conduct of defence. At that time Sir John French had issued a "lessons" instruction based on the results of some minor operations on 1 February that "although by no means entirely new ... merit the attention of all officers." He then listed 10 lessons that applied to minor and major operations, five of these being the importance of detailed planning, ensuring all raid participants knew their part, careful infantry-artillery co-ordination, the merits of surprise and the necessity for vigorous and determined offensive action. Raids offered in miniature form all the challenges inherent in planning and preparing a major attack and even more when the raid took place during the hours of darkness. Moreover, said one British brigadier, planning a raid greatly stimulated initiative "and offered great scope for ingenuity and cunning." A bonus was the training value raids provided for junior and sometimes field officers. Experience, after all, is the best teacher. His experience convinced Lieutenant W.D. Murray, 2nd Canadian Battalion, that:

> A minor operation demands as much careful thought and studious enquiry as a large one. There are still the hundred and one things to be considered. Information must be exact ... everyone must know exactly what the operation is, why it is done and when ... the whole reason for the latest operation being termed brilliant lies in the completion of the preparation.[52]

The hundred and one things taught junior officers a good deal about being an officer and measuring up to an officer's responsibilities and much else: recce and study of ground, map reading,

51 LAC, 6th Brigade War Diary, June 1918, orders and instructions for 3 and 25 June.

52 LAC, RG9IIIC3, Volume 4044, Folder 3, File 3, GHQ Instruction; War Diary, 2nd Battalion, September 1916; Hussey, *Fifth Division*, p. 142. In late March 1917 5th British Division came under the Canadian Corps, its 13th Brigade and Divisional Artillery joining 2nd Canadian Division for the attack on Vimy Ridge.

bomb resupply, siting of mortars and machine-guns, use of gas and not least, the training and leadership of soldiers.

Raids always had the potential to go from just unpleasantness to downright nastiness, a tendency that some neglect or shortcoming in preparation could greatly exacerbate.[53] In such instances death, always beckoning, drew even closer. The plan, therefore, had to be the epitome of sound thinking: precise and clear and, above all, invulnerable to misinterpretation. While not raid related, a good example of misinterpretation occurred in 35th British Division in December 1916. On the 14th, on the firing of an SOS signal by the infantry, divisional artillery responded with over 1,000 rounds before the firing could be stopped. Only then did the gunners learn that the infantry signal had been a test to see how quickly the gunners could respond. However, less than a week later clarity triumphed, 35th Divisional Artillery provided perfect support for a raid launched by 3rd Canadian Division. The raid itself was also nigh on perfect, many prisoners being taken at very low cost.[54]

A decision to raid could be taken at any level from battalion up. It is not surprising that a battalion commander would initiate a raid for he was charged with defending the ground assigned to him. Consequently, patrols and raids went out, for one thing, to dominate no man's land to the maximum extent possible, the aim being to prevent surprise. Part of this was domination of the enemy. As well, a CO simply had to know his sector, its strengths and weaknesses and the enemy situation. Some of this he got from the CO of any battalion that his battalion was relieving and some from intelligence, air photographs and scouts, but active patrolling and raiding provided a security these other sources could not. When a raid required support beyond his means then he had to seek brigade's assistance. Such inevitably came at a price for brigade then became more actively involved in the planning. Of course, a CO was often told when and where to raid and in such cases he knew the presence of higher command from the beginning. There being no force on earth as irresistible as the urge to change another man's draft any "paper" was sure to draw comment and amendment. A raid by 18th KRRC in February 1917, for example, saw the production of three editions of the Operation Order, this causing the chief scribe of the plan to remark somewhat ruefully "how interesting to see … the influence of the various brains that have worked on it."[55] The larger the raid the greater the interest of one's superiors.

Sometimes it went well beyond that. 22nd Manchester Regiment, planning a raid in mid-1916, soon found Brigade HQ well along the way to taking full charge of it. The problem in this instance was an ambitious brigade commander eager to make his mark. During the raid the 22nd got well into the German trenches, bombing dug-outs, securing prisoners and killing a good many Germans. However, on withdrawing the raiders unluckily encountered uncut wire and as the men bunched up enemy bombers struck. In the end, half the raiding force of 60 all ranks became casualties, including two officers killed, one

53 Any young man who completed officer training at the Royal Canadian School of Infantry would have no difficulty recalled the oft-repeated adage of that not-so-gentle institution that said "If you cannot get the little things right you will not get the big things right." (RCS of I Aide-Memoire for Platoon Commanders, Camp Borden, 1963).

54 Davson, *35th Division,* pp. 82-83; LAC, War Diary, 8th Canadian Brigade, December 1916.

55 Brown, *Imperial War Museum Book of the Western Front,* p. 111.

wounded and one missing: "A heavy price," said Captain Charles May, "that cast a shadow … a sad business."[56]

This same brigadier in June 1918 while commanding another brigade wrote an Appreciation for a raid by one of his battalions (10th Argyll and Sutherland Highlanders), which went to division (32nd) for approval. The extent to which said brigadier then became involved in the plan and the planning cannot be definitely stated, but odds are he became as "hands-on" as he had been in the Appreciation. Perhaps he was not aware of, or not in agreement with *The Solution to Tactical Problems,* which thought it important not to encroach on the "sphere of subordinates." Captain May does not say what the recipients thought of the brigadier's plan. Across no man's land *Leutnant* Ernst Junger found himself leading a raid in September 1917 based on a plan "that had been thrust on me ready-made, though there was much in it to take exception to," particularly, as Junger described it, the objective. Tactics, no matter the colour of the uniform, is sometimes the opinion of the senior officer present. Junger, ever the professional and a much admired thruster, selected the best men available and trained them very hard, running through every detail and contingency with them. In the event, the raid did not achieve its purpose, which was to take prisoners. Junger's account shows that the objective, a maze of parallel and crossing trenches, was simply too much for his small party. His regimental commander probably recognized this for despite failure he "distributed Iron Crosses and gave 14 days leave to each man." Junger summed up this raid as his "most uncomfortable" of the war.[57] Such interventions in raids were not limited to brigade commanders or German regimental commanders. Captain D.V. Kelly, MC, who served with 110th Brigade of 21st British Division, and had witnessed preparations for numerous raids, became convinced that raids demanded good knowledge of the ground and enemy dispositions. He believed that everyone in the line realized this, but right to the end corps commanders "persisted in ordering raids regardless of local conditions and with an arbitrary time limit – often twenty-four hours notice – and usually with a great artillery programme."[58] Little time to prepare was not uncommon, some senior officers oblivious to the impact (see Chapter 5).

One last aspect of the planning of raids is how the level of interest varied with the seasons, time and circumstances, just as the extent of raiding did. This is not to say that any particular raid would be ignored; it was just that like so many things there were peaks and valleys. In a lecture entitled "Notes on the Vimy Ridge Operations" the BGGS Canadian Corps, P. deB. Radcliffe, summarized the value of raids thus:

> Of equal or even greater importance than the training out of the line was the practical training in attack carried out by all Divisions in the line throughout the winter. Between 1st November and 8th April some 69 raids were carried out by the Corps … The total number of prisoners captured was 367 and most valuable information was obtained … But of even greater value was the atmosphere thus created … an atmosphere of ascendency …

56 Harrison (ed.), *To Fight Alongside Friends,* p. 187; Atkinson, *Seventh Division,* pp. 251, 323. The brigadier J.R.M. Minshull-Ford, had been a Captain in March 1915. In February 1916 he assumed command of the brigade, which consisted of 21st and 22nd Manchesters and two other battalions. He returned to England in November 1916 due to ill-health, but later returned to the front.

57 Needham, *The Solution to Tactical Problems,* p. 159; Junger, *Storm of Steel,* pp. 195-203.

58 Kelly, *39 Months With the "Tigers",* p. 40.

> which gave a feeling of the utmost confidence to all officers and men in the Corps … the effect on the subsequent operations can hardly be exaggerated.[59]

Radcliffe did not mention it in his lecture, but the period also shows a correlation between the extent of brigade commander involvement in the planning of raids and the proximity of a raid to the assault on 9 April. Of the 69 Canadian raids, 2nd Brigade made eight between 27 November 1916 and 8 April 1917. The last Canadian raid before the attack on 9 April on Vimy Ridge was launched at 0500 on 8 April by three officers and 85 ORs of 10th Battalion. The raid, planned and led by Captain Stanley Kent, came about because of uncertainty regarding the state of German wire. The CO of the 10th Battalion, Lieutenant-Colonel Daniel Ormond, in a postwar interview recalled his deep concern about the ground and the wire because due to deep and large craters less than a quarter of his 480-yard frontage was passable, the "only way to go [being] between these craters [that] the Boche had wired … very, very heavily." As the ground severely limited observation of the German defences, including the wire, Kent and others commenced recce patrols on 4/5 April, but by the 8th it could not be definitively stated that the wire was adequately cut, despite artillery observer insistence that it had been. According to Ormond, Arthur Currie, after personal study of the conflicting infantry and artillery reports decided that the only way to be sure was to raid. Accordingly, Kent and his raiders made final preparations for the job. The plan, as Ormond described it, was uncomplicated: a box barrage to isolate the objective, then a rapid assault, seize anyone or anything present and quickly withdraw. At a cost of five dead and 13 wounded the raid proved that the bombardment to that point had not "seriously damaged" enemy defences and the wire remained "virtually intact" in many places. Currie then ordered the battalion to vacate its trenches, so that the artillery could bring full weight down. Currie, said Ormond, "turned everything onto that, and when we went over on the morning of the ninth, the wire was no obstacle … We would have been ready to go over as it was … but he was right. The artillery went to it, and they did a first-class job." 2nd Brigade summed up the benefits of the raid: "it completely misled the enemy as to our main intentions and … very materially contributed towards the success of our main operation."[60] For this raid planning and execution were left to the CO and the OC Raid, except for a last minute intervention by GOC 1st Division (Currie) to resolve the impasse about the efficacy of the wire-cutting. The brigade commander, Frederick Loomis, and his staff seem to have had little, if any, involvement in the planning and preparation of this raid, which is understandable given the looming immediacy of the attack on Vimy Ridge. Loomis knew full well his main responsibility: he and his staff kept their eyes firmly on the main bout.[61]

59 LAC, RG9IIIC1, Volume 3846, Folder 51, File 7, 'Notes on the Vimy Ridge Operations'; Volume 3844, Folder 47, File 4, Summary of Raids by Canadian Corps (1 November 1916-1 April 1917). Of the 16 raids launched between 29 October and 26 December 1916 five were unsuccessful (RG9IIIC3, Folder 23, File 1). Between 1 January and 16 February 13 Canadian raids were launched. All were successful (Volume 4052, Folder 23, File 1).

60 LAC, RG9IIIC3, Volume 3844, Folder 47, File 4, summary of raids; RG 41, CBC Interview, Lieutenant-Colonel Ormond; RG9IIIC3, Volume 4919, Folder 373(2), Kent's report and Appendices A-C; RG9IIIC1, Volume 3846, Folder 51, File 2, report of 2nd Brigade; Dancocks, *Gallant Canadians,* pp. 107-109. Kent received his second MC for the raid. He died on 29 April of wounds suffered at Arleux.

61 Loomis, 44 in 1914, took 13th Battalion to war in 1914. In July 1916 he assumed command of 2nd Brigade, then in September 1918 on promotion moved on to 3rd Division. For more on Loomis see

In contrast was an earlier raid featuring 125 all ranks of Lieutenant-Colonel J.M. Prower's 8th Battalion raiding on 27 November 1916.[62] The archival records show that GOC 2nd Brigade (Frederick Loomis) and GOC 1st Division (Currie) had a great deal to do with the planning, Loomis being especially "hands-on" throughout preparation and planning of this raid. On 26 November Loomis toured brigade trenches and then visited HQ 1st Division that evening for further discussion. The following morning he and his BM, Captain W.H.S. Alston, toured again "to look over ground suitable for a raid."[63] Currie arrived at 8th Battalion HQ at 0750 that same morning and toured battalion trenches accompanied by Prower. "During the day," according to the battalion War Diary, "arrangements were perfected for the coming show." Loomis also called again later that day and "remained to dinner and discussed the situation with the CO." Currie and Loomis also conferred at some point during the afternoon. Loomis then conferred with corps and division artillery officers. Thus the senior commanders confirmed matters leaving Prower and his 2IC, Major J.P. Mackenzie, to get on with what Loomis described in his report on the raid as "arranging for all contingencies to the smallest detail."[64]

Loomis' close involvement in planning and preparation during the raid by 8th Battalion generally continued when it came to operations throughout his time as GOC. Another example came during the run-up to raids by 7th Battalion in February 1917 when he "spent considerable time in the forward area conferring with Battalion commanders and completing arrangements for further enterprises."[65] These raids show Loomis to have been something of a "details man," prone at times to over-direction and over-supervision and to some degree fusing command and control. Nevertheless, there can be no doubt that Loomis was an effective and successful brigade commander who deserved the divisional command he received in late 1918.

The fundamentals and process of planning described in this chapter became essential knowledge and skills for those who had to plan raids. What they planned could only be audited by execution which is fighting. This Robert Browning called the "soldier's art." The attitudes of those who had to do the raiding and the fighting is the subject of the next chapter.

Radley, *We Lead Others Follow,* and Trevor Harvey, *An Army of Brigadiers: British Brigade Commanders at the Battle of Arras 1917* (Solihull: Helion & Company Limited, 2017). Chapter 3 assesses Loomis as a brigade commander, including his views, approach and style of command and control in regard to raids.

62 John Prower was CO 8th Battalion from September 1916 to April 1918. He had been BM of 2nd Brigade from September 1915 to August 1916. A very astute officer, he was noted when CO for his thoroughness, tactical acumen and forthrightness. When in one case he believed divisional staff had not been as engaged as they might have been, he did not hesitate to make his concern known. For more on Prower see Radley, *We Lead Others Follow.*

63 LAC, War Diaries, 2nd Brigade and 8th Battalion, 26-27 November. Alston, a British officer, was BM of 2nd Brigade from August 1916 to July 1917. He had previously been GSO3 at 63rd British Division. In August 1917 he became BM 172nd Brigade, 57th British Division. Alston consistently demonstrated a very high level of competence as a BM, his efforts at Vimy being especially noteworthy. See Radley, *We Lead Others Follow* and Harvey, *An Army of Brigadiers,* Chapter 3.

64 LAC, MG30E100 (Currie Papers), Volume 35, File 176, 2nd Brigade report on raid. MacKenzie replaced Alston as BM 2nd Brigade, remaining until May 1918 when he was appointed BM Canadian Engineer Brigade. Loomis specially commended Mackenzie for his "concise orders and attention to detail" at Passchendaele.

65 LAC, War Diary, 2nd Brigade, February 1917.

7

The Balance of Profit

> Those higher up always see a clean map. The man who works in the mud can never see a clean map. So there was a difference in their viewpoint.
>
> Brigadier-General Victor Odlum

Odlum is saying that rank determined one's perspective, the lower down the ladder the less an individual sees; the private soldier, his concern little more than the trench a few yards either side of him, considered he and his mates "like fleas in a blanket ... seein' no more that the next nearest wrinkle."[1] Observation improved at the next higher rung and yet again as one climbed upward. As always, a chasm separated the Generals who offer battle, the lower ranking senior officers who conduct operations in which combat results and the rifle companies, officers and men, who fight. The same applies to how raids were viewed. Attitudes reflected personal characteristics such as aggressiveness, experience and, for some men, the incentives to raid such as promotion and decorations. Nor did regimental officers and men always share opinions about raids. Attitudes toward raids also depended to large extent on their outcome, individually, be it success or failure, and cumulatively, which is to say a record of repeated success or failure: "Successful operations raise the morale ... while costly failures lower it temporarily, perhaps considerably."[2] In short, as John Ruskin wrote, if people are to be happy in their work they need three things: "They must be fit for it. They must not do too much of it. And they must have a sense of success in it."

This chapter examines the attitudes of raiders, the "who" of the story, the officers and men, the units and sub-units, that made up the raiding parties. The raiders are the focus here, the planners of raids still influential, but not central, for plans are turned over to those who must do.

In the aftermath of any raid came assessment of value versus cost: the balance of profit. These words can be just as imprecise and inconstant in their applied meaning as "success" and "failure." When it comes to raids their values and the balance bring to mind the cliché about beauty and the eyes of the beholder. An early auditor, Cyril Falls, historian of the 36th (Ulster) Division, concluded in 1922 that whenever veterans got together the subject of raids arose and the conclusions of any debate would usually be along these lines:

1 Kipling, *The Irish Guards in the Great War: The First Battalion*, p. 154.
2 Terraine (ed.), *General Jack's Diary*, p. 166.

> Raids were frequently useful, and sometimes imperatively necessary; but the British raided too often. Raids to obtain identification of troops opposite, and even to keep the enemy 'on the stretch' were justifiable; those with the object of raising the moral[e] … were not because they did not succeed in their objective … And the raiders were always picked men … Many units had to deplore the loss of the very cream of their officers, NCOs and men … And the cold-blooded courage demanded … took a heavy toll of the nervous energy of even the biggest thruster.

Another of the divisional histories, published three years later, thought raids the means of identifying the enemy order of battle, a way to lower enemy morale by raising his anxiety and robbing him of rest and the best way to maintain own morale, a conclusion contrary to Falls' argument. A third divisional history, published in 1929, questioned the value of raids thus:

> There were for some time divided opinions as to whether these raids were worth their cost. They were supposed to be useful towards keeping up the fighting spirit of the men, but one may well wonder if any such tonic was needed. Sometimes they provided … precise details of the units in front and secured prisoners … But whatever was the balance of gain and loss they later on became fashionable, and a Division that did not report a number of raids each month was regarded as showing slackness and lack of zeal.[3]

In 1932 another divisional historian concluded that the cumulative effects of raids while "difficult to appraise at their true value now, will doubtless prove hereafter to have been considerable." He must have been disappointed with the conclusions that same year of the committee that had been formed to report on the lessons of the war. This report will receive further attention later, but for now suffice it to say that it, just like the conclusions reached in the accounts above, reflects ambiguity. This is not surprising since questions of value and profit achieved no consensus then amongst raiders and those who ordered raids, nor amongst those who had experienced raiding and subsequently wrote about it. Nor do modern assessments always agree.[4]

Lieutenant Wyn Griffith, 15th Royal Welsh Fusiliers, had his first experience of raiding, which he described as "cataclysmic upheaval," at Givenchy in May 1916. Despite repeated doses of assurance that raids ensured ascendency over the enemy, Griffith recalled how at the time "We were doubtful, sceptical even … for the balance of profit was not to be measured by our eyes." In fact, he realized that the balance would not be measured by battalions: unit officers could measure all they wished, but the balance that counted and drove events occurred at levels above battalion. Twelve years later, when he came to write *Up to Mametz,* he could see that raids, which to him had spelled "attrition," no longer had "many adherents … at any rate not among those who served in the infantry." As for the first raid he experienced, no prisoners, two officers missing, "many friends we would never see again." All in all, the night's work "not worth the cost."[5]

3 Falls, *36th (Ulster) Division,* p. 71; Sandilands, *23rd Division,* pp. 58-59; Atteridge, *17th (Northern) Division,* p. 69. Falls' comment about "picked" men was not the practice throughout the BEF.

4 Wyrall, *Nineteenth Division,* p. 25; *Report of the Committee on the Lessons of the Great War* (The War Office, October 1932; reprint ed., Uckfield, East Sussex: Naval and Military Press, n.d.), pp. 22-23. The President of the Committee, Lieutenant-General W.M. St. G. Kirke, had served at GHQ during the war.

5 Griffith, *Up to Mametz,* pp. 71-72, 111, 118.

Private John Becker, 75th Canadian Battalion, who wrote his war memoirs in 1930, recalled how in June 1917 he participated in a raid for the first time. He thought the balance pretty sorry. While the raiding party secured five prisoners, losses came to nearly a hundred killed and wounded: "We killed a number, but I don't believe the enemy loss was half ours … No one will ever convince me that the raid did us any good whatever." He asked bitterly "And what was it all for?" Lieutenant D.W.J. Cuddeford, 12th Highland Light Infantry, remembered how he and other Subalterns hated raids, their cost almost always more casualties that the results warranted. Thinking the whole idea of raiding just another indication that the "lives of infantrymen were cheap at that time," he was not shocked on hearing a story about two brigade commanders betting on whose brigade would capture the most prisoners in a trench raid competition. In view of this, perhaps he consciously intended the title of his recollections *And All For What?* to apply to raids and raiding.[6]

The balance of profit or a variant appears in modern accounts, too. G.R. Stevens in his history of the Loyal Edmonton Regiment (1964) describes a large-scale raid near Avion in June 1917 involving elements of the 7th and 11th Canadian Brigades and asks "Did this raid yield a credit balance? At this distance it seems doubtful." He also records some of the conflicting evidence, one account relating how the 49th Battalion went in perfectly aligned while another recorded how all was confusion, so much so that at Zero an officer ran up and down on the top of the jumping off trench shouting orders, rather a telling indication of something already gone wrong or preparations omitted or neglected. It is a fact, as Stevens concluded, that at night a man sitting tight, his weapon at the ready, has the advantage over an attacker stumbling in the dark across open and broken ground. In the end, German casualties were estimated at 100, probably an optimistic reckoning since enemy losses during night time encounters were usually inflated, no means existing to corroborate or confirm the numbers. Over 100 prisoners were taken, though. Canadian casualties totalled 100 killed or missing and over 600 wounded. The reader is free to answer Steven's question for himself.[7]

Siegfried Sassoon noted in late 1915 how certain "entertainments" (raids) had become very popular, thanks to "some Canadian toughs [who] had pulled off a fine effort." One side effect was that raids came to be expected, a second that they had also to be "roaring" successes. Since all battalions were expected to raid, and did so to varying degree, all officers and men had to master the tactical skills involved. *SS 107 Notes on Minor Enterprises* stipulated that officers and men "selected" to raid should "when possible, be volunteers." *SS 415 The Duties of an Officer* reiterated for the benefit of the officers of the BEF that "You are responsible for the successful leading of your men in battle; you are responsible for their safety as far as this can be ensured, while gaining success in battle; you are responsible for their health, for their comfort, for their good behaviour and discipline." The first, the officer's prime responsibility, included leading patrols and raids.[8]

6 Catherine Becker Monroe (ed.), *Silhouettes of the Great War: The Memoir of John Harold Becker 1915–1919* (Ottawa: CEF Books, 2001), p. 82; LAC, War Diary, 75th Battalion, June 1917, lists unit casualties as six officers wounded, 28 ORs killed, 112 wounded and 11 missing. Cuddeford, *And All For What?*, p. 124.

7 Stevens, *A City Goes to War*, p. 91; The figures are from brigade War Diaries and from Nicholson, *Canadian Expeditionary Force*, p. 281. This particular raid features in Chapter 13.

8 Siegfried Sassoon, *Memoirs of an Infantry Officer* (London: Faber and Faber, 1965), pp. 20. 24; *SS 107 Notes on Minor Enterprises; SS 415 The Duties of an Officer. Knowledge and Character* (London: HMSO,

What these responsibilities entailed in practise, and what the burden of command and expectations meant, is evident in the postwar reflections of many officers. One Subaltern soon learned how an officer's burden grew because of the general decline in the competence of NCOs and how this forced tasks upon officers that NCOs should have been capable of, but were not, the necessary confidence and credibility absent or inadequate. Lieutenant H.M. Butterworth of The Rifle Brigade recalled an instance when an NCO faltered and confessed his inability to take charge of a working party at night. Across no man's land the burden was much the same: as *Leutnant* Ernst Junger expressed it "I was always surprised and touched by the trusting reliance of the men on the ability of the officer to cope with the situation. 'Where shall we go, sir?' 'Help, sir, I'm wounded!' 'Where's the officer?'"[9]

How an officer or man became a member of a raiding party, whether volunteering or being selected, had a good deal to do with his record, experience, attitude and value as perceived by his superiors. Raiding could confirm or change perceptions thereby affecting how an individual saw himself and how others saw him. But before considering the avenue to membership certain preliminaries regarding the nature, organization and composition of raiding parties require description and clarification, the latter in regard to one or two recent accounts which contain some misapprehensions about command in general and the place and function of officers in particular.

A raiding party of any medium or larger size always consisted of at least one officer and any number of ORs. According to *SS 107 Notes on Minor Enterprises* "the number of men varies according to the nature and extent of the objective … from 30 to 300 men." On occasion, the number could be double or even more than that. The raiders, said the manual, should be volunteers, both officers and men. The manual also reminds that the objective had to be carefully selected and had to be "limited and definite." Ignoring this guidance could well lead to failure or at the very least make the raid additionally perilous for the raiders.

As a starting point to the misapprehensions mentioned a few lines above, there exists in a fairly recent (2010) account by John Lewis-Stempel a very dogmatic, completely erroneous and grossly insulting sentence: "Minor enterprises or not, British trench raids were always led by an officer; the Canadians once again left the dangerous aspects of the night shift to NCOs."[10] Seldom does one find a single sentence stuffed with such egregious, nonsensical scribbling. The falsity of the part of the sentence before the semi-colon would have been avoided had the writer been diligent and careful in his research. It is astonishing to see in the bibliography of his book, which is written by a Briton in Britain, not one single history of any of the British divisions of the Great War! Much can be learned from these histories, all of which are readily available in Britain and elsewhere. To offer just one example of a British raid led by an NCO we see in Gibbon's account of the 42nd (East Lancashire) Division a particularly daring raid led by

1917). This manual listed other useful attributes of an officer: mastery of weapons, ability to train as well as to lead and competent planning including allocating resources. Officers functioned as the thinking part of the Army.

9 Jon Cooksey (ed.), *Blood and Iron: Letters from the Western Front: Hugh Montague Butterworth* (Barnsley: Pen & Sword Military, 2011), p. 176. Butterworth served with the 9th Battalion, The Rifle Brigade. He was killed in action in September 1915. Junger, *Storm of Steel*, pp. 157-58. Radley, *Get Tough, Stay Tough*, illustrates the declining authority and standard of NCOs during the war.

10 John Lewis-Stempel, *Six Weeks: The Short and Gallant Life of the British Officer in the First World War* (London: Weidenfeld & Nicolson, 2010), p. 114.

Sergeant J. Sugden (10th Manchesters) who received a DCM and 14 days special leave for his very fine work which included the taking of four prisoners and a trench mortar.[11] Many more examples of raids led by British NCOs can be seen in the divisional histories and in the War Diaries if one cares to look.

Another aspect of Lewis-Stempel's erroneous use of the word "always" relates to several fundamentals of the organization of infantry battalions of the BEF and certain defining characteristics of the place and functions of the officers and ORs who made up the battalions. First, an infantry battalion consisted of four companies, each initially commanded by a Captain, but later Major came to be the usual rank of a company commander. Each company had four platoons, each commanded by an officer. Thus the officer establishment of a company came to be one Major, one Captain and four Subalterns, a Subaltern being an officer below the rank of Captain. Events such as casualties and absence on leave, training and temporary duties meant that not all six officers were always present. Lewis-Stempel seems unaware of normal trench routine which at company level included, day and night, a Duty or Orderly Officer (one of the four Subalterns) whose responsibilities included frequent checking of company trenches, manning company HQ and assisting the OC as required. Subalterns usually led raids, but given only a pool of four not all raids could be led by an officer. Common sense says that British raids could not possibly have "always" been led by an officer. The same is true of Canadian, Australian, New Zealand and other BEF raids.

An indefensible canard resides in the half of Lewis-Stempel's offensive sentence after the semi-colon. He must explain what he means by "once again." This unjustified character assassination is grossly offensive. But he cannot explain for never has there been a better example of hopelessly inadequate research! Given today's technology and the readily available published accounts there is no excuse for his neglect of the historical accounts. One would think a man whose research has been so shallow would be more circumspect rather than so highlight the absence of sufficient study. He must surely have seen how very thin it was as he went along. Would that Lewis-Stempel had heeded Somerset Maugham's wisdom which says "It is not necessary to eat a whole sheep in order to describe the taste of mutton, but it is advisable at least to have licked a lamb chop."[12] We do not know if Lewis-Stempel's careless contentions come to him from someone else, or whether it is self-generated nonsense, but either way it is incredibly cavalier and utterly unhistorical. He mentions on page 115 the well-known Canadian raid of November 1915. Had he read just the account of it in the British Official History he would have learned that 10 officers were on that raid. Failing all else, had Lewis-Stempel thought to just search out the numbers of DSOs and MCs awarded to Canadians for leadership of raids he would have been disabused of his misapprehensions. Twenty-one DSOs were awarded to Canadian officers for raids and over 200 MCs. These figures include only those awards where the citation includes the word "raid." There are many cases where the word "attack" is used instead of "raid." While the context of the citation indicates a raid, the word "raid" was not there so count has been kept strictly to those where "raid' is actually written. The real count of decorations for raids is likely higher than the 21 DSOs and the 200 MCs.[13]

11 Gibbon, *42nd (East Lancashire) Division*, pp. 94-95.

12 Quoted in Barrie Pitt, 'Writers and the Great War', *Journal of the Royal United Service Institute* (August 1964), p. 247.

13 Riddle and Mitchell, *Distinguished Service Order* and *Military Cross*, both volumes published in 1991; Brigadier-General J.E. Edmonds, *Military Operations France and Belgium, 1916: Sir Douglas Haig's*

Canadian NCOs, junior and senior, did lead raids, but in every instance of this found during the research done for this book such raids, with rare exception, were small, usually restricted to 10 or fewer men. In larger Canadian raids where the raiding force was organized in several parties we see NCOs, junior and senior, leading some sub-parties. During a raid by 3rd Battalion in December 1916, for example, NCOs led seven sub-parties of six to eight men each. The OC of the raid was a Major and the two assault parties to which the seven sub-parties belonged were each led by an officer. Likewise, the six sub-parties, each of less than eight ORs, that participated in a raid by 58th Battalion in December were led by NCOs. Again, the OC Raid and the assault party commanders were officers. What is irrefutably clear in Canadian archival documents and in published histories is that when it came to raids officers usually led them. Moreover, Canadians, whether subordinates or superiors, expected raids to be led by officers.

Given Sir Arthur Currie's views on command it would have been highly uncommon for an NCO to have led a platoon-sized or larger raid or a fighting patrol. In May 1917, in response to a proposal that warrant and non-commissioned officers should command infantry platoons (this suggestion stemming from the high rate of officer casualties), Currie rejected the idea since he considered "that all fighting units corresponding to a platoon of infantry should be led by a commissioned officer and that warrant and non-commissioned officers should not command similar units in a battalion." Such a scheme in Currie's view might be applied to "maintenance services," possibly artillery ammunition columns, non-fighting sapper establishments and service corps elements such as field bakeries, but never to infantry. It is evident that Currie saw the role of the NCO as supervision and the role of the officer as command and leadership. To him, the proposal put officer prestige and authority at risk, a development that could not be countenanced. A Canadian Corps instruction summed this up: "Men must possess discipline, officers prestige, all ranks morale."[14]

It is also evident in some of the recent literature that some confusion exists about the terminology applied to the categories of officers. An example in a fairly recent study of one British regiment illustrates this: "Raiding parties were generally commanded by Subalterns or trusted NCOs with a Captain in overall control who … more generally appears to have supervised from the front line … The actual raiding parties tended to be led by junior officers."[15] This is ambiguous – what exactly is the difference between raiding parties and actual raiding parties – but the bigger problem here is the contradiction between the first few words including "Subaltern" and the last few words including "junior officers." The facts are these. Three terms applied to the officers of a rifle company. First, as a collective the officers of a company were known as "Company Officers." Second, the term "Junior Officers" referred to Captains, Lieutenants and Second Lieutenants. Third, a Subaltern was an officer below the rank of Captain. The difference between a Subaltern and a Junior Officer (were he a Captain) was not insignificant and was important in the sense of command experience. Captains did command companies initially, and frequently did thereafter, and although a Subaltern could and did command a company during

Command to the 1st July: Appendices (London: Macmillan, 1932), Appendix 6, Organization and Execution of a Raid. (5th and 7th Battalions, 16th/17th November 1915).

14 LAC, RG9IIIC3, Volume 4008, Folder 7, File 4, Currie to Canadian Corps 8 May 1917; Volume 4079, Folder 8, file 6, 'Notes on Leadership for Company Officers', War Diaries, 3rd and 58th Battalions, December 1916.

15 Connelly, *Steady the Buffs!*, pp. 82-83.

times of high officer casualties, his usual command was a platoon, not a company. In short, the key difference was experience.

A number of factors determined who and how many officers and men would participate in a raid. First, the raiding party had to be large enough to cover the objective, the size of which had to be appropriate to the resources available. Second, the purpose of the raid had to be taken into account. A raid with one aim or purpose, and one where ground and circumstances made its execution straightforward, could be classed as simple, which is not to say it was easy to do. For a task, say, to take a prisoner from an outpost or sap, a platoon or even just half that might well suffice with no necessity for any outside assistance such as fire support. Organization in such a case could be simple, too, perhaps just a small covering party and a single assault party. When the raid involved entry to the enemy main line then planning and execution became more complicated. So, too, did a raid where the raiders had multiple tasks such as take prisoners, destroy dug-outs, penetrate more deeply into enemy lines and investigate other specific matters at different places within an objective. Here several officers might be required and a number of sub-parties would have to be organized to clear trenches and dug-outs, block trench junctions, provide flank protection, perhaps form a signals party, protection parties for sappers, reserves and other functional groupings dedicated to the specific requirements. Now the whole is complex, not simple; difficult, not easy. Clausewitz stressed that in war the simplest thing can be difficult, thanks to friction or the fog of war to which human failings such as misunderstanding, doubt and poor reactions to stress are added and accumulate.[16] An excellent example of a complex and difficult raid was one carried out by 11th Border Regiment (32nd British Division) in June 1916. This raid, one of a series that month just before the Somme, aimed to determine the condition of the enemy trenches, to secure identification of units and to confirm that the enemy was manning his trenches and in what strength. It involved deep penetration of enemy lines and multiple tasks spread over the objective and extending into the enemy support line. The OC Raid organized his officers and 80 ORs, all volunteers, into 13 sub-parties, a number necessitated by the complexity of the raid. An even more complicated raid was one by 3rd Canadian Division on the southern flank of Vimy Ridge in December 1916. It was the largest Canadian raid done up to that time (350 all ranks) and the second done in daylight. Because each section of the three companies involved had a particular task the organization of the raiders was very complicated. This being realized by the planners the raiders had a full month to prepare. These two raids are examined in later chapters in detail.

Having just mentioned "volunteers," which was how some men came to be on raids, it is appropriate here to examine this source together with the other primary means of obtaining membership in the fraternity of raiders. An officer or man volunteered or he was selected. He might volunteer on his own, or he might get "volunteered" (selected in a sort of press-gang fashion) because of his previous experience, or because he was known as a good man in a scrap, or, if sufficient volunteers were not coming forward, then simply to fill a hole, a clear case of standing about in the wrong place at the wrong time. Other nationalities had other means of selection. The Portuguese, for example, sorted men out according to this formula: best behaved men were kept in support, less satisfactory men held the front trenches and their worst did

16 Spartacus, 'Simplicity', pp.48-52; Howard and Paret (ed. and trans.) *On War* By Carl von Clausewitz, pp. 119-21.

tasks forward of their lines. An individual might also be selected simply because he was part of an existing organization, be it one of the early battalion "Bombing Parties," or because he was a member of a platoon or company that had been ordered to raid. When the task came from on high, the process often became a mix: when in May 1916 15th Royal Welsh Fusiliers went a-raiding it began with the corps commander wanting prisoners, the division commander selecting the brigade for the venture, the brigade commander selecting the 15th and the CO ordering company commanders to provide volunteers to make up the raiding force. Or a man got the nod because he was part of a "standing" raiding party, an organization favoured in some divisions during the first two years of the war.

In April 1916 Major-General H. Hudson, then GOC 8th British Division, directed that each battalion in the division would maintain a "special party" of two officers and 50 ORs trained as raiders. The object, as 25th Brigade posed it, was "to have ready to hand a body of men … who will, so far as is possible, always be ready to carry put a raid or counter-raid should necessity arise." Battalions in this brigade, and presumably in the other two brigades of the division, were ordered to submit by 2 May their training programmes for their standing party. Only one battalion of the 25th, the 2nd Rifle Brigade, seems to have met the deadline. In any case, brigade followed up with a demand, in addition to the training programme, for details as to special equipment required for the raiding parties and for a description of the methods which would be employed during raids from assembly prior to the raid through to completion.

The following month another division took up a variant of this. Battalions in reserve in 38th British Division were instructed to train one company each for raiding during the four days they were out of the line (at this time this division had two battalions forward and two in reserve). These companies, which were "to be as strong as possible," would be exempt from working parties. One brigade, the 114th, sought and received approval that when it was in reserve "two companies instead of one company from one battalion" would train for raiding. Brigade had received orders as to points to be raided and companies would train for these. COs would be informed which points they would reconnoitre. Battalions were to report as soon as possible the strength and composition of the raiding party and the names of the officers. This concept of standing and specialized raiding parties was part of the mania (some called it a disease) of specialization that had swept the BEF in early 1916, so much so that it worried regimental officers who saw fighting strength much reduced because of the drain of "detachments, whether specialists or employed men [men on other duties]." The concept of standing parties, like specialization itself, did not last. In February 1917 *SS 143 Instructions for the Training of Platoons for Offensive Action, 1917* pronounced "The guiding principles of this organization are that the Platoon shall consist of a combination of all the weapons with which the Infantry are now armed, and that specialist commanders for Infantry are undesirable."[17]

Those who volunteered for raids had various motives for doing so. Some sought promotion or other reward which would be reflected in what one officer called the "Book of Glory," the ribbons on one's tunic that set out a man's achievements for all to see. Private Stephen Graham's chum Fitz was one of "a number of fellows found eager for the affair [a raid in 1918] though none

17 Rees, *Schoolmaster at War*, p. 92; Griffith, *Up to Mametz*, p. 111; TNA: WO 95/1674: 8th Division, 30 April, 2-7 May 1916; TNA: WO 95/2557: 114th Brigade (38th Division), order to battalions, 23 May 1916; *SS 143;* Radley, *We Lead Others Follow*, p. 101, examines the negative impact of specialization upon the infantry.

could say how much or how little danger there was in it … Fitz … saw himself winning a VC or … distinction of some kind." The party as a whole, said Graham, "thirsted for blood." Some men just sought adventure, the more perilous the better. Graham Greenwell, in March 1917 just about to celebrate his 21st birthday (he had been at the front for two years), and a company commander with the Oxfordshire and Buckinghamshire Light Infantry, was ordered to lead a two-company raid. Describing in some detail his preparations for the raid, he recalled "weeding out the incapables … only the keen boys will do [and] they are all as pleased as Punch at the idea." As it turned out, the raiders entered empty trenches, the Germans having withdrawn.[18]

On occasion, there could be a hidden motive for volunteering. In one instance in mid-1916, it was "family with its … tawdry secrets." Robert Graves related how an officer of the North Staffordshire Regiment having learned

> from home that his wife was living with another man … went out on a raid that night and got either killed or captured; so the men with him said. There had been a fight and they came back without him. After two days he was arrested … trying to board a leave train; he had intended to go home and shoot up the wife and her lover. The officers who court-martialled him for deserting in the face of the enemy were content with a sentence of cashiering. He went as a private soldier to another regiment.[19]

At times units placed restrictions on those who could raid. The CO of 15th London Regiment, for example, having to turn away some men who had volunteered for a raid – a surfeit of riches – decided that "Married men with families, then those who had most recently been in bayonet reach of the Boche, were automatically ruled out. Company and platoon commanders sorted out the rest." Likewise, the CO of 9th East Surreys (24th British Division) in late 1917, tasked by brigade to get a prisoner, had to limit volunteers, many having come forward "at once." Sometimes intuition determined who volunteered. Captain James Dunn, Medical Officer of 2nd Royal Welsh Fusiliers, observed how "One comes to see that the older men, not the younger, volunteer for the bigger risks, and wonders at it." One theory voiced by a 19 year old Subaltern was that the youngsters saw their lives before them and wanted it, while the older men were mostly married and disillusioned about life.[20]

As time wore on line-ups to volunteer grew shorter. Lieutenant-Colonel (later Brigadier-General) J.L. Jack, in July 1917 CO 2nd West Yorkshires, noted that "the number of volunteers for raids is smaller than formerly, although courage in action is as common as ever." No surfeit shows here, nor in 19th Canadian Battalion in May 1918 when Private Deward Barnes wrote in his diary "Wanted volunteers for Brigade raid, *No compre.*" Here Barnes voted against stepping into danger unnecessarily. In February the GOC Canadian Corps had been made aware of the

18 Cloete, *A Victorian Son,* p. 197; Graham, *A Private in the Guards,* p. 261; Graham H. Greenwell, *An Infant in Arms: War Letters of a Company Officer 1914-1918* (London: The Penguin Press, 1972), p. 160.

19 Graves, *Goodbye to All That,* p. 103. This incident testifies to several motivations: possibly soldier loyalty to their officer, soldier views on the other world called the Home Front and what soldiers saw as right and wrong. The "so the men … said" can be taken as just statement of fact, or it can be taken to mean something quite different.

20 French, *Gone For a Soldier*, p. 53; Dunn, *The War the Infantry Knew,* p. 196.

declining number of volunteers. At that time the CO of the 3rd Battalion, J.B. Rogers, having been warned that a Court of Inquiry would be convened on the battalion's failure to secure a prisoner during a raid on 4 February, informed his brigade commander, William Griesbach, that every officer and man on the raid had volunteered for it. He warned that if a court went ahead it "would have a detrimental effect on men voluntarily coming forward for raids in the future." GOC 1st Division then requested an interview with the Corps commander. No court was held. Of course, reluctance to volunteer could be particular rather than general and may have been peculiar to a specific raid. That same month those directly concerned with planning raids would have been heartened by the ready response for a large-scale effort to be made by 10th Canadian Brigade: the raiding force consisted of one "regular" company from each of three battalions and one composite "volunteer" company from 47th Battalion, whose CO had decided on an all volunteer company and filled it with no difficulty.[21]

Even before the Somme some restrictions on which officers could raid, or even patrol, were in force as Second Lieutenant Bernard Martin, North Staffordshire Regiment, discovered on taking command of a company in May 1916. Amongst papers in his company HQ he found an order reading "Company commanders are prohibited from going beyond the front line trench." Another instruction warned that a junior officer intending to patrol had to notify his company commander of his intention. Seeking the guidance of an experienced officer Martin received this advice: "Panic orders. Someone … has discovered too many of us getting killed … No one is going to order you to go into No Man's Land … it's up to you to decide if and when you do. Forget it; at any rate till you are thoroughly familiar with all the routine and everyday responsibilities." However, to a young officer, challenge posed, challenge accepted. Martin very soon took out his first patrol. Later (early 1917) Major R.T. Rees, 4th Loyal North Lancashire Regiment, although well aware of orders that Captains and above who patrolled should expect immediate court-martial, decided, in view of a pressing need for information to go out anyway. On return, he covered his transgression so imaginatively that it either went unnoticed, or, more likely, his superiors chose not to take notice. As for raids, before Passchendaele when Rees' division, the 55th, was ordered to secure prisoners his battalion got the task and his company got the nod for the job. On the day of the raid 30 minutes before Zero Rees was told he was not to lead the raid, the brigadier saying that he could not afford to lose any more senior officers. The Subaltern who took his place was killed, one of many casualties suffered. No prisoners were taken. It is evident, however, that such restrictions were not universal. In July GOC 1st Canadian Brigade (Griesbach) asked battalion commanders to point out to subordinates that "the need of a prisoner is so great that in the event of success I should feel called upon to recommend … honours and awards."[22]

As the ranks of raid commanders were determined by the size of the raiding force and by policy, Majors and Lieutenant-Colonels did become active in the execution of raids. In October 1916 First Army (Horne) thought it better to slim down the size of raiding parties, but in the

21 Terraine (ed.), *General Jack's Diary,* p. 232; Cane, *It Made You Think of Home,* entry for 31 May; LAC, RG 9IIIC3, Volume 4017, Folder 35, file 18. Letter of 6 February, Rogers to GOC 1st Brigade and associated correspondence; 47th Battalion War Diary, February 1917; Pearse and Sloan, *East Surrey Regiment,* p. 81.

22 Rees, *Schoolmaster at War,* pp. 59, 64-67, 92; LAC, MG30E15 (Griesbach Papers), 'Book of Wisdom', Volume 2, 24 July 1917.

face of contrary views among his Corps he decided that Corps commanders should set their own policy providing strong raids did not entirely cease. Battalion officers were not generally in favour of their seniors being too involved. Alan Thomas, who served with the 6th Royal West Kents in 12th British Division, believed that patrols were no place for Colonels. The officers of another unit, the 4th King's Own Lancaster Regiment, seeing their CO foremost in such activities, became very uneasy about "Colonels crawling around in No Man's Land." The CO in question, Frederick Carlton, DSO, subsequently achieved brigade command.[23]

No matter which option a battalion commander took when it came to forming raiding parties, volunteers or selected men, formed or composite companies, there were disadvantages. Selection meant that invariably the best men were chosen and not just once. It was also recognized that using Captains and Majors as raid commanders would result in the loss of the very officers who would have to very soon command battalions and even brigades. Such extravagance did not bode well. The Committee on the Lessons of the War agreed: in "necessarily" selecting the best "irreplaceable material was thus expended."[24] Moreover, when the best were lost or were burnt out this damaged the units/sub-units from which the best had been selected. But reliance on volunteers also posed disadvantages. For one thing, such a recourse, while the easy route in making up a raiding party, became unfair for the simple reason that some men never volunteer. Nor were volunteers necessarily the best men for the task. In addition, as Lieutenant-Colonel J.L. Jack pointed out, eventually volunteers petered out and selection had to commence. The "happy warrior" extolled by Wordsworth eventually became less "ready, aye, ready."

As for what officers and men, top to bottom, thought about raids it is a fact that while an "attitude" is said to be a "settled" mode of thinking or behaviour, views on raids were anything but. The initial aspect to consider is this: whose attitudes are we talking about? First, look behind the camera at the directors that the Army calls senior commanders and their staffs. It would be wrong to call these "non-participants" since they always influenced, often instigated, frequently ordered and generally invigilated raids and assessed results. Next is the cast, the players being those officers and men who leapt into enemy trenches, sometimes their only catch, in *Leutnant* Junger's words, the "memory of a rapid and frantic glance into Vulcan's white-hot cauldron." The leading players, OC Raid and his officers, their number depending on the size and composition of the raiding party, had their personal views on raids and raiding in general and also on what they believed their men thought about raids. ORs in the raiding party also reflected upon raids in general, assessed their officers' actions and speculated about what their officers thought. Attitudes were cumulative since the cast would have to make any number of repeat performances. Outcomes, success or failure, also inspired attitudes. Attitudes were not immutable; a raider's before and after attitude usually differed, nor did they necessarily stand up to long-term reflection. In short, attitude was both photograph and moving picture.

Finally, military historians have views, too, and here a difference exists. Between the world wars, 45 of the divisions that served in the BEF became the subject of a history. Of these, 39 were written by former officers ranging in rank from Captain (three) to Major-General (one). Eleven were written by Lieutenant-Colonels. Some of the authors, like Cyril Falls (36th (Ulster)

23 Thomas, *A Life Apart,* p. 58; Shannon, *The Lion and the Rose,* p. 74. For the unfavourable views of ORs on such activities by officers see Radley, *Get Tough, Stay Tough.*

24 Falls, *36th (Ulster) Division,* p. 71; *Committee on the Lessons of the War,* p. 23.

Division), became distinguished military historians. These officer-historians could offer readers wisdom gained from war experience. We cannot say how many of them raided, planned raids, or otherwise were associated with raiding or with officers and men who had raided. Although those who had no military service did enjoy some benefit from contact with former soldiers they did not experience raiding and could not really appreciate the "cauldron" Junger spoke of above. Historians in more recent times have neither experience of raiding, nor the contacts available in former times, which probably explains why they came generally come out against raiding despite the fact that it was often useful and at times absolutely necessary. Not for nothing did Jomini proclaim passive defence pernicious.

It is historical fact, too, that commanders always want to know what looms beyond, that they fear surprise and that they cannot tolerate idle troops for these, in their minds, are soldiers who have lost or are losing their edge. Paddy Griffith stresses the fact that new troops must always be "blooded" and it is better to do so on a small scale rather than during a large operation. Working in gradually is always preferable to being suddenly savaged and left largely non-effective. Raids, as Chapter 4 related, were also training and testing, especially of new officers who all too soon, given officer casualties, would have to handle companies routinely and, more occasionally, battalions.[25] One has only to look at a list of the Principles of War, amongst them security and surprise, to comprehend why raiding has persisted.

Earlier this book discussed BEF raiding policy as conceived by French and then Haig. Although space does not permit an accounting of what each Army and Corps commander thought of the policy, one can say that all were expected to support it. An example of how one prominent Corps commander, Lieutenant-General Sir Richard Haking, GOC XI Corps, viewed raiding is evident in an essay by John Bourne. In a paragraph that opens with the disastrous failure at Fromelles in July 1917 he links Fromelles, raiding and Haking, a prominent exponent of the offensive spirit, as the General who "did more than anyone else in the BEF to encourage trench raids and the spirit of the bayonet." Hacking's superior, General Sir Charles Monro, GOC First Army, while he supported raids, insisted that if a raid did not serve a specific purpose then it should not be carried out. John Bourne rightly wonders how many of Haking's raids met this criterion. But Haking did not always get his way when it came to actual raiding within XI Corps; during the months November 1915 to April 1916 five of the 12 battalions in one of his divisions (19th) did not plan or execute a single raid. Moreover, total participation in the few raids the 19th actually did came to about 100 all ranks and total time spent in enemy trenches during these raids fell short of 60 minutes, a performance hardly in line with Haking's insistence that raids be big and raiders remain longer in enemy trenches. Frustrated, he remarked to Monro that the 19th had "got into bad ways when it first came out and it has been extremely difficult to get it out of them."[26]

James Roberts also informs us that by January 1916 the GOC of 19th Division and two of the three original brigadiers had been replaced and by July the "entire upper echelons" of the divisions (senior commanders and battalion commanders) had been "overhauled." This is not to

25 Griffith, *Battle Tactics of the Western Front,* p. 61.

26 John Bourne, 'Charles Monro', in Ian F.W. Beckett and Steven J. Corvi (eds.), *Haig's Generals* (Barnsley: Pen & Sword, 2006), pp. 133-34; James Roberts, 'Making the Butterflies Kill', *Stand To!,* 68 (September 2003), pp. 38-44. V. Wheeler Holohan, *Divisional and Other Signs* (London: John Murray, 1920), p. 52. 19th Division's sign, a butterfly of the peacock variety, was the personal choice of the GOC, G.M.T. Bridges, before the Somme.

suggest that raiding alone, or the lack thereof, drove all these changes. The author of the only biography of Haking describes Haking's "mixed" relationships with his division commanders and how "little" information in available about how he got on with his senior staff officers. Senior also cautions that Haking, as did every British corps commander, had to contend with the constant shuffle of divisions in and out of his corps. The shuffling influenced every level of command and raids as well. It would be extremely difficult, if not impossible, to know how many raids were demanded of units just arrived in a particular area and not yet knowing their way about, or in some cases in the process of recovering from attacking somewhere else.[27] Any conclusions about the general attitudes of division and brigade commanders regarding raids would be precarious, indeed. But one can say attitudes were not unanimous and could even be surprising.

In studying the British War Diaries it quickly became apparent, not surprisingly, that some divisions, brigades and battalions raided more than others. Some formations/units raided frequently, in some cases seemingly at every possible opportunity. Then, of course, others raided less frequently, just occasionally, certainly at a more measured pace. At the bottom end of the scale was 19th Division, but it was not alone in its infrequency. In researching a quite unrelated matter concerning the British Regular Divisions in due course each of the three brigades of 4th Division (a Regular Division) came to hand. One of the battalions of that division's 10th Brigade, 1st Royal Warwickshires, raided only once in each of 1916, 1917 and 1918 in the strength shown: April 1916, two officers and 25 ORs; November 1917, four officers and 153 ORs; and June 1918, four officers and 108 ORs. The aim of all three raids was to secure prisoners; only the 1918 raid did so.[28]

A battalion with a similar raiding record, 38th Canadian Battalion (4th Canadian Division), raided only twice: 22 February 1917 and 25/26 April 1918. The 1917 raid consisted of five officers and 85 ORs, the 1918 raid five and 116. The first took no prisoners and suffered four ORs killed and 27 wounded. The second took no prisoners, but did secure identifications in the form of enemy clothing. Two officers and 215 ORs were wounded. Five ORs were killed. Canadian raiding activity, like the British, varied from extremely active to infrequent.[29]

Raids, like the Army itself, were something of a Snakes and Ladders game, one that could get very personal in the event of failure or just not measuring up to expectations. The 6th South Staffordshires experienced the "high" of riding in September and October 1916. Following a great success in September, the unit received from its parent brigade and division (137th Brigade, 46th Division) "affectionate messages of gratitude and approval … from once irate higher authority." Both officers received the MC and MMs went to five men of the raiding party. While the GOC commented specifically on the thoroughness of raid preparation, the real message of official notice said "A capital affair! We must do this again." Responding to

27 Senior, *Haking*, pp. 252-53; Roberts, 'Making the Butterflies Kill', p. 43. In 1916 XI Corps hosted 14 different divisions, a mere 10 in 1917. This constant cycling in and out did not apply to the Canadian Corps which enjoyed divisional stability throughout.

28 TNA: WO 95/1484: 1st Royal Warwickshires; Dorrington, '"Live and Let Die" – The British Army's Experience of Trench Raiding 1915-1918', *Journal of the Centre for First World War Studies*, pp. 1-31. This does not seem to be available any longer at the web site. Dorrington uses the experience of the battalion "to examine the development of the raid as a specific operation."

29 LAC, War Diary, 38th Battalion.

cries of "Encore" the 6th raided again on 18 October, another success leaving "everyone pleased with the raiders and the raiders pleased with themselves." The 6th, now the "well-beloved" 6th, then went into divisional reserve for "rest," which usually included large doses of drill, general "smartening up," tighter discipline and training quite possibly for another raid, one that might add to their laurels or perhaps mark the "low" of raiding on the Western Front. The 6th had wrought, in Keat's phrase, a "thing of beauty," but not forever!

Occasionally, the ire of disappointed superiors could spread very far and to considerable depth, a reach that no doubt worried Second Lieutenant A.M. Brown, 15th Highland Light Infantry, OC of a raid in 1918 that failed to achieved its assigned purpose of diverting enemy attention from raids by a flanking division. In this case, failure was visible not only within the division, but outside it, publicity that did not please his superiors. Coming to the unfavourable notice of the GOC was not a reputation enhancing distinction.[30]

Reaction of brigade commanders to failure ranged across a wide spectrum, but some commonly seen elements were disappointment, concern about how to explain it when the raid had been demanded by higher command, embarrassment, and resigned recognition that the raid might well have to be repeated. The least negative reception given the OC of a raiding party was likely that accorded *Leutnant* Ernst Junger, who despite failure and the loss of half his raiding party, still received from his "very much disappointed" Colonel coffee and admiration "all the same for what we had done," then Junger had lunch with the divisional commander and the next day his Colonel awarded decorations Crosses and leave to all ranks. All this seems quite over the top, but as the Germans did not raid as much and the raiders had made a very determined effort, perhaps it was warranted; certainly, it was encouragement rather than condemnation.[31]

A very different situation faced W.D. Villiers-Stuart, CO in 1915 of 9th Rifle Brigade, a battalion of 14th British Division. In June when recce revealed that the objective chosen for a raid was very strongly held, he refused to raid, which made his brigadier furious. Nevertheless, he reiterated his refusal the next morning. Another battalion was then ordered to do the raid, although Villiers-Stuart had to provide bombers, a demand he could not refuse. The raid, when it went in, failed dramatically leaving him deeply angry "at losing such good officers and men for nothing. It taught the brigadier and his staff a lesson which should not have been necessary for them to learn in that way." When the brigadier visited the next day Villiers-Stuart expected trouble, but the GOC was "quite a lot tamer than before, being aware that he had made a fool of himself." Most likely Villiers-Stuart got away with his refusal in part because June 1915 was relatively early days. A year later his brigadier might not have been so tame, provided he retained command, of course.[32]

A failed raid could ruin one's personal reputation and spell the end of one's military career. The chain of events could be curious. After the 4th Suffolks (33rd British Division) failed to achieve the purpose of a raid on 13/14 May 1916 the CO, Lieutenant-Colonel F.W. Turner, was

30 Committee of Officers, *Sixth South Staffordshire Regiment,* pp. 159-60, 164; TNA: WO 95/2372: 32nd British Division, Operation Order 182; TNA: WO 95/2393: 15th Highland Light Infantry, June 1918; correspondence 14th Brigade and 32nd Division; Malcolm Brown, *Tommy Goes to War* (London J.M. Dent & Sons Ltd., 1978), p. 95.

31 Junger, *Storm of Steel,* pp. 194-203.

32 Maxwell. *Villiers-Stuart Goes to War,* pp. 82-83; Cooksey, *Blood and Iron,* pp. 65,77. Villiers-Stuart was well known for his irascibility and outspokenness.

four days later relieved by his brigade commander despite the divisional commander's appreciation of the raiders' spirit under "difficult" circumstances. The brigadier's grounds for relief were that Turner "owing to his wound had little war experience." According to the unit War Diary Turner had assumed command on 18 March. The reason for removal strikes one as reminiscent of the old complaint about inability to get a job because of lack of experience and cannot get any because of no job. The real reason for dismissal seems to be in Turner's report in which he describes the enemy trench being covered over by what appeared to be boards except for a few spaces about two feet wide and about 20 feet apart. This, and a ditch immediately in front of the enemy trench, apparently made entry into this trench impossible. One wonders if any recce was done before the raid. If not, then the stated reason for removal may have been kinder than a statement of incompetence or neglect. Or did the brigade commander see this raid as the last straw? In any case, Turner departed.[33]

A month later in another example of "degommy" (becoming ungummed) over a raid the CO of 11th Royal Sussex, Lieutenant-Colonel H.J.M. Grisewood, left the unit. Two very good accounts of the course of this dismissal are extant, one by a Subaltern and one by a company commander. The unit War Diary records that Grisewood took his battalion back into the line on 22 June 1916. Edmund Blunden, the Subaltern, described the CO as "very grave and conscientious," noting also "I seldom rise to the eminence of conversation with him." Major The Hon. Neville Lytton, OC C Company, who admired Grisewood, thought him "a positive genius for soldiering," but also an officer with a "troublesome" reputation, this probably based on his "complete intolerance of fools in high places." Blunden describes how "when Grisewood had been ordered to make a raid at once [against an area] fortified with the keenest intelligence, the thickest wire and emplacement, in the dark and without any preparation [he] demurred," was dismissed and another battalion had to do the raid. "Grisewood," he said "rescued us from this menacing plan." Lytton offers more detail as to how the CO after personal recce advised the GOC, M.L. Hornby, that to ensure success three or four days preparation was required. This reaction seems to have left Hornby thinking the CO lacking in aggressive spirit. He then got rid of Grisewood. In a farewell note to Lytton Grisewood wrote that brigade had ordered him "to clear off at once," which he did, stopping at division "to try and fix up staying on." Lytton called the raid made by the other unit a "hopeless" failure. Grisewood, obviously not a man to quit, presented 39th Division (Major-General R. Dawson) with an ultimatum: post him to another battalion or he would demand a Court of Inquiry. There must have been some sympathy for him at division and higher since rather than being summarily sent home he went to 17th Manchesters which he commanded until September. Hornby, GOC of the brigade since mid-April, had chosen to ignore the requirement for thorough preparation for a raid. While that decision was his, it seems the division commander was not entirely of the same mind about the raid.[34] The evidence available suggests that Grisewood's dismissal hinged entirely on Brigadier-

33 C.C.R. Murphy, *The History of the Suffolk Regiment 1914-1927* (London: Hutchinson, 1928), p. 145; TNA: WO 95/2424: 4th Suffolks, March and May 1916; Hodgkinson, *British Infantry Battalion Commanders*, p. 119. The brigade commander recommended Turner for command of a training battalion in England.

34 TNA: WO 95/2582: 11th Royal Suffolks, June 1916; Edmund Blunden, *The Mind's Eye* (London: Jonathan Cape, 1934), p. 61; Blunden, *Undertones of War*, pp.10, 23-24, 44; Major The Hon. N.S. Lytton, *The Press and the General Staff* (London: Collins, 1920), pp. 8, 32, 38-39, 41; Major A.F. Becke

General Hornby's speculation about Grisewood's aggressiveness. Major Lytton's remarks about Grisewood's reputation may have had something to do with it.

Rowland Fielding, who commanded two battalions in succession during the war, wrote that he knew of a "good many" battalion commanders who had become degommy. The always present possibility of that had a definite "looking over one's shoulder" impact. J.L. Jack's experience testifies to that. During the first December of the war when his battalion was ordered to raid, his CO and the brigade commander, considering conditions highly unfavourable, protested with vigour and division cancelled the order. By 1916 such a protest would likely have had a very different outcome. In September 1916 Jack, then CO 2nd West Yorkshires, reported on a raid on 15 September that became a "wretched affair" thanks to unreported belts of new wire. Consequently, he ordered the raiders to withdraw while he considered the situation: "It is intensely difficult to decide what to do next. The operation has been specially ordered … If we make no attempt we shall likely have to carry it out on another night, perhaps under peremptory orders and less favourable conditions. The enemy has apparently not been put on the alert by the first movement." He decided to go ahead, but at another location. But there the wire was too wide to be gapped by a Bangalore so the OC Raid selected another point, at which time a sentry sounded the alarm and the raid was aborted: "disappointing [but] the cool, determined courage of the officers and men has been admirable, as is admitted by High Command." The cost, amazingly, considering the ad-hockery, was just one killed and one wounded, sparing Jack the agony of complete disaster that could have resulted.[35]

Of course, brigadiers and their staff did not actively participate in raids. This fell to regimental officers and men who when their innocence of raids became experience, could and did weigh purpose. The Guards, for example, resented admonition about encouraging offensive spirit since Guards battalions needed no bracing up. In January 1916 Sir Henry Rawlinson, GOC First Army, expressing his pleasure with the Guards' frequent raiding, remarked upon their enterprise, sound planning and bold execution.[36] Resentment about raids ordered to increase offensive spirit was not limited to the Guards; in fact, it was general since an order to raid for such a purpose seemed a calumny against regimental honour and battalion fighting prowess. After the war one former CO of the 1st Gloucesters (1st British Division) recalled bitterly

> that raids for the sake of raiding were the worst part of the war. Nobody minded going over to get a necessary identification but the other kind to 'maintain fighting spirit' … was loathed by everyone. A unit that needed such an encouragement should have been disbanded, or at least its commander should have been replaced.[37]

Company officers, too, and ORs, recognized spurious reasons for raiding, wondering at times whether the origin of a raid was simply formation rivalry. While they realized the value of rivalry, they also knew that when overdone and carried to an extreme limit, such as seemed the

(comp.), *Order of Battle of Divisions Part 3B. New Army Divisions (30-41) & 63rd (R.N.) Division* (London: HMSO, 1945), pp. 91-100 (39th Division). Hornby commanded 116th Brigade from April 1916-March 1918 when he was wounded.

35 Feilding, *War Letters to a Wife*, p. 319; Terraine (ed.), *General Jack's Diary*, pp. 89-90, 167-68.

36 Headlam, *Guards Division*, Volume 1, pp. 106-107.

37 Pagan, *Infantry*, p. 140.

case all too often with raids, it had dangerous side-affects. Edmund Blunden believed that over time "the Great Unknown behind us [became] infatuated" with raiding. Whatever the reason for a raid, casualties were inevitable. The sense of loss, which often engendered in battalions strong animosity toward those who had ordered the enterprise, could not be assuaged by congratulations or awards, nor could these camouflage the insensitivity of some senior commanders. After a raid by 1st Royal Welsh Fusiliers in early 1915 Lord Moran, Battalion Medical Officer, remembered Major-General Sir Thomas Capper's visit to Battalion Headquarters:

> He was full of the raid which he said had been a great success. He warmly congratulated the Colonel who ventured to say that it had been very expensive. The General told him he must not worry about that … he had just come from the raiding party where he was told that the men had asked if he was coming to visit them. Evidently this had pleased him for he was in great good humour. The visitor and his remarks singularly failed to impress anyone.[38]

Rank, personality and the unit record of raiding largely determined officer views, assessments and sometimes assumptions as to the state of mind of their men. Many ORs were just as keen on raiding as their officers, nor were the less enthusiastic always ORs. Not all assumptions were wrong, some just statements of fact evident to anyone who had led or been closely associated with raiding. The consensus, for example, during a Commanding Officers' Course in September 1915 was that the men disliked raids because they did not see their value and especially hated giving up a position they had taken. It was fact, too, that raids begot retaliation, never pleasant, usually costly. While some officers continued to expound on how a successful raid improved the general morale, such a conclusion seldom featured at battalion or company level where the cost was all too obvious. Long before the postwar committee on the war's lessons concluded that raids failed to improve morale such a view had been the norm in front line trenches.[39]

When a raiding party consisted of hand-picked men, their attitudes well known to the officers who had picked them, then, in truth, they were "exceedingly keen" and afterwards had "good reason to think highly of themselves" for their successful hand-to-hand fighting in the enemy trenches. The officer ordered to raid with his company, if he was OC of the company, would not be reticent about wanting and accepting only keen men to the maximum extent possible. Graham Greenwell, in March 1917 leading his company on a raid, recalled the excitement of his men, this dampened somewhat by five days of postponements. In the event, the raid began as a "ghastly muddle" involving delay in getting into position, artillery fire that cut him off from his men and loss of surprise, but in the end by "piggybacking" on the fortuitous success of the neighbouring battalion, Greenwell's company did very well.[40] A month before that Lieutenant-Colonel (later Brigadier-General) Alexander Johnston, CO of 10th Cheshires, had been called to brigade HQ where he received orders to do a large raid (70 men from each of three companies) in daylight. It promised, he told his diary, "to be distinctly interesting. If we bring it off

38 Hitchcock, *"Stand To,"* pp. 229-30; Lord Moran, *Anatomy of Courage,* p. 150. Simpson, 'Capper and the Offensive Spirit', p. 55. Simpson described Capper as the epitome of the offensive spirit, this evident in his principle of "conquer or die." Blunden, *Undertones of War,* p. 163.
39 Senior, *Haking,* p. 103; *Committee on the Lessons of the Great War,* p. 23.
40 Nichols, *18th Division,* p. 26; Greenwell, *An Infant in Arms,* pp. 162-63.

successfully it will do the men a lot of good." Having selected the men he wanted, training commenced immediately, Zero day to be 17 February, 10 days away. Watching the selected men practising for the raid he thought them

> splendid, and it is a real treat to see how keen they are. It is refreshing when one remembers that these men are no enthusiastic novices who don't know what they are going in to but all are old soldiers … Most of them have been wounded and they all know well the inferno that they are entering. Yet they are all in tremendous fettle and are just itching to go over … I wanted about ten more men and called for volunteers … and could have got 50 if I had wanted.

The raid proved very interesting, but not so splendid, it being ruined by uncut wire. Casualties included 40 dead and 60 wounded, losses that made Johnston wish "we could have given them a better chance, and one grudges losing such splendid men … all the best men seem to have been lost." He estimated a hundred enemy dead, 35 having been confirmed by count. Preparations for the raid had been thorough: numerous rehearsals, careful air photograph study and detailed briefings of all officers and men.[41] The withdrawal across no man's land proved costly, men falling victim to interlocking machine-gun fire and heavy shelling, another example of the difficulty of that phase of raiding.

In early 1918 a long war continued grinding away at officers and men. On 28 January Sergeant John Becker, 75th Canadian Battalion (4th Canadian Division), speaking of a raid by the 54th Battalion, remembered hearing about a "success" but, as he put it, "everything was a success when our Publicity Department were reporting it. We likely lost double the casualties we inflicted, raids were supposed to be wearing down the enemy but they wore us down as much." Six months later Becker's skepticism had hardened: "the battalion to our right staged a spectacular raid … reported a success. I suppose that meant they lost most of the raiding party."[42]

Private Robert Crude, 7th Battalion, The Buffs (18th British Division), had no time for raids, or for those who ordered them. To him, they always meant the sacrifice of "decent chaps" in useless enterprises and the only return another "ribbon added to a full tunic" worn by a General. Crude could see, however, that there were times when a raid spelled value; Germans taken on 21 March revealed that all was ready for their all-out offensive that would erupt that very night.[43]

Private Thomas Dinesen, a Danish volunteer who had joined the 42nd Canadian Battalion in Montreal, thought his first raid in early April 1918 "most awfully thrilling." He had coaxed

41 Crookenden, *Cheshire Regiment*, pp. 97-98; Astill, *The Great War Diaries of Brigadier-General Alexander Johnston*, pp. 200, 202-204.

42 Monroe (ed.), *Silhouettes*, pp. 150, 191; LAC, War Diary 54th Battalion, January 1918, describes the raid as unsuccessful, the raiders unable to enter enemy trenches because of wire and alert defenders.

43 Brown, *Imperial War Museum Book of the Western Front*, pp. 110, 188. Crude's normal occupation was battalion runner, an appointment of great danger. Connelly, *Steady the Buffs*, p. 81, says the 7th did not raid during the war. Crude describes a "stunt" to get a prisoner as demanded by Corps. It is not entirely clear from his account that 7th Battalion did the stunt, nor does he date it, but he does mention that "half of our effectives" were lost. Moody, *Historical Records of the Buffs*, pp. 272, 279, notes that the 7th was to raid on 14 March, but this was cancelled. The next day a platoon of the 7th made a "recce in force" during which the platoon commander was killed and "some" other casualties were suffered. Crude does not say which unit made the 21 March raid.

his platoon commander to take him along even though he had no front line experience. Despite the failure to get a prisoner, Dinesen described the raid as "fun and merriment." Asked to join another raiding party a few days later he replied "I am delighted." In August, just after the start of the Amiens offensive, after 10 hours of hand to hand fighting during which he killed 12 men with bayonet and bomb, Dinesen also won a Victoria Cross. Here was a neutral not averse to fighting![44]

Private W.A. Tucker, who served with XI Corps Cyclists, held possibly the most negative view of raids, seeing these as "examples of murderous lunacy devised by short-moustached, over-medalled morons, who had never been nearer the trenches than distant Amiens and had assaulted nothing harder than French tarts." Others, like Guardsman Frederick Noakes, adopted a fatalistic stance, thinking it best not to dwell on the future, but rather to "take the cash in hand and waive the rest." Training with a raiding party for a week, listening to briefings and otherwise preparing, Noakes and his chums were then told the raid was off, no reason offered and

> we did not feel inclined to question the decision. I will not pretend that we were not profoundly relieved, for we knew only too well the hazardous nature of these enterprises … their main purpose to keep the war going … so the High Command evolved this plan of frequent pin-prick attacks, as a means of fostering the offensive spirit and of 'keeping the men on their toes' regardless of the useless waste of life involved.[45]

A raiding party of 5CMR, 3rd Canadian Division, on the other hand, when told on 14 January that their raid, for which they had trained daily, was off, expressed disappointment, this evident in an entry in the War Diary. The reason for disappointment seems more to do with the loss of a chance to show up 4CMR, the writer suggesting that that battalion did not raid, this being apparent in "that the enemy had been allowed to do a lot of work since [our] last tour."[46]

How officers perceived raiding also had much to do with the elements of officership, what was referred to as the officer spirit and the expectations held of them. This was reiterated in such publications as *SS 415 The Duties of an Officer: Knowledge and Character* which urged an officer to his primary responsibility, the leading of men in battle. Lieutenant Charles Douie, at 19 commanding a company on the Western Front, had come to realize the responsibility and pride of leadership: "I was an officer in command of men." Harry Drinkwater, told in June 1918 that he would lead a company-sized raid, admitted that he was "not too cheery" at this news, the odds being against one's safe return, but he realized full well that it does not become an officer to quibble "when there is a job to be done … so I take them over … with one intention – to bring back prisoners." For this he received an MC and, wounded, spent some time in England. Robert Graves, Royal Welsh Fusiliers, went out on patrol frequently knowing the men respected courage, but also because he coldly and fatalistically calculated that the best chance of lasting through to the end of the war was to get wounded and the best time to get

44 Dinesen, *Merry Hell: A Dane With the Canadians*, pp, 126, 134; Bishop, *Our Bravest and Our Best*), p, 112. Dinesen was commissioned in November 1918. He died in Denmark at 85 in 1974.

45 Tucker is quoted in Senior, *Haking*, p. 254; F.E. Noakes, *The Distant Drum: A Memoir of a Guardsman in the Great War* (London: Frontline Books, 2010), pp. 76-78.

46 LAC, 5CMR War Diary, January and February 1917.

wounded was at night and in the open by more or less unaimed rifle fire. Being wounded at such a time, when fewer casualties were seeking treatment, he reasoned that he would receive more medical attention and while on the way to the rear would not be exposed to as much artillery fire: "Best to get wounded, therefore, on a night patrol in a quiet sector."[47]

Some officers simply loved combat, including and even especially raids, this obvious to their comrades who dubbed them "thrusters." This distinction showed on their tunics: Captain "Bombo" Pollard, VC, MC and Bar, DCM, Honourable Artillery Company; Captain John MacGregor, VC, MC and Bar, DCM, 2CMR; Lieutenant George McKean, VC, MC, MM, 14th Canadian Battalion; and *Leutnant* Ernst Junger, *Pour le Merite* and multiple decorations. The record of the last is such that he may well have been the personification of the warrior.[48] A commonly voiced opinion among infantry officers said that while raids were risky they were also a challenge, even a pastime to be enjoyed, since they offered escape from the monotony of trench routine. Risk also offered a sense of achievement and enhanced standing amongst one's peers, an assuagement of "restlessness, not only a vague desire for action, but a definite wish to be given the opportunity of proving above all to themselves that they were as anxious as ever to meet the Bosche face to face, and confident of the result of the encounter."[49] Charles Edmonds [Charles Carrington] was much taken with raiding: "To lie breathless in the German wire with a storming party of volunteers, armed with clubs and made invisible … by having our faces blacked, was a splendid adventure … and what we did to them the Boche sought faithfully to do to us." Captain Herbert Read of the Green Howards, and holder of the DSO and the MC, expressing his delight at being chosen for "a death or glory job" (a raid), said this about his motives: "I am very glad – glad in the first place because it gives me the first chance I've had of doing anything – glad in the second place because it means that others recognise that I'm of the clan that don't care a damn for anything." But there is a note of caring: "All the same I intend to come through as full of life as anything." Lieutenant W. T. Colyer, Royal Dublin Fusiliers, echoes Read: "How different it feels to be doing something! Back there in the trenches I feel like a rat in a trap … I can't move out of it … can do nothing in my own defence." Edwin Vaughan, MC, Royal Warwickshire Regiment, describing one of his "little jaunts" said such forays made him very keen on no man's land and he now understood why such enterprises were the best "stiffener" of morale.[50]

47 Charles Douie, *The Weary Road: Recollections of a Subaltern of Infantry* (Stevenage, Herts: Strong Oak Press Ltd., 1980), p. 51; Cooksey and Griffiths (eds.), *Harry's War*, pp. 358-369; Graves, *Goodbye to All That*, p. 111.

48 Pollard served briefly in the RAF after the war and then became a writer. His first book, published in 1931, was followed by 59 others. His autobiography, *Fire-Eater: The Memoirs of a V.C.*, was published in 1932. See also the biography by N.S. Nash. Pollard died in 1960. MacGregor also served during the Second World War as CO of a training camp at Vernon, BC. He died in 1951. McKean wrote *Scouting Thrills* after the war and then went into the lumber business in England where he was accidentally killed in 1926. Junger also served in the German Army in the Second World War. For additional information see the Introduction, footnote 16.

49 Sandilands, *23rd Division*, pp. 58-59.

50 Edmonds [Carrington], *A Subaltern's War*, pp. 26, 28; Herbert Read, *The Contrary Experience* (London: Faber, 1963), p. 99; Brown, *Tommy Goes to War*, p. 96; Vaughan, *Some Desperate Glory*, p. 120; Stephen H. Hewett, *A Scholar's Letters From the Front* (London: Longmans, Green And Co.,1918), pp. 84-85; Neville, *War Letters*, p. 58.

A desire to compete and shine at centre stage inspired many. Captain Allan Thomas, 6th Royal West Kents (12th British Division), got a kick out of being out and about: "everyone had been warned that you were out. You were, as well as being in the dark, also in the limelight." This could even appear in the reaction of one's CO, as Second Lieutenant Kenneth Macardle, 17th Manchester Regiment, reported: "I love being out of trenches and searching for adventure ... They expect me to suffer from nervous strain bit I don't ... sometimes when I'm out ... the Colonel waits up for me!!" A taste for limelight, and the chance a raid offered to make a name for oneself, motivated many officers, a feeling expressed by Siegfried Sassoon after a raid in March 1916: "great fun ... most exhilarating ... No good being out here unless one takes the full amount of risks, and I want to get a good name in the Battalion. No Man's Land fascinates me ... something drives me to look for trouble." Decorations came to Sassoon and to many others who took the risk. "News of MC before lunch," is all he wrote for 29 June 1916 in his diary and about the same in letters to friends. His semi-autobiographical *Memoirs of an Infantry Officer* are more revealing, describing the day of his MC like this:

> For the rest of the day and, indeed, for the remainder of my military career, the left side of my chest was more often in my mind than the right – a habit which was common to a multitude of wearers of Military Cross ribbons. Much might be written ... about medals and their stimulating effect ... But ... nobody knew how much a decoration was worth except the man who received it.[51]

But attitudes are not static. Reality, driven by experience and cost, set in and for many with it came pessimism, cynicism and bitterness. A useful account of the anxiety that built up during pre-raid hours is one by Lieutenant Charles Douie, in March 1916 OC A Company, 1st Dorsets (32nd British Division). Initially on Zero day Douie felt himself in a state of "inexperienced optimism," but this soon turned to dread. In the end the raid failed. Casualties came to about a third of the raiding force of 68 all ranks. For Douie, the day ended with "anger and bitterness in his heart."[52]

Guy Chapman, a Subaltern with the Royal Fusiliers, and later to win the MC, briefly related his first observation of a raid in June 1916: a small party dashed across no man's land, took no prisoners, killed no Germans and on the way back lost two men to machine-gun fire and for Chapman and his platoon, brought home the realization that "these raids were a hundred to one chance." Bernard Martin, a Subaltern with the North Staffordshire Regiment, propelled by high officer casualties into command of a company in mid-1916, and unsure about orders prohibiting company commanders from going beyond the front line (see earlier in this chapter) sought advice, only to be told by another company commander "I'm damned glad of any order which positively bans me from crawling about in No Man's Land ... I reckon that game is played out, not worth the candle, as the gamblers say."[53]

51 Thomas, *A Life Apart*, p. 64; Brown, *Tommy Goes to War*, p. 96; Hart-Davis, *Siegfried Sassoon Diaries*, pp. 50, 82; Sassoon, *Memoirs of an Infantry Officer*, p. 52.

52 Douie, *The Weary Road*, pp. 126-29, 230-33; TNA: WO 95/2392: 14th British Brigade, Appendix, report on raid at La Boisselle. Chapter 9 describes this raid in detail.

53 Harrison (ed.), *To Fight Alongside Friends*, p. 161; Chapman, *A Passionate Prodigality*, p. 89; Martin, *Poor Bloody Infantry*, p. 68.

An account of a raid in August 1916 by a Canadian private soldier suggests, however, that some officers were either played out, or experienced enough to see the flies in the ointment surrounding any particular raid and could assess its chances and theirs were they to participate. Private Donald Fraser, 31st Battalion, recalled one raid especially well since it was the battalion's first. The purpose was to take prisoners. The essential prerequisite was surprise. Fraser was of a mind to volunteer since "any scheme with a fighting chance" appealed to him, but he began to sense no strong evidence of a plan and a "certain indefiniteness and lukewarmness developed as none of the officers appeared to be taking an active interest." When in sniffing about he heard the details as to how the raid would go in, he concluded that artillery involvement would alert the enemy and decided not to volunteer as the plan "spelt absolute failure." The raiders, 30 men under Captain Walter Jewitt, realized soon after the raid began that the Germans were ready and waiting. Hit hard by machine-gun fire and bombs from strongly manned enemy positions, the raiders could only withdraw. Jewitt and 15 men were wounded as they crossed no man's land.[54]

By the end of 1916 adverse opinions about raids were definite and hard. Edmund Blunden, for example, thought "raid" the word that caused the "greatest distress" in his battalion and such enterprises were simply "suicide operations." Even that intrepid fighting man, Ernst Junger, eventually admitted that wandering about in enemy trenches gave him the "blues."[55] Men were realizing that in some cases the rationale for a raid was nothing but the desire for a member of the "big brass" for a decoration or enhanced profile and reputation.

On occasion the aftermath of a raid might feature incongruity, bad luck, good luck, contrivance and subterfuge. What happened was this. In early 1918 Lieutenant-Colonel Harry Nelles, CO 4th Canadian Battalion, was ordered to identify the enemy opposite at any cost. Nelles assigned the raid to Captain Jolliffe's B Company. At dusk on the night of the raid Lieutenant James Pedley, having patrolled to check the state of enemy wire, reported it not demolished, the artillery claiming the opposite, but the raid went anyway. At Zero, 18-pounders and Stokes mortars commenced heavy fire on the enemy trenches and a hundred raiders were off. Thereafter no news, which in this case was not good news. Silence marked, in fact, failure, at a cost of two killed and a dozen wounded. One body was recovered, but the other had to be left in a tangle of German wire after the man's badges and any identifying papers had been removed. No prisoners were taken during the raid. One of the raid's officers did kill one German, but quite inexplicably he carried back only the man's worthless helmet instead of getting anything that showed identity: "how we cursed the luckless officer, and how he hated himself when he came to look back on his feat!" A garbled message to brigade HQ had convinced it that the Canadian body in the wire had on it identifications that would give the Germans valuable information. In fact, only the officers on the raid knew that there were no identifying items on the body hanging on the wire. Colonel Nelles decided that brigade would never hear of the confusion if he could help it, but the problem was how to explain the garbled message without giving away the officer's gaffe with the helmet. Brigade, having been told that 4th Battalion badges and identifying items were on the body, ordered their immediate recovery.

54 Roy (ed.), *Journal of Private Fraser*, pp. 184-87; Singer, *31st Battalion*, pp. 184-87. This raid was conceived at Brigade HQ. Jewitt later (1918) won the MC and then a Bar.

55 Blunden, *Undertones of War*, pp. 162-63; Junger, *Storm of Steel*, p. 203.

The only course open seemed to be organizing a recovery and being seen to do so, as well as to get a prisoner. Nelles "fussed and fumed" but had to pass on the brigade order. Thus the "Subaltern's Raid," Lieutenant McLean and eight men supposedly to recover the body while Lieutenants Ostic and Pedley supposedly created a diversion on the right. But this raid, based on nightly Subaltern assessments describing a moon supposedly too bright to risk more men, had repeatedly to be postponed. However, come the last night before the battalion was to go out to rest it appeared no more stalling would be tolerated and the game might be up. Here good luck struck in the form of two lost Germans who with all their equipment fell into B Company hands. Identifications! Christmas all over again! With prisoners in hand, and badges supposedly recovered, no further questions arose. A subsequent communique announced that the 4th had taken prisoners, but not how. None of this graced the War Diary and no report, fortunately, ever left the battalion. As Pedley explained

> Our attention had been fully occupied in making the most of a badly botched job, and in contriving some means of doing what the raid failed to accomplish. The amazing sequel, in the course of which identification was finally and most luckily thrown into our hands through a veritable act of God, changed the whole spirit of the battalion and sent us all out on our long summer rest with the feeling that if we had not indeed proved ourselves heroes, we had certainly done our job, by fair means or foul. The Fourth had put it across, and brigade was satisfied.

The whole matter, while somewhat ludicrous, does show that no officer or man wanted his unit to be tarnished in any way and COs usually acted to ensure that this did not happen.[56]

One of the best examples of how experience changes attitudes comes courtesy of Herbert Read, who was commissioned into the Green Howards in early 1915, then posted to the 10th Battalion where he later won the MC and the DSO. In his essay "The Impact of War" he described how in meeting the challenges of war he knew he had to be continuously active in the field, had to react to all manner of men, had to adapt to being an officer and had to command an infantry platoon, all this a learning curve sufficient for any man. He began, he wrote, in a spirit of adventure, which was followed by realization that the trenches were neither romantic nor novel, certainly not for very long. Soon the experience began to seem unreal, he being just part of a machine and consigned to just rub along or simply get killed. Resentment shows when he says "very little scope existed for individual initiative," this rather curious, even contradictory, since raids and patrols put a premium on officer initiative. Read had his chance at that scope during a daylight raid in April 1918:

> We suddenly confronted, round some mound or excavation, a German patrol … We were perhaps 20 yards from each other, fully visible. I waved a weary hand, as if to say: What is the use of killing each other? The German officer seemed to understand, and both parties turned and made their way back to their own trenches. Reprehensible conduct, no doubt,

56 Pedley, *Only This*, pp. 160-70.

> but in April 1918, the war-weariness of the infantry was stronger than its pugnacity, on both sides of the line.[57]

Having now employed Kipling's half-dozen serving men, the story turns to how the course of raiding developed and marked the rough and thorny road called experience from the early days of 1915 through to the Armistice. A Russian proverb says the road to war is very wide; the path home very narrow. This is also true of raiding. The next chapter sets us on that road.

57 Read, *Annals of Innocence and Experience,* pp. 140, 142-43.

Major-General David Watson, GOC 4th Canadian Division. (Library and Archives Canada/ PA002116)

Lieutenant-Colonel Edmund Ironside, GSO1 4th Canadian Division. (Library and Archives Canada/PA001352)

Lieutenant-Colonel Edward Hilliam, CO 25th Canadian Battalion, and later Brigadier-General and GOC 10th Brigade, 4th Canadian Division. (Library and Archives Canada/ PA000482)

Brigadier-General Victor Odlum, formerly CO 7th Canadian Battalion and later GOC 11th Brigade, 4th Canadian Division. (Library and Archives Canada/ PA002118)

Brigadier-General James MacBrien, GOC 12th Brigade, 4th Canadian Division (right) and Lieutenant-Colonel W.H. Clarke-Kennedy, VC, CMG, DSO and Bar, CO 24th Battalion. (Library and Archives Canada/PA006743)

Lieutenant-General Sir Arthur Currie, GOC Canadian Corps. (Library and Archives Canada/PA1370)

Lieutenant-Colonel Louis Lipsett, CO 8th Battalion and later Major-General and GOC 3rd Canadian Division. Killed in action while GOC 4th British Division. (Library and Archives Canada/PA007442)

Brigadier-General D.H.B. Ketchen, GOC 6th Canadian Brigade and to his right in trenchcoat Major A.H. Jukes, BM, May 1917. (Library and Archives Canada/PA001236)

Major The Hon. F.E. Grosvenor. (front row at left), BM 6th Canadian Brigade, March 1918. (Library and Archives Canada/MIKAN3522129)

Lieutenant-Colonel R.D.F. Hayter (front row, far left). GSO1 1st Canadian Division, April 1918, and later BGGS Canadian Corps. (Library and Archives Canada/MIKAN3522131)

Lieutenant-Colonel George Tuxford, CO 5th Canadian Battalion, later Brigadier-General and GOC 3rd Brigade. (Saskatchewan Archives Board Photo R-A10224)

Brigadier-General William Griesbach. (right), CO 49th Canadian Battalion and later GOC 1st Brigade. (Library and Archives Canada/ FA007103)

Major-General Frederick Loomis, CO 13th Canadian Battalion and later GOC 3rd Canadian Division. (Library and Archives Canada/PA002203)

Lieutenant-Colonel R.D. Davies, CO 44th Canadian Battalion, after award of DSO. (Library and Archives Canada/PA007009)

Lieutenant George McKean, VC, MC, MM, 14th Canadian Battalion. (Library and Archives Canada/PA006219)

Captain John MacGregor, VC, MC, DCM, 2nd Canadian Mounted Rifles. (Library and Archives Canada/PA004598)

Canadians leaving the line after a night raid, Avion, July 1917. Note black camouflage hands and face. (Library and Archives Canada/PA001814)

Canadian with prisoners after night raid February 1918. (Library and Archives Canada/PA002607)

Trench Mortar Battery, 2-inch mortar, "Toffee Apple" Bombs in front, 1917. (Library and Archives Canada/PA004921)

Heavy Mortar in emplacement, May 1917. (Library and Archives Canada/PA001409)

Damaged German trench with undamaged dug-out entrance, July 1916.
(Library and Archives Canada/PA000128)

Damaged German trench, dug-out entrance blown in, July 1916.
(Library and Archives Canada/PA000180)

Trench Mortar fire on German wire. (Library and Archives Canada/PA 001380)

Trench Mortar fire on German wire. (Library and Archives Canada/PA001381)

British officers watching rifle grenade demonstration, 1917. (Library and Archives Canada/PA004745)

Stokes 3-inch mortar and crew, not Western Front. Photo in Public Domain.

Canadians preparing hand grenades. (bombs) for use, reserve line, Bomb Storage Store, February 1918.
(Library and Archives Canada/PA002449)

Canadian machine-guns digging in, Vimy Ridge, April 1917. (Library and Archives Canada/PA001017)

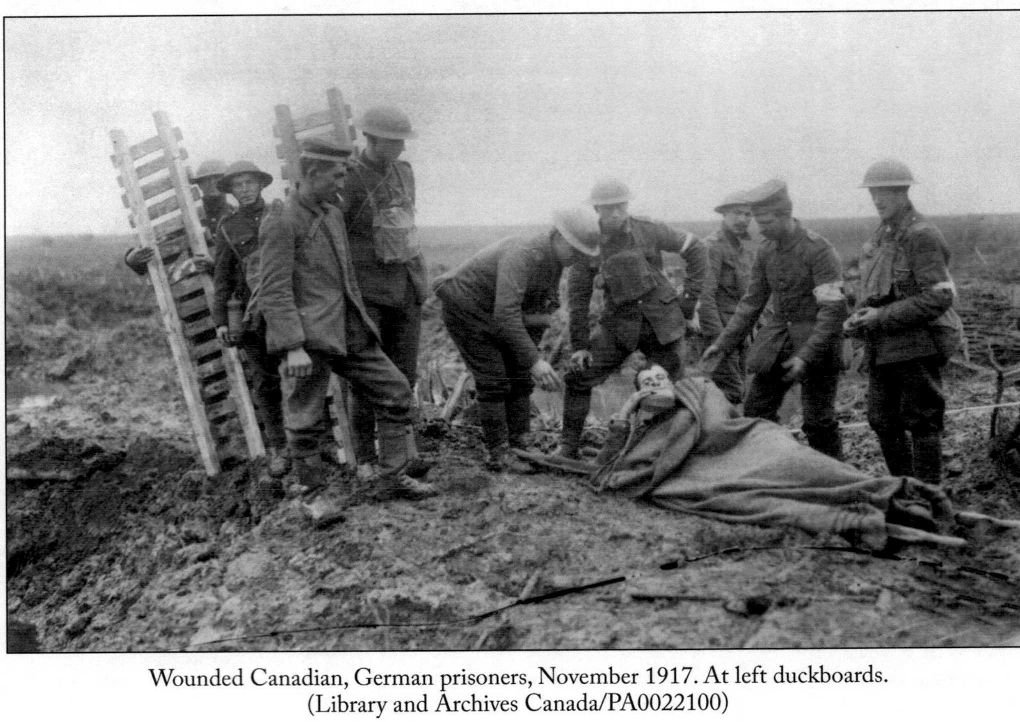

Wounded Canadian, German prisoners, November 1917. At left duckboards.
(Library and Archives Canada/PA0022100)

18th March. 1916. No. 82. Vol. 4.

THE WAR Illustrated

A PICTURE-RECORD *of Events by Land, Sea and Air.* *Edited by* J. A. HAMMERTON

COWARDLY "KULTUR."—A favourite ruse of the treacherously-inclined Hun is to hide behind a comrade who apparently is surrendering himself prisoner. With rifle ready and loaded, he is able to take in cold blood the life of the hesitant Briton. This cowardly conduct occurred recently during a Canadian night attack on the Prussian Guard. Fortunately the Maple Leaf man was too quick for the Prussians, and managed to get a revolver "bull" and bayonet thrust in first. In this engagement the Canadians took the enemy by surprise, and succeeded in wreaking considerable damage with bombs.

'Cowardly Kultur', *The War Illustrated,* March 1916. See Chapter 15, raids by 13th KRRC and 13th Battalion, The Rifle Brigade.

4th March, 1916. No. 81. Vol. 4.

THE WAR Illustrated

A PICTURE-RECORD *of Events by Land, Sea and Air.* *Edited by* J. A. HAMMERTON

CANADIANS THRASH THE PRUSSIANS.—Under the laconic official heading of a night bombing attack, a plucky affair took place recently on the western front. A company of Canadians went out under cover of dark to raid the trenches of the Prussian Guards. The Canadians launched their bombs full in the midst of the Guards, who set their flares going and turned a machine-gun on the nocturnal visitors. It would have fared ill with the Canadians had not a lucky bomb-thrower planted his missile right on to the Maxim, thereby allowing twenty-three out of the party of twenty-five to retreat.

'Canadians Thrash The Prussians', *The War Illustrated,* March 1916. See Chapter 9, raid by 6th Brigade. (28th Battalion), Spanbroekmolen, MSD 11.

The Last Alarm of a Hapless German Sentinel

Two parties of the West Yorkshires started on a nocturnal raid on the enemy's trenches after cutting through the German wire. An officer and sergeant came across an enemy sentry oblivious of immediate danger. The sergeant approached, and aimed point-blank, but his revolver missfired. He thereupon sprang at the throat of the sentry, who uttered a piercing shriek. The officer then crept up and endeavoured to club the German, but his weapon went off, the bullet passing through the sentry's neck and the sergeant's hand. By now the Germans were fully alarmed, and the raiders retreated.

'The Last Alarm of a Hapless German Sentinel', *The War Illustrated*, March 1916. See Chapter 9: possibly the raid by the West Yorkshires in March 1916.

Run to Earth! Enemy Trapped in Deep Dug-out

The Germans, judging by the depth to which they have "gone to earth" in some parts of the line, are developing a great respect for the power of the new British high explosives. In a spirited affair which took place recently on the west front cur men were surprised to find that the enemy dug-outs had been practically untouched by bombardment, owing to the fact that they had about eighteen feet of cover above a solidly-constructed wooden roof. Here large numbers of Germans took refuge, but were eventually induced either to surrender or submit to the ordeal of the grenade.

'Run to Earth! Enemy Trapped in Deep Dug-Out', *The War Illustrated*, July 1916.

'British Soldiers Great Trench Raid in the Snow;, *The War Illustrated,* March 1917. See Chapter 11: probably 6th London Regiment's raid on 20 February 1917.

Brave British Work with Bombs and Bayonets

Bombing a way into a German trench over a snowy parapet. Trench raids have formed a frequent feature of winter warfare on the western front. By means of them the British troops have kept the enemy ever nervously alert and in a "jumpy" condition.

Episode of one of the British "nibbling" advances. Progress was being held up by two hidden German machine-guns, when an officer picked a small party of bombers and bayonet men, penetrated the German line and destroyed the guns and their crews.

'Brave British Work With Bombs and Bayonets', *The War Illustrated*, March 1917.

1st September, 1917. No. 150. Vol. 7.

THE WAR Illustrated

A PICTURE-RECORD of Events by Land, Sea and Air. Edited by J. A. HAMMERTON

[British official photograph]

TWO GREAT LEADERS ON THE WESTERN FRONT.—General Sir Henry Horne, K.C.B. (right), with General Sir Arthur Currie, K.C.M.G. Sir Henry Horne invented the creeping barrage which has proved so valuable in successive British advances. Sir Arthur Currie, himself a Canadian, is in chief command of the Canadian Corps, having succeeded Sir Julian Byng in that position in June last.

'Two Great Leaders on the Western Front', *The War Illustrated,* September 1917.
General Sir Henry Horne and Lieutenant-General Sir Arthur Currie.

8

1915: Beginnings

> Wedges start with thin ends.
>
> Anon.

Relative quiet, when it came to raids, marked 1915, the first full year of the Great War. For most of the year the interest of commanders, senior and junior, and the men they commanded, resided mainly in major battles: Neuve Chapelle, Second Ypres, Festubert and Loos. Of the raids actually made during this time details are often scant and accounts generally rather sketchy; even the precise number of raids is elusive. One reason for this is the elastic and indefinite definitions meaning that it can be difficult, even impossible, to proclaim an enterprise small-scale attack or raid. It is evident, however, that raids identified prior to October 1915, were small-scale, perhaps 20 all ranks and usually fewer; they smack of mad dash and just fall on the enemy more than anything else; and they were also infrequent "the official [British] history [recording] only one raid for that year," a summation based, presumably, on the assessment that only one raid was of such magnitude that it warranted that description. This source describes this raid, launched on 16/17 November by two Canadian battalions, as the "model" raid.[1]

Another source notes that between 19 December 1915 and 30 May 1916 the BEF carried out 63 raids.[2] If we divide this sum by the number of months there might have been, say, 10 raids per month. But the December figure should fall by half, which fits a half-month. As for Canadian raids, the one on 16th/17th November was the largest of the six between 12 October and 31 December. The level of activity, Canadian and British, reflects the offensive policy determined upon in October and described in an earlier chapter. This present chapter surveys several raids conducted in the last quarter of 1915 and concludes with the "model" raid by 5th and 7th Canadian Battalions, 1st Canadian Division, in November 1915.

1st Cheshires conducted one of the small-scale raids of late 1915 south of Mametz on the night 6/7 December. The regimental historian called it "a model of its kind." His account and the unit War Diary show it was a well-planned and well-led enterprise. The latter source called

1 Ashworth, *Live and Let Live,* p. 185; Edmonds, *Haig's Command to the 1st July,* p. 156, note 1; John Lee, 'Some Lessons of the Somme: The British Infantry in 1917', in *Look to Your Front: Studies in the First World War By the British Commission for Military History,* Brian Bond et al (Staplehurst: Spellmount,1999), p. 80. Lee refers to the 6th (sic) and 7th Battalions as the raiding units.

2 Saunders, *Weapons of the Trench War*, p. 12.

it a "Bombing Expedition," presumably because bombs played a central role in the method of assault that night. Nowhere in the War Diary does the word "raid" appear, but by definition that is what it was. It is fortunate that in this instance we have the account by Colonel Arthur Crookenden, the regimental historian, since the War Diary sticks strictly to raid and post-raid events. Crookenden offers much more including pre-raid activity, information about the officers who led it and what is one of the most interesting aspects of the raid, the refusals by the CO and the OC Raid to accept the artillery preparatory fire initially insisted upon by brigade and division. Instead, the artillery provided only a box-barrage around the objective. In the event, the raiders surprised the Germans, reaching the objective "without being discovered."

Crookenden tells us that the CO, Lieutenant-Colonel R.D.F. Oldman, who had just assumed command, ordered the raid "to improve morale," the battalion just coming off 42 straight days in the line during which casualties had been heavy. This rationale probably struck some as akin to cancelling the rum ration until morale improved! After 42 days in the line others probably welcomed it. Second Lieutenant Geoffrey Harding, the unit Bombing Officer and OC Raid had under him a force of 50 ORs and Lieutenants Harper and Richardson, both known as "very stout men in a tight corner." It would have heartened Harding to have the assistance of two officers, who while senior to him, had volunteered to serve under him. He would measure up to their obviously favourable opinion regarding his abilities. Harding organized his raiders into three groups: an advance party he would lead, a support party under Harper and a reserve under Richardson. An aspect Crittenden did not mention was the support of a West Spring Gun, which from a position in the Cheshire trench would bomb the trench marked "Q" (see MSD 2). A machine-gun was also allocated in support, but was not used. The raiders, while the battalion was out of the line, repeatedly rehearsed on a spit-locked replica of the objective trench.

It is evident that pre-raid recce was thorough. The objective of the raid, selected after study of air photos, was confirmed by patrols, one finding a gap in the wire at the end of the sap leading to the main trench. The night before the raid (5/6 December) a final patrol led by Harding confirmed that the gap still existed, but the route selected across the crater could not be used since heavy rain had made the surface too treacherous. The patrol searching out a new route also discovered a sniper's post at the end of the sap. Clearly, the time spent on checking paid off! All in all, wrote Crookenden, "everything possible was done to ensure success."

At 0145 on the 7th the advance party moved off, soon reaching the sniper's post without being detected. Bombing killed one occupant, the other making off hotly pursued by Harding alone, his party having failed to understand that they were to follow him immediately. Harding as he returned to the party was taken for a German and received two bombs. Unhurt, he then led the party into the main trench at "C" where some of the men established a block at "D" while the remainder turned left killing some enemy, taking one prisoner and bombing three dug-outs. Two of these according to the prisoner were occupied. At this time he was escorted to the entry point at the sap where Richardson had established the reserve. A block was also established at "G".

Meanwhile, the support party under Harper had arrived in the main trench and reinforced the men holding the block at "D" before moving further on to a junction with a CT. Here a new block would be held, despite counter-attacks, for the whole time the raiders were in the enemy trenches. The enemy suffered numerous casualties at this block. Harper then relieved Harding at "G" and established a block at "H" before moving to "K." During this time the crew of the West Spring Gun put down accurate fire on "Q" which received 100 bombs in the space of an hour, this greatly assisting in keeping the counter-attackers at bay.

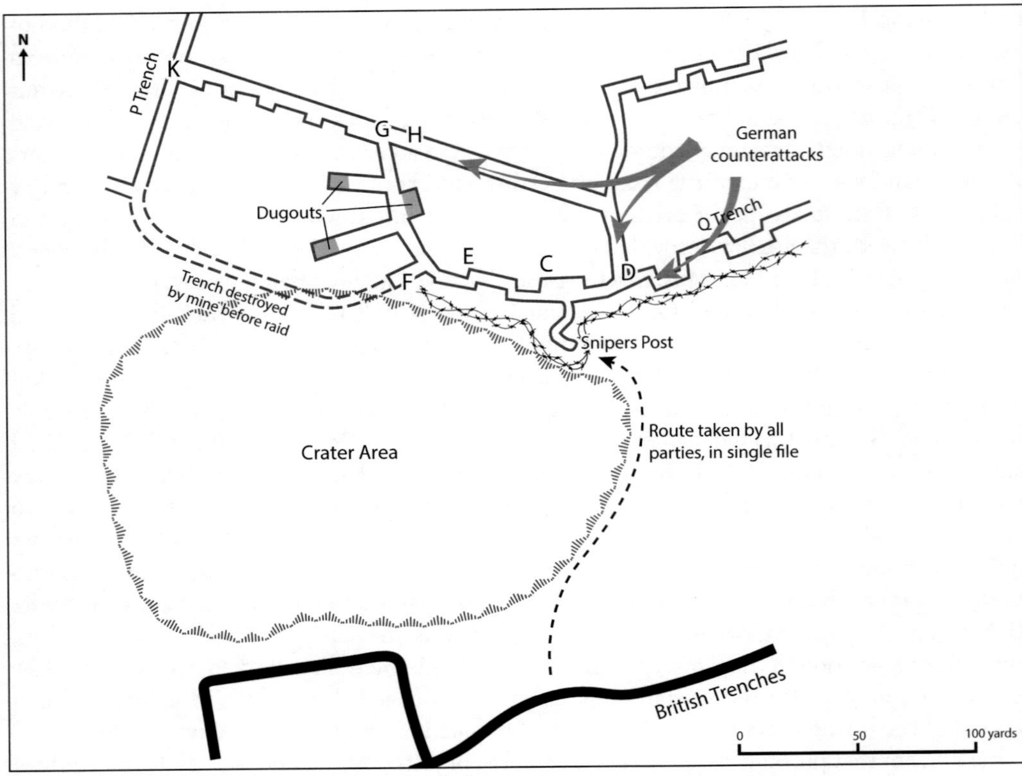

2 Raid Near Mametz, 6/7 December 1917, 1st Cheshire Regiment.

With the enemy now thoroughly aroused and bombs running short, with no probability of getting more forward, Harding ordered withdrawal according to the plan whereby Harper's party picked up all block personnel as it fell back. By five minutes past three, after 80 minutes in enemy lines, all raiders had returned to battalion trenches. During the raid two of the officers and five men were slightly wounded (one other man succumbed to serious wounds). The only hitch in the raid, according to the War Diary, was that the telephone carried by the raiders became unserviceable and a new one could not be gotten forward quickly enough to be of use. The raid report also noted that only "P" trench seemed in good condition; elsewhere mud knee-deep prevailed. Summing up, Crookenden called the raid successful in every respect including having "a marked effect on the morale of the battalion." Second Lieutenant Harding received the MC, the first to be awarded to the Cheshires during the war. Three men received the DCM. Visitors who came the next day to congratulate the unit included the Army Commander.[3]

3 Crookenden, *Cheshire Regiment,* pp. 61-63; TNA: WO 95/1571: reports on raid, 1st Cheshires (15th Brigade, 5th Division); Scott, 'The West Spring Gun'" S*tand To!,* p.16; This gun, the Great War version of a Roman ballista, was invented by Captain A. West early in 1915. It consisted of a long throwing arm controlled under tension of 24 springs. It could throw Mills bombs about 240 yards. Six hundred were ordered in May 1915, the first deliveries arriving in July. While silent and accurate, the gun could also be unpredictable; moreover, its bulk posed serious disadvantages. The weapon gave way to the far

The historian of the Guards Division remarked that during the first half of December 1915 raids became "quite popular," each battalion making "inroads" into enemy trenches, almost all enjoying "uniform success" and the congratulations of senior commanders including Lieutenant-General Haking, GOC XI Corps, who wrote to Lord Cavan expressing his appreciation for the raids made by the Guards while Cavan had been GOC the Guards Division. In his "Suggestions as to Winter Campaign 1915-1916" Lord Cavan had ordered constant offensive action to harass the enemy and keep him off balance. He also directed that raiding strength in future would be two companies and raiders would remain only briefly in enemy trenches.

One of the first of the Guards raids was initiated by Captain Sir Robert Filmer, a company commander in 4th Grenadier Guards, then in an area immediately northeast of Neuve Chapelle, the actual raid occurring about 500 yards northeast of that place. On 7th December a patrol by his company used a small gap it found in enemy wire to reach the enemy parapet where it learned much by listening and observing. The patrol leader told Filmer that from what he had seen the enemy could be rushed. While no useful map, sketch or diagram is available in any of the sources, including the unit War Diary, there is sufficient information to reconstruct the raid. On return to the line on 10 December the patrol leader took the two officers who would participate in the proposed raid, Lieutenant Frederick Ponsonby, Battalion Bombing Officer, and Lieutenant Nairn out for a look. This party also got right up to the parapet through the still open gap and also carefully reconnoitred the ground out to it. The next day Filmer briefed the CO, Lieutenant-Colonel H. Seymour, who ordered the raid for that very night (11 December). The raiders were ordered to determine the state of enemy trenches and in what strength they were held while doing as much damage as possible to posts and machine-gun emplacements. The only artillery involvement would be the laying down of a box-barrage around the objective area.

Immediately after obtaining the CO's approval Filmer gave preliminary verbal orders to the two officers and 33 volunteers of his company and the party of battalion bombers who would make the raid. These orders covered the organization of the raiding parties, the duties of every man, how the raiders would withdraw and the method of attack, the last to be confirmed once Filmer made a personal recce after dark, his intent being to reconnoitre the whole length of the objective area. During his absence the three equally sized raiding parties would assemble in a front line trench, the right party under Sergeant Higgins, the left party under Lieutenant Ponsonby and the centre party under Lieutenant Nairn. A small covering party under Filmer would remain at a midway point in no man's land to cover the withdrawal and pass prisoners and wounded rearward.

At 2015 Filmer, Sergeant Higgins and four men left on recce. He positioned one man at the covering party position halfway across no man's land and the others at the gap in the enemy wire. Filmer and Higgins then decided upon the exact route Higgins would take, his party being first in the order of march. At 2250 Filmer returned from his recce, briefed the CO and issued final verbal orders as to the exact point to be attacked, the order of march and the specific duties of each party. Nairn's party in the centre would clear the enemy trench 20 yards each way from the point of entry and hold that point. The left and right parties would bomb outwards

superior Stokes. Warrington, *Recipients of the Military Cross*, p. 289. Harding later transferred to the Royal Flying Corps. He received a Bar to the MC for escaping from enemy captivity.

from there, but would not go beyond the junctions of the main trench and the adjacent CTs. Only 20 minutes would be spent in the enemy trenches, withdrawal sounding (three whistle blasts) at the end of that time. The flanking parties would withdraw through the entry point, Nairn's party remaining until everyone had been checked through.

At 2300 Sergeant Higgins took his party out, Filmer following with two bomb carriers he intended placing at the gap in the enemy wire. Enroute he found Higgins and his party stationary, direction having been lost, but he set them straight quickly and got them moving forward. The box-barrage opened at this time, the noise helping the party reach the enemy parapet undetected. Immediately ahead lay a covered machine-gun post that Filmer had located. Higgins and his party entered the trench at this point whereupon bombing became general. Filmer then left matters in Nairn's hands and returned to where the covering party had settled (he had been ordered by the CO not to go beyond this, but the loss of direction had forced him to disobey in order to get the leading party to the point of entry). When a few minutes later the withdrawal signal sounded the raiders began passing through homeward bound. Filmer and his small partly remained until all were clear.

Given the short time in the enemy trench the raiders destroyed what little they could. During the withdrawal no enemy machine-guns engaged, a good indication that the Germans were simply not alert. It was some time before even rifle fire began, this causing five casualties, one being Lieutenant Ponsonby who went missing for a brief period, but was found and brought in by Lieutenant Nairn and Sergeant Higgins. Lieutenant-Colonel Seymour believed that the time in the enemy trench should have been longer, 20 minutes all too short a time to inflict substantial damage. The raiders reported sandbags unsuitable for the carriage of bombs and recommended that design and supply of a purpose-built carrier commence. Finally, the enemy had not been alert and the total surprise resulted in their confusion and ineffective reaction. One other comment, not accepted by brigade, concerned the issue of more revolvers to raiders, a point that for some time would be debatable. Overall, brigade, division and Corps HQs considered the raid satisfactory. While the preparations for the raid had been somewhat hurried, which posed a risk, the CO had been quite right to take the opportunity that the recce had revealed. Filmer's recce had been extraordinarily daring, but had paid off in up to date and accurate knowledge of the enemy position. Filmer received the MC for the raid.[4]

One Canadian raid in December 1915 drew considerable interest within Second Army, to which 1st Canadian Division belonged at that time, and within the wider BEF. The War Diary of the 1st Cheshires (5th British Division) for December 1915 contains a two-page account of this Canadian raid with a map dated 27 December summarizing the reports of 2nd Canadian Brigade (Louis Lipsett) and 5th Canadian Battalion (George Tuxford). The raid, mounted on the morning of 15 December, had as its objective a barrier the enemy had constructed across the north-south road between Ploegsteert and Messines (see MSD 3). The barrier, consisting of a large tree trunk and a thick wall of sandbags, would be the close and direct target of an 18-pounder field gun, this unusual support drawing great interest in the brigade. When it returned to the line on the night 10/11 December 2nd Brigade first saw the new barrier which

4 Headlam, *Guards Division,* Volume I, pp. 110-11; Ponsonby, *Grenadier Guards,* Volume I, pp. 346-49; TNA: WO 95/1190: Guards Division General Staff, December 1915, Appendix 118, XI Corps Winter Campaign; 3rd Guards Brigade War Diary, reports on raid by Filmer, Seymour and brigade HQ.

sat at about the halfway point of the 300 yards between Canadian and German lines. The Germans had linked it to the ruins of a house east of the road and as the River Douve rose and flooded each wing of the barrier became flanked by water. Based on patrol and other reports, and considering the extent of the barrier, 20 or so men were thought to be the garrison, supported by a machine-gun possibly sited in the ruins of the house. The barrier appeared to be well wired in. Because it offered considerable advantage to the enemy and possibly an opportunity to establish a large footing south of the river, Lipsett sought the approval of 1st Division to expel the enemy and destroy the barrier. Lipsett assigned the job to Tuxford's 5th Battalion, knowing how disappointed Tuxford had been at not being entirely successful during an earlier raid in November. At that time Lipsett had remarked to Arthur Currie, then GOC 1st Division, that the 5th "would have better luck next time."[5]

Lipsett, who was well known for his finely crafted tactical Appreciations (there are many by him in archival sources), recognized the narrow axis of approach and the dangers of enfilade machine-gun fire, so he set the raid for the hours of darkness. Having concluded that close artillery support and surprise would be crucial in such a raid, artillery arrangements underwent very careful planning. Artillery bombardment was requested for each of 12, 13 and 14 December to ensure accurate registration, to induce the enemy to withdraw any machine-guns and to cut wire. He also requested night bombardments on these same days, these being of 15 minutes duration, reducing to five minutes on the night of 14 December, the infantry assault to commence the second this fire, and that of the 18-pounder field gun firing from the front line, ceased. An armoured car of the Motor Machine Gun Battery would tow the gun to the rear.[6]

On 12 December the OC Raid, Captain E.C. Jackson, organized the raiders, all selected from B Company, 5th Battalion, into three parties, each of an officer and 14 ORs, the latter a mix of bombers, bomb carriers and bayonet men. B Company immediately began training on a practice barrier, together with an officer and several sappers of 2nd Canadian Field Company, whose task, if the 18-pounder's fire did not suffice, would be to blow up the barrier. The 18-pounder went into the front line the next night, it being taken within 200 yards of the line by the armoured car and then manhandled, its wheels wrapped in old rubber tires to muffle noise, into its prepared firing position on the road.

At 0400 on the 15th the operation began, the 18-pounder rapidly pumping 26 rounds at point blank range into the barrier, these punches being assisted by 4.5-inch and 6-inch howitzers and trench mortars. The assault force waited in their assault positions, one party left of the road in a ditch previously cleared of wire, another on the right side of the road in a sap that had been dug over several nights, and the third party acting as a flank guard further to the right. Five minutes after the 18-pounder opened, and as the artillery fire ceased, the infantry went in quickly securing the barrier, practically without opposition, though briefly delayed by some

5 LAC, RG 24, Volume 1825; TNA: WO 95/1571: War Diary, 1st Cheshires, December 1915.

6 Gilbert, *The Challenge of War*, p. 637, calls Lipsett the "inventor" of the raid as an operation. This is not so. But it is true that Lipsett was a skilled tactician. In the writing of *We Lead Others Follow, Get Tough, Stay Tough* and this present study the very high quality of Lipsett's operational writing has been evident. One comes away from the archives very impressed with the superior quality of anything he wrote, be it lessons and deductions drawn from operations, analysis of matters pertaining to organization, weapons and tactical doctrine, and especially Appreciations and plans, his work being classic examples of the mental process involved in their composition.

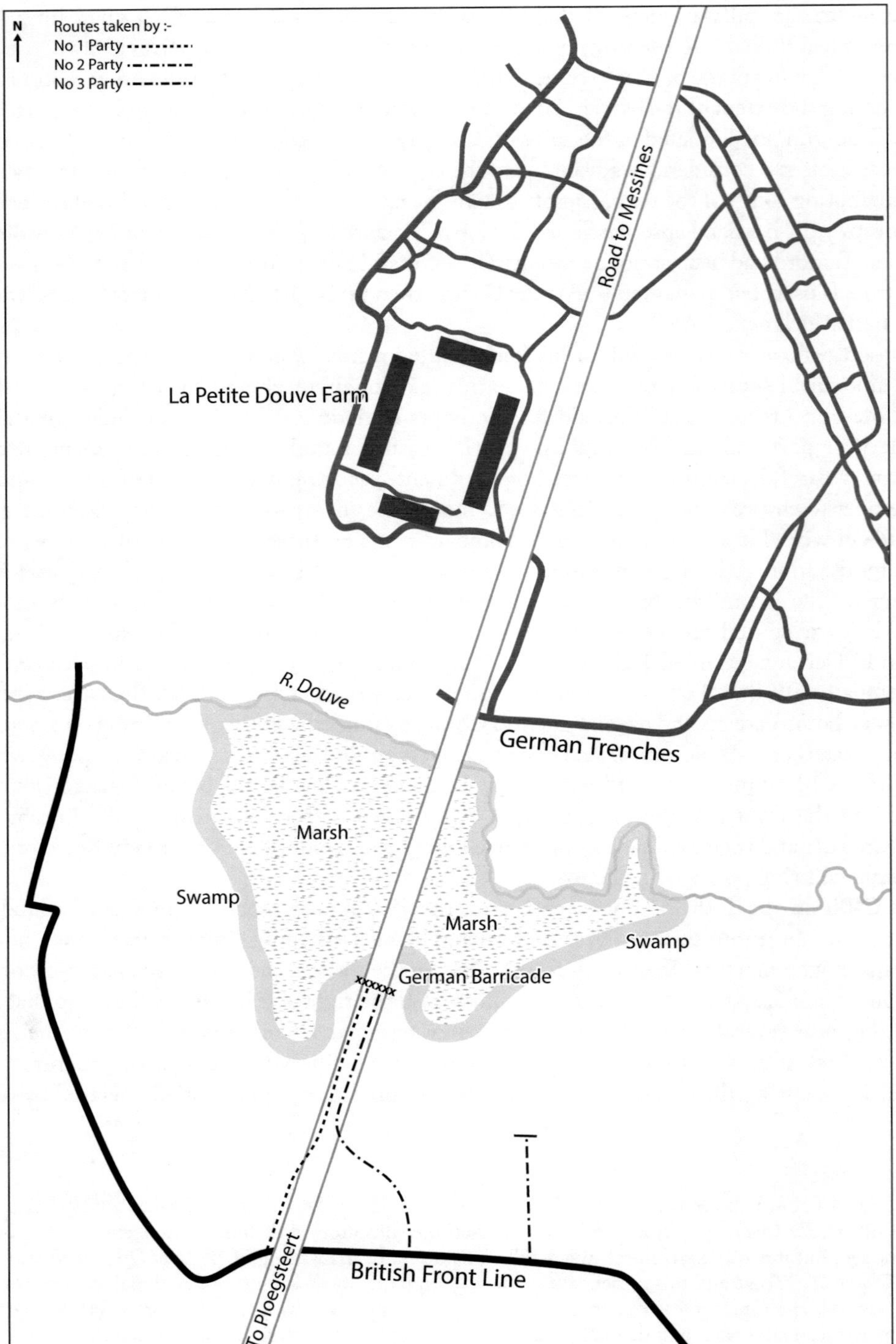

3 Raid at Messines Barrier, 14/15 December 1915, 5th Canadian Battalion.

remaining wire. Spoils included two prisoners, several rifles, including a Canadian Ross, a rifle that as early as May 1915 had proven unsuitable and unreliable as a general service weapon. The party did not remain long at the barrier, thereby avoiding enemy fire which quickly became accurate and intense. Before withdrawing a mine was placed in the barrier, this to be fired if the enemy tried to re-occupy it in any strength. When this enemy fire ceased around 0500, 5th Battalion re-occupied the barrier and established listening posts. Battalion casualties were two wounded. In his report on the operation Lipsett called surprise the main reason for success, the 18-pounder playing a key role in the surprise. He also praised the carefully prepared plan.[7]

The most notable British raid in the last two months of 1915 was conducted in the Laventie sector in mid-December by 59th Brigade, 20th Division. Describing and assessing this raid is difficult given the absence of a good map. Trenches and a dozen points are referred to in the description of the raid, but do not appear on the map. Fortunately, the division commander's report is clear and comprehensive, this being so because this GOC, R.H. Davies, was very hands-on in the conception and preparation of the raid. Careful reading of his text enables comprehension of the progress of the raid. A simplified version of the map in the War Diary of 20th Division has been inserted to give an idea of circumstances and concept (see MSD 4). The plan called for a night raid, Zero at 0100 (amended to 0200 to allow the moon to set) on 16 December, 10th Battalion of The Rifle Brigade on the right and 11th KRRC on the left, the raiders of each unit being in about platoon strength plus bombers, in all three officers and some 70 ORs per battalion. The two COs and the brigade commander selected the objectives. The latter defined the purposes of the two raids thus: "to inflict loss … capture machine-guns and documents, and to destroy wire and trenches as far as possible." Zero for both sets of raiders was to be simultaneous, but in the event one set was delayed the other would still assault at Zero. As it turned out, the 10th Battalion raiders, who had further to go than the 11th Battalion raiders, encountered wire that had been less thoroughly cut, which caused delay and noise that alerted the enemy. On learning this, the brigade commander cancelled the assault by the 10th. This he could do quickly since telephone lines had been laid to connect the raid commanders to each other and to their COs who could talk direct one to the other and both back to brigade HQ.

The artillery, during the week prior to the raids, cut enemy wire in several places in order to deceive the enemy as to the actual points to be raided. Despite being kept under continuous machine-gun fire, the gaps that had been created were repaired and had to be cut again by infantry wire-cutting parties. Machine-gun support by battalion weapons would provide the "usual" amount of fire on the gaps through which the assault parties would go commencing at 2100 and lasting until the assault troops began advancing. In addition, the Brigade Machine Gun Officer would arrange fire on the gaps that would not be used from dusk to Zero when fire would lift to cover enemy lines in areas adjacent to the objectives. Trench mortars would thicken the artillery curtain around each objective once these had been secured by the raiders. During the pre-raid period, recce repeatedly checked the state of the enemy wire. Finally, the GOC,

7 LAC, War Diary, 2nd Brigade, December 1915, report on minor operation night 14/15 December; 5th Battalion, Operation Order 61 and report; RG9IIIC1, Volume 3858, Folder 84, File 1, report on raid. TNA: WO 95/1571: 1st Cheshire Regiment, December 1915, 'Account of a Minor Operation Carried Out by 2nd Canadian Division, 15 December'. The raid was actually by 2nd Canadian Brigade.

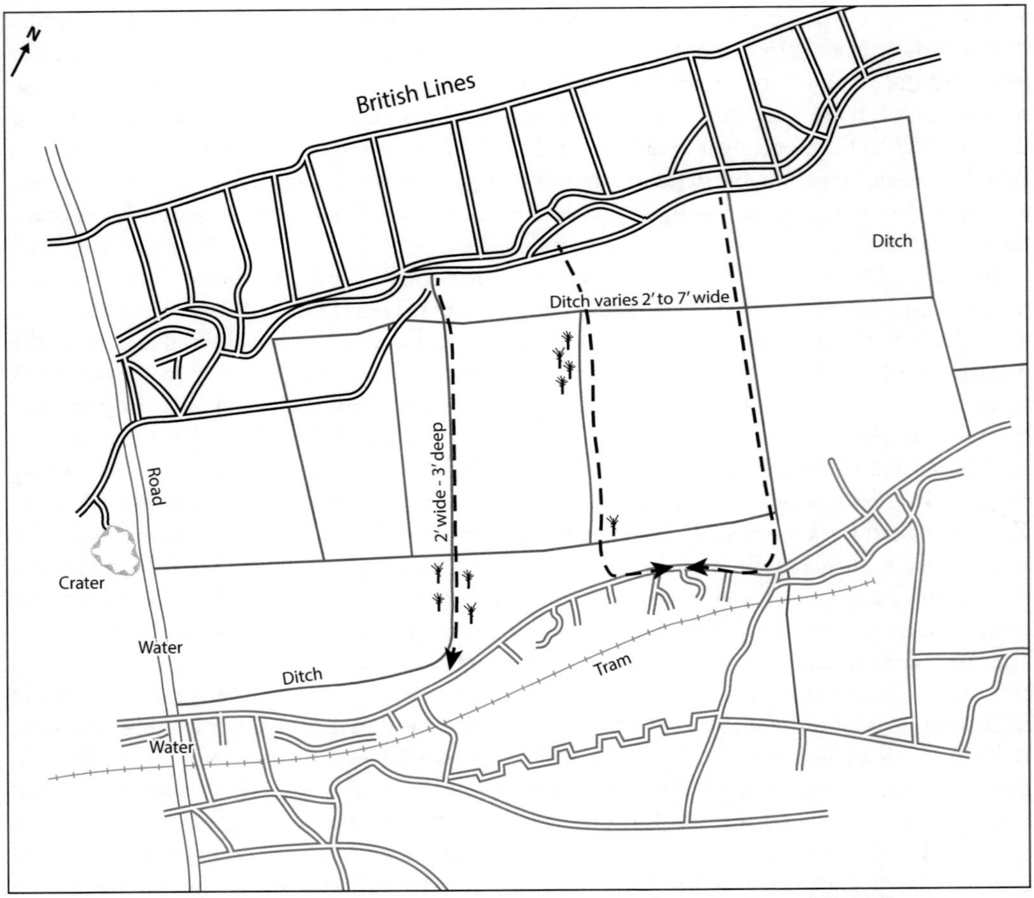

4 Laventie Raid, 16 December 1915, 11th King's Royal Rifle Corps (KRRC).

the COs and the raid commanders met to confirm all details. Raid commanders then wrote their orders, after which they briefed their raiders using air photographs to point out routes and locations.

Final preparations by 11th KRRC during the night of Wednesday, 15 December, included two recce patrols to check wire. The first, three men plus two wire-cutters and an NCO, went out at 1900, reporting on return that only one gap was open, the others having been plugged by new wire which the patrol had cut "under difficult circumstances" and without alerting the enemy. This made the second recce necessary, this time by an officer and four men plus two wire-cutters, at 2240. On return the officer reported no change in enemy wire. While these patrols were out, the raiders completed preparations, including the issue of sandbags in which to carry bombs and extra wire-cutters and axes. Immediately before moving out into no man's land at midnight the raiders fixed bayonets and were reminded of the vital targets: in the neck and if the opponent was retreating, then a liver jab. All ranks were cautioned that if they heard the word "Retire" they were to ignore it since this word would not be used during the raid. Finally, a password was made known to all.

By 0145 all three assault parties, one officer and about 20 ORs each, were in position, but some delay (unexplained in any of the relevant reports) then occurred since Second Lieutenant G.K. Baynes, OC Left Party, did not give the assault order until 0230. On this his party and the Centre Party, Lieutenant F.W. Warre, began entering the enemy trench, about 30 men in all succeeding in that. However, Second Lieutenant H.S. Gough's Right Party having been discovered while still cutting wire could not enter the enemy trench, but did bomb it from the parapet. Meanwhile, the other two parties, having turned inwards in the trench, bombed toward each other experiencing on the way to a link-up "very sharp fighting." As this was going on, the artillery curtain descended around the objective area thereby hindering or preventing enemy movement against it. Warre and his men worked in two groups, the bombers along the parapet and the bayonet men in the trench. A "brisk" struggle saw three of the party killed and another went missing, believed killed. The enemy lost 13 men, including an officer, either in the trench or trying to leave a dug-out. Bayne's party as it progressed toward Warre encountered a large, brilliantly lit dug-out where seven Germans were killed. Some of Bayne's bombers, as had Warre's, turned outward and blocked the trench while the remainder of each party continued on to link-up, killing more enemy as they pushed on. When the parties met having cleared the trench they then retraced their way to the entry point and left the trench unmolested, this being a tribute to the thoroughness of the clearing. While none of the reports say how long the raiders remained in the enemy trench it must have been quite some time since raid reports contain detailed descriptions of the trenches, size, depth and construction of the enemy dug-outs (the lighted one was six feet high inside), the composition of the firesteps (concrete-filled sandbags) the distance between revetted traverses, the extent of revetting overall and the thickness of the parapets. During the withdrawal bringing in the wounded proved difficult since the enemy opened heavy fire. Warre, who would receive the MC for "gallant conduct," was not only the last man to return, but went back under heavy fire to collect men who had been wounded. During his return he was wounded.

The GOC, Major-General R.H. Davies, offered a number of lessons in his report. First, the extreme cold had caused considerable difficulty in pulling the pins out of grenades, the men's hands being so numb they had resorted to extracting the pins with their teeth. The issue leather gloves had proven useless as they were sodden and could not solve the pin problem. Davies suggested a hook-type device attached to a wristlet, the hook to be easily inserted in the pins to extract them. Second, once again sandbags had not made good carriers for bombs, nor had the experimental "waistcoats" which became full of mud when the men had to crawl. The answer, as other divisions had also recommended, was a haversack fastened on the back by a belt and then slipped around to the front when required. This became the standard and can be seen in many photographs. Finally, Davies refers to the "trail of torn paper" dropped by the leading party as it traversed no man's land which guided the other parties and helped get all back during the withdrawal. He does not elaborate how the paper stood up to conditions, and he would certainly have realized the disadvantage of marking routes with paper. but as all got to where they had to go and then back again it seems to have been effective.

Summing up this raid the divisional historian called it a complete surprise achieved under difficult conditions including extreme cold. The Germans suffered 39 known dead, while raider casualties were five killed and 11 wounded. Overall, he considered the moral effect very good: "It was the first fighting that this brigade had seen, and keen as the men were it was a source of great encouragement to them to prove by experience that man for man they were better than the Germans." The GOC (Davies) gave the enemy some credit, saying they had fought with great determination and no surrenders of any kind were made, but such raids "makes them jumpy, causes then to increase their sentries and outpost line and [keeps] them in their front line trenches instead of in more comfortable quarters to the rear."[8]

To conclude this look at raids in 1915 we turn the clock back to the "model" raid of November mentioned at the beginning of this chapter. This raid by 5th and 7th Canadian Battalions (2nd Brigade, 1st Division) came on 16/17 November between Messines and Ploegsteert Wood. It made a name for the two units as "aggressive trench raiders," a reputation that also marked 2nd Royal Welsh Fusiliers, 1st Worcesters and 1st Grenadier Guards, units mentioned at the beginning of this chapter. Only Victor Odlum's 7th Battalion would actually enter the enemy trenches, George Tuxford's 5th getting within bomb-throwing range, but no further, the way being blocked by an unforeseen obstacle that could not be crossed.

It is not surprising that this raid which was (and is) commonly recognized as the first large-scale raid on the German trenches, originated, then was planned and executed by units of Louis Lipsett's 2nd Brigade. Lipsett, the first CO of the 8th Battalion, had been in command of the brigade since mid-September. By November he decided that conditions were perfect "for the proving of his belief that strong parties of determined troops, properly equipped and led … could enter the German trenches and inflict casualties out of all proportion to their own losses, make prisoners and get away."[9] Lipsett sought constantly for new ways to strike at the enemy and when he saw an opportunity he quickly seized it. Likewise Victor Odlum who on 4 November proposed a raid against what he called the "Petite Douve Fort" just north of the Douve River and immediately west of the Messines-Le Hutte Road (see MSD 6). Both officers thought it would be a good go at "annoying the enemy and disclosing how heavily he is holding the first line near the Petite Douve." Odlum recommended a simultaneous diversionary raid at some point opposite the right sector of the brigade front. That sector was George Tuxford's responsibility. The records show that he and Odlum had discussed and agreed on a joint enterprise which they then put to Lipsett. Not that the ever-aggressive Lipsett (and Tuxford) needed any great urging, but Odlum directed attention to several favourable characteristics of the proposed raid: the gaining of valuable information, low risk of serious loss, reduction of enemy morale, possibly prisoners and a rise in own troops morale.

Lipsett, considering the proposal sound, forwarded it to division with additional comment including restating the purpose of the raid thus: to decrease enemy morale, to take prisoners and to cause loss to the enemy by convincing him to move reserves and supports forward where they would be struck by artillery fire. On 9 November 1st Division passed the proposal to Corps HQ together with an estimate of additional artillery requirements, as well as noting that the proposed date for the raid was the same as an operation planned by V Corps. Two days later Second Army approved the proposal and the additional artillery support and advised that as the V Corps operation would be an artillery operation only no conflict existed between the two operations.[10]

8 Inglefield, *Twentieth Light Division,* pp. 30-32; TNA: WO 95/2111: 20th Division General Staff, December 1915, report dated 21 December; 59th Brigade Operation Order 18 and report, 14 December; TNA: WO 95/2115: 11th KRRC Operation Order and report 11 December.

9 Lord Beaverbrook, *Canada in Flanders* Volume II (Toronto: Hodder and Stoughton, 1917), p. 55.

10 LAC, War Diary, 1st Division General Staff, 4 November; Odlum to GOC 2nd Brigade; Lieutenant C.K.L. Pyman to CO 5th Battalion (undated recce report); 2nd Brigade to 1st Division, 7 December,

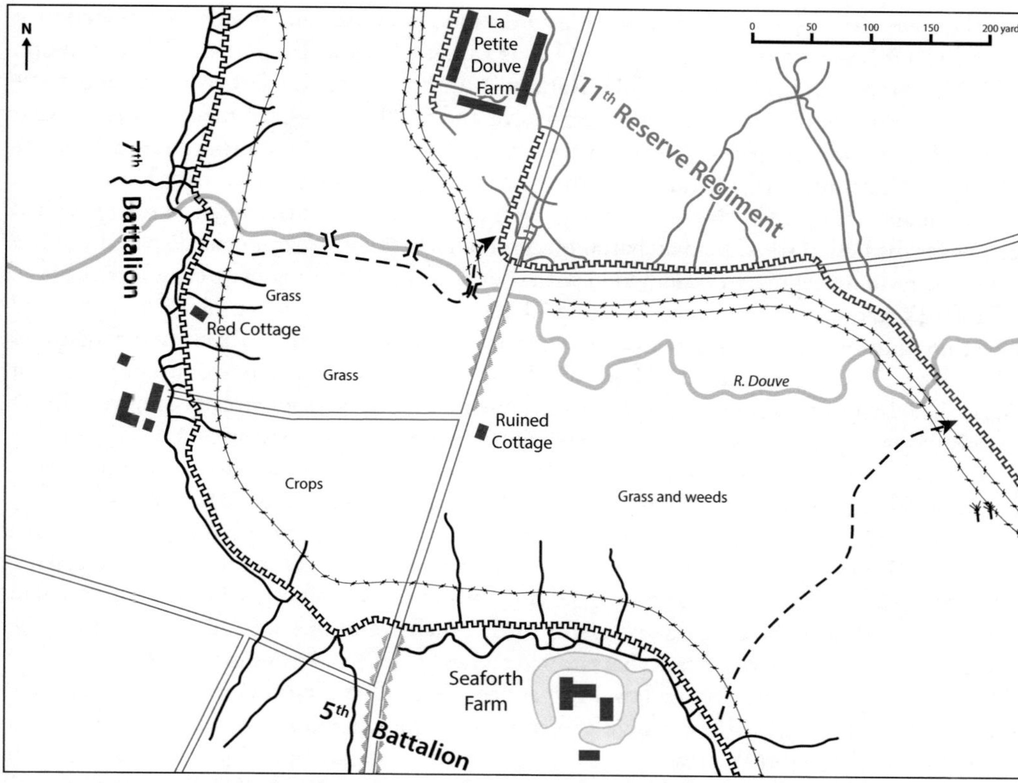

5 Raid at La Petite Douve, 17 November 1915, 2nd Canadian Brigade.

Mention should be made of 8th Battalion's contribution. Before it was relieved by Odlum's 7th Battalion, Sergeant Frank Iriam, a battalion scout, described the various reports on enemy wire and where listening posts were located before they were withdrawn after attempts had been made to seize the occupants. Iriam also reported the discovery of a path leading out from the enemy wire down to the river: "We saw here a possible entrance for a raiding party." During the relief this opportunity and the German inactivity was mentioned to the 7th Battalion. When this led to a raid Iriam remarked how it began a "regular craze' for raids, his battalion officers also becoming "infected with the germ."[11]

Before describing the pre-raid activity that commenced in 2nd Brigade it is appropriate here to say more about the major players – Lipsett, Odlum and Tuxford – the last two having heretofore been only briefly mentioned, and two other critical factors: first, the ground that a neighbouring brigade described as "difficult,"[12] and, second, the enemy, whose posture in the proposed objective area seemed to invite a substantial raid.

'Scheme for Small Offensive Operations 15/16 November'.

11 Glenn R. Iriam, *In the Trenches 1914-1918* (N.p.: Art Book Bindery, 2008), p. 95.

12 F.W. Bagnall, *Not Mentioned in Despatches: The Memoir of Fred Bagnall, 14th Battalion, C.E.F. 1914-1917* (Vancouver: North Shore Press, 1933; reprint ed., Ottawa: CEF Books, 2005), p. 77.

If there ever was a perfect fit of a brigade commander and his four battalion commanders it may well have been the formidable team of Louis Lipsett, George Tuxford and Victor Odlum, H.H. Matthews (8th Battalion) and J.G. Rattray (10th Battalion). The last two did not participate in this raid, but both were just as aggressive and would soon have their chance at what Haig had called winter sports. It is not surprising that Tuxford and Odlum would be Lipsett's weapons in this initial brigade raid since the three officers had commanded battalions, Odlum as a Major and acting CO 7th Battalion, during the hard fighting at Second Ypres. Lipsett had been by far the best of the Canadian battalion commanders there, a fact no one disputed and one that drove to some degree, in conjunction with friendship, the building of a very effective team.

Tuxford's role would be limited in this raid because of the unforeseen obstacle mentioned above, no fault of his or of his raiders, but simply an instance of the ill-luck that sometimes foiled plans. As Lipsett later said, "Poor old Tuxford was as sick as could be at not getting at the Boche!" Inability to come to grips with the enemy on this occasion greatly annoyed the 41 year old Welshman, an officer known for his outspoken nature, no prevarication ever, and his determination, two of the personal characteristics that saw him promoted to brigade command in March 1916. Tuxford, a shrewd man, knew full well that his unit's unique features (see below) "would build spirit and cohesion." Currie admired the former cavalryman who made the 5th a unit that had "never lost an inch of ground to the enemy, nor ever failed to take its objective." Before the war Tuxford had been a long-serving militia cavalry officer, CO of the 27th Light Horse, not a strange choice for a successful cattle rancher and one who in 1898 had led the longest cattle drive in history, a trek that covered endless prairie and three mountain ranges, over 1,700 miles in all, between Moose Jaw, in what became in 1905 the Province of Saskatchewan, and Dawson City in the Yukon where goldminers sought the gold that could buy steak and much else. At the outbreak of war Tuxford put together the 5th Battalion, an amalgamation of horsemen who would serve as infantry despite what their cap badge "5th Western Cavalry" proclaimed. Their sobriquet, "Tuxford's Dandies," and various retained habits such as cavalry bugle calls, gave rise to jibes such as "The Disappointed Fifth" and "The Fifth Mounted Foot," but there was admiration, too, of the unit's fighting ability. Tuxford's officers thought him a great "fusser" in running the ship, but the man who knew him best, his Adjutant F.C. Bagshaw, also described him as "selfish, bull-dozing and grabbing." After his promotion to brigadier some disliked Tuxford for his propensity to try to grab credit for himself.[13] Nevertheless, he was an able and dependable brigade commander, consistently so. Administration was not to his liking, a failing that his Adjutant remarked upon and he was at times a lax disciplinarian, the primary example being during the looting of Arras in March 1918 by British and Canadian troops. These shortcomings may explain why he did not get a division.[14]

Major Victor Odlum had been one of the four best Canadian battalion commanders at Second Ypres. His reward was promotion and command of the 7th Battalion shortly

13 LAC, RG 24, Volume 1825, GAQ 5-66, Lipsett to Currie, 20 November 1915; Imperial War Museum 76/170/1 Private E.W. Russell, 'A Private Soldier's View on the Great War, 1914-1918', p. 17; Baldwin, "*Holding the Line*", pp. 118-19, 140. Baldwin served with the 5th, which is fortunate, since there is not a substantial history of the battalion. LAC, RG 41, CBC Interviews, Volume 8, F.C. Bagshaw; MG30E100 (Currie Papers), Volume 52, Diary, 2 September 1918; Daniel G. Dancocks, Spearhead *to Victory: Canada and the Great War* (Edmonton: Hurtig,1987), p. 107.

14 For a full account of the Arras affair see Radley, *Get Tough, Stay Tough.*

afterward. He had at Second Ypres displayed "stamina, determination, battlefield sense and strong leadership."[15] While of undisputed competence he did sometimes tilt at windmills, an example being his abhorrence of liquor. He and Rattray of 10th Battalion, both being teatotallers, abolished the rum ration in their units, this lasting until Arthur Currie raised hell, demanding to know whose rum they thought it was. Currie, as he put it, did not like to see men "mucked about" needlessly. Rum and smiles were restored! Odlum, on taking over 11th Brigade on promotion in July 1916, seemingly remembered the lesson, but soon relapsed deciding that the 11th really needed pea-soup, not rum. The news spread like a prairie grass fire, this giving rise to the 11th being called throughout the BEF the "Pea-Soup Brigade." This title was short-lived. Very soon after the disastrous raid in early 1917 by 4th Division the GOC, Major-General David Watson, restored rum to the brigade. Odlum had some other unusual ideas. His was one of the few voices that did not condemn the Ross rifle. In his opinion "if the rifle is well-cared for and cleaned hourly during an action it will work easily." While this might have had some truth in it, getting the enemy to agree to the hourly time-outs would not have been so easily achieved. Another of his ideas was to do reliefs by companies instead of rotation by battalions. This did not pan out, an obvious disadvantage being how it put battalions half in and half out of the line all the time. Training also suffered until eventually common sense ruled.[16] However, Currie knew Odlum to be a good CO and when it came to this raid Currie thought "he had worked out the details very well," the assessment being that "The 7th has gone to the top of the class in this Brigade."[17] In an interview long after the war Odlum reminisced about organizing the raid:

> No man knows at the time when he's doing a thing of that sort that he's inventing anything at all. Each night I would go up and talk to the men in the line and the men would always tell me what the Germans had been doing in the night. They came up onto our trench, climbed up the face of it. They moved about here, they moved about there. And so I said to my men, 'I'm going to tell you something. What they have done we will do and a little bit more. If the Germans can come up onto our trenches we can go into theirs.' That's when I started raiding.[18]

Major P.F. Villiers in late 1915 the newly arrived GSO3 at 1st Division HQ, recalling the raid after the war, called it "an event … the importance of which cannot be over-estimated." He remembered Odlum's orders for the raid as so good they were translated and widely circulated within the French Army. Odlum and the officers who had been on the raid were invited to lecture within the BEF, Odlum himself becoming the recognized expert. To give just one example, when in February 1916 GOC Second Army wanted "notes" put together for a conference, his MGGS, H.B. Williams, wrote personally to Odlum asking for his comments, additions or

15 Radley, 'Inescapable Realities', in Jones (ed.), *Courage Without Glory.* During the South African War Odlum served initially as a private soldier with the RCR and then with 3rd Canadian Mounted Rifles (CMR) upon commissioning as a Lieutenant.

16 LAC. MG30E417 (Baxter Papers), p. 10; RG 41, CBC Interviews, Volume 8, F.C. Bagshaw; Pedley, *Only This* p. 57; Radley, *Get Tough, Stay Tough,* p. 213.

17 LAC, RG 24, Volume 1825, GAQ 5-66, 20 November 1915.

18 LAC, RG 41, CBC Interview, Volume 6, Victor Odlum.

alterations. Odlum's hand-written response and associated documents are discussed in the next chapter.[19]

As for Lipsett, George Tuxford, called him the "outstanding" one of the nine infantry battalion commanders who survived Second Ypres, a leader of "high ability in the judgement of his peers." Tuxford recalled how the four battalion commanders in Currie's 2nd Brigade had agreed that should Currie be lost, then Lipsett should command the brigade, despite not being the senior CO.[20] A born leader, and a fearless one, keen on recce well-forward, a habit that would cause his death in late 1918, and in the eyes of some a hard taskmaster, Lipsett was also approachable and able to inspire subordinates thanks to a keen sense of humour, a fine sense of the human touch and his obvious care for his men. Major Paul Villiers remembered a dinner where Lipsett's guests included J. Seely (GOC Canadian Cavalry Brigade) and Winston Churchill, CO 6th Royal Scots Fusiliers. Also in attendance was Private "Foghorn" MacDonald, an extremely "foul-mouthed man" there for only one purpose: "to horrify Winston and Seely!" Cyril Falls remembered Lipsett as "a charming man, as well as a good soldier," a sentiment shared by many. Major Lester Stephens, 8th Canadian Battalion, thought Lipsett "a good soldier, you know." Another officer called him "a wonderful soldier and a wonderful man."[21] Frank Iriam of 8th Battalion referred to Lipsett 17 times in his memoirs, some of his recollections lengthy tributes to Lipsett's ability, manner and character.[22] Will Bird, a soldier who disliked officers on sight, had much to say about Lipsett. He remembered one night while on sentry how Lipsett suddenly appeared and after a lengthy chat about many things gave him a signed photograph, a gift Bird treasured throughout his life.[23] Major C. Smellie, also 8th Battalion, went so far as to say that Lipsett rather than Currie should have been GOC the Canadian Corps. In any case, Lipsett, when he took command of 3rd Division in mid-1916, became the youngest of the Canadian division commanders and arguably the best. When he was killed in late 1918 while GOC 4th British Division it was said that "no officer lost by Canada in the whole war was more regretted by the men he led."[24]

19 LAC, MG 30E236 (Villiers Papers), Volume 4, Folder 7, Volume 1 of Villiers' Diary, 17 November 1915. Villiers became BM 3rd Brigade in October 1916 and was subsequently (January 1918) GSO2 of 29th British Division. LAC, MG30E300 (Odlum Papers), Volume 24, Folder 'Raids February 1916 to June 1917'.

20 Saskatchewan Provincial Archives, "The Great War As I Saw it," Memoirs of Brigadier-General George Tuxford, p. 64.

21 LAC, MG30E236 (Villiers Papers), Diary, entry for October 1915; Cyril Falls, 'The Best of My War', in George A. Panichas (ed.), *Promise of Greatness: The War of 1914-1918* (London: Cassell, 1968), pp. 230-31; LAC, RG 41, CBC Interviews, Lester Stephens, J. Pritchard and A.H. Fisher.

22 Iriam, *In the Trenches*, pp. 14, 41, 61, 68, 76, 89-90, 96, 99, 106, 109, 117, 145-46, 158, 213, 259. Iriam considered Lipsett the best soldier he ever saw.

23 Bird, *Ghosts Have Warm Hands*, pp. 14-15.

24 LAC, RG 41, Volume 8, Major C. Smellie. Smellie claimed that Victor Odlum told him that Lipsett was "put out and jealous" when Currie got the Corps, Lipsett supposedly saying to Odlum that he was more experienced, and if it had been "a straight forward thing" he would have gotten the Corps. Smellie's personal opinion and "of the troops that I knew' was that Lipsett should have gotten the Corps because while Currie "had the ability to keep good men around him … I don't think he had anything to write home about." Military Advisory Board, *Canada in the Great World War; an Authentic Account of the Military History of Canada From the Earliest Days to the Close of the War of the Nations.* Volume III: *Guarding the Channel Ports* (Toronto: United Publishers of Canada Limited, 1919), p. 66.

Ground was critical in this raid, it being, as noted earlier, "difficult." One early account gives a good picture of just what that meant:

> I was fortunate enough to visit the happy 7th Battalion on the morning after the raid. Later I went carefully over Petite Douve Farm [MSD 6]. The huge blocks of concrete and strips of railway iron, our raiders had reported were still there. It was the fortress which for months had stuck its nose, with Teutonic insolence, out into our lines. It commanded two splendid fields of fire down the valley of the Big and Little Douve, and continuous machine-gun volleys from it made life miserable for our working and ration parties. Through No Man's Land ran the smaller stream, passing diagonally through those of the enemy. Snarled and shell-scarred willows joined by stretches of barbed wire, both ours and the enemy's, lined the steep, crumbling banks. The Huns relied on this defence and seldom ventured beyond their own wire, which was gradually cut by our patrols, before the very eyes of the unsuspecting enemy.[25]

At the time of the raid heavy rain had caused the Douve, which ran east to west, to triple in depth and width (usually it was 10 feet or less wide and about a yard deep), but on the night of the raid the flood had subsided, returning the Douve to its normal state. Raid preparations by the 7th Battalion included building three "bridge-ladders" to span the Douve. These were kept as light as possible, but even so each weighed 60 pounds. Placing them where they had to go would prove slow and difficult, but they were in position in good time.[26]

Enemy inactivity brought about by complete Canadian domination of no man's land, made circumstances even more favourable for this raid. so much so that the 11th Reserve Regiment opposite Odlum's 7th battalion "had even given up … Listening Posts." In fact, it went beyond that, Odlum observing that the enemy "seldom ventured beyond his own parapet." Thus the enemy ceded the initiative and in doing so increased the possibility of raiders achieving a surprise. Private A. McGowan of the 7th remembered how quiet the enemy were: "Nothing happened last night, the night before that … or will happen tonight … Jerry was caught by surprise." Odlum's choice of objective, he thought, bettered the chance of surprise: "Right across from us was a very strong position … the last place they would be worried about." The river and double wire obstacle added to the German sense of solid security.[27]

While the Germans hibernated Canadian patrols roamed freely diligently searching for the best targets and how best to get at them. 5th Battalion's choice of a point of entry into the enemy trench was confirmed after the discovery of a gap 20 feet wide in the wire, this leading directly to the chosen point. As for the 7th Battalion, careful recce revealed a covered line of approach all along the bank of the Douve right to the objective. Patrols also discovered that near the point of entry a screen of trees protected the defences, a circumstance that would affect the method and efficacy of wire-cutting.[28]

25 *Ibid.,* pp. 228-29.
26 Tony Spagnoly, 'Canada at Ypres: La Petite Douve Farm, Messines, November 1915', *Stand To!,* 39 (Winter 1993), p. 23; Adkin, *Western Front Companion,* pp. 471-72.
27 LAC, War Diary, 7th Battalion, 6 November, 1915; Spagnoly, 'Canada at Ypres', pp. 23-24; LAC, RG9IIIC3, Volume 4051, Folder 19, File 2, report, 7th Battalion, 19 November.
28 LAC, RG 41, CBC Interview, F.C. Bagshaw; Lord Beaverbrook, *Canada in Flanders* Volume I, p. 55.

Recce was especially key in this particular raid. Privates McGowan and Rossiter both made special mention of Lieutenant H.H. Owen stating that the organization and planning of the "whole thing" was his based upon "the good work of his scouts." Major T.V. Scudamore agreed, saying that it was organized and planned "in its every detail, if it was not actually carried out by Owen, the 7th Battalion's first Scout Officer." Owen and his scouts on one patrol had even been on the enemy parapet. Owen was not to participate in the raid, much to his disappointment. While waiting for the raid his leave finally came up and he took it. As early as the end of October, Captain W.D. Holmes, who had replaced Owen, and the scouts had conducted very daring recce up to the Douve.[29]

Immediately after the five officers and 75 volunteers were settled upon and brought together Holmes moved them to the rear for a week where they were quartered in good billets and excused all other duties in order to focus on training. F.C. Bagshaw spoke of the numerous rehearsals during the week, day and night, on a facsimile of the German trenches: "A field was found where the natural configuration lent itself easily to adaptation to resemble the enemy trenches; a ditch served for the Douve River; a path for the Messines road; another ditch for the enemy trench … other trenches were turned up to make the plan complete."[30] Bombing attacks, blocking of trenches and the withdrawal, always a tricky stage, were thoroughly practised, as was handling of the specially built "bridge-ladders" that would get the raiders across and back from the Douve and the matts for crossing wire. Despite the weight and awkward size (two feet wide and 16 feet long) of the former gradually the men became comfortable with them. In addition, the scouts took small groups of the raiders out each night over the actual route to the enemy trenches.[31] Concurrently, the Douve was closely monitored as the flood water receded, likewise the state of enemy wire after the periodic strikes by artillery. Constant observation of the enemy continued right up to Zero to ensure their state had not changed.

A principle of battle procedure is concurrent activity and the 7th Battalion stuck to it, many activities going on simultaneously. Preparations made by the battalion also included some innovations. First, all the raiders surrendered all papers and insignia and identity discs. Second, Lee-Enfields were borrowed to replace the Ross rifles. Third, "flash lamps" with an on/off switch were attached to the rifles; Odlum called these "battery torches" a "wonderful thing" that would blind the enemy. Fourth, spools of wire were prepared for use by the blocking parties. Fifth, faces were blackened, or so Odlum recalled. Other sources say, variously, that men covered their faces with masks, black veils, or veils of crepe, the idea being that the covering would act not

29 Spagnoly, 'Canada at Ypres', p. 24; Major T.V. Scudamore, *A Short History of the 7th Battalion C.E.F.* (Vancouver: Anderson & Odlum, 1930), p. 16. Scudmore's account is 25 pages long. No proper history of the battalion has ever been done. He based his account on a brief item in *The Listening Post*, the trench journal of the battalion. The account notes that Owen was killed in action in January 1916.

30 LAC, RG9IIIC3, Volume 4051, Folder 19, File 2, 'Canadian Corps Report on Enterprises on La Petite Douve. IV. Report of OC 7th Battalion'.

31 LAC, RG 41, CBC Interview, F.C. Bagshaw, Volume 8; Spagnoly, 'Canada at Ypres,' p. 23. When it comes to the numbers of officers and men of 7th Battalion on the raid archival sources differ and so do published sources. LAC, RG9IIIC1, Vols. 3858 and 3860 agree on four officers and 75 ORs. The British Official History and Saunders' *Raiding on the Western Front* say four and 77. LAC, RG9IIIC3, Volume 4051, and the Canadian official historian (Nicholson) say five and 85. Both include the OC Raid which Vols. 3858 and 3860 do not. In all these sources no figures for 5th Battalion are evident; "similar" is all that is said about that battalion's raiders.

only as camouflage but as a means of recognition. Finally, the raiders placed white stakes from where they had done their training to their exit points from the forward trench to prevent any confusion while moving forward. Afterward, 2nd Brigade expressed complete satisfaction with pre-raid preparations, "everything and every party was in its place to the minute" and went on to say that every detail of organization and material required had been prepared.[32]

Well before they had first proposed the raid on 4 November to GOC 2nd Brigade Odlum and Tuxford worked hard planning the enterprise, separately and then jointly to ensure co-ordination. This continued as the proposal went up the chain of command, all comments and alterations being incorporated as they arose until finally a week later Second Army approval was received, followed immediately by 1st Division's Operation Order. Then commenced 2nd Brigade's final battle planning including preparation of Operation Orders by brigade and the two battalions. On Wednesday 15 November Lieutenant H.C.M. Clark, Adjutant of the 7th, signed off and issued the five-page manuscript Operation Order Number 59. There can be no doubt that Odlum had kept a close and sharp eye on the drafting of this order.[33]

People often prefer to save the best for last. This seems appropriate here, too, since one battalion, the 5th, failed through no fault of its own, while the other battalion, the 7th, achieved a resounding success, a blueprint or model for future endeavours and a considerable reputation as expert raiders. Before briefly recounting the 5th Battalion's disappointing foray as the right assault unit, the reader should know how it and the 7th, the left and primary assault unit, were organized in similar fashion with due regard for their particular tasks which differed somewhat. The left assault force founded by the 7th and its tasks looked like this:

> Commander. Captain L.J. Thomas. To remain in Canadian trenches, his functions being co-ordination, seeing the various parties went forward at the appointed times and to react to any emergencies.
>
> Wire-Cutting Party. Lieutenant Holmes and four ORs.

32 LAC, RG9IIIC3, Volume 4051, Folder 19, File 2, Canadian Corps report on Enterprise at La Petite Douve and report of CO 7th Battalion; RG9IIIC1, Volume 3858, Folder 84, File 5, Summary of Small Offensive Operation Carried Out By 5th and 7th Canadian Battalions; RG 421, CBC Interview, Victor Odlum; Military Advisory Board, *Guarding the Channel Ports,* p. 229; Griffith, *Battle Tactics,* note 57, p. 232; Spagnoly, 'Canada at Ypres'.

33 All documents pertaining to the proposal and its approval are in LAC, War Diary, 2nd Brigade for November 1915. Also see Appendix 6 of Edmonds, *Haig's Command to the 1st July. Appendices.* While this appendix contains some material from Operation Order 59 the title of this appendix indicates that it is much more than that: 'Organization and Execution of a Raid Carried Out By 5th and 7th Canadian Battalions, 2nd Canadian Infantry Brigade (Br.-General L.J. Lipsett), November 16th-17th, 1915'. The title suggests its origin. Appendix 6 is virtually word for word with LAC, RG9IIIC1, Volume 3858, Folder 84, File 5, 'Summary of Small Offensive Carried Out By 5th and 7th Canadian Battalions, 2nd Canadian Infantry Brigade, November 16th-17th, 1915'. The only difference is that Appendix 6 includes marginal subject headings. This version received wide distribution within the BEF; for example, Copy No. 33 is an appendix to the War Diary of 18th British Division for 8 December 1915. The cover page indicates that the brigades of that division received copies on 9 December. It is also clear that the Volume 3858 version and Appendix 6 were prepared from Lipsett's report to 1st Division dated 20 November, this being Part I 'General Report of Brigadier', RG9IIIC3, Volume 4051, Folder 19, File 2.

> Left Bombing and Blocking Party. Captain C.L. Costigan and 13 ORs: two bayonet men, two bomb throwers, two bomb carriers, one spare bomber, four wire men and two shovel men (each carrying 20 bombs). Allowing 20 bombs per carrier total bombs available 160.
>
> Right Bombing and Blocking Party. Lieutenant J.H. McIlree and 12 ORs: three bayonet men, only two wire men. Remainder as per Left Party. Total bombs available 120.
>
> Bridge Covering Parties (Left and Right). Three ORs at each. To take charge of prisoners and send them to Listening Post Support Party (see below). Remain in place until assault party had withdrawn.
>
> Trench Rifle Party. Lieutenant A.H. Wrightson (OC Assault) and nine ORs: five riflemen (carrying spare bombs), one telephonist, one linesman and two stretcher bearers. To direct operations in enemy trenches and see that communications were established with raid commander (Thomas).
>
> Listening Post Support Party. 13 ORs to reinforce assault if necessary. Escort prisoners and remove wounded.
>
> Trench Reserve Party. 22 ORs to remain with Captain Thomas in the Battalion trench.

The actual assault party, the men who would enter the enemy trenches, consisted of the two Bombing and Blocking Parties (Left and Right) and the Trench Rifle Party, all told, three officers and 34 ORs. It is noteworthy that this organization, while the numbers of men involved are different, generally reflects the tactics in *CDS 74 Training and Employment of Grenadiers* published in October 1915. For this raid the parties probably worked in accordance with that manual which shows a clearing party positioned at Traverse 2 and acting as per MSD 5:

> T1 (Thrower 1) would throw bombs into X and Y and over traverse 3 into Z. B1 (Bayonet Man 1) would then move so he could see progressively into X and then Y. If these were clear he so reported to the Leader (L) and the whole party moved to take up position at Traverse 3 as it had at traverse 2. On encountering a communication trench a second clearing party or T2, B2 and C2 would clear it.[34]

What is going on here became known as "rolling up" the enemy, fire bay by fire bay. Even the stoutest defenders would surely have experienced some degree of that "sinking feeling" found in fiction as the sound of fighting grew and drew relentlessly closer. This would slow and even stop for a time if blocks consisting of lashings of timbers or planks and wire, or knife rests, sometimes concertina, had been, or could be quickly put in place to block the trench and cause the attackers to bunch up and make good targets for the defenders' bombs. If this happened, the only options were to quickly get past the block or withdraw.

34 *CDS 74 The Training and Employment of Grenadiers* (GHQ: Stationary Services Press, October 1915), pp. 12-13.

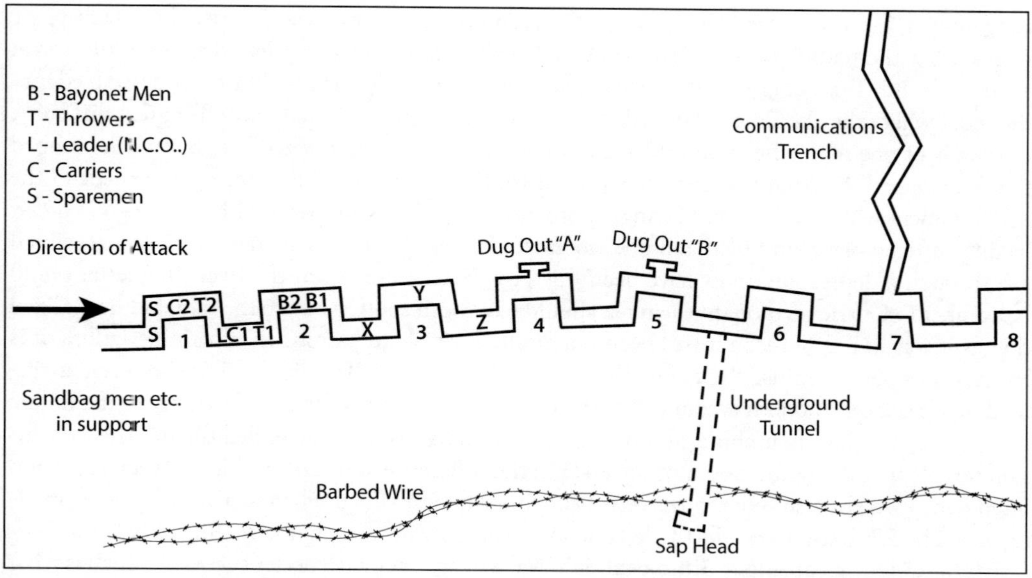

6 Trench Clearing Tactics, *CDS 74 Training and Employment of Grenadiers.*

Trench clearing tactics underwent frequent modification. In February 1917 GHQ announced that henceforth "The platoon should constitute a unit for fighting and training, and should consist of a combination of all the weapons with which the infantry is now armed." A week later GHQ laid down a "normal formation" for the attack. By April, *SS 143, SS 135* and *WO 3995 The Normal Formation for the Attack* had made the platoon the "unit of assault." A normal formation" for trench raiding, while it could vary, had this starting base:

> A party consisted of approximately seven men, trained to enter an enemy trench and work along it in single file, with each man carrying out specific duties. Roughly, the usual plan was: the leading man was a Bayonet Man whose duties were to clear the way between the bays of the trenches and protect the party following him from surprise [next] a Bomb Thrower who supports the Bayonet Man by bombing ahead of him and thus helping to clear the way … third man carried a rifle, but also bombs to keep [second man] supplied … [next man] was usually the NCO in charge of the party … [next] spare Bayonet Man … spare Bomb Thrower … No. 7 carried extra bombs and was to join in anything required … this system adapted as necessary, proved most effective.[35]

5th Battalion's assault, while entirely separate from that of the 7th Battalion, had to arrive in the enemy trench at the same time (0230), this necessary to convince the enemy that a large attack was in progress and he should move his reserve. The assault force reported that enemy wire had been satisfactorily cut and proceeded quickly to the enemy trenches, "very little opposition' being

35 LAC, RG9IIIC1, Volume 3864, Folder 99, File 3, GHQ, O.B./1919, 7 February 1917; Volume 3868, Folder 109, File 10, 14 February 1917; Fetherstonhaugh, *The Royal Canadian Regiment,* pp. 287-88, note 1; Stevens, *A City Goes to War,* p. 89.

encountered, but then immediately before them and directly before the parapet the assault party struck what the battalion War Diary called a "moat" 12 feet wide, six feet deep and filled with water and wire. This being entirely unexpected the two officers leading and three men tumbled into the moat where they became entangled in the wire. Rescue was effected only with great difficulty, especially of one man who went under the water. The enemy had opened fire, but when bombed the fire stopped. Seeking another entry proved fruitless, the Douve preventing movement to the left and uncut wire to the right. Having no other option, the assault party withdrew in good order, having suffered one man killed and one wounded. In his report Lipsett thought the moat, which ran through a depression, must have been filled by "back water" from the river. In a letter on 20 November to Currie he thought the moat should have been spotted before the raid, but he realized that as it was in a depression it had been practically invisible to patrols. In explaining failure, it is entirely possible to confuse the cause. This is so in this case. 5th Battalion's failure has been attributed in at least one modern account to a "deficiency in intelligence [that] led directly to the failure … Assaulting troops [stumbling] onto a previously undiscovered water-filled ditch." This conclusion reveals that the writer does not understand the difference and relationship between recce and intelligence which is simply that recce collects information which when analysed becomes intelligence. The 5th Battalion's effort failed due to a deficiency in recce, not in intelligence![36]

7th Battalion, according to 5th Battalion's War Diary, "met with better success," which is what the results show, but just as many future raids would reveal wire-cutting as a headache usually featuring conflicting viewpoints, their tenor depending upon one's cap badge, be it artillery or infantry. For this raid the artillery began firing at 0900 to cut wire at several points in addition to those selected for the raid and fire continued throughout much of the day. Howitzers also hit the enemy front line and the CTs in rear of the points of attack. Trench mortars bombarded Petite Douve Farm. The fire of 1st Canadian Field Brigade (18-pounders) and the British 118th Howitzer Brigade pleased the infantry: "splendid work … perfect … the enemy parapet … badly damaged." However, Odlum's report was less complimentary when it came to A Battery of the Royal Canadian Horse Artillery (RCHA) tasked to cut wire entanglements in front of the point of entry. Here the screen of trees along the Messines Road caused premature detonation of 75 percent of the shells fired, the result being no appreciable damage to wire. Lieutenant Huntley MacPherson, RCHA, remarked at some length on the problem in his diary for that day:

> We started firing at 9 and kept it up till about 12 … chats over the phone to see what actual effect we are having on the wire … some trees were bursting a good many of our shells prematurely and the battalion commander whose men were going to attack got very angry. However we started again at about 2:30 and put in a lot more … Buzz says he is afraid we didn't do the job thoroughly … We will certainly have it rubbed in pretty hard if we didn't.[37]

36 LAC, War Diary, entry for 16 November and Appendix (report); RG9IIIC3, Volume 4051, Folder 19, File 2, 20 November, 2nd Brigade report; Dan Richard Jenkins, 'Winning Trench Warfare: Battlefield Intelligence in the Canadian Corps, 1914-1918'. Doctorial Thesis, Carleton University, Ottawa, 1999, p. 119.

37 LAC, 5th Battalion War Diary; RG9IIIC3, Volume 4051, Folder 19, File 2, Canadian Corps report, Appendix IV Report by 7th Battalion; MG30E23 (Papers of Lieutenant Huntley Wilson MacPherson, RCHA), Diary.

According to MacPherson the RCHA continued intermittent firing until 1600. As the infantry scouts saw it the wire was still not sufficiently cut and it was evident that the mats the raiders would carry would not get them across the wire. At this point, Lipsett and Odlum reviewed the situation: "the artillery had not cut the wire … success was not very sure but [Odlum] told me his scouts would cut it and set his old jaw!" It was agreed that two lanes would have to be cut by hand that night.[38]

After dark Lieutenant Holmes, Sergeant W. Merston and Corporals H. Odlum and P.I. Babcock crept out into no man's land and by 2100 were cutting wire, doing so until midnight, lying flat when the moon was clear and cutting when it clouded: "as the task … caused both muscular and nervous fatigue, hot cocoa was carried out to the cutters at intervals during the three hours … two lanes were cut … diagonally so as not to be observed from the German parapet, and converged on the point of attack." In his diary Lieutenant MacPherson made these entries:

> 17 November (Wednesday). It appears that they had to do a bit of cutting. However, it could not have been much.
>
> 20 November (Saturday). We were informed today that our wire-cutting was not satisfactory and that it was due to faulty recce.
>
> 22 November (Monday). The Major went to look for a position for the new wire cut … for Wednesday. Hope we have better luck than last time or our name will be mud.[39]

Once he was satisfied with the cutting Holmes and his party proceeded to place the three bridges, a slow and difficult job, but one completed by 0200, 30 minutes before Zero. Even the placing of the last bridge, a mere 16 yards away from the enemy parapet, went undetected because as Holmes put it, "the bridge lay without a shadow, a move or a sound beyond the ken of sleepy sentries."[40]

Zero, initially set for midnight, had been postponed so that the assault would be in darkness (on the 16th the moon went down at 0100). At Zero plus two the assault began. Throughout, the guns fired on the enemy rearward trenches in order to isolate the objective and then hit all roads and tracks by which support could reach the objective area. Once all friendly troops had

38 *Ibid.*, RG9IIIC1, Volume 3860, Folder 87, File 1, Summary of Operations Canadian Corps 15th to 22nd November; David W. Love, *"A Call to Arms" The Organization and Administration of Canada's Military in World War One* (Calgary: Bunker to Bunker Books, 1999), pp. 300-301.The standard field gun of British and Canadian Horse Artillery in 1914 was the 13-pounder. With the onset of trench warfare, it proved too light to effectively engage defensive positions and Horse Artillery not in support of cavalry gradually converted to 18-pounders. Horse Artillery in support of cavalry brigades retained the 13-pounder.

39 Lord Beaverbrook, *Canada in Flanders,* Volume 1, p. 56; LAC, RG9IIIC3, Volume 4050, Folder 19, File 2, Canadian Corps Report, Appendix IV, report of 7th Battalion; MG30E23 (MacPherson Papers).

40 LAC, RG9IIID1, Volume 4691, Folder 48, File 7. A detailed account of the wire-cutting and bridge placement by Holmes himself came to the attention of Lord Beaverbrook in mid-1917 when he received a copy from Holmes' father who described it as unpublished and given only to friends in confidence. Holmes, who received the DSO for the raid, and later also won the MC, was killed in action in June 1916.

withdrawn, the artillery would open on enemy trenches to catch any reserves that did manage to get forward.[41]

When immediately before Zero sudden heavy rain began, it impacted adversely on enemy activity and alertness. The dark and the storm's noise helped get the assault parties silently to the parapet. Captain Costigan and Lieutenant McIlree from the enemy parapet saw immediately below them, as the Calgary *Daily Herald* put it,

> A large white platform [subsequently found to be a sheet of corrugated iron] ... which looked solid [but] to their horror it gave way and they were precipitated headforemost ... on to the heads of three German sentries. The latter were more surprised than the Canadian officers and before they could recover themselves, Captain Costigan and his pal had shot two sentries dead and the third, wounded in the leg, ran down the trench screaming for help.[42]

Another report said that McIlree on leading his party into the trench shot one sentry, brained another and threw a third to the ground. At this point his party joined him and all moved down the trench to the left, bombing, bayoneting and shooting as they went, a process Costigan was also hard at as he and his party moved to the right, shooting three of the enemy before the third bay along the trench.[43] The trench being strongly garrisoned, and the enemy beginning to come out from their dug-outs, general mayhem ensued, it becoming a "miniature massacre," the two assault parties killing many, taking prisoners, bombing dug-outs and eventually controlling about 40 yards of trench, blocks being established left and right to prevent any enemy interference.[44] Lieutenant Wrightson and his party had been in the trench for some time, having followed the assault parties into it. On arrival he had sent some of his party left and right to cover the bombers and help defeat any counter-attack that might develop. He also telephoned the OC Raid (Thomas) to report "all going well." Thus "complete success" was known to Corps HQ before the raiders were even out of the German trench. Some prisoners were already being taken rearward by the Bridge Covering Parties who then passed them along to the Listening Post Support Party which had the responsibility of escorting prisoners to the Canadian lines.[45]

Time in enemy trenches had been limited to 20 minutes, a restriction that the OC Assault Party stuck to, giving at the 19th minute the stipulated signal (whistle) whereupon the blocking parties got out and headed back to his location at the entry point. In short order, all raiders had withdrawn from the enemy trench, Wrightson being the last man to leave. The return across no man's land proved uneventful and casualty free. During the withdrawal two of the three bridges were removed, the last being recovered the following night.[46]

41 LAC, RG9IIIC3, Volume 4051, Folder 19, File 2, Appendix II, Scheme for artillery action and report of 7th Battalion.
42 Calgary *Daily Herald,* 22 April 1919, quoted in Dancocks, *Gallant Canadians,* pp. 65-66.
43 Lord Beaverbrook, *Canada in Flanders,* Volume 1, p. 58.
44 Military Advisory Board, *Guarding the Channel Ports,* p. 230; LAC, RG9IIIC1, Volume 3858, Folder 84, File 5, Summary of Small Offensive Operation, p. 5.
45 *Ibid.*
46 *Ibid.*

And what of the enemy response? Odlum characterized it as confused, twice over: first, the enemy seemed to think his front "badly pierced" by the left assault and it appeared as if he was evacuating Petite Douve Fort as initial fire from there ceased abruptly; and, second, he did not seem to realize what direction he was under fire from, this being evident in that all of his fire was directed down the Messines Road probably because of 5th Battalion's effort. While that unit's raid had not been a success, it had diverted enemy fire and attention. 2nd Brigade reported snuffing out a "very weak local bombing" counter-attack; no enemy officers seen and NCOs present displayed neither initiative nor leadership. Otherwise, as Colonel Nicholson says, local counter-attacks did not materialize. No organized deliberate and determined counter-attack occurred until 40 minutes after the Canadians had departed, the only result being more German casualties as the attackers were greeted and hammered by artillery fire. As for the German artillery response, when it did finally come, it fell mostly between the Canadian front and support lines. All in all, the response was ineffectual and slow.[47]

The post-raid focus of raiders and commanders (and the Germans) shifted to determining and assessing why the raid had been such a success and the defence such a failure. When it comes to answering the first some accounts, like Colonel Nicholson's, for example, present a list of reasons for success: "the thoroughness with which the enemy's position had been scouted in advance, the careful selection of personnel and equipment, the thorough training and rehearsal … the explicitness of the orders for the operation, and the excellent co-operation which the infantry had received from the artillery." The equipment mentioned included the rifles with the attached torches, the portable bridges and the mats. All of these are valid, to be sure, but they are also part and parcel of what Odlum attributed success to in just four words: "careful recce and preparations." After the raid Tuxford expressed his conviction that "the essence of a good raid is first to have a good plan." Saunders and Adkin see enemy shortcomings as the primary reason for the Canadian success.[48] Neither highlights how the shortcomings conferred surprise; in fact, in only one official report of the raid do we find a direct statement on surprise: "The attack was a complete surprise." *SS 107 Notes on Minor Enterprises* had been more emphatic when it described surprise as "probably the most important factor" in raids. The enemy must always be considered in any operation, of course, which is what one official account did when it concluded with what it called the "Positive Lessons" (which brought success) and the "Negative Lessons" (why the enemy failed), the latter being an inherent corollary of the former:

> The success appears to be due to the following:
>
> First class diligent scouting, as a result of which a distinct moral superiority had been obtained and the chance of discovery much reduced.

47 LAC, RG9IIIC1, Volume 3858, Folder 84, File 5, Summary of Small Offensive Operation; RG9IIIC3, Volume 5051, Folder 19, File 2, Canadian Corps report and Appendix IV, report of 7th Battalion; Nicholson, *Canadian Expeditionary Force,* p. 124; Saunders, *Raiding on the Western Front,* p. 20. Tim Cook, *At the Sharp End* (Toronto: Viking, 2007), p. 293, is alone in placing the deliberate enemy counter-attack only 20 minutes after the raiders withdrew.

48 Nicholson, *Canadian Expeditionary Force,* pp. 124-25; Saunders, *Raiding on the Western Front,* pp. 20-21; Adkin, *Western Front Companion,* p. 474.

Careful selection of personnel, careful study and arrangement of every detail connected with the organization of the attacking parties and the material required for the operation.

Careful training and rehearsal over similar ground and preparations to meet every contingency.

Good artillery co-operation and utilization of all methods of attack and surprise to the same end.

Although the enemy's trench was very strong and was heavily manned (about 8 men per 10 yards in the front line) and despite the bright night and other conditions favourable to them, the enemy absolutely failed to meet the attack. His failure appears to have been mainly due to the following:

Complete lack of active patrolling and the surrender of the initiative.

Lack of protection by listening posts.

Bad discipline. Sentries too few and not alert. Sentries allowed to take cover from the rain.

Lack of co-operation between adjoining sections. Immediate local counter-attack was not attempted outside of our blocks.

Lack of initiative by NCOs and men when officers absent.[49]

This report concluded "The whole of the left attack went so smoothly and was carried out so entirely in accordance with the prearranged plans that even the commanders immediately concerned are not able to suggest any improvement."[50] This, and the lessons, positive and negative, brings to mind the adage that says to be lucky you must be good and to be good you must be lucky. But a raid, like any other operation, could not rely solely on luck. Nor was there a place for complacency.

While it is hard to criticize such a success one or two questions do arise. The most important one concerns Lieutenant Wrightson and his nine men of the Trench Rifle Party, the only reserve immediately at hand (in the trench). Could it have adequately assisted either Bombing and Blocking Party in holding their respective block had a serious challenge been mounted? If these parties had suffered some or serious casualties in the trench clearing up to the blocks then the question is even more pertinent. Perhaps there should have been a rifle party per Bombing and Blocking Party. The planners may have considered one such party adequate given the anticipated stay of only 20 minutes.

49 *SS 107 Notes on Minor Enterprises;* LAC, RG9IIIC1, Volume 3858, Folder 84, File 5, Summary of Small Offensive Operation; RG9IIIC3, Volume 4051, Folder 19, File 2, Canadian Corps report and report of 7th Battalion; RG 24, Volume 1825, GAQ 5-66, Lipsett to Currie, 20 November. Lipsett met with German prisoners taken in the raid. According to them the raid had been expected, which is why the trench was heavily manned.

50 *Ibid.*

What, then, did the raid achieve? First, it took 12 prisoners from the 11th Prussian Regiment, Lipsett describing these as "not a bad looking lot," meaning they were of soldierly appearance. Each prisoner had a new rubber gas mask, an item of high interest to intelligence. Raid reports claimed 50 enemy dead, an estimate Lipsett reduced to 30 since at night in a trench in the midst of chaos such estimates were usually more assumption than hard fact. Claims about damage to enemy morale were also speculative, founded on the poor enemy response, but this may have been an indication of the absence of officers and poor leadership by NCOs rather than low morale. Despite the brief stay in the enemy trench, the raid gained considerable knowledge about German trench and dugout construction methods, trench revetting and flooring, depth and location of dug-outs and their interiors (floored and lined with lumber). German house-keeping impressed the raiders: clean and dry trenches, covered rifle racks in every bay and well-maintained revetting and flooring. Little damage to the trenches by artillery fire was apparent.[51]

The raid pleased everyone, raiders, planners and senior commanders. General and fulsome praise and congratulations (and visitors) descended upon the battalion. Odlum had made his mark, most certainly with his brigade commander (Lipsett) who remarked that when the 2nd Brigade was relieved the newcomers would have to go some to top Odlum. Clearly, Lipsett attributed to Odlum the fact that, in his words, the 7th had gone to the top of the class. Lipsett summed up the 7th Battalion's raid as a "good night's work." Within the BEF the raid reports circulated widely and the French and Italians translated and distributed one account. More tangible rewards were the decorations. Captain Holmes' citation for the DSO referred to his supervision of wire-cutting and the laying of the bridges over the Douve. Costigan's DSO came because of his conspicuous gallantry in the enemy trench where he killed three men and for his leadership. Lieutenant Wrightson received the MC for his coolness, good judgement and gallantry during the clearing of the enemy trench.[52]

Some thought the raid marked "a new branch of the science of trench warfare" and even the possible beginning of a "break-up" of trench warfare. While this did not happen, it did begin to seem that raiding had become almost a phase of war on its own between defence and attack and as such every battalion would participate: "the staff became greatly excited over the Canadian raid. It was exceedingly well-planned – the Canadian Corps possessed that genius which is the aptitude for taking infinite pains … raids became part of the ordinary duty of fighting battalions … these raids, miniature battles, soon became most unpleasant."[53]

The raid also intensified competitive spirit, especially in a brigade as good as the 2nd. With a GOC like Lipsett, COs were keen to show their unit to best advantage. As a former, and the first, CO of 8th Battalion, Lipsett would have looked to see the 8th in action. His replacement, H.H. Matthews, now into his second month as CO, was looking, too, for an opportunity.

51 Saunders, *Raiding on the Western Front,* p. 20; Nicholson, *Canadian Expeditionary Force,* p. 124; LAC, RG 9IIIC3, Volume 4051, Folder 19, File 2, Canadian Corps and 7th Battalion reports.

52 S. Douglas MacGowan, Harry (Mac) Heckbert, MM, and Byron E. O'Leary, *New Brunswick's "Fighting 26th": A History of the 26th New Brunswick Battalion, C.E.F. 1914-1919* (Saint John: Neptune Publishing Company Limited, 1995); Riddle and Mitchell, *The Distinguished Service Order,* pp. 24, 45-46; *The Military Cross,* p. 363; Dancocks, *Gallant Canadians,* p. 66, states that Costigan was recommended for the VC, but received the DSO. LAC, RG 24, Volume 1825, GAQ 5-66, Lipsett to Currie, 20 November.

53 Dudley Ward, *Royal Welsh Fusiliers,* p. 163.

As for J.G. Rattray's 10th Battalion, at the end of 1915 it had yet to make a raid, this causing him concern that his unit lacked "sufficiently high profile" despite it being "one of the best in France."[54] This, to some extent, was a factor in 10th Battalion's raid in early February. This raid is examined in the next chapter along with some others during the first half of 1916.[55]

54 Dancocks, *Gallant Canadians*, p. 68.
55 The Canadian Letters and Images Project, *An Archive of the Canadian War Experience,* Vancouver Island University and the Canadian War Museum, Corporal Alfred Andrews, Diary, February 1916; LAC, RG 24, Volume 1825, GAQ 5-66, Lipsett to Currie, 20 November 1915.

9

1916 – First Half

> He leads a little party through the darkness …
> And creeps to catch the Deutschers unaware.
> Eric Cooper, "The Night Attack"

Deutschers attacked or raided, and found unaware, were Deutschers surprised and disadvantaged. As *SS 107* said, surprise was the most important factor in achieving a successful raid. This manual also echoed "lessons" issued earlier in 1916 by Second Army and other formations (see below).[1] A Canadian officer, who had been central in the highly successful Canadian raid in November 1915, directly influenced Second Army's contribution to these lessons documents. But before looking at the part played in raid doctrine by this officer, Lieutenant-Colonel Victor Odlum, the course of this chapter must be set out.

In a lecture he made just after Vimy, P. deB. Radcliffe, BGGS of the Canadian Corps, mentioned that the Corps had raided 69 times between 1 November 1915 and 8 April 1917. To attempt here description and discussion of all 69, plus relate the events of over 100 British raids during the first half of 1916 would be nigh on impossible and likely to end only in lifeless list. What can be done is an accounting of selected raids, British and Canadian, during that period. This applies also to subsequent chapters. As the Introduction said, this book does not present a picture of every raid. Nevertheless, a reader might well ask why this or that raid is not included, or he may ask why this or that formation or unit is not included. The short answer is that a process of selection had to be applied and when it comes to lists and selections unanimity can only be found in churchyards. First off, since a line had to be drawn somewhere inclusion or not was based on the definition of raid settled upon in Chapter 4. To begin, one looked for the word "raid" in the primary accounts, the War Diaries, British and Canadian. These contain numerous instances of minor attacks, which aimed to seize and hold ground, being dubbed "raids," but close reading usually made it obvious that this tag was not warranted. Also, any given period might feature several virtually identical raids, of which one was chosen to represent the lot.

1 *SS 107 Notes on Minor Enterprises,* 'General Principles'; LAC, RG9IIIC3, Volume 4052, Folder 23, File 2, G. 535/14K, 'Lessons to be Drawn From the Various Minor Operations Carried Out by the Second Army Up to the 9th February 1916, General Principles', paragraph 7. This document was widely circulated within the BEF; for example, 8th British Division's War Diary (TNA: WO 95/1674) for that month includes a copy. The 8th at that time was in First Army.

Raids were also selected on the basis of some especially interesting feature, perhaps unusual size or composition or purpose, or on the extent of available source material, the ideal being War Diary plus published history plus personal accounts. Such a package usually highlighted why a raid failed or succeeded or what was the key to success. Consequently, not all Canadian battalions find a place in these pages, nor do all British battalions and divisions. Another key consideration was balance; after all, the title says British and Canadian.

This chapter examines only two Canadian raids. One reason for this is that during the first half of 1916 only two Canadian divisions were engaged in raiding. Another reason for the seeming imbalance is that the chapter concludes with a detailed account of the large Canadian raid at Spanbroekmolen in February 1916.[2]

After the Canadian raid in November 1915 at La Petite Douve Victor Odlum, who had conceived and executed that raid, became something of a celebrity, as did his 7th Battalion, officer and unit now seen as worth consulting when it came to raiding. And so Major-General H.B. Williams, MGGS Second Army, did on 10 February when he sent Odlum a copy of a "Lessons Drawn" draft and requested comments and suggestions by 12 February as the draft was to be presented at the Army Commander's Conference. Odlum's response suggested re-arranging the text so that it flowed from pre-raid preparations and activities to specific arrangements and tasks for the raid and then to action during the raid. His comments (italics shown as per the original) bear repeating:

> Is it [the draft] not too comprehensive … as it deals with many things which are incidentals and not essentials, and I have found a very general weakness … is inability to distinguish between the two … My suggestion is that this … should be re-examined so as to bring the essentials out clearly and then the rest of the ideas could be given as aids to success … *Most* precautions are non-essentials – but are good aids to success. *Certain* ones are absolute essentials. These should be emphasized … I consider them to be:
>
> 1. *Careful recce* and training in inter-trench work (This must be carried to the point where domination of No Man's land is secured.)
> 2. *Sound allotment* and limitation of tasks.
> 3. *Thorough practise and rehearsal.*
> 4. *A full knowledge* on the part of every NCO and man on the entire plan and the part to be played by each man.

These four "essentials", subsequently dubbed "General Principles," appeared largely untouched with eight others in the issued document. Curiously, the word "recce" does not appear anywhere in the list of 12 principles, and although it is in a later section of the document entitled "Preparations for Minor Operations" the wording is neither precise nor emphatic. The Canadian Corps response on 1 February to Second Army's request stressed the "absolute necessity for thorough and perfect recce" describing this as a matter that had to be "most strictly insisted

2 Christopher Duffy, *Through German Eyes: The British and the Somme 1916* (London: Weidenfeld and Nicolson, 2006), pp. 121, 269. In the first half of 1916 the British launched 106 raids. Ashworth, *Live and Let Live,* p. 185, breaks this figure down thus: 19 December 1915 to 30 May 1916, 63 raids and in June 1916 another 43. Canadian figures are at LAC, RG9IIIC1, Volume 3846, Folder 51, File 7.

upon." Canadian Corps and divisional responses to the request are far too lengthy to be recorded here, as is the complete text (14 foolscap pages) of Second Army's "Lessons Drawn," but the 12 "General Principles to be Observed in Designing and Carrying Out Minor Operations" are indeed "Essentials" and warrant space especially since they were not always observed:

1. Superiority in patrolling must be established before any minor operation can be attempted. The preliminary training of patrols is therefore just as important as the preliminary training of the men who are to take part in the actual raid.
2. Patrols cannot be expected to bring back prisoners from enemy trenches.
3. Time is the determining factor in the scope of all minor operations. A small raiding party can usually stay from 8 to 15 minutes in enemy trenches, i.e. until the Germans send up their supports and turn on their artillery fire. Three to five minutes, according to the distance between our trenches and those of the enemy, must be allowed to enable the raiders to get back to our line. A larger raiding party, owing to it being able to offer more resistance to a local counter-attack, can stay in enemy trenches for 20 or 30 minutes.
4. The objective of a minor operation must be strictly limited and the utmost care should be given to its selection. It must be suitable to the size of the force to be used and the object which it is hoped to obtain. An objective should not be avoided simply because it is a strong point. A successful blow at a strong point has great moral effect. It is no use attacking a trench which is not held by the enemy. A raiding party of 50 men can generally deal with about 100 yards of trench.
5. The preparation and working out of the details of a minor operation should be left as much as possible to the unit engaged upon the enterprise. But the Brigade or Divisional Staff must check the scheme when it has been prepared.
6. Success will be in proportion to the care given beforehand in working out its details. Ample time – at least a week – should be given for preparation.
7. As surprise is a most important factor consideration of how surprise can be best affected, and loss of life avoided, must be carefully borne in mind. An officer planning an operation of this kind cannot be absolutely bound by any rules, but, after observing how other attacks have succeeded or failed, he must use his imagination in planning, and also in carrying out the enterprise. The more a plan differs from that of any previous attack the more successful it is likely to be.
8. Every endeavour must be made to deceive the enemy as to the point of attack or from where it is coming.
9. Every NCO and man who is to take part should have full knowledge of the plan and of the part he is to play in it.
10. Combined attacks, particularly at night, are most difficult to synchronize, owing to the variations in the ground and the vigilance of the enemy. The failure of one attack may interfere with the success of the other. Combined attacks, therefore, are not to be recommended unless one of them is intended to be merely a feint to distract the enemy's attention from the real attack. If it is decided that a minor operation is to consist of 2 separate attacks each party must be practised many times over the actual distance over which it will be necessary to advance. Every effort must be made to ensure the two parties reaching the enemy's parapet at the same time.

11. Secrecy must be maintained regarding preparations. The men engaged should be kept as long as possible in ignorance of the date and time it is to take place. No conversation with regard to the enterprise must be held over the telephone or in the vicinity of the trenches.
12. A minor enterprise should seldom be persevered with if the enemy is found ready and prepared.

Of these principles four (2, 3, 8, 9) do not appear in *SS 107*. The omissions seem, at least in part, to have been made in order to stick to "general" and avoid particular. Number 5 is in the manual, but not as a principle. Numbers 10 and 11 appear only in part as principles. In fact, these principles were not immutable; as number 7 points out an officer planning a minor enterprise could not be "absolutely bound" by them. Time and experience would dictate that.[3] As a whole these documents, the request of Second Army to its corps and the responses, battalion and upward, reflect the BEF's careful, thoughtful and usually well-considered response to minor operational situations and requirements. This activity also typifies the learning curve experienced by the officers planning and conducting raids, by units and formations and by the BEF as a whole. Finally, Second Army's "Lessons Drawn" suggested, and *SS 107* confirmed, that there were "no definite rules" and offered instead "a guide in future operations."[4]

Minor operations in 1916 began a few minutes after 1915 became 1916 when men of the 9th Yorkshire Regiment (69th British Brigade), the 10th Northumberland Fusiliers (68th Brigade), a party of 128th Field Company RE and divisional artillery of 23rd British Division raided. As conceived, the raid had two objectives, both being salients relatively close together in the same general area of the Armentieres front. The reason for ignoring the recommendation in point 10 (see above) about separate attacks was likely what the division's historian thought: "the enemy were still unprepared for raids … trenches had been entered where … general slackness was apparent." There being two objectives the plan called for elements of two battalions to assault simultaneously, each to kill Germans, take prisoners and destroy any "important works."[5] Two weeks before the raid the raiders occupied billets in the rear area where they commenced intensive training including rehearsals by day and by night on a replica of the enemy line. Other training included rifle grenade firing, bomb throwing and wire-cutting plus large doses of route marching, bayonet fighting and running. Concurrently, frequent patrols under the officers who would lead or participate in the raids looked closely at approach routes and the immediate vicinity of the objectives. Needless to say, air photos became favourite reading.

The 10th Northumberlands, tasked to raid the right salient, organized six officers and 110 ORs under command of a Captain, into three parties, a covering party, an assault party and a blocking party each under a Subaltern. Against the left salient were the 9th Yorkshires, six officers and 109 ORs, under Major H.A.S. Prior. He organized three parties as well, an assault

3 LAC, RG9IIIC1, Volume 3858, Folder 82, File 1, Canadian Corps to Second Army, 3 February, and divisional responses; RG9IIIC3, Volume 4052, Folder 23, File 2, 'Lessons Drawn'; MG30E300 (Odlum Papers), Volume 24, Folder: Raids, February 1916; *SS 107 Notes on Minor Enterprises*, 'General Principles'. Second Army's 'Lessons Drawn' might well have been placed in an earlier chapter concerned with policy, but because they mark the zenith of practices of early 1916 they serve best in this chapter.
4 *Ibid.*
5 Sandilands, *23rd Division*, p. 39.

party, a support group and a reserve. The first consisted of two assault groups, one officer and 18 ORs per, who upon entering enemy trenches would bomb left and right down the enemy trenches for roughly 75 yards each way at which points blocks would be installed. The covering party (one officer and 21 ORs) would remain at the entry point ready to take charge of any prisoners. An RE party of an officer and 15 men would prepare demolitions to destroy the important "works" that were thought to exist. Two small flank guards would remain in no man's land ready to advance to defeat any enemy counter-attacks. Finally, a reserve of an officer and nine ORs would stand ready at a listening post near the exit point from the battalion's home trench.[6]

Artillery preparation, which commenced on the 27th, continued the next day, 18-pounders cutting wire at both points of assault, howitzers thickening up the fire, as well as at two additional points by way of a feint. During the days remaining before the raid this fire continued intermittently. Patrols reported wire at the right salient thoroughly cut, but less so at the left salient. Two nights prior to the assault another patrol led by an officer of the 9th Yorkshires reported wire still not adequately cut, but thought it "inadvisable" to continue firing for fear of alarming the enemy. At this point it was decided that parties would complete wire-cutting manually on assault night.[7] Final preparations continued apace, all going well until late in the afternoon of the 31st when an explosion during preparation of the demolitions killed the engineer officer and four of his men and wounded 28 others. Time did not permit organizing more sappers. The raid would go without any.

On New Year's Eve as the Northumberlands prepared to enter no man's land the enemy became active and alert, flares rising continually all along the right salient and three searchlights sweeping no man's land. A covering party under a Subaltern had earlier moved out into position. The assault party plus the blocking party followed at just past midnight. When 45 minutes later the enemy spotted the blocking party up went more flares and down came rifle, machine-gun and artillery fire. With the OC wounded, casualties mounting and surprise gone, this raid was aborted (point 12 above). To what extent it distracted the enemy could not be known.

Earlier, at 2130 to be precise, a 9th Yorkshires Subaltern took out a wire-cutting party. On return two hours later he reported the wire gapped, the way clear right up to the enemy parapet and the enemy none the wiser. Just after midnight the assault parties moved to a pre-determined forming-up position in no man's land and were then guided forward to the gap in the enemy wire by members of the wire-cutting party. Even so, during the move many men of the assault parties lost contact with the guides and hence direction and drifted off to the left of the gap where they were held up by wire. Consequently, only 35 or so raiders entered the enemy trench just after 0130. At this time artillery fire began on enemy CTs. One assault party, turning right as per the plan, found only four Germans. The other party moving to the left encountered more resistance, killing 15 Germans of a party about to counter-attack. At 0148 the raiders withdrew. Casualties were "trifling" (seven slightly wounded) during the raid, but heavy retaliatory artillery fire caused 24 casualties during the return to home trenches.

Results were disappointing. Of the three prisoners taken, all had attempted escape and were killed. Nor were any demolitions carried out. Fifteen Germans were claimed as killed. Still, the raid was pronounced "success" in that it continued dominance of no mans land.

6 TNA: WO 95/2183: brigade Operation Order; WO 95//2184: 9th Yorkshires, report of raid 31 December; Sandilands, *23rd Division,* p. 115. Prior, on promotion, took command of the 9th.

7 TNA: WO 95/2184: 9th Yorkshires.

Lieutenant-Colonel Sandilands' account suggests careless handling of the prisoners including poor reaction to their escape attempt: "to secure prisoners demands considerable skill and judgement … as the war continued … with greater experience and a better appreciation of the value of prisoners, the number captured in such operations increased."[8]

A month later 10th Canadian Battalion (1st Canadian Division) made its first ever raid. The story of this raid, which began in early December 1915, was summarized in Chapter 3. What follows is a detailed account. In his history of the 10th Daniel Dancocks related the concern at that time of the CO, Lieutenant-Colonel John Rattray, that his battalion's profile was not high, the unit, in his opinion "over-shadowed by the advertising" of men of another western Canadian battalion, a reference to the 7th Battalion that had done so well in the La Petite Douve raid. However, on 1 January Rattray received the DSO for his "tireless efforts to improve combat proficiency." While no doubt welcome, this probably did little to assuage Rattray's concern about unit profile.[9] Two days later when the 10th went into divisional reserve it began planning a raid based on earlier recce that had observed the enemy paying special attention to putting in machine-gun emplacements, strengthening their parapet and making general trench improvements. Recce had also suggested a good objective as the junction of the main enemy trench and a CT from Messines (see MSD 7), this being a point of heavier traffic and presenting a better chance of taking prisoners. Rattray ordered the raid for the first suitable night, but for one reason or another considerable time would elapse before the plan could be executed. On returning to the line on 9 January bright moonlight made raiding impossible. On the 15th the battalion went into brigade reserve where it was fully engaged in working parties until return to the line on 21 January. Out and in went the battalion – twice. Not until 2 February did conditions largely satisfy, but as it turned out moonlight was just the first of the challenges this raid would face.[10]

The raid was set for the next night. The plan called for a wire-cutting party under Lieutenant Stanley Kent, together with a covering party under an NCO, to go out first while an assault party of 50 waited in battalion trenches for word from Kent to join him and then enter enemy trenches. Kent set out at 2100 Thursday evening. Six hours later he returned to report that the enemy had thickened his wire and appeared to have instituted roving patrols to ensure that it remained intact. By this time, daylight not far off, the raid was aborted and re-scheduled for the following night (5/6 February).

During the late afternoon of 4 February Major Charles Stewart, acting CO of the 10th (Rattray was absent on leave), seeing it "very dark with clouded sky ands slight rain" ordered the raid to proceed. Its purposes, as defined in the "Intention" paragraph of the Operation Order, were to gain information on enemy strength, dispositions and the state of his trenches, to take prisoners and to secure a German machine-gun. In overall charge of the raid was Captain Allan Connors with Lieutenant Kent as OC Assault Party. The raiders were organized into five parties: a wire-cutting party (Sergeant Milne and five men) who would work under the direction of Lieutenant Kent; a right bombing party of two bayonet men, two bombers, a bomb carrier, seven spares and a three-man covering party; a left bombing party organized as per

8 *Ibid.*, Sandilands, *23rd Division*, pp. 41-42.
9 Dancocks, *Gallant Canadians*, p. 68; Riddle and Mitchell (comps.), *The Distinguished Service Order*, p. 88. Rattray's award is described as "New Year award. No Citation."
10 Dancocks, *Gallant Canadians*, pp. 69-70; LAC, 10th Battalion War Diary, February 1916.

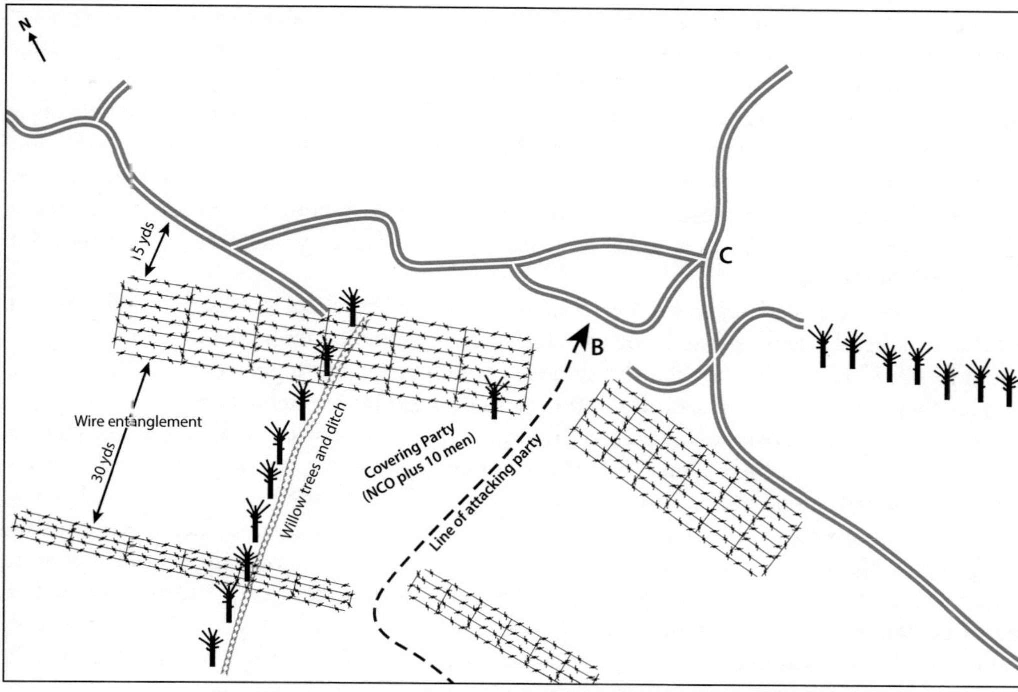

7 Raid Douve Sector, 4/5 February 1916, 10th Canadian Battalion.

the right party under an NCO and a centre bombing party of six men under Lieutenant A. Trimmer. The left and right bombing parties would bomb outward from the point of entry (see "B" on MSD 7), the centre bombing party then passing through and proceeding to the junction at "C" and onward for about 30 yards. A covering party of 11 under Sergeant J. Pringle would take up a position in no man's land from which the withdrawal of the bombing parties could be covered. In support were three signallers, two stretcher bearers and two sappers.[11]

At 1845 Lieutenant Kent took out the wire-cutters, the covering party and the three signallers and soon had the first and the last at the enemy wire. On then returning to where he had left the covering party he could find no sign of it, nor did a search locate it. Over an hour later Sergeant Pringle appeared explaining that the party had been forced to move to avoid discovery by two enemy patrols, but was now secure at a patch of shattered trees along a ditch a short distance away. Kent seems to have had some doubt about Pringle's state of mind for on leaving him to rejoin the wire-cutters, he cautioned "Don't fail us, Sergeant, we are absolutely dependant upon you." Because of the delay it was 2130 before Kent could send a telephone message advising that the covering party was now in place and that the wiring party had only the main wire barrier to

11 *Ibid.* 'Report of Minor Operation Carried out on Night 4-5 February 1916'. The initial Operation Order (Number 42) was prepared on 3 January and amended on 3 February, the amendments naming officers to replace those no longer available. Rattray's report on the raid was very brief (one page) owing to his absence on leave. Stewart's report was comprehensive and detailed. Dancocks, *Gallant Canadians*, p. 70.

cut as the cutters had found gaps the enemy had cut in their outer barrier to permit passage for departing patrols. Unknown to Kent, all was not well with Pringle and party. Sometime after Kent rejoined the wire-cutters two of Pringle's party returned to the main trench to warn that Pringle was "somewhat excited." Hearing this, Captain Connors sent the Regimental Sergeant-Major (RSM), Duncan Stuart, to investigate. On encountering Pringle, and hearing a wild and implausible story that the covering party, the wire-cutters and Lieutenant Kent had all been captured, Stuart arrested Pringle and took him back to the battalion trench. Captain Connors then sent Lieutenant A. Younger and seven men out to join the covering party, which they did shortly after midnight.[12]

Meanwhile, Kent had reported the inner wire barrier breached, but cutting then ceased because of several enemy patrols, one of which nearly stumbled upon the covering party. It would be 0337 before Kent advised the anxious 50 men of the raiding party that the wire was cut and they were to come ahead. By 0400 the raiders led by Lieutenants Kent and Younger and Sergeant Milne were crawling through the gap in the wire. Just short of the parapet chance forced another halt for there along the parapet an enemy working party, guarded by sentries spaced at intervals along the trench, was hard at work. This put the raiders in a terrible spot, the men being in single file and some still in the gap. Withdrawal without alerting the enemy being impossible, Kent decided to wait 10 minutes in hopes that the working party would quit and return to their trench and the raiders could advance. Failing this, he decided at the end of the 10 minutes they would rush the working party and bring back as many prisoners as possible. But before the time expired the enemy had his say, a party of 30-40 men coming from the left ran into the raiders whereupon a general "mix-up" ensued:

> They began to fire and threw bombs. Our men then went for them, throwing their bombs and using their bayonets and clubs, and seized four or five of them for prisoners. The alarm thus being raised, the working party jumped into the trench … An exceedingly heavy fire of machine-guns, rifles and bombs then came from the German trenches all round … the prisoners were all killed, either by the German fire or through reluctance to accompany their captors.

No chance of entering the enemy trench remaining Kent ordered withdrawal, this being covered by two field batteries which put down such heavy fire on the enemy trenches that most of the enemy fire ceased. Major Stewart described the gunner's effort as "excellent shooting [which] undoubtedly prevented many of the Attacking Party from becoming casualties." In all, casualties came to two officers slightly wounded, one OR killed and three others missing, believed killed, and 15 wounded, only one severely. Enemy losses could not be confirmed, the consensus in the various reports estimating their casualties as some 40-50. Given the enemy's participation in the hand-to-hand fighting, the heavy shelling of his trench during the raiders' withdrawal

12 *Ibid.*, LAC, RG9IIIC3, Volume 4070, Book 23, Summary of Evidence, 11 February 1916. Pringle was court-martialled, convicted and sentenced to death, a sentence later commuted to five years' imprisonment, this subsequently suspended. He continued to serve as a Private with the 10th and survived the war. In December 1916 D.M. Ormond, CO of the 10th from September 1916 to April 1918, reporting upon Pringle, said that he had "carried on in a most satisfactory manner … and on at least one occasion behaved exceptionally well." (LAC, RG9IIIC3, Volume 4071, Book 39).

and the general absence of enemy small arms fire thereafter, this estimate may not have been too far off the mark.[13]

As for success (or not) of the raid, Lieutenant-Colonel Rattray's report somewhat disingenuously describes it as "not entirely successful in that they did not get into the enemy trench." It also inflated the claim of "severe" enemy casualties, adding that the large covering patrol "were all but annihilated." None of the purposes of the raid were achieved: no prisoners, no useful information and no machine-gun. Corporal Alfred Andrews' diary summed matters up more directly:

> The raid didn't succeed … Our platoon and in fact the whole company was very much worked up … they felt it was a useless waste … and that it was put on for the glorification of the CO and to show he could do as much as the 7th [Battalion]. We were joshed over this for weeks. Every time we went in, the 7th would say 'Are you taking a machine-gun this trip?'[14]

Putting the best face upon it, the GOC 2nd Brigade, Louis Lipsett, wrote that

> All ranks seem to have behaved very well and achieved a good result, in spite of the fact that luck was against them and considering the difficult position in which they were and the heavy fire which they experienced … they were fortunate in not having greater losses.

Arthur Currie, then GOC 1st Canadian Division, made a point of visiting the 10th to see the party that had made the battalion's first raid. The Corps Commander, Lieutenant-General Alderson, in his report to Second Army wrote that the 10th had "behaved very well in a critical situation."[15] Given the results of the raid, the plethora of decorations that followed does seem exorbitant: MCs to Captain Connors, Lieutenants Kent, Younger and Trimmer and RSM Stuart; a clasp to Sergeant Milne's DCM and DCMs to four others, including Lance/Corporal Frank Cox (see jacket photo). However, it was early days, a first raid and expectations were not as high as they would become. Still, as Siegfried Sassoon later wrote, while the distribution of decorations became "fortuitous and debased" decorations did have a stimulating effect and in the final analysis their worth to the recipients could not be doubted.[16]

In February/March 1916 another 10th Battalion officer would become the leading character in an unusual minor enterprise. This officer, Captain Charles Costigan, DSO, had begun the war as a paymaster, but requested transfer to the battalion and subsequently volunteered to lead a bombing party during the La Petite Douve raid in November 1915. Costigan received

13 LAC, 10th Battalion War Diary, February 1916, Reports of Lieutenants Kent and Younger; 2nd Brigade 'Narrative of Minor Enterprise Night 4/5th February'; RG9IIIC1, Volume 3860, Folder 87, File 1, "Summary of Canadian Corps Operations 1st to 7th February 1916'.

14 LAC, 10th Battalion War Diary, February 1916, Appendix 3; Vancouver Island University, *The Canadian Letters and Images Project,* Diary of Alfred Herbert John Andrews, 10th Battalion, 1916.

15 LAC, 2nd Brigade War Diary, February 1916, 'Narrative of Minor Enterprise Night 4/5th February'; MG 30E100 (Currie Papers), Diary, 6 February 1916; RG9IIIC1, Volume 3858, Folder 84, File 6, Canadian Corps to Second Army, 6 February 1916.

16 For the officer citations see Riddle and Mitchell, *The Military Cross,* pp. 67, 171, 322, 335, 366; Sassoon, *Memoirs of an Infantry Officer,* p. 52.

the DSO for his part in this raid (see also Footnote 52, Chapter 8). In March 1916, as part of a "demonstration" in the same area, Costigan became a one-man river flotilla reminiscent of the fireships of old. Strictly speaking this was not a raid, but taking shameless advantage of point 7 of Second Army's "Lessons Drawn" – do not be "bound by any rules" – this present soldier-historian simply cannot forego reporting on Costigan's novel "naval" endeavour.

Costigan's cruise came about in February when 1st Canadian Division received orders to demonstrate as a deception for an attack to be delivered by V Corps. 10th Battalion got the task. The demonstration included exploding smoke bombs forward of battalion listening posts, firing rifle grenades and machine-guns at selected points and making "an ally of the Douve River which has been for so long our enemy. So a small raft was made and on it a mine of seven pounds of gun-cotton was fastened and in the gun-cotton was attached six cases of smoke bombs." It had been thought that once launched the raft would float down nicely on its own to the enemy line on the Douve, but Costigan realized immediately after launching that he would have to guide the raft all the way which he did to within 30 yards of the enemy bridge. Here he lit the fuse, swam clear and from the river bank watched the raft floating down in mid-stream. As far as he could see, it reached the bridge, or very near to it, and then exploded. The battalion report called it "a new method of scare" and an effective one, the explosion a bright flash seen from battalion lines, followed by a rain of enemy flares of various colours. Overall, judging from enemy reaction the demonstration got the enemy's "wind up at once." Arthur Currie's report to Corps HQ made special mention of Costigan's fine work.[17]

Returning to land operations, in March the 1st Dorsets of 32nd British Division raided the infamous "Y" Sap at La Boiselle northeast of Albert on the Bapaume Road (see MSD 8).[18] The raid sought to take prisoners and do as much damage as possible. To signal the assault a mine opposite La Boiselle would be fired at 1227 on 27 March whereupon the raiders organized in four parties under Captain W.B. Algeo, OC B Company, would enter the enemy trenches at two points. "W" Party of 38 men under Lieutenant H.G.M. Mansell-Pleydell would enter at "A", then split into two groups and clear to points "C" and "E", the trench being blocked at the latter. "X" Party (Second Lieutenant N.C. Blakeway and 28 ORs) would enter at "F", work toward a rendezvous with "W" Party at "C" and toward "D" where the trench was to be blocked. "Y" Party was to remain at "K" ready to provide support and take charge of prisoners and any casualties. "Z" Party (10 men) would remain in reserve in own trenches. For several days prior to the raid the artillery worked at wire-cutting opposite the two entry points and elsewhere so as "to confuse the enemy as to our intentions." On the night of the 26th patrols reported the wire well cut, but the Germans continued to repair it despite being under machine-gun fire.

As it turned out, premature explosion of the mine did not affect the raiders who attacked immediately it went up and reached the entry points simultaneously and without casualties. There they found wire outside the parapet no obstacle, but on the inner slope thick wire caused serious delay and bunching that resulted in most of the casualties. Mansell-Pleydell and his men met considerable opposition on entering the trench, this continuing as the two sub-parties

17 LAC, RG9IIIC1, Volume 3858, Folder 84, File 11, report on demonstration by 10th Battalion night 1/2 March; Costigan's report and letter Currie to Corps HQ.

18 Peter Barton, *The Somme: The Unseen Panoramas* (London: Constable In Association With the Imperial War Museum, 2011). The panorama and map at pp.130-37 portray the "Y" Sap and La Boiselle.

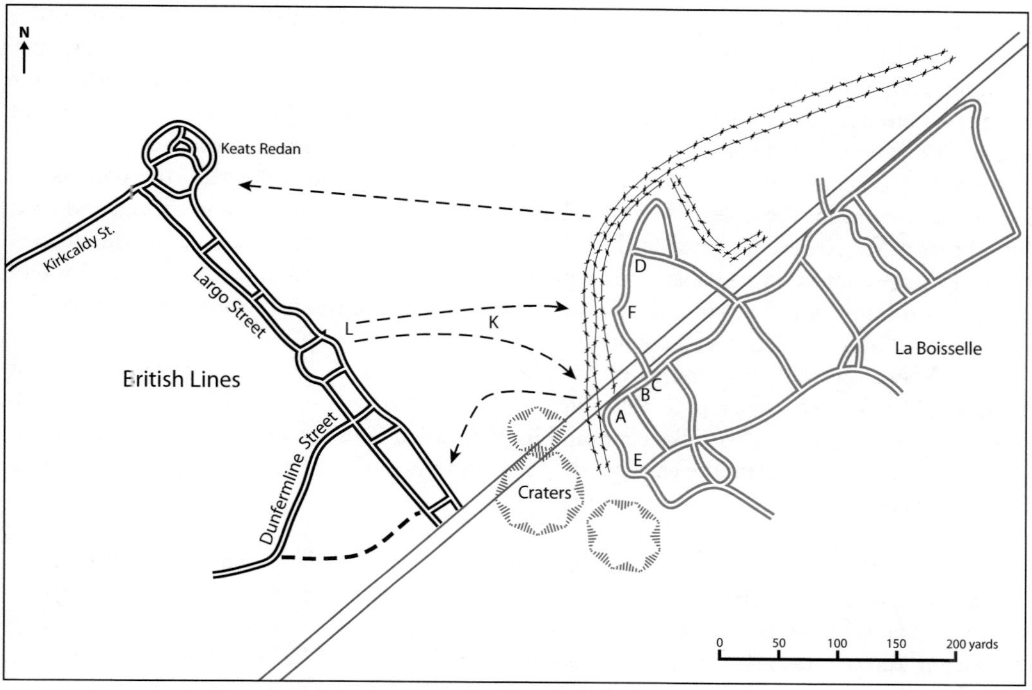

8 La Boiselle Raid, March 1916, 1st Dorsets.

worked toward "C" and "E". At "A" the depth of the trench, 12-15 feet, caused some hesitation to enter. Blakeway and his men met little opposition, "Y" sap being empty, less one or two men who rapidly withdrew. But heavy artillery fire and an immediate shower of grenades led this party to conclude that the enemy had been withdrawn so that the sap could be a killing zone. Knife-rests that had been set firmly in the sap checked further movement. Here Blakeway was wounded and could not be rescued. Withdrawal proved very difficult for both parties. Casualties included Blakeway missing, later reported dead, three ORs killed and 17 wounded.[19]

Attitudes regarding raiding, as noted earlier in this book, were neither static nor consistent. An account particularly useful on the anxiety that built up during pre-raid hours is one by Lieutenant Charles Douie, in March 1916 OC A Company of the 1st Dorsets. Initially on Zero Day Douie described being in a state of "inexperienced optimism," but he became "less sanguine" as there were indications that the enemy knew the raid was coming, this evident in the obvious registration of support and CTs. As his CO passed through the raiding party's

19 British War Diaries, 1st Dorsets and 14th Brigade, 32nd Division, 'Report on Raid and Sketch'. The Brigade War Diary for May includes a report on an enemy raid on the Dorsets on 7/8 May. Battalion casualties included one officer killed and one wounded, 12 ORs killed and 30 wounded, plus 24 others missing. Among the missing were Captain Algeo and Lieutenant Mansell-Playdell. According to the brigadier's report, which notified division that a Court of Inquiry was investigating, these officers had left the trenches on recce without telling anyone of their intention and Algeo had done so "in direct disobedience of repeated orders."

assembly area, Douie saw the "grave anxiety" on his Colonel's face. When the enemy immediately answered the fire to take out their wire with an intense counter-barrage, Douie knew that "beyond a doubt German batteries had been standing to their guns and that every detail of our attack was known." Nevertheless, both raiding parties reached the objective simultaneously and without casualties, but thick wire on the parapet caused congestion and "a very serious check." The primary objective of the raid, the taking of prisoners. was not achieved. The unit report listed two reasons for the failure. First, the loss of secrecy. The practice ground chosen and used for rehearsals for 10 days was next to the billets of other troops and the raiders had "free access" to local village shops that a sizable civilian population also patronized; in essence, loose lips had probably sunk the "ship." Second, the artillery fire in support of the raid ruined the "surprise by which means only can success be obtained."[20]

On 6 May a sap was again the objective of a raid, this time by 5th King's Shropshire Light Infantry (14th British Division) at Ronville near Arras. This venture, as proposed by the CO, featured quite imaginative use of deception. His plan called for a demonstration against one sap (designated sap "Y") to draw the enemy's attention and the raid to be on a second sap designated Sap "Z" under cover of the demonstration:

> I suggest that from 30-40 4.5-inch and about 100 H.E. 18-pounder be fired on Sap Y followed by some 50 shrapnel for wire-cutting … thus making a big show … The firing should be timed to finish just before dark, but it is essential that the wire be cut and the enemy know it. D46 [battery] would bombard Sap Z using 50-75 H.E. followed by some 25 shrapnel for wire-cutting. No 4.5-inch should fire … The idea should be to cut the wire for certain, but to use only sufficient H.E. to make it appear … only a demo … by this means it is to be hoped that the enemy would be drawn to Sap Y.

During the demonstration 18-pounders, 4.5-inch howitzers and 6-inch howitzers blasted "Y" Sap, the result as reported by the OC Raid and the artillery as wire satisfactorily cut. But at "Z" the wire was not cut, it apparently being "40 yards thick and very strong with iron stakes driven in at an angle instead of vertically, which gave the impression from a distance that the wire was composed of knife rests." By 0130 manual cutting still only half way through it and daylight due before 0230 the raiders withdrew. 14th Division HQ considered failure due "entirely to the wire not being cut as planned [this] no doubt due to the difficulty of observation." The enemy seemed unaware of the attempt on Sap "Z" since he did not open fire and his artillery fire was "feeble." In responding to the report, VI Corps expressed a hope that "after careful preparation another attempt will be made at this or some more favourable point." This seems to hint at a perception of inadequate recce, but if such was intended Corps HQ nevertheless expressed satisfaction with the attempt and wished the battalion better luck next time. [21]

But to return to April that month featured a number of more complex raids by elements of two battalions. The first of the examples offered here involved two battalions of 10th Brigade (4th British Division), the 1st Royal Warwickshire Regiment and the 1st Royal Irish Fusiliers.

20 Douie, *The Weary Road*, pp. 126, 128; TNA: WO 95/2389 and 2392: 14th Brigade, 32nd Division, 'Report on Raid and Sketch'.

21 TNA: WO 95/1865: 14th Division, May 1916: 'General Ideas for a Raid', 19 April; division report, 7 May and VI Corps response 8 May.

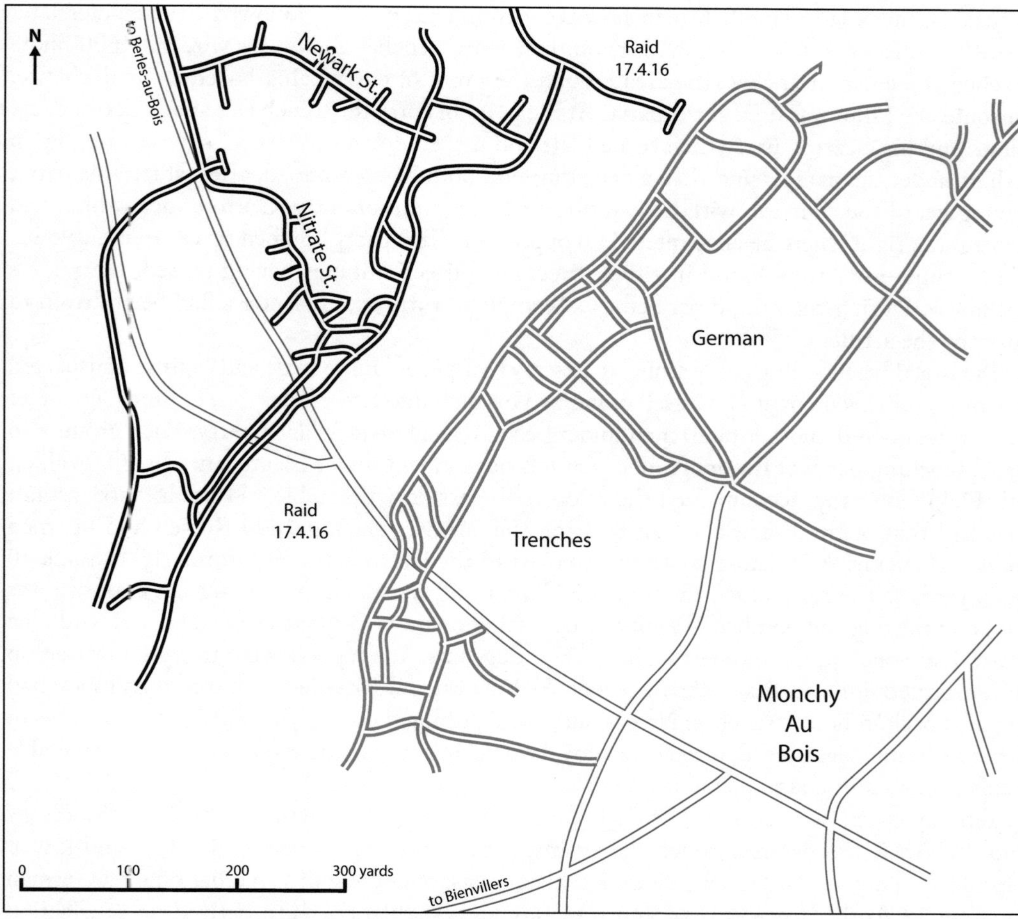

9 Monchy Au Bois Raid, 17 April 1916, 10th British Brigade.

These units would launch simultaneous raids northwest of Beaumont Hamel, the Warwicks at a point near the junction of the Beries – Monchy au Bois road and the enemy trench, and the Royal Irish about 500 yards north of that at a point opposite the British "T" Sap (see MSD 9). This raid would be in daylight "an innovation [that] will show the Germans that our men do not have to trust to darkness to enter their lines."[22]

Raider tasks included capturing two machine-guns that had been observed, killing Germans, taking prisoners and securing any items that would identify enemy units. The Warwicks organized three raiding parties, one of 12 men under Lieutenant J.L. Shute, a second of eight men under Second Lieutenant R.W. Gorton and a covering party of five men tasked once in the enemy trenches to place three ladders for use during withdrawal. At 1535 on the 17th Shute and his party moved to the assembly area at the "Y" junction of the Beries – Monchy road.

22 TNA: WO 95/1865: 10th Brigade, congratulations of GOC VI Corps.

Fifteen minutes later (1550) 6-inch howitzers commenced firing followed five minutes later by 18-pounders and 4.5-inch howitzers on the enemy trenches and on his wire. At 1600 Shute reached the enemy trenches, the area around the point of entry being boxed by artillery fire. Enroute not a shot was fired at the party. At the point of entry the trench was about 12 feet deep. Shute and his clearing party then turned left and moved down the trench, soon coming upon a shaft under the parapet and then a deep dug-out, both being bombed, after which this party, having heard the signal to withdraw, returned to the point of entry. Gorton, meanwhile, had gone to the right where he encountered no opposition. This party bombed seven deep dug-outs. No machine-guns were found in either direction. Fifteen minutes having passed, the raiders withdrew. During the raid, described as a "complete" surprise, all sentries had been driven to cover by the artillery.[23]

The Royal Irish raiding party aimed to destroy a suspected mine shaft and capture a suspected machine-gun. Lieutenant N. Russell organized his men into two groups, one of nine men under his command and another of 10 men under Second Lieutenant W.H. Crotty. Each group also had a blocking party of five more men. An RE detachment under Lieutenant H.C.C. Walker, 9th Field Company, accompanied the raiders. The artillery timetable and the infantry assault matched that of the Warwicks. On entering the enemy trench at 1600 Russell and his men found no enemy. A blocking party then moved to the left and another to the right. Some 10 or so yards to the right along the trench a German officer standing at a dug-out entrance was shot and the dug-out bombed. Twenty yards further on more Germans were met, and while the alarm had gone up, more were caught in their dug-outs. The sappers went to work blowing up the suspected mine shaft and the dug-outs. At 1610 Russell signalled withdrawal and soon had his men back in home trenches. No casualties were suffered during the raid or the withdrawal. Later a German deserter reported 63 enemy dead during the raid, this quite likely a considerable exaggeration designed to please his captors.[24]

Ten days later two battalions of 54th British Brigade (18th Division), the 12th Middlesex and the 7th Bedfordshires, raided the enemy, their aim being to demoralize him and kill or capture as many as possible. The divisional history describes the raid as retaliation for a German foray on 13 April. If it was that, and the aims suggest this, the 12th derived no satisfaction since the raiders failed to even enter the trenches. The CO, Lieutenant-Colonel H.P. Osborne, thought failure due to an error in judgement by the OC Raid. This raid by the 12th, which is fully described in Chapter 5, is mentioned here only to remind that the best of plans can come unstuck in the execution and that not all can be foreseen.[25]

Nichols relates the experience of the Bedfordshires at some length, the raid "admirably planned" by its CO, Lieutenant-Colonel G.D. Price, and the raiders, after 30 minutes of hand to hand fighting in the enemy trenches, coming away with "good reason to think highly of themselves." The brigade commander described Price's Operation Order as being "based" on the brigade order, an unnecessary emphasis on an inherent characteristic of Operation Orders

23 *Ibid.*, "Preliminary report on Raid by 10th Brigade on 17th April, Operation Order and reports.

24 *Ibid.*, Burrowes, *The Faugh-A-Ballaghs*, pp. 65-67. Lieutenants Shute and Russell both received the MC.

25 Nichols, *18th Division*, p. 26, says the GOC, Ivor Maxse, ordered the raid because it "would be good for morale." TNA: WO 95/2044: 12th Middlesex, Osborne to GOC 54th Brigade, 27 April; GOC 54th Brigade report to 18th Division, undated.

in general. The statement also seems superfluous and somewhat self-serving for a battalion order could hardly entirely ignore a brigade order. He also referred to Price's "able manner" in carrying out his orders. These comments suggest that this was a raid where the brigade commander was very much hands-on in planning and preparation.[26]

The night before the raid the OC Raid, Second Lieutenant H. Driver, and the two NCOs of the raiding party, carried out a careful recce of the route to the objective and its immediate area. In addition, each raider was shown the position he would occupy when the artillery began firing during the raid. The fire support consisted of three phases, the first hitting at enemy trenches and wire, followed by a box barrage around the objective and then counter-battery fire. Machine-guns featured in the raid, 11 Vickers machine-guns from 54th Machine-Gun Company and numerous Lewis guns intensely engaged the enemy parapet. All of the raiders (30 men) entered the enemy trenches, then moved left and right, bombing as they went. The alert enemy reacted quickly and effectively, fighting being heavy during the entering and the leaving of the enemy trench. Consequently, tempers were up and "the desirability of taking prisoners" again got forgotten, a not uncommon lapse during the heat of fighting. Eight raiders were wounded, but all got safely home. Driver, who was wounded in three places, was last out of the enemy trench. His strong personality and determination were instrumental in the raid's success, as it was proclaimed despite the failure to secure prisoners. For his efforts Driver received the MC.[27]

A party of the 15th Royal Welsh Fusiliers of 38th (Welsh) Division in May 1916 near Laventie in the Givenchy sector of the front prepared equally well for a raid. On returning from leave Wyn Griffith learned that the corps commander's desire for prisoners had filtered down through division and brigade to settle upon one of the other company commanders in the 15th. Griffith had no direct involvement in the venture since it was only two days away. His company had a minor part to play, the cutting of gaps in the wire through which the raiders would enter no man's land. But his company might suffer casualties since the raid's objective was opposite his lines and German retaliation would likely strike at his company.[28] On the day of the raid (7 May) Griffith observed artillery cutting the enemy wire and then watched that night as events unfolded. At 2230 an NCO and four men left to reconnoitre enemy wire, do any cutting necessary and then return. Nothing was heard from this party until 0030 when one man returned to advise that an enemy working party of 12-15 men was repairing wire at the point chosen as the objective of the raid. The OC Raid, Captain G. Owen, having consulted the CO, took the raiders, 51 ORs plus two Subalterns, organized into left and right assault parties, out to a position some 40 yards in front of the enemy wire from which the enemy workers could be rushed. But here the NCO of the recce party told Owen that the enemy had returned to his trenches. Captain Owen then moved forward, cut the last few feet of wire and reached the enemy parapet where he could see about 20 men in three bays standing about without weapons or equipment.

26 Nichols, *18th Division,* pp. 26, 131. Price was promoted to command 55th Brigade in October 1916. TNA: WO 95/2043: 54th Brigade, April 1916, GOC to 18th Division. Once preliminary matters were settled a final conference was held at brigade HQ where the whole scheme "was gone into in the greatest detail."

27 Nichols, *18th Division,* pp. 26-28.

28 Griffith, *Up to Mametz,* pp. 111-12.

The raiding parties then advanced, bombed the trench and made their entry, the 20 or so Germans being killed or dispersed. The left and right assault groups, each of 20 men under a Subaltern, began bombing outward, but immediately became aware of and were surprised at the large number of enemy in neighbouring bays: "the Germans sandwiched together, some without arms and equipment which seem[ed] to show that they did not constitute the ordinary garrison." While these mostly unarmed men could offer little opposition, they did block the trench. Seeing this, the bombers on the parapet began bombing successive bays from above, thereby clearing them in front of the battalion bombers who were in the trenches and bombing around the traverses. The right assault party, as it continued to bomb outward, reached a CT crowded with enemy who were then heavily bombed and prevented from reaching the main trench. Enemy casualties in both directions were estimated as heavy. After 15 minutes of severe fighting Captain Owen decided to withdraw. To this point no casualties had been suffered, but once back out in no man's land the raiders received heavy machine-gun and rifle fire, the result being two Subalterns wounded and missing, two ORs killed and eight wounded and one missing. While no enemy were captured the raid provided valuable information. In Captain Owen's opinion the large number of unarmed men about without any equipment were probably miners awaiting shift change. Despite the raiders consequent inability to clear more than 50 yards of enemy trench, the brigade commander (113th Brigade) praised them for their very successful outing.[29]

Numerous small raids continued throughout May and June 1916. One by 20 men of the 13th Durham Light Infantry (69th Brigade, 23rd British Division) on 2 June in the Souchez area was notable for two reasons. First, artillery did no systematic wire-cutting for fear of warning the enemy; instead, a short, sharp bombardment at 1930 covered registration by mortars (six trench mortars and six Stokes). At Zero (0100) the mortars, plus four batteries of 18-pounders and two of 4.5-inch howitzers, opened intense rate for one minute before the 18-pounders lifted to enemy support lines. The Stokes continued firing for another minute, the raiders moving forward under this cover to the enemy wire where a gap had been made and then into the enemy trench where 12 Germans were killed. The brigade commander attributed success to the fine work of the artillery and mortars and "especially to the fact that there was no apparent lift as the howitzers fired [throughout] on the enemy support line … and the Stokes … continued to fire on the front line while the advance was starting." Moreover, the raid being launched only one minute after the start of the bombardment "probably surprised the enemy." The brigade report also made special mention of Captain G. White, acting CO of the 13th, who "carried out the plan in every detail and chose the objective." This wording suggests that brigade HQ had a prominent part in the planning. Of the two Subalterns on the raid, Lieutenant D.H. Clarke received the MC.[30]

Three days later (5/6 June) 11th Battalion, The Border Regiment (32nd British Division), executed a somewhat larger raid on the Leipzig Salient about 1,300 yards south of Thiepval

29 TNA: WO 95/2556: 15th Royal Welsh Fusiliers, Operation Order No. 14, 'Notes on the Raid and Narrative'. Over 800 bombs were expended during the raid.

30 Sandilands, *23rd Division*, pp. 59-60; TNA: WO 95/2167: 13th Durhams, Reports of 68th Brigade and the 13th. Lieutenant Clarke was later Lieutenant-Colonel Clarke, DSO, MC and Bar and, at 26, CO 13th Durhams. The other Subaltern, Lieutenant N.A. Target, was killed two months later. He received a posthumous MC.

List of Plates

Major-General David Watson, GOC 4th Canadian Division. (Library and Archives Canada/PA002116)

Lieutenant-Colonel Edmund Ironside, GSO1 4th Canadian Division. (Library and Archives Canada/PA001352)

Lieutenant-Colonel Edward Hilliam, CO 25th Canadian Battalion, and later Brigadier-General and GOC 10th Brigade, 4th Canadian Division. (Library and Archives Canada/ PA000482)

Brigadier-General Victor Odlum, formerly CO 7th Canadian Battalion and later GOC 11th Brigade, 4th Canadian Division. (Library and Archives Canada/ PA002118)

Brigadier-General James MacBrien, GOC 12th Brigade, 4th Canadian Division (right) and Lieutenant-Colonel W.H. Clarke-Kennedy, VC, CMG, DSO and Bar, CO 24th Battalion. (Library and Archives Canada/PA006743)

Lieutenant-General Sir Arthur Currie, GOC Canadian Corps. (Library and Archives Canada/PA1370)

Lieutenant-Colonel Louis Lipsett, CO 8th Battalion and later Major-General and GOC 3rd Canadian Division. Killed in action while GOC 4th British Division. (Library and Archives Canada/PA007442)

Brigadier-General D.H.B. Ketchen, GOC 6th Canadian Brigade and to his right in trenchcoat Major A.H. Jukes, BM, May 1917. (Library and Archives Canada/PA001236)

Major The Hon. F.E. Grosvenor. (front row at left), BM 6th Canadian Brigade, March 1918. (Library and Archives Canada/MIKAN3522129)

Lieutenant-Colonel R.D.F. Hayter (front row, far left). GSO1 1st Canadian Division, April 1918, and later BGGS Canadian Corps. (Library and Archives Canada/MIKAN3522131)

Lieutenant-Colonel George Tuxford, CO 5th Canadian Battalion, later Brigadier-General and GOC 3rd Brigade. (Saskatchewan Archives Board Photo R-A10224)

Brigadier-General William Griesbach. (right), CO 49th Canadian Battalion and later GOC 1st Brigade. (Library and Archives Canada/ PA007103)

Major-General Frederick Loomis, CO 13th Canadian Battalion and later GOC 3rd Canadian Division. (Library and Archives Canada/PA002203)

Lieutenant-Colonel R.D. Davies, CO 44th Canadian Battalion, after award of DSO. (Library and Archives Canada/PA007009)

Lieutenant George McKean, VC, MC, MM, 14th Canadian Battalion. (Library and Archives Canada/PA006219)

Captain John MacGregor, VC, MC, DCM, 2nd Canadian Mounted Rifles. (Library and Archives Canada/PA004598)

Canadians leaving the line after a night raid, Avion, July 1917. Note black camouflage hands and face. (Library and Archives Canada/PA001814)

Canadian with prisoners after night raid February 1918. (Library and Archives Canada/PA002607)

Trench Mortar Battery, 2-inch mortar, "Toffee Apple" Bombs in front, 1917.
(Library and Archives Canada/PA004921)

Heavy Mortar in emplacement, May 1917. (Library and Archives Canada/PA001409)

Damaged German trench with undamaged dug-out entrance, July 1916.
(Library and Archives Canada/PA000128)

Damaged German trench, dug-out entrance blown in, July 1916.
(Library and Archives Canada/PA000180)

Trench Mortar fire on German wire. (Library and Archives Canada/PA 001380)

Trench Mortar fire on German wire. (Library and Archives Canada/PA001381)

British officers watching rifle grenade demonstration, 1917. (Library and Archives Canada/PA004745)

Stokes 3-inch mortar and crew, not Western Front. Photo in Public Domain.

Canadians preparing hand grenades. (bombs) for use, reserve line, Bomb Storage Store, February 1918. (Library and Archives Canada/PA002449)

Canadian machine-guns digging in, Vimy Ridge, April 1917. (Library and Archives Canada/PA001017)

Wounded Canadian, German prisoners, November 1917. At left duckboards.
(Library and Archives Canada/PA0022100)

19th March, 1916. No. 82. Vol. 4.

THE WAR
Illustrated

A PICTURE-RECORD *of Events by Land, Sea and Air.* *Edited by* J. A. HAMMERTON

COWARDLY "KULTUR."—A favourite ruse of the treacherously-inclined Hun is to hide behind a comrade who apparently is surrendering himself prisoner. With rifle ready and loaded, he is able to take in cold blood the life of the hesitant Briton. This cowardly conduct occurred recently during a Canadian night attack on the Prussian Guard. Fortunately the Maple Leaf man was too quick for the Prussians, and managed to get a revolver "bull" and bayonet thrust in first. In this engagement the Canadians took the enemy by surprise, and succeeded in wreaking considerable damage with bombs.

'Cowardly Kultur', *The War Illustrated,* March 1916. See Chapter 15, raids by 13th KRRC and 13th Battalion, The Rifle Brigade.

4th March, 1916. No. 81. Vol. 4.

THE WAR Illustrated

A PICTURE-RECORD of Events by Land, Sea and Air. Edited by J. A. HAMMERTON

CANADIANS THRASH THE PRUSSIANS.—Under the laconic official heading of a night bombing attack, a plucky affair took place recently on the western front. A company of Canadians went out under cover of dark to raid the trenches of the Prussian Guards. The Canadians launched their bombs full in the midst of the Guards, who set their flares going and turned a machine-gun on the nocturnal visitors. It would have fared ill with the Canadians had not a lucky bomb-thrower planted his missile right on to the Maxim, thereby allowing twenty-three out of the party of twenty-five to retreat.

'Canadians Thrash The Prussians', *The War Illustrated*, March 1916. See Chapter 9, raid by 6th Brigade. (28th Battalion), Spanbroekmolen, MSD 11.

The Last Alarm of a Hapless German Sentinel

Two parties of the West Yorkshires started on a nocturnal raid on the enemy's trenches after cutting through the German wire. An officer and sergeant came across an enemy sentry oblivious of immediate danger. The sergeant approached, and aimed point-blank, but his revolver missfired. He thereupon sprang at the throat of the sentry, who uttered a piercing shriek. The officer then crept up and endeavoured to club the German, but his weapon went off, the bullet passing through the sentry's neck and the sergeant's hand. By now the Germans were fully alarmed, and the raiders retreated.

'The Last Alarm of a Hapless German Sentinel', *The War Illustrated*, March 1916. See Chapter 9: possibly the raid by the West Yorkshires in March 1916.

Run to Earth! Enemy Trapped in Deep Dug-out

The Germans, judging by the depth to which they have "gone to earth" in some parts of the line, are developing a great respect for the power of the new British high explosives. In a spirited affair which took place recently on the west front our men were surprised to find that the enemy dug-outs had been practically untouched by bombardment, owing to the fact that they had about eighteen feet of cover above a solidly-constructed wooden roof. Here large numbers of Germans took refuge, but were eventually induced either to surrender or submit to the ordeal of the grenade.

'Run to Earth! Enemy Trapped in Deep Dug-Out', *The War Illustrated*, July 1916.

BRITISH SOLDIERS' GREAT TRENCH RAID IN THE SNOW.—Our soldiers in a German trench, where they "trapped" a number of Wurtembergers by the daring suddenness of their attack. One of the most notable features of the winter warfare on the western front as revealed in the daily official despatches has been the frequency of the trench raids with which our men have kept the enemy in a nervous and "jumpy" condition. These raids have, however, frequently served more immediately valuable purposes than that, sometimes resulting in the capture of many prisoners. In the case illustrated, at half-past five in the morning, our guns broke into a terrific crash of firing, which the Germans regarded as "just a morning strafe," and so sought the supposed security of their dug-outs. In about four minutes—says Mr. Philip Gibbs in his graphic account of the exploit—our troops were over the hundred yards of frozen No Man's Land and in the trench, capturing "Kamerads" from every dug-out. And, what is more, they continued to hold the trench.

'British Soldiers Great Trench Raid in the Snow;, *The War Illustrated*, March 1917. See Chapter 11: probably 6th London Regiment's raid on 20 February 1917.

Brave British Work with Bombs and Bayonets

Bombing a way into a German trench over a snowy parapet. Trench raids have formed a frequent feature of winter warfare on the western front. By means of them the British troops have kept the enemy ever nervously alert and in a "jumpy" condition.

Episode of one of the British "nibbling" advances. Progress was being held up by two hidden German machine-guns, when an officer picked a small party of bombers and bayonet men, penetrated the German line and destroyed the guns and their crews.

'Brave British Work With Bombs and Bayonets', *The War Illustrated*, March 1917.

1st September, 1917. No. 159. Vol. 7.

THE WAR Illustrated

A PICTURE-RECORD *of Events by Land, Sea and Air.* *Edited by* J. A. HAMMERTON

[British official photograph

TWO GREAT LEADERS ON THE WESTERN FRONT.—General Sir Henry Horne, K.C.B. (right), with General Sir Arthur Currie, K.C.M.G. Sir Henry Horne invented the creeping barrage which has proved so valuable in successive British advances. Sir Arthur Currie, himself a Canadian, is in chief command of the Canadian Corps, having succeeded Sir Julian Byng in that position in June last.

'Two Great Leaders on the Western Front', *The War Illustrated*, September 1917.
General Sir Henry Horne and Lieutenant-General Sir Arthur Currie.

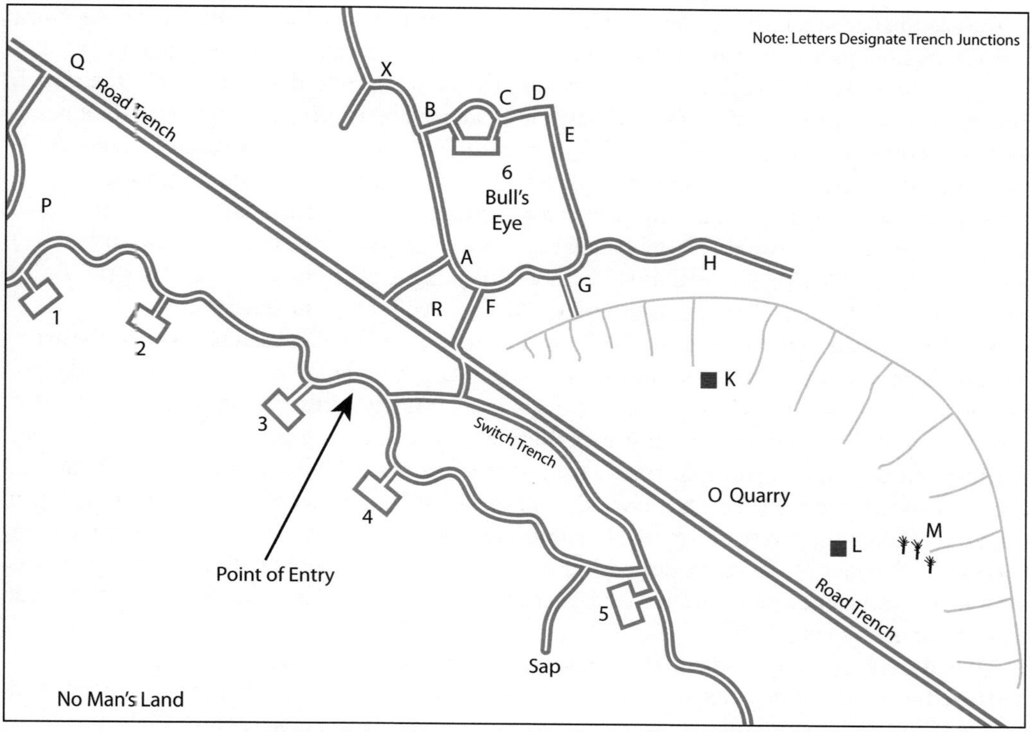

10 Leipzig Salient Raid, 5/6 June 1916, 11th Border Regiment.

and east of Authville.[31] Air photography had highlighted some unusual activity and deployment in the Salient: first, earthen mounds near the head of the salient hinted at mining underway; second, a quarry fronting on the enemy line appeared to house emplacements for machine-guns; and, finally, a quadrilateral trench dubbed the "Bull's Eye" that lay behind the front line appeared to be a strongpoint (see MSD 10).

Lieutenant W.S. Barnes, OC Raid, set out the raid's purposes thus: "ascertain what was going on in the quarry, determine activity and its purpose in the 'Bull's Eye' and capture prisoners in order that a picture of deployment and activity could be compiled." Having considered all aspects of the raid, including entry, establishment of blocks left and right to prevent enemy access to the objective area, dealing with dug-outs in the enemy line, seizing, guarding and escorting prisoners, plus exploring the Bull's Eye, Barnes determined that he required three more Subalterns and a total of 83 ORs. These he organized into 13 groups according to function. Training commenced three weeks before Zero day, the focus on careful rehearsals at night on a trench replica and close study of aerial photographs. A bonus gratefully accepted by Barnes and Lieutenant M. McKerrow was a flight arranged to give them a good look at the objective from above.

31 Barton, *The Somme: The Unseen Panoramas*, p. 114 (map).

The plan called for Barnes, plus a taping party that had marked the route to the objective, and a Bangalore party that would finish the wire-cutting, to remain at the entry point to receive prisoners and escort any back to home trenches. The raiders would depart not from the trench directly opposite the nose of the salient, but from a trench about 100 yards to the north, it being thought best to avoid the most direct route to the salient as it would likely receive heavy retaliatory fire. The Germans did exactly that. Barnes' left and right parties were to investigate dug-outs in the main trench while a third party would check Switch Trench, and a fourth the Road Trench where a block would be established beyond the junction with the short (10 yards or so) trench to the Bull's Eye. Finally, a party under Lieutenant McKerrow would enter the Bull's Eye and dug-out No. 6. Part of this group would also reconnoitre the quarry.

At 2220 the tape men followed by the Bangalore team, left friendly trenches. When the artillery bombardment began at 2300 the tapes had been laid, the Bangalore was in place and close behind were the raiding parties in assault formation. Enemy artillery had quickly responded with fire on the battalion front line: "the rapidity with which their heavy guns opened was very striking." At 2315 a Bangalore destroyed the last few feet of the German wire and the raiders at once gained entry to the enemy trench. Dug-outs 4, 3 and 2 were checked, prisoners being taken from each before they were destroyed. In the Bull's Eye Lieutenant McKerrow took three prisoners from dug-out No. 6 before destroying it. At 2330 his party rejoined Lieutenant Barnes, as did the left and right assault parties, and 10 minutes later the raiders with their prisoners were crossing no man's land.

All had gone according to plan. The raid secured 16 prisoners (11 reached the British trenches), destroyed most of the dug-outs and met the other objectives set out by Barnes. Unfortunately, he was killed by enemy artillery during the return to home trench as were three ORs. From the report written by one of the other officers on the raid it is evident that Barnes' sound plan and the numerous rehearsals for the raid were what brought success. As for the report itself, it is a fine example of military writing at its best. In 10 pages the author set out in detail the events and progress of the raid, carefully described the enemy wire, all trenches and the Bull's Eye and provided good diagrams of the objective and dug-outs (front line and Bull's Eye). McKerrow had found the latter "badly knocked about," but work clearly in progress, large mounds of earth suggesting more than just repair. All in all, this raid displayed solid planning and determined and professional execution.[32]

Another raid two nights later by three officers and 60 men of the 14th Gloucesters (35th British Division) was described by the divisional historian as "entirely successful," although he added that "the battalion cannot be said to have been favoured by fortune." The first shell of the enemy retaliatory barrage killed the CO and severely wounded, then hit again and killed the OC Raid. In all, two officers and three ORs were killed, one officer and 15 ORs wounded and four ORs were missing. No prisoners were taken, but the raiders did return with one machine-gun and had bombed several dug-outs. Casualties at roughly 40 percent of the raiding force was a high price to pay. The divisional historian also reminds that on 8 June 1916 compulsory service was instituted in Great Britain.[33]

32 TNA: WO 95/2399: 11th Border Regiment, report on raid and map. Martin Middlebrook, *The First Day on the Somme: 1 July 1916* (London: Purnell, 1971), p. 91.

33 Davson, *35th Division,* pp. 22-23; TNA: WO 95/2485: 14th Gloucesters, report of raid 8/9 June 1916.

A raid on 16/17 June by B Company, 4/5 Black Watch (118th Brigade, 39th British Division), was more notable for its preparation than for the results. Its purpose was prisoners and/or identifications. The objective trench was anchored on the north bank of the La Bassee Canal immediately southeast of Givenchy.[34] The raiding force, two Subalterns and 81 ORs, was organized into six parties: four small assault parties (9-10 men each) consisting of bayonet men, bombers, bomb carriers and one spare man and an officer with the lead party, No. 1 Assault Party; a covering party of one officer and 14 men to remain at the point of entry; and a strong reserve (one officer and 28 ORs) to remain on standby outside the enemy trench. Ten minutes was set for the "stay," withdrawal to be on the "watch" and by runners from the point of entry to the parties. Fire support included field artillery, trench mortars and Stokes. The operation was to commence at 0100, Saturday, 17 June with a brief bombardment, the raiders to advance eight minutes later and a mine to be exploded as a diversion near Ducksbill Craters about 1,000 yards northwest of the objective at 0109. To what extent this drew off any enemy attention cannot be said. It received only bare and nebulous mention in the brigade commander's report.

The raid package in the battalion War Diary is a delight to read because of its organization and its clarity throughout. Pre-raid instructions include "General Orders and Timetable" and "Schedule of Armament" prepared by the CO, Lieutenant-Colonel G. McL.Sceales, and "Orders to Raiders" prepared by Captain T. Stevenson (OC B Company) who directed the raid from a point in the British lines. A logical division of writing labour had the CO "write up" all pre-raid requirements and arrangements including communications, signals and telephones, bomb issue, cutting of own wire, location of a control post, instructions for trench mortars, the mine explosion and the manning of the line at the departure point. The last had to be carefully arranged since raiders from one unit were not keen on departing from and returning to lines held by another unit. This meant moving men of one unit out of the front line and moving the raiders into their place and then reversing this at the end of the raid. This went to and was approved by GOC 118th Brigade. For how Sceales arranged this to ensure it went smoothly, and for other examples of such arrangements, see the last third of Chapter 5. The "Timetable" shows major activities/events from Zero minus 60 when the switch in manning began, to Zero plus 20 when the withdrawal from enemy trenches would begin.

Sceales' "Schedule of Armament" (MSD 10A), while not referred to directly in the brigade commander's report, explains his statement that "It will be seen that he [Sceales] has taken great pains … and set the example … to this I attribute the success." This document shows at a glance the organization of the raiding parties, their composition, some of the equipment carried and by whom, and even the number of knives, bayonets and bombs carried, 630 of the last, and who carried them and how many. This "Schedule" would have pleased Stevenson no end. It allowed him to keep his orders to a page and a half.

Stevenson's "Orders to Raiders" is an Operation Order by another name. It is confined to the actual execution of the raid. It tells the raiders everything they had to know: entry point, objective, organization of parties, movement, dress and armament, signals and one matter not seen in any other such order: "all ranks will wear trousers." If this seems rather trifling consider the disadvantages of a kilt during a raid. To mention just one, kilts would have delighted enemy intelligence. Not all tartans are alike! The package also included the reports of Stevenson,

34 Barton, *The Battlefields of the First World War*, p. 220 (map).

SCHEDULE OF ARMAMENT.

	Officers	N.C.Os.	Bayonet men	Throwers	Carriers	Spare men	S.Bearers	Signallers	Officers	N.C.Os.	O.Rs.	Total	Knives	Bayonets	Stretchers	Blkg.Mtls	Buckets	Torches	Bombs		
									Summary.												
A.1st.party	1	1	3	3	2	1			1	1	9	11	3	7		x	5	2	94	(2 bombs per man) = 22 (3 throwers 12 each) = 36 (2 carriers 18 ") = 36 (3 throwers carry knives) (1.spare man wire)	94
B.2nd.party		1	3	3	2	1				1	9	10	3	7		x	5	2	92	(Bombs and knives as A.) (1.spare man wire.)	92
C.3rd.party		1	4	3	2	1				1	10	11	3	8		x	5	2	94	(Bombs and wire as A.)	94
D.4th.party		1	2	1	1					1	4	5		4			2	1	40	(Bombs as A.)	40
E.5th.party	1	1	10				2	2	1	1	14	16		11	4		10		144	(2.bombs per man) = 24 (10. with 12 each) =120 (2.small Roger stretchers.) (2.long R.A.M.C.Do.)	144
F.6th.party	1	2	10	10			4	4	1	2	28	31		20	4		10		166	(2.Bombs per man) = 46 (10 with 12 each) =120 (2 Roger and 2 long stretchers)	166
	3	7	32	20	7	3	6	6	3	7	74	84	9	57	8	3	37	7	630		630

N.B. Torches with leading Bayonet men of A.B. and C. and N.C.Os. of A.B.C. and D.

16/6/16

Sgd. G.McL. Sceales, Lt-Col.,
4/5th.Black Watch.

10A Givenchy, 16/17 June 1916, 4/5 Black Watch.

Sceales and two by the GOC. All in all it is certainly one of the best, perhaps the best of all the "paper trails" for smaller raids seen during the research for this study of raiding. Would that the whole could grace this study, but the one-page "Schedule of Armaments" will have to stand for all. This document (MSD 10A) may not be unique, but it is certainly one of the earliest examples of such time and space savers seen in use by an officer charged with crafting Operation Orders. It is striking in its practical utility.

The raid did not do as well as had been anticipated. An extract from Captain Stevenson's report explains why:

> The raiders reached the enemy trench at 1:10 a.m. and entered … The first party immediately commenced to bomb to the right, the second party commenced bombing to the left. The third and fourth parties [entered] and followed on the first party … The first party were stopped about 40 yards from the point of entry by a solid block … the second party bombed along for about 40 yards and there encountered a similar block … The third and fourth parties were unable to reach their objectives owing to No. 1 Party being held up and blocking the trench … communication round the blocks was by means of dug-outs.

Lieutenant-Colonel Sceales and the GOC both remarked on this, the latter saying the German practice seemed to be to block CTs near the front parapet and use dug-outs to pass to and fro. This "frustrated the scheme," said Sceales. His reference to the "unusual number" of men in the German front line is explained by the one prisoner who during interrogation stated this was because a raid was in preparation. Given the presence of more Germans than usual the Black Watch "may have forestalled the Bosches in a raid by a short time." Twenty Germans were counted as killed and many more were thought wounded. Black Watch casualties were only eight wounded. Sceales also praised Stevenson's well-thought out plan, calling it another example of the untiring energy he had displayed in eight months as OC B Company.[35]

The pace of raiding picked up as 1 July and the opening of the Somme drew closer. Just before the "Big Show" several large-scale raids occurred, the idea being, supposedly, to prevent the enemy accurately appreciating where the super-offensive would commence. One of the most interesting of these raids was that by 2nd Royal Munster Fusiliers, a unit of 3rd Brigade, 1st British Division, in the coal-mining area of Lens, specifically at Calonne, one mile north of Lievin near Lens. Peter Barton called this area a "quintessential industrial battleground." Having been in residence since October 1914 the Germans had worked hard to make their defences formidable.[36]

This raid, set for 2310 on 25 June, aimed to take prisoners, gain unit identifications, reconnoitre defences and inflict losses at two saps each about 330 yards distant from the Munster lines and separated from one another by about 200 yards. The distance raiders would have to cover seemed to offer a possibility that this would make the enemy less likely to anticipate raids at the two points; rather, their focus would be areas where the opposing trenches were closer. Also wire at the two selected points had been reported as not as thick as elsewhere. The raiding

35 TNA: WO 95/2588: 118th Brigade, 39th Division, instructions, orders and reports for raid on 17 June 1916; Wauchope, *History of the Black Watch,* barely mentions the raid, a single short paragraph offering nothing.

36 Barton, *The Somme: The Unseen Panoramas,* pp. 256 and 262 (map).

force, eight officers and 152 ORs, formed in two equal parties, would act independently but simultaneously.

The general idea stipulated that following artillery preparation and any necessary wire-cutting two raiding parties, "Northern" and "Southern," would enter enemy trenches at or near the junction of a sap and the main trench at each objective point. First in at each would be what the CO and chief planner of the raids, Lieutenant-Colonel W.B. Lyons, called "Picquets," his term for the two blocking parties of nine men each. In both cases, the Picquets would be closely followed by the two trench parties (each one officer and 24 ORs). Both types of party consisted of a mix of bayonet men, bombers and bomb carriers. Next came the wire-cutters who on entering the trench became the parapet party at each entry point, their task being custody of any prisoners and assistance to any wounded. A reserve of 24 ORs under the OC Raid would remain just outside the wire ready to prevent any interference from the flanks. Once in the trenches the Picquets and the Trench Parties would work outward left and right to where the Picquets would establish blocks at the junction with the first CT encountered. Thirty minutes would be "stay" time in the enemy trench, retirement being signalled by klaxon horn and a green Very light.

For two days prior to the raid trench mortars cut wire at the head of each sap and five other selected points, as did the artillery on Zero day, this shelling ceasing before 2300 daily. At 2250 the raiders moved forward to a ditch conveniently running parallel to the German front line and about halfway across no man's land. There they waited until the end at 2305 of an intense bombardment on the two objectives by four batteries of 18-pounders and one 4.5-inch howitzer battery. Another 18-pounder battery struck three other points. Also at 2305, a heavy box barrage by five 18-pounder batteries and one howitzer battery descended on the flanks and rear of the two objectives.[37] Both sets of raiders then rushed the gaps, neither experiencing any difficulty in finding a wide gap, the enemy wire being generally demolished, but the saps were filled with wire which meant the raiders had to enter via the parapet of the main trenches. At these points, rifle fire and rifle grenades caused casualties in the Southern Party and in the Northern Party, including its OC, Lieutenant Arthur Batten-Pooll, and Second Lieutenant Beevor.

Once in the trenches (about 2320) Batten-Pooll, despite his wounds, got his two Picquet Parties and two Trench Parties moving outward left and right, bombing as they went. They experienced considerable difficulty due to intense enemy bombing from behind the parados. The right group lost Lieutenant W.S. Clarke (killed). The raiders got no further than 40-50 yards along the trench, the enemy "standing to arms … fully prepared for the attack and offer[ing] strenuous resistance." With their bombs all gone, the party had to return to the entry point. Here the two prisoners offered such resistance they had to be killed. The left group, which became heavily engaged and severely bombed as to it moved to the left, also soon had to return to the entry point. With casualties mounting, the OC Parapet Party, Second Lieutenant J.H. Jordeson, and Lieutenant Batten-Pooll conferred and the withdrawal signal was sounded.[38]

37 TNA: WO 95/1279: 2nd Royal Munster Fusiliers, June 1916, Appendix 13, 'Scheme for Proposed Raid', 21 June; WO 95/1279 3rd Brigade, Appendix 16, 'Scheme for Proposed Raid', 18 June. For the raid 1,800 rounds of shrapnel and 3,000 rounds of HE were allotted to the 18-pounders and 600 rounds to the howitzers.

38 Graham Saville, 'Night Attack: 2/Royal Munster Fusiliers at Cite Calonne 25 June 1916', *Stand To!*, 56 (September 1999): 25-26. Batten-Pooll, age 24, joined the 2nd Battalion in February 1916 on

The Southern Party under Major Lancelot Shildrick entered the enemy trench about 2320. His Picquet and Trench Parties quickly moved outward left and right. The right group bombed about 70 yards along the trench passing through six firing bays, five to seven Germans in each, to a junction with a CT. Throughout they were bombed continuously from behind the parados, the enemy quite indifferent to the presence of their own men in the front trench. One dug-out about halfway along their path was bombed, it appearing by the noise to be filled with many Germans. Beyond the CT junction, where a picquet had been left, fighting became fierce, the officer and his NCO severely wounded as were many others. Now leaderless, and with bombs running short, this force fell back closely pursued by the enemy. On reaching the junction no trace of the Picquet could be found (all its men were later reported as missing). About 20 yards from the entry point they heard the withdrawal signal at about 2340. Casualty evacuation proved extremely difficult due to the depth of the trench. One prisoner in attempting to push his escort into a dug-out was clubbed, while the other three were "dispatched" as it was all the raiders could do to get the wounded out. The left party experienced similar hard times, as did its Picquet Party which suffered many casualties. No prisoners were brought in.[39]

Lieutenant-Colonel Lyons' report is illuminating and comprehensive. While no prisoners or identifications of units were secured, it was confirmed that IV German Corps still held the sector. Enemy losses were estimated at 50 dead. The very deep enemy trenches, up to 12 feet in depth, had not been foreseen during the planning. As for own losses, Lyons reported these as very heavy, half the officers and NCOs and a third of the men (raiding strength was eight officers and 152 men). Stretcher cases (24) were brought back. In all, one officer and two ORs were killed, two officers and 34 ORs wounded, one officer was missing, believed killed (the body could not be recovered) and 10 ORs were missing.[40]

Enemy reaction was described as very quick and their defences solid. Both saps, for example, were filled with barbed wire as were the traverses on either flank of the gaps where bombing posts had been established. Storming these took a great deal of time. Some wounded had to be left as they could not be extracted from the barbed wire. Also evident were rifle grenade batteries sited so as to cover the gaps. As for the strength in the main trench:

> every fire bay had its garrison and it would appear the enemy were standing to in large numbers awaiting the attack. The fact that our parties were allowed to come right inside the gap before a shot was fired or a flare sent up, suggests enemy planned to capture the entire party [but] did not contemplate such large numbers being employed by us.

Despite the heavy losses (one-third of raiding strength) and the absence of prisoners on the whole the attack went as planned. Surprise had not been achieved, the enemy on the alert and ready in all respects. It seems that both sides realized where a raid could best be made. The preparatory artillery fire may well have steered them in the right direction, or perhaps poor

transfer (requested) from a cavalry regiment. TNA: WO 95/1279: 3rd Brigade, June 1916, Appendix 1, report on raid by CO (26 June) and Appendix 15, further report by CO on 27 June.

39 Saville, 'Night Attack', p. 25.

40 TNA: WO 95/1279: 3rd Brigade, June 1916, Appendices 1 and 15 (CO's reports).

telephone security had given the game away. In any case, a high price had been paid for very little gain. The balance of profit stood wanting.[41]

As usual reportage at higher levels was mixed. The GHQ Press Bureau called the raid "particularly successful." A First Army Intelligence Summary described enemy casualties as heavy and British losses as light, an assessment originating in a I Corps Intelligence Summary. However, a supplement to the former, obviously reflecting closer assessment, concluded with some "details" of the raid that would certainly influence future planning:

> The enemy appears to have been prepared … his system of defence being to vacate the portion of his front line opposite … where wire had been cut, and to establish barricades some 30 or 40 yards down his front trench on each side, with possibly a second barricade further on, then to await the attack without rifle or other retaliation until our parties were well into his trench, and having retired to above-mentioned barricades, bombed them with rifle grenades from the support line and with bombs from the flanks.[42]

As Lyons said, the enterprise reflected the highest credit on the officers who directed it and on all who participated. Lieutenant Batten-Pooll received the VC: "When in command of a raiding party he was severely wounded, but continued to direct his men until the withdrawal … In spite of his own injuries he assisted two wounded men until he himself was further wounded, at which time he fainted within yards of safety." MCs went to Second Lieutenants John Jordeson and Charles Ryan. Three DCMs and nine MMs were also awarded. Perhaps Second Lieutenant Clarke, whose final resting place is unknown, should have the last word:

> Dear Parents, when you get this letter, I shall be either missing or dead. Anyway, I shall not be able to communicate with you again … I'll have gone out with what is probably the pick of the Battalion. We are out on a little job which is going to help in anything that may be happening. I'll at any rate have had the satisfaction of dying in the open … I am sorry to have to die so soon. I had hoped to have done great things after the war. Still I am doing what I think to be my duty. Remember me to all.[43]

To conclude this survey of selected raids during the first half of 1916, we return to January and a Canadian raid that were it summarized in only two words would echo the first half of a line from the third act of Goethe's *Egmont*: "Heavenly joy." A Canadian raid a year and two weeks later, and equally restricted to two words, would echo the last two words of Goethe's line that express the antonym or downside of raiding: "Deadly Sorrow."

The joy, more earthly than heavenly, began with Private Ted Brown, a scout in the 29th Canadian Battalion of Brigadier-General H.D.B. Ketchen's 6th Brigade, 2nd Canadian Division, at this time in the line southeast of Kemmel, the "great hill of Flanders," the area of interest being the Spanbroekmolen Salient (see MSD 11). Brown, considered to be one of the

41 *Ibid.*
42 *Ibid.* War Diary, 1st Division, June 1916, clipping dated 27 June, First Army Intelligence Summary No. 532 (26 June) and supplement (29 June), I Corps Intelligence Summary 26 June.
43 Saville, 'Night Attack', p. 26, copy of Clarke's letter originally published in the *Alfreton and Belper Journal,* 7 July 1916; Harvey, *Monuments to Courage,* Volume 1, p. 381.

best scouts in the battalion, spent most of his nights exploring no man's land; perhaps he, like the historian of the 4th Battalion Seaforth Highlanders, Lieutenant-Colonel M.M. Haldane, thought no man's land "pleasant enough … Experienced soldiers knew that during a bombardment the safest place was the middle of No Man's Land. And to get out and move about in the open after the confinement of trenches … to be able to look in other directions than skywards, was an inexpressible relief."[44]

On one of his nightly jaunts Brown spotted what he thought a good opportunity to winkle a prisoner. How this mushroomed into an extravaganza involving officers and men of two battalions and held the brigade commander's rapt attention is a classic example of what happens when an avalanche starts:

> In conversation with Clynne, Brown stated that there were but two or three men in the enemy trenches opposite the 29th, and that he thought he could get into the trench if the sergeant would help him. Clynne agreed but thought it should be a platoon show, with an appropriate covering party. The NCO then asked permission of the OC D Company … but [he] felt it should be a company raid, with a supporting platoon … When Col. Tobin heard of the plan he considered the idea … excellent but wanted it to be a 29th show … next came the brigadier, equally enthusiastic, but of the opinion that the 28th Battalion should raid simultaneously on the left, under the brigade bombing officer as a brigade affair. Fortunately … the divisional Commander was not notified … otherwise [it might] have snowballed into a major BEF operation with the French Army involved as well.[45]

In a post-war unpublished account the scout officer of the 28th, Captain Duncan Macintyre, who was appointed OC Raid, related his version of the planning that then went on, comparing it to that of the La Petite Douve raid in late 1915. During that enterprise artillery had cut the enemy wire, but the Spanbroekmolen raid would not include that since it was designed to be the "first stealth raid." Here Macintyre takes up the story. According to him, early in January he formed a plan to which his CO agreed, but only after considerable explanation and with some reluctance since he would then have to sell the idea to the brigade commander. This proved to be no problem since the Brigadier was all for the raid, so much so that he was not content to leave matters there, instead, according to Macintyre, he expanded the scheme to include the 29th:

> I did not like the arrangement because the success of the operation depended to a large extent on the effect of surprise. Perfect synchronization of the two attacks was essential … but I could see many conditions that might arise to frustrate the efforts of either party and make perfect timing impossible. In spite of my protests the top brass decreed that the raid be a two-party effort, so I had to make the best of it.[46]

44 Military Advisory Board, *Guarding the Channel Ports*, p. 278; H.R.N. Clynne, MC, *Vancouver's 29th* (Vancouver: Tobin's Tigers Association, 1964), p. 8; Haldane, *Fourth Battalion Seaforth Highlanders*, pp. 86-87.

45 Clynne, *Vancouver's 29th*, pp. 8-9.

46 LAC, MG30E241 (Macintyre Papers), 'Men of Valour', Chapter 1, pp. 2-3. This account was never published in book form, but in March 1970 *Legion Magazine* published a four-page article by Macintyre entitled 'The Trench Raiders'" This has recently (2016) been republished in *War Stories*

Brigadier-General Ketchen's amendments to the plan put these concerns to rest. As Ketchen later reported:

> I decided, after careful consideration, to arrange for the carrying out of two Minor Offensive Operations, to be put through simultaneously. After going over my ideas with the Officers Commanding 28th and 29th Battalions, I requested each to select an objective … and to have the necessary recce made and to prepare and submit their suggestions for the … enterprise.

The purposes of the raids, as he defined them, were: prisoners, see if any mining was in progress, ascertain if gas cylinders were in place, securing one if any were found, kill the enemy and destroy his works.[47]

In his General Plan for the raids Ketchen decided to carry out the enterprises at the extreme flanks of the brigade front, meaning the two raids would be about 1,100 yards apart. This put a raiding force on each side of the Spanbroekmolen Salient. The separation, he thought, would ensure that any indentifications obtained would include at least two units and possibly the corps identity. Realizing the danger in such a wide separation, he stressed that the two raids must be simultaneous and he demanded the most careful preparation in order to secure surprise. It would be no exaggeration to say that he kept a very close watch indeed on developments. In August, a Canadian Corps survey of Canadian raids during the first half of 1916 would say this about Spanbroekmolen: the two raids entered enemy trenches 1.5 minutes apart. This is a tribute to the training for the raid.[48] With achieving surprise foremost in his mind, Ketchen also placed certain restrictions on the two COs during the planning. First, wire would be cut by hand, without artillery preparation on either objective. Covering fire (artillery, mortars and machine-guns) would be on call once the raiders entered enemy trenches, initially to box off the

(Kanata: *Legion Canada's Military History Magazine,* 2016), pp. 26-35. Macintyre's book *Canada at Vimy* was published in 1967 in Toronto by Peter Martin Associates. Macintrye was born in 1885. He enlisted in 1914. As a Lieutenant-Colonel in 1917 he was GSO1, 2nd Canadian Division.

47 Ketchen, age 43, assumed command of 6th Canadian Brigade in May 1915. He was a graduate of Sandhurst and had served as a Subaltern with the British Army from 1890-1893. He went to Canada in 1894 where he served with the North-West Mounted Police until 1900. Ketchen commanded a troop with Lord Strathcona's Horse during the South African War. For his service see Carman Miller, *Painting the Map Red: Canada and the South African War 1899-1902* (Canadian War Museum and McGill-Queen's University Press, 1993). Prior to appointment to command 6th Brigade Ketchen had not commanded a battalion. Nicholson, *Canadian Expeditionary Force,* p. 145, notes that after the "St. Eloi fiasco" in April 1916 the GOC the Canadian Corps (Alderson) had written an adverse report on Ketchen, but GOC 2nd Division (Turner) "refused to associate himself" with it, a position that aggravated the very strained relationship between Alderson and Turner that had begun at Second Ypres. Ketchen remained GOC 6th Brigade until April 1918, a period of 35 months. During the middle third of 1918 Sir Arthur Currie replaced three other long-serving brigade commanders, Robert Rennie, James Elmsley and Frederick Hill, thinking that they were worn out. (Rennie GOC 4th Brigade for 34 months, Hill GOC 9th Brigade for 30 months and Elmsley GOC 8th Brigade for 23 months). The only other brigade commander to achieve the 30 month mark was George Tuxford, GOC 3rd Brigade for 32 months. But Ketchen remained in place. See LAC, RG9IIIC1, Volume 3858, Folder 84, File 3, General Report of GOC 6th Canadian Brigade, 3 February 1916.

48 LAC, MG30E61 (Mitchell Papers), Volume 16, 1916-1918, 'Trench Raids. Based Upon Raids Done By Canadian Corps'.

objectives and then concentrate on entry points once the raiders had withdrawn. Second, the parties of scouts and bombers for each raid had to be under selected officers and parties were not to exceed 30 men.[49] Third, if one party failed to cut the wire it was to withdraw quietly so as to allow the other party to carry on. Fourth, to further emphasize time and simultaneous execution Ketchen instituted other control arrangements: first, to ensure the actual time of the two assaults would be simultaneous a "Central Control Point" would open at brigade HQ; and, second, both parties would be allowed a specific time to cut wire, the aim being synchronization as closely as possible. Ketchen decided to limit time in enemy trenches to eight minutes. Corps Intelligence Staff thought time in enemy trenches should depend on the size of the raiding party; for example, a party ranging in size from 20-40 men should count on staying 5-10 minutes at night. Experience said that for the Germans to get organized, move support forward and crank up artillery took 10-15 minutes from the sounding of "alarm," depending on "communications and their state of bewilderment." As it turned out, both raiding parties at Spanbroekmolen spent less than 10 minutes in the enemy trenches.[50]

Most of this direction appeared in the Brigade Operation Order, some aspects being further amplified therein. First, in addition to the desirable characteristics of an objective as later listed in the Corps survey – limited and definite objectives and avoidance whenever possible of points exposed to flanking fire (this making the closest study and recce even more critical) – Ketchen cautioned that careful recce included determining where enemy wire was thinnest. The survey later again referred to Spanbroekmolen (and the earlier La Petite Douve), calling these raids cases where "a strong point need not be avoided because it is strong since a success there would have great moral effect." This echoed point 4 of Second Army's "Lessons Drawn." Second, Ketchen added further direction on timings, co-operation and synchronization and on the role and functions of the "Central Control Point." The "time of assault" he defined as the time at which the assault parties reached the enemy parapet after having completed all preliminary tasks such as wire-cutting. Completion of cutting had to be advised to the "Central Control Point" which would be co-located with advanced brigade HQ. On receipt of reports from both parties, "Control" would order "Proceed" and specify "time of assault." On receipt of this, the raiders would advance at a pace that would put them at the enemy parapet at the "time of assault."[51]

Well before the issue of the Brigade Operation Order the two COs had begun their own battle procedure. On 14 January when the 28th and the 29th returned to the line especially careful recce commenced. Here Captain A.H. Jukes, Staff Captain (Intelligence) of 6th Brigade, provided splendid support, his intelligence files compiled throughout his time with the brigade offering a wealth of knowledge on previous raids as well as descriptions of enemy trenches, their methods of blocking trenches, notes on German grenades and telephones, where enemy soldiers carried their paybooks, description of gas cylinders, reports of enemy machine-gun

49 *Ibid.* According to the August Corps Survey the Canadian norm during the first half of 1916 was 30-40 men per raid, this based on the estimate that "the proportion of men to front attacked seems to be about 25 men to 40 or 50 yards." This norm continued into the second half of 1916. Of 12 raids between 1 July and 18 August the average number of men per raid was 25.

50 *Ibid.* The Brigade Operation Order (No. 47), which at two pages is very brief, could be so since the closest consultation prevailed throughout between Ketchen and his two battalion commanders. MG30E61 (Mitchell Papers), Volume 16, 1916-1918, 'Trench Raids. Based Upon Raids Done By Canadian Corps'.

51 *Ibid.*

emplacements, identifications of units and numerous other matters useful to officers and men about to go raiding. Ketchen's report notes that scouts of both battalions had patrolled very actively over a four-month period and their reports, collected and collated by Jukes and his small staff, had built up a solid picture of enemy habits and activities. Air photos supplied by Corps, specially taken for the purpose of the raids, added to Jukes' files.[52]

After thoroughly assessing the possibilities, the CO of the 28th, Lieutenant-Colonel John Embury, selected as his objective a point on the western edge of the salient where considerable enemy activity had been observed (see MSD 11). Although the point chosen had strong wire it did appear somewhat thinner and a hedge and some dead ground provided good cover and a well-defined approach. Lieutenant-Colonel H.S. Tobin, CO of the 29th, selected an objective on the eastern edge of the salient. His jumping-off line was a hedgerow parallel to the enemy trench. The area chosen resembled a "U" that greatly assisted navigation, the base of the "U" being the easily-identifiable hedgerow. On the left, another hedge led directly to the entry point in the enemy line. On the right another hedgerow, albeit a shorter one, provided a well-defined guide toward the enemy line. Just past it lay a fallen tree, another recognizable point but, as it proved, one that also posed an obstacle.

The objectives settled upon, the COs selected the OCs and the other officers for the raid.[53] As noted earlier, Macintyre would be OC Raid for the 28th. Captain Kenneth Taylor, the acting Brigade Grenade Officer, when asked to participate, the incumbent being absent, agreed to do so. "Glad we were," wrote Macintyre, for Taylor was "a great leader and terrifying warrior in combat." Lieutenant-Colonel Tobin selected Lieutenant Lemuel Wilmot, Battalion Scout Officer, as OC 29th Battalion raid, and to assist him Lieutenants Nigel O'Brian and G.I. Gwynn. Alexander Ross, then 2IC of the 28th Battalion, later described the general feeling about making this first raid: "The First Canadian Division had started the fashion … and it now devolved upon us to show that we were just as keen and clever as were our Elder brethren."[54] Ross also recalled that both battalions selected men "from the hundreds of volunteers," but the report of the CO 29th Battalion says only that the men were "detailed," while the OC 28th Raid (Macintyre) later wrote that he made no call for volunteers; rather he hand-picked the men he wanted, assembled them and told them what was on, adding that those who did not wish to go did not have to do so. However, all 20 bombers and nine scouts were keen on it. Lieutenant Wilmot selected 30 men, all either bombers or scouts.[55]

52 Files such as those compiled by Jukes were becoming common and by their very nature they expanded apace and demanded constant amendment in order to remain current. Later Jukes became BM 6th Brigade.

53 Seeing CO and OC so close together makes this a good place to highlight the difference for the non-military reader. At the time these terms were used interchangeably, COs often referred to as OCs, a practice that appears strange now. The most senior officer in a battalion was the CO, normally a Lieutenant-Colonel. A battalion had only one CO. A lesser rank could be appointed acting CO when necessary. But there were four OCs commanding companies (for example OC A Company) and 16 OCs commanding platoons (for example OC 1 Platoon). In Louis Lipsett's 8th Battalion the rule was "The CO is thy Colonel, thou shalt have no other CO before him." (LAC, MG30E60 (H.H. Matthews Papers), Volume 3, Folder 12, the first commandment of the 8th Battalion's "The Ten Commandments."

54 Major D. G. Scott Calder, *The History of the 28th (Northwest) Battalion, C.E.F. (October 1914–June 1919)* (Regina: privately printed, 1961), p. 47; Macintyre, 'Trench Raiders', p. 29.

55 LAC, RG9IIIC1, Volume 3858, Folder 84, File 3, reports of COs and battalion Operation Orders. Henry Tobin graduated from RMC, Kingston in 1897, thereafter serving in the Klondike and then with Lord Strathcona's Horse in South Africa.

The parties of both battalions moved on 22 January to the Brigade Grenade School where intensive training continued for a week. Based on the latest air photos, spitlocked representations of the enemy trenches were rehearsed upon day and night. Captain Jukes, whose files had been so useful, helped supervise the training. Here, too, dress and equipment for the raid was finalized. Bombers would carry 12 grenades, the grenade carriers 16 in the new issue three-pocket apron, and all other personnel six grenades each. Every man received an electric torch,

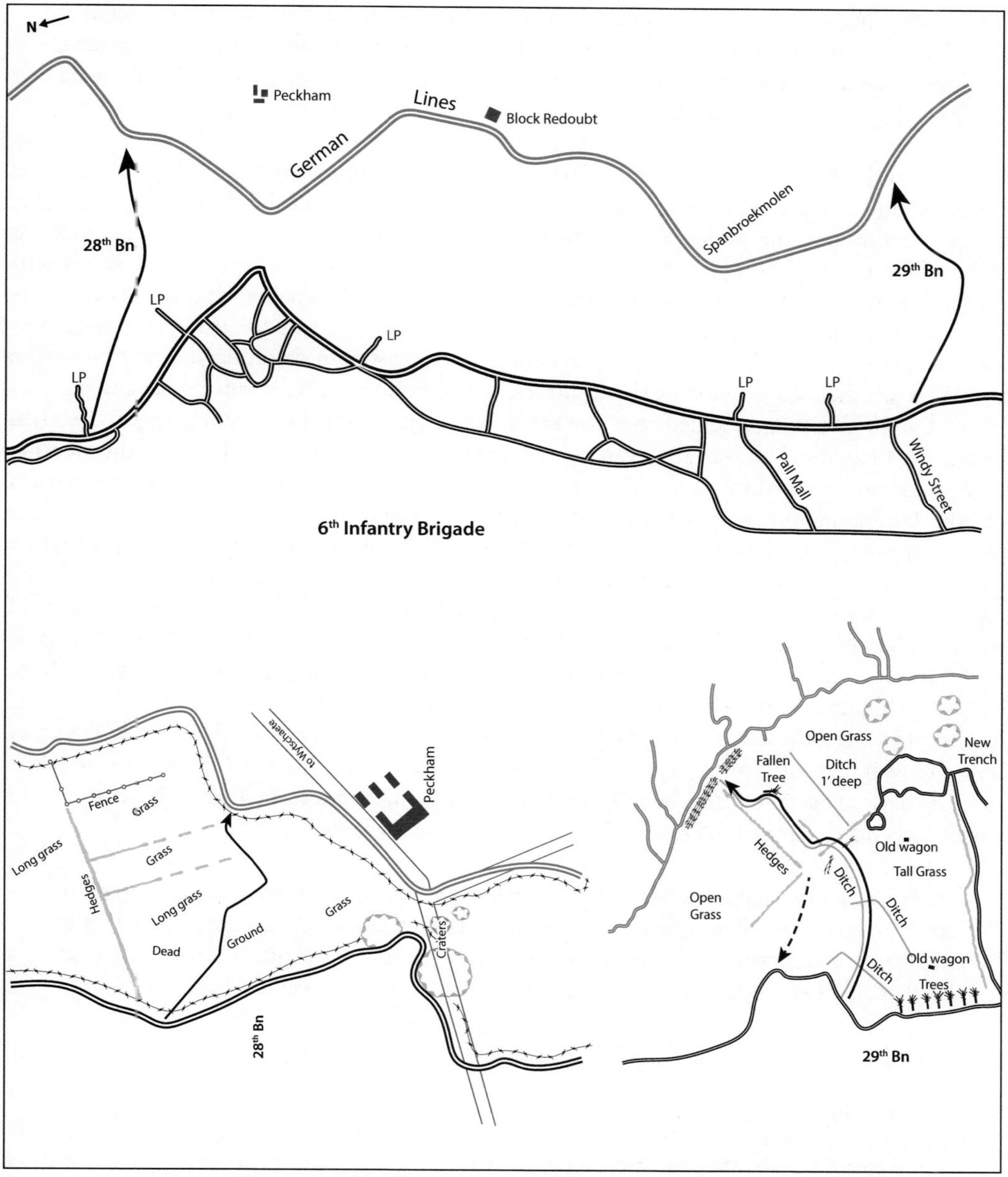

11 Spanbroekmolen Salient Raid, 30/31 January 1916, 6th Canadian Brigade.

bayonet men taping theirs to their rifles. At this time the Ross rifle was still in use by Canadians, a weapon few men liked or had any confidence in. In this instance, the men clearly expressed their assessment of the Ross:

> We asked for the Lee-Enfield as it was shorter, the magazine held ten cartridges and the men had confidence in it ... The General came down and said it had to be the Ross or the raid was off and gave us till the next day to think it over. We thought it over to some purpose for Ken [Captain] Taylor ... rode off to see a friend of his in the Divisional Mounted Troops and made a deal to exchange ... We told the general not to bother anymore getting Lee-Enfields, that we would raid. Later when he saw us drilling with the Enfields he, being a good sport, asked no questions.

Bombers and others carried revolvers. On the night of the 26th all ranks went forward to the trenches and reconnoitred the ground, afterward returning to the Divisional School where training continued, the raiders going repeatedly over the replica whose dimensions matched those of the actual assault plan, their times being recorded, the aim being to ensure synchronization. The recce on the 26th had involved going twice up to the enemy wire, the actual times taken to reach it being recorded. While these movements presented considerable risk, they all went undetected and, as Ketchen later said, greatly assisted in determining the time of the actual assault that was ordered by the Central Control Point after wire-cutting concluded.

On the 28th, having decided that the raids would go on the first suitable night, Ketchen issued his Operation Order. Then during the afternoon of Monday, 30 January, the weather being foggy and everything favourable, he ordered the raids for that night. At 1900 the parties of both battalions moved forward to within a short distance of their start points. Here final preparations such as blacking faces began. Two hours later Ketchen visited the 29th Battalion party to see that all was well, Captain Jukes doing the same at 28th Battalion. At 2130, the night now very dark, the 29th Battalion wire-cutters moved out, followed at 2200 by those of the 28th, Sergeant George Turner, Corporal Stewart Conlin and Private J. Haylock. Their task, said Captain Macintyre, was a tough one, the wire being very thick and about 15 yards deep, but it was thought cutting could be finished by a half-hour past midnight.[56] Two hours later Macintyre moved the assault party out to the hedge that bisected no man's land. Here the party lay up to wait for word from Sergeant Turner and the signallers connected the telephone cables running back to battalion trenches. By 0030, nothing being heard from Turner, Macintyre sent a man forward. On return he reported a run of reasons for the delay:

> More wire had been put out by the enemy during the day, [it] had been materially strengthened: indeed, more than doubled. In addition, a large tree had fallen across the wire [this was mentioned above] and had to be crossed ... thus increasing the risk of being discovered. Further ... a Relief was in progress and consequently very little wire could be cut.

56 *Ibid.*, MG 30E241 (Macintyre Papers), Diary. A few nights before the raid the men who were to do the cutting the night of the raid went out to test if it was possible to cut wire without being detected. They reported that they had cut through two belts of wire and got close to the enemy parapet without him being any the wiser.

Hearing all this, Macintyre wondered why he had ever suggested such a "mad enterprise." However, at 0149 he received the magic words "Wire Cut," which he immediately reported to battalion. Six minutes later, the assault party of the 29th, which had earlier moved into no man's land, also reported wire cut. The Central Control Point then ordered the assault for 0230.[57]

A few minutes later one of the wire-cutters came back and told Macintyre that the Germans were "nervous and there seemed to be a lot of them in the trenches." This reinforced in everyone's mind the absolute necessity of silence and maintaining great caution when moving forward. The main problem for the assault force was the fallen tree, but as Macintyre wrote later "These Huns are a sleepy bunch" and before long a third of the 30 raiders were over the tree. However, with 20 men still the wrong side of the tree, the enemy suddenly woke up. Alexander Ross recalled how "There and then ensued a terrific encounter, no quarter asked or given." There can be no better description of this struggle than Macintyre's, he being in the thick of it:

> Instantly the air was full of flare rockets and the jig was up. There we were all tangled up in the wire, the alarm had been given, men were running along the walks inside, sentries were speeding up their fire so I had to act quick. Turner, Conlin, Captain Taylor and I crawled up the great high parapet and each threw a bomb over. I looked into a trench 10 feet deep. About 30 feet to my left I spotted a sentry [who] took a pot shot at me but his aim was bad. He was yelling 'Alarm' at the top of his voice, but I got him good with my second shot. Conlin was shot through the head and fell at my feet. A Hun was coming at me head on. I shot him through the stomach. Turner, Haylock and I got Conlin out.
>
> After that our casualties kept coming fast … our bombs are deadly … and the Germans were bombing us back and they got a machine-gun in the trench and killed three men in one corner. We got them all out. One of the bombers shot at me point blank, but his safety catch was on. He thought I was a German coming out … Pretty soon I noticed nobody but big Sergeant Cameron at my right and Ken Taylor on my left. I told them to beat it and we all jumped. We had been in six minutes. What happened was that our men spread right and left and cleaned up three or four bays. We had run slam into a "Stand To" and men were thick. We killed between forty and fifty of them. The men were so wild about Conlin that they killed everyone. We got two prisoners and they were both killed getting them out. Well, we ran out of their wire. Taylor was with me and said he was all right, but he had eight wounds and I did not know it. All the way back … the Germans cut loose with everything they had, but I had been figuring this out for two months and knew exactly where they would fire if surprised and carefully kept out of those places, so I got the whole party home without any losses on the way.
>
> It must have looked an awful trench the next morning … Who do you think we had the luck to thrash so well? Nobody but the troops of the Second Reserve Division of the Prussian Guards, just moved in … for a rest after being … on the Russian Front … General Turner said the information we got was invaluable. Everybody up to the Army Commander seemed tickled to death.[58]

57 LAC, RG9IIIC1, Volume 3858, Folder 84, File 3, reports of the COs; MG30E241 (Macintyre Papers), Diary; Macintyre, 'Trench Raiders', p. 31.

58 LAC, MG30E241 (Macintyre Papers), Diary, pp. 111-13. In a note he added later Macintyre wrote that the 64th Regiment, Prussian Guards was in the process of relief by the 22nd Regiment, this

Battalion casualties were one OR killed, two died of wounds and the wounded being Captain Taylor and five ORs. During the short stay in the enemy trenches Taylor killed three Germans with a bayonet and another with his revolver. As always, it was extremely difficult to assess the extent of enemy casualties, but "as the trenches were thick with men … the loss was heavy." By actual count 39 were killed and perhaps as many as 50. While no prisoners reached battalion lines several identifications were secured, thereby achieving one of the main purposes of the raid.[59]

Ketchen's report highlighted the central facts about the raid. First, the enemy was surprised, it being noticeable in 28th Battalion's area that he did not put up an unusual number of flares, no shower of red and/or green, and no "golden rain" for some time, he not seeming to realize what was happening. It was several minutes before his first flare showed and another four minutes before his first artillery fire; in all 14 minutes elapsed before his artillery retaliated. Canadian artillery fired only when the signal had been received that the raiders of both battalions were clear of enemy lines. This fire was effective. Another indication of the surprise came from one of the prisoners who on interrogation revealed that the raid was a surprise since one had been expected the night before, this knowledge gained by listening to Canadian telephone conversations, a fact that served as a warning that more care had to be taken during use of telephones. Second, the report, dated three days after the raid, reflects a more considered and reflective account of enemy resistance:

> Neither party found any organized resistance put in hand to evict them from the trenches … the 28th Battalion found a large number of men in the front trench, some "Standing To," and others coming out of dug-outs wrapped in blankets and in their stocking feet. These latter had no rifles which, however, were seen in racks against the parapet with bayonets fixed. With exception of one sentry none of these men made any great resistance … Retaliation was however very heavy from a machine-gun enfilading the trench and from bombs from the support trench and men in communications trenches. A machine-gun in the main communications trench was responsible for the majority of our casualties.

Third, Ketchen described all arrangements as working out "perfectly," noting especially the "synchronization of these two entirely separate enterprises": the two wire-cutting parties completed their cutting within six minutes of each other and the two assaults were delivered within 60 seconds of each other. The fallen tree (see earlier) delayed the 28th Battalion's assault by roughly a minute. Finally, from the two raids Ketchen drew five deductions that

being why "the trench was doubly manned … this accounts for all the movement the scouts had seen earlier and also for … the trenches being so crowded." Conlin's body was lifted out of the trench, but could not be gotten through the wire and was never recovered.

59 LAC, RG9IIIC1, Volume 3858, Folder 84, File 3, report of CO 28th Battalion. Taylor's conduct in the enemy trenches was reported in Foster and Duthie, *Letters From the Front,* p. 87, and in Roy (ed.), *Journal of Private Fraser,* p. 89. Fraser, a Private in the 31st Canadian Battalion, got a good many things wrong. Macintyre, not Taylor, was OC Raid, nor did the raiders of the 28th stay 25 minutes in enemy trenches. Ketchen's report has the first bombs exploding at that battalion's objective at 0243 and Canadian artillery striking that objective at 0248. This fits with Macintrye's statement that the raiders stayed six minutes. Calder, *28th Battalion,* says the raiders stayed eight minutes. Fraser also thought the enemy unit was Silesian, not Prussian.

he thought had been "clearly established." Three of these were universal: thorough recce and study of enemy habits had good results, as did carefully planned fire support, artillery and mortars, and thorough planning and training. Alexander Ross thought the plans more meticulously "worked out … than later would have been those for a major operation." This was necessary since "the slightest slip or mistake … meant complete failure and the possibility of the loss of the entire party." A fourth deduction – it was possible to cut wire by hand and without artillery which, if employed, "does away with surprise" – applied more to small raids and could not be said to be universal. The last deduction, which was not that at all, it being just comment, thought the enemy demonstrated poor morale during this particular raid. No evidence was offered for this.[60]

Turning now to 29th Battalion during the week before the raid a nightly patrol kept an eye on enemy wire. These patrols were mounted by men not involved in the raid. Lieutenant Wilmot, meanwhile, had organized his raiders into three parties, a Right Party (Lieutenant Gwynn and 10 ORs) and a Left Party (Lieutenant O'Brian and 10 ORs) and his party of signallers, scouts and wire-cutters, 10 ORs in all. He and the scouts would guide the assault parties forward to the enemy parapet either side of a known enemy machine-gun emplacement. Here they would enter the enemy trench, the Right Party marking their entry point with white tape that designated the line of retirement. Of the Left Party, the first two men in, O'Brian and an NCO, landed practically on top of two sentries, who were completely surprised and, no doubt, utterly shocked. O'Brian on entering a dug-out then captured one man and took him to the entry point. At this time (0242) an alarm sounded and the Germans began firing and throwing bombs. The Right Party, meanwhile, on entering the trench discovered a CT immediately opposite their entry point. Four Germans coming down the trench were shot by Gwynne and one of his men. Three prisoners were taken from a dug-out. The enemy nest now buzzing, Wilmot, who had been wounded, ordered retirement. All of his party got out. Enemy dead totalled 11 (body count) and possibly 20 more killed in dug-outs. No gas cylinders were found, nor did any new works appear to be underway.[61]

Captains Macintyre and Taylor both received the DSO, Lieutenants Wilmot and O'Brian the MC. As well, five DCMs were awarded. All participants got 14 days special leave. But what of Private Ted Brown who had spotted the opportunity? Curiously, and ironically, he was not permitted to participate in the raid because he was too young![62]

These two raids are especially well-documented, the 28th battalion particularly so. For both, we have the Operation Orders and fulsome reports by the COs, seven foolscap pages for the 28th and six for the 29th. Ketchen's report totals 11 pages. For the 28th, we also have the diary of Captain Duncan Macintyre, DSO, MC, OC Raid, his entries about the raid beginning on 18 January and culminating in an eight-page entry on 3 February, plus his "The Trench Raiders" and his unpublished "Men of Valour." All of the available accounts indicate that Plate 31 illustrates this raid. A bonus is the "Narrative" of Alexander Ross, who in January 1916 was 2IC of the 28th Battalion. The value of this package is obvious. The reports mentioned – those of Ketchen and Lieutenant-Colonels Embury and Tobin are among the best written and most comprehensive of all the reports reviewed in preparation for this book. This raid reveals

60 *Ibid.*, Ketchen's report, 3 February; Clynne, *Vancouver's 29th*, p. 8; Calder, *28th Battalion*, p. 48.
61 *Ibid.*
62 Clynne, *Vancouver's 29th*, p. 8.

Ketchen as an officer of ordered and precise mind with the ability to craft both an excellent plan and relate it in a splendidly coherent account of a complicated raid, the flow being impeccable: Objects Aimed At, General Plan, Preliminary Arrangements, Selection of Personnel, Preliminary Training, Additional Recce, Covering Fire, Narrative of Events, Action of Enemy, Results, General Conclusions and Deductions. Taken together, all these reports offer a picture of the most thorough and exacting planning, every conceivable eventuality being considered, even the smallest matter being weighed and acted upon. This raid strengthened Ross' conviction that when it came to raiding, the BEF could not be surpassed, and while the enemy did occasionally achieve good results, such was the exception rather than the rule.[63]

This raid and the others in this chapter highlight the necessity to pay close attention to even the smallest details during planning. Once a raiding party reached no man's land there existed no remedy or supply of what had been neglected or forgotten. Planners and raiders alike had always to think to a finish. That principle applies just as well to the last half of 1916, the subject of the next chapter.

63 LAC, RG9IIIC1, Volume 3858, Folder 84, File 3, Ketchen's report; Calder, *28th Battalion*, p. 48.

10

1916 – Second Half

And ye that love fighting shall soon have enough.
Song of the Redcoat

1 July marked the first day of the gigantic struggle on the Somme, a struggle that would last several months. For the three Armies not involved, normal trench warfare, including raiding, continued, these formations being "called upon to wear down the enemy formations opposed to them, and, by initiating such … minor enterprises as their means allowed to prevent the free reinforcement of the Germans on the Somme." The number of minor enterprises – raids – launched by the three Armies would set a record not afterward exceeded. During the 18 weeks from 1 July to mid-November the First, Second and Third Armies raided 310 times, 65 percent being considered successful. German raids during roughly the same period totalled 65 of which a third succeeded.[1] The total of 310 was almost three times the 106 raids made during the months mid-December 1915 to end June 1916.[2]

The most precise figures for Canadian raids during the last half of 1916 are those of the BGGS of the Canadian Corps, P. deB. Radcliffe. Of 69 raids between 1 November 1916 and April 1917, 55 entered German trenches, a success rate of 80 percent. Radcliffe defined success as "entering enemy trenches." For the period 29 October-31 December the Corps made 16 raids of which 11 matched Radcliffe's definition.[3] Figures for the period 1 July to 31 October 1916 are less definitive due to ambiguities in reporting, in the varying definitions of success in use and,

1 Edmonds, *2nd July 1916 to the End of the Battles of the Somme*, pp. 543-44.
2 Edmonds, *Haig's Command to the 1st July*, p. 242. From 19 December 1915 to 30 May 1916 there were 63 British raids of from 10 to 200 men of which 47 were considered successful. Ashworth, *Live and Let Live*, p. 185, says there were 43 British raids in June 1916. Hence, the total of 106. During the December-May time frame the Germans made 33 raids of which 20 succeeded.
3 LAC, RG9IIIC1, Volume 3846, Folder 51, File 7, Lecture Notes, p. 8; Volume 3844, Folder 47, File 4, 'Summary of Raids', 1 November to 8 April. During this period the number of raids per division were: 1st Division, 14; 2nd Division, 12; 3rd Division, 32; and 4th Division, 11. The 16 raids are described in text and located on a map in RG9IIIC3, Volume 4074, Folder 2, File 9, 'Raids Carried Out by the Canadian Corps'. Senior, *Haking*, Table 1 (p. 286), shows four Canadian raids in November and three in December. The Canadian figures per month in RG 9IIIC3 are one in October, four in November and 11 in December.

at times, the differing opinions as to whether a minor enterprise was raid or attack. However, a reasonable figure based on Canadian War Diaries during those months was 23.[4]

This chapter continues the survey of selected raids, British and Canadian, during the last half of 1916. These raids illustrate the increasing sophistication of raiding and how the learning curve stretched ahead, always lessons having to be learned. It must also be said that it is one thing to see what is wrong, but quite another matter to put it right. The path forward, to paraphrase Vitruvius, demanded both talent and instruction, not just one or the other. In this regard, and of raids as a whole, the Subaltern was ever more the key to success. So, too, his training since by late 1916 it had become evident, as Lord Cavan would remark in January 1917, that "victory depends more on the leadership of platoon commanders than on anything else." *SS 143,* in listing the requirements to be attained by training, could be said to have been referring directly to raids when it included offensive spirit, initiative, confidence and discipline.[5]

The Canadian opening play for the period came in Flanders on the night of 30 June 1916. At 0400 that day the GOC 5th Brigade, A. H. Macdonell, visited 22nd and 26th Battalions to arrange raids for that very night. During the afternoon these units issued their Operation Orders, the intention being, in the case of the 26th, to take prisoners or otherwise secure identifications of opposing enemy units. The manual cutting (no artillery for this raid) of enemy wire commenced at 2230, this task taking longer than expected, but at 0130 on Dominion Day the raiders entered the enemy trenches finding them vacant except for three men who immediately withdrew up a CT. The two officers and 20 ORs remained for 10 minutes during which time they found marked equipment that identified two enemy regiments. 22nd Battalion did not do as well, thick and uncut wire preventing entry to the enemy trenches. Neither unit suffered any casualties.[6]

British units were equally quick off the mark. A 2nd Division Operation Order issued on 28 June tasked 6th Brigade to raid and take prisoners and to ascertain the nature of "important works" (a suspected mineshaft) where the enemy appeared to be busy. Artillery began striking immediately at wire and enemy trenches to prepare the way for the three officers and 199 ORs of the raiding party of the 13th Essex. At Zero, set for 0039 on 2 July, artillery and mortars would establish a box barrage around the objective and fire on suspected weapons positions and CTs throughout the raid. By 0030 the entire party occupied a start line some 60 yards from the enemy trench. At Zero the Stokes commenced fire at intense rate (the Stokes could fire 20 bombs per minute) and as their one minute burst ended, the raiders rushed the trenches which were entered with only one casualty being taken enroute. But the trenches being full of Germans a fierce fight began. However, on eventually gaining the upper hand the raiders worked as left, centre and right groups. The first in checking an adjoining sap found it unoccupied while on the right the suspected enemy "work" turned out to be a mine shaft. Meanwhile, the centre party had killed 11 Germans and taken one prisoner. Most of the garrison, however,

4 Sources for the estimate also include LAC, MG30E61 (Mitchell Papers), Volume 16, 'Western Front Orders and Instructions 1916-1918'.

5 Lord Cavan quoted in Col. W.N. Nicholson, *Behind the Lines: An Account of Administrative Staffwork in the British Army 1914-1918* (London: Jonathan Cape, 1939), p. 136; *SS 143,* p. 11.

6 LAC, War Diary, 5th Brigade, 30 June; Operation Order No. 7, Appendix 12 and Operation Order No. 4 (22nd Battalion), Appendix 13; MG30E61 (Mitchell Papers), Volume 16, 'Western Front Orders and Instructions' and 'Typical Trench Raids'" 1 July-20 August 1916.

began withdrawing eastward. During a running fight 12 more prisoners were taken. Captain Arthur Hayward, OC Raid, then ordered withdrawal, the raiders having been a quarter of an hour in the trench. Casualties included Hayward and another officer wounded and 40 ORs wounded, most of these suffered during the return across no man's land, enemy artillery beginning just as the withdrawal began. Mortars, 2-inch and Stokes, played a prominent part in this raid, no doubt in the interests of saving artillery ammunition for operations on the Somme. The divisional historian later pointed out that the raid "reflected considerable credit" on the 13th, a New Army battalion that had not been long with the BEF. All three officers on the raid received the MC.[7]

1 July also featured preparations for a raid by the 2nd Worcestershires of 33rd British Division about 2,000 yards south of Bethune, the 33rd then in the line on both banks of the La Bassee Canal. During the day artillery struck hard at the enemy. When darkness came volunteers laid white tapes across no man's land and up to three gaps in enemy wire. At this time eight Stokes mortars occupied forward firing positions in battalion lines. Through the gaps would pass the raiders of A and C Companies of the 2nd, the first under Lieutenant Arthur Roberts MC and the second under Captain Charles Pigg. At midnight the raiders occupied their start line in no man's land. At 0010 a diversionary mine about 1,000 yards north of the intended objective detonated, this being effective since the enemy, thinking the explosion heralded a raid there, opened fire on that point. British guns then blasted the enemy reserve line and another mine exploded at the real objective. The eight Stokes then unleashed intense fire, the signal for the assault to begin, C Company on the right and A Company on the left, each company organized in two parties, in all four groups of raiders charging on and into the enemy trench, both first and second lines. Blocks were quickly established either side of the entry points and a systematic bombing of dug-outs and mineshafts commenced using large explosive charges the raiders had carried with them, unlike 2nd Division's raiders who seemed not to have taken heavy charges along. The enemy proved stubborn and energetic, his bombing parties repeatedly attacking the blocks at both sides of the British-held trench, but to no avail. Parties not defending the blocks freely surged up and down the trench destroying at will as they went. Lance-Corporal W. Davis, a signaller with the raid, used his telephone to keep the British front line in the picture, thereby enabling the assault to be easily directed. At the 60-minute mark he received the signal to retire which then began. The raiders got home with 11 prisoners. Casualties were two killed and a few wounded, most only slightly.[8]

Three days later 2nd Royal Welsh Fusiliers, also in 33rd Division, launched a strong raid, 200 men in all founded by A and D Companies, Captains John Higgins and Percy Moody respectively. This retaliatory raid, so Robert Graves pronounced it, came about not only because of a "general wish for a return blow" (Captain James Dunn, Battalion MO), but because of a

7 TNA: WO 95/1290: 2nd Division Operation Order 104, 28 June; Wyrall, *Second Division*, pp. 258-59. For characteristics of the Stokes see Radley, *We Lead Others Follow*, Chapter 3, footnote 57, and Hudson, 'Trench Mortars' p. 19. None of the sources describing this raid, which took place in the Carency area (Souchez), relate what the raiders did about the mineshaft, but presumably it was damaged as much as possible.

8 Stacke, *The Worcestershire Regiment*, p. 160. Davis received the DCM for his work. Two of the officers on the Raid, Captain Pigg and Lieutenant Thomas Wilmost (killed in action a month later) received the MC. Roberts had won his MC at Gallipoli in 1915.

marked map taken off a dead German raider showing every dug-out and feature of the objective salient. This caught the attention of the CO, Lieutenant-Colonel W.H. Stanway. Brigade and Division in approving the raid also arranged substantial fire support of which Stanway took full advantage. The gunner contribution was an imaginative scheme:

> A barrage of shrapnel would shift forward and backward from the front line to the supports. The intention was that the Germans should go down into dug-outs at the first bombardment, leaving only sentries in the trench and reappear as soon as the barrage lifted. When it started again they would make another dash for the dug-outs. After this happened two or three times they would be slow in emerging. Then, under cover of a smoke screen, the raid would be made and the barrage put down uninterruptedly on the support and reserve lines to prevent reinforcements coming up.

Captain Dunn recalled how the expenditure of shells ran "into the thousands. The Battalion never had anything remotely approaching the artillery cover given for this raid in any of the battle pieces." The unit War Diary recorded the expenditure as 10,000 shells in 45 minutes.[9]

The plan allowed the raiders two hours in enemy lines, sufficient time to "completely wreck" with explosives any mineshafts, saps, mortar pits and dug-outs and return with prisoners, weapons and equipment, food, correspondence and anything of consequence.[10] The assault would be two-pronged, D and A Companies from the west and northwest respectively, the latter pushing through to the enemy reserve line while the former mopped up and assisted the sappers of 11th Field Company RE in their work of destruction. B Company would provide 20 men to carry bombs and other explosives forward to each of the two assault companies.

By dusk, all preparations being complete, the two companies had only to await Zero. At 2230, 18-pounders, 4.5-inch and 6-inch howitzers opened, their fire supplemented by Stokes and rifle grenades. As this began the raiders left the assembly area, "away like a pack of hounds," as Stanway remembered it. D Company, using craters as cover, got well forward and waited while A Company moved forward, it having to cover about 600 yards to reach the northern side of the salient. Here it laid up awaiting the box barrage set for 2315, at which time both companies made a full out run to the enemy trench. Resistance while "stout," according to Captain Dunn, was soon overcome. "Our fellows fought like demons," read Captain Higginson's report. All went without a hitch, so much so the bomb carriers of B Company joined in the fray and then helped carry off enemy weapons and other equipment. In all, 43 prisoners, some wounded, became British guests, one revealing how the raid caught them during distribution of rations and mail. The prisoners, said Robert Graves, had packs full of "good lootable stuff," they having just returned from leave in Germany.[11] Welsh casualties were one officer and six ORs killed and one officer and 40 ORs wounded, most from A Company. Senior commanders from GHQ down thought the raid a terrific success, GOC 33rd Division (H.J. Landon) remarking how the Royal Welsh Fusiliers "got their own back."

9 Graves, *Goodbye to All That*, pp. 170-71; Dunn, *The War the Infantry Knew*, pp. 218-19, 221; TNA: WO 95/2423: 2nd Royal Welsh Fusiliers, 4-5 July. Stanway left the 2nd to command 6th Cheshires after the raid.

10 *Ibid.*

11 Dunn, *The War the Infantry Knew*, p. 219; Graves, *Goodbye to All That*, p. 170.

The C-in-C expressed his delight with the raid, emphasizing the "great material assistance" of raids to the main operations on the Somme.[12]

By this time diversions had become important and a concern of those directing, planning and executing raids. So 52nd and 58th Battalions of 3rd Canadian Division learned in early July. The background to their raids included the attempts to recover ground lost earlier at Mount Sorrel. On 8 July GOC 1st Canadian Brigade (G.B. Hughes) ordered the 4th Battalion (Lieutenant-Colonel Willian Rae, DSO) to re-establish the Canadian position on Mount Sorrel. Rae planned to consolidate once the line was gained by linking up the regained trench with four saps that extended into no man's land from the present Canadian line. In the event, this attack "failed solely because the wire was not cut. That you cannot capture trenches from a brave and unshaken enemy behind uncut wire is an oft proved lesson." Julian Byng, then GOC the Canadian Corps, thought failure due to insufficient fire support and the difficulty of observation of enemy wire. During this attack 20th British Division and 3rd Canadian Division launched four "strong" raids hoping to divert enemy attention.[13]

3rd Division's diversionary effort made by 52nd and 58th Battalions of Frederick Hill's 9th Brigade on 8/9 July, aimed to obscure the real objective and obtain prisoners. 52nd Battalion's first raiding party, 50 men under Lieutenant Harold Fryer, had as its objective a post the enemy had established in a former Canadian post. Fryer organized his men into six parties: Left and Right Bombing Parties, a Rifle Party of 10 men to advance between and in line with the bombers and two smaller Flank Parties, one at either side of the bombers. Fryer and a small reserve followed the Rifle Party. Uncut wire soon proved a significant obstacle, little damage showing from the artillery fire. Nevertheless, all of the raiders entered the post only to find it vacant and clearly not having been occupied for some time. The second party, 50 men under Lieutenant William Dougall, encountered uncut wire but entered the trench only to find it very thinly populated. Only two prisoners were taken. During the whole of the diversion no enemy retaliation of any kind occurred.[14]

Of 58th Battalion's two raiding parties, the first, 40 men under Lieutenant Charles Howard, entered enemy trenches, but on finding no enemy withdrew. The second party, Lieutenant N.C. Pearse and 28 ORs found its objective heavily manned and covering a large party, 40 or so men, working in an area not usually occupied. Entry not being possible, Pearse ordered bombing and then withdrawal. He was the only casualty during the raid, suffering a slight wound. To what extent these raids diverted the enemy cannot be said. GOC 3rd Division (Louis Lipsett) thought the efforts "satisfactory," while General Byng "hoped" they made the enemy retain troops that might have been used for other operations. Why Pearse had as his objective a trench known to be usually unoccupied is not explained. Second Army's "Lessons Drawn" had included comment (see Chapter 9) on the futility of such raids.

Likewise, a diversionary raid in the Festubert area by a platoon of 17th Sherwood Foresters (117th Brigade, 39th British Division) on 3/4 July seems not to have achieved much, no claim being made that it affected a real raid by 16th Battalion, Rifle Brigade, that same night. This raid featured two companies, one either side of a salient known as the "Pope's Nose," the whole

12 TNA: WO 95/2423: 2nd Royal Welsh Fusiliers, 4-5 July.

13 LAC, Canadian Corps General Staff War Diary, 8-9 July; RG9IIIC1, Volume 3842, Folder 43, File 2, reports by Corps, 1st Division, 1st Brigade and 4th Battalion.

14 LAC, 52nd Battalion War Diary, Operation Order and raid report.

objective being about 350 yards wide. The company assaulting the northern face encountered a fully alert enemy "waiting at the parapet" (there had been a preparatory artillery bombardment) and many casualties were suffered as the leading elements entered the enemy trench. The other company moving against the western face of the salient also met "formidable" opposition. No demolitions could be carried out, nor were any prisoners taken. During the hour the raiders were in the trench heavy close combat fighting raged. All 10 officers on the raid became casualties: three killed, two missing and five wounded, one dying of his wounds, a deplorable loss of expertise and experience of company officers who would in due course have been ready to command companies and even battalions. Unquestionably, these officer losses shook the CO and the brigade commander, while the effects in the companies would have been equally devastating and a shock to morale. While the GOC brought to division's notice Major H.C. Bridges, OC Raid, and Second Lieutenant R. Page, their names do not appear in Warrington's register of MC winners. But then decorations were more likely to accompany success than failure, circumstances notwithstanding.[15]

A week later the 5th Yorkshires (The Green Howards) of 150th Brigade, 50th British Division, occupying a sector about four miles south of Ypres and west of Wytschaete, were preparing to raid an enemy occupied crater on the night of 9/10 July. "Fortunately," wrote the divisional historian, "there exists a full narrative of the raid … the first real narrative … of ops with the diaries for it was about this period that [units]were ordered to send in full reports with sketches and maps (if possible) of any operations." In this case a clear sketch, see MSD 12, is extant.

The OC Raid, Captain Harold Brown, DSO, had 33 men and two other officers to gain identifications and to determine if there was a mineshaft in the crater, a feature of "considerable proportions" (dimensions not known as sketch does not mention scale). To do this Brown organized seven parties. "A" Party (Brown and six men) would enter the CT that led to the crater at point "A" and block that trench at "X". "B" Party (Second Lieutenant Henry Bagge and five ORs) would follow "A" Party, then move to the other CT and block it at point "Y". Two other parties (four men each) would clear the west side and the centre of the crater. "D" Party would remain at the entry point with rope ladders and take charge of prisoners. "E" Party, five men under Second Lieutenant Edwin Saltonstall, would move independently to point "B" to cut wire to provide an alternative withdrawal route. Finally, a four-man covering party would remain in no man's land at a point from which they could cover withdrawal.

The crater was recognized as a tough place to raid. Stealth having been decided upon, no artillery became involved. At 0115 the parties moved out in alphabetical order and soon reached the enemy trench undetected, the gamble to go without artillery having enabled surprise. Brown, at the head of the raiders and peering over the parapet, could see no one in the fire bay at the entry point, but as he moved to enter the trench a sentry who suddenly appeared below him, looked up right into his face and fired from the hip. He missed. Brown did not. "A" and "B" Parties joined Brown in the trench where bombs had begun to fly in both directions. Under attack by two Germans, their bayonets flashing, Brown did for them both before he and his men cleared another bay and proceeded to the crater. Here Brown shot a German officer or NCO and one other man, then took one prisoner. This fellow, not knowing that Brown's pistol was now empty, was then taken to the entry point.

15 TNA: WO 95/2584: 39th Division General Staff, 5 July, and brigade report of 4 July.

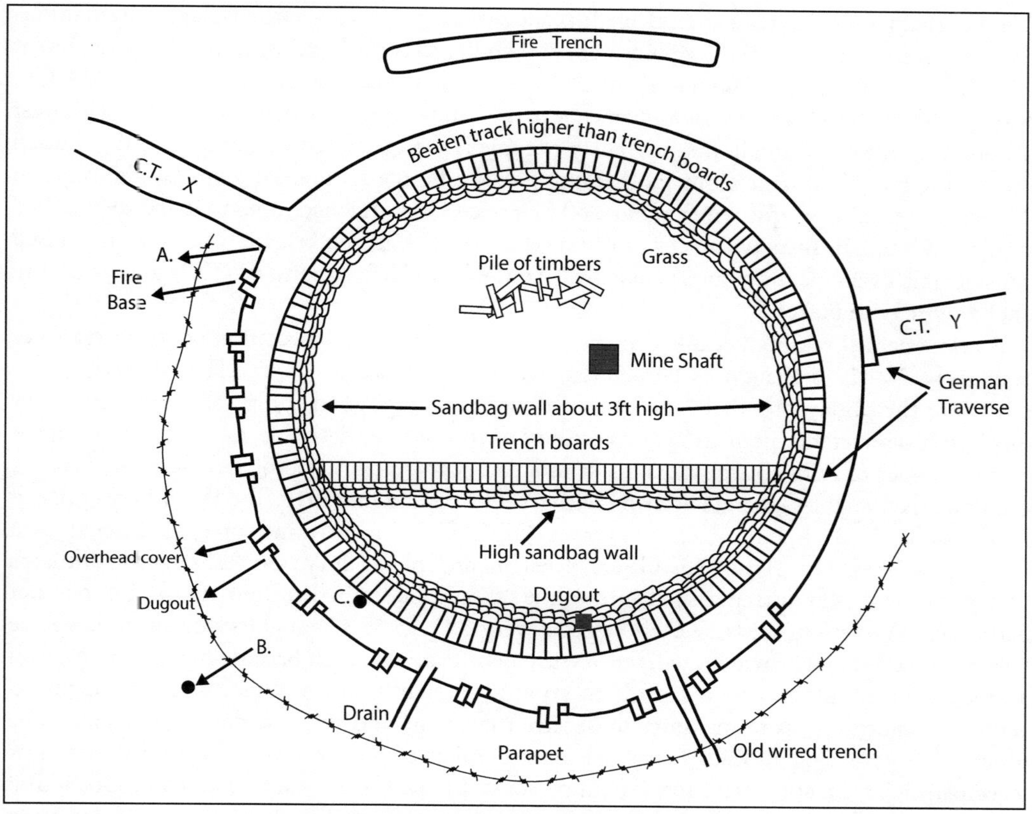

12 Crater Raid, 9/10 July 1916, 5th Yorkshires.

On entering the crater with his party Lieutenant Bagge crossed to point "C" where his party did some bombing. There he realized, there being Germans ahead, that the eastern CT could not be reached, and given the increasing opposition he took his party back to the entry point and then out, they being the last to leave the crater. Saltonstall's party on arriving at "B" discovered the wire there so strengthened that it could not be cut. Hearing the action at point "A", and it being nearly 0145, the time for withdrawal, he, too, returned to the entry point where hearing Brown shout "Get back everyone" he withdrew in company with the other parties.

While Brown's report confirmed the existence of a mineshaft (he could hear pumps working) the raiders could not pinpoint its exact location. The whole crater, had been "admirably consolidated," as he put it, everything in and around it "exceedingly well constructed" with good overhead cover and the crater itself boarded, sandbagged and revetted. Both officers were slightly wounded, as were 11 of the men. One prisoner was taken and 15 killed, Brown accounting for the prisoner and seven of the dead. The enterprise received high praise from every level of command. All three officers received the MC.[16]

16 Wyrall, *Fiftieth Division,* pp. 129-30; TNA: WO 95/2836: 5th Yorkshires, report on raid.

Later that month 7th Canadian Brigade made several small raids, two displaying solid initiative, one overcoming initial disappointment at inability to come to grips. In this instance, uncut wire foiled an officer and 50 men of the RCR. Realizing there was no time to cut it, the OC Raid withdrew to where a German working party had been observed and savaged it with over 40 bombs. Given the small area the party occupied, the concerted bombing probably caused many casualties. That same night another unit pulled off quite an unusual coup. Two officers and 35 men on reaching enemy wire cut out a 60 foot wide slice, attached ropes to it and then pulled it to the Canadian lines where it fit very nicely. "This," said the brigade War Diary, "caused considerable excitement among the enemy." No doubt embarrassment, too. It is always best to anchor wire with pickets![17]

As time passed raiding became expected and, lo and behold, expectation never decreases or goes away. Nor is satisfaction a permanent state of mind. Senior commanders did not generally share the philosophy that "you can have too much of a good thing." Consequently, they displayed no reluctance in making "suggestions" as to what was desirable, or what was an appropriate number of raids. Suggestions most usually became policy, a progression evident in, for example, Lieutenant-General Richard Haking's XI Corps in July 1916. The War Diary of one of his divisions, the 39th, is illustrative of how its GOC, G.J. Cuthbert, interpreted and acted upon Haking's wishes. On 21 July his GSO1, Lieutenant-Colonel F.W. Cosset, issued Cuthbert's policy: each brigade during a spell in the line "should be limited to four [raids], i.e. one per battalion." While four raids by each brigade every 12 days was thought sufficient to keep the enemy unsettled and provide intelligence with identifications, each brigade had also to prepare a scheme for an additional raid ready to go at a moment's notice. This instruction included several "suggestions" as to measures to deceive the enemy and two mandatory measures to be observed in preparing all raids: rehearsals over a replica of the trenches to be raided and prior recce patrols of the approach routes to an objective by the OC of the raid and a proportion of the raiding party. Nine days later Cosset forwarded amended policy that had come down from Corps: "four to six raids, really good ones – one company to a battalion – a month on the Corps front, would be sufficient and of course more if we can get the ammunition. This would mean one raid for each division every fortnight." This policy also cautioned that raids, if they were to succeed, demanded very careful thinking and planning, not forgetting means of subterfuge.[18]

This last comment likely referred, without saying so, to raids on 19 and 20 July in the Festubert area. On the 19th a raid by 1st Cambridgeshires failed due to uncut wire. Those reading the report might well have wondered about the adequacy of recce for the raid and whether the state of enemy wire had been monitored as closely as it should have been. In any case, the raid cost two officers missing. The next night a raid by 1st Hertfordshires resulted in more officer casualties and nothing else. On entering the enemy trench the raiders found it empty and blocks either side of the entry points. Clearly, the enemy was ready for visitors. Two days later one party of raiders of 6th Cheshires took two prisoners, but the other party accomplished nothing. This angered Cuthbert, whose report to XI Corps read "The raid appears … most disappointing … no determined attempt to enter the trench appears to have been made. This want of resolution can hardly be accounted for by the fact … that Captain Smith was wounded. I am making

17 LAC, War Diaries, RCR and 7th Brigade, July, 1916.
18 TNA: WO 95/2564: 39th Division General Staff to brigades 21 and 27 July.

further enquiries."[19] Equally disturbing was the raid on 31 July/1 August by 17th Notts and Derby Regiment of 117th British Brigade, the purpose being prisoners. The plan called for bombardment by heavy and medium trench mortars and 10 minutes intense fire by artillery, a pause and then further bombardment on the raider's entry point. This fire proved effective, the raiders getting to and into the enemy trench which was found so wrecked by the mortar fire that it was more craters than trench. However, the raiders bombed what dug-outs they could find and in doing so took four prisoners, but these were lost when enemy counter-attacks came in, one casualty being the OC Raid who was killed. Shortly afterward the sapper detachment reported a mineshaft that had been wrecked by heavy artillery. At about this time someone ordered the sappers to withdraw, which they obeyed along with some of the infantry. When the originator of this order could not be determined, the infantry returned to the enemy trench and continued bombing. By then retaliation had become very heavy "by all calibres up to 5.9-inch." All the officers became casualties.

R.D.F. Oldman, GOC 117th Brigade, summing up the raid, said "it cannot be claimed that the objects of the raid were entirely achieved." Quite so, no prisoners or identifications being secured, and only one mineshaft located, but the trenches had been entered and the raiders spent 70 minutes ruining what they could. No detailed report on the raid was possible because of the death or serious wounding of every officer. The more than 70 ORs killed, wounded or missing, equated to a casualty rate of 75 percent. Oldman believed such heavy casualties were inevitable at this time since heavy fighting seemed to be the only way to obtain entry to German trenches. This comment cannot be said to have been universal at this time.[20]

Before leaving July behind a raid by a battalion of 2nd Canadian Division on the 29th opposite St. Eloi warrants a close look. This is not because of its strength (only four officers and 18 ORs), or because it was especially difficult or complex, although it did demand (and received) elaborate artillery support and, of necessity, dedicated and efficient communication to control that fire, but because the raid occurred in broad daylight, 0855 to be precise. Clearly, for such an innovation to have any chance of success surprise was essential. It was achieved. Colonel Nicholson thought this raid marked the third stage of raiding, the first having been the more or less "casual" encounters in the dark and the second the "organized" raids also at night.[21]

The genesis for this raid was a signal from 2nd Division HQ on 15 July to 4th Brigade, the parent formation of the 19th Battalion:

> First and Second Divisions have been ordered to carry out wire cutting at selected points today and tomorrow … 4th Brigade south of Canal [Ypres-Comines Canal east of St. Eloi] … Any gaps will be kept open and advantage taken of them for enterprises by patrols and raiding parties.

19 *Ibid.*, War Diaries of units involved. No further mention of Cuthbert's "enquiries" appears in the Cheshire War Diary or in Crookenden, *Cheshire Regiment.* This is not surprising.

20 TNA: WO 95/2587: 17th Notts and Derby Regiment.

21 LAC, War Diary 19th Battalion, July 1916. The artillery fire plan set out precise fire tasks for each of the five supporting batteries. Each was allocated a specific target, either front line trench, a CT or the support trench. One battery would shift fire from CT to support trench on receipt of an order from a gunner officer located in the Canadian front line. One other battery would engage its assigned target twice, the second time on order by that officer. See also Nicholson, *Canadian Expeditionary Force,* p. 136.

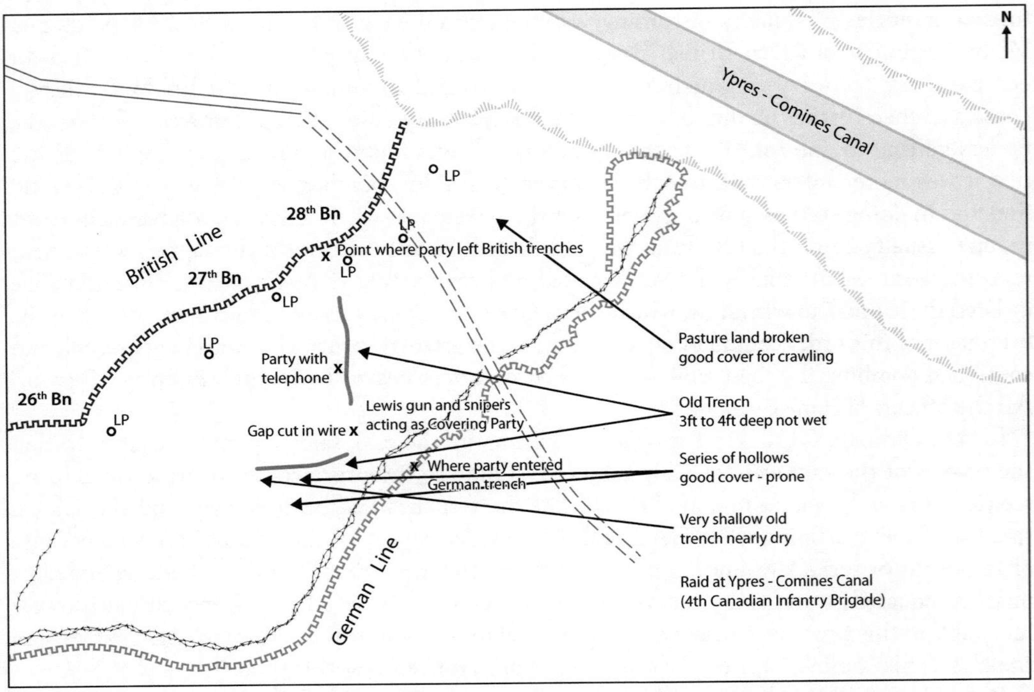

13 Raid at Ypres-Comines Canal, 29 July 1916, 4th Canadian Brigade.

This, more or less, equated to what is today called a "Warning Order." It got the usual pre-raid activity underway: selection of objective and raiding party, forecast as to when, training, planning and recce. The map at MSD 13 shows the immediate area of the raid, scale 1:2500. By the time Lieutenant-Colonel W.R. Turnbull, CO 19th Battalion, issued his Operation Order on 28th July Lieutenants B. Hooper and S.S. Burnham, two of the officers who would participate in the raid, had reconnoitred for the whole of the previous week. That night a gap was made in the enemy wire opposite the selected point of entry. All stood ready for Zero.[22]

At Zero the OC Raid, Captain C.R. Kilmer, led his party forward along an old ditch for 120 yards to a point within 45 yards of the enemy parapet. Here Lieutenant Burnham placed his party to cover the entry point. Lieutenant Hooper and a few men, including a telephonist, would hold the ditch and govern the artillery barrage in concert with the gunner officer in the battalion front line. All being set, Kilmer signalled the assault. Not until the Canadians were in the objective trench did the enemy become aware of the raid. During the next few minutes the raiders killed several defenders, bombed four large dug-outs filled with men and then withdrew, thereby avoiding a large group of counter-attackers coming on the run down a CT. As the withdrawal began, heavy fire fastened on the German front line. Kilmer and one man were wounded during the return home.

22 *Ibid.* 4th Brigade War Diary, order from division; Barton, *Battlefields of the First World War*, p. 133; 19th Battalion Operation Order, 28 July (Appendix 21); recce report for CO 19th Battalion (Appendix 24); Artillery Operation Order 24, 28 July.

This daylight experiment succeeded thanks to surprise, and while this was encouraging, clearly such raids could only be staged at irregular and infrequent intervals. Had it been in greater strength more would likely have been achieved, perhaps by way of prisoners, or the enemy attackers might have been more roughly handled, but the whole idea being experimental it seemed best to limit the raiding party to 20 men and three officers.

Turnbull and his battalion were a cagey lot, it seems, for on 15 August they put on a dummy raid that sought to draw Germans into wasteful firing on their own wire. This scheme began with strong wires being attached to enemy wire at two points. Then for an hour flares were sent up at irregular intervals, rifle grenades were fired, artillery hit enemy trenches very briefly (one minute) and mortars fired a few bombs at selected points. Finally, the enemy wire was shaken very hard. Immediately the enemy bombed his own wire along a front of 600 yards and then began heavy artillery shelling, some of this falling into his own trench. Division praised the "Ingenuity, careful preparation and co-operation. Novelty fooled the enemy. Undoubtedly casualties to enemy by his own guns as well as ours."[23]

August was less active when it came to raiding. 46th British Division then in the Albert area closed the month on a happy note. On the 30th Captain Howard Mander, MC, 6th South Staffords, took his B Company, plus a platoon of A Company and some of the battalion bombers, in all 104 men, rearward for training for a raid to be launched on 2 September, the purpose being to take prisoners. How he organized his force suggests he also made the raid a vehicle to train and/or to test newly arrived or inexperienced Subalterns. Each of his three assault parties, average strength 25 men, had two officers, the reserve assault party one and 14 men. The day of the raid the guns commenced intermittent fire to create gaps in enemy wire, two being confirmed as adequate by officer patrols that night. These were led by Subalterns who were to participate in the raid. At 2200 the raiders were lying up near the enemy wire awaiting Zero at 2235. When the intense artillery barrage ceased they passed through the gaps and entered the enemy line. Mander and the reserve remained at the entry point. Surprise had been achieved. During trench clearing four prisoners were taken and within 15 minutes raiders and prisoners headed for home. Casualties were light, one man dead and five wounded. Two MCs and five MMs were awarded.[24]

That month 4th Canadian Division (less artillery) joined the Canadian Corps on the Somme. After settling in the division launched seven raids, the first on 16/17 August by 12th Brigade and three each by 10th and 11th Brigades. All consisted of four or fewer officers and an average of 37 ORs. Only one of these raids failed to enter the enemy trenches. In this instance the raiders found the enemy fully alert, direct evidence of this being the detonation of two small mines under the raiding party as it moved forward. Five of the seven raids reached enemy trenches without being detected and four of the seven took prisoners. The rest reported enemy resistance as slight and in one instance as very feeble. 54th Battalion made the largest raid, four officers and 58 ORs. All four officers were wounded almost at once and although the raiders reached the objective, some loss of direction and control occurred. One party met with considerable resistance. Overall, though, the raids were judged a "distinct success due to the care with which details were worked out … the ground constantly patrolled

23 LAC, War Diary 19th Battalion, August 1916.
24 Committee of Officers, *Sixth Battalion South Staffordshire Regiment,* pp. 155-59.

and arrangements made to prevent the enemy repairing any of the damage caused by the artillery preparation."[25]

On 15 September, the night before the 4th Canadian Division raids, units of 29th, 36th and 51st British Divisions launched raids.[26] One by the 29th featured three officers and 30 ORs of the 4th Worcesters, the purposes being to take prisoners, inflict loss and shake enemy morale. This venture became rather misadventure beginning with the approach to the objective when driving rain and extreme darkness caused loss of direction. Realizing what had happened the OC Raid attempted to correct the situation, but his order not reaching the Bangalore Party and one of the Blocking Parties, these continued on their errant way. As the main party moved forward it found wire but no gaps. A Bangalore party came forward, but then discovered that the detonators were with the missing parties, meaning the enemy wire could not be gapped. Meanwhile, the missing parties did gain entry, threw a few bombs and then withdrew. Enroute home they surprised an enemy patrol and took prisoners, but the encounter caused the party to again lose direction. Eventually it approached wire protecting another unit, which opened fire on the raiders, resulting in one prisoner killed, another wounded and not found and one escaped, leaving only one bird in hand.[27]

That same night two units of 36th (Ulster) Division also launched raids. One by three officers and 41 ORs of 9th Royal Irish Rifles took one prisoner and suffered no casualties; quick and remarkably easy, a raid distinguished, said Cyril Falls, by "neatness." The second raid by a similarly sized party of the 11th Royal Inniskilling Fusiliers met significant enemy strength and resistance. At 2045 the raiders formed up unobserved in a large shell crater 25 yards from the enemy lines. At Zero the party rushed the enemy trench. Having entered it the two parties that went to the right forced the enemy to retreat, but on being held up by the box barrage they turned on their pursuers and fought it out until most of the enemy were killed. One prisoner was taken. The parties that went to the left reached the second line but could not penetrate further. Enemy dead were estimated at 30. Own casualties totalled four missing and nine wounded.[28]

51st (Highland) Division launched four raids on the night of the 15th. Two failed due to faulty Bangalore detonators. The third raid (7th Black Watch) saw the raiders enter the enemy trench, but there they encountered only two Germans, one being captured, but then killed by German artillery fire during the withdrawal. The divisional historian, describing the fourth raid, called it an "unqualified success" despite some difficulty with Bangalores, going on to say

> As raiding became so marked a feature of the war, space forbids that each raid should be described in detail. General Harper [GOC] was therefore asked to select the raid he

25 LAC, 10th Brigade War Diary, September 1916, Operation Order 7; 4th Division War Diary, 'Report on Raids Carried Out'.

26 Ninth (Scottish) Division specifically 8th Black Watch and 5th Cameronians, also raided to get prisoners, but of more interest was that this raid was also specifically ordered as a vehicle to test the Stokes mortars. This being so, and because of what was learned about them, this raid and this reason to raid were examined in Chapter 5.

27 TNA: WO 95/2281: 29th Division General Staff, Appendices 3(a) and 3 (b).

28 Falls, *36th (Ulster) Division,* pp. 74-75; TNA: WO 95/2503: 109th Brigade, Operation Order 72; TNA: WO 95/2510: 11th Inniskillings, Appendix 2, report on raid; TNA: WO 95/2503: 9th Royal Irish Rifles, raid report.

considered most suitable for description, and he has chosen that carried out by the 6th Seaforth Highlanders.

The historian responded with six pages. What follows must be shorter, but brevity does not come at the expense of the significant aspects of the raid.

The target, a prominent salient, which at its apex had running at right angles the Armentieres-Lille Railway, featured at its base a well-defined trench. The plan called for raiders to enter the salient close to its base, one party from each side. At each of the entry points a blocking party would remain to prevent any enemy ingress while the two assault parties drove the enemy toward the apex, thereby, it was hoped, "doing" for the entire enemy garrison. Sticking to what had been the norm for some time, the raiders, two officers and 32 men divided into two equal parties, then trained behind the front on a replica, this to give them a good sense of direction at the entry points and of the distances they must cover. Each party would cut enemy wire with Bangalores, a decision that made these devices of central importance, success being dependent upon adequate gapping of enemy wire. No artillery or mortar support would be involved until Zero when a barrage would begin, every gun, howitzer and mortar having a target allocated so that the enemy would be prevented from withdrawing or counter-attacking, or moving about in their trench within about 800 yards of the point of entry. Every trench junction and mortar position on a front of 1,500 yards was also a target. Nor was security neglected, the plan and the Brigade Operation Order both stressing that watches were not to be checked by telephone; rather, a brigade staff officer would come to the unit the day of the raid with the correct time.[29]

Recce had determined the extent (depth) of enemy wire to be such that the Bangalores would have to be 75 feet long. The two officers, Lieutenant James Sainter, OC No. 1 Assault Party, and Lieutenant Donald Jenkins, OC No. 2 Assault Party, each accompanied by two men, would place the Bangalores 30 minutes prior to Zero, At the time, according to the divisional historian, many thought Bangalores 75 feet long, the brigade commander's idea, overly "ambitious," it being hard to see how even several shorter sections, each still an awkward burden, could be man-handled across no man's land and placed under the wire. As it turned out, the GOC was half-right, but then so were those who questioned his idea.

At 2005 Jenkins and his party with the Bangalore left the trench and headed for the enemy wire. This party, and Sainter's, had to place the Bangalores, metal tubes three inches in diameter, under the wire, which lay 70 yards short of the enemy trench, and this under the glare of a constant blaze of enemy lights overhead. Moreover, the placing had to be done quietly, a daunting challenge since the nose of the device had to be forced through undergrowth, the bottom strand of wire would scrape against it and its forward movement would cease if it hit one of the posts that secured the wire. Should this happen the tube had then to be withdrawn and pushed in again on a new course. Despite all this, Jenkins placed his Bangalore in good time without being detected and then returned to unit trenches where he picked up his party and moved it forward to within 30 yards of the Bangalore to await Zero.

For Lieutenant Sainter, OC No. 1 Party, luck was less of a lady. While crossing no man's land his Bangalore separated several times at several joints. However, the German overhead lights

29 Bewsher, *Fifty First (Highland) Division*, pp. 90-91, 95-96; TNA: WO 95/2871 and 2877: 153rd Brigade raid 15 September.

worked to raider advantage in that they provided light sufficient to effect the necessary repairs. On reaching the placement point the Bangalore was inserted, but becoming stuck had to be removed and inserted at another point. All then went well, but the delay meant Sainter could not return to bring his party forward which left him hoping that his 2IC would realize the situation and bring it forward. His party joined him two minutes before Zero.

At Zero both Bangalores fired almost simultaneously, followed immediately by the barrage whose results exceeded expectations preventing not only any enemy reinforcements getting forward, but also any attempt by the garrison to escape rearward. Nor did any enemy fire from the flanks occur. Once in the trench, bayonets flashing and bombs flying, the raiders killed many Germans and took one prisoner. Enemy inability to interfere in any way enabled the salient to be completely cleared. It helped that the enemy had been surprised. Sainter's party suffered no casualties. When on return to Seaforth trenches Jenkins learned that his party had five wounded, three seriously, he and one man returned to the enemy trench three times, rescuing one man each time, this in itself evidence of enemy confusion and inability to respond. All in all, it is clear why General Harper thought this raid warranted description in the divisional history.[30]

A raid that went even more smoothly involved five officers and 136 men of A Company of the 8th Sherwood Foresters (46th British Division) and a sapper detachment on 21/22 September against a sap and its junction with a main trench. The purposes of this raid were securing prisoners and causing damage. Ten days before the raid Captain Bernard Vann, MC, had his men training hard on a spitlocked replica of the enemy sap and trench. Eight parties were necessary because of the multiple tasks assigned the raiders, four of these being assault parties: one to deal with the sap; a left and a right party to clear the main trench, block CTs, bomb dug-outs and obtain identifications; and a small party (one officer and four men) to find and deal with a possible company HQ in a small dead-end trench near the sap. Two other parties were to provide flank protection and a third would remain at the entry point to keep it open for the withdrawal and to manage wounded and any prisoners. One other party would escort the sappers of the Bangalore party who would carry two short Bangalores for blowing up the suspected company HQ if it was found and two 24 foot Bangalores for use if the wire was not adequately cut. The detailed description of the duties and actions of these parties contained in his raid orders show that Vann knew what he was about. His plan was the product of a good deal of thought and foresight and careful writing. Its execution was flawless.[31]

30 TNA: WO 75/2867: 6th Seaforths, Report on Raid; Bewsher, *Fifty First (Highland) Division*, pp. 94-95. Both officers received the MC and four men the MM.

31 TNA: WO 95/2695: 8th Sherwood Foresters, report on raid and brigade Operation Order 81, 20 September; Warrington, *MC Register*, p. 693; Harvey, *Monuments to Courage*, Volume Two, p. 171. Lieutenant-Colonel The Rev. Bernard Vann, VC, MC and Bar, was an ordained clergyman when he enlisted in 1914. He won his first MC in 1915, the Bar for this raid and the VC at Canal du Nord in 1918. While Lieutenant-Colonel and CO 6th Sherwood Foresters he led his unit across St. Quentin Canal on 29 September. He was shot and killed by a sniper a few days later. Charles Beresford, *The Christian Soldier: The Life of Lieutenant-Colonel The Rev.Bernard William Vann V.C., M.C. and Bar, Croix de Guerre avec palme,* (Solihull: Helion & Company Limited, 2017), p. 194, says the raiders were in six, not eight parties. Vann's hasty report (he left for a Senior Officers' Course at Aldershot four days later) lists the eight parties described here. Vann married Doris Beck of Peterborough,

On the 21st 2-inch mortars put 600 bombs down on the wire. Patrols after dark found adequate gaps. At 2320 the raiders entered no man's land and moved to a point 25 yards short of the wire. At 0015 intense artillery fire (18-pounders and 4.5-inch howitzers) struck the enemy, this ceasing three minutes later at which point the raiders rushed and entered enemy lines. The sap assault party, after checking its entire length, found no enemy and only one dug-out which they destroyed. The left and right assault parties, meanwhile, had bombed outward, established blocks where necessary and consolidated control of the length of trench occupied. No company HQ was found. Of the six prisoners five survived the trek under German artillery fire to British lines. Captain Vann, reporting on his own movement during the time spent in the German trench, described how he, two buglers and his runner had gone "along the parapet … to help [the right party] along the trench." Regarding this tactic Vann said

> a raid can be materially assisted if provision is made for strong parapet parties to clear the trenches. Officers or determined NCOs can push the bombing parties along the trench much more quickly in this way as they [the parties] are sometimes inclined to hold back. To do this it is necessary for enemy wire to be cut all along the parapet. This was done.

While such a tactic was not confined to this battalion or raid, such a course of action presupposed that enemy flanking fire, or fire from their support line, had not the observation and lines of fire necessary to hit raiders on the parapet, or that such fire had been suppressed. This could not always be the case. After 10 minutes or so the enemy sent up white lights which on bursting turned red, clearly the signal for artillery fire on their own trench, a portion of which was temporarily British. This arrived quickly. Vann had ordered the withdrawal and soon all were home safe. Casualties for the raid totalled eight men wounded. For the raid Vann received a Bar to his MC. One of the five Subalterns also received the MC.[32]

The British were also making daylight raids. In early October a sapper officer watched an officer and 20 men of a battalion race across no man's land "like a pack of hounds," then disappear into enemy trenches and then return at a "dog trot" with the officer in the rear, "all safe, thank God." This observer, Second Lieutenant H.L. Morton, DSO, 255 Tunnelling Company RE,

> met them as they came out of the communication trench, panting after run … fit and happy but disappointed at not getting a prisoner, which meant six days leave … It is considered an absolute insult to Boche so I'm told for a party of men in broad daylight to raid a trench and return unscathed, and has hardly ever been attempted before. He is evidently a bit peeved as he has been strafing us ever since.[33]

Later that month (23 October), according to the historian of the Cameronians (Scottish Rifles), having concluded that after each night raid the odds in favour of success declined, the unit then had "the idea of a short sharp raid in full daylight, when the enemy might be … less

Ontario in December 1916. Her uncle, Robert Dennistoun, served with the Fort Garry Horse and later commanded the 53rd Canadian Battalion.

32 TNA: WO 95/2695: 8th Sherwood Foresters.

33 Barton, *Battlefields of the First World War*, p. 242.

alert or asleep." It would be February before the 9th Battalion could try it on for size. The RCR had had experience of the declining odds in August during a night raid by one officer and 16 ORs. This raid began with a Bangalore creating a good gap in the wire and the raiders moving through it quickly, but on leaving the gap the whole party, less the officer, was killed or wounded. Lieutenant Lawrence Bole, OC Raid, assisted by another officer from the covering party, worked under fire for 45 minutes clearing the casualties, all being evacuated, an example of bravery and determination that earned Bole the MC. "It would appear," said the War Diary, that the enemy were awaiting our attack as the enemy trench was very strongly held and they were waiting for us as immediately our men were wiped out."[34]

In mid-October the 6th South Staffords (46th British Division) received orders that Captain Howard Mander, whose raid on 2 September had been so successful (see earlier), should do an encore, he having "become famous for his luck." Encores can be very tricky. Undaunted, Mander set about improving on his earlier effort, two "novelties" being limiting gaps in enemy wire to only one and having the raiders "get there by their own momentum and morale; that is to say … no cover or comfort from a preliminary or accompanying artillery bombardment." He organized the raiders in much the same way as before, three assault parties averaging 20 men and two officers each, a small reserve and a Lewis gun group of two teams under an officer, this grouping being an innovation. Of the officers, five had been on the 2 September raid.[35]

On raid day the gunners put down on enemy wire what would seem to the defenders as nothing more than the usual day's "hate." Immediately after dark Second Lieutenant James Sheddon (he had not been on the September raid) took out a patrol to check on the wire and any gaps and to lay tapes from the gap back to the start point.[36] Just short of the wire Sheddon spotted a work party busy replacing wire destroyed by the artillery. On being advised of this the CO thought to abandon the raid, but Mander convinced him to let it proceed. More artillery fire removed the working party, but failed to make a gap. A Bangalore being the only resort one accompanied the raiders when the party left friendly trenches at 2145 and advanced to the enemy wire. Here Sheddon and his patrol detonated the Bangalore, the ongoing artillery fire hiding the detonation. When the firing ceased the raiders were up and through the gap and into the enemy trench. Left and right the assault parties hurried clearing as they went. By and by six prisoners were bagged. By 2245 all raiders, plus prisoners and a mass of documents found in a dug-out, were back in friendly trenches. While the enterprise had not gone exactly according to plan determination brought success. Mander had done it again![37]

Such was not the case for a raid by 35th British Division on the night of 25 October. Extant documents (Operation Orders, fire plan, timetable of messages during the raid and the brigade (105th) report and that of the CO of the unit (15th Sherwood Foresters) indicate the raid was thoroughly planned and organized and the four Subalterns and 124 ORs had spent several days rehearsing. But only one prisoner was put in the bag. Casualties included one officer killed, one

34 LAC, War Diary, The RCR, 18 August 1916.

35 Committee of Officers, *Sixth South Staffordshire Regiment*, pp. 159-60.

36 Sheddon, who would receive the MC for his night's work, is shown in Warrington as "Shedden." As a Major he would receive a DSO in 1918. Committee of Officers, *Sixth South Staffordshire Regiment*, p. 154, lists him as one of 13 Scottish Subalterns who joined the South Staffords in July 1916. Five of these were on the September raid. Sheddon and two others were on the October raid.

37 *Ibid.*, pp. 161-63.

seriously wounded and two missing, one found later by a patrol so seriously wounded he had to be carried in. OR casualties included two dead, 18 wounded and eight missing.

The brigade report indicates what went wrong: "there was considerable loss of direction, and only one of the [three] bombing parties got in [the enemy trench]." The battalion report related specifics about navigation. Despite the guide tapes laid by scouts, and their efforts to keep the raiders within the tapes, the right and centre parties had strayed. The OC of the centre party had gone missing at this time and his party played no further part in events. One of the three clearing parties also went astray. The officer with this party, Lieutenant Dunn, OC Raid, eventually got the party to the enemy trenches where hand to hand fighting ensued, but as the party had no bombs left it had to withdraw. The two clearing parties that actually entered the trench took the only prisoner. No search could be made for a suspected mineshaft or for documents. The CO concluded that the failure of the two bombing parties to reach the point of entry "interfered considerably with the whole raid and was partly responsible for the failure." He went on to say that the raiders met little resistance and no counter-attack was made, nor did the enemy retaliate to any appreciable degree. In the absence, then, of any other contributory factors, the "partly" should read "solely" responsible. In getting lost, despite tapes and guides, the two bombing parties wrecked the raid.[38]

On 3 October Second Army had issued a "Summary of Raids" for September. During that month Second Army had made 20, three of these by 38th (Welsh) Division, its GOC being C.G. Blackader and the Corps Commander being Lieutenant-General Sir A.G. Hunter-Weston, widely known as "Hunter-Bunter." The considerable correspondence in the division's War Diary for September shows a "push" on for raids, the pressure filtering down from Second Army through VIII Corps and the 38th to brigades for action.[39]

What this "push" sought (and achieved) was a firmer divisional grip on raiding, one that entailed divisional control measures including a more precise system of reporting on raids while delegating responsibility of "hands-on" supervision to brigades. During the first half of September a series of orders and instructions on raids flowed from divisional HQs. One of the first ordered that brigades on going into divisional reserve must order each battalion to form a raiding party of one or two officers and 30 or so ORs. On return to the line each party had to reconnoitre an assigned area to the extent necessary to work out a definite plan to be finalized on going into reserve. The parties would then return to the reserve area to train. On 14 September

38 Davson, *35th Division*, pp. 69-70; TNA: WO 95/2488: 105th Brigade and 15th Sherwood Foresters, reports on raid.

39 Hunter-Weston, 50 years old and a brigade commander in 1914, took command of VIII Corps in May 1915. He came away from Gallipoli with a poor reputation, the consensus being that he seemed to care little for his men: one comment attributed to him was "Casualties, what do I care about casualties." Many considered him excessively optimistic and overly ambitious, routinely asking too much of his men. To some, his speciality appeared to be frontal attacks without artillery support in broad daylight. The GOC 52nd Division (Granville Egerton) had been outraged by Hunter-Weston's comment to the BM of the shattered 156th Brigade that he had been glad to have the opportunity of "blooding the pups." Sir Ian Hamilton rebuked him severely when during a visit to the 52nd he persisted in introducing each unit as "the remains of the ---th Battalion." See Robert Rhodes James, *Gallipoli* (London: Papermac, 1989), pp. 210, 231, and Richard van Emden and Stephen Chambers, *Gallipoli: The Dardanelles Disaster in Soldiers' Words and Photographs* (London: Bloomsbury, 2015), pp. 208, 216. Also useful is Peter Hart, *Gallipoli* (Oxford: Oxford University Press, 2011).

114th Brigade, for example, having ordered its battalions to form a party, assigned each party the section of the front it would raid, suggested two suitable objectives, ordered recce of these (all members of the raiding party to participate) and demanded the submission of a scheme as soon as recce was "sufficiently advanced."

Three days later brigade HQ expressed the "Brigadier's desire" for full information on enemy wire, machine-guns, approach routes and trenches, all to be marked on a map to be submitted to brigade with a "definite scheme" by 22 September. Each of 38th Division's brigades would have issued similar instructions. A further instruction ordered that the reports on raids to be submitted by the commanders of raiding companies must include the times when raiders entered no man's land, when they entered enemy trenches, when they withdrew and when all had returned, plus the number and identification of prisoners, number of captured and destroyed machine-guns and casualties, enemy and friendly. On return from a raid the two most senior officers of the raiding party had to ascertain the facts needed for a "good" report and then proceed to a given point where they would be met and taken to divisional HQ to have their report taken down. They would remain at HQ for the night. Firmer control, indeed.

On the 18th, division passed an order from Hunter-Weston that each battalion must be ready to raid at 12 hours notice and their "detailed schemes" must reach divisional HQs the next day. Not surprisingly, the brigade commander of 114th Brigade, as an example, demanded the schemes by "8 p.m. tonight, 18th instant," the scheme to be per an attached "Headings and Sequence" proforma: object of raid, strength, distribution of parties, general scheme, duties and composition of parties, report centres, signal and order for withdrawal and line of direction. Later that day brigade directed that 13th and 15th Welsh would raid. The BM advised the CO 14th Welsh that since he had had no opportunity for recce and therefore could not raid, he must choose an objective (one of two suggested by brigade), form a raiding party and submit his plan for a raid "when in a position to do so." CO 13th Welsh submitted a "provisional" plan that day advising that he, too, had had no time for recce and would submit a revised scheme in two or three days. This the GOC accepted, but ordered the raid to be made on an objective he had chosen. The tenor, objective and impact of these instructions hardly needs elaboration.

On the 17th the 13th Royal Welsh Fusiliers, a unit of 113th Brigade, had submitted a detailed plan for a raid to be conducted on the night 19/20 September. This raid was postponed because on the 20th VIII Corps advised divisions that Second Army wanted each division to raid in a strength of 40-100 men. As it turned out, the raid by the 13th would be one of only two raids by 38th Division in September.[40] It actually occurred on the night 28/29 September in a strength of four officers and 73 men. The raiders entered enemy lines unhindered in any way, but met very few enemy, only two being killed for certain. Their papers were given to the OC Raid who subsequently went missing, no trace of him being found.[41]

On 5 November 38th Division issued an instruction describing what it considered the lessons drawn from raids during September and October. First, officers commanding raids seemed inclined to take more men than needed, even though "there was no advantage to have more

40 TNA: WO 95/2555: 38th Division General Staff. The other raid was by 11th South Wales Borderers (115th Brigade) on 29/30 September. The only mention of this raid in the War Diary of the 11th (TNA: WO 95/2562) is 'Raid carried out. 7 Casualties'. Second Army 'Summary of Raids' called it 'Satisfactory as far as can be ascertained. No prisoners'.

41 *Ibid.*

than one man per every five yards of trenches to be entered." Second, placing men at the point of entry to check raiders as they withdrew was "useless in the dark and in the confusion." No alternative was suggested. Finally, more thought had to be given to the means of keeping direction in no man's land. Not everyone would have agreed with the first two, which do not seem to have been well considered by the writer of the instruction.[42]

British raids during the first half of November had mixed results. On the 3rd, two officers and 32 ORs of 17th West Yorkshires (35th Division) used Bangalores to gap wire and were in and out of enemy trenches quickly, having secured identifications; all in all a typical "smack and back," not spectacular, but productive. Conversely, raiders of 9th Royal Scots, 51st (Highland) Division, barely reached enemy wire before volleys of bombs fell upon them, plus heavy rifle and machine-gun fire, the enemy clearly alert. The raiders withdrew.[43]

A week later 11th Inniskillings of 36th (Ulster) Division launched a stronger raid (four officers and 184 ORs), a raid described by Cyril Falls as the most important of the series of raids by that division between 15 September and 16 November. The objective, the Spanbroekmolen Salient, was hit on a frontage of 200 yards, the ratio men to yards being rather more than 38th Division's suggestion above. One of the reasons for the choice of target was the opposition, a newly arrived Saxon division that was considered "less formidable" that its predecessor.[44] As for intentions, securing identifications was top priority, but Corps also wanted to know if any gas cylinders had been emplaced and if a tunnel reported by patrols actually existed. Four equally sized parties were formed, one by each rifle company, the composite being designated G Company. It then went rearward for intensive day and night training. Each party consisted of a Bangalore sub-party, including an NCO of 150 Field Company RE, and an assault sub-party of bayonet men, bombers, bomb carriers, searchers and a Lewis gun team. Zero was set for 2200 on 16 November. After dark the four parties left home trenches at intervals, each led by Bangalore men, and moved to a pre-selected position near the enemy parapet. All four were in position undetected just before Zero at which time the four Bangalores would be detonated and the raiders would rush the trench.

Once in the trench one group of No. 1 Party went up a CT until it reached the enemy line where the junction was found to be blocked. There the group inserted its own block. A second group that had moved to the right along the main trench reached its objective where it inserted a block. Only four enemy were encountered. A third group moving along a trench off the main had a spirited fight with a counter-attack party, but defeated it after expending 600 bombs. No. 2 Party on being detected before entering the trench suffered casualties and the destruction of its Bangalore, but the OC of this party was able to link up with No. 1 Party and from there worked its way to its objective, blowing up several dug-outs and capturing one Saxon. No. 3 Party encountered strong opposition – "plenty of fighting" – on entering the enemy trench and then beat off a counter-attack after which it bombed a mineshaft. One prisoner, a miner, being a high interest catch, was immediately escorted to brigade HQ. No. 4 Party, on being discovered early on, did not enter enemy lines. None of the parties found

42 *Ibid.*, 38th Division, 'Further Lessons'.

43 Davson, *35th Division*, p. 71; TNA: WO 95/2887: 51st (Highland) Division General Staff, Appendix A, raid orders and report.

44 Falls. *36th (Ulster) Division*, pp. 74-75.

any gas cylinders.[45] Cyril Falls summed it up nicely: the Saxons were dealt with in "terrible" fashion, "terror-stricken [they] deserted their front line on a wide front, and the Inniskillings had their pleasure with it for half an hour, looting, wrecking everything they could not carry and blowing up all the dug-outs. Three prisoners were taken."[46]

The next night, 17 November, the 14 Welsh (38th Division), launched a raid almost as strong, seven officers and 158 ORs. In most respects this raid was similar to that of the Inniskillings except that two wounded and 18 unwounded prisoners were taken together with a machine-gun and other equipment. An intelligence party with the raiders had time to enter and search a dozen dug-outs and came up with a large haul of documents. The very pleased brigade commander attributed success to a careful artillery fire plan and good counter-battery work that accounted for the lack of any enemy gun retaliation. The haul of prisoners made this raid really stand out.[47]

Three nights later seven officers and 77 men of 5th West Riding Regiment of 49th British Division raided enemy lines. No prisoners or identification were secured and only nine enemy killed. Enemy response was slow and slight. The brigade report lists a few lessons, one well-known and always a consideration while another may have been new to this division. First, "surprise was undoubtedly the essence" in this instance, this being so it was recommended that whenever possible wire should be cut by Bangalores. Second, the raid proved "undoubtedly" the advantage of some officers remaining outside the trench where they could better direct and control the situation. In this instance the OC Raid, the OC Bangalore Party and one other officer remained with the parapet party at the point of entry. Another aspect of this important matter of control centres around the question of to what extent officers should be directing as opposed to fighting. This is examined in Chapter 16.[48]

In the fall of 1916 the four divisions of the Canadian Corps occupied the Vimy Ridge sector of the British front. Initially this period, as described by Colonel Nicholson, allowed time for "recuperation, training and strengthening," but as October drew to a close the pattern became one of "limited hostilities" featuring numerous patrols and raids. Identification of enemy units became a pressing requirement as 1917 approached and thoughts turned to the spring campaign. Most raids prior to Christmas consisted of 40 or so officers and men with fire support limited at times due to shortages of ammunition.[49]

One such raid by 2CMR (3rd Division) – two officers and 47 ORs – came on 30 November after several patrols reconnoitred approaches to the objective and ascertained the state of enemy wire. Initially trench mortars tried to break it up in two or three places, but limited ammunition meant they could do no better than create one partial gap, a situation that left planners seeking some other means of getting over the wire. When additional recce located one spot where wire appeared to be thinner, and the inner wire low and only about eight feet in depth, mats to lay over it seemed to be the solution. At 2330 Lieutenants Charles Douglas (OC Raid) and Frank Heather led the raiding party out to a position close to the wire where the men awaited the end

45 TNA: WO 95/2510: 36th Division General Staff, Appendix 1, 109th Brigade Operation Order, Appendix 2 and Appendix 3, Inniskilling report.
46 Falls, *36th (Ulster) Division,* p. 76. One OR was killed, one was missing and 14 wounded. Saxon dead were 23 by actual count and probably twice as many more in the dug-outs.
47 TNA: WO 95/2557: 114th Brigade reports.
48 TNA: WO 95/2766 and 2800: 49th Division General Staff, 147th Brigade report.
49 Nicholson, *Canadian Expeditionary Force,* p. 233; LAC, War Diary, 2 CMR.

of a brief preparatory barrage. As it ended, they threw the mats on the wire and were quickly over and in the trench. Hard fighting ensued, but working left and right the raiders reached their assigned objectives on a frontage of 150 yards and commenced bombing dug-outs. One prisoner was taken. Raider casualties were very light. The whole of the raid went according to plan, testament to its soundness. Both officers received the MC. Two DCMs and five MMs were awarded.[50]

Three days later 26th Battalion (2nd Division) launched a punitive raid, the sole purpose being to "maintain supremacy," identifications having been already secured, against a 175 yard-wide section of the enemy trench east of Souchez. The OC Raid, Captain Gerald Anglin, assisted by Lieutenant R. MacKay, organized the raiders into four parties: a storming party of nine ORs under the OC, a wire-cutting party of four men, two flank guards of five men each and a rear party of nine under Mackay which would remain at a shell crater about 30 yards short of the enemy trench. From there a telephone line would be laid back to battalion trenches and to battalion HQ. When the wire-cutters went forward that night they found a good gap had been cut by trench mortars. On signal the stormers moved through it and deployed in a line along the enemy trench with the flankers either side. On "ready" they threw grenades and then all quickly entered the trench, clearing it and bombing several dug-outs. After 10 minutes Anglin gave the withdrawl signal followed 30 seconds later by a box barrage on the objective. Surprise had been achieved, the enemy unaware until the raiders were on their parapet. Own casualties were light, one man wounded and one killed and Captain Anglin, who received the MC for the night's work, slightly wounded. The raid was another of the flawless smaller raids.[51]

On the 27th, 8th Canadian Battalion (1st Division), Lieutenant-Colonel John Prower, DSO, commanding, raided in a strength of four officers and 120 men. Both the brigade commander (F.O.W. Loomis) and the division commander (Arthur Currie) displayed great interest in this raid and could afford to do so since the attack on Vimy Ridge lay some months away. Zero for the raid, 2150, coincided with the detonation of two mines under the German lines, one opposite 2nd Brigade and the other opposite 3rd Brigade. Also at Zero, 7th Battalion would lay down rifle, machine-gun and rifle grenade fire on the enemy hoping to deceive him as to the 8th Battalion's objective.[52] 2nd Brigade's Operation Order defined the primary purpose of the raid as securing identifications. The raid, as it turned out, proved notable in three respects: first, a lapse in judgement by one of the officers; second, the expression by Canadian formation commanders of conflicting opinions about raids and third, the unusual use (in Canadian raids) of numerous light signals.

50 Johnston *2nd Canadian Mounted Rifles,* pp. 37, 41; LAC, 2CMR War Diary, November 1916, Appendix D. In February 1917 Johnston experimented with a sawed-off Lee Enfield (11 inches were removed) to see if this would increase the range when firing rifle grenades. The experiment doubled the range to about 180 yards, which more or less matched the German rifle grenades. After approval by Corps, numbers of rifles were cut in many battalions, these remaining in service until the Mills rifle grenades were improved. The sawed-off rifles proved very useful during raids.

51 MacGowan et al, *26th New Brunswick,* pp. 146-47; LAC, 26th Battalion War Diary, Appendix 12 (Operation Order).

52 LAC, RG9IIIC1, Volume 3858, Folder 84, File 4. 14th Battalion consolidated the resulting crater on 3rd Brigade's front. Loomis' involvement in the planning of the raid by 8th Battalion is discussed in Chapter 6.

Prower's plan called for two entry points, each to be used by two officers and 60 ORs. At 2020 scouts advised Prower that wire at the two points had been satisfactorily cut. The two assault parties then moved forward to their jumping-off points. At Zero up went the mines and the raiders made their way into enemy trenches where the parties moved right and left down the trench, bombing as they went, including the two saps as per the battalion Operation Order. However, the right party, having encountered no enemy and finding only one dilapidated dug-out, did not remain long in the trench. The left party were fired on before reaching the trench, the officer being wounded, but some of the men did enter it. Meanwhile, the officer having encountered a formidable tangle of wire and thinking the raid impossible "his wounds [probably] interfered with his judgement gave the order to retire … [another officer] attempted to rally the party, as it was evident to him that the raid should be attempted, unfortunately, retirement had commenced and the operation had to be abandoned." No identifications were secured. Casualties included the officer and 10 men wounded and two killed.[53]

In a memorandum covering the brigade report submitted to Corps HQ Currie stated "I am satisfied with the plan, the preliminary preparations and the artillery co-operation. The results were disappointing." Regarding results, Loomis mentioned only that the enemy seemed to be holding the front with just posts. He made no mention of prior recce that might have picked this up; raiding empty trenches hardly seemed worthwhile where the purpose was identifications. As for the lapse in judgement, Loomis referred to the large proportion of new officers who "have not been tried out on this kind of work … Prower, therefore, was obliged to use some officers who have not had experience." This remark seems a statement of the obvious. His other comments reveal the differences in opinion. In his view, he considered "surprise raids of this nature have now had their day, and are not sound or advisable." First, he thought the novelty of such raids gone since the enemy was now alert and had adopted counter-measures. Second, having been warned by preliminary activity such as patrols, hand cutting wire or cutting it by artillery, the enemy now on the "qui vive," would either vacate and lay a trap or take other precautions. Finally, the "work requires special knowledge, faculties, and experience, and men of this class are very valuable and difficult to replace." Currie said only that for a raid to be a complete success surprise was necessary: "if that is lacking or unobtainable, it would be better to make a regular attack." Byng, for his part, did not think the day of surprise raids over, although "they had become more difficult and as difficulties increased so was fire support to the point where with block barrage, counter-battery and wire-cutting, surprise was lost." He concluded with a paragraph relating to a large raid (over 400 men) that will be mentioned again later in this chapter:

> Real surprise raids without artillery fire are still possible but their results are not far reaching, but I am now endeavouring to organize raids which really come under the head of minor operations, that is, the capture and occupation of the enemy's system for some hours by a force of at least half a battalion or more. With this strength the destruction to the trenches would be more complete and full utility gained of the artillery and trench mortar

53 LAC, RG9IIIC3, Volume 4065, Folder 2, File 16, 8th Battalion Operation Order A, 25 November; MG30E100 (Currie Papers), Volume 35, File 176, 'Report on Raid by 2nd Brigade', 27 November. This raid report is one of only a few in Currie's papers probably because of the differing opinions on this raid.

> co-operation. In addition, being organized on the lines of an attack, it will accustom young soldiers to the necessary formations and tactical requirements of the offensive.[54]

Loomis concluded his report with one other matter "deserving of notice," the rocket signals employed by the raiders on a scale not seen before during Canadian raids. These, he wrote, worked perfectly and "could be utilized to a much greater extent for communications from the Front Line to rear than at present."[55]

The first British raid in December began on the 1st. It had been in preparation since 30 October, about two weeks after the 23rd Division joined Second Army in the Ypres Salient. On the 30th the GOC 70th Brigade ordered battalions to prepare and submit a plan for a raid. These then went to division, two being approved and final plans and Operation Orders demanded by 10 November. The units whose plans received approval were the 11th Sherwood Foresters and the 8th York and Lancasters, their detailed schemes and orders reaching brigade HQ on the 8th. The GOC, H. Gordon, then had the two COs, plus the OCs of the raids, in on the 11th to review all preparations. Zero would be between 29 November and 3 December.[56]

Lieutenant-Colonel H. Watson, CO 11th Sherwood Foresters, ordered his raiding party, two officers and 40 ORs, to seize the occupants of a post situated at the junction of a sap and the main enemy trench. The OC Raid organized his men into seven parties, so many being necessary as a CT would have to be blocked, as well as the main trench at two places, plus the junction of the main with a secondary trench. Another party would have to clear the sap right to its head. In addition, there would be a parapet reserve party and a small reserve to remain outside the enemy trench. The artillery would supply a box barrage and cover for the withdrawal. On the 28th Zero was set for 0030 on 2 December. All went well until the heavy artillery began firing two minutes early, this shooting catching the assault party moving forward, wounding both officers and several men, and rousing the Germans who began intense bombing of the party. The raiders had no option but to withdraw.[57]

The raiding party of the 8th York and Lancasters, Lieutenant-Colonel S.L. Whatford, also sought prisoners. Gordon made only one change to Whatford's plan. Instead of sappers accompanying the party and detonating the Bangalore in the enemy wire the raiders would do so. Before the raid the infantry Bangalore party would train on the Bangalores at 102nd Field Company RE. The artillery would only be involved during the withdrawal and then only on request. MSD 14 shows the objective, which was the length of trench between Sap A and Sap B, and the start point for the raid opposite the two knolls marked "E" where the raiders would

54 LAC, MG30E100 (Currie Papers), Volume 35, File 176, Currie to Canadian Corps HQ, 2 December; Loomis to 1st Division, 29 November; RG9IIIC1, Volume 3858, Folder 84, File 4, Byng to First Army, 7 December. The tactical changes Byng refers to have been discussed earlier in this book.

55 LAC, MG30E100 (Currie Papers), Volume 35, File 176, Loomis to 1st Division. Signals used during this raid to indicate timings were these: at Zero one rocket showing coloured stars and gold and silver rain; at Zero plus 15 one red rocket followed by four more at one minute intervals, the last at Zero plus 19; and Zero plus 20 one green rocket (all parties to return). When all parties had returned another rocket like the one at Zero went up.

56 All of the pertinent documents, which form a complete package are at TNA: WO 95/2185: 70th Brigade, 23rd Division.

57 *Ibid.*, 11th Battalion plan and report.

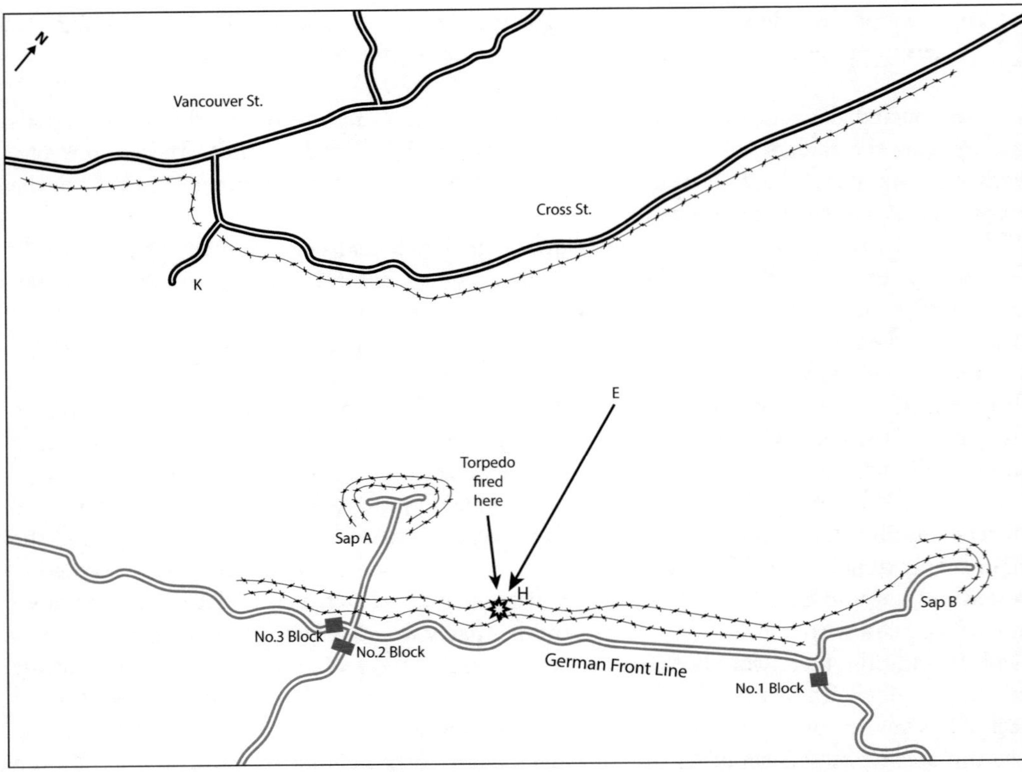

14 Raid near Ypres, 2 December 1916, 8th York and Lancasters.

await detonation of the Bangalore at "H". At "K" a Lewis gun would be placed to cover the right flank and a Vickers machine-gun (not shown) to the left of Sap "B" to provide flank cover.

Lieutenant H.A. Spalding, OC Raid, organized the men into four parties. First, a Bangalore Party of one officer and four men that would move first to "E" and then on to "H" to place the Bangalore and at Zero fire it. Second, the Assault Party (30 ORs) divided into Right and Left Parties of equal strength and composition (bombers and bayonet men) and each under an NCO. Spalding and four men would remain at the entry point, Finally, a Bomb Carrying Party of 13 ORs would cross to the entry point once it was secure, supply bombs as required and place ladders for the withdrawal. The Left Party would operate in two groups, the first moving along to Sap "B," which it would clear, followed by the second group which would block the main trench at "No. 1". The Right Party, similarly organized, would clear Sap "A" and establish blocks at "No. 2" and "No. 3".

At 0015 the Bangalore Party, followed by the remainder, moved to "E." The ground described as being very frosty caused some delay for the Bangalore party, the Bangalore not being placed until nearly 0400. Enemy fire caused more delay when it wounded two men plus the OC Raid. At 0450 when the enemy attempted to pull the Bangalore through the wire it had to be fired. It created a satisfactory gap. Immediately the raiders were up, through it and into the trench, bombing outward left and right and executing all their assigned tasks. However, counter-attack came swiftly, left and right "the enemy in fairly large numbers running along the top of their trench throwing bombs to catch our men in the trenches and bomb them from above ... to meet this Spalding ordered his men to the top of the trench and a bombing fight ensured." It soon became apparent that the counter-attack could not be contained and to avoid encirclement Spalding ordered withdrawal, which came off well, only one man being killed on the way home. Spalding received the MC for the night's work. Given what had to be done – clear a trench, clear two saps and install three blocks – the size of the raiding party hardly seems adequate and it is not surprising that no prisoners were taken, this being the purpose of the raid. It might have turned out better had the assault party been stronger and had each of the two assault parties been under an officer. Moreover, as the CO of the 8th wrote, "The enemy seemed to be expecting something and was fairly well on the alert."[58]

The next night 32nd Royal Fusiliers made the first raid ever by the 41st British Division which had arrived in France in May 1916. It struck at German lines northwest of Wytschaete (south of St. Eloi), the raiding party consisting of four officers and 90 ORs under Major E.T. Cooper. The raiders, organized in two parties, left and right, the former under 19 year old Second Lieutenant Wilfred Trotter and the latter under Second Lieutenant Arthur Davis, trained intensively from 16 November onward at the Divisional Trench Warfare School. During this time both Subalterns went out on several patrols thereby becoming thoroughly familiar and comfortable with the ground.[59]

Cooper's plan was simple. Zero would be at 0035 on 3 December. Forty-five minutes prior to that the raiders would enter no man's land in file, the left party (Trotter) leading would move to a previously marked point about half-way across no man's land. There he would halt, the two parties wheeling on him, left and right, would crawl for 50 yards and halt, an extended line about 100 yards long having been so formed. This manoeuvre complete, the OC (Cooper) at the centre of the line and behind it would be so advised. White tapes would then be laid forward, one on each flank and one at the centre point of the extended line. Signallers with each party would provide telephone communications from the enemy trench rearward to the OC Raid. No preliminary artillery fire would occur, fire only opening at Zero. Beginning on 16 November the artillery, trench mortars and Stokes would shoot daily at wire along the enemy front.[60]

On Saturday, 2 December, the raiders made final preparations. Here Trotter in his letters and notes made a number of interesting observations. Divisional staff, he wrote, had ordered the issue of flare pistols to several men. Trotter ordered these discarded as soon as possible. A man hit with a flare would be set on fire. The probable consequences for any man captured with any flares or a flare pistol on his person would surely be drastic and savage retribution. At 2100 three London buses took the raiders forward to Battalion HQ just behind Vierstraat where rum was issued and the CO spoke briefly to them. On arrival at the departure point in the front trench the raiders had a half-hour wait. Here Trotter faced what he called the "first hitch," the discovery that the NCO in charge of the stretcher bearers was drunk, as were his men. Trotter

58 Sandilands, *23rd Division,* pp. 128-29; TNA: WO 95/2185: 70th Brigade, details of raid and report of CO 8th Battalion.

59 TNA: WO 95/2644: 32nd Royal Fusiliers, reports of Lieutenant-Colonel R.E. Key, Major E.T. Cooper and Second Lieutenant W.P. Trotter. Laurence Hopkinson, 'Night Raid on the Hollandscheschuur Salient', *Stand To!,* 102 (January 2015), pp. 3-6.

60 *Ibid.*

then forced each man to make himself sick and "when they sobered up a trifle" he warned them that if there was any further trouble he would immediately shoot them.[61]

At midnight the raiders entered no man's land where they shook out into assault formation. With Zero came the barrage and off they went, the two assault parties through the wire without much difficulty and into the enemy trench where all went well, three prisoners being taken and several dug-outs blown sky high. Withdrawal came at the end of 15 minutes. Casualties included four killed, six wounded and one missing. For the raid Trotter received the first of his two MCs.[62]

British and Canadian divisions conducted fewer raids in December, most not particularly striking. Often weather forced cancellations, frost and snow making for poor visibility and going. Moreover, as Haig wrote "throughout December our energies were principally directed to the improvement of our own trenches and of roads and communications."[63] A table in one source shows only three Canadian raids in December, but archival records say 11. Of these, three failed to enter enemy trenches due either to Bangalore failure or enemy alertness. Two others were very minor, eight men in one case and nine in another. The former (a stealth raid) did, however, take two prisoners and suffered no casualties.[64]

Another Canadian raid in December came on the night 5/6 December when two officers and 44 ORs of the 52nd Battalion (9th Brigade) were said to have had a "very successful" night, but to what extent this raid achieved its purpose, to distract the enemy from another unit that was to raid on a large scale, is hard to say. Lieutenant Burdett Harmon, OC of the deception raid, organized the raiders into five parties. The two largest, each of one officer and 12 men, would clear the enemy trench left and right for a set distance and then block each end. Two smaller parties would block a CT and a secondary trench where these joined the main trench. The last party would remain at the entry point. Bangalores would cut the wire, artillery being involved after that only to put down a box barrage.

At 0355 the raiding parties, led by the Bangalore Party left the trench. At 0515 the 40-foot Bangalore blew a gap five feet wide in the enemy wire and immediately the raiders hurried forward into the enemy trench. Five enemy dead were found and four prisoners taken within 10 minutes. Only two made it to the Canadian trenches, one Prussian and one Saxon who under interrogation stated that such a mix was common, a statement of much interest to intelligence. Common sentiment considered Saxons less aggressive and generally easier to deal with. Likely the mixing, if it was general, aimed to instill Prussian virtues in the Saxons. Casualties were slight. Lieutenants Harmon and George Millican received the MC. For the raid the battalion received additional slots for leave and some of the raiders left soon afterward.[65]

61 Hopkinson, 'Night Raid', p. 5. Some men refused rum before a raid thinking it best to be fully in possession of one's wits. For full discussion of the merits and otherwise of rum see Radley, *Get Tough, Stay Tough,* pp. 225-29.

62 TNA: WO 95/2644: 32nd Royal Fusiliers, Key's report; Warrington, *MC Register,* p. 685. Trotter received the second MC in March 1918.

63 Boraston, *Haig's Despatches,* p. 66.

64 Senior, *Haking,* Table 1, p. 286; LAC, RG9IIIC3, Volume 4074, Folder 2, File 9, 'Raids Carried Out by the Canadian Corps 29 October-31 December 1916'.

65 LAC, 52nd Battalion War Diary, December 1916, Appendix 2, Operation Order 81 and raid reports by CO and OC Raid.

Three days later 3rd Canadian Battalion of 1st Division staged what the battalion historian called the "principal event of the month."[66] On 7th December GOC 1st Division (Arthur Currie) had proposed the raid to Corps HQ, describing it as a surprise raid and therefore no "previous artillery preparation." In order to deceive the enemy as to the exact location of the raid a diversion by artillery fire would occur on 4th Battalion's front to the right of the 3rd Battalion. The objective of the raid had been chosen partly on the results of the interrogation of a prisoner some days earlier in which the soldier revealed that usually one-third of each company manned the front line. Zero was set for 0400 on 9 December.

Major Henry Cooper, OC Raid, organized his raiders, four Subalterns and 80 ORs, into three assault parties, left, centre and right, each a mix of bayonet men, bombers and bomb carriers as well as a party of mat carriers, who would place their mats on the wire, and ladder carriers, necessary since the enemy trench was known to be 10 or more feet deep. The plan called for the raiders to enter the enemy trench at three places along a 100 yard front, the three parties working left and right to clear the stretch and link up. Blocks would be required at either end and at three trench junctions. Cooper's orders clearly defined action to be taken should any one of the parties fail to enter the trench.

Shortly before 0400 Zero was postponed for 35 minutes because of the bright moon. At 0435 Cooper led the raiders out, guides heading each party, the move so carefully done that all parties were before long within 20 yards of the enemy wire and still undetected. In the final charge to the trench the right and left parties crossed the wire on the mats. At its entry point the right party experienced a rain of bombs, which partially disorganized it, but it rallied and entered the trench, clearing it after hard fighting. The left party entered the trench so quickly it captured a machine-gun which had time to fire only a few rounds. The centre party on encountering thick wire that could not be surmounted then spread out along the wire and began throwing bombs into the heavily manned trench. Major Cooper signalled withdrawal after eight minutes and the barrage to cover it began, it being thickened by the fire of 1st Canadian Trench Mortar Battery. The withdrawal proved uneventful, German artillery being very slow to respond.

Friendly casualties consisted of three officers wounded, two ORs killed and 29 wounded, three dying of wounds. Major Cooper and Lieutenants Harry Coombs and Arthur McCormick received the MC. Two DCMs were also won. Raid results included a machine-gun and the death of 20 Germans (counted). It was thought that in the blowing up with gun cotton of 14 dug-outs more Germans were probably killed. The CO of the 3rd, Lieutenant-Colonel J. Rogers, believed morale had soared because of the raid; as he pointed out, 70 percent of the raiders had never been in action before and they now knew they were superior to the enemy.

Currie, as he usually did after any action, listed a number of lessons to be drawn from the raid. First, it had demonstrated that success attends a well-considered and well-rehearsed plan carried out with determination. Second, constant patrolling was always necessary; if the enemy had done so then the raid might not have succeeded. Third, wire had to be properly placed. In placing theirs so close to their parapet the enemy had made it possible for the centre party to bomb their trench from the far side of the wire. Moreover, the lack of depth of most of the wire had made mats a viable way of crossing it. Finally, he raised the question of artillery support, this drawing comment by First Army and Corps HQ:

66 Goodspeed, *Battle Royal*, p. 168.

> Co-operation with artillery is not yet close enough with us, although those batteries … covering the raiding party were all that could be desired. It took too long – six minutes – to commence the "diversion." The German Artillery were too slow in getting into action. This division has never had its trenches raided. If they were, I wonder how much time would elapse before our artillery opened up.

The report of the acting GOC 1st Brigade, Lieutenant-Colonel W. Hodgson, had this to say about the artillery diversion: the fire was late because the signal to open "had to pass through two Artillery Brigades and then to the batteries." In his Operation Order Lieutenant-Colonel C.H. Sykes, commanding the Left Group Lahore Divisional Artillery, noted that the signal to open had to be sent from the front line to the Liaison Officer at 3rd Battalion HQ and then transmitted to the Artillery Brigade that would fire on 4th Battalion's front. First Army commented thus: "The Army Commander presumes that the complaint as regards the tardy artillery support is being attended to. The means of communication referred to in Lieutenant-Colonel Hodgson's report seems to have been too complicated and bound to lead to delay." Corps HQ, in forwarding these remarks to 1st Division, also "presumed" that all necessary action had been taken.[67]

A raid by an officer and 40 ORs of 58th Canadian Battalion (3rd Division) took place the following night. Of the two raiding parties, the left one on arriving at what it supposed was the enemy trench discovered that it was not that at all. It was a rudimentary trench that had been prepared in front of the actual main trench. This party found the main trench heavily wired along the parapet and at both ends, the wire having also been brought across over the protective dummy trench to connect with the wire in front of it. What they faced was a canopy of wire. The party had no way to enter the trenches, but it did bomb the main trench for 10 minutes hoping to prevent the opposing enemy from moving along the trench to assist in defending against the other assault party. Lieutenant Allen Shortt, OC Raid and commanding the other party, got it into the enemy trench where it commenced clearing. Some of the party moved into a CT and continued up it to the enemy second line, but could not penetrate any further and had to block the CT. Some of the party had been blowing up dug-outs with gun cotton as they cleared. No signal for withdrawal could be made since those who were to sound it were missing, but the party did exit through their entry point when the time to stay had elapsed by the watch. While the raid was deemed successful, no prisoners had been taken, Lieutenant Shortt and two ORs were missing and nine others were wounded. The CO concluded that had the raid not surprised the enemy the raiders would probably have suffered very severely.[68]

The largest Canadian raid to this point in the war came on 20 December when 12 officers and 410 ORs of 1CMR (3rd Division), supported by Division and Corps Artillery firing on enemy front and second lines, raided at 1518 on a frontage of 400 yards on the southern flank of Vimy Ridge near the corps right boundary (see MSD 15). It was, in fact, the second Canadian daylight raid, the first having been the small raid by 19th Battalion on 29 July near St. Eloi (see earlier in this chapter). The 1CMR operation included a diversionary raid by four officers and 70 ORs of 4CMR. This December raid drew the attention of the BEF, copies of General Byng's

67 LAC, MG30E100 (Currie Papers), Volume 35, File 176. All of the documents referred to in description of this raid are in this file.

68 LAC, War Diary 58th Battalion, Operation Order 34 and report of CO.

post-raid "Notes" being distributed to all BEF Armies, then down to divisions and brigades and, no doubt, to battalions as well.[69] The first paragraph of his "Notes" outlines his concept for the raid (see also his comments in the indented material that precedes footnote 54):

> The raid was done on an idea I had for some time, viz:- that the 40 or 50 man raid was a thing of the past and what was wanted now was … to go in by daylight and stay until dark damaging everything … as far back as the Support Line. So we set to work and trained the 1st C.M.R. practically as a battalion for it. About 350 all ranks in three Companies. Each divided into platoons and sections and each allotted a particular task.

Byng later defined "the good feature of the show as the very careful preparation lasting nearly a month." In parsing this first paragraph of his "Notes" we see his intent and most of the basics, intent being simply to do as much damage as possible and the basics, as they worked out, were 422 all ranks of 1CMR raiding in daylight and occupying the enemy trench for 90 minutes. As Byng stipulated, 1CMR's raid would be "in the form of an attack so that all the new men should [become] accustomed to crossing No Man's Land in formation."[70]

This large raid is notable for the excellence of the planning and recce and for the adroit co-ordination of support elements. This shines through in both the brigade Operation Order and the brigade reports. The choice of objective resulted from an Appreciation done by the GOC 8th Brigade, J.H. Elmsley.[71] He concluded that the area from the Lille Road to the "Snout" (see MSD 15) offered the best ground; for one thing along this front the wire was easily distinguishable, less the strips behind Craters XIX, XIXA and XXIV, meaning that cutting would be relatively straightforward. Second, the craters between the lines offered good jumping-off positions. Finally, no man's land was mostly hidden from the enemy support line. He decided, then, on a battalion daylight raid between Lille Road and the "Snout" and a diversionary night raid on the brigade's right sector by 4CMR. Time, of course, featured in his Appreciation, one

69 LAC, RG9IIIC3, Volume 4074, Folder 2, File 9, 'Raids Carried Out by the Canadian Corps, 29 October-31 December 1916'. This particular document was also in TNA: WO 95/2540: 38th British Division General Staff. The documentation shows this division had the "Notes" distributed to all brigades and battalions.

70 By late 1916 the organization of an infantry battalion and company and especially the platoon was a pressing interest in the Canadian Corps. So, too, was formations during trench-to-trench attacks. Byng was instrumental in the organizational development of the new platoon in the Canadian Corps, his BGGS, P. deB. Radcliffe, noting that a new organization was instituted early in the winter of 1916/17 some six weeks before GHQ instructions on the matter were issued. (LAC, RG9IIIC1, Volume 3846, Folder 51, File 7, 'Vimy Ridge Operations', a lecture Radcliffe gave to various BEF audiences). As early as 12 January the War Diary of 25th Canadian Battalion (2nd Division) noted "Day spent on re-organization in accordance with instructions from Canadian Corps." The same had commenced in 1st Division well before Christmas. In February 1917 Second Army issued 'General Principles' (O.B./1919/T) of the normal formation for the attack and *WO 3995 The Organization of an Infantry Battalion and the Normal Formation for the Attack* and *SS 143 Instructions for the Training of Platoons for Offensive Action, 1917.* These organizational matters were discussed in Radley, *We Lead Others Follow,* especially Chapter 3. See also Chapter 11 of this present study.

71 Miller, *Painting the Map Red*, pp. 161, 273, 275-76, 394. Elmsley assumed command of 8th Brigade in June 1916 and remained with it until May 1918. He had not previously commanded an infantry battalion. Before and during the South African War he commanded a troop of the Royal Canadian Dragoons. He was seriously wounded at Liliefontein.

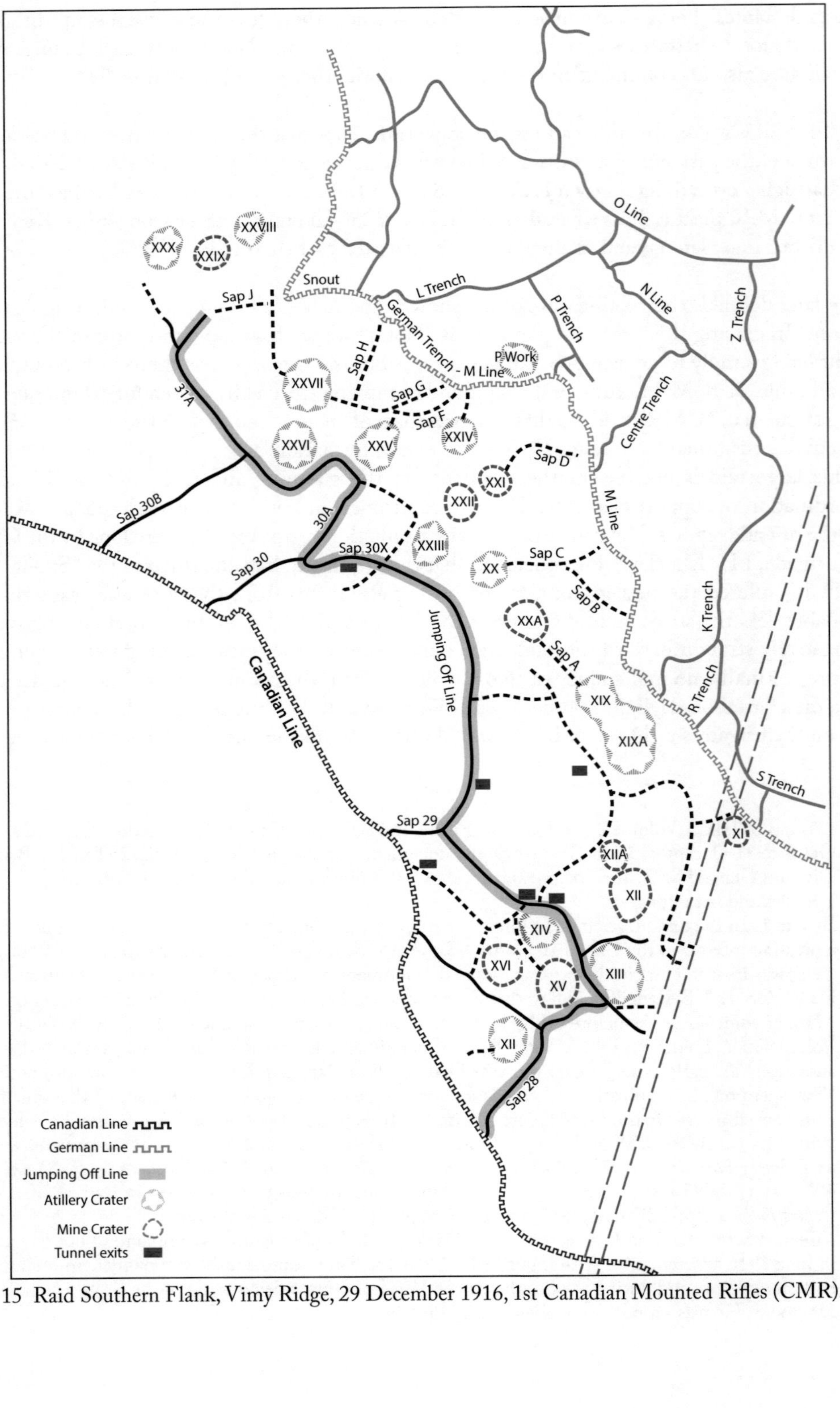

15 Raid Southern Flank, Vimy Ridge, 29 December 1916, 1st Canadian Mounted Rifles (CMR).

question being the length of stay in enemy trenches. To withdraw in daylight meant the enemy seeing and striking at the retiring raiders. On the other hand, remaining too long would invite counter-attack by troops with superior knowledge of the trenches. Elmsley opted for a leap-frog withdrawal as soon as it was dark: second wave assault troops withdrawing through the first wave and then that wave withdrawing through the reserve holding the crater lines and saps. This "proved to be satisfactory," he wrote, "the Germans not aware that we had evacuated until 7 p.m., two hours after the withdrawal had been completed."[72]

As for the plan, 1CMR formed in three parties, left, centre and right, each featuring a number of waves. The Right Party (A Company), four officers and 107 ORs, consisted of three waves. The first (56 all ranks) would jump off from Craters XII, XIII and XIV and from the exit of the tunnel 20 yards south of XIX, its task being to clear XIX (enemy occupied) and XIXA. The 28 all ranks of the second wave would clear "K" Trench and occupy "N" Line from the Lille Road to the junction with "Z" Trench. Wave 3 (14 ORs) would follow the first wave.

Centre Party (B Company), four officers and 96 ORs in three waves, would jump off from Craters XX and XXIII and from the sap in rear of Sap 30X and the tunnel exit immediately south of it. Wave 1 of B Company (42 all ranks) would occupy the enemy front line from Sap B to the "P. Work" and then clear up "P" Trench to "L" Trench. Wave 2, 14 men, would clear up Centre Trench to "N" Line and link up with the Right and Left Parties.

The latter (C Company), four officers and 115 ORs, would jump off from Craters XXV and XXVII and the sap to their rear. The first wave would clear the trench between "P. Work" and "Snout" and block the main and support trenches 40 or so yards north of "Snout." Wave 2 would clear up "L" Trench and link up with centre Party in "N" Line. Each of the three parties would have Lewis guns with their second waves. In the battalion trench a platoon per party would be posted to meet any counter-attack.[73]

Given the circumstances – daylight and a fairly complex plan – support was key. Byng's "Notes" identified the essence:

> Registration as usual. 5 days wire-cutting slow, with Trench Mortars 6 days, then two hours hard with 18-pounders. Creeping barrage. Ordinary box barrage, 18-pounders, 4.5-inch, 6-inch and Trench Mortars [Support] and all Communication Trenches blocked with 8-inch and 9.2-inch. An extra lot of medium trench mortars, Stokes and Machine-Guns were brought in and Machine-Gun barrages under central control … Smoke bombs from Stokes along the front.[74]

In execution, this coalesced into an extensive fire plan involving Canadian Corps Heavy Artillery, Divisional Artillery, 8th and 2nd Canadian Trench Mortar Batteries, 8th Canadian Machine-Gun Company, No. 1 Special (Smoke) Company RE and medium (2-inch) mortars. The day before the raid the heavy artillery and medium mortars carried out a deliberate bombardment of selected targets, followed on Zero day by an intense bombardment of the objectives for 35 minutes (1330 – 1415) prior to Zero at 1515. Medium mortars (2-inch) worked

72 LAC, 8th Brigade War Diary, 'Report on Minor Operation 20 December 1916'.
73 *Ibid.*
74 Byng's "Notes".

at wire-cutting for eight days, cutting about 500 yards of wire, 400 by the 2-inch mortars which expended 1,500 bombs, the result being adequate cutting "without arousing suspicion." Under covering fire of Divisional Artillery and a 4-inch Stokes smoke barrage in the rear of the objective area, the infantry reached all objectives in the front and second enemy lines. The gunners and Stokes (3-inch) crews also provided an effective box barrage for the assault, this being added to by 8th Canadian Machine-Gun Company. All barrages began as planned and proved very effective, especially near the Lille Road. Fire control was good throughout. On 19 December a forward brigade HQ had been established from which lines were laid as far forward as possible into no man's land ready to be connected with the company HQs of the assault troops. On Zero day, and well before Zero, CRA and his HQ joined the net, communications being established on dedicated lines to the fire units. Also at the brigade HQ a Corps Heavy Artillery Liaison Officer had lines connected to the heavy artillery groups. From this HQ the Brigade Machine-Gun Officer had direct control over all his weapons.[75]

Other pre-raid preparations were as comprehensive and careful. All craters and saps, which prior to the raid had only been visited by patrols, were occupied and saps were cleared and repaired to ensure rapidity of movement. For protection during the intense preliminary bombardment three mine galleries were allotted to the raiders. "Step-ups" from the tunnels into the advanced craters were also constructed, as was an exit from the tunnel 20 yards south of Crater XIX. Thorough practise getting out of the galleries quickly and into position in the jumping-off craters featured in pre-raid training. Because 1CMR would not be in the line on Zero day additional arrangements had to be made. Battalion raiders would begin and end their raid in 5CMR lines, this battalion having relieved 1CMR in the line. To prevent any inadvertent friendly-on-friendly fire when the raiders returned during the raid the line behind the raiders would be held with sentries only, the rest of the garrison being withdrawn or placed in dug-outs. In addition, 5CMR men in sap heads and crater posts would be withdrawn at 1300. On receipt of a message "Normal Situation" 5CMR would resume normal defence of its line.[76]

As for the diversion by 4CMR, for once there is ample and measurable evidence to say that the diversion did what it aimed to do. Elmsley considered it a "decided success." 4CMR made no effort to conceal wire-cutting which was in full view of the German rear lines. During the intense bombardments by the heavy artillery practically all the enemy artillery and machine-gun retaliation was directed at 4CMR, not 1CMR. The War Diary of 4CMR in explaining why its raiding party was unable to enter the enemy line highlights the enemy's focus on 4CMR:

> The barrage placed around 1CMR when it began to withdraw drew heavy retaliation on our trenches, especially on Sap 20 down which our raiding party had to go to their jumping-off trench. The party started at 4:15 pm, went through the enemy barrage but suffered several casualties and [so] delayed them that they were unable to assemble in the jumping-off trench in time to go forward under the artillery barrage … arranged for 5 pm. The wires to the jumping-off trench were all so cut that the OC raid could not ask for postponement. As the main object had been accomplished, namely drawing the enemy's attention

75 LAC, War Diary 8th Brigade, Operation Order 69 and 'Report on Minor Operations'; RG9IIIC3, Volume 4074, Folder 2, File 9, 'Raids carried Out by the Canadian Corps'.

76 LAC, War Diary 8th Brigade, 'Report on Minor Operations'. Other examples of such procedure are at Chapters Five and Nine.

from the attack of 1CMR … the OC decided to retire … this carried out without further casualties.[77]

Prior to Zero the artillery and mortars executed the fire plan perfectly: the heavies struck hard at the objectives and enemy trenches, the Stokes commenced on time and the 4-inch Stokes masked the objective trenches from observation from enemy rear trenches. At 1518 the barrage shifted to the enemy support line and the infantry assaulted. The Right Party (A Company) took Craters XIX and XIXA, opposition being met only at XIX and at 1345 runners advised that all elements had reached their objectives and had linked up with C Company on the left. Several dug-outs were destroyed and five prisoners were taken at the junction of "R" and "S" Trenches. A large dug-out in "Z" Trench was also blown up. Centre Party (B Company) met little resistance. Eight dug-outs and "P. Works", found to be an ammunition dump, were blown up. This party took 23 prisoners. Link-up with Left and Right Parties was quickly achieved. The former destroyed 13 dug-outs, defeated an enemy bombing party and took 31 prisoners including one officer. In all, 59 prisoners including two officers were taken. Every weapon emplacement and dug-out found were wrecked. At 1630 the signal to withdraw went up; fitting that it was a celebratory "Gold and Silver Rain Rocket." By 1700 all raiders and their haul of prisoners had returned to 1CMR lines.[78]

Byng's "Notes" included three other comments. "Going in by daylight had surprised them," he wrote, "as we caught the garrison including the Company Commander napping." While this officer did have time to summon his support company, artillery fire prevented it getting forward. Second, the enemy thinking the raiders were going to stay put heavy fire down on their trench from 1700 on. Of the two German companies in the enemy front trench Byng estimated their total strength as 150-200 and he believed "none got away and their support company must have got a bad mauling." The two other reasons for the great success as Byng saw it were the very careful preparation lasting nearly a month and the very excellent fire support by artillery, trench mortars, Stokes and machine-guns. Canadian casualties came to six killed, two died of wounds and 45 wounded, the last including 11 men of 4CMR. Men who had distinguished themselves received special leave.[79]

On Christmas morning at 0245 one of the last Canadian raids of the year began. Five officers and 100 ORs of the 25th Battalion (2nd Division) under Captain William Cameron raided on a front of 350 yards. Each of the four raiding parties consisted of one officer and 25 men and each party entered enemy trenches through its own entry point. Prior to the raid no concentrated fire was directed at wire in front of the objective; rather for three weeks before Zero Day Stokes mortars occasionally cut the wire without attracting any attention. Divisional artillery (18-pounders) joined in this from time to time, but Stokes did most of the cutting. By 0215 that day the raiders were lying up 30 or so yards from the enemy parapet. When the guns opened they charged, three of the four parties experiencing no difficulty with wire and surprise was complete. The fourth party had to contend with a tangle of wire that caused some delay. Once in the trench the work of destruction began during which seven men of the 21st Bavarians were captured and escorted to battalion lines. Canadian casualties amounted to one officer and six

77 LAC, War Diary, 4CMR, 20 December 1916.
78 LAC, War Diary, 8th Brigade 'Report on Minor Operations'.
79 Byng's "Notes."

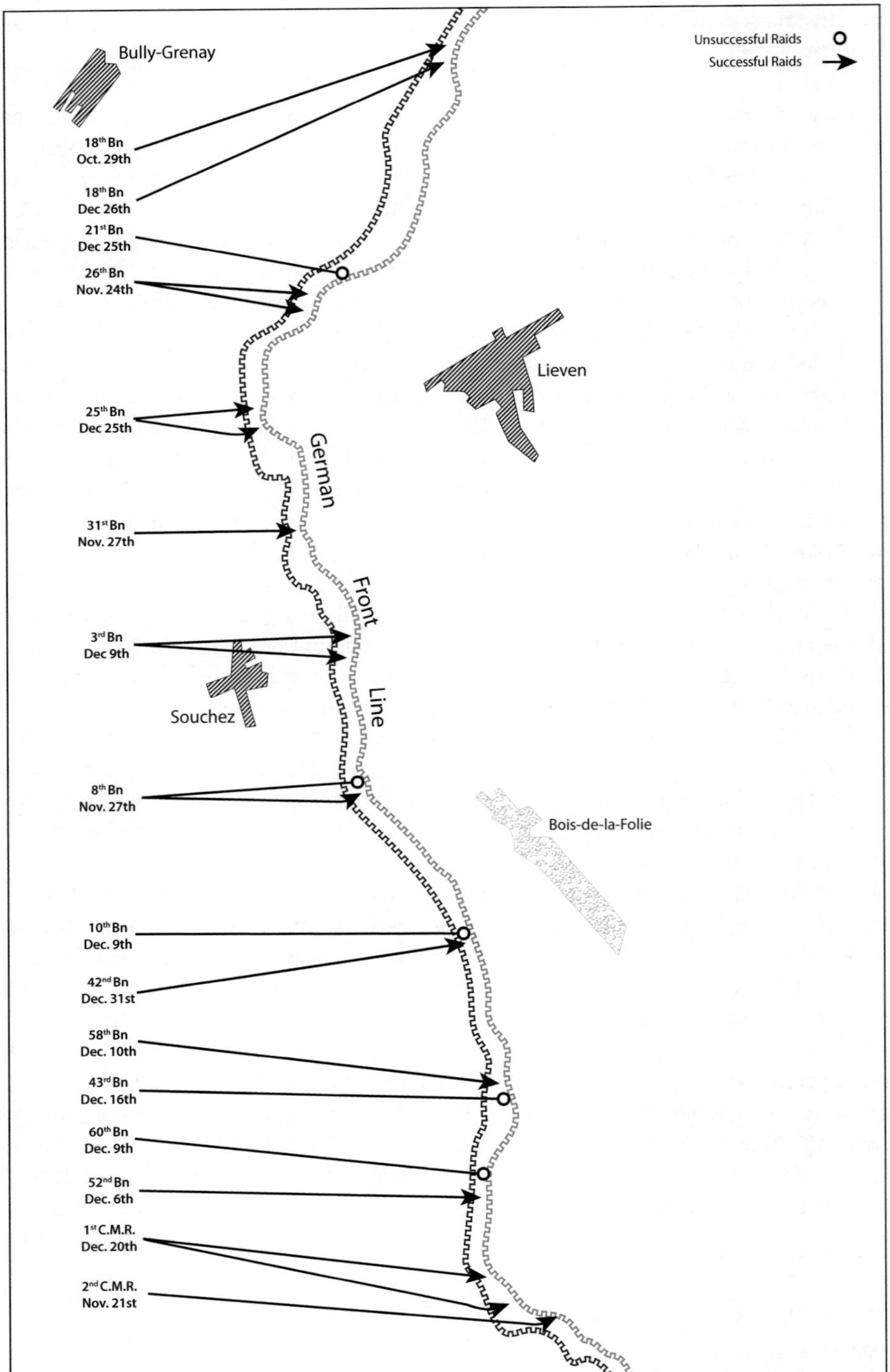

16 Canadian Corps Raids October-December 1916.

men wounded and one OR killed. The spoils included numerous Christmas parcels, their loss so infuriating the Germans that their gunners spent most of Christmas Day hammering the 25th Battalion.[80]

In early January 1917 Canadian Corps HQ issued a report and map (see MSD 16) entitled "Raids Organized By the Canadian Corps During October, November and December 1916." The report included a summation "Points to be Noted" by the BGGS, P. deB. Radcliffe. Of the seven points, three relate to wire. First, several raids had failed due to unsatisfactory wire-cutting. Second, to avoid having the enemy simply withdrawing more than one gap had to be cut, or the raiding party had to be in such strength that it could penetrate to the enemy support line as 1CMR had done. Finally, in one case a second row of wire (uncut) held up raiders. Had recce been more thorough this might have been observed before the raid. Signals again proved problematic. In two cases explosions (in one case a Bangalore and in the other a number of bombs) were the signal for Canadian artillery to open, but German explosions were mistaken for these signals and Canadian artillery opened too soon. This forced the raiders to withdraw. One point concerned German deployment. Prisoners had revealed that most machine-guns were in second and third line trenches. Artillery barrages on these had been found to reduce enemy machine-gun fire. The sixth point related to tactics in enemy trenches. During one raid the raiding party had destroyed a Company HQ dug-out after the company commander and three men had been taken prisoner. One revealed that in the just wrecked dug-out was a German slide-rule code. A frantic search was fruitless. The lesson was obvious: search, then destroy.

1916 ended with numerous small raids, British and Canadian, most just 10 or fewer men and an officer. One of these, a Subaltern and seven men of the 42nd Canadian Battalion (Black Watch), just before midnight 31 December 1916 cut through two rows of concertina wire and entered an enemy trench a few minutes into 1917. There two sentries were spotted, one in an improvised shelter and the second just coming around the corner. Both surrendered and were escorted to Canadian lines. This raid was all so easy and uncomplicated. Radcliffe's Point 7 refers:

> Stealth raids, such as that by the 42nd, seem to be especially adapted for the purpose of getting identifications, while the enemy is holding his front line so lightly. With skilful scouting and resourceful officers and men they should produce excellent results with very few casualties.[81]

1916 was the busiest of the war years when it came to raiding. Prior to Vimy in April 1917 there was no reduction of the pace; indeed, from 20 March onward British and Canadian units raided the enemy every night. After Vimy the pace varied depending on the frequency and scale of major operations. The next chapter surveys minor enterprises during early 1917.

80 LAC, War Diary, 25th Battalion. Tennyson, ed., *Merry Hell*, p. 160. Captain Cameron received the MC for the raid.

81 LAC, RG9IIIC3, Volume 4074, Folder 2, File 9, 'Raids Carried Out By the Canadian Corps'.

11

1917 – Early Days

> One lives calmly on the brink of the abyss.
> Lt. Col. Winston S. Churchill

According to the Canadian Official Historian the winter of 1916/17, a period with no major operations in progress, was a time to recuperate, train and simply hold the line.[1]

This is not to say that all went quiet for once firm on the ground opposite Vimy Ridge the Canadian Corps commenced active and vigorous patrolling and raiding, the pace gradually quickening so that by 20 March with the attack on Vimy Ridge just three weeks away Canadians were raiding the enemy every night, the purpose being to give the Corps the latest and most accurate picture of the enemy and his defences. These raids did this and more, but at a cost of 1,400 casualties during the first two of the three weeks before the attack. While the pace was slower before 20 March several of the raids were large-scale ones. In December 1916, 400 officers and men of 1CMR had enjoyed a considerable success, blowing up 26 dug-outs and taking 59 prisoners. Building on this, in mid-January 20th and 21st Battalions of 2nd Canadian Division, raiding in twice the strength of 1CMR, destroyed 40 dug-outs and took 100 prisoners. A raid by 4th Division a month later in about the same strength scooped up 50 more. Then on 1 March 4th Division launched 1,700 raiders against enemy lines, perhaps a case of once too many times to the well for the Germans had by far the best of it, Canadian casualties being very heavy, almost 700 all ranks, including two battalion commanders killed. Colonel Nicholson summed the venture up as almost "complete failure." The nearly 40 percent casualties, almost twice the losses during the earlier 2nd Division raid, severely shook planners and raiders alike. The next chapter describes this raid in detail.[2]

During this first quarter of 1917 British raids show a similar pattern of smaller raids gradually building to larger and more frequent forays. Two examples of substantial efforts in the quarter came in February, first a raid by 600 all ranks of the 6th London Regiment (47th Division), followed by 350 officers and men of the 9th Cameronians (9th Division), success in the last due, according to the divisional historian, to the "most painstaking care" in organization and tactics. Ewing also described a smaller raid by 8th Black Watch and 10th Argyle and Sutherland

1 Nicholson, *Canadian Expeditionary Force,* p. 233.
2 *Ibid.,* p. 234.

Highlanders near Arras on 6 January.[3] The acting brigade commander, Lieutenant-Colonel J. Kennedy, DSO, blamed changes in the "object and character" of the raid and the uncertainty about Zero Day for the short notice given the raiding party. For one thing, as the Adjutant of the Argylls remarked, his unit had only 24 hours warning because the proposal for the raid initially involved only the 8th Black Watch.

The purposes of the raid also became more complex adding taking prisoners, locating trench mortar and machine-gun emplacements and destroying dug-outs to the original purposes which were essentially of a recce nature: to see how effective heavy artillery had been in wire-cutting, especially in front of the enemy second and third lines, and to determine if a strong point known as "The Harp" rearward of the enemy fourth line could be observed from the enemy front and second line. This strong point posed a formidable obstacle to any possible later advance.

The raid, a daylight operation (Zero at 1508 on 6 January) commencing with heavy preliminary bombardment and an infantry advance covered by smoke, aimed to penetrate as far as the third line after securing the first two lines which were to be held for 30 minutes. Lieutenant-Colonel Kennedy directed that the raiders not be specially selected; rather a company from each battalion should be chosen just as it stood; in short a "normal" company organization and composition. The Argyles complied, A Company being chosen, four officers and 77 ORs forming four small platoons, but the Black Watch formed a composite company of four officers and 80 ORs, 20 from each of four rifle companies. Comprehensive and effective artillery support was provided for wire-cutting, bombardment of enemy front line trenches and the lift to enemy rear lines, the box barrage, the creeping barrage to cover the withdrawal and smoke during the assault. As for the raid itself, the raiders penetrated to the enemy third line quite rapidly, the opposition "practically nil" according to the brigade report, because most of the enemy remained in dug-outs in the first three lines and only a few were seen in the fourth line. Stokes bombs destroyed many dug-outs plus a mineshaft discovered in a sap. One man was captured. The raiders had only one killed and 14 wounded.

Kennedy's report is notable for its assessment of the lessons of the raid. Regarding the two specific purposes assigned, he reported that heavy artillery had effectively dealt with enemy wire, all in front of the enemy second line being "smashed up" and easily passable by day, although it might have posed a serious obstacle at night. Wire protecting the third line proved "fairly" well cut presenting only a slight check to movement by day, but a considerable obstacle at night. As for observation, "The Harp" was clearly visible from the enemy front line, likewise the German rear area for as much as a mile. The three enemy trenches and CTs connecting the three lines proved thoroughly damaged. Dug-outs in the front line, however, were intact as they were under the parapet, but in the other lines where they had been set in the rear wall of the trenches many were blown in. When it came to reasons for success Kennedy thought that the chance for surprise had been somewhat compromised by premature firing from machine-guns, by the smoke barrage which should have been closer in time to Zero and by the lifting of much of the heavy artillery before Zero, although regarding this he later wrote that keeping some of them firing on the front trench until Zero did keep the defenders in their dug-outs thereby affording a measure of surprise. One prisoner stated that he had not

3 The account of this raid is based on Ewing, *Ninth (Scottish) Division*, pp. 179-80, and TNA: WO 95/1762: War Diary of the General Staff of that division for January which includes the Operation Orders of both battalions and the reports of the parent brigade (26th).

detected any difference in the shelling and on leaving his dug-out to answer a call of nature he had no idea raiders were present. Kennedy concluded that premature firing and the lifting of fire at the very least hinted at the "exact moment" of the infantry assault and "NB. Enemy barrage was on our front line within two minutes of Zero," a quick response, indeed, and one indicative of alertness.

Another interesting aspect of these lessons is the reiteration – twice – of the definition of Zero.[4] First, he said "It should be clearly understood that Zero is the hour at which infantry leave their own trenches, and all timings worked from that." Later he elaborated: "The [fire] programme should be calculated on Zero, not on the moment of arriving in Hunland, which is uncertain." Both battalion Operation Orders echo Kennedy. The Argylls' order, for example, states that the infantry had to be formed up in the battalion front line by Zero minus three and ready to leave that line at Zero. Kennedy's version of Zero had not yet become general practice.[5] For example, the author of several articles on the development of artillery tactics wrote that at the end of 1916 Zero was commonly regarded as the "hour at which the artillery barrage opened." By early 1917 the historian of the 29th Division, reflecting upon training at the schools of instruction at Army, Corps and Division level, found in a current pamphlet the following nebulous definition: "Zero is only an approximation. Watch the barrage." Both definitions were recipes for trouble.[6]

Raiding-wise January was also a busy month for 24th British Division. In the 16 days commencing on the 10th the division launched five substantial raids in the right sector of the Loos Salient. The first (10 January) featured the 2nd Leinsters of 73rd Brigade, five officers and 80 ORs, 20 from each of four platoons, tackling "The Triangle," a target described by the OC Raid, Captain Francis Hitchcock, MC, thus: "the trenches curved down across Hill 70, coming to an abrupt turn at the famous triangle to straighten themselves out towards the Double Crassier – huge mammoths of waste slag and charcoal."[7] This daylight enterprise (Zero at 1620) involved no preliminary bombardment, but did place box barrages opposite neighbouring units in hopes this combination of surprise and deception would achieve surprise for the two platoons assaulting the eastern face of the salient formed by The Triangle and for the two going against the western face.[8] The raid aimed, ostensibly, at obtaining identifications of opposing units, their disposition and activities, including mining, but what really drove it was reprisal for a "brilliantly" carried out enemy raid that had netted 50 prisoners from the 8th Buffs, a unit of the 17th Brigade of 24th Division, and 3rd Australian Tunnelling Company. The denouement to this was swift and decisive. The CO of the Buffs was sacked. His boss, the brigade commander, left "sick" on

4 As far as can be determined the first use of the term Zero was in First Army Operation Order 95 for Loos in 1915 (Becke, 'The Coming of the Creeping Barrage', p. 22).

5 TNA: WO 95/1762: 9th (Scottish) Division, January 1917, brigade commander's report.

6 Broad, 'The Development of Artillery Tactics', pp. 79-80; Gillon, *29th Division,* p. 101. It bears reiterating that today Zero, now known as "H Hour," is the time at which the infantry crosses the Start Line. All timings are reckoned from that.

7 A large-scale map of the area is at p. 252 of Barton, *Battlefields of the First World War.* Maps showing the Leinsters lines, details of the triangle complex and the plan are at pages 204 and 233 of Hitchcock's "*Stand To.*"

8 *Ibid.,* 'General Plan', pp. 335-37.

30 January.[9] The GOC 24th Division at the time was J.E. Capper, a strong believer in the offensive spirit.[10]

It is evident in Hitchcock's account that the Leinsters raiding parties were carefully organized and prepared for the raid, including thorough training for six days. As OC Raid, Hitchcock chose to accompany the two platoons assaulting the eastern side of the salient. He describes how initially the raiders faced only sporadic fire, but on reaching the intended entry point they found it full of coils of barbed wire that air photographs had not revealed. However, on moving slightly to the right they easily entered the trench at the apex of the triangle exactly according to where the plan had intended he go since a position there would enable him to control both western and eastern parties as they moved to secure their sectors. "There is no doubt," he wrote, "that we greatly surprised the enemy … I landed right on top of a Boche sentry … occupied in reading a newspaper!" Four prisoners immediately on capture were hustled back to battalion lines. As the party moved toward the eastern point of entry, Hitchcock discovered that wire and stiff opposition had prevented the eastern party from entering the trench. Still, with the trench occupied by the western party it was secure, and with the enemy confused and not yet organized to counter-attack, Hitchcock and his men hung on until 1710 when he signalled withdrawal. All in all, the raid succeeded, eight prisoners and considerable information on enemy dispositions and activities acquired. Casualties were four killed and 18 wounded. Hitchcock received the MC.[11]

Four days later four officers and 110 ORs of the 1st Royal Fusiliers, 17th Brigade, did a night raid. Captain William Burdett, OC Raid, had organized the raiders into four bombing parties, four search parties, two bomb carrier parties, a covering party and Lewis gun teams on each flank. His plan differed in that these would enter the enemy trenches in the order listed. Once in the trenches one quartet (a pair of bombing parties and a pair of search parties) would go left and one would go right. Tail end in each case would be a bomb carrier party. Two officers would remain at the point of entry with the covering party. The quartet to the left soon encountered stiff resistance, suffering "many" casualties during hand-to-hand fighting, but did force the enemy back, this freeing the infantry and RE party to get on with blowing up dug-outs. No progress could be made up a CT since from a loopholed traverse machine-gun fire raked the trench. The quartet that had gone to the right encountered equally strong opposition, but did take three prisoners. Total casualties were eight ORs killed and 26 wounded. One officer was wounded. The reports prepared by Burdett, who received the MC, and his CO contain useful lessons. The CO thought Burdett should have combined the bombing and searching parties and moved as such, i.e. two parties, not four. As to tactics Burdett thought that next time the

9 The GOC, Brigadier-General J.W.V. Carroll, who assumed command of 17th Brigade in September 1915, is shown as "sick 16/1/17" on page 128 of Becke (comp)., *Order of Battle of Divisions Part 3A New Army Divisions (9-26)*. As of 16 January Lieutenant-Colonel A.M. Tringham was acting GOC. TNA: WO 95/2204: 17th Brigade, entry for 30 January says: "Brig General JWV Carroll CMG left brigade." It may be that his departure was due to illness rather than the events of the enemy raid, but the time between it and 16 January is short. Carroll is listed as "Lt Col (Temp Brig Gen), CMG, Norfolk Regiment" in *The War Gazettes* (DVD-ROM, Naval and Military Press) for 1917. He does not appear in the 1918 listing. This DVD-ROM includes all "British" (the term includes all Dominions and Colonies) awards for gallantry, orders, medals and decorations, and "tens of thousands" of appointments, transfers, promotion and foreign awards.

10 Moody, *Historical Records of the Buffs*, p. 231, makes no mention of the 8th Battalion's losses.

11 Hitchcock, *"Stand To"*, pp. 237-42.

parties should work one on the parapet and one in the trench rather than both in the trench. He also noted that casualty removal would have been easier had the parapet at the entry point been "stepped" since the trench was very deep and the ladders too short.[12]

A few days later 73rd Brigade's 13th Middlesex took a turn. This raid, launched at 0930 under cover of smoke, consisted of four officers and 52 ORs, plus eight sappers. The preliminaries included using "The Triangle" as a diversion. For a few days prior to this raid it was the target of brief artillery and trench mortar fire and Bangalores were fired in the vicinity. On the day of the raid more diversionary fire hit it, this time including smoke. In addition, two red Very Lights were fired above the smoke, the idea being that the enemy might think these an SOS call from the front line for fire. This apparently worked since for some time after Zero the enemy put down heavy fire on the front of "The Triangle" and on British lines in that area.

With all this going on 13th Middlesex entered enemy trenches without difficulty and began bombing every dug-out it found. Despite some resistance the bombing parties held their ground and repulsed a bombing counter-attack. Given the success of the diversion, the excellence of fire support and the easy entry and the very light casualties (one killed, four wounded and one officer missing) it was unfortunate that the raiders had only 15 minutes in the enemy trenches to exploit their good fortune. This came about when a telephone message sent by a signaller in no man's land was misunderstood and the signal to withdraw was given early. "It shows," said the brigade commander, "the importance of very careful detailed instructions being given to everyone on the enterprise."[13]

On 25 January the 9th East Surreys of 72nd Brigade had their turn.[14] At the time, the 9th occupied trenches opposite Hulluch, a small village about two miles northeast of Loos and about three miles south of La Bassee.[15] This raid, the first large-scale one by the unit, had Zero at 12 noon, raiding strength being three officers, 50 ORs and six sappers. The raid sought to obtain identifications, to inflict casualties and to obtain a sample of German ration bread, an acquisition that could possibly help confirm reports of acute food shortages in Germany. The OC Raid, Second Lieutenant E.W. Davies, organized two "fighting squads," one under Second Lieutenant Lackmere Thomas and the other under Sergeant Summers; two mopping-up parties; and two "blocking and connecting" parties. The third officer, Second Lieutenant William Lindsay, would remain at the entry point where he could best control the blockers and connectors. On entry Summers, with one fighting and one mopping-up party, would go left clearing the trench and blowing up dug-outs. Thomas would take his two parties to the right and do likewise. Over several days artillery and trench mortars cut several good gaps in enemy wire. By Zero minus ten Davies had his men formed up in a sap awaiting Zero. However, when seconds before Zero Davies realized that the smoke barrage had not developed quickly enough

12 TNA: WO 95/2207: 1st Royal Fusiliers, January 1917.
13 TNA: WO 95/2217: 73rd Brigade, brigade and battalion reports.
14 Michael Lucas, *The Journey's End Battalion: The 9th East Surrey in the Great War* (Barnsley: Pen and Sword, 2012), pp. 183-85. R.C. Sherriff, author of *Journey's End,* served as a Subaltern with the 9th. Lucas notes that Sherriff told C.A. Clarke, a former Adjutant of the 9th, that he based the play on the battalion's raid in January, a carefully planned and executed raid that was far more successful than the one portrayed in the play. Lucas' book also presents a good account of the officers of the 9th who inspired the main characters in Sherriff's play.
15 Barton, *Battlefields of the First World War,* Panorama P117 (pp. 234-35) and map at p. 244.

he exhibited good judgement by delaying the advance. By Zero plus four with the smoke now sufficient the parties moved forward the 100 yards to the enemy trench and then quickly into it, entry being made at 1205. This must have gone unobserved since no fire was directed at the first wave. Some fire directed at the second was wild and short-lived. Neither party suffered any casualties.[16]

Thomas' parties as they moved to the right found the trenches in very bad order, the only dug-out seen being flooded. In this area the party killed several Germans and captured three, several others escaping rearward and alerting the enemy. Summers' parties moving to the left found only two dug-outs. Realizing that the now alert enemy was moving toward the raiders down the flanking CTs, Thomas and Summers warned Lindsay that they were returning to the entry point. At 1215 withdrawal commenced, six casualties (two killed) being suffered while crossing no man's land. During the crossing Lindsay particularly distinguished himself by his care of the wounded and his attempts to rescue one of the men. The Adjutant, C.A. Clarke, later described Lindsay as "very efficient and very brave." An MC was his reward. One also went to Thomas who was well known as "Tommy the Bomber." Clarke called him "one of the most courageous men" he had ever met, an officer "Never happy unless he was in the thick of it. Would volunteer for any job … men would follow him anywhere, so cool, so calm, so inspiring." Thomas and Summers, he wrote, formed the "best combination" in the unit for raiding.[17]

The battalion report put the difficulty with smoke down to a large number of misfires and the smoke drifting further to the south than had been anticipated, wind direction being "most unfavourable." The delay did not affect artillery and mortar support because of the way the fire plan had been programmed. The artillery during the morning had fired intermittently at points in the vicinity of the area to be raided, this not sufficiently heavy to arouse suspicion, but enough to force enemy sentries to take cover. At Zero minus five slow barrages commenced on support and reserve lines and on the flanking CTs. Not until Zero plus 13 did enemy artillery react. Of the raid as a whole, the brigade commander thought it demonstrated "the possibilities of surprising the enemy by day … the inadequacy of the enemy's alarm signals and his communication with his covering artillery [and] that every precaution should be taken to guard against being, ourselves, surprised by similar enemy enterprises." What this had translated into for the raiders was very slow enemy artillery response, no hostile rifle fire, a minute amount of machine-gun fire during the advance and no friendly casualties.[18]

The next day units of 17th Brigade, 8th Buffs and 12th Royal Fusiliers, launched a joint raid committing 120 and 113 all ranks respectively, the 8th, no doubt, still smarting from the enemy raid earlier in January that had made off with 50 prisoners, cost their CO his command and may well have led to the departure of J.W.V. Carroll, the brigade commander. Carroll's last report, written before his departure on 30 January, said the raid was made as a "Somme attack," it being delivered in line, 8th Buffs right and 12th Royal Fusiliers left, the general idea being that the left sub-unit of the latter unit would use a CT to enter the enemy support line while most of

16 TNA: WO 95/2211: 9th East Surreys, January 1917. Noon was chosen on the theory that the raid would coincide with the mid-day meal and the enemy might be less alert. Decades after the war Thomas recalled that brigade was not keen on a daylight raid, but division gave the nod to the plan on the grounds that those doing the raid should have the final say (Lucas, *Journey's End Battalion,* p. 84).

17 Clarke, quoted in Lucas' *Journey's End Battalion,* pp. 83-84.

18 TNA: WO 95/2211: 9th East Surreys, battalion and brigade reports.

the 12th and all of the 8th would limit their attack to the enemy front line securing it as well as blocking all CTs.

For five days prior to Zero Day heavy artillery and 18-pounders shelled the wire and enemy front line, the results being excellent, this confirmed by air photographs taken on the 24th that showed wire no longer an obstacle. After the usual training in rear areas the raiders moved forward during the afternoon of 25 January to deep dug-outs in Loos. The next morning (Zero Day) both raiding parties began moving forward to the jumping-off trench. According to the brigade report both were late arriving there. The War Diary of the 8th Buffs admits to being "slightly late." That of the 12th Royal Fusiliers makes no mention of late arrival. None of the reports state the time set for the raiders to be in the jumping-off trench, nor is a time of departure from Loos shown. Colonel Moody's brief account notes only that the 8th "started at 6:30 a.m. for the German trenches." Zero being set for 0845 using Moody's time the raiders had two hours and fifteen minutes to get from dug-outs in Loos to the jumping-off trench and make Zero. Carroll's report says flatly that neither party "started at the time given them" nor moved "on the route laid down."

One of the mental gymnastics involved in the movement of units, formations or raiding parties meant making a time appreciation, which sounds exotic, but is not that at all since we all make these in our daily lives, they being nothing more than a means of ensuring that deadlines are met and nothing gets forgotten. But when time appreciations are made during operations if they are faulty the consequences can be deadly, even disastrous. The methodology is simply to work backwards from Zero to the time at which every preparatory measure should begin, in this case from the dug-outs in Loos to the jumping-off position. A rough outline of such a sequence and the relevant timings might look like this:

0845	Zero
0835	Commence final preparations, assault formation, weapons check
0820	Arrive jumping-off position, check equipment, final instructions
0630	Depart dug-outs in Loos
0610	Form up for move
0530	Hot meal, rum issue

One would think that brigade (Carroll and/or his BM) determined the time given to the raiding parties to begin the move forward based on a recce of the route assigned and a time trial of how long it would take using this route to reach the jumping-off position. Either the time given was insufficient (see below), or the 8th, which Moody says started at 0630, actually started late (the departure time had been set earlier than 0630 and the raiders did not meet it), or the route actually used was longer than that assigned by brigade. We do not know if the commanders of the raiding parties or their COs did time appreciations. If they did, then these were faulty and made them late. In any case, Carroll's final comment said more attention should have been paid to the arrangements for the move of the raiders forward.

Carroll describes the consequences of being late into the jumping-off position: "although they [the two parties] joined up in the jumping-off trench … when Zero came there was a gap of 80 yards between them." It would have been "safer," he admits, to have allocated more time for the movement forward, but it being "a very cold morning … unnecessary waiting in [that] trench had to be guarded against." This argument is unconvincing: even 10 minutes earlier in the jumping-off trench would probably have seen the gap identified and closed. By definition a jumping-off trench (in modern terms a "forming-up place") is where men shake out into attack formation ready to go at Zero (H Hour). Then (and now) this takes time. Carroll then related the unfortunate consequences of the 80 yard gap: "it allowed the Germans to remain in their front line and bomb the left of one party and the right of the other." Fortunately, the raiders held their ground, German bombing being "feeble," but they could not close the gap.[19]

Still, at Zero the "show" began, the raiders in their white winter smocks and with their helmets painted white (helmets on raids were not the norm), were off, passing easily through the wire and into the trenches where they began blowing up dug-outs, in so doing taking 18 prisoners. Under interrogation these revealed that the raid had surprised them, nor were they aware their wire had been cut, this being possible since their unit had only come into the line the night before. German artillery, however, responded very quickly, one report stating that fire began within two minutes. When the signal for withdrawal sounded the raiders had only been in the enemy position for 15 minutes, another case of the signal being given too early. This raid, like many others, confirmed for Carroll that withdrawal was the most difficult time during a raid. Initially, it had been decided to retire on the sounding of a klaxon horn, but this was changed to a bugle. Few heard it. Over all, though, the raid was judged satisfactory, 20 or so Germans killed, several dug-outs destroyed and a good haul of prisoners. The raid elated the Buffs who thought they had got some of their own back. Casualties included one officer killed and four wounded, three ORs killed, 25 wounded and six missing. Most of the raider casualties occurred in their own trenches on the return because most of the party withdrew down the two CTs which had been previously registered by the enemy and were now heavily shelled.[20]

The previous chapter described the large-scale and successful daylight raid (over 400 all ranks) by 1CMR (3rd Canadian Division) on 20 December 1916. To provide maximum cover for the raiders a smoke screen had been provided plus box barrages, machine-gun barrages and deceptive measures such as demonstrations and firings of Bangalores and small mines. Prior to the New Year, and aiming to build on the 1CMR raid, 2nd Canadian Division planned a daylight raid to be executed by two battalions of Robert Rennie's 4th Brigade and one battalion of A.H. Macdonell's 5th Brigade.[21] Rennie, a pre-war CO of the First Battalion, The Queen's Own Rifles of Canada, and first CO of 3rd Battalion (September 1914-November 1915), would command the 4th Brigade until September 1918. As CO, and then as GOC, he enjoyed a reputation as a highly professional officer and a precise and diligent one. Prior to re-commencing the winter 1917 raiding "season" Rennie reminded battalion commanders of several matters that

19 TNA: WO 95/2190: 12th Royal Fusiliers, 8th Buffs and 17th Brigade; Moody, *Historical Records of the Buffs*, p. 232. Moody does not mention the late arrival.

20 TNA: WO 95/2190: 17th Brigade, brigade report; Moody, *Historical Records of the Buffs*, p. 232.

21 A.H. Macdonell should not to be confused with his cousin A.C. ("Batty Mac") Macdonell, who took command of 1st Canadian Division in June 1917. A.H. Macdonell , was a long-serving Regular officer who began his service in 1892 with the RCR. During the South African War he was a prisoner of the Boers for six weeks before escaping and rejoining his regiment. He was awarded the DSO and the rank of Brevet Major during the war. In 1901 he served with the British Army during the Southern Nigeria Expedition. At the outbreak of war in 1914, following a period on the staff of 1st Division, he commanded the RCR (August 1915 to April 1916) and then 5th Brigade until July 1917. Macdonell's career is described fully in Fetherstonhaugh, *The Royal Canadian Regiment 1883-1933*.

had always to be a focus of attention when it came to raids, among them every detail during preparation must be attended to, every aspect of the plan had to be made known to every man and the chain of command down to the last man had to be explained.[22]

On 8 January 4th Brigade submitted proposals for a daylight raid on enemy trenches north-east of Cite Calonne near the Lens-Bethune railway in the coal-mining region of Lens. The proposals, which outlined the brigade concept for a major raid, included intention, objective and plan, the last covering all major aspects of how the raid would be executed.[23] The purposes of this large-scale raid – 860 officers and men of 20th and 21st Battalions – were to cause maximum casualties, take prisoners, booty and documents and wreck as much as possible in the objective area. This raid would feature several of the elements of the 1CMR raid and some additional ones. First, it would be a joint raid. About one mile southwest of the objective area a battalion of 5th Brigade, the right flanking brigade, would raid supported by field artillery, trench mortars, Corps Heavy Artillery and 4th Canadian Trench Mortar Battery. Second, over 40 machine-guns of 4th Canadian Machine-Gun Company, Canadian Corps Machine-Gun Brigade and 7th Machine-Gun Squadron, 7th British Cavalry Brigade, would also be in support. Third, RE would provide smoke both sides of the objective and mortars would provide smoke as a diversion south of the objective. Finally, a mine would be fired south of the objective as a diversion.

Zero was set for 0745 on 17 January.[24] The brigade report shows that a good deal of thought was given to a morning start. While a late afternoon time had the great advantage of darkness to cover the withdrawal, the enemy was known to "stand down about 0830 and a prior raid by 19th Battalion had shown the enemy to be less alert around the time of his stand down." Moreover, since the assembly and jumping-off trenches were under observation from the Double Crassier a morning start would mean that forming up would be covered by darkness. Daylight also made passage through any obstacle easier and enabled precise movement. Finally, morning seemed to enhance chances of surprise. Consequently, morning it would be. As for the objective, three factors determined the choice: first, ground dictated that enemy machine-guns could only be brought to bear from a distance, no commanding ground being closer than 800 yards; second, some cover for troops moving in the open existed; and, third, no man's land narrowed at the point chosen, varying from 200-300 yards along the front of the assaulting battalions and then widening considerably opposite 18th and 19th Battalions. Moreover, enemy observation could be further limited, perhaps even prevented, by use of smoke.

Pre-raid recce received its due. During training for the raid officers and NCOs frequently visited the front line to observe the ground and all ranks participated in patrolling no man's land, the idea being to see the wire close-up, a standard Canadian practice by 1917. As always, time spent on recce would pay huge dividends. Recce also involved close checking of enemy wire

22 LAC, War Diary, 3rd Battalion, January 1917, Appendix 11.

23 LAC RG9IIIC3, Volume 4106, Folder 22, File 6. The account of this raid is based on the following: 4th Brigade proposal for raid, 8 January, Operation Orders of 20th Battalion, 21st Battalion, 4th Brigade and engineers, trench mortars and machine-guns; reports of brigade and battalions and artillery fire plan including tables of guns available and ammunition expenditures. Corrigall, *Twentieth Canadian Battalion,* pp. 99-105.

24 LAC, War Diary 20th Battalion. The raid was set initially for 11 January, then postponed first on the 14th and again on the 15th due to "unfavourable wind." On the 17th the diary read "wind north by west; snowing steadily about one inch on the parapet."

during the week prior to Zero. Destruction of enemy wire had begun well before 8 January and damage had to be repeatedly ascertained (see below as to the effort and the results). 4th Brigade insisted upon this in an instruction to battalions on 12 January. It also demanded a report on wire to be submitted daily by 2130. If this could not be done then answers to the following questions had to be submitted: "Do you consider enemy front line wire sufficiently cut? Do you consider enemy second line wire sufficiently cut?"[25]

Communications received close attention as well. The Brigade Signals Officer arranged communications with the jumping-off trench and with machine-gun positions while battalions would arrange telephone and other communications from enemy lines back to the jumping-off trench. In the event, communication was such that from 0743 to 0915 battalion HQs, brigade HQ, machine-gun groups and the artillery were all working satisfactorily on net. During this period 64 situation reports were passed rearward. 4th Brigade HQ received 38, some of these being forwarded from the enemy front line to HQ 2nd Division in as little as four minutes. Smooth as silk!

The general concept called for an advance of four companies, two from each battalion, on a front of about 800 yards, the 20th Battalion's companies left assault and the 21st Battalion's companies right assault. The advance would be in three waves, intervals of 50 yards between them, the first and second waves each of eight platoons, four per battalion, and the third consisting of carrying parties and other support elements. Each of the assault platoons constituted a self-contained force, one officer and 50 ORs, composed of 11 riflemen, 12 bombers, four rifle grenadiers, eight bomb carriers, three Lewis gun teams, two signallers and two runners. 20th Battalion's second wave would include a section of battalion bombers tasked to hold the block that would be established on the left flank of the battalion. With that battalion's first wave would be a bomber section carrying a reserve of rifle grenades, 10 per man. Two sappers carrying pre-prepared explosive charges accompanied each of the platoons of the first two waves. Company commanders would move with the third wave and control operations from the enemy front line once it was reached.[26]

The tasks of each wave were clearly detailed. First wave would capture and mop-up the first objective, the enemy front line, then form a covering party for the withdrawal. Second wave would leapfrog the first objective, moving to assault the second and final objective, the enemy support line. Two platoons of the first wave would accompany the second wave. Third wave support elements would follow second wave and execute tasks as assigned. Withdrawal from the enemy trenches would commence at Zero plus 45, parties in the front line holding their positions until all had passed through.

25 LAC, 4th Brigade War Diary, January 1917, Appendix 29.

26 In early 1917 infantry platoons were being re-organized. Canadian divisions enjoyed considerable discretion in this, the only restrictions being that establishments be uniform and that every rifleman be trained as bomber, rifle grenadier or Lewis gunner. 1st Canadian Division adopted the organization shown in *SS 144 The Normal Formation for the Attack:* standard nine-man sections and specialization by sections: No. 1 Section – bombers; No. 2 – riflemen; No. 3 – rifle grenadiers; and No. 4 – Lewis gunners. 2nd Division preferred two identical rifle and rifle grenadier sections, a bomber section and a Lewis gun section. Re-organization proved to be a work in progress. Platoon strength and composition subsequently varied for a time. See also Chapter 10 of this present study. In British divisions, too, variations were common. 4th King's Own Royal Lancaster Regiment, for example, preferred one rifle, one Lewis gun, one bomber/rifle and one rifle grenadier section (Shannon, *Lion and the Rose,* p. 127). This was also the general choice in 1st British Division (Pagan, *Infantry,* p. 140).

Other preparations for the raid included the standard extensive training on reproductions of the enemy trenches. Training began with the formation of the two assault companies of 20th battalion and the three companies of the 21st Battalion. The practice trenches were even signed with their German names that had been garnered from captured maps. Platoon commanders received copies of the most recent air photographs. Rehearsals occurred at least twice a day, always at 45 minutes past the hour. Training included instruction in the use of explosive charges and Stokes bombs, the latter proven bunker busters. Rennie frequently reminded that every man had to know all aspects of the plan and his role in it. Training even featured refreshers in first aid including the "Fireman's Lift" which proved useful in casualty evacuation. One rehearsal was done for the Corps Commander after the usual rehearsals for brigade and divisional commanders.

20th Battalion's No. 1 Company, under Major Cuthbert Wansbrough, formed the right assault company of the battalion. Major Harold Foster, MC and Bar, led the left assault company, the battalion's No. 2 Company. Foster was also OC Raid.[27] Both these field officers were well-experienced. First wave platoons were under Captain Harold Parke and Lieutenants Harper Gillham, Reginald Ferguson and J.J. Walters. Second wave platoons were under Lieutenants George Marr, Thomas Stagman, R.G.H. Travers and Benjamin Nicholls. Captain W.H. Keslick, MC, had a single but crucial task in the raid, his responsibility being to ensure that the raid started at Zero, precision being vital given the range and scope of the fire support programme. These officers, in what was to come, would prove an impressive group, the raid for some perhaps their first experience of raiding. This enterprise, clearly something more than "minor," offered in reality a pretty good slice of what a really "big show" looked like.

21st Battalion's three companies totalled 420 officers and men, about the same as the 20th Battalion's two companies. Thirty-two year old Major George Bowerbank, a former bank accountant, who had been with the battalion since the outbreak of war, had been appointed OC battalion raiders.[28] He and one of the other company commanders, Major Frederick Raymond, would receive an MC for the raid. Captain P. Brocklebank commanded the third company.

Artillery and mortar support involved considerable assets and prodigious expenditure of ammunition. Field artillery, 102 guns and howitzers, expended over 35,000 rounds, 2-inch and Stokes mortars adding 15,000 bombs to the downpour of metal. Corps Heavy Artillery contributed nearly 4,500 rounds to which mortars added 600. Given this, and the 327,000 rounds fired by the 41 machine-guns, it is no wonder that many Canadians dubbed the raid the "Million Dollar Scrap," the figure being the rumoured tab for the array of fireworks.[29] The initial state of enemy wire as reported at end-December described it as a thick and formidable mix of staked wire, concertina and "some five or six rows of angle-iron knife rests closely laced together." Based on this, mortars hammered it for a week, this rather in vain since recce determined that

27 DVD-ROM, *The War Gazettes* (Naval and Military Press). Foster would receive the DSO for the raid. Afterward he became a Brigade Major. Wansbrough received the MC in June 1917, this award not relating to the raid, and the DSO in August 1917.

28 Foster, ed., *Letters From the Front,* pp. 47-48.

29 LAC, War Diary, 4th Brigade, brigade report, 'Table of Field Gun and Trench Mortar Ammunition Expended', 'Heavy Artillery Co-operation' and Appendix A 'Conclusions, Recommendations and Notes;' Will R. Bird, *The Communication Trench* (Ottawa: CEF Books, 2000), p. 19. This book is a collection of articles written in 1933.

"very little damage" had resulted.[30] Divisional artillery and Corps Heavy Artillery then battered the enemy lines, known and suspected machine-gun emplacements and points further to the rear. Diversionary tasks included wire-cutting on the southern sector of 2nd Division's front, several lanes being opened by mortars.

At the centre of that sector opposite 5th Brigade wire was cut in several places along a 500 yard front, this in preparation for a diversionary raid by 26th Battalion simultaneously with 4th Brigade's major effort. However, this "not found to be feasible" the 26th instead raided the previous day (16 January). This diversion had been reduced from three companies to three platoons (three officers and 135 men) and it was limited to the enemy front line, the raiders not to remain more than 20 minutes. One platoon failed to enter the enemy trench, it being heavily manned, while the other two on entry found the trench empty. The battalion historian, quoting the 31 January 1917 issue of *Canadian Daily Record,* a tabloid that circulated in the Canadian Corps, claimed it distracted enemy attention from the major raid and "was an essential factor in its success."[31]

Diversionary shelling at Zero would also hit the Double Crassier, this to be followed at Zero plus 15 by a mine detonation, the work of 173rd Tunnelling Company RE. It was hoped these activities would convince the enemy that the raid would be on this tactical feature, the enemy knowing full well that the British desired it. Persistent wire-cutting also went on in that area. Other sappers, a company of 4A Special Battalion RE, made ready smoke barrages on the flanks of the real objective and north of it. Likewise, diversionary activities by 18th and 19th Battalions on 20th Battalion's left flank may have caused some distraction. One diversionary activity, a small raid by 18th Battalion, netted several prisoners at low cost.[32]

Wire-cutting continued on the front where 4th Brigade would raid. On the 12th and 14th mortars (2-inch and Stokes) hit enemy front line trenches while howitzers and heavy artillery struck at selected points. The firing on the 14th was limited to 25 minutes, followed on the 15th by continual Stokes fire on enemy wire. During the night this slackened to allow the enemy to effect some repairs; to continue heavy fire might make him think this area the point of attack. That night patrols reported wire sufficiently cut. That same night each battalion sent out small work parties to cut gaps in own wire, which was left in position with ropes attached so that it could be removed quickly prior to Zero on the 17th. "This completed our preparations," said the 20th Battalion's historian, "nothing possible to foresee [having] been left to chance."[33]

After a hot breakfast at 0400 on Wednesday 17 January the raiders began moving forward from the brigade reserve area arriving at the jumping-off trenches by 0700, the first wave in the front line, the second in CTs and the third in the support trenches.[34] Here with 30 minutes to wait officers and men had time for weapons and equipment final checks: smoke bombs, pistols

30 Corrigall, *Twentieth Canadian Battalion,* p. 100; LAC, War Diary, 4th Brigade, brigade, divisional and Corps Artillery reports.

31 MacGowan, *26th Battalion,* pp. 152-56; LAC, War Diaries, 2nd Division, Operation Order 95; 5th Brigade, Operation Order 110 and 26th Battalion, Appendix 2, raid report.

32 LAC, War Diaries, 4th Brigade reports and artillery reports, and 18th Battalion.

33 Corrigall, *Twentieth Canadian Battalion,* p. 102.

34 LAC, War Diaries, 4th Brigade and the two battalions. The brigade report gives the relevant timings as 0400 and 0700, but both battalions had the move forward beginning at 0430. Corrigall, *Twentieth Canadian Battalion,* says the raiders were in position "about 7:15 a.m."

and rifles, bayonets and for those who had to carry them, heavy hand wire-cutters, mats for crossing wire and light ladders.[35] All was quiet in Canadian and German trenches.

Precisely at Zero the artillery, trench mortar, machine-gun and smoke barrages began, the assault troops up at once and out through the several gaps in own wire and then quick to the enemy wire, a brief pause until the artillery lifted and then the final rush into the trenches, time elapsed less than five minutes during which enemy reaction was slight and ineffective. The first wave, Major Foster's company of 20th Battalion on the left, and to his right Major Bowerbank's company, had no difficulty securing the enemy front line, the first objective, it being only lightly held by a few sentries. These trenches appeared ramshackle, fallen in and badly damaged by shelling, no revetting and few firesteps, likewise the dug-outs, very poor, most full of water and no evidence of recent occupation except for two where several prisoners were taken. No signs of any recent trench maintenance were seen.

As the second wave passed through it picked up the two first wave platoons tasked to reinforce it (given the slight resistance some of the third wave also joined in) and advanced on the second line, the final objective. Most of the men went overland, the wire that had protected the second line proving no obstacle, the guns having done fine work. The parties moving up the CTs found them in a state as bad as the front line. Any dug-out that appeared habitable was blasted apart as the party moved along, so quickly, in fact, that a brief halt was necessary until the barrage lifted and began establishing the protective box barrage around the objective area. By Zero plus 24 the final objective was secured. As they withdrew, many Germans were killed by Lewis gun fire. The sappers now had their way with dug-outs. One sapper described the process of bunker-blasting like this: "light the fuse-drop the charge in-run like hell-look over your shoulder and see the dug-out come out of the door."[36]

21st Battalion's experience on the right flank was similar. Major Raymond reported reaching the enemy front line at 0748 where he found only sentry groups, took several prisoners and then quickly moved on to the second line, the final objective. At 0812 he reported it secure. The good communications that had been arranged worked well, the FOO with the company allowed rapid correction of fire and the FOO had also passed back a stream of messages as to progress, enemy reaction, prisoners taken, casualties and other important information. Even the light signals were good; the white fired to signal first objective taken and the green for second objective were easily perceived by those watching from battalion lines.[37]

Helpful, too, was the mine exploded at the Double Crassier at 0815. Enemy artillery reacted swiftly and strongly to it: "intense fire of all calibres" near the crassier, intensity increasing over 20 minutes and by 0845 "very intense … the only concerted [enemy] bombardment." 4th Brigade rightly concluded that this diversion "produced the desired result."[38]

What remained was the withdrawal, a phase of war (and of raiding) that always presented the danger of counter-attack in strength that could result, things not going well, in a running fight, those withdrawing not able to break free, and the whole of the operation jeopardized. If by day the withdrawal was even more difficult and had to be covered by fire which dictated that troops

35 LAC, 4th Brigade, brigade report. Raiders carried the following bombs: officers, four; carriers, 15; all others, 10. Each company also carried 150 rifle grenades and 50 smoke bombs.

36 Corrigall, *Twentieth Canadian Battalion*, p. 103.

37 LAC, War Diary, 4th Brigade, raid report.

38 *Ibid.*

that had penetrated enemy lines deeply had to withdraw through those that had remained in the enemy front line. This study has offered numerous examples of why withdrawal was so tricky. One major problem was how best to signal it to start, indicators whether by sound or sight often being missed or misunderstood. This raid employed both means. First, sappers drove an underground ammonal tube forward 100 feet from the jumping-off trench. The firing of this at Zero plus 45 would not only signal withdrawal, but would provide a trench for the use of some raiders. Second, it had been arranged that coloured rockets would be fired at intervals along the battalion support trench simultaneously with the ammonal detonation. Even with these means effectiveness proved debatable and hard to quantify given the varying accounts.[39]

Some may have thought the 45 minutes spent in enemy trenches too long, but given the frontage of the raid (800 yards) it is hard to see that anything less would have sufficed to achieve the purposes of the raid. 4th Brigade's report included this conclusion. The balance of profit suggests 45 minutes was appropriate, not that it was strictly adhered to. 21st Battalion, for example, spent 47 minutes in enemy trenches.[40]

In any case, as the Germans began to recover from their confusion caused by the diversions, the loss of telephone lines, the rapid penetration by the raiders and the destruction of company HQs, opposition picked up. Around 0830 artillery retaliation had significantly increased and 20th Battalion raiders had beaten off two small counter-attacks. Before withdrawing at about 0845 the raiders had established covering parties in good positions to hold off any determined counter-attack until such time as all troops in the enemy second line were back in his first line. Then the covering parties withdrew, their movement being overseen by the platoons of the first wave that had held the front line throughout the whole of the raid. Neither raiding party reported any serious difficulty during the return home, there being no dramatic running retreat by "several units" as was supposed in a journal article published long after the war. Who these "several units" were is not clear since elements of only two "units" participated in the raid. The withdrawal seems to have been done in part at section level, meaning several sections would have been observed moving toward battalion lines. This is where the confusion probably arose. During the war the word "unit" was commonly applied to every organization from section up to and including division. Modern terminology is more precise: "sub-unit" now denotes section, platoon and company, while "unit" refers to battalion and above that are formations, brigade, division, corps and above. One must be careful, then, in reviewing archival material and books published at the time and in quoting material from these sources for the units mentioned in the original may not be units at all, but rather sub-units. Context is critical. In the case of this raid by two units of 4th Brigade (20th and 21st Battalions) none of the reports mention any running fights.

As always, there was a bill to pay. Total casualties in the brigade were three officers wounded, 35 ORs killed, seven more dead of wounds, two missing and 133 wounded; in all, 180 of the 875 participants, or about 20 percent. Brigade noted that "a very considerable number of the casualties occurred in our own lines after the withdrawal." One other aspect of withdrawal that could result in difficulty was how easy it was in a strange enemy trench to "confuse one's orientation." Lieutenant Marr and Captain Parke experienced this. After a debate about which way led

39 Corrigall, *Twentieth Canadian Battalion*, p. 103.
40 LAC, 4th Brigade War Diary, battalion and brigade reports.

home Parke went the wrong way, but luckily another officer homeward bound with prisoners set him straight. As for prisoners, Corrigall credits 20th Battalion with 57, including one officer, and one mortar. 21st Battalion reported over 30 prisoners and the capture of one mortar and one machine-gun. The brigade report lists 99 prisoners in all, including the one officer, all from various companies of 22nd Reserve Infantry Regiment. German casualty figures say 18 dead, 51 wounded and 61 missing. The German report described the raid as "an extraordinarily forceful undertaking." This it certainly was, and, moreover, one finely tuned in every detail.[41]

Even so lessons surfaced, but fewer in this case since the raid had been so successful. Of the 35 numbered paragraphs that fill five pages of the section "Conclusions, Recommendations and Notes" of the brigade report, most are really just notes peculiar to this raid. The salient "Recommendations" (lessons) were these. First, the Stokes had been most efficient because they had been placed under the artillery for co-ordination of targeting. Second, anything less than a 45 minute stay would not have sufficed to achieve the raid's purposes. Third, the best withdrawal signal proved to be a watch (many had been issued). The ammonal explosion and the light signals "were observed by few." The latter, however, effectively signalled the capture of the first and final objectives. Finally, despite the unfavourable wind, the smoke barrage was good.[42]

Of interest, at the time this raid took place certain changes underway in German defensive doctrine became for them the subject of debate and tentative and incremental implementation beginning in late 1916 and extending well into 1917. Essentially these marked a transition from linear and rigid defence to one of a zone of fortified localities or strong points consisting of machine-gun posts and "islands" held by garrisons in all-round defence and allowed freedom of movement with counter-attack forces held ready to strike at enemy penetration. In mid-November 1916 the Germans had published *Manual of Position Warfare for All Arms. Part 1a. General Principles of the Construction of Field Positions.* When in early January opposition arose to some of the content the freedom of movement provision was withdrawn and the machine-gunners and "islanders" were told they must hold their ground. Amendments to come would impact on the planning, tactical development and execution of raids by the BEF. Where matters stood doctrinally at that time in the German 12th Reserve Division, the parent division of the 22nd Reserve Regiment, can only be surmised, but from the history of the raid it appears some of the doctrinal changes had been undertaken.[43]

February, too, would prove an active raiding month. As the historian of the British 2nd Division points out, the month opened clear and cold, the frozen ground hampering digging and trench maintenance, but making life easier for the carrying parties that had to lug everything forward to the trenches. Jack Frost also helped those who had to plan and execute raids, these being part of preparations for the coming major offensive. On 1 February HQ 2nd

41 Corrigall, *Twentieth Canadian Battalion,* pp. 103-105; LAC, War Diary, brigade report; Nicholson, *Canadian Expeditionary Force,* p. 234.

42 LAC, War Diary, 4th Brigade, brigade report.

43 After the capture of a copy of *Part 1a* it was published in the SS series of manuals. Another part of the German manual entitled *The Principles of Command in the Defensive Battle in Position Warfare* would become available later. A study of these by Captain G.C. Wynne was published in 1937 in *The Army Quarterly* and then later in his book *If Germany Attacks.* The impact of German changes on British defensive doctrine makes fascinating reading; see, for example, Ian Beckett (ed.), *The Memoirs of Sir James Edmonds* (Brighton: Tom Donovan Editions, 2013), Chapter XXVII.

Division issued Operation Order 187 ordering 99th Brigade to raid. 1st Royal Berkshires got the job, the objective being the salient at the point of two trenches in the Courcelette sector. Three days later division ordered a second raid, this one by 5th Brigade, the raid to be on "similar lines" on the night of 8/9 February (amended on the 7th to 9/10 February). 17th Royal Fusiliers was so tasked.

The former raid, while not of large-scale and scope, is none the less interesting in that it provided some useful lessons for planners of subsequent raids. The other raid offers no particular lessons. It entered enemy lines, took seven prisoners, had 12 wounded and returned to battalion lines.[44]

1st Berkshires aimed to take prisoners or obtain identifications and do as much damage as possible. Two officers and 60 men under Second Lieutenant Burgess immediately commenced training in preparation for Zero set for 0300 on 5 February. Training included rehearsals by day and by night. Artillery would not be involved before Zero, but then the gunners would provide a box barrage around the objective which had been chosen after careful recce and study of air photographs and Intelligence Summaries. Four Stokes mortars would open rapid fire on the objective for one minute starting at Zero, one of the mortars concentrating on a known enemy post. The assault itself would feature two waves, each organized in groups corresponding to the various tasks such as clearing, inserting trench blocks, searching and destroying dug-outs. Time in enemy trenches would be 20 minutes. 99th Machine-Gun Company, assisted by Lewis guns, would deal with any counter-attacks.[45]

At 1800 on 4 February the raiders moved forward to dug-outs near the support line for rest prior to the raid. Later (no time stated in the raid reports) they moved forward to Regina Trench, their jumping-off trench, being firm in it prior to Zero at 0300. Earlier that afternoon recce had reported the state of the wire at the salient and along part of the eastern face as unsatisfactory, a condition that had been foreseen. Consequently, the entry point to the trench shifted by about 100 yards to where the wire "was known to be insignificant." Not content to trust to that analysis the CO, Lieutenant-Colonel A.C. Harris, DSO, who had been closely involved in the planning, decided to go forward in advance of the raiding party, reconnoitre the wire and place the raiders at the point where they would begin the assault. Harris thought this necessary in order to avoid the possibility that the raiders might miss the position opposite the new entry point. Raid reports do not mention when the raiders began moving from Regina Trench to join Harris, but all were in place before Zero. At Zero plus 1 the Stokes would cease firing and the raiders would go hard across the 75 yards to the enemy trench.

This is precisely what transpired, there being, fortunately, no hostile fire during that frantic minute. As Harris wrote

> The leading wave jumped the east arm of the Salient on a front of about 40 yards … and went for the west arm [while] the rear wave crossed the enemy wire, jumped the trench, turned to the left and ran down outside the parapet until they met the enemy, most of whom, including two officers they found near the point of the salient … men then jumped into the trench and in a few minutes all resistance came to an end.

44 Wyrall, *Second Division,* Volume II, pp. 361-63; TNA: WO 95/1371 and 1350: 1st Royal Berkshires and 17th Royal Fusiliers.

45 *Ibid.,* Operation Order 187.

Prisoners were very soon on their way under escort to battalion lines along with the wounded. Twenty minutes having passed the withdrawal began. No enemy counter-attack came in during the raid; in fact, the blocking party at each end of the salient's legs had nothing to do, the enemy apparently ignorant of the location of the raiders. Of the 65 or so members of the salient's garrison, 51, including two officers, were now prisoners. Casualties included Burgess, severely wounded, command having devolved to Second Lieutenant Alec Aveline who would receive the MC for his leadership. Burgess received the DSO for his part in the raid. Other casualties included one man killed and 11 wounded.[46]

Harris thought several lessons were apparent. For one, had raid orders included the positions of the OC and the 2IC delay would not have ensued after Burgess was wounded. Second, so many prisoners had not been expected, the number almost equalling the strength of the raiding party. It might have been better had the escort party remained outside the trench and otherwise uncommitted. Third, the decision that officers would wear helmets with brown covers (probably a sandbag) while the men had white helmet covers (all personnel wore white smocks since the ground was snow-covered) could have been costly and tragic. Finally, Harris closed with this: "Each man carried two bombs, but were told to use their rifles. This gives more dash to the attack and prevents hesitation. No bombs were thrown." This comment reflects the "new" thinking, the wheel well on the way to coming full circle. While the rifle had given way over time to the cult of the bomb, its place in the scheme of things was becoming clear again and increasingly dominant:

> Alf is old as a soldier goes
> With hair that is rapidly turning grey;
> Ever since Mons he has strafed our foes
> In his own cool, calm, methodical way.
> He learned to shoot on a Sunday range,
> His aim is steady and quick and true.
> 'Bombs,' says Alf, 'are good for a change,
> But it's the rifle will pull you through.'[47]

Subsequent chapters will offer more examples of raids marking the return of the rifle, but one comment made at a very high level is appropriate here, albeit it jumps ahead about five months. "Alf" would find his opinions about bombs and bullets shared by many. In July Second Lieutenant Arthur Hodge, 7th Manchesters (3rd British Division) would lead his platoon against an enemy party protected by a covering party and wire: "He rushed the party … killed several with the bayonet and point blank rifle fire, and brought back two unwounded and one wounded prisoner. The raiding party suffered no casualties." Louis Vaughan, MGGS, on behalf of Third Army Commander, congratulated Hodge for his skilful leading and determination (Hodge received

46 TNA: WO 95/137: 1st Berkshires, report of Lieutenant-Colonel Harris; Wyrall, *Second Division,* p.363.

47 *Ibid.;* Dunn, *The War the Infantry Knew,* p. 355, quoting verses circulated by GHQ, author unknown. For the story of the resurgence of the rifle see Radley, *We Lead Others Follow.*

the MC) and ended with this: "The rifle and bayonet were used, and there was no futile bomb throwing." "Futile" is the operative word.[48]

On 10 February 230 officers and men of the 1st West Kents of 13th Brigade (5th British Division) then in the Givenchy sector launched a daylight raid on an 800 yard frontage, the division's first daylight and the most famous of the raids it made, according to the divisional historian.[49] Careful and protracted preparations beginning in early January prefaced this raid. Even before that Lieutenant-Colonel H.D. Buchanan-Dunlop, CO of the 1st, had begun planning it. On the same day the raid had been approved he designated the companies that would do it and briefed the two OCs as to his concept: a daylight affair supported by field and heavy artillery. During the unit's next tour in the line (14-20 January) the ground was carefully studied, this being even more crucial given the more than 50 mine craters that cut up the ground. When thorough recce determined six places where passage would be comparatively easy the two companies were organized in three parties each. Party leaders, four subalterns and two NCOs, then observed the relevant ground by day and patrolled it at night to ensure that they knew the routes across no man's land. On leaving the line on the 20th six days of intensive training began, emphasis being put on the necessity to make the final rush of all six parties simultaneous. As the raid drew closer, artillery registration began, but carefully so as not to tell the enemy that more guns than usual were at it. The fire plan would include six batteries firing a creeping barrage, three firing frontal and three enfilade, while other 18-pounders and 4.5-inch howitzers would concentrate on machine-gun posts. Corps Heavy Artillery would fire counter-battery for 30 minutes before Zero, which was set for 1500 on 10 February. In addition, before the raid medium mortars would hit the enemy front line at about 1500 every afternoon. Some of the bombs were deliberate "shorts" so they would land in and cut the wire. It was hoped that this scheduled "hate" would train the enemy to get their heads down.

On Zero day instead of the usual mortar fire the enemy received the artillery barrage which, according to prisoners, caused them to seek cover. The barrage impressed the prisoners who belonged to a reserve division lately come from the Russian Front. They had not experienced such fire before. The fire was such that one officer thought the spring offensive had started.[50] The CO attributed success to complete surprise and to the excellent wire-cutting by the mortars. Enemy resistance was so feeble the raiders quickly overran the front line and took an officer and 26 men prisoner. The final objective, the support line, also fell sooner than expected. There sappers accompanying the infantry blew up dug-outs, four mineshafts and a bomb dump. Buchanan-Dunlop reduced by half the number of casualties claimed to have been inflicted. Counter-battery fire must have been very effective since enemy artillery did not fire until 23 minutes had passed and never became severe. Battalion casualties, however, equated to 30 percent, 70 of 230 participants (11 killed, 54 wounded and five missing). The CO qualified this, writing that the total included not only raiders but men holding the front line. Most of the wounded were able to remain on duty. He then pointed out what he considered the only mistake made: half the casualties were due to friendly fire because many of the raiders had followed the barrage too closely

48 TNA: WO 95/2661: 3rd Division General Staff, report on raid and memorandum Third Army to III, IV, VI and XVII Corps, 14 July 1917.

49 Hussey, *Fifth Division*, p. 144.

50 *Ibid.*, p. 145; Major C.V. Molony, *"Invicta": With the First Battalion The Queen's Own Royal West Kent Regiment in the Great War* (London: Nisbet & Co. Ltd., 1923), pp. 164-65.

and some had even passed through it. Overall, though, the raid had been carefully planned and prepared, an aspect that impressed senior commanders.[51]

Another daylight raid, this one on Valentine's Day by 9th (Scottish) Division, then in the Arras sector south of the Scarpe, enjoyed equal if not more success, the raiding unit, 9th Scottish Rifles, visiting the Germans with 20 officers and 320 ORs. Several weapons and 43 prisoners were taken. The planner, Major H.W. Forsyth, MC (and later DSO) set Zero for 1100 (1200 German time). After treating the enemy to an intense 60 second artillery and trench mortar bashing, the raiders were up and made good use of ground as they advanced on the selected objective, which being in a shallow dip could not be observed from either flank. Forsyth had planned a two-phase operation. Immediately the short barrage ended two parties would enter enemy trenches through two gaps in the wire cut earlier by trench mortars, push up two CTs, one either side of the objective which was about 350 yards wide, link up in the enemy third line (about 300 yards from the first line) and box the enemy in. The remaining parties, moving right on the heels of the first two, would clear all trenches between first and third line and all dug-outs. Time in trenches would be limited to 40 minutes. During this period smoke would shroud the sides of the box. The whole enterprise, which achieved surprise, the enemy being focussed on his lunch, went so well that Haig sent personal congratulations. Losses were light, two killed, 13 wounded and one missing.[52]

Not so successful at all, surprise not having been achieved, was a night raid west of Serre (about two miles north of Beaumont Hamel) on 11 February by the 10th Worcestershires of 57th Brigade, 19th British Division. "Lessons Learnt" would receive the close attention of the GSO1, Lieutenant-Colonel R.M. Johnson. What got the raid rolling was a brief memorandum on 29 January from the MGGS of V Corps advising that the Army Commander, Sir H. Gough, "wishes the 19th Division to make one or more raids at an early date."[53] The then GOC 19th Division, Major-General G.T.M. Bridges, responded with a proposal for a daylight raid (as it turned out it was done at night) by 150 all ranks of the 10th Worcesters in two waves tailed by moppers-up, the enemy front line being the initial objective and their second line the final objective. The raiders, whose aim was prisoners, would remain in enemy trenches for 30 minutes. Artillery support would consist of an intense barrage on the frontline beginning at Zero minus 1 and then lift to the second line at Zero plus 3, plus a box barrage from Zero plus 5 and reducing in intensity from Zero plus 10 until the raiders were reported as home.[54]

51 TNA: WO 95/1549: 1st West Kents, report by CO.

52 Ewing, *Ninth Division,* pp. 178-79; TNA: WO 95/1738: 9th Scottish Rifles.

53 Wyrall, *Nineteenth Division,* p. 72. Wyrall mentions nine raids by the division between 21 March 1916 and the 10th Worcesters' raid on 11 February 1917. Between 21 March and the date of the MGGS memorandum (29th January) to 19th Division Wyrall mentions five raids. The only prior raid by the 10th was on 15 September 1916 (p. 59). In 'Making the Butterflies Kill', *Stand To!,* 68 (September 2003), pp. 42-43, James Roberts states that nine of the 14 raids by 19th Division were cancelled by battalion commanders before Zero, or by OC Raids after Zero, but before engaging the enemy. Of the remaining five raids, two engaged the enemy, but did not enter enemy trenches. Only three of the 14 raiding parties actually fought in the enemy trenches.

54 TNA: WO 95/2083: 57th Brigade, memo from BGGS and divisional proposal. Wyrall, *Nineteenth Division,* p. 63, mentions Bridges' "exploits in the cavalry" in late 1914 as a Major. The story is in Radley, *Get Tough, Stay Tough,* p. 85. Bridges assumed command of the 19th Division on Christmas day 1916.

Well before Zero (2315 on 11 February) the assault force organized in two waves, the leading wave under Captain G.C.N. Sturt and the second under Captain E.W. Butler, arrived at the jumping-off trench. The advance when it began under cover of the barrage took fire while still about 90 yards from the enemy front trench from a post well in front of the trench. The CO, Lieutenant-Colonel D.M. Sole, explained what transpired: "If our troops had shown more dash this post would undoubtedly have been taken … as it was Capt. Sturt went forward, but the men did not back him up close enough." As the occupants of the post withdrew, the raiders followed them into the trench which appeared greatly damaged and showed no signs of use or occupation. While the first wave secured the trench, an easy task since no enemy were to be had, the second wave moved toward the final objective. There heavy machine-gun fire erupted from beyond the second line. This fire struck so hard at the centre party that it could not enter the second line trench. The other parties on entry found no Germans, but did bomb one occupied dug-out. This party, which did not see the coloured rocket withdrawal signal at 2345, remained in the trench for 30 additional minutes without being bothered and without any sign of enemy. Raid reports concluded that the defence consisted only of machine-gun posts beyond the second line and outposts forward of the first line.

Lieutenant-Colonel Sole concluded with a summation of casualties and an assessment of the state of training. Casualties included 46 wounded, many seriously, three of these being officers. NCO casualties were very high. He anticipated about 60 casualties in all, there being 13 missing. His final comment, which raised a larger issue, did not make pleasant reading:

> It is more apparent than ever, that if the rank and file are to take an active part in operations they must have more training at their work, and their own officers must get more chances of handling them, otherwise the fighting all falls on a few gallant men and the bulk do not do their share, although in this case … there was no enemy to get at.[55]

Sole was not alone in his criticism of training standards, this being widespread throughout the BEF, which helps explain the rapid proliferation of schools of instruction from division up and the concern about officer training expressed by many senior BEF officers.[56] His comment suggests that during the raid there may have been other problems that went unreported. The full page of "Lessons Learnt" from the raid by the GSO1, Lieutenant-Colonel R.M. Johnson, reflects the concerns of his GOC. Johnson mentioned four lessons. First, the enemy probably detected the troops forming up for the raid: "It would have been better had more time been allocated for the move from home trench to the forming-up trench." Second, the men did not get as close to the barrage as they should have. Third, they did not rush to the enemy post behind the company commander, this "a good object lesson for instructional purposes." Finally,

55 TNA: WO 95/2054: 10th Worcesters. Soles' report; Stacke, *Worcestershire Regiment,* Volume 1, p. 242, speaks of little enemy resistance.

56 Radley, *We Lead Others Follow.* A third of this book concerns training including standards, the school system, officer training, training problems and remedies and much else. In February 1918 Sir Arthur Currie expressed his regret about how the inexperience of platoon commanders and the necessity for close supervision of platoon training distracted formation commanders. The GOC 1st Canadian Division at that time considered training of platoon commanders his most challenging training problem.

because enemy machine-gun fire came from between the second and third lines, the box barrage was probably too far out. Three of the four have training implications, as do some of his other comments and all would have been the subject of discussion within and beyond the division.[57]

In the first volume for 1917 of the British Official History Captain Cyril Falls noted certain characteristics of Second Army's front, which for the first half of 1917 ran from east of Laventie to Boesinghe, three being heavy and frequent use of mortars by both sides to compensate for lack of heavy artillery, frequent mining and considerable raiding activity.[58] One raid by Lieutenant-Colonel W.F. Mildren's 6th London Regiment (140th Brigade, 47th British Division), on 20 February involved 20 officers and 640 ORs, these figures including one officer and 20 sappers of 520 Field Company RE and one officer and four ORs of 2nd Australian Tunnelling Company. The objective, south of Hill 60, had a 500 yard wide frontage just north of the Bluff and halfway between the Ypres-Commines Canal and the railway (see MSD 17). Alan Maude, who edited the divisional history, called this raid the "outstanding event of the winter in the Ypres Salient."[59]

Falls wrote that the raid "is said to have brought in the largest number of prisoners ever taken in a raid by a British battalion on the Western Front." Maude agrees, saying the haul set a record never equalled by another British battalion. Will Bird called the haul "the biggest ever by one battalion." It included one officer and 117 ORs, two heavy and three light machine-guns and bags full of documents and maps. In addition, large numbers of enemy were killed or wounded as they tried to escape, and 44 dug-outs, a mineshaft, several weapons emplacements and ammunition dumps were blown up.[60]

Maude attributes success to surprise, this being achieved despite imperfect security:

> The raid was planned and rehearsed long before its actual execution; in fact, it was reported that the proprietors of any estaminet in Poperinghe were prepared to tell you the date, time and personnel of the projected operation for some months before it took place. If this was so, either the German Intelligence Service had deteriorated or the accuracy of the information was doubted, because when the raid was eventually carried after a week's wire-cutting … prisoners admitted that they were completely surprised.[61]

The careful and thorough plan developed for this raid on an enemy salient also had a good deal to do with the outcome. Would that space permitted the inclusion of the whole of Mildren's Operation Order 97. In a word, it is a gem, complete in every respect and logically and precisely sequenced. The first six pages (of nine) are familiar and similar to today's version of an Operation Order that relates sequentially situation, mission, execution, administration and logistics and command and control. With Mildren you know exactly where to look despite the different

57 TNA: WO 95/2054: 19th Division General Staff, 'Lessons Learnt from the Raid on Enemy Trenches west of Serre, 11/2/17'.
58 Falls, *German Retreat to the Hindenburg Line,* p. 533.
59 Maude, *47th (London) Division,* pp. 89-90.
60 Falls, *German Retreat to the Hindenburg Line,* p. 533; Maude, *47th (London) Division,* p. 91; Bird, *The Communication Trench,* p. 20; TNA: WO 95/2702: 140th Brigade, report by GOC. Ewing, *Ninth (Scottish) Division,* p. 322, refers to an Australian raid in June 1918 that surprised the enemy during a relief and netted five officers and 250 ORs.
61 Maude, *47th (London) Division,* p. 89.

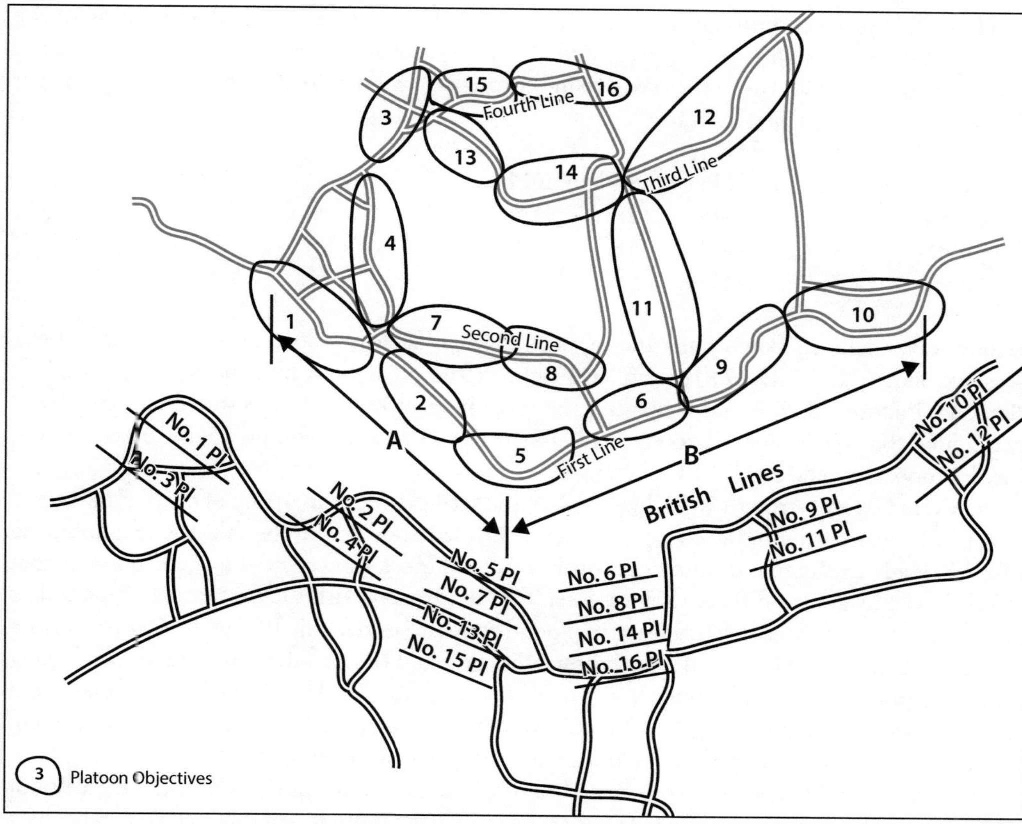

17 Raid South of Hill 60, 20 February 1917, 6th London Regiment.

terminology of the headings. His Operation Order highlights the fact that the present version is a product of a century of incremental improvement that began in the Great War and continued in peace, in a Second World War and since. Mildren's work displays the essential elements of good military writing: clarity, accuracy and "brevity," as much as that was possible given that this division was a Territorial Division and he, like many of the officers who served with the division as brigade and/or battalion commanders and as staff officers, were also Territorials. Very few began with the training and experience of Regular officers, most starting at the bottom of a steeply rising learning curve.[62]

Mildren settled on a daylight raid, Zero at 1700, a time when light was still good enough to ensure good control, but close to the dusk that would hide the withdrawal an hour later. The raid, beyond the usual purpose of kill and destroy, sought precise information as to enemy defences and had specific tasks: locate and destroy mineshafts, search for gas cylinders and find and destroy a light gun that in firing from a suspected position just behind the enemy third line, had caused considerable disruption. In the event, none of these specifics were found. Mildren,

62 TNA: WO 95/2702: 6th London Regiment, Operation Order 97; Maude, *47th (London) Division*, p. 211.

who based his plan on thorough study of air photographs and on a careful Appreciation of the ground, allocated his 16 platoons, weighted to the right in four waves, the first to secure the nearest enemy line with the rear waves passing through to those more distant, "leap-frog," as per *The Normal Formation for the Attack:*

First Wave	5Pl	6Pl	9 Pl	10Pl	
Second	2Pl	7Pl	8Pl	11Pl	12Pl
Third	1Pl	4Pl	13Pl	14Pl	
Fourth	3Pl	15Pl	16Pl		

Second wave included Lewis guns and sappers. Platoon deployments once secure on the objectives are shown at MSD 17. The left and right of the objective would be held by 1 and 10 Platoons, Platoons 2, 5, 6 and 9 holding the remainder of the first objective. Platoons 4, 7, 8 would hold the second line, Platoons 3, 12, 14 the third line and Platoons 15 and 16 the fourth line. Platoon 11 would hold the CT at right.

Diversion features strongly in Mildren's plan, the artillery fire plan, firing of mines, smoke and rockets all contributing to deceiving the enemy. Immediately before the raid the neighbouring 142nd Brigade executed a dummy raid on Hill 60. At Zero miners fired a small mine in that area followed by a second three minutes later. Simultaneously with the first mine, 18-pounders and 2-inch mortars fired a barrage in the vicinity of the mine, this lifting at Zero to form a box barrage. During this time 4.5-inch howitzers targeted trench junctions and known strong points behind the line and smoke was put down on Hill 60. At various points Stokes and coloured rockets added to the show. In addition, 4th Division artillery south of the raid swept the high ground south of the Ypres-Commines Canal with heavy fire.

47th Divisional Artillery also contributed to the deception. During the week before the raid it cut wire daily along the whole of the divisional front with 18-pounders and 2-inch trench mortars and on the morning of the raid intense wire-cutting was done on the front of 142nd Brigade to the left of the raid area. On the front of the raid field artillery could not be put down as the enemy line was too close. Consequently, Stokes worked on the wire at the first enemy line at Zero and continued for three minutes. Field artillery then crept back to the second objective remaining on it for nine minutes, lifting then clear of the second line and forming the box barrage. In addition, until the withdrawal mortars kept firing at enemy lines on both flanks and on junctions and strong points. Corps Heavy Artillery during this period in maintaining counter-battery fire expended 1,900 rounds (6, 8 and 9.2-inch howitzers and 60-pounders). Field artillery expenditure amounted to 24,672 rounds, the Stokes adding over 1,400 bombs. [63] The Stokes proved instrumental in the success of the raid. Will Bird and Alan Maude both described how hurricane fire not only cut the wire – what remained posed no obstacle – but drove the enemy into their dug-outs and the raiders were into the enemy trench before a single machine-gun could get into action.[64]

Brigade reported the enemy completely taken by surprise, neither his men nor his machine-guns in concrete recesses ready. An officer, who proved to be the sector commander, was caught

63 TNA: WO 95/2728: 140th Brigade, brigade report, Operation Orders 125 and 141 and Appendix 'Total Ammunition Expenditure'.

64 Bird, *The Communication Trench,* p. 20; Maude, *47th (London) Division,* pp. 90-91.

unarmed on a tour of inspection of his line.[65] Prisoners were taken in every line within the salient, the raiders having been so quick and the whole so well-organized and conducted that most of the garrison of the salient became prisoners. The diversions, described as being "of the greatest assistance … materially helped the enterprise," and appeared "to have defeated attempts of the enemy artillery to locate the attack until it was too late." Enemy retaliation proved ineffective, most of his fire during the early part of the raid falling on Hill 60 and when he eventually focussed on the raid area, most of his fire hit battalion lines and not the raiders. The enemy, of course, had his own view claiming that only a few raiders entered his lines, most being quickly ejected and prisoners all so drunk they could not be interrogated.[66] As for the cost, the 6th London had 76 casualties, about 11 percent of raid strength. Of this number two-thirds were wounded. In March Lieutenant-Colonel Milden received the DSO for the raid. In January 1918 on promotion he took command of 141st Brigade and ended the war as GOC.[67]

The British Official History offers an useful comparison, describing the largest German raid, 500 all ranks, as one on Hill 60 against the 23rd British Division on 9 April. A four hour bombardment did great damage, the 23rd suffering 278 casualties, including 58 missing, but the raiders failed to destroy the mine gallery that was thought to have been the primary purpose of the raid. The Germans left 40 dead and two prisoners behind.[68]

41st British Division, which had provided a diversion to assist the 6th Londons, launched a raid almost as large on 24 February near Hollandscheschuur Farm northwest of Wytschaete (Ypres Salient). Here, too, the objective was a salient. The raiding party under Major R.V. Gwynne consisted of 17 officers and 550 ORs of the 10th Royal West Surrey Regiment, plus a detachment of two officers and nine ORs of 250th Tunnelling Company RE.[69] Brigade initiated the raid, the 10th being "selected" to do it in accordance with the "plan of operations issued by the Headquarters 124th Infantry Brigade." The BM received due credit: "Captain C.G. Ling, RE, Brigade Major, who by his careful study of past raids and the very clear orders given by him, which left nothing to chance, contributed very largely to the success of the operation." Brigade also arranged for training assistance, seconding Second Lieutenant F.W. Smith, whose "past experience of raids was of the greatest assistance to the CO of the 10th in the training for the raid." The very close "hands-on" of brigade HQ is obvious throughout the raid report.[70]

On 11 February the battalion moved to the rear where training commenced the following morning and would continue for 11 days beginning with practise of individual skills and progressing to rehearsals on a replica of the enemy trench. One aspect, the move forward to assault position, received special attention: "As the raiders were to go into our front line trenches at midday [Zero was set for 1655] down a communication trench on the forward slope of the Vierstraat Ridge, in full view of Wytschaete, very careful training had to be given … every

65 TNA: WO 95/2728: 140th Brigade, GOC report; Maude, *47th (London) Division*, p. 91.
66 *Ibid.*
67 *Ibid.*
68 Falls, *German Retreat to the Hindenburg Line*, pp. 533-34.
69 TNA: WO 95/2641: reports of 124th Brigade and Major Gwynne.
70 *Ibid.* An engineer officer as BM of an infantry brigade was uncommon, the great majority of BMs being infantry officers who had line and staff experience, often as a Staff Captain at brigade and/or as a GSO3 at division before being appointed as a BM; for example, the BM of 2nd Canadian Brigade in June 1918 had served previously as Staff Captain 2nd Brigade June 1917-January 1918 and then as GSO3 4th Division until June 1918.

man was made to realize the vital necessity of the assembly [being] unobserved." On the 23rd the battalion moved to a camp closer to the front leaving from there the following morning for the jumping-off trench. By 1400 the raiders were settled in their jumping-off position, absolute stillness being critical: as the brigade report noted, the presence of 550 men along 450 yards of front and along a CT for over two hours without detection was due to "careful preliminary arrangements and training, and excellent discipline."[71]

At Zero minus 15 a dummy bombardment in a neighbouring sector succeeded in drawing off some enemy fire. Shortly thereafter the guns began a box barrage and at Zero the creeping barrage began. At this time three aircraft of No. 6 Squadron Royal Flying Corps dropped smoke bombs over three points, their effect not observable, but the hope being that fire and smoke would provide some cover for the advance across no man's land.

The infantry, advancing at Zero, encountered little difficulty enroute to the objective where the heavy damage caused by British artillery and mortars showed plainly, "very little" left of the trenches over the whole of the salient. Prisoners (one officer and 54 ORs) speaking of the heavy casualties caused by the fire appeared demoralized. All in all, the riders thought the defenders put up a very poor fight. Sappers destroyed many dug-outs and a mineshaft during the 60 minutes in the enemy trenches. At 1800 a coloured rocket (seen by all) signalled withdrawal. Casualties during the raid came to three officers and 18 ORs killed, 15 ORs also missing and six officers and 105 ORs wounded, or 26 percent casualties. Most occurred during the withdrawal during which time the raiders were under severe artillery and mortar fire. This led to a suggestion in the brigade report as to how this might in future be avoided:

> It is thought that … our artillery [might cease] fire before the withdrawal takes place. The enemy could be led to think the withdrawal was taking place by sending up rocket signals similar to those employed on this raid, but the actual withdrawal would not begin until a certain period after the rocket had gone up and after our artillery had ceased fire.

There is an obvious difficulty here. More counter-battery fire was the better option. Major Gwynne during one of his telephone calls (communications during the raid worked perfectly) had requested at 1735 more counter-battery effort, which on being given had immediate marked effect on the intensity of enemy fire.[72] Another and unrelated comment was this:

> As it is very rare for the same battalion to carry out more than one raid in several months … there should be an officer in each corps who would keep himself in touch with all the latest tips gathered from raids in other parts of the line, and who would be available to assist and advise the battalion commander in preliminary training.[73]

71 *Ibid.*, report of 124th Brigade.
72 *Ibid.*
73 LAC, RG9IIIC1, Volume 3843, Folder 44, File 1, GHQ, 14 February 1917. On 14 February GHQ promulgated staff responsibilities for training, a GSO1 (Training) was established at Army and a GSO2 (Training) at Corps. See also *SS 152 Instructions for the Training of the British Armies in France* (London: HMSO, June 1917), Appendix XIV, 'General Staff Officers (Training)'. Maude, *47th (London) Division,* pp. 44, 58, 85, 89. The division's first experience of raids was being raided twice in December 1915. In June 1916 the division made its first: "a new kind of amusement invented by the

During the first quarter of 1917 the Canadian divisions launched a considerable number of raids large and small, "the pressure of the seemingly never-ending series of raids … against Vimy Ridge during the weeks up to mid-March were by now a cause of concern" for the enemy. Of the five raids launched by 3rd Division, the smallest, a stealth raid of two officers and seven ORs of 42nd Battalion, launched at 0200 on New Year's morning. On entering the enemy trench the party split, one group moving along to the junction of the main trench with a CT. There a sentry surrendered as did another when called in German. The raiders then withdrew: time elapsed 10 minutes, no casualties, no shots fired and for the two men of the 23rd Reserve Infantry Regiment the war was over. Later that month two officers and 25 men of the RCR again surprised the 23rd whose trench they entered at 0730, breakfast time. Five prisoners were taken. Not a shot was fired in the whole of the 10 minute raid. Five days later (28 January) an officer and 20 ORs of 49th Battalion had a turn at the 23rd, entering the enemy trench undetected at 0700 and then protected by a box barrage proceeded to grab eight prisoners and kill nine others. At the 15 minute mark the party returned home with the prisoners. Smack and back! A raid four days later was not quite as tidy, the party of two officers and 28 men had a very stiff fight in the German trench, but did manage to take one prisoner.[74]

3rd Division's largest raid of the first two months of 1917 came at 0915 on 13 February when three officers and 47 ORs of 42nd Battalion under cover of a strong artillery and trench mortar barrage again set upon the hapless 23rd Reserve Infantry Regiment. Fire support included a two-minute barrage of rifle grenades fired by 19 rifle grenadiers. The combination raining down forced many of the defenders to their dug-outs, three of the four assault parties entering the trench unopposed. However, Lieutenant Frederick Gillingwater's party met with heavy rifle fire and flurries of stick bombs that prevented entry for a time. During the bombing Gillingham was twice wounded, first on entering the trench and then again so seriously he had to be carried out. At this time another enemy party attacked. The FOO with the assault party, Lieutenant Conn Smythe, seeking a better spot for observing fire, had just joined Gillingwater's party. Seeing what was going on, he led the raiders in a charge, personally killing two Germans and wounding another. Having driven the enemy off, he organized the bombing of a very large dug-out with five entrances. In his report the brigade commander remarked on how unique it was for an artillery officer to lead a raiding party, but Smythe "proved the right man in the right place at a critical moment … and acted in a most gallant manner." Meanwhile, the other parties, no opposition in sight, bombed 10 large dug-outs, most with three entrances, with grenades and Stokes bombs. Two prisoners were taken. Withdrawal posed no difficulty, all personnel home by 0935. Casualties were only nine wounded. Gillingwater and Smythe both received the MC. Summing it all up, the brigade commander described the enterprise as "a good plucky raid that worked smoothly."[75]

Canadians [this was not so] … the raid was done by the 19th London Battalion." The division raided again on 3/4 July (twice, night and early morning), on 8 July and on 22 December 1916. Its next raid was the one described here.

74 Sheldon, *German Army on Vimy Ridge,* p. 248; LAC, RG 9IIIC3, Volume 4077, Folder 4, File 1, 'Raids Carried Out by the Canadian Corps'.

75 LAC, War Diaries, 7th Brigade and 42nd Battalion, reports of GOC and CO. Topp, *42nd Battalion,* offers no additional information, his account virtually duplicating the War Diary. Conn Smythe is a name familiar to ice hockey fans. In 1927 he and several others purchased the Toronto Maple Leafs,

4th Canadian Division, although equally active in February, preferred raiding on a larger scale, six of seven raids nearing or exceeding 100 all ranks and the seventh just over half that. Three of the raids featured 10th Brigade and four 12th Brigade. One of the 10th Brigade raids in February was described in detail earlier in this book with special mention of the fine planning of the CO of 44th Battalion. An eighth raid by 4th Division was executed on the night 28 February/1 March in a strength of over 1,700 all ranks. As it ended in March it will be examined in the next chapter.

10th Brigade made the first of these February raids on the 3rd. Participants included three officers and 72 ORs of 44th Battalion under Captain C.S. Belcher and six officers and 93 ORs of 50th Battalion under Major H.L. Keegan. Zero was at 2100, the barrage bang on time and the assault parties moving close behind it to the enemy lines. The right party under Lieutenant Kaufman (44th Battalion) reached the wire in good order, but at the gap a machine-gun firing from the right not only seriously wounded Kaufman, but all NCOs of the party as well. Two scouts got this party into the trench where clearing began. Meanwhile, bombers of the covering party disposed of the machine-gun. The left party under Lieutenant Norman Pawley, according to a Canadian Corps report, entered the trench without opposition, there capturing a machine-gun and silencing another with a Lewis gun. In this part of the trench 14 prisoners were taken.[76]

Major H.L. Keegan, OC of the 50th Battalion raiders, organized his men in six parties each under an officer. During the approach to and the entry into the enemy trench the raiders came under severe machine-gun fire, both frontally and enfilade, from the enemy line to the north. Clearly, the enemy had stood to immediately the barrage ended and offered stiff resistance including a determined counter-attack. However, the raiders prevailed and bombed 17 dug-outs; the raiders had been instructed to ask for surrender only once, time being short, and "no time was wasted at dug-outs in waiting for men to come up." The enemy in the support line strongly supported the first line. Seven prisoners were taken. Casualties for both battalions included one officer missing, believed killed and four wounded. OR casualties included five missing, one killed and 15 wounded.[77]

The next day (4 February) 73rd Battalion of 12th Brigade had a turn in the form of a daylight raid at 1400, the purposes being to take prisoners, to determine whether mineshafts were being dug and to report on how the enemy was holding his line, it being suspected that by day it was lightly held. The raiders began training on the morning of the 2nd on a replica of the enemy trench marked out in the snow. Initially four assault parties, each of one officer and 20 men, and two covering parties, 15 men each, were organized, but this was changed the next day to only one covering party and "all the parties were finally selected and every man familiarized with his task." At this time fire support was finalized, the enterprise to be covered by artillery, trench mortars and Stokes. A final conference at brigade HQ confirmed that nothing had been neglected. One the morning of the 4th the raiders moved forward where final preparations commenced.

At Zero all went well, wire no difficulty and no casualties being suffered enroute enemy trenches which all four parties entered by Zero plus seven. Lieutenant R.G. Vincent's party

Smythe remaining with the ownership until 1961. He also served during the Second World War, being severely wounded during that struggle.

76 LAC, War Diary, 10th Brigade, report of 44th Battalion; Russenholt, *Six Thousand Canadian Men*, pp. 72-73. Lieutenant Pawley's citation for the MC refers specifically to the capture of the machine-gun as well as to his leadership.

77 LAC, War Diary, 10th Brigade and 50th Battalion, reports of GOC and CO.

working to the left soon found a mineshaft which they destroyed with 30 pound explosive charges. At a junction with a CT two prisoners were taken. Lieutenant Harold MacGregor's party, which had worked right on entry, encountered no enemy, but destroyed a second mineshaft. Lieutenant Walker's party, finding no enemy in the sap that was its objective joined MacGregor's party. Lieutenant E. Grestock's party moved quickly along the trench to a junction that had to be blocked, but there bombs killed Grestock and 10 men and wounded five. On being so informed MacGregor with his party moved to the junction, got the survivors out and then blocked the trench. His quick action prevented much worse happening and for it he received the MC. The 20-minute limit having arrived withdrawal began. No two accounts agree as to casualties during the raid, but it seems that one officer was killed and another wounded and 13 ORs were killed, two were missing and believed killed and 14 were wounded. While the raid had achieved its purposes, the cost exceeded 25 percent of raiding strength.[78]

Two days later at 2200 on 15 February two officers and 54 ORs of 72nd Battalion (12th Brigade) raided enemy trenches on Vimy Ridge. During the preceding three weeks the two officers and some of the party had reconnoitred the approach to the objective several times in order to become thoroughly familiar with the ground. For the raid two parties had been formed, Lieutenant William Ross and 30 men in one and Lieutenant Thomas Barrie and 24 men in the other. All went smoothly during the raid. Barrages by artillery and Stokes forced the defenders into cover, leaving the attackers free to enter the trench without being fired upon. There 11 prisoners were "taken very easily and showed no fight." Six other Germans were killed. Casualties were three wounded.[79]

A raid about twice the size was made by three officers and 93 ORs of 46th Battalion of 10th Brigade during the late afternoon (Zero at 1730) of 19 February. Few Germans were found, 10 or so being killed trying to escape rearward. While no prisoners were taken a good lot of shoulder straps was gathered to provide identifications. The trenches appeared generally heavily damaged. The raiders withdrew without incident.[80] Four officers and 80 ORs of the 78th Battalion (12th Brigade) also raided that day, Zero at 0930. The course of events was much the same, but the results more rewarding in the form of three prisoners. One of the bombed dugouts probably contained explosive stores for simultaneously with the explosive charge came a huge explosion "a large crater forming and large quantities of debris thrown as far as our own trenches." The NCO who laid the charge was killed 20 yards from the entrance. Later that day more explosions were heard and smoke arose from the scene of the great explosion.[81] Three days later (22 February) the 78th Battalion contributed a platoon to a 38th Battalion raid by 88 all ranks on an objective not far distant from the raid on the 19th. No prisoners were taken during a

78 LAC, War Diaries, 73rd Battalion and 12th Brigade, brigade preliminary and final reports, battalion report and Operation Order 39.

79 LAC, RG9IIIC3, Volume 4077, Folder 4, File 1, 'Raids Carried Out By the Canadian Corps', 12th Brigade War Diary, report on raid and Operation Order 48. Ross received the first of this three MCs here, the other two being awarded in 1918. Barrie received the first of his two MCs, the second coming later in 1917.

80 LAC, War Diaries, 46th Battalion and 12th Brigade.

81 LAC, War Diary, 12th Brigade. The BM at this time, Major Richard Partridge of the Devonshire Regiment, had served as Staff Captain with a British brigade earlier. In July he went to a British division as GSO2. The progression – Staff Captain, then BM, then GSO2 – made for a well-experienced officer. Partridge was awarded the MC and the DSO during his war service.

struggle with an enemy aroused and willing to fight hard. The bill came to three men killed and 27 wounded. The one party that had to conduct a running battle during its withdrawal suffered most of the casualties.[82]

This leaves four raids that conveniently close out this chapter and the month of February. Here it is more accurate to speak not of four raids, but of two pair of raids, each pair, one Canadian and one British, hitting the same objective twice within a 24-hour period. Such double raids were uncommon, but not novel since 47th (London) Division had done a double in July 1916.

During the early morning of Tuesday 27 February, and again late that night, the Germans were at home to 1st Canadian Division, at that time the southern most of the four divisions of the Canadian Corps facing Vimy Ridge. On the division's right was 51st (Highland) Division and to its left stood 2nd Division, then 3rd and, finally, 4th Canadian Divisions. 2nd Canadian Brigade did the pair of raids, the first at 0330 and the second about 19 hours later at 2230. The early birds, five officers and 60 ORs of Lieutenant-Colonel William Gilson's 7th Battalion, were supported by a covering party of 20 and a smaller party (one officer and 16 men) whose target was the tip of a salient a short distance away. From Zero minus two to Zero heavy artillery and Stokes "stonkered" the objective, some of the latter also firing on the flank. As the barrage lifted to the enemy support line, the larger party quickly entered the front trench without much by way of hindrance, there killing 10 Germans and seizing three prisoners.[83] The smaller salient party, supported by Stokes only, received fire from the wire protecting the salient and had to withdraw. During the morning raid casualties were "very slight."

Lieutenant George Allan led the night raid consisting of 32 ORs and an engineer officer and six men, the party being shot in by artillery and Stokes much like the morning raiders had been. Thereafter matters progressed somewhat differently starting with "very heavy resistance" at the point of entry. Allan, although wounded immediately on entering the trench, carried on getting the two raiding parties moving left and right, each with three sappers working along the trenches. The left party covered about 75 yards bombing five dug-outs as it went and the sappers destroying three others with large charges. Voices, lights and cooking in progress indicated that these were all occupied. The right party got about 90 yards down the trench where it was checked by an enemy party firing and throwing bombs from a dug-out. One of the sappers managed to reach this dug-out and hurled an explosive charge in the door. Twenty minutes having passed, the raiders obeyed the signal to retire. A vigorous and prompt enemy response, including artillery retaliation, began within four minutes of their infantry SOS signal that had been fired even before the raiders entered the trench. In addition to Allan 12 others were wounded and two were missing believed killed. Captain William Alston, the BM, concluded his report by saying the raids provided "an occasion of coming to grips with the enemy and experience of making an attack. In respect of both … valuable results were obtained."[84] In view of the forthcoming major attack on Vimy Ridge the two raids were no doubt beneficial in a general sense.

82 LAC, 12th Brigade War Diary, Operation Order 51 and report on raid.

83 LAC, War Diary, 2nd Brigade, 'Preliminary Report on Raid by 7th Battalion'. For three days prior to the raid field and heavy artillery and medium and light mortars had cut wire.

84 LAC, War Diary, 7th Battalion, 'Report on Raid'. William Alston, a British officer, was one of two Captains who served as BM of 2nd Brigade, the other being William Herridge, a Canadian. Alston was BM from August 1916 until July 1917. He joined 2nd Brigade from 63rd British Division where he had been a GSO3. On leaving 2nd Brigade he became BM of 172nd Brigade, 57th British

The first of the pair of British raids by the 2nd Worcestershires (33rd Division) on the Pekley Bulge on the Clery Spur west of Peronne came at 2043 on the night of 27 February, followed by the second four hours later at 0100 28 February. The first raid consisted of two officers and 57 ORs under Second Lieutenant Edward Hopkins, accompanied by a sapper officer and seven men. Hopkins organized his men in three parties for the raid which was covered by Stokes, rifle grenades and Lewis guns. After a brief fight in the enemy trench, the parties withdrew with seven prisoners. Casualties included one officer and 10 men wounded. German artillery retaliated strongly for a brief period after which comparative quiet prevailed except for Lewis guns firing to prevent or hinder the enemy making repairs. No time was wasted in preparing the second visit, the new party under Second Lieutenant Eric Durlacher consisting of five officers and 150 ORs, plus 15 sappers and their officer, being assembled as quietly as possible. At 0043 the raiders passed through their own wire and lay down just in front of it. Shortly after 0100 mortars and Lewis guns began heavy firing whereupon the raiders raced forward, some enemy fire striking at them, but mostly this was wild, and they were soon in the enemy trenches and into a vicious fight. An enemy counter-attack launched very quickly and strongly was defeated and the trench was blocked. For 30 more minutes the raiders blasted dug-outs and rampaged until the withdrawal sounded at 0200. The raiders and their 16 prisoners, later found to be Prussians of the 2nd Guard Grenadiers, headed home. Casualties included one officer killed and two wounded, six ORs missing believed killed and 47 wounded. Six sappers were also wounded. The historian of the 33rd Division, Graham Hutchison, quite rightly described this second raid as "particularly fine." As for the brigade commander, he thought smacking Prussian Guards twice in one night worth special mention! Certainly, the night said a good deal about the 2nd Worcestershires.[85]

These pairs of raids shared several characteristics: they were smaller in scale, they were simple, they were "easy" to plan and execute and they all succeeded, which is to say they entered enemy trenches, did considerable damage and, with one exception, took prisoners. Finally, they present a sharp contrast to a very large raid to come that would share none of the characteristics just listed. It would prove novel, however, in a number of ways. This raid opens the next chapter.

Division. By 1917 staff work in 1st Canadian Division was of a very high standard. For the Vimy Ridge attack 2nd Brigade's plan, the work of the GOC, F.O.W. Loomis and Alston, comes off as best in the division. Arthur Currie, then GOC 1st Division, and his GSO1, Lieutenant-Colonel R.H. Kearsley, had only five comments on 2nd Brigade's plan (there were 24 on 1st Brigade's plan and 21 on 3rd Brigade's plan). If one reads these the reason is obvious. Alston's work is just simply superior quality: plan, preliminary instructions, Movement Order and Operation Order, the whole package finely done. Afterward, Loomis, who demanded much from subordinates and was not given to empty display, singled Alston out for his "work throughout." Kearsley, a much-admired British officer and one thoroughly liked within 1st Division, was GSO1 from July 1915 to August 1917. He had joined the division from the Indian Cavalry Corps where he had been a GSO2. He left the Canadian Corps on appointment as BGGS VI Corps. For further information on Alston and Kearsley see Radley, *We Lead Others Follow*, pp. 228-30.

85 Stacke, *The Worcestershire Regiment*, pp. 238-39; Hutchison, *Thirty-Third Division*, p. 30; TNA: WO 95/2406: War Diary, 33rd Division General Staff, 'Scheme I'.

12

1917 – High Expectations

> Oh, ye brave who rush to glory, or the grave!
> Thomas Campbell, *Hohenlinden*

In February 1917 the Canadian Corps could look back at a string of successful small and large raids, some observers seeing the latter as the Canadian forte. And why not given 3rd Division's 400 man raid on 20 December that netted 60 prisoners; 2nd Division's daylight endeavour by 800 men on 17 January, the haul being 100 prisoners; and the 13 February raid by 800 men of 4th Division – specifically Brigadier-General Edward Hilliam's 10th Brigade – that had scooped up 50 prisoners. The last had been planned by Lieutenant-Colonel Reginald Davies, of 44th Battalion, an officer suddenly and widely deemed *the* raiding expert. To be sure, there had been casualties, but, nevertheless, the record was solid. With everything coming up roses there was no reason to think the string would not continue.

The next large-scale Canadian raid, 4th Division's major effort on the night 28 February/1 March, would prove the thorn in the bouquet. This raid, the first in this chapter, will be followed by examination of several other significant raids, Canadian and British, that occurred during March 1917, thereby closing the first quarter of the year. Before looking at 4th Division's monster raid it is appropriate and useful to consider a raid that was proposed but never happened. It involved a technology that would also feature on 28 February/1 March in 4th Division's raid.

On 13 January Major Thomas Morrisey, BM 8th Brigade (3rd Division) signed off and issued Operation Order 71 which began "In accordance with instructions received from 3rd Canadian Division gas will be discharged on this Brigade front." The instructions referred to came from Lieutenant-Colonel R.J.F. Hayter, GSO1 3rd Division. The information that formed the basis of these instructions came from Canadian Corps HQ, specifically from the BGGS, P. deB. Radcliffe, who had become involved in 8th Brigade's undertaking for the simple reason that neither 3rd Division nor the Canadian Corps controlled the special asset that featured in 8th Brigade's plan. Consequently, Corps asked Army to arrange the assistance of the Special Brigade RE. As it turned out, the request was for naught.

There was nothing unusual in such a request. It adhered to the hierarchy and the organization of the BEF and the staff system: what went up and down was part and parcel of not only the chain of command but of the staff chain: BM to GSO1 at division, then to BGGS at Corps and then to MGGS at Army. The staff was the lubricant that made the command wheels go round, it being the instrument through which a commander exercised command. It provided a commander with the relevant facts needed to form ideas and decisions, it informed a commander about the possible consequences of his decisions, it converted a commander's decisions into orders and it conveyed these orders to those who had to execute them. While staff and commander relationships were critical so, too, were inter-staff relationships. A BM, for example, while directly responsible to his commander, had also to work closely and well with the GSO1 at division. Close and frequent liaison between the staff levels was critical since this was what enabled trust to develop and be maintained. Conferences, too, made for an efficient relationship and system. In a corps as close knit as the Canadian Corps the BGGS became closely involved in the guidance of GSO1s and his ideas, methods and personality indirectly influenced BMs and even division and brigade commanders. The BGGS, for example, attended the weekly conference of his staff superior at Army. On return to his HQ he appraised his commander of developments and he conferred with divisional GSO1s who on return to their HQs briefed BMs. Staff levels did not and could not work in isolation, most certainly not in the Canadian Corps with its permanent four divisions where commanders and staff officers had time and continuity to develop the strong relationships that enabled solid co-ordination, co-operation and routine and constant sharing of ideas and information.[1]

So when in February 4th Division planned a raid using assets not under Canadian Corps control, just as 8th Brigade had thought to do, the GSO1 of 4th Division, Lieutenant-Colonel Edmund Ironside, forwarded raid requirements to the BGGS. He probably followed up personally with Radcliffe, the relationship no doubt helped by the fact that both were British officers and they may well have previously known each other. It is inconceivable that Radcliffe, an enormously talented officer, would not have mentioned 8th Brigade's proposed raid and he may well have suggested that Ironside confer with Hayter about it, including why the raid never came off.

That brigade had planned release of gas followed by smoke to simulate a second release followed by "Battle Patrols" founded by 4CMR and 5CMR, each of two officers and 35 ORs to enter enemy trenches to see what damage the gas had done, do more damage and bring back gassed Germans dead or alive. The preliminaries, including the labour-intensive movement forward of the heavy (150 pound) gas cylinders and their installation in the trenches by Special Companies RE, went well as did the other preparations such as fire planning. But Mother Nature intervened. Commencing on 14 January wind began blowing east to west into the face of the Canadian infantry and the RE personnel standing by to release the gas at 2000 on Tuesday 16 January. No change in the wind meant no gas and no raid, but the raiders remained in the line while the rest of the brigade was relieved as planned. Two days later, it being apparent that the wind would not soon co-operate, the raiders were withdrawn, but only to begin a shuttle forward and back, each move up a reaction to a momentary lull in the wind that seemed to offer opportunity, and then, hope dashed, another trek to the rear. This went on for two exhausting weeks until 8th Brigade and the raiders had to move elsewhere, the "show" now put amongst the things that would never be. Not surprisingly, little of this appears in the War Diaries.[2]

1 For details of the careers of Hayter and Radcliffe and for the staff system of the BEF see Radley, *We Lead Others Follow*. In contrast, 46th British Division, for example, served in 10 different corps during the war: I, II, III, V, VII, XI, XIII, XIV, XVII and XVIII (Beresford, *The Christian Soldier*, p. 225).

2 LAC, War Diary, 8th Brigade, January 1917, Appendix B, Operation order 71, 13 January; Sheldon, *German Army on Vimy Ridge*, pp. x-xi.

To what extent 8th Brigade's frustrating experience became a subject of discussion between 3rd and 4th Divisions, either by the GOCs, Louis Lipsett and David Watson, or by GSO1s Hayter and Ironside, we cannot say. No doubt, there was some conferring, 8th Brigade at this time being the only Canadian formation that had experienced the process of preparing for the use of gas. At the very least, the 8th could offer an infantry perspective on what such preparations entailed. But consultation or not, there then being no artillery gas shells available to the Canadian Corps, and the Livens Gas Projectors not yet in service, 4th Division would, perforce, have to "muck in" with the sappers and their nefarious devices, in this instance Major-General C.H. Foulkes and his Special Brigade RE. The infantry did not see sappers as pals for whenever they appeared it meant additional labour for the infantry. Getting the sapper's devices forward would just add to the load, for sappers were "Boss" and the infantry beasts of burden. 8th Canadian Battalion's "Ten Commandments" summed up the relationship: "Remember that thou workest on the Sabbath … six days shalt thou labour and do more than thy oughtest, but the seventh is the day of the C.R.E. [Commander Royal Engineers], on it thou shalt do all manner of work."[3] Thus 4th Division was left to getting on with the Special Brigade and to other planning. This chapter further explains the raid.

One part of the explanation is the officers who would plan and execute the largest Canadian raid of the Great War. These officers included the division and brigade commanders and their primary staff officers, the GSO1 at division and the BMs at brigade HQs. Of the four battalion commanders most closely involved in the raid two would stand out because of their opposition to the raid and their tragic deaths. The GOC 4th Division and his GSO1 also warrant the closest attention since their actions and decisions were decisive.

One of the most heralded commander-staff officer relationships of the Great War was the Hindenburg-Ludendorff collaboration, the first a genial and calm strategist, the latter somewhat highly strung, but untiring and inspirational. Such matches were critical, the ideal being that the pair be different: if one was a generalist then the other should be a man of detail; if one was reserved then the other should be outgoing. In the Hindenburg-Ludendorff case the fit was excellent. Their relationship and its results have been much examined. Hindenburg's summation of it is instructive of what such a relationship should be:

> the relations between the chief of staff and his general, who has the responsibility, are not theoretically laid down. The way in which they work together and the degree to which

3 LAC, MG 30E60 (Matthews Papers), Volume 3, Folder 2, 'The Ten Commandments'. Andrew Rawson, *British Army Handbook 1914-1918* (Stroud: Sutton Publishing Limited, 2006), pp. 94-95; Major-General C.H. Foulkes, *"Gas!": The Story of the Special Brigade* (Edinburgh: Blackwood, 1934), pp. 94-95 and Adkin, *The Western Front Companion*, pp. 312-13. These sources are most helpful in describing the Special Brigade. On re-organization in January 1916 the brigade consisted of 208 officers and 5,306 ORs organized in four Special Battalions numbered 1 through 4, each battalion of four companies, seven officers and 218 ORs per company. Each company was capable of installing and operating gas cylinders along 1,500 yards, this being the usual frontage of a division. For the raid M Company was allocated to 4th Division. The Special Brigade also had a Stokes 4-inch Mortar Battalion of four companies, each with 16 4-inch mortars manned by 18 officers and 315 ORs. Finally, the brigade included a separate company designated "Z Company" consisting of 18 officers and 300 ORs organized in four sections that were initially equipped with manpacked flame projectors.

> their powers are complementary are much more a matter of personality. The boundaries … are therefore not clearly demarcated. If the relations … are what they ought to be, these boundaries are easily adjusted by soldierly and personal tact and the qualities of mind on both sides … They are at one in thought and action … harmony formed the basis … as to proper use of our resources. Differences of opinion were easily reconciled without our relations being disturbed.[4]

While this relationship existed on a much higher plane and it reflects the German Army's concept, it does offer useful ideas and a striking contrast to the state of relations between the GOC 4th Division, Major-General David Watson, and his GSO1, Lieutenant-Colonel Edmund Ironside, the former a Canadian and the latter a Briton. This was not unusual in the Canadian Corps which prospered thanks to generally good commanders and a generous giving by the British of their very best when it came to filling the senior staff appointments in the corps that Canada could not. As Andrew McNaughton later said, "We had … the pick of the British Army. They were absolutely superb … we had … staff officers … the like of which no other corps had … We owe them an immense debt of gratitude."[5] At the time of the raid the commanders of the formations involved – 4th Division and its three brigades – were all Canadian except Edward Hilliam, 10th Brigade, who was British born, had served in the British Army and would later return to it. Their senior staff officers were all British. All three brigade commanders, Hilliam, Victor Odlum (11th Brigade) and James MacBrien (12th Brigade) saw action during the South African War. Hilliam, the newcomer to 4th Division, had assumed command of 10th Brigade on 18 January. Odlum would be a central figure in the raid.[6]

Watson, the first CO of the 2nd Battalion and then GOC 5th Brigade as of August 1915 had taken command of 4th Division in April 1916. His division arrived on the Somme on 10 October 1916, remaining there under command of II British Corps, its task being to capture Regina Trench, while the rest of the Canadian Corps moved to an area between Arras and Lens. Not until late November did the 4th rejoin. Watson, a pre-war newspaperman and a Militia officer, had led his battalion at Second Ypres with distinction: "His lean, seamed face, with its twisted, sardonic smile … had been seen at every crisis point." His battalion had the highest number of casualties in 1st Brigade. During the withdrawal, the last man to leave, he found and carried a wounded man out. Second Ypres made him an obvious choice for a brigade.[7]

There is some evidence to suggest that after the St. Eloi fiasco in 1916 Watson's priority as a brigade commander became self-interest and self-promotion, seeking always to grab undue credit, this and "bad judgement" completely alienating at least one battalion commander to the point where he demanded a meeting with higher command to express his grievance. However,

4 Paul von Hindenburg, *Out of My Life*. F. Holt, (trans.) (London: Cassell, 1920), pp. 84-86.
5 John Swettenham, *McNaughton*. Volume 1: *1887-1939* (Toronto: The Ryerson Press, 1968), p. 67.
6 At the outbreak of war Hilliam became Adjutant of the 5th Battalion, later commanding the 25th Battalion, then 10th Brigade as of 18 January and, finally, a British brigade. MacBrien, a Regular cavalry officer (Royal Canadian Dragoons) from 1907 on, commenced training at Camberley in 1912, but did not attain his psc since the Staff College was closed in August 1914. He then became a GSO3 at the War Office in 1914. Thereafter he was a staff officer with 1st Canadian Division and the Canadian Corps, being promoted to command of 12th Brigade in September 1916. Odlum, initially 2IC of 7th Battalion, and then its CO as of April 1915, took command of 11th Brigade in mid-1916.
7 Herbert Fairlie Wood, *Vimy!* (London: Corgi Books, 1972), p. 69; Cassar, *Beyond Courage*, pp. 132-33.

as he later regretted, he did not pursue the matter. In 1917 another battalion commander, this one in 11th Brigade, developed a similar opinion, describing Watson as "mercenary" and a politician who used his division to enhance his profile and reputation.[8]

Watson, a not particularly well-educated officer, did not express himself well in terms of his personal philosophy as a formation commander and seemed to have trouble defining concepts. Postwar, G.J. Farmar, a former Deputy Adjutant and Quartermaster General of the Canadian Corps, recalled his acute embarrassment listening to Watson attempting to explain his concept of operations in response to a question from Currie during a Corps Commander's Conference. The other part of Farmar's recollection of the question, and the stumbling response, is even less flattering to Watson the man and Watson the General: as Watson was attempting to answer Currie his GSO1, Edmund Ironside, "contradicted him at every point."[9] Such gross disrespect, and Watson's toleration of it, went well beyond the immediate audience. E.L.M. Burns, then a junior officer, had this to say about Watson:

> We frequently saw him about. But his personality was rather put in the shade by that of Ironside. The general opinion was that Ironside was the real commander of the division. It is not surprising that this view was current – whether it was true or not – when one recalls Ironside's subsequent career, toward the end of which he became Chief of the Imperial General Staff.[10]

Nor does the incident Farmar recalled say much for "Tiny" Ironside, but it does fit Brian Bond's description of him as "not so much the archetypal 'gentle giant' [he was six foot four inches tall] as a supremely self-confident, forceful and opinionated commander."[11] Overweening confidence would drive 4th Division to its nadir.

Another aspect of this unpleasant incident is this: Watson, evidently, had not been actively prepared to consider seriously and deeply the formulation of his concept of operations, which is a fundamental element in command and control. One must wonder, then, to what extent he was prepared to direct, monitor and influence the detailed thinking involved in thorough planning, a process running from concept to Appreciation of the situation including ground and the preliminary and final planning of any operation.

8 Patrick H. Brennan, 'Byng's and Currie's Commanders: A Still Untold Story of the Canadian Corps'. *Canadian Military History,* 11. 2 (Spring 2002), pp. 5-16. Brennan attributes these opinions and remarks to Lieutenant-Colonel J.A. Gunn, DSO, CO 24th Battalion, expressed in a letter to Colonel A.F. Duguid in 1938. The second CO, Lieutenant-Colonel John Warden, DSO, 102nd Battalion, is quoted in Stephen Harris, *Canadian Brass: The Making of a Professional Army* (Toronto: University of Toronto Press, 1988), pp. 113, 117-18.

9 McGill University Archives (MUA), Urquhart Papers, C.1, File 13, response of Farmar to a circular letter. Known as "Jolly" Farmar for his sense of humour and ready wit, Farmar had friends everywhere. This very gifted British officer was much admired for his great efficiency and energy. See Radley, *We Lead Others Follow,* p. 237.

10 Lt. Gen. E.L.M. Burns, *General Mud: Memoirs of Two World Wars* (Toronto: Clarke, Irwin and Company Limited, 1970), p. 15. During 1917 Burns was Signals Officer of 11th Brigade.

11 Brian Bond, 'Ironside' in *Churchill's Generals,* John Keegan (ed.). (London: Warner Books, 1992), p. 18.

Such characteristics no doubt influenced Watson's style and performance, as did the fact that at the time of the raid he and his staff were strangers to Julian Byng's Canadian Corps. Watson's initial experience of divisional command had been with II British Corps on the Somme. Consequently, he likely felt some pressure to do well for his new boss. Given the inevitable pull of competition and rivalry, one can surmise that in looking to make his mark with Byng and with his peers, Watson was drawn to a raid, and not just more of the same, but a large-scale raid featuring some innovation to add to the profile. With whom the idea of a gas raid originated cannot be said. 3rd Division's experience did not deter him or Ironside for that could be seen as simply bad luck. Clearly, the risk inherent in an experiment with gas just a few weeks before the biggest Canadian attack of the war did not deter either. Nor would the reservations of some senior officers in the division, an obvious concern in their minds being the lack of any training with gas and an almost complete absence of knowledge of it from top to bottom within the Corps. Complications and limitations would soon surface.

Terry Carroll, the author of a fine journal article concerning the death of a relative who was killed while serving with the Special Brigade RE and 4th Division, refers to the raid as a "recce in strength." He does not provide the source of this quotation, but it might well be a recollection of Pierre Berton's book on Vimy wherein this inaccurate statement appears: "a raid, or, as it was called at the time, a 'recce in force.'" Had Berton kept in mind the fact that recce is only one of the numerous reasons why raids were made he might not have made such a statement, providing, of course, he was aware of the 1902 manual *Combined Training (Provisional.):*

> When it is uncertain whether a position is occupied in strength or not and it is impossible to determine the fact by any other means, recourse may be had to reconnaissance in force. But this method of clearing up a situation involves so many disadvantages that it should never be employed unless the necessity is urgent. If only a portion of the force is used it may be exposed to attack … if the whole is used success or failure will depend to great extent on chance … if no weak spot exists the consequences may be disastrous.[12]

In any case, the plan's the thing, as an ancient Staff College expression cautions. The objectives of the raid were four in number: to test the defences of Hill 145 to see whether or not it was held in strength; to reconnoitre the position with a view to facilitating the actual assault in First Army plan of operations; to destroy enemy lines, dug-outs and wire; and to kill and capture Germans. The critical point, Hill 145, was also the highest point on Vimy Ridge. One might well question the large numbers of officers and men involved were it not for the fact that the raid was intended to be made on a 2,000 yard front. The plan stipulated one man every two yards, a strength that though weaker than for a regular assault "appeared sufficient" even if the gas effects should not be as great as expected.[13]

12 Terry Carroll, 'A Wexford Soldier Dies With the Canadians at Vimy Ridge'. Western Front Association *Bulletin,* 98 (March 2014), pp. 15-17; Pierre Berton, *Vimy* (Toronto: McClelland & Stewart, 1986), p. 126; *Combined Training (Provisional.),* Section 58.

13 LAC, 4th Division War Diary, March 1917, Appendix A, 'Report of Operation With Gas on Night of February 28th/March 1st'; *German Retreat to the Hindenburg Line: Appendices,* Appendix 11. Byng planned to take Vimy Ridge sometime after 15 March. 3rd and 4th Divisions were already in the sector of the Canadian front from which they would attack. Early in March he would order 1st and

4th Division's plan designated 11th Brigade (Odlum) as right assault and 12th Brigade (MacBrien) as left assault. Assault battalions from south to north were the 54th, 75th, 72nd and 73rd, total raiding strength almost 1,700 all ranks. Hilliam's 10th Brigade would play a minor diversionary role by providing a smoke barrage and strong patrols to enter enemy lines to ascertain the effect of the gas.[14] The assault would be a wave followed by strong "patrols" accompanied by sapper demolition parties. Instead of a preliminary bombardment, which would ruin any chance of surprise, gas would be released along the entire front in two lots: "White Star" (chlorine/phosgene mix) at Zero (0300 1 March), followed by "Red Star" (chlorine only) at Zero plus 120, the infantry assault 40 minutes later. Because phosgene required a propellant upon release, chlorine had to be added to the first release. The other essential propellant was a strong and constant wind to drive the gas up the hill and in the right direction. Without such a wind then all the low-lying areas in no man's land would fill with gas, a decidedly unhealthy environment for the raiders who would have to cross it twice. "M" Company, Special Brigade, would install the gas cylinders that infantry work parties would bring forward over several days and initiate the gas releases.[15] E. L.M. Burns, Signals Officer of 11th Brigade, later wrote about how gas would provide surprise, "knocking out those defending the forward trenches, force them to put on their gas masks, or take refuge in gas-proof dug-outs [either course enabling] the raiders to enter their positions with little or no opposition." Enemy wire would be cut by Bangalores. Heavy artillery and the fire of 70 machine-guns would isolate the enemy and 4-inch Stokes would fire "SK" lachrymatory bombs at areas not intended to be occupied by raiders. Withdrawal would commence 90 minutes after the raiders entered the enemy trenches, meaning that 0700 or so would see all raiders back in Canadian lines.[16]

Neither the plan, nor the very idea of using gas, universally impressed. Several senior officers had no reluctance in expressing their deep concern about the raid, chief among these the 37 year old GOC 11th Brigade, Victor Odlum, an officer who after the enormously successful raid by his 7th Battalion in late 1915, became known as the expert planner of raids and the master raider. While a decidedly competent officer, and one much admired for his courage and fine leadership

2nd Divisions to take up their attack positions on the Canadian right, 1st Division on the right of the line, a fitting tribute given the division's history.

14 Raiding strengths per battalion according to their War Diaries (LAC) were as follows (first figure is number of officers): 75th Battalion, 15/390; 72nd Battalion, 15/300, and 73rd Battalion, 18/450. 54th Battalion reported only a total of 481 all ranks This comes to 1,669 in all.

15 As only one Special Brigade officer was attached to each brigade, brigade commanders had to decide which battalion the officer would be attached to. Whichever the choice, the officer still had responsibility for the gas release on the entire 1,000 yard brigade frontage. The two sapper officers were to advise divisional HQ at midnight if weather conditions were favourable or not. That HQ would then tell brigade HQs "Go" or not and battalions would then be so informed. While the Operation Orders do not say so, it is likely that the sapper officers would have received the order to release the gas through the HQ of the battalion to which each was attached. In addition to the usual slate of officers at Advanced Brigade HQ there was to be an officer of M Special Company and an officer of No. 4 Special Battalion, RE (see footnote 3).

16 LAC, War Diary, 4th Division, Appendix A, report on operations. As it turned out "faults" with the 4-inch Stokes meant that only 60 bombs were fired. Burns, *General Mud,* p. 39; Foulkes, *"Gas!"*, pp. 111-14, 198. Chlorine and phosgene both inflamed lung tissues and caused victims to drown. Unlike chlorine, phosgene could be breathed in fatal doses without undue discomfort or coughing. It also had "remarkable delayed action" causing symptoms (and death) 24 or even 48 hours after taking it in.

– he was wounded three times, twice while GOC – he had at times exhibited some contrary and peculiar ideas about things such as the Ross rifle and the rum issue (see Chapter 8).[17] Prior to the attack at Vimy he favoured a unique system of relief within his brigade. It was not a good one. For one thing, rotation by company meant that a battalion was always half in the line and half out of it all the time. The negative impact on training is obvious. Battalion training should have been done under the eyes of the CO but, as Burns wrote, "if he was responsible for a sector of the front his eyes would generally be turned in that direction and the training would be left more or less to the company commanders, whose standards might not be so high." Moreover, as Burns also pointed out, the relief system meant that Odlum was constantly forward.[18]

Despite all this, Odlum retained the confidence and respect of his brigade. His concern for his men was well known, so, too, was his loyalty to his officers, this, according to Burns perhaps "somewhat excessive. Junior officers on the staff thought he retained certain battalion commanders when they might better have been replaced. He was not a ruthless man, although his manner sometimes made people think he was." It seems Odlum also knew a lame horse when he saw one for as the raid drew closer he strongly objected to it. Burns recalled listening (he was the Brigade Signal Officer) to Odlum "using very stiff, almost insubordinate language" urging divisional HQ to cancel the raid. In subsequent visits to divisional HQ he met with Ironside with whom he forcefully argued for cancellation, presenting not only his own concerns, but those of the two COs who had vigorously protested the raid. The CO of the 54th, Arthur Kemball, CB, DSO, had been a long-serving officer in the British Army before emigrating to Canada. He had been CO since the 54th formed in November 1915. Kemball thought that the unpredictability of the wind made postponement necessary until conditions stabilized. Second, he considered the allocated artillery support inadequate should the wind not be a friend. Another CO, Samuel Beckett of 75th Battalion, believed his men were at great disadvantage as they had no familiarity with gas, this being, in fact, true of the entire division. Odlum also protested vehemently at what he and others recognized as the major fly in the ointment: no preliminary bombardment. If the gas did not negatively affect the enemy by creating casualties and/or forcing them to take cover then they would be able to savage the raiders approaching across no man's land. The question was this. If the gas did not do as expected, would sufficient numbers of men survive to settle with the enemy in his trenches? As Zero drew closer, the postponements began night-by-night for more than a week. Each time the wind was neither in strength nor blowing in the right direction. Many officers in the division concluded that as this had ended any possibility of surprise the raid should be cancelled. There does not seem to be an account of what GOC 12th Brigade, James MacBrien, thought or said about the raid beforehand, but given his background he no doubt recognized, as Odlum had, its primary flaw. But nothing swayed 4th Division or Corps. The time for argument over, the raid would go as planned.[19]

Once all the "rats" (sapper-speak), or "lunch baskets," as the infantry called the gas cylinders, were in place the sappers of M Special Company would prepare to do their part. The first cylinders

17 Radley, *We Lead Others Follow*, p. 261; *Get Tough, Stay Tough*, p. 213; Burns, *General Mud*, pp. 14-15.

18 *Ibid.*

19 MacBrien, a more reserved man and an invariably calm one, commanded 12th Brigade to the end of the war. Postwar he became Canadian CGS. Burns, *General Mud*, pp. 14-15, 39-40; LAC, MG30E300 (Odlum Papers), Volume 19, "'Gas Attack, Vimy'; 11th Brigade War Diary, February/ March 1917.

arrived forward on the night of 19 February, more arriving during the next two nights, the BM 11th Brigade, Major M. Ferrers-Guy, DSO, Lancashire Fusiliers, remarking on the "big" working parties the brigade had to provide to carry the cylinders forward.[20] Carroll describes the intense labour involved in getting over a thousand 150-pound cylinders forward to the release points. Canadian work parties, 48 men per party, met the cylinders at the points to which they had been brought from the railhead. The men lugging them forward from there used various methods, one being toboggans that once loaded they dragged overland to their release positions. There M Company installed them in "rat traps" (frames) half-buried in the trenches and protected them with sandbag wrappings. The last cylinders arrived and were placed on 26 February. At the designated time, they would run the discharge pipes out into no man's land and await Zero to open the stoppers.[21] As much as they hated the labour what really bothered the infantry was having to live beside the cylinders, which at any time could be shattered by enemy fire. Private Frank Richards, for example, recalled his experience with gas on returning from leave a year earlier. He and his pals "thoroughly hated the sight of those cylinders and knew the danger." When enemy shelling smashed some cylinders, Richards' company had suffered many casualties.[22] On the night of the 25th February 1917 a few broken cylinders in 11th Brigade's area caused some casualties, but it could have been far worse for the enemy was "active with minenwerfers on our front."[23]

4th Division's War Diary for 1 March reported the raid in four lines, the essence being the first gas release was at 0300, but owing to a change in the wind the second set for 0445 was cancelled and the assault troops advanced under cover of artillery. 11th Brigade's War Diary is virtually the same, adding only that while "some" of the raiders gained the enemy line, "in the face of intense rifle and machine-gun fire [they] had to retire." Two COs were killed, Lieutenant-Colonels Kemball (54th Battalion) and Beckett (75th Battalion). 12th Brigade's War Diary said the infantry advanced, entered enemy trenches, killed many Germans and destroyed a bomb dump and numerous dug-outs.[24]

Kemball's 54th Battalion, the right assault battalion of 11th Brigade (immediately to the right or south of the 54th was 3rd Division), reported enemy reaction to the first gas release as prompt. At Zero plus two enemy flares went up, followed within a minute by red rockets and rifle and machine-gun fire, their artillery joining in five minutes later, this fire not heavy, but continuing for considerable time, thereby indicating that the gas "apparently had no effect." At 0540 the raiders of the 54th commenced the assault. The battalion historian described what happened:

> Unfortunately after the first lot of gas … the wind shifted, and instead of drifting across to the Hun lines [it] went down No Man's Land and entered the Hun lines opposite 3rd Division on our right … Consequently, the Bosche was ready for us … we advanced through a heavy barrage up to the enemy wire, but were unable to penetrate his trenches in face of the terrible machine-gun fire and grenades.[25]

20 *Ibid.*
21 Carroll, 'A Wexford Soldier', p. 16; Hayes, *The Eighty-Fifth in France and Flanders*, p. 44.
22 Richards, *Old Soldiers Never Die*, p. 100.
23 LAC, War Diary, 11th Brigade, February 1917.
24 LAC, War Diaries, division and 11th and 12th Brigades.
25 LAC, War Diary, 54th Battalion; *Cinquante-Quatre: Being a Short History of the 54th Canadian Infantry Battalion By One of Them* (N.p.: Privately published, 1919), pp. 13-14.

Both the 54th and the 75th Battalions referred to the unfavourable wind that prevented a second gas release on 11th Brigade's front. The 75th, whose neighbour to the north was 12th Brigade, reported that at 0445 the 12th did make a second gas release. This "rolled down No Man's Land and came back to 11th Brigade's support trench and respirators had to again be fixed." To this release enemy reaction echoed that made to the first release. Most enemy fire had ended by 0515. The assault parties began moving to the jumping-off line in no man's land at this time. Thereafter enemy flares and rifle fire commenced, followed by red rockets and then rifle and machine-gun fire that became general by 0530 when artillery began falling on Canadian front and support trenches. 12th Brigade reported fire on its assault troops when the enemy discovered 11th Brigade moving forward. Ten minutes later the Canadian barrage began, as did the 54th Battalion's raiders. What happened then to the 54th as related above was not quite the whole picture. Thick wire entanglements also explained the failure to enter enemy trenches: "no headway could be made." The 54th also found supporting artillery fire not adequately concentrated, "very short" at left and centre which was where it suffered most of its casualties.[26]

75th Battalion's raiders, split into seven parties, each under an officer, moved forward to the jumping-off position immediately behind the battalion support trench at 10 minute intervals, all being in position just before Zero. To the gas release at 0300 the enemy promptly responded. While only one shell hit the support trench it did force the raiders to don respirators for about 30 minutes. 12th Brigade's second gas release again forced the 75th into respirators. At 0515 the raiders occupied the jumping-off line in no man's land. When the Canadian barrage began at 0540 the enemy responded with heavy machine-gun fire. As the raiders moved to the assault, the enemy in his strongly manned trenches inflicted severe casualties. Only on the left could significant entry be gained, three parties penetrating beyond the frontline and heavy fighting ensuing. These parties, which remained only very briefly, bombed several dug-outs, thought 75 Germans had been killed and then withdrew with eight prisoners; unfortunately, many wounded raiders, including an officer, could not be evacuated. At the centre, only a few men, including the battalion 2IC, Major Langstaff, who was killed, gained entry. Those who survived did get out with one prisoner. No enemy gas casualties were observed in either area. Several of the raiders believed that the enemy exploded small land mines in the gaps in their wire as the raiders passed through. If this was so, then this, too, said "no surprise."[27]

In summary, then, none of the raiders of the 54th made it into enemy trenches. Caught in the wire they were savaged. Those men of the 75th that did enter enemy trenches were too few to tarry long. 11th Brigade had put in 825 men and suffered 425 casualties, or, in effect, every second man who participated.

Advancing north of the 75th Battalion were the raiders of 72nd Battalion (12th Brigade) under Major R.K. Johnston who would be killed. He had organized his raiders into a first wave of three officers and 100 ORs and five "patrols" each of two officers and 40 men plus sapper demolition parties. Prior to Zero the whole force sheltered in gas-proof dug-outs and tunnels, emerging after 0500 to occupy jumping-of positions. All stood ready to go by 0540. The first wave (A Company), tasked to secure the first objective (the enemy front trench), moved off on time and secured the trench handily, there being little immediate opposition. However, when

26 LAC, War Diaries, 54th and 75th Battalions and 11th Brigade report, Appendix A, March 1917.
27 LAC, War Diary, 75th Battalion.

a strong enemy party emerged from a large dug-out vicious bombing fights began, the raiders eventually prevailing and taking 14 prisoners in the process. D Company also got off to a good start, following the first wave into the enemy trench, but B and C Companies were not so fortunate, heavy artillery fire on their jumping-off positions making things very difficult. While perhaps half of B Company got promptly away, the other half experienced gas leaking from cylinders which caused such delay that B and C Companies had to abandon the raid. The patrols of B and D Companies that did join A Company in the enemy front line moved off quickly toward their objectives, a line of craters about 300 yards beyond the enemy front line, but soon encountered a swamp of water-filled craters. There some disorganization and loss of direction occurred as the patrols tried to find pathways forward. One patrol ended up becoming mixed with men of 73rd Battalion and subsequently did not reach its objective. Another patrol became surrounded and had to surrender. A third party that did reach its objective found it vacant.

In the end, none of 72nd Battalion's patrols got as far as had been intended. Damage inflicted was mostly to the first line trench. Most casualties occurred as the patrols withdrew to that line, the enemy being in large numbers and closely pursuing; in short, running fights. The battalion report on the raid concluded by directing attention to two particular points. First, the gas had little impact, only one German found to be suffering from gas. Second, while the front line was lightly held as soon as the patrols left it they immediately came under fire of numerous machine-guns.[28]

73rd Battalion assaulted in similar fashion: a first wave of about 100 all ranks followed by four patrols each of an officer and 40 ORs, the former to secure the front line and the patrols to move on from there up two CTs destroying dug-outs as they went and then clearing up and down the enemy support trench. Shortly after the first release of gas at 0300 heavy enemy machine-gun and rifle fire began and hundreds of flares went up, this continuing for 30 minutes, sure notice that "the gas was not effective." A few minutes later heavy artillery fire erupted across the whole of the battalion front continuing to 0400. Several damaged cylinders released gas killing six men of M Special Company and preventing the infantry using this area, about 300 yards long. In addition, gas drifting back toward the Canadian trenches interfered with the assembly of the raiders and forced them to proceed to the jumping-off positions overland instead of by the trench. While assembly was in progress, fire opened upon the front and support trenches because 11th Brigade raiders in occupying jumping-off positions in front of their wire had been detected. Despite all this, the raiders moved at 0540. As soon as the strongly held enemy front-line was secured, the patrols began moving up the CTs to the enemy support line. One patrol encountered heavy machine-gun fire just as 72nd Battalion had, while another did not leave the enemy front line since it had to reinforce the first wave which had suffered heavy casualties. Another patrol encountered heavy fire, part of it, including the OC, disappearing and "not been heard of since." It made no progress due to superior enemy strength. Only one patrol reached its objective and there the patrol commander suffered severe wounds.[29]

28 LAC, War Diary, 72nd Battalion, report on raid; McEvoy, *72nd Canadian Infantry Battalion,* pp. 38-41.

29 LAC, War Diary, 73rd Battalion, report on raid; Alexander McKee, *Vimy Ridge* (London: Souvenir Press, 1966), p. 41. 102nd Battalion, which did not participate in the raid, also found its trenches full of drifting gas.

Victor Wheeler, 50th Battalion, learned after the first gas release that rats were not keen on gas either. Sitting in a gas-proof battalion bunker there suddenly came to him a sound "like water rushing over rocks":

> To my horror dozens of terrified rodents were rushing down the steps … tails and whiskers twitching [they] had somehow gotten beneath the heavy gas curtain at the dug-out entrance … Instinct, I supposed. Or had they detected gas? Strangely, I shared a measure of sympathy with these bedeviled rats.[30]

12th Brigade's report, signed off by the BM, Major Richard Partridge, MC, Dorsetshire Regiment,[31] is an excellent account of the raid, its six pages so well-written and comprehensive that the GSO1 (Ironside) seems to have incorporated three of it pages virtually verbatim in the divisional report. The "General Remarks" that opened the brigade report primarily concern gas, as does a part of the fifth section entitled "Narrative." Both are summarized here. First, gas had no effect on the enemy except to make him come up out of his dug-outs and man his trenches and machine-guns. It also gave him a definite idea as to where the attack would likely be made.

Second, the gas attack failed. Many of the first release cylinders were not let off and none of the second release were (here this report erred since as related earlier some of the second release occurred). Finally, only one enemy casualty caused by gas was known. When the raiders advanced they saw no masks on the enemy, nor except in a very few places did the raiders smell gas in the enemy lines. Prisoners from four companies reported practically no casualties due to gas. Gas was also the primary topic in the section entitled "Lessons." First, gas is "most unreliable in its effect." Second, gas personnel did not seem to be in sufficient numbers to quickly release the gas; in one brigade area there was only one sapper officer to control a front of 1,000 yards "too much work to do from … when the emplacements commenced to the liberation of the gas." Of greater concern the final decision to release gas rested with the sappers of the Special Company. Finally, owing to the great demand for labour the report recommended that gas should not be used on more that a 500 yard frontage.[32]

12th Brigade's Intelligence Summary of 2 March said only that a raid had been made, the raiders had entered enemy trenches and pushed patrols forward and "the enemy managed to get on gas helmets quickly and came out of dug-outs before gas actually reached their front lines." In short, the gas had no negative affect on their readiness. 4th Division's Intelligence Summary No. 71 of 1 March included details that should have been left to further careful analysis. The following are perhaps the most egregious and inaccurate assertions about this "successful" raid.

30 Wheeler, *50th Battalion*, pp.102-103. It is not clear in Wheeler's account what bunker he was in. As a signaller he could have been at an Advanced Brigade HQ, several having been established in 11th and 12th Brigade areas. 50th Battalion did not participate in the raid.

31 DVD-ROM, *The War Gazettes 1914-1919* (Naval and Military Press). Partridge was later in the war awarded the DSO. Appointed a Staff Captain in January 1916 he became BM 12th Brigade in May. In July 1917 he was appointed GSO2 in a British Division.

32 LAC, War Diary, 12th Brigade, report on raid. Partridge is describing what occurred in 12th Brigade. If what he says was the situation, then it was not what was intended. Footnote 15 states that each brigade had a Special Brigade officer attached. He was responsible for the whole of the frontage of the brigade. That footnote also describes the release procedure. While engineer personnel would physically release the gas, it would be on the order of the infantry HQ.

First, "weather conditions were ideal for release of gas, but it did not appear to be as effective as we had expected." Second, prisoners report that the raid was "not expected [see next paragraph], nor did they know that gas cylinders had been placed in our line." Finally, full details were not yet available, "but our casualties are not thought to be very heavy." In fact, casualties were almost 700. Of these, 12th Brigade suffered 275. Such editions further demonstrated to many readers the shortcomings of Intelligence Summaries and those who produced them.[33]

In summary, both battalions of 12th Brigade entered the enemy trenches, despite the enemy "undoubtedly expecting" the raid. The line opposite 73rd Battalion was most strongly held which accounts for casualties being twice that of the 72nd Battalion (see below). Prisoners totalled 37 from three companies of the 11th Bavarian Infantry Regiment and from one company of the 261st Reserve Infantry Regiment.[34]

Why, then, did the raid fail? Or did it fail? It certainly tested enemy defences, it reconnoitred, it did some destruction and it killed some Germans and captured others, achieving to some degree the four objectives assigned to it. The rub was the cost, almost 700, which made it, depending on what source you have at hand and which one you agree with, "complete fiasco, disaster, almost a complete failure, near disaster, an utter debacle, appalling disaster, notoriously unsuccessful or most costly failure of its type of the whole war". 4th Division's report called it a "partial failure."[35] The balance of profit says this raid failed.

The two most credible reasons for the failure, and the ones that appear most often, were loss of surprise or gas. In contemporary accounts the raid is frequently referred to as the "Gas Raid." Private Fraser of 31st Canadian Battalion, the biographer of Lieutenant-Colonel Cy Peck VC, and the Military Advisory Board all call gas the culprit.[36] Looking at the loss of surprise, the last account (1920) thought "surprise entirely lacking" because of the escape of two German prisoners who "obtained" details of the raid and got this information back to German lines. No source is given for this, and in any case, it seems apocryphal and can be dismissed out of hand. Pierre Berton claimed that "everybody" in the rear areas knew about the attack; he offers one account in which French villagers supposedly repeatedly asked a soldier of 75th Battalion "When's the gas attack?" Again, we do not know where this comes from and even if we did, did this soldier really get asked this question about a gas attack?[37] However, this does raise the question of security. An earlier chapter related how the Germans were very good at listening in to men talking in the trenches, or on telephones about matters they should not have been. Significant information may have come to them in such ways. Sheldon gives an example of

33 *Ibid.*, Intelligence Summary No. 63; 4th Division War Diary, Appendix B, Intelligence Summary No. 71; Murray, *2nd Canadian Battalion*, p. 235; Hamilton, *War Diary*, p. 171.

34 LAC, War Diary, 4th Division. A supplement of 2 March to the divisional report stated that 47, not 37 prisoners, had been taken.

35 The thumbnail sketches are from the following: Brereton Greenhous and Stephen J. Harris, *Canada and the Battle of Vimy Ridge: 9-12 April 1917* (Ottawa: Department of National Defence, 2004), p. 76; Singer, *31st Battalion*, p. 187; Nicholson, *Canadian Expeditionary Force*, p. 234; Sheldon, *German Army on Vimy Ridge*, p. 241; Carroll, "Wexford Soldier," p. 17; 'Raids' by Colonel W.W. Murray ["Kultus Nanich,"], p. 338; LAC, War Diary, 4th Division, report on raid.

36 Roy (ed.), *Journal of Private Fraser*, p. 252; Edward Peck, *Cy Peck, VC: A Biography of a Legendary Canadian* (Winnipeg: privately printed, 2008), p. 75; Military Advisory Board, *The Turn of the Tide*, p. 119.

37 *Ibid.*, p. 120; Berton, *Vimy*, p. 128.

how a proposed German raid at the end of March would be cancelled because the night before an intercept of Canadian telephone conversation revealed that the Canadians were expecting it. He also mentions a sort of conspiracy theory: "a story [that] spread (and persists to this day) that somehow the defenders must have had advance information and set a trap." He sees no truth in this whatsoever. According to the theory, Canadian prisoners told their captors that German advanced knowledge caused the failure, a handy explanation when a man does not want to blame his own side.[38] The author of the history of the 85th Canadian Battalion surmised that the enemy became "fully informed" of the plan, but how this came to be he does not say. Presumably he concluded this for the same reason that then Lieutenant (later General) Burns did: the postponements over a week "must have allowed the Germans to learn what was intended," an opinion shared, he says, by the raiding battalions and brigades.

Frank Underhill, author of the *Canada* volume (1923) of Lucas' *Empire at War,* thought the raid failed "chiefly through having too broad a stretch of No Man's Land to cross." The only other reference to such a cause is in Major-General Watson's diary where he wrote that the Canadian and German trenches were too far apart. This must surely have been recognized during the planning of the raid, but it would seem that distance was not considered a disadvantage strong enough to appreciably change the raid or cancel it. Yet it appears prominently in Watson's diary. Ground, it should be remembered, is a critical element in any tactical Appreciation.

Sheldon thinks it "far more likely that the raid failed because it was too large and unwieldy, was poorly prepared and badly executed." Not all of this can be accepted. He goes on to say "the use of gas seems ... to have been particularly incompetently handled."[39] This strikes a chord, reminding us of Major Partridge's "lessons" above about gas: unreliable, insufficient personnel to use it, lack of supervision and decision delegated to M Company (see also footnotes 15 and 32). All of Partridge's points are about poor handling of gas; grief, indeed, considering that the critical element in this raid was gas! 4th Division's report concluded with this: "The partial failure of the operation and the consequent heavy casualties" was due to the following causes: the ineffectiveness of the first gas release; the change of wind, which prevented the greater portion of the second wave from being discharged; and the enemy discovery of the 11th Brigade's advance before it got well clear of own wire. While the last point affected what the brigade's raiders could do in the enemy trenches, what failure really came down to is gas. Everything depended upon it. When it failed, the raid failed. Watson wrote that over-estimating the effect of gas led to too much reliance being placed on it.[40]

Drawing any conclusions on the impact of the heavy casualties requires some arithmetic. Precise calculations are only as good as the figures in the reports. This also applies to the number of participants on any raid. Figures for wounded can also be misleading; 73rd Battalion, for example, mentioned that a "very large proportion" of battalion casualties were "slightly wounded" and the proportion of killed to wounded was "about 1 to 7."[41]

38 Sheldon, *German Army on Vimy Ridge,* pp. 241-42, 261.

39 Hayes, *85th Battalion,* p. 44; Burns, *General Mud,* p. 39; Sir Charles Lucas, gen. ed., *The Empire at War.* 5 vols. Oxford: Oxford University Press, 1921-26. Volume 2, *Canada* by Frank Underhill (London: Clarendon Press, 1923), p. 165; LAC, MG30E69 M-10 (Watson Papers), Diary; Sheldon, *German Army on Vimy Ridge,* p. 243.

40 LAC, 4th Division raid report.

41 *Ibid.,* 12th Brigade report.

Starting with 54th Battalion, the War Diary says 15 officers and 390 ORs took part in the raid. Of the six officers killed, one was the CO, two were company commanders, Captain W.L. Tooker and Major F.T. Lucas, who was recommended for the VC, and three were Subalterns.[42]

Two other officers later died of wounds. The wounded included the other two company commanders. Of the four company commanders on the raid all were casualties! Such figures represent a savage cull of the senior leadership of the 54th. The figures for ORs were 83 killed, 10 died of wounds, 89 wounded and seven missing. Total battalion casualties were 204, a casualty rate of 50 percent. The casualty picture in 75th Battalion is no better. No figure appears extant for the number of officers who participated, but of those that did the CO and his 2IC, Major J.M. Langstaff, were killed. One officer was reported missing. Seven others, including two company commanders, were wounded. Again, a tragically high cost to bear. OR casualties included 68 killed, 112 wounded and 31 missing. Of the 481 participants, casualties came to 221, a casualty rate of 45 percent.

Of 12th Brigade's 783 raiders, 243 were casualties, including 14 officers. 72nd Battalion lost Major R.K. Johnston, who led the battalion, and a Subaltern killed, two Subalterns wounded and missing (believed prisoners), one other Subaltern missing and two more wounded. Of 72 OR casualties (figures vary) 15 were killed, 24 were missing and 33 were wounded, a rate of just under 25 percent. Of 73rd Battalion's raiding strength of 18 officers and 450 ORs, 158 all ranks became casualties, a rate of about 33 percent. Of the officers on the raid four were missing and four wounded, one subsequently dying of his wounds. OR casualties included 26 killed, 37 missing and 99 wounded.[43]

In summary, 4th Division's raiders consisted of 1,569 (figures vary), plus sappers of M Special Company RE, 12th Canadian Field Company and 176th and 182nd Tunnelling Companies RE, all together something just over 1,700 officers and men. The infantry suffered 37 officer and 630 OR casualties, a casualty rate of 42 percent. Of the 60 infantry officers on the raid, 61 percent became casualties. Another source lists 41 officer casualties; if this was so, the rate rises to 68 percent.[44] In either case, the raid resulted in a very severe cull of middle-ranking officers, the very category that would have seen some of these very soon as battalion or even brigade commanders. It also seriously ate away at the seed corn, the Subalterns. A military index that has historically signalled failure of an operation has been any report speaking of heavy losses

42 *Cinquante-Quatre,* p. 14; Greenhous and Harris, *Battle of Vimy Ridge,* p. 77. This book quotes a conversation in no man's land during the two hour truce after the raid between Captain D.S. Elliot, 73rd Battalion, and a German officer, the latter "loud in his praise of Major Travers Lucas who had led his men so gallantly right up to their wire." Sheldon, *German Army on Vimy Ridge,* p. 238, quotes from the report of a German Colonel, 261st Reserve Infantry Regiment: "Not one single enemy soldier got into our trenches. Only the English [sic] Major Lucas was hanging on the barbed wire." The Germans frequently, if not habitually, referred to all BEF as "English." Had the raid been a resounding success Lucas may well have received a VC.

43 LAC, RG 9IIIC1, Volume 3861, Folder 90, File 3. Not all battalion officers and men participated. Some were always Left Out of Battle (LOB). The purpose of LOB was that in the advent of decimation LOB personnel would reform a unit. The policy directed that not more than 20 officers per battalion would accompany an attack. A year later amendments said not more than 21 would accompany an attack, including either the CO or the 2IC and either the OC or 2IC of each company, but not more than two company commanders in all. LOB policy was also set out in *SS 135 Instructions for the Training of Divisions for Offensive Action.* The contemporary tern for LOB was "the nucleus."

44 LAC, War Diary, 4th Division; Roy (ed.), *Journal of Private Fraser,* p. 252.

"particularly" or "especially" of officers. Such modifiers in relation to losses are striking and always indicative of extremity. In this raid, we learn of 54th Battalion being stripped of the CO and four company commanders and 75th Battalion's loss of the CO and the 2IC. Sometimes policy, LOE or otherwise, got the back seat. However, there is another factor. In such an undertaking, and knowing the risk, it is not surprising that Lieutenant-Colonel Kemball, CO 54th Battalion, went with his best, two Majors and two Captains, all well-experienced company commanders. Had he survived, their loss would likely have broken his heart. The same applies to Lieutenant-Colonel Beckett's decision to take his 2IC with him. Kemball died on enemy wire, Beckett killed very quickly in the attack trying to rally his men.[45]

But the raid while over on 1 March did not end. On the night of the 2nd volunteers recovered some bodies from no man's land. It seemed impossible for more to be brought in, but with morning came a surprise:

> About 8 a.m. a German Major, OC German front line, bearing a Red Cross Flag, came over their trenches into No Man's Land and called for our CO to come out and see him. Lieutenant Sinclair went out. The German Major offered an armistice for a few hours in order to give an opportunity of collecting the bodies of those killed ... The armistice was carried out between 8 and 12 a.m. in good order. The Germans bringing the bodies of those killed of the 54th and 75th Battalions half way across to be carried the remaining distance by our men. The German Major, who spoke English fluently, stated that his object in offering the armistice was that there might be fewer missing men and that those at home might gain some consolation from the fact of their relatives having Christian burial.[46]

26th Battalion in neighbouring 3rd Division also observed some of what went on, remarking on the many Germans and Canadians carrying bodies to and from the centre of no man's land. 11th Brigade's War Diary includes this:

> Enemy allowed us to collect our dead and carried those behind their firing line halfway across No Man's Land for us to take in. Brigade Major [Major Ferrers-Guy] was ordered by divisional commander to see the Colonel of the German regiment and thank him. Brigade Major saw him and thanked him and asked him to convey thanks to his division commander.

Ferrers-Guy later recalled the German officer mentioning that his brother-in-law was a Major Elliott of Canadian Engineers. Ferrers-Guy was probably the officer mentioned in this German account:

> An English officer of the divisional staff appeared at our trench. He was there to pass on the thanks of the divisional commander and to state that the gesture would be reciprocated if a similar situation arose in future. I must state that the Canadians by their upright military

45 LAC, War Diaries of 54th and 75th Battalions.
46 LAC, War Diary, 87th Battalion, entry for 3 March.

> bearing and their behaviour made an outstanding impression on us. They could almost have been from the 261st! [the defending regiment].

Another German officer recalled how "anyone who was present for this remarkable episode, the like of which never occurred on any other occasion during the war, will certainly often have pleasant memories of it." *Cinquante-Quatre* considered that day "one of the most memorable and pleasant features of our fighting record."[47]

Nor did the story end there. Of the four Canadian divisions that attacked at Vimy Ridge only the 4th failed to achieve all its objectives. It did have the hardest nut to crack, but that is not the whole story. Why the shortcoming has periodically been a recurring question among those who study, or those who are just interested, in what happened there. Lieutenant-General Burns attributed that division's performance on 9 April to the heavy losses sustained during the raid.[48] Desmond Morton, Jack Granatstein and Pierre Berton share his opinion in respectively *When Your Number's Up, Marching to Armageddon* and *Vimy.*

Bill Rawling contends the opposite: the raid, he says, had "little effect" on 9 April. He also states "the battalions involved in the raid did better on 9 April than the 87th, which had not been part of the 1 March operation." Looking first at his second contention he says that the 75th Battalion remained in its trenches on 9 April because of a tactical error by 87th Battalion. This being so, how then did the 75th do better? The 54th Battalion, despite its partial withdrawal, which occurred because of the 87th Battalion's error, did do better than the 87th. The 72nd Battalion had only 88 casualties (some sources say 82) on the raid, the lowest casualty count of the four raiding battalions. While 88 casualties can hit hard at a unit, the number is still small enough not to have had much effect on 9 April. The 72nd Battalion did better than the 87th. As for the 73rd Battalion, which took all its objectives, the 1 March losses seem not to have had any ill effect. It is worth noting that most of this battalion's casualties on the raid were "slightly wounded," meaning that many of these probably "remained at duty" with the battalion. The 73rd, too, did better than the 87th.

Regarding Rawling's first contention – the raid had "little effect" – we have seen that one of the four battalions did not do better than the 87th. But this was not a consequence of the raid. Strictly speaking, then, the desired results on the 9th April being largely achieved, Rawling is right as far as he goes.[49] But there is another aspect to consider. It is what heavy losses can do to morale and subsequent performance. The nearly 700 casualties out of a raiding force of 1,569, a casualty rate of 45 percent, meant that many comrades and trusted, experienced leaders had "gone west." In an infantry battalion this means the loss of many of the guiding hands at battalion, company, platoon and section levels. We know that two battalion and at least six company commanders were casualties. We do not know exactly how many platoon commanders were casualties, but the battalion reports indicate a good number. Private Fraser thought 41 officers had become casualties.[50] There would have been at least that number of NCO casualties.

47 LAC, War Diary 11th Brigade and 4th Division; Sheldon, *German Army on Vimy Ridge,* pp. 240-41; Sheldon offers a fascinating account of the episode. *Cinquante-Quatre,* p. 14.

48 Burns, *General Mud,* p. 40.

49 Bill Rawling, *Surviving Trench Warfare: Technology and the Canadian Corps, 1914-1918* (Toronto: University of Toronto Press, 1992), p. 128.

50 Roy (ed.), *Journal of Private Fraser,* p. 252.

The impact is obvious; performance was adversely affected. The "disaster" quickly became widely known in the Corps, as did the fact that a brigade commander and at least two experienced and respected battalion commanders had strongly opposed the raid. Lieutenant Burns, 11th Brigade Signals Officer, had overheard the strong objections of the former; so, too, did the signallers and they were likely not averse to relating the story to others. If senior officers that the men trusted thought the planning for the raid shaky, and then were proven right, dead right for two of them, then some doubt crept in. To those who knew, the raid seemed to have defied common sense. Such was bound to negatively impact morale and affect views about leadership in 4th Division and to lesser extent within the Corps. Lieutenant Stuart Tompkins, OC 6th Trench Mortar Battery, 2nd Canadian Division, for example, added the following to his Diary: "2 March. Heard disquieting rumours of the 4th Division … numerous casualties. 3 March. Bad rumours … hundreds of casualties … gas never reached the German lines. 4 March. Armistice … to recover dead and wounded."[51]

Burns brings out another very significant point about the raid's impact on 9 April, one that has been missed in some accounts. He could not remember to what extent the battalions of 11th Brigade trained for the Vimy offensive, particularly on the taped replica of the objectives, but he offered two scenarios. First, if this training was done before the raid then the key officers and NCOs were probably killed and wounded in the raid. Second, if the training for the offensive was done after the raid the replacements that brought battalions up to strength would be new to battle and to their officers and comrades. Consequently, training for the offensive was negatively impacted.[52]

One sign of a decline in morale that brigade and battalion commanders can recognize in action is what a divisional commander in a later war described as "stickiness," which could be defined as the adoption of a degree of caution beyond prudence and a readily observable hesitation: "It is most noticeable that the standard of minor tactics and unit tactics has deteriorated … opposition now causes untold delay and stickiness." What shows is slower reaction and/or less effective reaction to events. Little things get forgotten or are ignored and the harm accumulates.[53] There must surely have been some signs and impact of this in 4th Division at Vimy and some stumbling, a dilution in skills associated with minor tactics, a hesitation and uncertainty that dulled the "edge." How could it have been otherwise? This is not to proclaim 4th Division no longer effective, or a crippled formation, for this would be gross exaggeration considering that it achieved much of what it was tasked to do in the offensive. Nevertheless, it must be said that the raid on 1 March did have considerably more than "little effect" on 4th Division on 9 April.

History tells us that hubris can slip easily into nemesis. While the raid was not that, it did give a much-needed jolt to the Canadian Corps whose long record of successful raids had bred a degree of over confidence. The failure did engender a renewed and sharper focus on the planning of raids, which from 2 March onward were for a time very much smaller and executed without

51 Stuart Ramsay Tompkins, *A Canadian's Road to Russia: Letters from the Great War Decade* (Edmonton: University of Alberta Press, 1989), p. 181. Tompkins was commissioned in 1916 and badly wounded in April 1917. He later volunteered for and served with the Siberian Expedition.

52 Burns, *General Mud,* p. 38.

53 LAC, RG 9IIIC3, Volume 4016, File 1, Section VI, Lessons; Bill McAndrew, 'The Soldier and the Battle', in David A. Charters, Marc Milner and J. Brent Wilson (eds.), *Military History and the Military Profession* (Westport: Praeger, 1992), p. 65.

the use of gas. Instead, conventional fire support would cover raiders going in and out. This is not to say that no more casualties would be suffered during raids for the nightly excursions between 20 March and 9 April, for example, would cost an additional 1,653 Canadian casualties, but the string of successes would do much to restore the confidence of those who planned and executed minor enterprises.[54]

4th Division's assessment of the raid as "valuable" had some truth to it as it did, strictly speaking, achieve to some degree the assigned objectives, but at terrible cost. More Canadians than Germans died. The division's report also concluded, in a stock and expected remark, that "all officers and men showed the highest moral [e]."[55] The Germans that helped move Canadian bodies saw the results of machine-guns versus morale. "Kultus Nanich," writing a decade and a half later, bitterly recalled the raid: "one does not like to speak of this affair and perhaps the least said the better … as far as we others … could understand it, it was the most inconceivably stupid thing that it is possible to imagine." He then dismissed the other possible result: "Had it been entirely successful one can't see where it was worth the risk."[56] In short, Murray saw the game as not worth the candle. Ivor Gurney's lines about another matter appear a good fit here:

> A man might rave, or shout, or sob;
> And God he takes no sort of heed.
> This is a bloody mess indeed.[57]

Beyond the 1,653 casualties suffered during the raids up to 9 April that sought the most and latest information on enemy defences, units and anything else that would assist the attack on the ridge, the Canadian Corps gave away information on its intentions, dispositions, units and attack preparations. Such went to the enemy during Canadian raids and also during enemy raids, this simply an example of the proverbial two-edged sword. It should not be supposed that the Germans did not take prisoners. In November and December they winkled some from 3rd Canadian Division. From these they learned Canadians were opposite them. In late December prisoners from 4th Division confirmed that division's presence. In March two prisoners were lifted from 3rd Division and four from 2nd Division, the first lot revealing that the ridge would be attacked during the spring offensive and the quartet from the last singing a song about that division's objective and the deployment of all four Canadian divisions. Nor did the enemy miss the significance of the constant and aggressive Canadian raiding. This did cause the Germans to focus on their defensive posture, artillery response times and counter-attack procedures including rehearsals and routes forward.[58]

Such captures by the Germans were not unexpected, of course. This did not, nor should it have, deterred Canadian and British raiding. At 0400 on 2 March officers and men of two

54 Don Farr, *The Silent General: Horne of the First Army* (Solihull: Helion and Company Ltd., 2007), p. 153; Nicholson, *Canadian Expeditionary Force,* p. 234; MacGowan et al, *26th New Brunswick,* p. 165.
55 LAC, War Diary, 4th Division, report on raid.
56 Colonel W.W. Murray ["Kultus Nanich"], "Raids," p. 338.
57 Ivor Gurney, 'The Target', in David Roberts (ed.), *Minds at War: Poetry and Experience of the First World War* (Hurst: Saxon Books, 2014), p. 131.
58 Sheldon, *German Army on Vimy Ridge,* pp. 169-70, 254, 261.

battalions of 1st Canadian Division launched a raid determined to prove that what had gone on in 4th Division's raid was an anomaly. This raid, a join effort by 14th and 15th Battalions of George Tuxford's 3rd Brigade, had been set to go on 1 March, but at a conference on 26 February at 3rd Brigade HQ the divisional commander, Arthur Currie, ordered it postponed by 24 hours since 4th Division had been allocated the Corps Heavy Artillery.[59]

The reason for the 3rd Brigade raid was, in a word, retaliation for two German raids on the 25th, one on the 15th Battalion coming in at 0400 and neatly winkling an NCO, and shortly afterward a raid on 14th Battalion, this netting two more prisoners at no cost to the raiders. Major Paul Villiers, BM 3rd Brigade, noting the reaction at division and at corps, recalled the awkwardness of a visit by Byng and Currie to Brigade HQ on the 25th: "I need hardly say that we were not popular."[60] At 1300 Currie again visited, a conference being convened with Tuxford and Lieutenant-Colonels G. McCombe and C.E. Bent to discuss retaliation. Given the circumstances Tuxford became very interested in this raid. So, too, did his BM, so much so that Villiers became heavily involved even taking the shopping list for support to Corps Heavy Artillery HQ, specifically to a chum there then commanding a heavy brigade, who promised and delivered all to be at 3rd Brigade's disposal: "they laid themselves out to help us," wrote Villiers, "and right good support they gave to the raiding parties." While not innovative in any way the raid was noteworthy for it being very much smaller than 4th Division's effort and for its success, which very much pleased division. Four MCs were awarded.[61]

To the south, the British 1st Division of III Corps (Fourth Army) had also been planning retaliation. On the night of 6/7 March enemy trenches at Barleux Quarry were assaulted by five officers and 137 ORs under Captain Edward Nichol, who had organized the raiders in four parties. None entered the enemy trench. Of the right party only the officer and three men even reached the enemy wire. Neither of the two centre parties got beyond the gap in the wire, one reaching the wire with only the officer and six men, nor did the left party. It is evident from the War Diary that surprise had not been achieved. First, the raiders were hit by "most effective" mortars, rifle grenades and machine-gun fire that began one minute after Zero. Second, an alert enemy was holding the trench "particularly" strongly. The right party had to contend not only with a strongly held trench, but with men lying out behind the wire, these accompanied by a machine-gun. The other parties were heavily bombed, the left party suffering especially heavy casualties, the survivors being only "remnants." Casualties included Captain Nichol and 45 men wounded, one officer and 10 killed and six missing; in all, a casualty rate of 44 percent. The brigade report noted that the Quarry was "a natural raiding point and our wire cutting must

59 LAC, War Diary, 3rd Brigade, 26 February.

60 LAC, MG30E236 (Villiers Papers), Volume 4, Folder 7, and Volume 3 of Diary; 3rd Brigade War Diary. Villiers, in 1914 a 30-year old expatriate Londoner who had served eight years in the British Army, began the war as a Subaltern with 15th Battalion. From May 1915 onward he served as a Staff Officer: Staff Captain, 3rd Brigade, May-Jul 1915; BM, 3rd Brigade, July 1915-January 1916; GSO3 1st Division, January-October 1916; BM 3rd Brigade, October 1916-January 1918; GSO2, 29th British Division, January-November 1918. Villiers enjoyed a solid reputation drawing high praise from his superiors wherever he served. On the two German raids see Beattie, *48th Highlanders,* p. 204, and Fetherstonhaugh, *14th Battalion,* p. 135, who described the German raid as daring and reflecting "credit on those who planned it and on the party which carried it out."

61 LAC, MG30E236 (Villiers Papers), Diary, Volume 3; War Diaries, 3rd Brigade, 14th and 15th Battalions; Beattie, *48th Highlanders,* pp. 205-207; Fetherstonhaugh, *14th Battalion,* pp. 137-38.

have shown that a raid was probable." One must, therefore, question the extent to which pre-raid recce was done and, indeed, the very selection of such an objective. In short, the planning seems suspect.[62]

On 5 March 6th Gordon Highlanders of 51st (Highland) Division, 1st Canadian Division's immediate neighbour to the south, launched a daylight raid. On 17 March the 8th Argyll and Sutherland Highlanders of the 51st also raided. Both raids were part of a series designed to inflict serious damage to enemy wire and trenches prior to the April offensive. Despite the 12 day interval these raids were closely linked as will be shown below.

The Gordons planned an assault by the leapfrog method to clear the front and support trenches on a frontage of nearly 500 yards and hold them long enough to ensure destruction of the garrison and their dug-outs. Wire would be cut by artillery and 2-inch trench mortars along the whole of the divisional front in order not to draw attention to the gaps cut in the wire opposite the Gordons. The jumping off position, an old French trench in no man's land, had been cleared earlier. It would also serve as a staging point during the withdrawal, it being unlikely, and so it proved, that enemy artillery would target it. Artillery support would be in three phases: a preliminary bombardment at Zero minus one to Zero (0610); support for the assault on the front line Zero to Zero plus three; and then support of the assault on the enemy support line and during the time in trenches until Zero plus 30. Heavy howitzers and 4.5-inch howitzers, 18-pounders, 2-inch trench mortars, Stokes and machine-guns would all be involved. Artillery and mortars of 9th (Scotttish) and 34th Divisions on the right and 1st Canadian Division on the left would create diversions. The OC Raid, Captain Ian Fleming, MC, organized his 11 officers and 303 ORs into 11 parties, each allocated a specific objective and each consisting of three sections. Air photographs were carefully studied in order to locate dug-outs clearly in the mind. The plan was to thoroughly destroy these with 20-pound explosive charges accompanied by "P" grenades and one-gallon tins of petrol, the charge to blow in the dug-out entrance, the petrol and grenades to cause fires.[63]

Despite fierce enemy resistance the raid was a complete success: many dug-outs destroyed, 66 Germans counted dead and 21 prisoners taken, including one officer. It had been thought that the 164th Saxon Regiment was in residence, but the garrison proved to be 2nd Bavarian Regiment. Prisoners revealed that the Bavarians had relieved the Saxons the previous night, the relief not ending until midnight. The newcomers had been warned to expect a raid, but coming so soon in their stay it surprised them. Bewsher gave the Bavarians full credit, describing them as "magnificent fighters," especially given that they had only been in place for six hours prior to the raid. This, he said, also "showed how well the line must have been handed over by the outgoing battalion and what a sound system of defence existed."[64] Thus in this instance the usual advantages of catching the enemy during a relief or very soon after it did not pay as big a bonus

62 TNA: WO 95/1268: 2nd Brigade report, 7 March, Appendix A; Colonel H.C. Wylly, *The Loyal North Lancashire Regiment. Volume II. 1914–1919* (London: Royal United Services Institution, 1933), pp. 47-48.

63 TNA: WO 95/2862: 152nd Brigade, Operation Order 122, signed by Captain F.W. Bewsher, BM (later the historian of 51st Division). The "gifts" thrown into the dug-outs included eight Stokes bombs, 660 pounds of ammonal, 16 tins of petrol and 164 "P" grenades, a type filled with phosphorous which was very good at starting fires. Some dug-outs were still burning 12 hours after the raid. (Bewsher, pp. 145-46).

64 *Ibid.*, p. 147.

as might have been the case had the German units been less professional and efficient. These qualities also showed in other ways.

But there were benefits beyond destruction and prisoners. What the raiders learned enabled a map to be prepared showing every feature of the enemy trenches. A lesson in trench fighting also surfaced. While the enemy resisted with men throwing bombs in the open trench, those in dug-out entrances used their rifles as well as bombs. The raiders also learned that from loopholes cut in trench traverses, and from the entrances to deep dug-outs cut in the side of the traverses, short stretches of trench could be enfiladed. These doorways could not be seen until attackers were almost beside them. The best counter was to stay out of the trench and shoot and bomb the enemy from above, but this not always possible if subsequent enemy lines had good observation and fields of fire. The previous fall, after a raid by his company of 8th Sherwood Foresters (46th British Division), then Major Bernard Vann in the last paragraph of his report on the raid had recommended strong parapet parties because they could enable quicker clearing of enemy trenches.[65]

The cost to the Gordons was one officer missing and five wounded, plus 10 ORs killed, six missing and 32 wounded, a casualty rate of 17 percent: "Our losses" according to the War Diary, "entirely due to the fighting qualities of the German Regiment found in the trenches." Awards included two MCs, one DCM and six MMs.[66]

As for the link mentioned above, it entailed a bold experiment. The raid the Gordons made on 5 March was repeated by the 8th Argyll and Sutherland Highlanders 12 days later, the aim being the "utter destruction" of the same objective and the lowering of enemy morale prior to the imminent April offensive. This repeat performance was also by day (Zero at 0615), the 12 officers and 378 ORs of the Argylls occupying the old French trench at 0400. Artillery support very similar in scope and extent to the earlier raid, was "perfectly accurate" in the words of the CO of the 8th, Lieutenant-Colonel R. Campbell, who went on to say "our party was at the enemy wire before the barrage lifted and I did not see a single casualty." However, things then changed, the 8th meeting with harder fighting than the Gordons had. On the left, the raiders discovered that the wire had been repaired and on the right flank, too, meaning both parties were held up for some time. In the centre the raiders entered the enemy trench without much trouble and caught the enemy leaving his dug-outs. In the very savage fight that ensued the raiders used rifles rather than bombs, this "extraordinarily effective and [this] should be strongly impressed on all ranks taking part in attacks and raids." On the left, meanwhile, all three officers had become casualties. Learning this, and with no officers immediately available, the OC Raid sent the Company Sergeant-Major to see what could be done. CSM McKinnon got the party into the enemy trench using a gap that the Gordons had used and despite some delay still caught the enemy in his dug-outs. At left and right many dug-outs were destroyed using the Gordons' recipe for explosions. Only 10 prisoners were taken by the Argylls, the CO attributing this to the intense fighting that did not allow for much prisoner taking.[67]

Casualties totalled 110, a rate of 28 percent. Eight of the 12 officers are in that total: two killed, one missing and five wounded. Of the ORs, 14 were dead, 12 missing and 76 wounded, many only slightly. Lieutenant-Colonel Campbell believed that the enemy suspected another

65 *Ibid.*, Beresford, *The Christian Soldier*, p. 197.
66 TNA: WO 95/2868: 6th Gordon Highlanders, 'Special Operation Order', 27 February 1917.
67 TNA: WO 95/2865: 8th Argylls, raid report.

raid and had reinforced the trench. Bewsher thought the raid of great value since during the coming offensive they would pass over the same ground. Also, the many men of the Argylls who had not previously been under a barrage were now experienced and had gained in confidence. But Bewsher also concluded that given the "fairly heavy" casualties that affected chiefly one company per battalion, "when the day of attack came, these companies contained an undue proportion of inexperienced drafts."[68]

The rest of March and early April featured many more raids, the aims always being more information, prisoners and destruction and each reflecting a desire to keep the enemy off balance and retain the "edge" on one's own men. Raids by this time were generally well-organized and planned and thoroughly rehearsed, but certain imponderables remained; plans, for example, do not always survive contact and there are other Clausewitzian frictions that cannot always be foreseen, such often related to chance, which does not always come to the well-prepared. One culprit was weather which can prevent an enemy force being seen, delay a battalion or ruin a charge. Weather, as the historian of the Cameronians tells us, "could gravely upset the accuracy of our artillery support. A sudden unexpected fall in temperature would cause 'short' shooting." [69] This was so on 24 March, a sharp frost hardening the ground upon which B and D Companies of 10th Cameronians, a battalion of the 27th Brigade, 9th (Scottish) Division, sat for 90 minutes before Zero at 0400. The objective was almost the shape of a square box, at either side a CT, at the bottom the enemy front line and at the top his support line. B Company would enter at the bottom right corner and send one party left along the front line and another up the CT to the junction with the support line. There one group would clear left along that line. D Company would enter at the left bottom corner and send one party right along the trench, the other up the CT to the junction with the support line. There one group would clear right along that line to link-up with B Company. Artillery and trench mortars would hit hard at the front trench for five minutes during which time the raiding parties were enroute to their entry points, fire would then lift and lay down a barrage for 30 minutes.

At Zero the barrage fell and the raiders moving single file ("worms") in two columns were off.[70] But friendly fire played a deadly card. Before the head of B Company reached enemy wire several "shorts" hit the tail of the column, severely wounding the OC Raid, killing another officer and causing numerous other casualties. Second Lieutenant A.S. Pratt, at the head of the column, being unaware of this, pushed on accompanied by only five men into the enemy trench and up the CT. Near the third of four dug-outs Pratt was killed. His five stalwarts, having no means of destroying anything, then withdrew. D Company also experienced "shorts," only an officer and four men actually entering the trench. Moving up the CT several dug-out sites were destroyed, but no enemy were seen until the small party reached the junction with the support line and then only a few, these posing no impediment to clearing along the support trench. No prisoners or identifications were secured. As for casualties, all except for Pratt, were due to British "shorts" caused by "the effect upon the guns of the sudden drop in temperature." In all, two officers were killed and one died of wounds and three ORs were missing and 22 wounded.

68 Bewsher, *51st Division*, pp. 148-49; TNA: WO 95/2865: 8th Argylls, raid report.
69 Story, *Cameronians*, p. 152.
70 One of the lessons of the Somme that appeared in *SS 119 Preliminary Notes on the Lessons of the Recent Operations* (Army P & S Service, July 1916) was "lines for fighting and worms for movement," worms able to move more quickly than lines.

While "shorts" were not uncommon (see Chapter 5) it was especially hard that the raiders were hit so early in the raid.[71]

Two days later Private T. Flatt of the 10th got what the raiders had not. Observing from a wrecked building the enemy trench some 30 yards distant, Flatt, using the cover of debris, crossed over and into the enemy trench. After a short walk he discovered one German so intent on watching the British line through a loophole that he did not hear Flatt approach. He then invited the man along and shortly thereafter "26518 Private T. Flatt reported to his OC with his prisoner, a Private of the 104th Reserve Infantry Regiment, attached to the 133rd Regiment". For this coup he received the DCM and 10 days special leave. Certainly, Flatt's raid was long remembered by the 10th Cameronians.[72]

Eight days before the 10th Cameronians endured friendly fire, raiders of the 44th Canadian Battalion (4th Division) got a taste of such fire. On the night of 15/16 March four officers and 95 ORs set out to take prisoners to confirm unit identifications. The battalion report has much to say about the artillery supporting fire, noting that starting at Zero it "appeared irregular." The right assault party on getting close to the enemy line had "artillery fire falling all around them." The irregularity became such that the OC of the party decided to withdraw on account of it. None of this party entered the enemy trench. Similar fire beset the left assault party, the OC, Lieutenant T.G. Robertson, stating that it could "not be recognized as a distinct barrage." Only 20 or so of this party actually entered the enemy trench. Once in it, this party lost all its leaders in a struggle against strong opposition. No prisoners were taken. Captain Francis Caldwell, OC Raid, described the raid as "almost entirely unsuccessful" due to "irregular barrage fire" and the loss of all the leaders of the left assault party. No reasons were advanced for the fire, but barrel wear comes immediately to mind. Caldwell concluded his report by saying the raiders "were mostly new men, having only a few weeks experience in France. The effect of casualties from our own shell fire on the morale of these men was most serious and great credit is due to the officers for their efforts to control them."[73]

During the last week of March several more Canadian raids took place. On the 26th 13th and 14th Battalions received from HQ 3rd Brigade (1st Division) orders to raid on the 28th, the purpose being to obtain "very urgently needed" identifications. The raids were to be simultaneous, but on different objectives.[74] Lieutenant D.M. McRae, who had led 14th Battalion's raid on 2 March, led the new raid consisting of one other officer and 55 ORs. The end of a preliminary barrage signalled the assault. No difficulty was faced reaching the enemy front line trench and on entry not a German was in sight. But from somewhere between the front and support lines came flurries of grenades, these causing the death of one man, the only casualty during the raid. Seeing no prospect of any further penetration, McRae withdrew his party. The battalion report concluded that the enemy, anticipating the raid, opted to withdraw behind his line and then bomb the raiders. In so doing the defenders also avoided the Canadian artillery barrage. This raid, then, was of considerable disappointment given the extensive training done for it and the allocation of strong fire support including field and heavy artillery, trench mortars and Stokes. Once again McRae was commended for his good judgement. A month later while

71 Story, *Cameronians*, pp. 152-54.
72 *Ibid.*, pp. 154-55.
73 LAC, War Diary, 44th Battalion, report on raid.
74 LAC, War Diary, 3rd Brigade, Operation Order 138.

commanding another raid he would win the MC.[75] The raid by 13th Battalion, Major I.M.R. Sinclair (OC), two Subalterns and 67 ORs, also commenced at 0300. After a perfect barrage the raiders were quickly in the enemy line and made their way to the support line destroying several dug-outs as they went. At the end of 15 minutes, having secured identifications, they withdrew. Casualties were three wounded. While the more adventurous in the party may have thought the evening rather a bust, it achieved what it set out to do and at virtually no cost.[76]

6th Canadian Brigade (2nd Division) raided on 28/29 March, the raiders from 27th and 31st Battalions. The former unit had no difficulty entering the enemy trench, but found it empty and so deep in mud that it was thought to be held only by a few sentries who had quickly withdrawn. Nothing was gained. 31st Battalion had much more than a walk. Zero was set for 1920 on the premise that this might catch the enemy unprepared since most of the previous raids had come at dawn or in the dark. The raiders, two officers and 60 ORs under Major W.F. Seaton, were in two parties commanded by Subalterns, Lieutenants Norman Appleby and W.R. Barnes. Neither party had any problem entering enemy trenches, but once in "luck did not favour the right party which suffered rather heavily." Initially no enemy could be seen. Close by was a dug-out too large for destruction by bombs so a Stokes bomb was thrown into it. It was fielded and tossed right back and on explosion killed Appleby. One group of his party while moving along the trench toward Barnes' party was bombed, some being killed and the survivors scattered. The left party had an easier time of it, immediately defeating a counter-attack, bombing numerous dug-outs and taking two prisoners. Barnes found the trenches so battered that they were almost unrecognizable as that. On the whole, this raid was successful, the two prisoners surviving the trek back across no man's land. Casualties came to six killed or missing and 14 wounded. In the aftermath of this raid we see, when it came to information, the give and take nature of raiding. In the War Diary of 6th Brigade we find an example of "take":

> Information received through examination of prisoners captured in our raid by 31st Battn. proved valuable and the report by Pte. Painter, W., one of the raiding party, who spent the night of the 29th March behind enemy front line trench and most of the 30th March in No Man's Land, was most interesting and his information of great value for troops going over at this point in future operations.[77]

The "give" came, in part, from four men of the 31st Battalion captured by 263rd Reserve Infantry Regiment during the raid and interrogated thereafter. A German intelligence report of 31 March referred to information gained "From statements by prisoners belonging to 2nd Canadian Division." This information was graded as "probably reliable." Prisoners were only one element of the assessments in the report, some of which were unlikely to have been known by four Privates. Other information provided the Germans with 2nd Division's axis of advance

75 Fetherstonhaugh, *14th Battalion,* p. 140; LAC, War Diary, 14th Battalion, report on raid night 28/29 March.

76 R.C. Fetherstonhaugh, *The 13th Battalion Royal Highlanders of Canada 1914–1919* (Montreal: The 13th Battalion Royal Highlanders of Canada, 1925), p. 161.

77 LAC, War Diary, 6th Brigade. Painter was one the men in Lieutenant Barnes' party who went missing during the enemy bombing.

and confirmation of Canadian Corps deployment for the attack. The Germans were compiling a picture of the coming attack. But there was more to come. The next day a supplementary report detailed 6th Brigade's training from 13-23 March for the attack including training hours, content of training, attack formations, battalion objectives and other information. What was underway here was the collation phase of intelligence production, the process during which information becomes intelligence.[78]

10th Canadian Brigade closed March with a large-scale raid founded by elements of three of the brigade's four battalions. The officer chosen to plan it was Lieutenant-Colonel H.J. Dawson, CO 46th Battalion. At first sight it seems strange to see three Operation Orders for the raid, all numbered number 54 and all two pages long. The first, dated 13 March, expressed the intention to raid on or about 17 March, the purpose of the raid being to take prisoners and mop up the area. An addendum described the timings and routes each battalion party was to take to the three assembly areas and specified where and when bombs and rifle grenades would be issued. 46th Battalion would arrange for and distribute these. But at some point after the 13th several fundamental changes having been made to the plan, Dawson, probably thinking a new order better than a chain of amendments, issued a new version on 26 March. One of the changes added 47th Battalion to the 46th and the 50th. Each of the first two would provide four officers and 200 ORs and the 50th would double its commitment from two and 100 to match the other two battalions. This meant a change to battalion frontages and to the fire plan since Corps Heavy Artillery now joined divisional artillery and mortars for the raid. Raider organization remained the same: "Battle Platoons" and an advance in two waves at 20-yard intervals as laid down in *The Normal Formation for the Attack.* The leapfrog system would be used, second wave passing through the first objective, the enemy first line, leaving it to be secured by the first wave, and move directly on the second objective, the support line. The "Identification" paragraph warned that no papers of any kind were to be carried, a caution that sits rather awkwardly given what follows nine pages later: "Each officer and NCO will carry ... a nominal roll of men in his party. Rolls will be called and reports made after the return of the party." An earlier chapter in this present study details the system of raider identification that was eventually established. Thereafter the two versions of the Operation Order are virtually identical. The third version mirrors the second except in minor matters of equipment. A memorandum would probably have sufficed. Given the many changes Dawson felt he had no option but to write new orders. All three orders are clear and highlight the changes made, thereby avoiding any confusion.[79]

As for the raid itself, 47th Battalion's party entered the enemy trench easily and found only sentries. Two prisoners were taken. Lieutenant O.R. Matthews, the OC Raid, reported the front trench badly damaged and unoccupied. The support line was almost as badly damaged, most dug-outs appearing to be flooded. 50th Battalion's party reported the front line as being in fair condition. Thirteen prisoners were taken. Of these, only four reached 50th Battalion's lines, the rest falling victim to enemy artillery. 46th Battalion met with strong enemy resistance, only

78 Sheldon, *German Army on Vimy Ridge,* pp. 261-62.
79 LAC, War Diary, 46th Battalion, Operations Orders 13, 26 and 28 March; *SS 144 The Normal Formation for the Attack.* Dawson issued the three orders using 46th Battalion's designated numbers, leaving the other two battalions to use their numerical designations for their orders.

one party being able to enter the trenches. Overall, Canadian casualties were two officers and six ORs killed and one officer and 50 ORs wounded.[80]

As the impending offensive drew closer raiding slipped well down the list of priorities, but this is not to say that it ceased entirely. After Vimy it would begin again in earnest. The next chapter picks up the course of raiding at that time.

80 LAC, War Diaries of 10th Brigade and the participating battalions and Operation Orders for the raid.

13

1917 – Spring Into Summer

Oh, how full of briers is this working day.
As You Like It

Before and during the spring offensive British and Canadian divisions continued to raid and would do so throughout the spring and summer, albeit at a reduced pace. By this time the planning for a raid had generally become thoroughly professional, but never quite "routine" since a primary challenge remained how to achieve surprise, the key to success. Imaginative minds had bent to the task. One of the ideas of early 1917 had been the "repeat" raid. In February 7th Battalion of 1st Canadian Division had hit the same objective twice in one day, first in the early morning and then again that night. 2nd Worcesters (33rd British Division) had done likewise, hitting hard at mid-evening on the 27th and then again early the next morning. A few days later 51st (Highland) Division changed the recipe somewhat, going for a longer interval between strikes on the same objective, the first "show" on 5 March and then waiting for 12 days to renew the lightning.

On 20 February 6th London Regiment had struck hard at the enemy, a force of 20 officers and 640 ORs almost completely achieving surprise, this accounting for the never equalled take, at least by Canadian and British units of the BEF, of 118 prisoners. Stokes mortars, which had driven the enemy to his dug-outs and kept him there, thereby allowing the raiders to enter the trenches virtually casualty free, also played a significant role in the battalion's success. This endeavour, in the words of the divisional historian, was "the outstanding event of the winter in the Ypres Salient." (see Chapter 11 for a detailed account). Before and during the 6th Battalion's raid HQ 47th British Division paid close attention to the planning. Throughout the concurrent activity good battle procedure was evident. Come the end of March "it was determined to repeat the raid of the 6th Battalion."[1] Who determined what, while it reflects the normal chain of command, should not be seen as uninteresting; for one thing, the relevant correspondence reveals the formal, yet seemingly casual expression, of life and death decisions by, in Victor Odlum's description, those who "always see a clean map." Further down the chain the map gets grubby with mud and blood.

1 Maude, *47th (London) Division*, pp. 89, 92.

The genesis of this repeat raid came on 1 March when C.H. Harington, MGGS Second Army, advised Lieutenant-General T.L.N. Morland, GOC X Corps, that "The Army Commander will be glad to know as early as possible what raids … Corps have in preparation … and the approximate dates they will be ready to carry them out."[2] On receipt, BGGS X Corps (A.R. Cameron) directed each division in the Corps to "submit a scheme for a large-scale raid – strength about one battalion – to include what artillery support from Corps would be required." In due course (two days later) GOC 47th Division, G.F. Gorringe, in offering two objectives for a raid, suggested that the best choice was "the place where the last raid was carried out … if same is to be at an early date." Corps agreed. Gorringe advised Corps on 10 March that 18th London Regiment of 141st Brigade would do the raid and he requested as much artillery support, field and heavy, and ammunition as the 6th Battalion had been given for the 20 February raid. On 16 March X Corps ordered the raid for 7 April.[3]

On 19 March GSO1 47th Division, Lieutenant-Colonel A.J. Turner, issued Preliminary Instructions for the raid. Corps had agreed that guns and ammunition would equal that given the earlier raid. Stokes mortars would include those of 140th and 141st Brigades, plus four from 142nd Brigade and four from a neighbouring division. Dummy raids would be conducted by neighbouring divisions on both flanks. The purposes of the raid were kill, capture and destroy, especially any repairs done by the enemy after the earlier raid. The objective, a salient, contained three lines. The first had been described after the earlier raid as a breastwork with frequent traverses and a weak and broken parados. The state of the intermediate line had been described as "nearly ruinous," but thereafter recce had reported it under extensive repairs. The support line was thought to have been thoroughly restored and strengthened.[4]

On 5 April the Brigade Operation Order confirmed arrangements including the fire plan. Four days earlier Lieutenant-Colonel D.B. Parry, CO 18th Londoners, had issued his Operation Order 155 for the raid. Raider strength totalled 20 officers and 500 men of the 18th, plus 10 men and an officer of 517th Field Company RE, in all somewhat less than the 20 February raid. While Parry was OC Raid, the assault would be led by Captain Charles Watson. The plan, like the earlier version, stipulated an assault in four waves, plus moppers up. Once again, a mine would be detonated outside the divisional sector, this and dummy raids designed to attract enemy attention. Fire support arrangements duplicated the earlier raid. Zero was set for 2000 on 7 April, three hours later than the February endeavour. As the divisional historian later wrote, the preliminaries were similar to the February raid.[5]

Thereafter things were not similar at all. Even as the raiders moved forward to the front line enemy shelling caused casualties, including one company commander killed, but by 1930 the raiders were ready in the jumping off trench. Twenty minutes later, and right on time, barrages could be heard from north and south as the dummy raids began, heartening sounds for those awaiting Zero.

2 Harington was BGGS of the Canadian Corps from September 1915 to August 1916. He began the war as a GSO1 with a Territorial Division. Within 14 months he was a Major-General. A description of his stellar record is in Radley, *We Lead Others Follow*.

3 TNA: WO 95/2702: 47th Division. All correspondence pertaining to this raid by 18th Battalion on 7 April is in Folder 90/10/2.

4 *Ibid.* Artillery report on raid. Ammunition expended included 18-pounder (20,000), 4.5-inch howitzer (3,500), 2-inch mortars (1,600) and "heavies" (1,900). The Stokes fired 1,324 bombs.

5 Maude, *47th Division*, p. 93.

At Zero, 2000 hours, the Stokes, plus all the allocated artillery and trench mortars opened on the enemy line which "through the gathering gloom appeared as a mass of flames, explosions and smoke," the fire being deadly accurate along the raid frontage including the area where only 40 or so yards separated the lines. Nevertheless, the enemy reacted ominously quickly: up went bouquets of SOS rockets and down came intense and accurate artillery fire, indications that the enemy had not been "taken unawares" and that he "fully expected" the raid. A sure sign of this came even before Zero in the form of signals sent up by the enemy on each flank of the objective area.[6]

At Zero plus three the raiders advanced, the ground, described by Parry as "incredibly bad," was a quilt of water-filled craters, scattered wire and shattered trees, the whole a bog caused by bad weather extending over a week. Consequently, the advance took much longer than had been calculated, a delay that meant an increase in the fire that came at the raiders as they crossed no man's land, mud and water flying up and about and casualties steadily increasing. As for the defenders, they were resolute and stubborn, keeping up their fire until the raiders began to break through the remaining wire, whereupon they made their way rearward to the support line where they resumed firing. On leaping in the dark into the enemy trench the raiders encountered not only waist-deep mud, but enfilade machine-gun fire. Almost immediately enemy shells began dropping into the now raider-occupied trench, incentive, not that they needed it, to get on to the intermediate line. But there was no respite there since the strongly manned support line now engaged the oncoming raiders who had also to contend with ground "perfectly indescribable," such that the brigade commander wrote "in advancing, the infantry could not keep pace with the barrage." Parry also remarked that the British barrage on each objective had lifted "for an appreciable period before the troops had reached it," a lift advantageous to the enemy. Nevertheless, the raiders reached all objectives and many enemy were thought killed. Of the 18 prisoners taken, only seven reached battalion lines, German artillery killing the others.

The withdrawal proved arduous and costly. Many wounded had to be carried across the very bad ground, all the while raiders, wounded and prisoners subject to intense machine-gun fire and unrelenting artillery fire that caused the death or wounding of many of the survivors of the severe struggle at the objective. As if this was not sufficient evil for the night, the rearguard had to contend with Germans eager to cut off and kill yet more raiders. The whole withdrawal, said the divisional commander, became a "severe test" of the battalion's "excellent discipline." A Division Intelligence Summary of 7/8 April summed up matters somewhat glowingly, ending with a short sentence hardly likely to please those who had done the raiding: "Our casualties were moderate."[7] At least it made no claim (nor did any of the raid reports) about how the night's work had caused a decline in enemy morale. Such was always an unverifiable contention that angered battalion commanders.

The raid proved a hard night's work. Two officers had been killed and three wounded. Of the men, 32 were dead, 25 were missing and 139 had been wounded, a casualty rate of about 38 percent. Congratulations on the raid came from the corps and divisional commanders and in due course so did decorations. Captain Watson received the MC as did two Subalterns. Twenty MMs were awarded. As the divisional historian wrote, the enemy infantry and artillery were

6 *Ibid.*, Matthew Richardson, 'The Ypres Raid-7 April 1917'. *Stand To!*, 44 (September 1995), p. 11; TNA: WO 95/2702: Folder 90/10/2, 47th Division, reports of brigade and battalion commanders.
7 *Ibid.*

alert and prepared. Another sign that he knew of the raid was evident in the move forward into close support of a storm troop battalion that at the appropriate time took a hand. This "repeat" raid, while most certainly a gamble, might well have succeeded had surprise answered the roll call.[8]

By early April the BEF was well up to the main Hindenburg Line at most places, the ground having been cleared for the spring offensive opposite Arras and Vimy Ridge. South of that the enemy still held several villages and covering positions forward of their main defences. That month Fourth Army had made further advances, XV Corps taking Gonzeaucourt, Villiers Guislain and Gonnelieu, the 8th and 40th British Divisions prominent in these successes which put the corps right up to the Hindenburg Line. In the former division's sector there remained only one enemy held village in front of that line, the village of La Vacquerie (see MSD 18). At the end of April XV Corps ordered the 8th and the 40th to capture the village and nearby positions and then consolidate. On 4 May this attack was cancelled, the two divisions instead to make an "extensive raid" on a wide front on La Vacquerie, enemy trenches northwest of it and Sonnet Farm on the road to Cambrai. Zero would be 2300 on 5 May, withdrawal two hours later at 0100 6 May. The purpose of the raid was to impede enemy attempts to strengthen the position, but, as the historian of the 40th Division put it, other purposes were those "that were usually at the bottom of [such] operations, namely to inflict loss, damage defences and, above all, to obtain identifications."[9]

8th Division (Major-General W.C.G. Heneker) was allocated the southern half of the objective area, the 40th Division to handle the other half to the left (north). In 8th Division's area 23rd Brigade would carry out the raid, 2nd Scottish Rifles on the right and 2nd Middlesex Regiment on the left. Both units would assault with two companies and have two companies in support. 2nd West Yorkshires would provide one company as moppers-up, their task to assist sappers in demolition of dug-outs and general clean up. 40th Division, assigned the wider slice, employed two brigades. Beside 23rd Brigade would be 119th Brigade, 12th South Wales Borderers on the right and the 17th Welsh on the left, organized as per 23rd Brigade and with one company of moppers-up from 19th Royal Welsh Fusiliers. Next in line was 121st Brigade, 20th Middlesex right and 12th Suffolks left, with one company of moppers-up from 18th Welsh.

At Zero weather influenced both divisions, for the full moon "which had been relied upon" made no appearance, the night being black and cloud overhead, plus rain starting immediately after Zero, but according to 40th Division's report "not heavily." 8th Division, on the other hand, experienced "driving rain beating in the faces of the attackers." Matters for the 8th worsened as its raiders reached the sunken roads that ran diagonally across their front. In his report Heneker related their impact: "The natural tendency of the Infantry was to line the banks of these roads before continuing the advance. The consequence was that there was a great tendency to advance in a South Easterly direction after meeting these roads." Tendency became event. Heneker went on to say" Companies immediately began to lose direction … which at once threw them half-right to the true bearing of their advance." This tendency, says

8 Richardson, 'The Ypres Raid-7 April 1917,' p. 12; Maude, *47th Division,* p. 93.
9 TNA: WO 95/2702: Folder 90/10/2 and 95/1676: 8th Division Operation Order 189, 3 May, and Operation Order 190, 4 May; TNA: WO 95/1709: 23rd Brigade Operation Order 44, 4 May; TNA: WO 95/2592: 40th Division, Operation Order 77, 3 May; Whitton, *40th Division,* p. 76; Boraston and Bax, *Eighth Division,* p. 117.

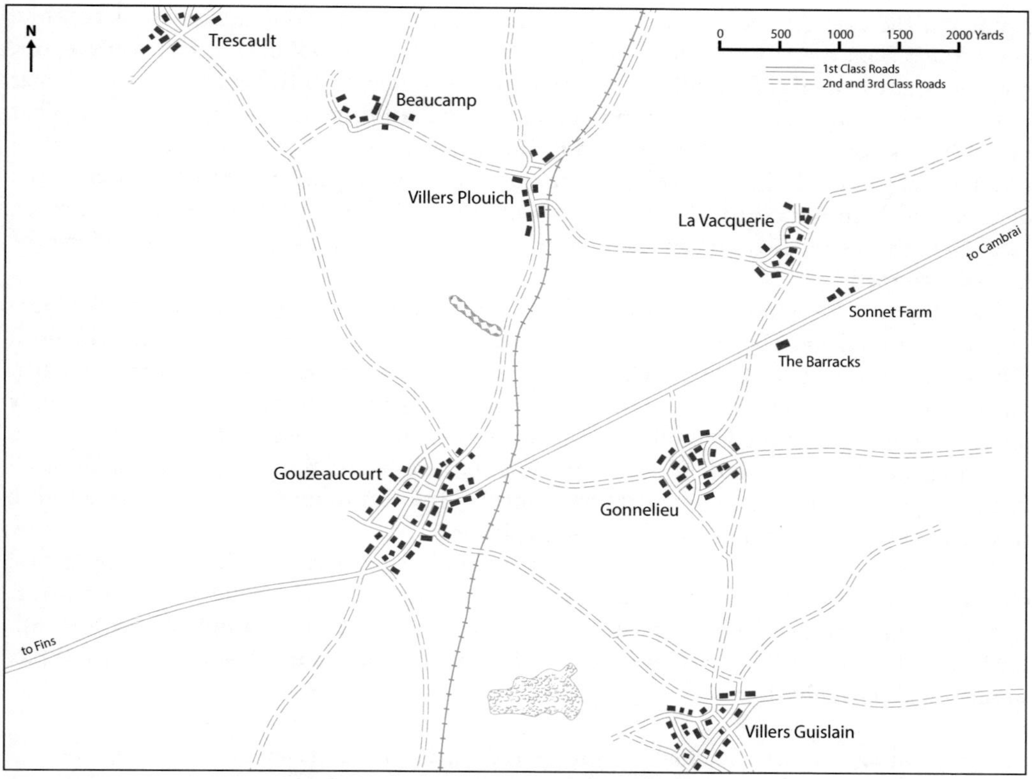

18 La Vaquerie Raid, May 1917, 119th British Brigade.

Colonel Boraston, the divisional historian, "ought to have been provided for, but was not and the [Infantry] lost direction." Heneker also noted that weather the night of the raid was as bad as it could have been, the driving rain upsetting all calculations and making cohesion and direction keeping difficult since all landmarks were obscured. It was unfortunate that the raid had to go ahead, it having to be "coincident ... with a final effort by the French on the Aisne front." As if all this was not enough, enemy artillery hit 2nd Middlesex while it was trying to regain direction, this fire taking out all the officers and many men of the right assault companies. When these companies did not further advance, a gap "of considerable width" opened between that unit and 2nd Scottish Rifles.[10]

The lesson here, one of several Heneker stressed, was "attacking infantry must form up on tapes." His remark suggests this had not been so, which leaves us to think that the raiders did not make use of a tape, or, more likely, no tape had been placed despite 23rd Brigade's Operation Order that had assigned responsibility for tape: "A Section of 2nd Field Company RE will be placed at the disposal of 2nd Middlesex [for] destroying buildings, laying booby traps and in

10 TNA: WO 95/2702 and 1676: 8th and 40th Divisions, reports on raid; Boraston and Bax, *Eighth Division*, p. 117. Heneker assumed command of the division on 10 December 1916. His GSO1, Lieutenant-Colonel E.H.L. Beddington, arrived that same month.

taping out the assembly positions." Furthermore, the 2nd was to arrange to mark with white tape a track from the front line to the enemy wire. This is not mentioned in Heneker's report, nor is it clear whether 2nd Middlesex was to mark the 2nd Scottish Rifles assembly position as well as its own. Such a connection is not mentioned in 23rd Brigade's Operation Order. What Heneker says about 2nd Scottish Rifles' direction keeping forces us to conclude that unit had no tape to align on: "2nd Scottish emerged from the sunken road and pressed on with some loss of direction. Their right drifts ... their left in common with the rest of the line had been much delayed ... the loss of direction and consequent confusion, caused by their alignment along the first sunken road."[11]

The left or northern most companies of 2nd Middlesex did keep on and reached their objectives where they demolished buildings. They also established and maintained contact with 40th Division as they advanced. At Sonnet Farm they killed several enemy and took one prisoner. The company commander wisely chose not to move further forward as he realized no friendly forces were to his right and no other troops were in support. Heneker refused his request to launch a general advance on the Farm as time did not permit. 2nd Scottish did eventually reach its first objective, but found the trench unoccupied. Time fast running out no further advance was made. Withdrawal commenced at 0100 as planned.

23rd Brigade, then, had little to show for the night's work. Eleven officers were casualties: one killed, one missing and nine wounded. Six ORs were dead, 121 wounded and 53 missing. In all, 191 casualties marked an expensive evening, one that would have weighed heavily on 8th Division, which was a Regular Division, one of ten such divisions in 1914. Boratston and Bax summarized the night thus:

> This raid was the last operation of any magnitude that was undertaken by the 8th Division on this front. It may well be regretted that it did not meet with better fortune; but it was after all but a single semi-failure to set off against a long series of successes which had earned the division the frequent commendations of higher command.[12]

The raiding units of 40th Division experienced no difficulty keeping direction. 17th Welsh Regiment formed on "tapes laid parallel to the objective" while 12th South Wales Borderers' CO and Adjutant personally laid the tape on the jumping off line. The divisional report relates how at Zero the infantry, which had formed on a taped line, moved forward closer to the barrage. All well and good, but both brigades of the 40th soon had other worries. 119th Brigade after leaving the tape experienced considerable difficulty getting through the gap in the wire and at La Vacqueries found wire thick and uncut. The division's history described gaps as "insufficient," a state that caused delay, a "serious thing" in a raid. Nevertheless, both battalions reached most of their objectives where they found very few enemy, only 14 counted as dead. At 0100 the withdrawal began and went smoothly and unhindered. No prisoners were taken during the raid. Brigade casualties included one officer killed and three wounded, 15 ORs killed, 76 wounded and 12 missing. [13]

11 TNA: WO 95/2702: 8th Division, report on raid.
12 Boraston and Bax, *Eighth Division,* p. 117.
13 TNA: WO 95/2592: 40th Division, division, brigade and battalion reports; Whitton, *40th Division,* p.78.

John Campbell, GOC 12th Brigade, discussed the raid with the COs of the assault battalions and based his report on their accounts "as far as can be ascertained although a good deal must remain obscure." Some confusion is apparent in the reports of 20th Middlesex and 17th Welsh (119th Brigade) as to why no contact was established between the units – neighbours during the assault – until the withdrawal began. Lieutenant-Colonel F.S.B. Johnson, CO 20th Middlesex, reported that at 2230 the officer he had sent to contact the 17th could not find that battalion. At 2309 he tried again, but "found no signs" of the 17th. At 0055, with withdrawal just about to begin, contact was finally made. Campbell thought the OC of the right hand company of the 20th committed "an error of judgement" and demonstrated 'a lack of experience" in failing to ensure "that touch was obtained on his right before moving off." Johnson's report mentions none of this. The 20th did not get as far as the final objective, the village, since at 0020 the company commander on the right, considering it impossible to enter the village, ordered withdrawal. The brigade commander considered this another "error of Judgement [resulting from] the initial error in not starting with and keeping touch with the battalion [17th Welsh] on the right." Failure to reach and clear the village meant that the sappers were left with nothing to do. The third assault battalion, the 12th Suffolk (Lieutenant-Colonel T.E. Wilmot) did enter the enemy trench through satisfactory gaps in the wire, but then became so heavily engaged in a bombing match it could not penetrate deeper. The left companies, encountering no enemy, then moved to assist the right companies. About 40 men, not hearing the order to change direction, pushed straight on into the enemy's rear area. Some of the group, realizing their error, eventually corrected their course, but others were not again seen. The very dark night hindered movement and created considerable confusion, Wilmot calling the situation "extremely obscure." Withdrawal, however, was unimpeded and without incident. Prisoners taken totalled 11. Casualties came to one officer killed and five wounded, plus 14 ORs killed, 87 wounded and 37 missing. Total 40th Division casualties came to 12 officers and 245 ORs. Of the 49 missing, one man turned up and a few having been reported as killed, not missing, reduced the unaccounted for to 35.[14]

The divisional historian said the raid "fell short" of expectations. A closer look at Major-General Heneker's (GOC 8th Division) "lessons" section of his report raises some fundamental questions that go well beyond that. Previously mentioned were the negative effects of weather and the failure to mark the jumping off line properly (or at all). "Obscure" seems to have been a word in frequent use. His third lesson described the distance to the enemy trenches as simply "too long." Heneker believed that troops forming up for a large operation should not be further than 200 yards from the enemy front line, the factors determining the distance being visibility and the need to keep indications of an attack hidden. An advance at night over a long stretch negatively impacted order and cohesion. All this was true, but there was nothing for it. The distance was what it was. Distance and weather made route marking even more critical, but little attention was paid to this in 8th Division whose assault units left the jumping off line either without tapes, or with tapes not parallel to the objective. Tapes would have also been useful along unit boundaries during the advance and forward of the gaps in enemy wire. The risk to proper direction keeping posed by the sunken roads running diagonally in a "Southeasterly

14 TNA: WO 95/2592, 2600 and 2601: 121st Brigade, 20th Middlesex, 17th Welsh, 12th Suffolk, and reports of Major T. Miller, OC 224 Field Company RE and Major J. Johnson, OC 231 Field Company RE.

direction," and the tendency Heneker referred to, seems not to have been realized in 23rd Brigade. The other major lesson was shockingly revealing:

> a raid must be treated with the same respect as an attack for although it is intended to withdraw after the objectives have been achieved, still the enemy lines have to be entered and his strong points taken before any results justifying the raid can be obtained. I find that in this Division there is a tendency to consider the operation in a less careful and serious spirit because it is a raid. This is obviously wrong.[15]

6th British Division, also a Regular Division, was in the Loos sector in May. Two of its smaller raids that month drew considerable attention, not so much for events during the raid, but for the lessons they offered. Consequently, the GSO1 had the raid reports distributed to all battalions in the division. The first raid, conducted by the 1st West Yorkshires on the night 20/21 May, consisted of two officers and 45 ORs divided into two parties, one per gap in the wire, the gaps having been cut the previous afternoon. The objective trenches were found vacant and not until the parties reached the support line did any fire come their way. The CO, Lieutenant-Colonel A. Boyall, expressed regret that no "tangible results" were obtained, but as half of the raiders had not raided before, and they had gained confidence in closely following the barrage, he thought the endeavour had been worthwhile. Casualties were one officer and one OR wounded and one missing believed killed.

The 6th Division's second raid, executed by the 1st Leicestershires at noon on 22 May, consisted of four officers and 132 ORs organized in two waves, the first of an officer, a rifle party and 10 squads (five bombing and five mopping-up) and the second of two officers and three Lewis gun detachments. Three gaps had been cut in enemy wire before the raid. While the raiders quickly gained the enemy trenches they arrived to find only one sentry who quickly vanished into a dug-out. Fifteen unoccupied dug-outs were blown in. The second objective was also unoccupied. Enemy artillery fire, while not severe, wounded nine men. The only hitch in the raid occurred when one of the squads announced withdrawal, a cry taken up and passed along. An NCO thinking this an order from an officer ordered all to withdraw, but the OC Raid who happened to arrive at precisely this moment got any rearward movement stopped. The battalion report remarking on this incident thought it occurred "because so many NCOs are inexperienced and not well trained, it would have been better to have employed more officers."

Such complaints about NCOs had become frequent and common. Many were killed, of course, and many had to be commissioned to replace dead officers. In early 1917 British divisions had to send 10 NCOs per month for officer training. No figure for Canadian Divisions appears extant, but the high officer losses would have meant a similar levy. So much bleeding-off of NCO talent took its toll. What often remained were the less capable, meaning the NCO corps became reduced in authority and especially in prestige. Overall, NCOs remained a weak link in the chain of command. Care had to be taken that men recommended for commissioning had to be the best available. William Griesbach, GOC 1st Brigade, frequently cautioned his battalion commanders about this, warning that a poor or fair NCO might make a good officer,

15 TNA: WO 95/1676: 8th Division. The raid was the division's first since Heneker became GOC in mid-December 1916. See footnote 10.

but "the fact that a man is a good NCO does not necessarily qualify him for commissioned rank." He had rejected many recommendations fearing that accepting some of the nominees "would have had the result of losing a good NCO to gain a poor officer."[16]

The GSO1, Lieutenant-Colonel T.T. Grove, offered several lessons drawn from the two raids, not all of which can be said to be universal. First, it was clear that the enemy, if he realized that more gaps in wire had been cut, routinely withdrew his men from his front trench in expectation of a raid meaning that in the case of a small raid if surprise was to be achieved the wire should be cut with Bangalores. Grove also thought that a daylight raid when properly prepared made crossing no man's land by day just as easy as by night. Third, the methods used in the two raids did not give the desired result, this being "to make certain of getting hold of the enemy." The thinking at divisional HQ was that bigger raids, which had the capability to penetrate more deeply, offered "far greater chances of success while not increasing the proportion of casualties." But this pre-supposed two essentials. The first was getting enemy wire into "ragged condition on wide stretches." This would offer greater chance of surprise by day or night and greater possibility of getting at the enemy before he could withdraw. The second concerned recce, the acquiring of intimate knowledge of enemy dispositions and habits:

> To raid trenches in which it is doubted if the enemy will be found is to risk casualties without any prospect of a proportionate result. Further, in order to outwit the enemy, we require to know his normal precautions for his protection, and to be able to predict his probable action to meet any given conditions.[17]

In June the virus called "loss of direction" hit 6th Division twice. On the 27th as 1st Buffs, 12 officers and 314 ORs, left their jumping-off line, the right flank of the raiders veered off to the right. The brigade commander, W.L. Osborn, observed how unfortunate that "when all other arrangements are complete that loss of direction should mar, as it often does, the success of an assault." The CO 1st Buffs recommended more use of compasses. A good deal of planning and preparation had gone into this raid including the involvement of considerable artillery and mortars providing conventional and smoke barrages, dummy raids by neighbouring formations and support by 40 machine-guns. Still, the raiders spent over two hours in enemy trenches destroying numerous dug-outs using heavy charges and took six prisoners. A searchlight assisted the withdrawal at 2345. Half of the 12 officers on the raid were casualties: one killed, one missing and four wounded. OR casualties included three killed, 46 wounded and 22 missing, of which four later returned. The next night 2nd Durham Light Infantry and 11th Essex Regiment raided in a strength of one company each. Here, too the brigade commander (R.J. Bridgeford, 18th Brigade) commented on loss of direction. Half the Durham company went too far south, which meant an enemy strong point could not be dealt with, this in turn preventing a link up of the 2nd and the 11th. The 2nd reported killing 25 Germans, but secured no prisoners. Despite

16 TNA: WO 95/1583: 6th Division, 1st West Yorkshires and 1st Leicestershires; LAC, MG30E15 (Griesbach Papers), Volume 3, File 16A; Hanbury-Sparrow, *The Land-Locked Lake,* p. 214; Terraine (ed.), *General Jack's Diary,* p. 195. Jack's diary entry for 18 February 1917 says each month battalions had to submit the names of five men for commissioning. For more on this particular problem see Radley, *We Lead Others Follow.*

17 TNA: WO 95/1583: 6th Division General Staff, divisional report 25 May 1917.

every man carrying bombs the supply proved inadequate during the bombing fight. One officer was killed, 16 ORs wounded and 12 missing believed killed. 11th Essex reported an "alert and very aggressive" defence that posed a severe challenge the whole time the raiders were in the enemy trench. Constant enemy bombing and repeated counter-attacks caused heavy casualties in one party, so much so that the other had to abandon its tasks and rush to aid the first. Two officers were known to have been killed. Exact numbers of other casualties had yet to be ascertained at the time the GOC wrote his report. The 11th took one prisoner.[18]

The first Canadian raid in April was made by the 42nd Battalion on the first day of that month. This smaller enterprise, an officer and 30 men, visited enemy trenches for 15 minutes starting at 0645. There the raid achieved its aim, one prisoner accompanying the raiders home. Another 3rd Division unit, 43rd Battalion, doubled the ante four days later, three officers and 63 ORs. The target was La Folie Farm south-east of Hill 145. At 1400 the raiders, closely following a barrage by 4.5-inch howitzers and 18-pounders, entered enemy trenches at three points. The varying enemy response typifies the fortunes of war. One party met only one German who made off at speed, closely pursued by the officer in charge, but he could not overtake the German who was obviously a runner of some note. The second party met only "slight" resistance and took two prisoners, thereby satisfying the purpose of the raid. Number Three party, the largest of the three, faced a "very stubborn and bloody fight" resulting in four ORs and the officer leading the party dead, three men missing and 17 wounded.[19]

After Vimy Ridge and the subsequent operations at Arleux, against which many patrols were mounted, and Fresnoy, the Canadian Corps and I British Corps were ordered to attack astride the Souchez River and penetrate the enemy salient between Avion and Lens. The attacking Canadian formations would be 3rd and 4th Divisions. Preliminary operations in May seized several positions, but as both Corps was short of guns at this time, which meant the enemy could concentrate overwhelming fire on captured positions, First Army (Sir Henry Horne) decided that since additional captures would be too costly to hold further operations would consist only of large-scale raids. I Corps and the Canadian Corps were then so tasked, the former to raid at 2030 on 8 June and the latter that same night at a time to be set by the GOC Canadian Corps.[20]

How attack came instead to be large-scale raids appears in the entry for Monday 4 June in the Canadian Corps General Staff War Diary which notes that Byng and the commanders of 3rd and 4th Divisions conferred at 1730. Arthur Currie was not present. On 6 June he would be told by Byng that he was to take over the Corps. Byng and the two division commanders reviewed the artillery shortage and a suggestion arose "that the object might be obtained equally well by [a] big raid … to be carried out in full strength … the whole operation to take place under the cover of darkness." Nicholson says Currie suggested this to the GOC First Army (Sir Henry Horne), but if Currie made such a suggestion it would seem more likely that he would have made it to Byng. At 1830 General Horne visited Canadian Corps HQ and approved the proposal. Currie's diary entry for 4 June shows he visited hospitals in the morning and in the

18 TNA: WO 95/1583: reports of 1st Buffs, 2nd Durhams, 11th Essex.
19 LAC, War Diaries 42nd and 43rd Battalions. The OC of the 42nd raid, Lieutenant Ralph Willcock, MC, received a bar to his MC for the raid and in 1918 would also receive the DSO. A feature of this raid was the use of cut-down rifles.
20 LAC, Canadian Corps General Staff War Diary, First Army Order No. 125, 5 June 1917, Copy No. 4 to Canadian Corps.

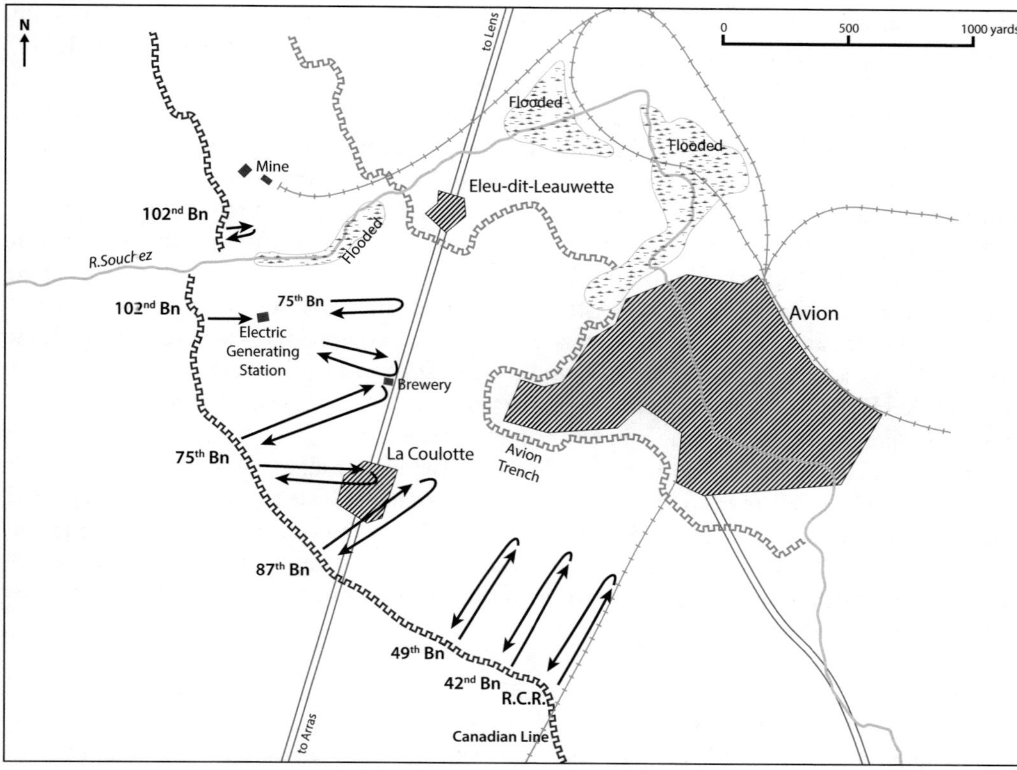

19 Avion Raid, 8 June 1917, 4th Canadian Division.

afternoon had visitors including GOC 1st Brigade and Byng. The 1st Division General Staff War Diary (Currie was still GOC on 4 June) makes no mention of him attending the 1730 meeting at Corps HQ, nor does his diary.[21]

On Tuesday 5 June Canadian Corps Operation Order 123 confirmed the raid, advised that the objectives and inter-corps boundary in the First Army Operation Order "held good," and that the two divisions were to submit revised schemes forthwith. Operation Order 124 the next day confirmed that I British Corps would also carry out a large-scale raid and 4th Canadian Division must establish and hold a contact point immediately north of the Souchez River until relieved by 46th British Division of I Corps (see MSD 19, Avion Raid). The stay in enemy lines was set at 90 minutes, Zero Hour to be advised.[22]

Divisional Operation Orders were issued on 6 June, brigade orders a few hours later. The Canadian raid would involve elements of six battalions, three each from 7th and 11th Brigades. Artillery support would include Canadian, British and Australian field artillery and heavy artillery (6-inch and 9.2-inch howitzers). 3rd Division Trench Mortar Group and 11th Canadian

21 LAC, Canadian Corps General Staff War Diary; Nicholson, *Canadian Expeditionary Force,* p. 281; LAC, MG30E100 (Currie Papers) Diary entry for 4 June; 1st Division General Staff War Diary, 4 June.

22 LAC, War Diary, Canadian Corps General Staff, 5 and 6 June.

Stokes Battery would also be in support, as would four machine-gun companies. The raid would be on a two-mile front from the railway leading to Avion to just north of the Souchez River, on the right 7th Brigade (south of La Coulotte) and 11th Brigade at and to the north of La Coulotte, a village that split the frontage roughly in half. 3rd Division's order stipulated that no signal would be made for general withdrawal. Instead, such orders would be issued by company and platoon commanders at the specified hour. A special signal would be arranged for withdrawal of the Rear Guard. On the night of 7/8 June 7th Brigade would relieve 8th Brigade in the line, less one battalion of the 8th that would come under command of 7th Brigade. 4th Division's Operation Order contained precise instructions as to the boundary with 3rd Division, including direction that sufficient strength had to be on the right in order to ensure contact with 3rd Division, and the measures necessary (password and signal flag) to ensure recognition between the 4th and the flanking 46th Division. Also, 7th and 11th Brigades would establish a joint "Battle HQ." Given that raid orders were based on previously prepared attack orders, each divisional Operation Order for the raid was only two pages long.[23]

Brigades trained hard for the raid. L. Gould of 102nd Battalion (11th Brigade) recalled training as "very severe" over a replica of the objective trenches, this accompanied by repeated explanations to all ranks of what had to be done and how. By the time his unit returned to the line he thought it a "well-instructed" one. The GOC (Victor Odlum) wrote later that his battalions "are unanimous in stating that the success of the operations was due to the training." As an example he offered this:

> One section in the practice attacks [had been] sent to the junction of two trenches in the second objective. In the raid every man in the section, except one, became a casualty before reaching the objective. The one man left, however, was found on duty at his post at the proper time. It is also worthy of note that many of the men had never been in the trenches before.[24]

7th Brigade (Brigadier-General A.C. Macdonell) having already issued orders for the cancelled attack issued an Operation Order that was simply an amendment list, following up the next day (7 June) with Operation Order 95 which specified signals for withdrawal and other matters that had not been decided upon the day before. Macdonell tasked the RCR, 42nd and 49th Battalions to conduct the raid, the RCR on the right, 42nd centre and 49th left on a frontage of about 1,200 yards and raiders to penetrate to a depth of about 800 yards. Withdrawal would begin at Zero plus 90, troops in the final objective withdrawing through those in the first objective, some of the men there being tasked as Rear Guard to cover the withdrawal. It would then withdraw on sight of a "golden rain" of rockets put up by the Brigade Report Centre. Tapes daubed with luminous paint were to be laid as a guide for the return to battalion lines and to first aid posts. Will Bird of the 42nd thought the very effective tapes looked like "pathways for ghosts." During the actual assault tapes were extended right up to the final objective.[25]

23 LAC, War Diaries, 3rd and 4th Division General Staff War Diaries.
24 L. McLeod Gould, *From B.C. to Baisieux: Being the Narrative History of the 102nd Canadian Infantry Battalion* (Victoria: Thos. R. Cusack Presses, 1919), p. 54; LAC, War Diary, 11th Brigade, report on raid.
25 LAC, War Diary, 7th Brigade, June 1917; Bird, *Ghosts Have Warm Hands,* p. 35.

The acting CO of the RCR, Major Charles Willets, planned a two-company assault astride the railway embankment. Objectives were the enemy first, support and reserve lines. D Company, two officers and 70 ORs, in two groups would assault left of the railway embankment. To D Company's right (and to the right of the embankment) would be C Company, three officers and 93 ORs, in three groups. D Company would maintain contact with the right company of the 42nd Battalion whose CO, Major Bartlett McLennan, DSO, decided to assault in greater strength, three officers and 420 ORs. His B and D Companies would secure the first objective, the enemy front line, A and C Companies then passing through to the battalion's final objective, the enemy intermediate line about 800 yards beyond the front line. The 49th Battalion, Lieutenant-Colonel Robert Palmer, DSO, on the left flank had a 500 yard frontage, this reducing to about 400 yards at the final objective nearly 500 yards beyond the enemy front line. Strength for the raid was 14 officers and 514 ORs. Each of the three assault companies went three platoons up.[26]

At Zero (2345) immediately following the barrage the RCR crossed to the enemy trench without difficulty except to the right (south) of the railway embankment where a machine-gun opened on the raiders, but was quickly put out of action. To the left of the embankment Captain Charles Thompson's party established contact with the right company of the 42nd and his second party drove on to the second objective, pausing only to establish blocks in the CTs. Determined opposition was met and overcome and several strong points were destroyed. To the right of the embankment Captain J.S. Wood's men made equally rapid progress onto their final objective, Lieutenant Milton Gregg distinguishing himself by taking out an enemy machine-gun. While no prisoners were taken, enemy losses were thought to be considerable. Throughout the RCR sector trenches, wire and dug-out entrances were found generally heavily damaged. At 0115 upon the arranged signal troops at the final objective withdrew back through the first objective. Thirty minutes later the signal for Rear Guard withdrawal was given. While no direct rifle fire struck at the raiders as they withdrew, enemy mortar fire was heavy across the front, only very rapid movement averting heavy loss. During the raid RCR casualties amounted to one officer and 12 ORs killed, two ORs missing and 54 wounded.[27]

42nd Battalion's three companies, advancing immediately at the heels of the barrage, were clear of their assembly areas before enemy artillery got into action. Little fire was encountered during the advance to the enemy trenches which were entered within 15 minutes. The barrage was such that the raiders were able to keep up with it and prevent enemy machine-guns getting into action. While the barrage caused some casualties it was considered satisfactory. In short order B and D Companies secured the enemy front line, A and C Companies pushing on to the final objective. Thereafter as much damage as possible was done and 26 prisoners were taken. Withdrawal proved uneventful. Battalion casualties (79) included two officers and 71 ORs wounded and six killed.[28]

26 LAC, War Diaries, The RCR, 'Scheme for Raid', 7 June and 42nd Battalion, entry for 8/9 June; Fetherstonhaugh, *Royal Canadian Regiment,* p. 287; Topp, *42nd Battalion,* pp. 137-42.

27 LAC, War Diary, 7th Brigade, report on raid. Gregg was awarded the MC, later in the war a Bar and in another action the VC. Captain Thompson received the DSO later in the war while acting CO of the RCR.

28 LAC, War Diary, 42nd Battalion, entries for 8-10 June. The battalion revised its list of prisoners stating that while it had receipts for 26 it believed others had been turned in giving a total of 43.

49th Battalion reported that when at 2345 a "splendid barrage was laid down" the raiders were over the top and well beyond the jumping off trench before the first enemy artillery response at Zero plus four. In crossing to the enemy trench some casualties were caused by "shorts," there being "possibly too much high bursting shrapnel" and the light being poor. Wire posed no obstacle throughout. At the badly damaged enemy first line opposition was slight, the same true at the final objective which was reached within 20 minutes. The raid netted 35 prisoners, some then being employed as stretcher-bearers. The withdrawal, initially unhindered, did not end quite so well due to heavy enemy fire: in the words of one severely wounded officer, who was the last to withdraw, the moppers up "were themselves mopped up." Battalion losses included one officer killed and one wounded, 24 ORs killed or dead of wounds, 26 missing and 120 wounded. Some of the missing later returned.[29]

Lieutenant-Colonel Topp, historian of the 42nd, thought the brigade's raid "the most thoroughly organized and brilliantly carried out minor operation." However, another battalion historian (49th Battalion) stated that battalion records told two stories, one described the assault as being in perfect order, but another said all was in confusion, with an officer "running along shouting orders." He then asked "Did this operation yield a credit balance?" And answered "At this distance it seems doubtful."[30] Prisoners taken by the brigade totalled 62. According to the double conditional in the brigade report "German casualties may, we think" be summed up thus: dead in trench, 250; dead in dug-outs, 312; prisoners, 60; wounded by barrages, 100; and total 722. No confirmation is possible. The estimate, especially of the killed at nearly 600, is doubtless more wish than fact. Of the 335 Canadian casualties, about 10 percent were fatal. The reader can judge the balance for himself.[31]

11th Brigade (Victor Odlum) of 4th Division was to the left of Macdonell's 7th Brigade. Odlum's Operation Order 57 (Preliminary Instructions) issued on 25 May for what was initially to be an attack designated the assault units (75th, 87th and 102nd Battalions), set out some guidance for training and demanded battalion plans within 48 hours. A second page, entitled "Outline Scheme of Attack," described the objectives and unit boundaries. On 6 June Odlum's Operation Order 61 for what was now a raid repeated the objectives and boundaries, adding the raid plan, assembly areas and artillery support. Attached were "Administrative Instructions," if not the first use of this term then certainly an early example of usage. This dealt, as one would expect, with matters such as ammunition and stores, carrying parties, casualties, straggler posts and prisoner evacuation.[32]

Odlum's plan stipulated a three-battalion assault under cover of artillery and Stokes mortars, the first objective being the enemy first and support lines and the final objective their reserve line. 87th Battalion, the right assault battalion, Lieutenant-Colonel James O'Donahue, DSO, would assault on a three-company front of about 600 yards, sufficient strength to be on the right to ensure junction with 7th Brigade. The battalion's main objectives were front and support line trenches near the village of La Coulotte and south of a coal pit. The centre battalion, Lieutenant-Colonel Colin Harbottle's 75th, would assault in a northeasterly direction on a two-company

29 LAC, War Diary, 49th Battalion, 'Narrative Report on Raid' and diary entries 8-10 June; Stevens, *A City Goes to War*, pp. 90-91.
30 Topp, *42nd Battalion*, p. 137; Stevens, *A City Goes to War*, p. 91.
31 LAC, War Diary, 7th Brigade, report on raid.
32 LAC, War Diary, 11th Brigade.

front weighted to the right to mop up the Brewery area including a sunken road and the second objective, the reserve line north of La Coulotte. On the left was 102nd Battalion, Lieutenant-Colonel John Warden, DSO, which in accordance with Battalion Operation Order 52 issued on 8 June, would attack on a one-company front. Its objectives differed little from those set out in the order issued earlier when the raid had been an attack: capture and secure The Triangle trenches in co-operation with 138th British Brigade, capture a concrete machine-gun emplacement in the railway embankment and capture and hold a line east of the Electric Generating Station between there and the Souchez River. While all troops were to destroy as much as possible and then withdraw, those parties attacking immediately east of the Station and those attacking The Triangle were to hold what they took. The platoon attacking the latter would be assisting the 138th Brigade and had to link up with two platoons of the Leicesters.[33]

On the night of the raid 75th Battalion got off to a bad start – no fault of its own – enemy artillery hitting it well before Zero (2345). This fire preceded and followed 46th Division's raid whose Zero was 2030. Losses, according to Odlum's report, were about 40 percent, this "greatly disjointing operations." John Becker, a Corporal with the 75th, recalled the bombardment very clearly:

> suddenly a shell hit immediately in front of my parapet ... the concussion knocked me flat in the trench. I was unhurt and jumped to the step just as another shell lit on the parapet and down I went ... almost completely buried only my head and one arm clear ... Lieutenant Langford happened along and he and Corvin pulled me out ... our part of the trench was by now almost filled with more shells still plowing in.

No doubt Becker found this personally "disjointing." Many men found the ten bombs they were to carry all buried by the shell fire, plus other equipment, which meant all had to be drawn again. Becker remembered it as one of the worst bombardments he ever experienced. While the raiders got off on time, things did not improve, Becker and his mates experiencing incoming shells and machine-gun fire as they crossed the 100 or so yards to the enemy front line. On reaching the wire, no longer an obstacle, he found himself "seemingly alone," but once in the trench ended up beside his platoon commander and an NCO. In all, Becker thought perhaps half the platoon had made it across no man's land. The enemy posed no initial threat, but this changed abruptly when flurries of bombs began arriving, one wounding both his officer and the NCO.[34] Becker's company did not take its final objective. On the whole the 75th had stiff fighting and heavy casualties, especially on the right where progress toward the final objective was roughly checked. But the centre and left companies did reach their objectives where they blew up several dug-outs. Five prisoners were taken, the price per captive a high one: six officers wounded, 11 ORs missing, 28 killed and 112 wounded.[35]

33 LAC, War Diary, 11th Brigade, Operation Order 61, 6 June; 75th Battalion Operation Order 50, 87th Battalion Operation Order 39 and 102nd Battalion Operation Order 52; Gould, *From B.C. to Baisieux,* p. 54.

34 LAC, War Diary, 75th Battalion, Appendix I, 'Account of Raid, 8/9 June'; 11th Brigade, report of 21 June; Monroe, ed., *Silhouettes,* pp. 75-76.

35 LAC, War Diary, 75th Battalion, Appendix I, 'Account of Raid'.

At Zero the 87th, in the words of the battalion diarist, "got away in fine style." It found enemy wire adequately cut all along the battalion front. At the 16 minute mark the raiders were on their first objective and in 15 more were clearing the final objective. In the mine pit area some 200 drums of burning oil had been projected during the barrage, an expenditure that Odlum described as having "a marked moral effect, but the physical effect was not material because the oil burnt up almost instantaneously." Several dug-outs were destroyed, but more impressive was the count of prisoners, over 100 according to the unit War Diary, half of that being counted in by unit control posts, the rest having been turned over to other units. Odlum likely based his assessment of the effect of the oil on the fact that the area where the oil was projected was where most of the prisoners were taken. He also thought the capture of so many might have had something to do with the fact that the 87th had not suffered from the enemy bombardment to the extent the other battalions had. This may have raised some degree of charity in the raiders' minds. Raid casualties included three officers and 101 ORs wounded, nine ORs missing and 19 killed. Seven of the wounded later died.[36]

102nd Battalion's two objectives presented rather a unique challenge in that raiders attacking The Triangle north of the Souchez River would move south to north while the rest of the force would move west to east against the Electric Generating Station. No. 6 Platoon, B Company, Lieutenant G. Lowrie, would attack and secure The Triangle and then hand over to the 5th Leicesters of 138th Brigade. When a few minutes after Zero (2030) Lowrie was killed, Lieutenant John Knight took his place. Under a hail of machine-gun and artillery fire "the men cut through the wire and bombed their way … resistance very stubborn, but The Triangle was eventually captured, together with 15 unwounded prisoners, and handed over to the Leicesters, and No. 6 Platoon returned to its starting point." The platoon had taken the position within 40 minutes, killing 30 Germans at a cost of one officer and one OR killed and five wounded. Odlum lauded 6 Platoon's achievement thus: "as brilliant as anything I have seen in France." Knight received the MC for his fine performance.[37]

Phase 2 of the battalion's tasks began at 2345. The officers moving their raiders eastward against the area of the Electric Generating Station may well have mused upon the fact that what they were about had gone two revolutions, attack had become raid and then for their specific task had again become attack since any ground seized would have to be held. Major Richard Burde's A Company and one platoon from each of B and C Companies set off making good progress initially toward the Station, but at 0110 he reported wire too thick to get through. Because the jumping off trench and the enemy line were so close, the artillery had become fearful of hitting the 102nd and had overshot. Despite Lieutenant-Colonel Warden sending Major Ryan forward with orders that the men had to make "further endeavours to reach their objective," and the desperate attempts of Sergeant Z. Kirby to cut the wire, the attack permanently stalled. Consequently, Burde was told to consolidate where he stood and a platoon of D Company moved to reinforce him. Two hours later came disquieting news: the enemy had recovered The Triangle north of the Souchez. Not realizing this, one platoon of A Company

36 LAC, War Diary, 87th Battalion, 8-9 June; 11th Brigade, report of 21 June and 'Report on Operations from 5th to 12th June, Minor Operation No, 5', para 10. See Foulkes, *"Gas!"* for other examples of the use of projected oil.

37 LAC, War Diary, 11th Brigade report, 21 June.

suffered 30 casualties from fire delivered by the enemy who had retaken The Triangle. Battalion casualties included two officers and six ORs killed and 67 wounded.[38]

Canadian Corps reported one officer and 109 ORs admitted to the Corps Cage and Casualty Clearing Stations, concluding that the raids had been "very successful ... very high casualties were inflicted ... our casualties quite moderate."[39] Colonel Nicholson said only that the raid had gone as planned with more than 150 dug-outs bombed and 136 prisoners taken. German casualties were estimated variously as about 700. Reports of "relatively light" Canadian casualties ranged from 709 (108 of these fatal) to as high as 1,000.

During the 7 May conference with his Army commanders the C-in-C had directed that those Armies not engaged in the attack on Messines-Wytschaete Ridge were to do what they could "with a view to wearing out as many of the enemy troops as possible." First Army had directed the joint I Corps/Canadian Corps raid that half of this chapter has focussed on. One participant, Corporal Becker. 75th Canadian Battalion, had a less positive view of "wearing out":

> What was it all for? Our Battalion alone lost almost 100 ... I don't believe the enemy loss was half ours. The idea was to get identifications and to wear down their defence ... just one of those crazy ideas that cost us men and wore ourselves out. No one will ever convince me that the raid did us any good whatsoever.[40]

Private Bert Cooke, also 75th Battalion, but in a different company, recalled "light casualties with only nine killed and a small number slightly wounded ... Several of our boys were new men. It was a critical experience for them because it was their first time in the battle line."[41]

For the Canadian Corps the second half of 1917 began with another raid that had initially been an attack, the change coming because of a suggestion by the new GOC, Sir Arthur Currie. This raid, and several others, British and Canadian, the emphasis on the former, are the concern of the next chapter.

38 *Ibid.*, Gould, *From B.C. to Baisieux*, pp. 55-56.
39 LAC, War Diary, Canadian Corps General Staff Summary of Intelligence.
40 Nicholson, *Canadian Expeditionary Force*, p. 281; Brigadier-General Sir James E. Edmonds, *Military Operations France and Belgium 1917: Volume II 7th June–10th November: Messines and Third Ypres (Passchendaele)* (London: MacMillan, 1948), pp. 24-25; Monroe, ed., *Silhouettes*, p. 82.
41 Milly Walsh and John Callan, *We're Not Dead Yet: The First World War Diary of Private Bert Cooke* (St. Catharines: Vanwell Publishing Limited, 2004), p. 118. The figures are just those of Cooke's B Company.

14

1917 – Second Half

> Yet still the fields at home are green
> Though here the grass is red.
> M.A. Bell

The first part of July 1917 was not especially notable when it came to raiding. 7th British Division staged a series of small raids in response to "higher authorities" demands for an "active" policy in order to "detain as many Germans as possible on the less active parts of the front." On the night of 14/15 July 20th Brigade of the division raided twice, three platoons of 2nd Gordon Highlanders striking at an area opposite the brigade front and three platoons of the 1st South Staffords of 91st Brigade hitting another. A detachment of sappers to carry out demolitions accompanied the Gordons, the sappers in kilts "possibly for the only time in the history of the RE." The objective being both sides of a sunken road dictated one platoon (an officer plus 29 men) per side and the third in support. On the left uncut wire caused delay that gave the enemy time to move more defenders to the entry point, but the platoon prevailed after a short, sharp fight. The "Highland" sappers, their kilts no obstacle to the work, blew up the dug-out to which the defeated enemy had retreated. The explosive charge that destroyed this dug-out was followed by a massive explosion and then a fire, evidence that it was probably a bomb dump. The platoon on the right had a relatively quiet time of it, few enemy about. At the end of 15 minutes the Gordons, with one prisoner and 18 wounded Gordons, including two officers, headed home.

The Staffords did not fare so well, their objective proved a little too much to chew on for it was really three points: on the left a "Mebus" with a trench behind it, in the centre another trench and on the right another "Mebus" plus trench.[1] The raiders taking on the last could not enter the objective area, the enemy being too alert, not only very prompt to bring down fire, but also actively trying to outflank the raiding party. In the centre, the officer and one man of the party did enter the trench, but with a strong enemy group advancing from the right "Mebus" and trench the party had to withdraw very quickly. Heavy rifle and machine-gun fire from the "Mebus" prevented the left party entering the trench. Casualties in the Staffords came to five

1 TNA: WO 95/1633, 1656, 1667, 1670: 7th Division General Staff, 20th Brigade, 2nd Gordons, 91st Brigade and 1st Staffords, raid reports; Fraser and Gibbons, *Soldier and Sailor Words*, p. 154. "Mebus" stemmed from "Mebu" or Pill Box, "Mebu" representing the German for "Machine-Gun Iron Concrete Emplacement (*Maschinengewehr Eisenbeton Unterstand)*".

ORs killed and one missing, plus one officer and 15 ORs wounded. The brigade commander, R.T. Pelly, thought the raiders fell between chairs: either the barrage should have been heavier, or there should have been none at all; as it was, it alerted the enemy and failed to drive him to ground. A week later 7th Division launched a second pair of raids, both finding the objective vacant, leaving nothing to do but blow up a few dug-outs and withdraw.[2]

Given the lack of notable successes in July, 7th Division implemented a questionnaire to be completed by brigades immediately after a raid, nine of the 11 questions requiring only Yes or No, the other two requiring Yes/No and a word or two, no more:

A. Did raiders enter enemy positions?
B. Were enemy found there?
C. Was raid successful?
D. How many prisoners brought in?
E. What is estimated enemy dead?
F. How many machine-guns captured?
G. How many trench mortars captured?
H. How many dug-outs destroyed?
J. What are our officer casualties?
K. What are our OR casualties?
L. Have raiders all returned?[3]

7th Division was not the only division providing additional guidance to brigades. IV Corps had distributed that division's "Some Notes on Raids," an undated three-page compilation of the lessons of the several raids made by that division. This document seems to have been widely distributed, British and Canadian. While a few of the notes are peculiar to the 7th Division's experience, most are universal, reflecting general experience and the state of the art to that time. First, recce of the objective had to continue up to and including the night the raid would be made. The notes remarked that when raids failed this was often attributed to loss of direction, new wire or machine-guns when the real cause was just as often poor recce. Second, the notes recommended organizational changes, one being that every raid should include a strong support party close at hand, but not in the trench, standing ready to intervene if necessary and, second, parties of rifle bombers, distinct from the assault parties, should be either in no man's land close to the objective or at any blocks that had been established. One particular task of the support party should be to escort prisoners across no man's land immediately they were captured. Third, regarding arms and equipment raiders should travel as light as possible, helmets, for example, were not usually required, and rifle and bayonet were "invariably … the most effective weapons. Bombs … a last extremity." Fourth, the best signal to withdraw was a "time signal" by the watch of leaders. Fifth, if the returning raiders were to avoid retaliatory fire they should not pause in their front line, but move through it quickly to a rearward rendezvous. Sixth, fire support comments mainly concerned barrages, a creeping barrage before a raid entered the enemy trench was "inadvisable;"

2 Atkinson, *Seventh Division,* pp. 399-400; TNA: WO 95 War Diaries (as above).
3 TNA: WO 95/1654:7th Division General Staff, 'Some Notes on Raids'. The letter "I" was not used in orders and reports as it could be confused with the number "1".

better a standing barrage on trench junctions at time of entry and a box ("block") barrage beyond the objective. Of course, this depended on guns available. Finally, execution of a raid depended on two "dominant" qualifications: first, determination to reach the objective, no stopping to assist wounded, throw bombs or take cover, all such activities could cause failure; and, second, trench fighting "depends for success on the individual soldier's skill with the rifle and bayonet."[4]

A IV Corps memorandum on raids issued on the same day had considerable to say about setting another rendezvous that would assist in withdrawal. It pointed out that during night raids wounded men could inadvertently be left behind and men could go missing. This being so "Some well defined feature on the line of withdrawal must be occupied, such as a sunken road, cross roads or embankment, and held until daylight, or longer if possible, on which wounded or missing men can retire." Also, the night after a raid a patrol should search the scene of the raid for missing and wounded men. This second point was not something new as many units routinely made such searches. Both suggestions had obvious limitations.[5]

2nd British Division also launched a series of raids in July hoping to take advantage of information gained from two deserters about an upcoming relief. Quick action was necessary since the shorter the time between the relief and the raids the better. On 12 July divisional HQ ordered each brigade to make one raid of 100-150 men before the end of the month.[6] A raid by 23rd Royal Fusiliers of 99th Brigade came eight days later at 2230 on 20 July.

That night forming up of the raiders forward of the battalion wire went undetected. Shortly after Zero three officers and 115 ORs organized in eight parties reached enemy wire, which they found well-cut, and entered the trenches unopposed. Very few enemy were about, eight being killed in a brief skirmish. Sappers destroyed a mineshaft, two dug-outs and an ammunition dump. Nor were enemy encountered in the support line. Summing up the raid the division's historian commented on the "sheer bad luck" not to have met any appreciable body of enemy. Of this raid the GSO1 thought that if the main object had been to secure identifications then "perhaps some simpler form … would [have met] the case better." Eight days between information and action leads one to share his opinion; a much smaller and simpler raid could have been cranked up much faster. Also, it was not so much "sheer bad luck," but inadequate recce that resulted in nothing being achieved. Either the deserters had been wrong or had lied, or the relief had taken place before the raid. Given the eight day interval one is left to wonder how much patrolling was done.[7]

2nd Highland Light Infantry (5th Brigade) made the third raid at 0040 on 28 July (the second is left to last as it drew the most "friendly" fire). Results were little better for the 2nd, a few dug-outs destroyed or damaged, no prisoners taken, nothing really achieved because the wire so delayed the party that was to have captured the enemy garrison that the enemy had ample time to evacuate.[8] 5th Brigade thought that wire-cutting had been so obvious that it

4 TNA: WO 95/1379: 3rd Division General Staff, 9th Brigade, IV Corps instruction, 26 June. A similar but larger compilation issued by 19th Division General Staff in February 1918 is discussed in Chapter 15.

5 *Ibid.*

6 TNA: WO 95/1297: 2nd Division General Staff, instructions 12 and 13 July to 5th, 6th and 99th Brigades.

7 Wyrall, *Second Division,* p. 463; TNA: WO 95/1369: 99th Brigade.

8 Wyrall, *Second Division,* pp. 466-67; TNA: WO 95/1297: 5th Brigade.

warned the enemy. The GSO1, Lieutenant-Colonel E.D. Giles, strongly criticized what he thought was brigade carelessness, one example being the escape of a prisoner who was left to find his own way to battalion lines. This left Giles thinking 5th Brigade did not attach "great importance … to securing prisoners."[9]

Of the second raid, that of 1st King's Regiment (6th Brigade) on the night of 25 July, the entry for that day in the brigade War Diary says it all: "Raid was not successful. No prisoners taken or identifications obtained." Why the raid failed is answered by the published divisional history: when the barrage began the enemy immediately replied with heavy fire including minenwerfers, causing casualties and confusion that ended the raid. Lieutenant-Colonel Giles was scathing about the raid. First, he thought the plan for the raid lacked precision. Second, despite what was claimed to be thorough recce one of the raiding parties bumped into an enemy post, another did not know where it was and the others were held up by wire. "Thorough" hardly seems appropriate. Third, the plan made "no mention of any special training … beyond nightly recce." Here one wonders about the extent of 6th Brigade's involvement in the planning. Nor did Giles share 6th Brigade's contention that the forming up of the raiders had gone undetected: "To expect to get 120 men out into No Man's Land, form them up, keep them there for half an hour undetected, however quiet they may try to be, seems to be expecting a good deal. The only thing is that if any were observed, their losses were certainly extraordinarily light." Finally, he offered a comparison. If it was possible for the enemy to surprise a post in a sap and take two prisoners (this happened on the night of 23 July), "it should be equally easy for us to raid his saps, where the primary object is to obtain an identification that would seem to be the best and easiest way of getting it." This report, which was in manuscript and signed only with initials, these somewhat indistinct but appearing to be those of Giles, was in the divisional HQ "Raids Register" In view of its content it appears this report was simply "PA" (Put Away). [10]

Looking now at Canadian raids, in July a battalion of 3rd Division made one of the most interesting raids of the second half of 1917. One reason for this is that the battalion chosen to do the raid, the 116th of 9th Brigade, had only been in France since February and had seen no action as a unit before the raid, which became its initiation, its rite of passage, its virgin status, no doubt, a significant factor in its selection as the raiding battalion. The battalion historian later wrote how untiring the CO, Lieutenant-Colonel S.S. Sharpe, had been in getting the battalion to France, and while he does not say so, Sharpe probably lobbied hard to get the raid for his battalion.[11] Second, this raid is another case of an attack becoming a raid, here the instrument of change being Sir Arthur Currie, GOC the Canadian Corps. It offers a good example of how subordinates viewed the "wishes" of senior commanders and how these sometimes underwent negotiation and considerable amendment as they filtered down the chain of command.

The story of 116th Battalion's first raid began on 7 July when First Army (Horne) advised the Canadian Corps of Field Marshal Haig's orders "to take Lens with a view to threatening an advance on Lille from the South." Horne wished consideration of such an operation to capture

9 *Ibid.*, War Diary, 2nd Division General Staff, report on raid.
10 *Ibid.*, 6th Brigade and 2nd Division General Staff, 'Raids Register' and attached manuscript divisional report. Wyrall, *Second Division*, pp. 454, 466-67. Giles became GSO1 in early May.
11 E.P.S. Allen, *The 116th Battalion in France: By the Adjutant* (Toronto: Hunter-Ross Co. Ltd., 1921), p. 16. Sharpe became CO of the battalion when it began forming in October 1915, remaining as such until January 1918 when G.L.R. Pearkes, VC, DSO, MC, took command.

certain objectives in that area to begin at an early date.[12] Having duly considered these objectives, Currie was unhappy. At a conference three days later he voiced his concern and presented a case for making Hill 70 the "immediate main objective," not Lens. Horne, seeing Currie's proposal as eminently sensible, agreed and so amended Canadian objectives, the Canadian operation to start on 23 July and be so carried out as to give the impression that it was a preliminary operation to a First Army attack on its entire front. As part of this, 3rd Canadian Division (Louis Lipsett) was to attack on 22/23 July, the objective being to destroy enemy works at the railway embankment near Avion (see MSD 20). On the 11th, First Army had at hand Canadian Corps Operation Order 135 wherein 3rd Division would prepare "a large raid" south of the Souchez River to give the impression desired. First Army responded immediately:

> The Army Commander wishes you to consider the advisability of establishing posts so as to retain the ground gained, and not to come back as appears to be implied by the word 'raid' in your order. The retention of the ground will … increase the pressure on Lens, and such action is indicated by the wording of the Commander-in-Chief's instructions which were read out at the conference … on 10 July, viz:- all ground gained must be held by rifle and bayonet alone if no assistance is available from other Arms.[13]

Four days later Currie submitted an "outline of the operations" to be carried out by 3rd Division on the 23rd, including the objectives and forces to be employed and he refers to the "wishes" of the Army Commander:

> It is not considered advisable to try and occupy permanently the line of the Railway Embankment which forms the main objective, as in that position we should be very unfavourably placed from the tactical point of view. The line there is commanded from the high ground in front and enfiladed from commanding positions on both flanks … Moreover, in view of the … transfer [of] guns … it would, therefore, be difficult to guarantee that the position could be held against a determined attempt to take it back.

At this point "operations" by 3rd Division are about to be reasonably modified by First Army which approved the proposals as outlined by Currie, viz: the main objective of the "raid" was the dug-outs and trench mortar emplacements behind the Railway Embankment. The plan saw the slag heap and the CT running north of it as the left boundary of the raid and the CT on the right of the objective would serve as the right. As for the assault force, it would consist of one battalion, the 116th.[14] The battalion historian provides a good description of the main features of the raid area. The railway embankment, some 300 yards behind and parallel to the enemy front line, stood about 24 feet high. Roughly halfway to the first objective lay Quebec Road,

12 LAC, War Diary, Canadian Corps General Staff, First Army GS 658/1(a) to GOC, 7 July 1917.

13 Nicholson, *Canadian Expeditionary Force*, p. 285; LAC, War Diary, Canadian Corps General Staff, First Army GS 658/4 (a) to GOCs I, XI, XIII, Canadian Corps, 10 July: Canadian Corps Operation Order 135, 11 July; First Army GS 658/13 (a) to Canadian Corps, 11 July.

14 *Ibid.*, Canadian Corps G178/23-15-1 to Advanced HQ First Army, 16 July; First Army GS 658/17 (a) to Canadian Corps 16 July.

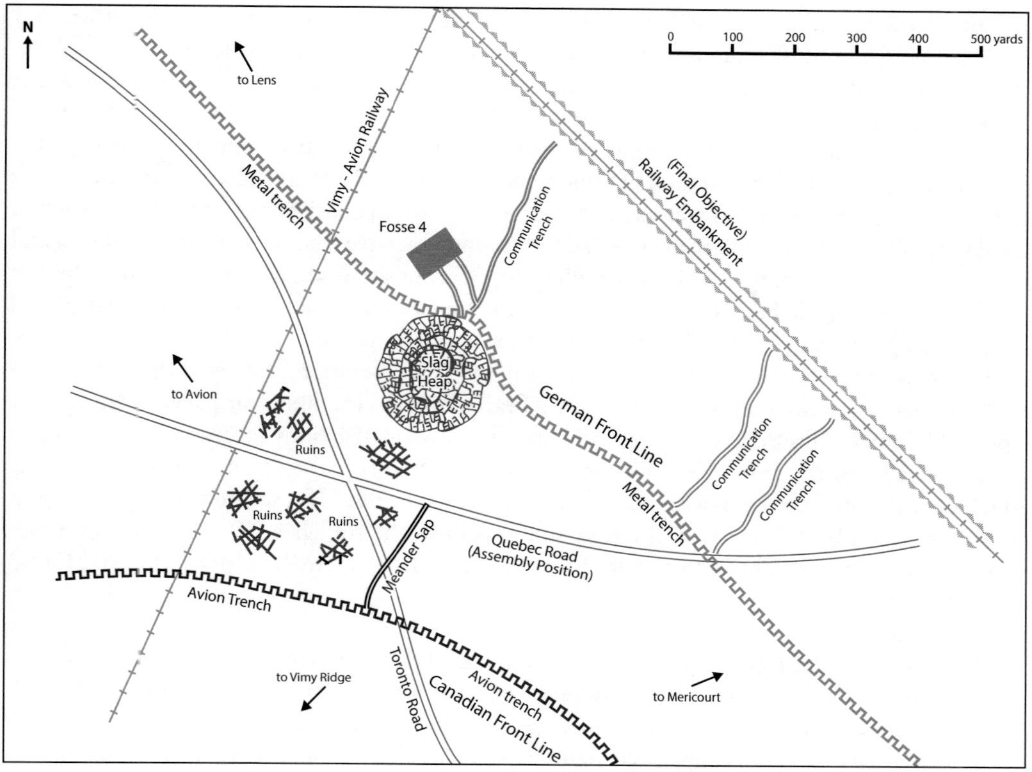

20 Northeast of Vimy Ridge, 23 July 1917, 9th Canadian Brigade.

partly sunken and full of wire, but once cleared a good jumping off line. Machine-guns apparently infested the slag heap.[15]

On the 17th, HQ 3rd Division issued Operation Order 119 giving the objectives as first the Metal Trench (enemy front line) and second the enemy dug-outs and trench mortar emplacements in the railway embankment. 9th Brigade, which would run the operation, was directed to issue plans and orders in accordance with the already approved divisional outline plan. A paragraph of the Operation Order reflected the Army Commander's "wishes" and Haig's instructions on retention of ground: "Arrangements will be made for posts to be left in the enemy's line which will be held in the event of the enemy not endeavouring to re-occupy his trenches in force." Allen explains how the BM, Captain Richard Stayner, MC, and not the battalion, came to write and issue the outline plan: "Having no plan of our own, it was evidently the duty of 9th Brigade HQ to devise some scheme for us … on 12 July we received orders to practise for a raid."[16] Initially, Stayner provided "Preliminary Notes on Scheme for Raid (Tentative)." By

15 Allen, *116th Battalion*, pp. 31-32.
16 LAC, War Diary, 3rd Division Operation Order 119, 17 July; Captain S.G. Bennett, MC, *The 4th Canadian Mounted Rifles 1914-1919* (Toronto: Murray Printing Company Limited, 1926), p. 171. Stayner, age 40 in 1917, began his war service with 1CMR in 1914. Later he was Lieutenant-Colonel and DSO, CBE, MC. He served 1898-1908 with the Royal North West Mounted Police and with

way of introduction he cautioned that the notes could not be considered definitive since they had been worked out by map. A "proper" scheme based on recce and air photos would follow. He reiterated the two objectives defined in the divisional Operation Order and assigned one company to the first objective, two to the second and one as a reserve and covering party for the withdrawal. The jumping off line, Quebec Road, was about 150 yards short of the first objective. Leapfrog would be the method of attack, the first wave being three platoons for the assault and mopping up of the first objective. The second wave would consist of one platoon for each of the flanking CTs and four platoons to seize the second objective (the railway embankment) and mop up dug-outs and emplacements. Artillery support consisted of 18-pounders and 4.5-inch howitzers firing on the first objective, CTs and rear trenches. Quebec Road would be taped and occupied by posts founded by 52nd Battalion prior to the raid.[17]

Six days later (the 18th) Stayner issued "Instructions for Operation," followed the next day by an "Administrative Instruction" prepared by a Staff Captain. The first four pages of the former repeated Stayner's "Preliminary Notes" and added precise instructions for the move forward to Quebec Road and the time (Zero minus 60) when all troops had to be assembled there. The attack details stated where blocks were to be established in the CTs, where Lewis guns would be positioned on both objectives, the time to be spent in the trenches (20 minutes) and directions for the withdrawal including that of the posts that had to remain as per Army and GHQ instructions (see previous paragraph):

> Rear Guard will establish standing patrols in the final objective where the communication trenches on right and left of the raided area intersect with the railway embankment, with instructions to prevent the enemy re-occupying the final objective, except in force. These standing patrols will be supported by posts established in communication trenches on either flank and in Metal Trench. The two companies assaulting final objective including rear guard sections minus standing patrols referred to, will withdraw through company holding first objective after which that company will also withdraw.

The artillery fire plan had four phases: fire on the first objective, then between the two objectives, then on the second objective and then beyond it. The signals plan called for lines forward to both objectives. Battalion HQ would signal the withdrawal at Zero plus 35 by rockets. On 21 July two days before Zero Stayner issued Operation Order 106 which reiterated the purpose of the raid, the troops participating, instructions for the withdrawal and Zero, which was set for 0100 on 23 July.[18]

Summing up, 9th Brigade BM provided Preliminary Notes, Operation Instructions, Administrative Instructions and an Operation Order for the raid. Chapter 6 described the differences between Operation Orders and Operation Instructions and their usage. Captain Stayner clearly understood these. While the titles of some of the staff papers are now slightly different, they reflect a purpose and sequence not unlike those today's staff officers would be required to prepare. A seeming omission in 9th Brigade's staffing is the document now called a

the Fort Garry Horse. He also served in South Africa 1899-1902 with 1CMR and 2CMR. In 1918-19 he was with HQ Canadian Expeditionary Force in Siberia.

17 LAC, War Diary, 9th Brigade, 'Preliminary Notes Scheme for Raid (Tentative)', 12 July.

18 *Ibid.*, 9th Brigade, 12, 18, 19 and 21 July.

"Warning Order," but the "Preliminary Notes" serve that purpose. The term "Warning Order" does not seem to have been in general use at this time, although HQ Canadian Corps did issue "Operation Order 137 Warning Order" directing liaison to adjust a boundary.[19]

The CO, Lieutenant-Colonel Sharpe, was then left "to arrange the details." Concurrently, the raiders were trained on a taped replica where they endured the usual rehearsals including a final witnessed by brigade and division commanders. Sharpe also took a party of raid officers and NCOs on a carefully arranged daylight recce into Avion where they could have a good view of the area.[20] The raiding parties consisted of A Company (three platoons) under Captain Harold Gould to secure the first objective; B and C Companies, Captain E.P.S. Allen and Major Martin Currie respectively, to pass through to the second objective; and D Company, Captain Ritchie, in reserve and prepared to cover the withdrawal.[21]

At 2130 on the night of the raid all four companies moved forward to the front line where each man received an "electric torch-light" and had a large white patch attached to his box respirator. It then remained only to wait for guides to take them forward to Quebec Road. Suddenly gas alarms sounded in the enemy trenches and gas fumes began drifting into Canadian trenches. Respirators had to be donned. The impact can well be imagined. As Allen described the situation, "It is hard enough to find your way about in the dark under ordinary conditions, but with a gas helmet on it is absolutely impossible, and the greatest confusion arose … the whole operation hung in the balance." As the men milled about, platoon formations broke apart, some men moving forward, some backward, all seeking to escape the gas. The battalion War Diary reported how for 30 minutes the situation was critical, re-assembly of the platoons being slow and difficult with raiders' respirators on and off – chances had to be taken – and then on again, the changes several and frequent, but as the gas dissipated most of the raiders got sorted out under guide control and reached Quebec Road before Zero.[22]

Promptly at 0100 as the guns opened on the enemy front line A Company moved forward, Captain Gould well in front, through the gaps previously cut by scouts. At Zero plus three as the barrage lifted to the rear of the first objective A Company rushed the enemy trench, closely followed by B Company on the left and C Company on the right. Gould and his men reached the enemy line just in time to meet the Germans leaving their dug-outs. Hand to hand fighting began in earnest. As this continued, B and C Companies began passing through, paying no attention to the carnage, intent only on reaching the railway embankment. As had been anticipated, during the rush to the embankment fire from the flanks did inflict fairly heavy casualties. The enemy also put up stiff resistance on and behind the embankment, but once blocks were established left and right in the CTs and north of the embankment the fighting decreased. With the fumes now blowing back over the German lines gas again became a problem. However, those tasked to destroy dug-outs and emplacements went hard at it. "Refractory" prisoners posed another headache. Those who continued to resist or attempted to escape left their captors no choice.[23]

19 LAC, Canadian Corps General Staff, Operation Order 137 Warning Order, 13 July.
20 Allen, *116th Battalion,* p. 32.
21 LAC, War Diary, 116th Battalion; Allen, *116th Battalion,* pp. 32-33.
22 *Ibid.,* pp. 34-35.
23 LAC, War Diary, 116th Battalion.

When time to stay elapsed B and C Companies, covered by a rear guard, began to withdraw. Both companies left posts on the embankment where CTs intersected it and on each flank. Neither company experienced any difficulty returning to the enemy front line and then through it to home trenches, A Company remaining in possession as a covering force. D Company had arranged parties to relieve the B and C Companies' posts at daybreak, but at 0445 German counter-attacks on both flanks came in such force that the posts had no choice but to withdraw. A running fight ensued. For a time, confusion became such that the occupants of the posts were reported as missing. Such was not the case. The War Diary and Allen later related how the posts got out.[24]

As usual enemy losses could not be accurately determined, but Lieutenant-Colonel Sharpe believed them heavy; in one case of 48 enemy holding a position 11 were captured and the rest killed or wounded. In all, 53 prisoners were taken, 60 according to Allen's account. Battalion casualties included two officers and 10 ORs killed, three officers and 42 ORs wounded and two officers and 15 ORs missing, the two officers later reported as killed.[25] But the raid had been successful, the battalion historian thinking "we had at last won the right to our place in the 9th Brigade and in the Canadian Corps." Given the interest expressed by GHQ, Army and Corps from the beginning in the holding of the lines by "posts" the brigade commander, F.W. Hill, carefully noted the situation that pertained at the end of the raid: while every effort had been made to establish and maintain posts in order to prevent enemy re-occupation they were untenable, being enfiladed from both flanks and commanded by high ground, this also applying to the first objective and the slag heap. Consequently, he had ordered Quebec Road to be held, it being on commanding ground and free from enfilade fire. He considered this the furthest forward position that could reasonably be retained.[26]

Many of the Canadian raids in August, mostly smaller in size and scope, aimed at securing identifications. 4th Division, for example, in the ten days between 9 and 19 August launched four raids against enemy lines in the Lens area. Only one of these secured prisoners (two), the other three finding enemy trenches unoccupied. 12th Brigade also launched two raids, neither obtaining the required identifications, but no further attempts were necessary as the information was garnered elsewhere.[27] 12th British Division also made a series of raids in August, but on a much larger scale. On the 9th two of its brigades, the 35th and the 37th, sent out a total of 790 raiders, 360 from the 7th Suffolks of the 35th and the balance from 37th Brigade's 6th Buffs and 7th East Surrey Regiment. These took on six objectives in enemy trenches 1,000 yards east of Monchy Le Preux and about the same distance northeast of Guemappe.

The 7th Suffolks raided three objectives on a frontage of about 1,000 yards after a lengthy bombardment that began at 0630 on the 9th and continued intermittently in varying intensity until 1945 when the raiders advanced under cover of a creeping barrage. Wire proved no obstacle. "A" Raiding Party, 180 strong, went over in two waves, the first to secure and hold the front line while the second passed through to the enemy support line. Little resistance was met, the trenches in very bad condition, many dead in the debris. A Lewis gun team then prevented an enemy counter-attack from the south. "B" Raiding Party, somewhat smaller (100 officers and men) encountered no resistance, the enemy front line "very much knocked about" and many dead

24 LAC, War Diaries, 9th Brigade and 116th Battalion; Allen, *116th Battalion,* p. 37.
25 LAC, War Diary, 116th Battalion, report of CO; Allen, *116th Battalion,* p. 38.
26 *Ibid.,* LAC, War Diary, 9th Brigade, report of GOC, 23 July.
27 LAC, War Diaries, 11th and 12th Brigades, 4th Division.

evident, most seeming to be the result of shelling. "C" Raiding Party, 80 strong, encountered opposition only beyond the front line, but even there it was neither determined nor protracted. Some men fell victim to machine-gun fire from the south, this fire continuing during the withdrawal. By 2030 all three parties had returned bringing 69 prisoners with them. On the down side, all four company commanders were casualties, one killed, one missing believed killed and two wounded, a matter of "great regret" to all.[28]

In 37th Brigade the 6th Buffs, which raided 80 strong, had as an objective "Devil's Trench" and so it proved, one party coming under such severe enfilade machine-gun fire that it could not enter the enemy trench. The other party did enter, but could not reach its final objective due to machine-gun fire. This party reported the trench as "practically flattened," but cleverly defended by machine-guns they could not locate. The three parties of the 7th East Surreys, 350 officers and men, were more fortunate, doing, in the words of the brigade commander, "splendid work," all three parties gaining all objectives, in two cases meeting only slight opposition and in the other only short-lived resistance before the enemy slipped away. In all, 37th Brigade brought home 26 prisoners. By actual count enemy dead totalled 100 killed by shelling and perhaps 60 more killed by the raiders.[29]

In all, 12th Division lost two officers and 33 ORs killed. Wounded and missing came to 12 officers and 205 ORs. The divisional historian related that fire support was provided by "a group that were moved to any required locality, being known as The Circus." For the raids, "The Circus" expended the following ammunition: 18-pounders, 22,800 rounds; 4.5-inch howitzers, 10,100; 2-inch trench mortars, 1,358; and Stokes, 2,700.[30]

The 12th British Division continued raiding in the Monchy Le Preux area in September. On the 2nd, 100 men of the 9th Royal Fusiliers under Captain George Baudains raided an area immediately adjacent to where the 7th Suffolks had. Sharp at 1915 artillery began putting down a box around the objective, this signalling the start of the infantry advance across the narrow stretch between friendly and enemy trenches. The enemy having been taken completely by surprise meant no immediate opposition; many simply fled. Some bombing took place on the right flank where one blocking party had set up. Here captured stick grenades proved useful. Sappers destroyed three dug-outs, a chained down machine-gun and a mortar. Eighteen prisoners accompanied the raiders back to battalion lines. The Army Commander thought the raid "excellent … one of those dashing enterprises which reflect the highest credit on the leaders and the men." Captain Baudains received the MC.[31] The series ended with a raid on 22 September by four officers and 65 men of the 9th Essex on an area near to where the Fusiliers had struck. While surprise was complete, the objective was manned only by sentries. Of the 23 Germans seen, five were captured, all, plus their captors, returning to battalion lines within 10 minutes. Only one man was wounded during the raid.[32]

28 Scott, *12th (Eastern) Division,* p. 122; TNA: WO 95/1848: 35th Brigade and 7th Suffolks, raid reports.
29 Scott, *12th (Eastern) Division,* pp. 122-23; TNA: WO 95/1859: 37th Brigade, 6th Buffs and 7th East Surreys, reports of GOC and COs.
30 Scott, *12th (Eastern) Division,* p. 123.
31 *Ibid.,* p. 124; TNA: WO 95/1825: 36th Brigade, report on raid by 9th Royal Fusiliers and memorandum 7 September 12th Division to 36th Brigade.
32 TNA: WO 95/1825: 9th Essex, report by CO 22 September 1917.

58th Battalion of 3rd Canadian Division made one of the last Canadian minor operations in August. This operation on the 30th, a preliminary to a larger raid by 52nd Battalion of that division, was variously dubbed a "bombing attack," a "minor operation" and a "raid." Strictly speaking, the last term did not apply since the aim was to hold some ground, but as the ground to be held was only a single post at a block it appears in most reports as raid rather than attack. The CO decided to call it a "bombing attack, with the intention of driving the enemy out of Nun's Alley and establishing a block and advanced post in that trench" (see MSD 21). In his report, F.W. Hill, GOC 9th Brigade, describing the endeavour as a "minor operation," elaborated:

> At approximately 200 yards up Nun's Alley there is a crest which commands a portion of our front line. In order to deprive the enemy of this advantage, and to secure for ourselves a similar command of the enemy's trench system, and to enable us to construct our proposed trench east of our present front line, the 58th … was ordered to clear Nun's Alley as far as the crest and to establish a post there.

The battalion War Diary called this operation a raid carried out by Lieutenants Frank Gray and Warner Cusler and 34 bombers and rifle grenadiers of C Company, the operation directed by Major R.A. Macfarlane, DSO, who decided on a daylight operation without artillery support.

At 1330 the enemy block (see MSD 21) was bombed and taken, its garrison of eight killed and a machine-gun captured. When Lieutenant Gray was wounded Lieutenant Cusler took over, the raiders overcoming two more enemy posts of eight men each and continuing down Nun's Alley to within 50 yards of the junction with Nabob Alley and Cinnabar Trench. Here an enemy counter-attack suffered defeat. Blocks having been established, and Nun's Alley having been wired in, the bombers and grenadiers fell back to their original positions. Several more counter-attacks were beaten off during the afternoon and night, each time with rifle grenades. The post established at the crest enabled good observation of Cinnabar and a good field of fire, the whole covered by Lewis guns and a Stokes mortar. Thirty enemy dead were counted and three prisoners, one an officer, were taken. Canadian casualties were six wounded and one killed.[33]

The larger raid began at 0030 on 4 September, 14 officers and 180 ORs of 52nd Battalion, Lieutenant-Colonel William Foster, DSO and Bar, MC, raiding Nabob Alley and Cinnabar Trench, and then withdrawing to the new line that had been prepared after the raid on 30 August. The intent was to advance battalion positions and establish posts in advance of the new line, to render Cinnabar Trench useless by wrecking dug-outs, strong points and weapons emplacements and to take prisoners and obtain identifications. At the 50 minute mark all troops had to be behind the newly established advanced posts. To cover the assault, artillery would fire a rolling barrage in three stages: Zero to Zero plus two intense rate on a line 50 yards west of Cinnabar Trench, then two minutes intense on Cinnabar and from Zero plus four to 50 rapid rate initially, then normal and then slow. At Zero, a Stokes mortar would enfilade Nun's Alley for one minute. As a diversion, at Zero minus five 20 projectors north of the raid area would launch drums containing a mixture resembling a gas discharge. To strengthen the deception,

33 LAC, War Diary, 9th Brigade, reports of Major MacFarlane and GOC.

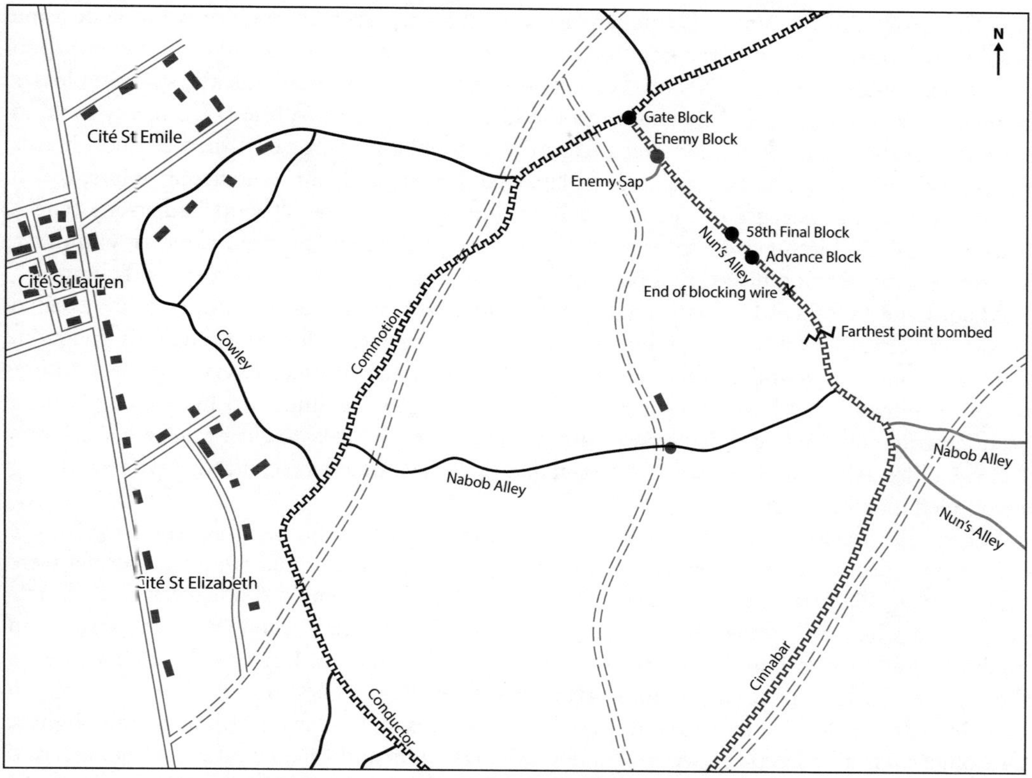

21 Raid near Lens, 30 August 1917, 58th Canadian Battalion.

black powder charges would be fired to create the impression of a large-scale gas discharge. A real gas discharge (200 drums) was also planned, but not done.[34]

A Company, plus one platoon of B Company, 90 men in all, attacked on the right. Almost immediately the company commander was killed, his place filled by Lieutenant William King who within minutes was wounded, his arm broken in two places, but he retained command and led the way into the enemy trench. During the severe fighting there King was again wounded, but continued to command his company which defeated the garrison and thoroughly wrecked trench works, dug-out and weapons emplacements. Cinnabar Trench featured deep dug-outs every 75 or so yards. Eight prisoners were taken. King, despite his injuries, was the last man to leave the trench and assisted a wounded man back to battalion lines.

34 LAC, War Diaries, 9th Brigade and 52nd Battalion, Operation Order 116 and Appendices, and Battalion Operation Order 143, 2 September; RG9IIIC1, Volume 3843, Folder 46, File 5, 'Artillery Instructions No. 3', issued by First Army, 22 March 1917. This instruction stipulated rates of fire for divisional and heavy artillery. For 18-pounders the rates per gun per minute were: intense, four; rapid, three; normal, two; slow, one; and very slow, one-half. Rates for 4.5-inch howitzers were half the 18-pounder rate and rates for 60-pounders half the howitzer rate.

B Company, 30 men under Lieutenant Edward Abbott, reached its objective in good time despite encountering wire at the junction of Nabob Alley and Cinnabar. The enemy in Nabob and at the double junction – Nabob, Nun's and Cinnabar – withdrew quickly, suffering losses as they went and more when they ran into the Canadian barrage. While B Company took no prisoners, it did collect shoulder straps from the dead, these being confirmed as 2nd Guards Regiment. Abbott reported Cinnabar and Nabob badly damaged, but some strong points, which could not be got at because of intense machine-gun fire, remained. Abbott had strong blocks placed at the double junction to prevent any interference when the time came to withdraw. While these were being placed moppers up destroyed dug-outs with large 30-pound charges.

Major Ernest Collier's D Company (60 men) in its attack on the right on Nun's Alley created havoc with rifle grenades and bombing. Surprise was complete. For a time, the only enemy in sight were dead or wounded. One unwounded German was captured. Every dug-out encountered was blown in with heavy charges. Collier, ignoring his wounds, led his men against an eventual counter-attack and defeated it, this allowing the company to clear almost all of Nun's Alley. Collier, who like King, was the last man out, was wounded a second time while carrying a wounded man to safety.

When withdrawal began at Zero plus 30 the assault parties did so under the cover of the covering parties which then withdrew 10 minutes later. By Zero plus 50, all personnel were consolidating the new line with advance posts forward. The enemy did not react until shortly after dawn when he bombed his way into Cinnabar, but did not occupy it in any force, and established a block in Nun's Alley in front of the double junction. Raid results, in addition to the prisoners, were the obtaining of a better sited front line, a good observation line and also posts in Nabob Alley and Nun's Alley. Battalion casualties were 60 wounded, most only slightly. One officer was killed and five were wounded. Major Collier and Lieutenant King both received the DSO, an uncommon award by mid-1917 for a Subaltern, but in this instance fully deserved. Three MCs, two DCMs and several MMs were also awarded.[35]

Raiding was always a learning process. Lessons could always be drawn, some peculiar to local circumstances, and while these were of significance to the unit and formation involved, some of the lessons did not travel well in the sense of being "global" in import. Conversely, some lessons had universal applicability. The "double raid" at Cherisy in September 1917, offers something of both. It was also one of the "named" raids, a name often being affixed because of the proximity of a village or a prominent geographical feature, but sometimes because the raid in some fashion was unusual or spectacularly good or bad.

Back in April the British attack had eventually created a salient south of the village of Monchy le Preux (see MSD 22). To straighten the line Third Army advanced southward. In due course 50th Division reached a line in mid-June opposite Cherisy and short by 250 yards or so of Narrow Trench which the enemy had determined to hold, his support line being adjacent to the village and his reserve line being in and behind it.[36] The GOC, Major-General Sir Percival Wilkinson, had two brigades up to hold the 3,000 yards of the divisional sector, relief within

35 LAC, War Diaries, 9th Brigade and 52nd Battalion, brigade and battalion reports and Operation Orders, brigade Intelligence Summaries for 3 and 4 September and citations for DSO and MC awards. Radley, *Get Tough, Stay Tough,* describes the distinctions between these awards and award criteria and procedures.

36 Cherisy was 10 miles south of Arras and roughly 4,000 yards south of Monchy.

22 Cherisy Raid, 15 September 1917, 50th British Division.

brigades being on a battalion basis more or less every four days following a cycle of front line, support, reserve and rest. On 1 September 151st Brigade, Brigadier-General N.J.G. Cameron, went into reserve. That same day it had become evident that an enemy relief had also occurred, which raised the question of who twice over: who had taken over and who was going to get an answer? At Narrow Trench the slight curve of the ridge made observation of the opposing positions almost impossible. The German decision to hold Narrow Trench, a straight-line trench without the bays and traverses of a properly constructed trench, would cost them dearly. The 151st had raided twice in August, neither raid meeting any enemy to speak of, no prisoners or identifications being secured in either. This, no doubt, played a part in giving the brigade the starring role, the objective being the section of Narrow Trench immediately opposite the village (this area is boxed on MSD 22).[37]

The officer who planned the raid, Lieutenant-Colonel Henry Karslake, GSO1 50th Division, came up with an imaginative concept for a raid in three phases: first, a three-company assault by 9th Durham Light Infantry, Lieutenant-Colonel Roland Bradford, VC, at 1600 hours on Saturday 15 September, then a one-company assault by 8th Durhams on the northern third of the same objective at 1940, followed at 0400 the next morning by a projection of the gas from 552

37 Wyrall, *Fiftieth Division,* p. 234.

drums into enemy lines, then 10 minutes later by an intense 18-pounder barrage for 10 minutes and, as a finale, 10 more minutes of equally intense 4.5-inch howitzer fire. Support would also include 70 machine-guns, light, medium and heavy trench mortars and extensive deception measures including smoke and thermit, Very lights and deployment of dummy figures.[38]

In initially referring above to this raid the word "unusual' was used. Stephen Badsey's fine article on the raid begins with one reason for such a summation: it was the only British raid on the Western Front during which air photographs charted its progress.[39] Another reason was the disparity in ages between the three levels of commanders involved. At 52, Wilkinson, GOC 50th Division, was more than twice the age of the battalion commander, Bradford being only 25. In the middle at 43 was Cameron the brigade commander. All three were well-experienced: Wilkinson had been GOC for almost two years. Cameron and Bradford had held command for 12 months each. Cameron would be promoted and appointed GOC 49th Division a month after the raid. In October Bradford would be promoted Brigadier-General and appointed GOC of a brigade in 62nd Division, this making him at age 25 the youngest General Officer in the British Army. He was, one could say, an iconic figure. A Subaltern at 22 in 1914, he received the MC in 1915 and then in October 1916 as CO 9th Durhams won the VC on the Somme, the citation relating how he took command of a second battalion after that battalion had suffered appalling losses, including its CO and most of its officers, and then led the two units into a renewed attack. Unfortunately, Bradford would be killed in action in late November 1917. Wilkinson had joined the Army at 18 in 1883. In December 1915 he became GOC 50th Division. Under him, it was praised for its "fine fighting" on the Somme and he had been personally praised for his initiative which was instrumental in the capture of High Wood.[40]

Another key player, Henry Karslake, the GSO1, had been 15 months in that appointment. Commissioned as a Regular artillery officer in 1898, he had won the DSO in South Africa. A Staff College graduate (1913) at the outbreak of war he was posted as a Captain with his battery to France, but given the shortage of trained staff officers he became in December a BM, moving on in 1915 to Third Army as GSO2 and then in June 1916 he was appointed GSO1 of the 50th.

38 TNA: WO 95/2810: 50th Division General Staff, Operation Order 121, 6 September; Foulkes, "*Gas!*", pp. 194-95.Thermit, a metallic mixture of powdered aluminum and iron oxide, when ignited, rose to a temperature of 5,000 degrees centigrade, The metals became molten. By fitting artillery time fuses to 4-inch mortar bombs these could be burst in the air 50-100 feet up: "the cascades of molten metal descending must have been terrifying." Statements by prisoners spoke of how much the thermit bombs were dreaded.

39 Stephen Badsey, 'The Trench Raid at Cherisy, 15 September 1917', *Imperial War Museum Review*, 4 (1989), p. 87. Captain Donald Stevenson and his observer, Lieutenant John Webster, were over Narrow Trench when the raid began. As the assault troops left their trenches on went the camera. The three plates illustrating the article show artillery shells bursting, this being obvious even on the small 2-inch by 3-inch photographs, and 9th Battalion soldiers advancing, these very difficult to see. Of the 12 photos taken only the three survived.

40 *Ibid.*, p. 88; Wyrall, *Fiftieth Division*, pp. 153, 223. Bradford's VC citation is in Wyrall (pp. 168-69) and in Harvey, *Monuments to Courage*, Number 761. His brother, Lieutenant Commander G.N. Bradford, RN, also won the VC during the war. Trevor Harvey, *An Army of Brigadiers: British Brigade Commanders at the Battle of Arras 1917* (Solihull: Helion & Company Limited, 2017), pp. 33, 291. Cameron did not command a battalion, but had considerable line and staff experience. In December 1915 he relinquished his appointment as GSO1 34th Division on promotion to command 103rd Brigade of that division.

Despite keeping the initial planning and co-ordination of the raid at divisional HQ Wilkinson was not expressing any distrust of Cameron and his BM, Captain C.C.M. Kennedy. It is clear from the divisional history that he had no complaint with the performance of 151st Brigade. The decision reflected Wilkinson's hands-on approach to command and control.[41]

In his report on the raid Cameron closed by thanking the General Staff of the division "for the infinite pains taken by them to ensure success." He complained, in jest, that such had left him nothing to do, which, of course, was not so since he, as the brigadier, would naturally have been deeply interested and involved in co-ordination of a raid to be made by half his brigade. Undoubtedly, his interest in Karslake's Operation Order would have been as high since its excellence (or not) meant the life (or death) of his men, but a year's observation of Karslake's abilities as GSO1 would have convinced him that things were in good order and he need not worry. And so it proved for the two pages of Operation Order 121 and its eight appendices reflect the enormous and careful work that had gone into preparing and co-ordinating every aspect of the raid. It is significant that the order required only one amendment, this being simply a change in the location of the Prisoner Interrogation Centre. Also, there had been only one addition to the order, this coming six days after the issue of the order, Zero for the raid and for the three phases not having been decided until then. The Operation Order specified intention, objectives, phases, forces and fire support and prisoner handling. The appendices detailed in one or two pages each the programmes for machine-guns, trench mortars, field artillery, smoke screens and thermit shells, heavy artillery and deception measures. All in all, the order would have made the life of the BM 151st Brigade, Captain Kennedy, much easier. In fact, Karslake's Operation Order and other instructions epitomize solid staff work. There are no errors or ambiguities in the order: it is simple, direct, concise and clear. Clarity, above all, is the essential ingredient of military writing.[42]

Captain Kennedy crafted an equally fine Operation Order at four pages plus three timetables, his order being longer, of course, since it had to include the detailed instructions for the battalions to prepare for the raid. The order also had to get the 9th Battalion from where it was in reserve forward to the front line to relieve one of the other battalions. As he translated the divisional Operation Order into a brigade Operation Order Kennedy put data from the division's appendices into three timetables of brigade events, one for each phase. These made every activity – infantry, artillery (field and heavy), mortars, machine-guns, deception and 12th Division's contribution – stand out clearly. Such timetables were more and more becoming standard practice. Indeed, Cameron testified to their usefulness: "as the timetables were so clearly adhered to it will not be necessary to describe the sequence of events in detail." Kennedy stuck as closely as he could to the format and sequence of the divisional Operation Order, not forgetting the requirements necessary to the differing level of command. Neither assault battalion would have found any difficulty translating the brigade order into battalion orders. Kennedy being clear in his mind and in his order about the difference between object and objective, carefully set out both for the first and second phases: first phase object to kill Germans, secure identifications,

41 Karslake finished the war as BGGS of the Tank Corps. Thereafter most of his service was in India, one appointment of note being Commandant of the Staff College at Quetta. Lieutenant-General Sir Henry Karslake retired in 1936, but on recall at the outbreak of war he became GOC Lines of Communication of the BEF, his last active appointment. He died in 1942.

42 TNA: WO 95/2810: 50th Division General Staff, Operation Order 121, 6 September.

destroy dug-outs and bring back or destroy weapons; second phase to kill more Germans; first phase objective (here he directed readers to a map co-ordinate); second phase, northern third of the objective of first phase.[43]

Turning now to pre-raid activities, wire cutting began on 3 September, first by medium and heavy mortars, then on the 7th field artillery (18-pounders and 4.5-inch howitzers) joining in, the whole effort being circumspectly done sticking to the typical intermittent and seemingly mere searching fire that marked most days. Anything more could well warn the enemy. The Divisional Trench Mortar Officer reported that during the first nine days of September, 272 medium and 39 heavy mortar bombs hit enemy wire, the guns adding 1,950 shells.[44] On the 5th, the raiders of the 9th Battalion moved into an area south of Arras where they trained for the raid. The next day C Company, the raiding company of the 8th Durhams under Captain Bennett Williams arrived and began training. Meanwhile, the Commander Royal Engineers (CRE) of 50th Division had decided that 7th Field Company RE would provide 12 men and a Subaltern for the raid. This detachment then began preparing the gun cotton and Stokes bomb charges for dug-out demolition. On the 12th, Second Lieutenant William Rebbeck and his sappers joined the Durhams in the training. That afternoon a final rehearsal was witnessed by GOC Third Army, General Sir Julian Byng, and the divisional and brigade commanders.[45]

Other preliminaries for the raid began on Tuesday the 11th. The artillery switched its fire from the wire to Narrow Trench, the Heavy Artillery of VI Corps adding to that fire and also striking at Night Trench forward and north of the elbow of Narrow Trench. That same day 151st Brigade issued Operation Order 117, followed next day by Lieutenant-Colonel Karslake's addendum to divisional Operation Order 121 advising Zero Day and Zero for the three phases. No timing could be given for the third phase – the gas – since its release would depend on favourable weather. The timings had also appeared in the brigade Operation Order. On Thursday 13 September C Company of the 8th Durhams returned to the trenches, followed on the 14th by the brigade, 9th Durhams going into brigade reserve. On the afternoon of the 14th, the day before the raid, the three assault companies of the 9th replaced C Company of the 8th in the front line, but men of the 8th continued to patrol, taking along the elements of the 9th who were to cut gaps in the British wire. Throughout these last pre-raid days field and heavy artillery continued shelling Narrow Trench to prevent repairs and replacement of cut wire and weapons. Later that day medium and heavy mortars put down 302 medium and 10 heavy bombs on enemy wire.[46]

On raid day, Saturday the 15th, final preparations commenced including the usual checking to ensure each man had all the necessary equipment and his share of bombs, two to each rifleman,

43 *Ibid.*, TNA: WO 95/2839: Operation Order 117, 151st Brigade Operation Order, 11 September. Having read a very large number of Operation Orders in preparation of this present study it became clear that the difference between object and objective was not always appreciated. These terms are defined in Chapter 6 of this study.

44 *Ibid.*, 50th Division, trench mortar and artillery ammunition expenditures.

45 Badsey, 'The Trench Raid at Cherisy', p. 89. C Company, like all companies of the 8th, was understrength and was brought up to five officers and 110 ORs by adding 10 men from each of the other companies.

46 TNA: WO 95/2840: 9th Durham Light Infantry, entry for 14 September; WO 95/2839 151st Brigade Operation Order 117; 50th Division Operation Order 121; WO 95/2841 8th Durhams Operation Order, 7 September; ammunition expenditure tables of 50th Division Trench Mortars.

five to bombers and 10 to bomb carriers. The gunners re-checked their calculations for placing a box barrage and for the creeping barrage that would shoot the assault troops onto the objective. The 70 Vickers machine-guns Lieutenant-Colonel Karslake had begged and borrowed also made ready. It seems only fitting to let the 9th Durhams describe the grand opening at 1600: "the heavy creeping barrage came down and A, B and C Companies raided the German front and support lines in front of Cherisy. A was left, C centre and B right company. Flank parties covered the flanks. Raid a complete surprise to the enemy."[47] Parsing this succinct account shows the fine co-ordination that marked this raid. Sharp at 1600 the 70 Vickers began their drumming, 250 rounds per minute winging their way above the British front line. Mortars chimed in. Captain Francis Buckley, the Brigade Bombing Officer, recalled the din caused by 22 Stokes firing at intense rate, one bomb every five seconds per tube, plus two heavy and 18 medium mortars getting off three bombs per minute.[48] The gunners' 48 eighteen-pounders put down four rounds per minute (intense rate) on Narrow Trench, assisted by 4.5-inch howitzers (17 of these) also at intense rate of two rounds per minute. VI Corps "heavies" thundered, too, their fire slower, but powerful and destructive.[49] Smoke from 4-inch Stokes and 4.5-inch howitzers enriched the mix, this aiming to hinder enemy observation of the area. The brigade report noted that while the wind drove the smoke and dust in such a way that enemy ability to see was ruined, it did not hinder the raiders. Thermit, called "flame-shells" by some, (see earlier in this chapter) added terror, bursting as they did, over the occupants of trenches. Such intensity leaves one to say woe betide the waiting ones!

When at Zero plus two the fire lifted from Narrow Trench and began creeping toward the enemy depth, the three companies of 9th Battalion moved forward into the unknown, unknown since they were unable to see the enemy because of the curve of the ridge mentioned earlier. As they moved, above them Lieutenant Webster (see footnote 39) turned his camera on. The assault parties advanced on a three-company front, each company consisting of two platoons one behind the other (the third platoon of each company remained in battalion trenches as a reserve), each platoon moving in one wave of two lines, 15 yards between the lines, in accordance with *The Normal Formation for the Attack*. But because the raiders were in less than normal company strength no moppers up moved between the two platoons. Instead, two sections of the first line of the second platoon would act as moppers up in the assault and then as a rearguard during the withdrawal. As per the manual, each flank was protected by a party of one Lewis gun team, one rifle grenadier section and two snipers. Lieutenant Rebbeck and his sappers moved with the second platoon. For this raid the company commander, rather than being between the platoons, moved at the centre of the fourth line. The two platoon commanders advanced at the centre of the first and third lines, the company 2IC moving at the centre of the second line. Thus in this formation each of the four lines had an officer with it, one of their responsibilities being to ensure that the intervals between the waves and lines were maintained.

During the advance the first line would fire from the hip, this at the insistence of the brigade commander who believed the advantages of this outweighed its disadvantages. The first and second lines would go directly to the enemy support line, which was the furthest objective. The

47 TNA: WO 95/2840: 9th Durhams, entry for 15 September.

48 Francis Buckley, *Q.6.A. And Other Places* (London: Ballantyne & Co. Ltd., 1920), p. 98. Buckley said Q.6.A. was a map reference for a location on the Somme.

49 See footnote 34 for artillery rates of fire.

third line would go to and remain at the enemy front line. The fourth line was tasked to reinforce the first and second lines as necessary. Company HQ would remain in the enemy front line. This methodology adhered to the manual which stated that when there were only two objectives, as in this raid, the preferred method was for the leading wave to go directly to the furthest objective. On the withdrawal (timed for 1630) the first, second and fourth lines would withdraw by sections through the third line which once in the enemy front trench had remained there. The third line would then withdraw followed by the flank parties.[50]

Cameron's report on the raid described the formation as satisfactory in every way. Going was good in no man's land and enemy wire proved no obstacle, the gaps being adequate. A machine-gun opened as the raiders advanced, but was silenced immediately, no appreciable damage having been done. Within a remarkably short time Narrow Trench was secured and the support line as well by Zero plus five, the trenches being in poor condition, not even revetted. The first prisoners, 24 in all, reached battalion lines by 1610. Only one casualty was suffered during the rush to the final objective. "There seems to be no doubt," wrote Cameron, "that the raid was a complete surprise." Little resistance was offered, a single and "feeble" enemy bombing attack being easily defeated. The sappers blew up a dozen dug-outs, all that were located. Enemy dead were estimated at 70. The raiders thought that the dummy attacks north and south of the raid area drew off considerable enemy fire, two sections of dummies in the southern "attack" suffering heavy casualties. The dummy tank received little enemy attention because it broke down very soon after starting. Enemy artillery had been slow to respond and appeared weak and ragged. 9th Battalion had one officer killed and five wounded, five ORs killed and 20 wounded, two of these having been initially reported as missing and killed.[51]

Captain Bennett Williams led the second phase, a raid by five officers and 110 ORs of C Company, 8th Durhams, on the northern third of the objective. Zero at 1940 meant that the raiders would have daylight for the assault and failing light for the withdrawal. The formation and methodology were similar to those used in the raid by the 9th Durhams except that the first two lines would merge on crossing the enemy front line. As the raiders crossed the British wire enemy artillery struck. While this did not stop the assault, it indicated an alert enemy and signalled that achieving surprise was unlikely. Williams and his company reached Narrow Trench quickly, there finding only five defenders, one being captured. In all, only 22 unwounded enemy were present. Withdrawal commenced on time at 2015. Captain Williams received the MC for the night's work.[52]

Phase 3 kicked off at 0404 the next morning, the wind, "SW by W strength six miles an hour," helpfully blowing the gas from the hundreds of gas drums well into enemy lines. Captain Buckley thought the gas caused more enemy casualties than the two raids had since the next day the Germans were seen burying or removing large numbers of men from the areas covered by the gas. Observers in his unit reported seeing 200 gas casualties being moved. Adding in the numbers seen by other observers it was thought the gas caused something like 400 casualties. Buckley believed this to be accurate since "Gas casualties were easily distinguished, as the

50 TNA: WO 95/2839: 151st Brigade, report of GOC; *WO 3995 The Organization of an Infantry Battalion and The Normal Formation for the Attack* (General Staff, April 1917), Part II, VI and Plates A and B.
51 TNA: WO 95/2839: 151st Brigade.
52 *Ibid., WO 95/2841:* 8th Durham Light Infantry Operation Order (unnumbered).

Germans removed them in blankets slung between two men on a pole. Besides … the gas cloud drifted north and caught the Germans during a relief nearly half a mile away from the scene of the two raids … the Germans were burying dead all day … some distance from Cherisy."[53] When the gas release ended relative silence ensued for about 10 minutes at which point the 70 machine-guns opened fire, as did the 18-pounders at intense rate, followed by the howitzers. One can only speculate about the casualties caused. Cameron described enemy retaliation as slight. A patrol some hours later found Narrow Trench unoccupied; the enemy had called it a day.[54]

On Monday, 17 September *The Times* published a GHQ statement which simply noted the success of the raids, the regiment that had made them, the time of the raids and the number of prisoners taken. A German official press release had an opposite view: both raids failed, slight penetration of German line was quickly defeated, the enemy retiring after "great losses."[55]

Brigadier-General Cameron's comprehensive report reflects a good deal of thought, especially in the three pages headed "Notes and Comments," which would have been better titled "Lessons." Some of his remarks were peculiar to the raid, others were of universal applicability. Anyone planning a raid would have profited from reading his report's lessons:

> Surprise. If surprise is to be preserved it is a good thing if no unusual fire of any kind is begun before Zero.
>
> Smoke. The infantry unanimously liked the proportion of smoke (one in three) in the creeping barrage [the report by the CRA said it was one in six].
>
> Snipers. Snipers on the flanks proved effective against advancing infantry.
>
> Training. It is essential that RE personnel live and train with the infantry for some days. In this case they trained for only three days. Sapper opinion was for longer attachment, seven days preferred.
>
> Maps. Every officer and NCO should be issued a good map.
>
> Medical. RAP (Regimental Aid Post) remained in reserve line. Some thought it should have been in support line. Fortunately, it was not since the support line was heavily shelled.
>
> Firing From the Hip. All ranks attach great importance to this. The battalion commander thinks it improves morale, lowers that of the enemy and inflicts a certain number of

53 Buckley, *Q.6.A.*, p. 98.

54 TNA: WO 95/2810: 151st Brigade, Operation Order 117, Appendix A, Timetable for Gas Attack, and Cameron's report; CRA report (20 September) listed total ammunition expended as 18-pounders, 7,558 rounds; 4.5-inch howitzers, 2,318; 9.45-inch trench mortars, 152; and 2-inch trench mortars, 966.

55 *The Times* Archives, 17 September 1917, p. 8, 'Persistent Raids By British. Durham's Double Success'; TNA: WO 95/2823: 245th Machine-Gun Company, 50th Division, manuscript appendix to Intelligence Summary No.102, 17 September. The full German statement suggests deception for the raid had some effect.

> casualties. He has not the same faith in firing the Lewis Gun from the hip. In both opinions I agree.
>
> Fire Support Allocation. The concentration of a large number of medium and light trench mortars in a fairly small area is a factor in determining the proportion of Heavy Artillery to be devoted to Counter-Battery work and the proportion to be devoted to enemy forward trenches. The plastering of enemy forward trenches aims at knocking out Machine Guns, the chief enemy of the Infantry. The interests of medium and light trench mortars rather ask for Counter-Battery work: the enemy's artillery is their chief enemy, as their [short] range ties them to being in or near trenches on which the enemy barrage is nearly sure to fall, whereas the Infantry is soon within the enemy barrage line. It is submitted that in such case one should devote more attention than one otherwise would to Counter-Battery work for the sake of the Trench Mortars.
>
> Assault Formations. It is debatable as to whether it would not have been better if the leading line only had been in extended order whilst the others followed in lines of sections or half-sections in file or single file … this in order to negotiate the gaps in wire or barrages while retaining the power to extend very rapidly when coming under fire. The battalion commander in the first phase now thinks this would have been a better formation and I agree.
>
> Mortar Protection. It seems highly desirable that their ammunition dumps should be divided into strongly traversed sections.

Regarding assault formations, a pattern in general use after the Somme was lines for fighting, worms for movement, worms denoting columns. During an advance or assault, support platoons moved in column, while the assault platoons including moppers up advanced in line. Worms could move faster and remain close to the waves thereby being readily available to support the assault.[56] Control was also enhanced. As for mortar protection, Cameron is referring to the casualties suffered by a trench mortar battery borrowed from 62nd Division. A mortar emplacement in the Durhams support line took a direct hit, killing eight men and detonating the dump of bombs. The support line was hit twice, once during each raid. Each time mortar crews suffered casualties.[57]

Cameron did not comment on the slight opposition encountered in the enemy front line, especially during the first phase. Perhaps he thought it unnecessary since the "new" German defence in depth was becoming well known, a central feature being lightly held forward lines. His remarks and those of the CO of 9th Durhams on firing from the hip are not entirely convincing. As for lowering enemy morale and causing casualties, no means existed to quantify these suppositions; "a certain number of casualties" is hardly quantitative or definitive and does not suffice. The disadvantages, which are obvious, hardly need exposition.

56 This had been promulgated in *SS 119 Preliminary Notes on the Tactical Lessons of the Recent Operations* issued in July and again in September 1916 and further amplified during the remainder of 1916 and into 1917.

57 TNA: WO 95/2810: 151st Brigade, Cameron's report.

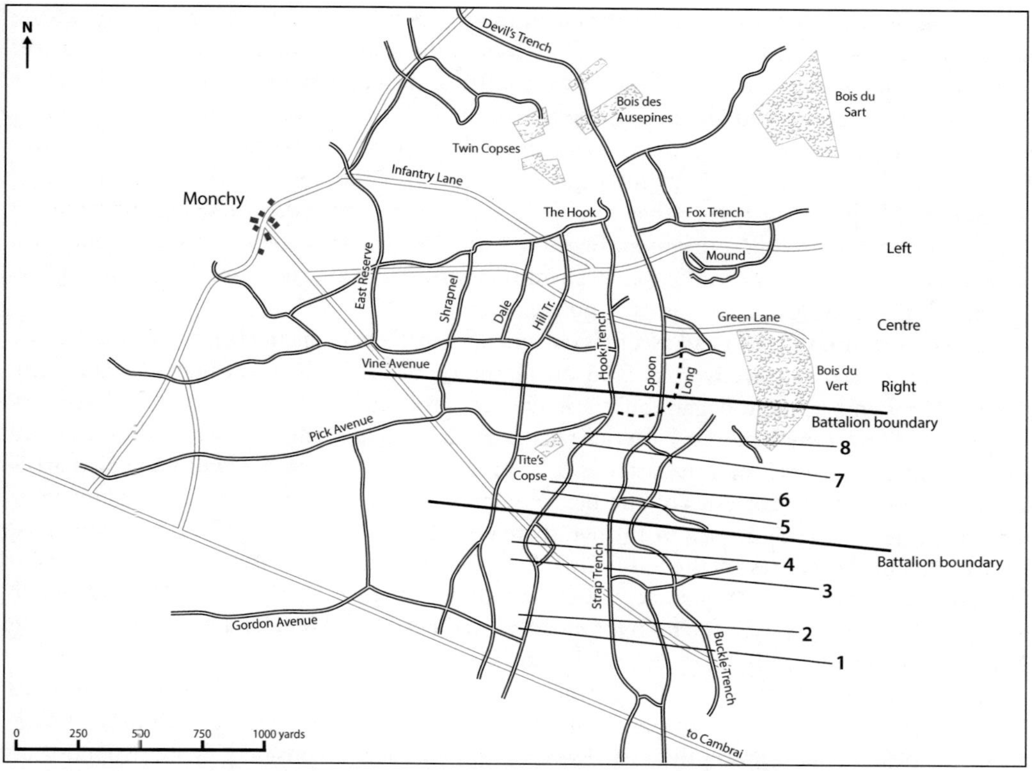

23 Raid east of Monchy, 14 October 1917, 12th British Division.

A daylight raid by 750 officers and men of 35th and 37th Brigades of 12th British Division a month later (14 October) encountered little opposition in the enemy front line, but considerably more in the support line just as 151st Brigade had and for the same reason: the change in German defensive doctrine. The unusual aspect of the 12th Division raid was the enemy machine-gunning and bombing of the raiders by low-flying aircraft. Three battalions participated in the raid. On the right from 37th Brigade were four 50-man parties of Lieutenant-Colonel N.T. Rolls' 6th Queens, each party under a Subaltern and Captain J.M. Pike as OC Raid. These parties were designated 1, 2, 3 and 4 and are shown as such on MSD 23. Accompanying the 6th Queens were 20 sappers of 87th Field Company RE. To the north were Parties 5, 6, 7 and 8 founded by Lieutenant-Colonel W.R.A. Dawson's 6th Royal West Kents organized as per the first four parties. OC Raid was Captain L.C.R. Smith.[58] Due east of Monchy were 330 raiders of 7th Norfolks (Major R. Gethen) organized in three parties (right, centre and left) plus a sapper detachment. The Centre Party would advance astride Green Lane, the Left party opposite The Mound and the Right Party from near the junction of Vine and Hook.

58 Scott, *12th (Eastern) Division*, p. 222. Dawson was a highly decorated officer: DSO and three Bars. A Captain in March 1915 he became on promotion CO of his battalion in December 1916. He was killed in action in late 1918.

The raid by the 7th Norfolks was very much the secondary effort. The Left Party met little opposition in the enemy front line and at The Mound, the trench immediately east of the latter being unoccupied. An estimated 30 enemy were killed and eight prisoners were taken. Trenches were found "much knocked about." In the centre the raiders found the front line only lightly held except on the right where a stronger party was engaged and defeated. The Right Party found Spoon Trench strongly held initially, but the enemy withdrew upon the raiders reaching the trench. Many were killed as they ran. Several prisoners were taken. During the whole of the raid no enemy machine-guns fired. Battalion casualties (none of the sources give a number) were due to enemy artillery and action by enemy aircraft. All in all, the raid achieved very little. Estimates of enemy dead appear greatly inflated.[59]

Parties 1 – 4 (6th Queens) had as a first objective Strap Trench (enemy front line) and Buckle Trench as the second objective. At 1055 on the morning of the raid, six hours before Zero, the artillery bombardment began. Substantial assets produced it, including two field artillery brigades and four trench mortar batteries plus Army level field artillery. Borrowed for the raid were two medium trench mortar batteries. Flanking divisions co-operated with one field artillery brigade plus three batteries of another. Numbers of barrels were impressive: of howitzers ranging in calibre from 4.5-inch to 15-inch there were 144; 60-pounders, 17; and 18-pounders, 74. Mortars of all calibres totalled 20. The CRA (Commander Royal Artillery) reported 12th Division expenditures as 18-pounders, 14,900 rounds; 4.5-inch howitzers, 7,750; and trench mortars (all calibres), 1,778. Stokes light mortars fired over 1,220 bombs. During wire-cutting 2-inch and 6-inch mortars expended 810 bombs.[60]

Parties 1-4 all reached their assembly trenches 30 minutes before Zero. At Zero they advanced in two lines to find opposition in the enemy front line feeble, many Germans still in their dug-outs, which the sappers promptly started wrecking. Once again, considerably more opposition met the raiders in the support line. There they killed a "considerable number." Those who put up their hands only to start firing again were "dealt with in the usual way." The raiders found front and support trenches "largely obliterated," so much so they could not locate parts of the support line. Wire posed no obstacle. An orderly withdrawal commenced at the 30-minute mark despite aircraft machine-gunning and bombing. Numbers of prisoners taken ranged from 44 (battalion report) to 64 (divisional history). Enemy dead were estimated at 100.[61]

Lieutenant-Colonel Dawson's report on Parties 5-8 (6th Royal West Kents) explains why the raid by both battalions went so well: "our artillery preparation was perfect and our barrage could not have been better." All four parties reported enemy wire and trenches "almost obliterated." Two parties reported destruction such that they could not accurately locate the support line. One party found some Germans in shell holes "about where" it was supposed to be. Many

59 *Ibid.*, pp. 126-27; TNA: WO 95/1848, 1859: 35th and 37th Brigades, 12th Division, and the three battalions.

60 *Ibid.*, report of CRA 12th Division, 18 October 1917. To manage this array of fire support the GOCRA XVII Corps was appointed to command. In dividing up the frontage among fire units 50 yards of trench was allotted to each howitzer and trench mortar. Howitzer and medium trench mortar fire was concentrated on the front trench and CTs while 18-pounder fire was to hit at areas close up to the enemy front line. Heavy trench mortar fire was concentrated on large dug-outs and trench junctions in and behind the support line.

61 *Ibid.*, TNA: WO 95/1825: report of CO 6th Queens; Scott, *12th (Eastern) Division*, p. 127.

dead, obvious victims of artillery, littered the area. No enemy machine-gun fire occurred during the raid, probably due to destruction or burial of the weapons. Very little enemy trench mortar firing occurred likely for the same reason. As for opposition, the parties reported as follows: very slight and short-lived, enemy thoroughly demoralized, 10 prisoners taken (Party 5); nil resistance at either objective, 22 prisoners taken (Party 6); no resistance at front line but some fighting at where support line was thought to be, some casualties suffered, six prisoners taken (Party 7); and some resistance at front line, none at support line, 11 prisoners taken (Party 8). Dawson thought as many as 50 prisoners were started toward battalion lines, but only half could be accounted for and he suspected some duplication in accounting. Most battalion casualties were due to enemy artillery during the withdrawal. As for enemy air activity, he said only "Our aeroplanes did not seem to be sufficiently far forward."

There is no question that both raids were successful, due in large part to the artillery, but the cost was high, six officers and 17 ORs killed and 144 ORs wounded or missing, most of these during the withdrawal. Counter-Battery seems not to have been as effective as the CRA concluded. He noted that the British barrage intensified when the withdrawal began at Zero plus 30, but so did enemy fire, it appearing that "the enemy realized that our infantry was withdrawing." Nevertheless, General Byng praised the raid: "as usual the 12th carried out a most successful operation."

An equally successful raid occurred just over a mile south of Lens by 137th Brigade of 46th (North Midland) Division at the end of October. This raid, executed by 250 all ranks (about a third of the strength of 12th Division's raid), was initiated on 10 October by the GOC, Major-General William Thwaites who, wrote one of his staff, "wishes you to make preparations to carry out a daylight raid with one battalion to be ready by 30th October." In conjunction with the raid a demonstration with dummies would be made by a neighbouring formation to the north shortly before the real raid. An artillery barrage with smoke would accompany the dummies and wire-cutting on the raid front. Three days later 137th Brigade submitted its raid proposal: 6th North Staffords would raid with four companies in depth and attacking in three waves against the enemy front line, Horton Trench and Hobart Trench (see MSD 24), and remain for 60 minutes. 4th Special Company RE would provide a smoke barrage on the left flank of the objective and would fire gas bombs into southeast Hulluch at Zero plus ten. Divisional engineers would also accompany the raiders. GOC 137th Brigade requested some assistance from division: first, that wire-cutting for the real and dummy raids begin immediately; second, that the Divisional Machine-Gun Officer (DMGO) plan barrages on the flanks of the raid and on the ground between Hobb's Alley and Honey Alley; and, finally, that 139th Trench Mortar Battery co-operate with his Stokes battery in dealing with selected targets.[62]

46th Division's Operation Order 252 reached 137th Brigade on 17 October. The purpose of the raid was the standard kill, capture, destroy as much as possible. In addition to immediate wire-cutting by 4.5-inch howitzers and 6-inch mortars, heavy artillery would cut wire in front of the enemy second and third lines. The heavies would also strike the trench and trench junctions at the points on MSD 24. The brigade Operation Order (173), issued on 27 October, added aircraft participation, specifically the bombing of Hulluch and the machine-gunning of Hobb's

62 TNA: WO 95/2664: 46th Division, instruction to 137th Brigade, 10 October; 137th Brigade proposal, 13 October and Operation Orders, division, brigade and battalion.

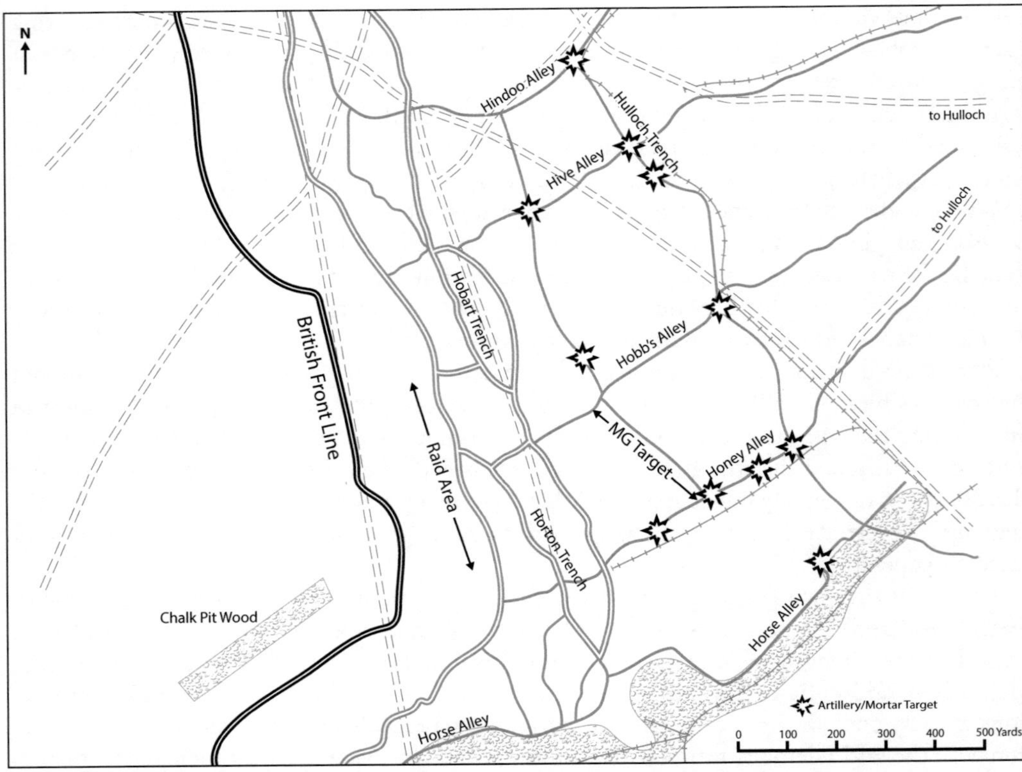

24 Raid Hulloch Area, 14 October 1917, 46th British Division.

Alley, Hive Alley and Hulluch Trench after Zero. The battalion Operation Order (33) added the details necessary to assemble the raiders, get them to the jumping off trench and then into the assault.[63]

Zero came at 1632 on 31 October. Each of the four companies had a specific area with three objectives to clear. Each company attacked in three waves as per *Normal Formation for the Attack*. In recognition of the change in enemy defensive doctrine the first wave was smaller than the other two since it was expected that the front line would pose the least resistance. All officers wore OR tunics with rank badges on the shoulder straps. The 6th North Staffords on return to the trenches the night before the raid patrolled to confirm that enemy wire was adequately cut, which it was. On raid day the three assault companies assembled in the front line by 1600, these trenches having been deepened to afford cover from observation from Hulluch. Where necessary, camouflage screens had also been erected. The assembly drew no reaction. At 1628 the barrage opened on the area of the dummy raid and thermit and gas bombs were projected into Hulluch. Sappers raised the dummies at this time, these being promptly greeted with copious machine-gun fire plus artillery within five minutes, this fire continuing intermittently for some time afterward. Division assessed the dummy raid a complete success since it drew "nearly all"

63 *Ibid.*

enemy machine-gun and artillery fire. Only one machine-gun opened against the real raid and this not until the end of the withdrawal.

Bang on Zero the three waves advanced covering the 250 yards to the first objective in two or three minutes, this allowing the waves to close before the barrage lifted to the second line. No live enemy sentries were found in the front line, probably because when the smoke came down on the dummy raid area they expected gas and had gone to the dug-outs to warn the garrison. Some enemy were seen withdrawing. At Zero plus three the barrage lifted and the front line was secured. The lifts to the second and third lines each came at the two minute mark which put the raiders on top of the enemy before they could fully man their trenches. All objectives were gained. Many of the enemy had remained in their dug-outs in the first two lines and on trying to withdraw suffered many casualties. Sappers destroyed four machine-gun emplacements, four mortar emplacements and ten large dug-outs. Stokes mortar bombs tossed down the stairs of 13 others blew the entrances in. Withdrawal, which began at 1710, was unhindered. Fifty prisoners were in tow. Enemy dead, unit confirmed by shoulder straps, totalled 81. Casualties were very slight, three officers and 10 ORs wounded. Fire support during the raid especially pleased the GOC. Heavy artillery and Stokes fire had silenced enemy machine-guns and had prevented the enemy enjoying any fire support from the flanks. Likewise, the Stokes had prevented enemy movement across the open and down the trenches on the flanks of the objective area. The raid, he said, went like clock work. While there was nothing spectacular about this raid, the participation of aircraft, whose fire he thought had disconcerted the enemy in their rear area, was notable.[64]

46th (North Midland) Division had been the first complete Territorial Division to arrive in any theatre of war. Some of its units had actually reached Egypt in early 1916, but were returned immediately to France where the bulk of the division had been assembled. The second complete Territorial Division to arrive in France was the 47th (2nd London) Division.[65] In September the 47th took over a sector of the Gavrelle-Oppy front (see MSD 25) described at that time as a quiet front. But, as the divisional historian wrote, the division had no intention of letting the enemy rest and soon began wire-cutting to enable a series of raids. The division's first effort in mid-October, a small one, went off well and not long after – 4 November – the 47th made what Maude called "the chief event" of the division's time on this front, a raid by four companies and sappers, 505 all ranks, of the 23rd and 24th Battalions of the London Regiment (Major T.C. Hargreaves, DSO and Lieutenant-Colonel G.E. Miller, DSO, respectively) of 142nd Brigade.[66]

This large-scale raid was most notable for careful preparation and staff work, especially the latter, that went into it. The divisional War Diary presents a comprehensive package of all Operation Orders and the reports thereafter, plus a set of clear maps showing the objectives, the creeping barrage, the machine-gun and Stokes barrages and the 4.5-inch howitzer and Heavy Artillery targets. The excellence of this package says much about the professionalism at this point of the war of the 47th Division, a Territorial Division. Of special note must be the undoubted competence and drive of the GSO1, Lieutenant-Colonel A.J. Turner, who began "on temporary appointment," but immediately after the raid was confirmed as GSO1. There was keen interest in this raid, obviously at divisional HQ, but no less at Corps (XIII), the GOC,

64 TNA: WO 95/2665: 46th Division, report on raid, 4 November 1917.
65 Becke, *Order of Battle of Divisions. Part 2A,* 46th and 47th Divisions.
66 Maude, *47th Division,* pp. 112, 114, 116.

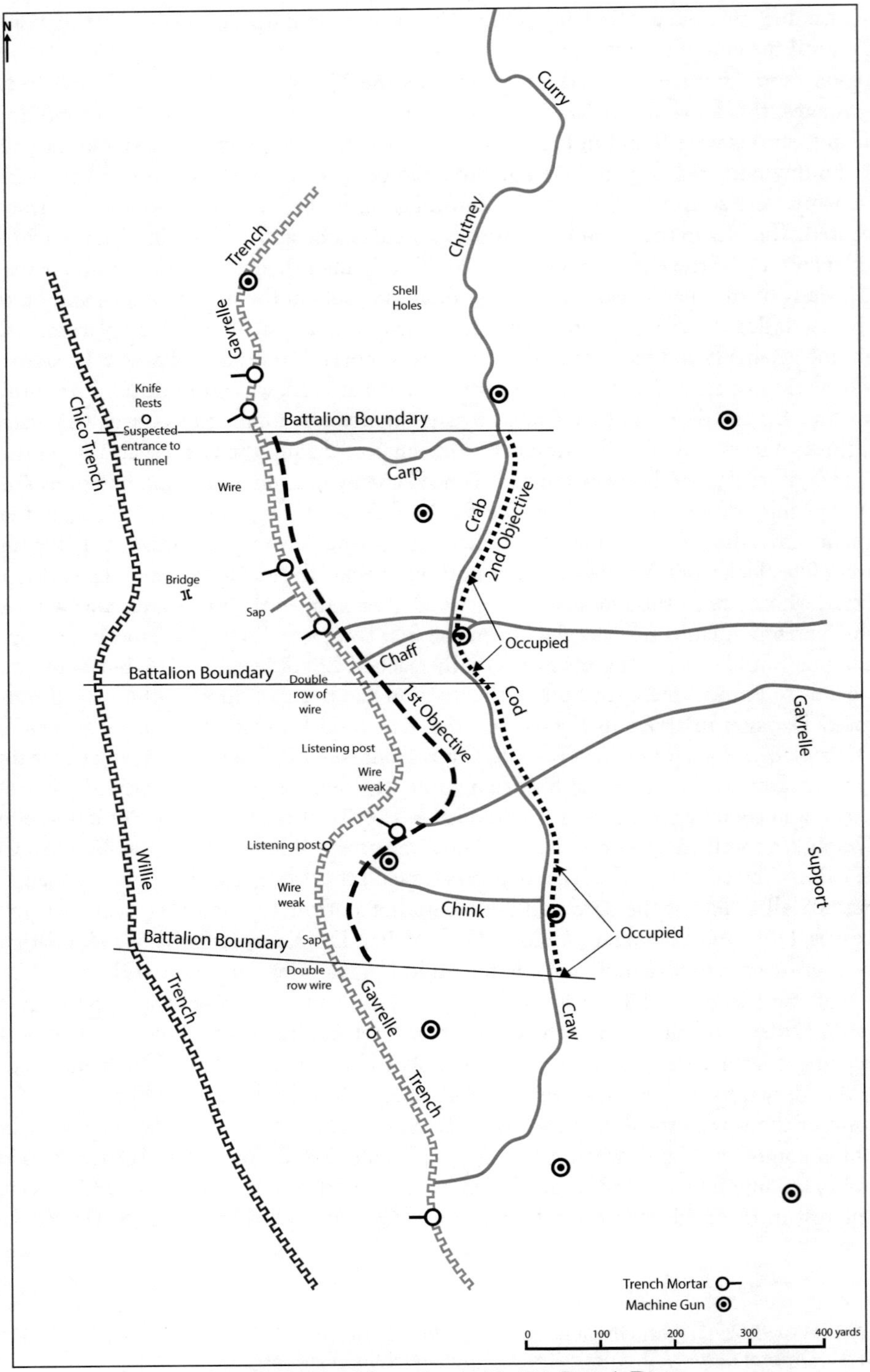

25 Gavrelle Raid, 4 November 1917, 47th British Division.

Lieutenant-General Sir W.F.N. McCracken, forwarding to Army a comprehensive report on the raid plus his own comments. This raid again reflects how the change in German doctrine influenced raids, one indication being how statements of intention in raid orders now speak of raiding in depth.[67]

Looking first at divisional instructions, the GSO1 had warned that the division had to prepare a raid by 15 October, the purpose being to attract attention away from the real point of attack by First Army to the north. 142nd Brigade would do a dawn raid, date to be advised, on a front of three battalions, the brigade commander to decide upon strength of the raid and its boundaries, to a depth as far as the enemy support lines. Artillery support would include three field artillery brigades and possibly one heavy artillery brigade. Wire-cutting would start immediately on the divisional front, but not on the objective front. Cutting on the latter would start at Zero minus seven days, this cutting to be done as far as possible by field artillery and trench mortars. Concurrent activity, always an essential in battle procedure, began at once at brigade level, the GOC's plan to be available as soon as possible to permit early co-ordination. Considerable co-ordination began even before division's Preliminary Instructions and maps were issued on 25 October. By that date the intention had been refined: raid the enemy trench system within boundaries, including Carp CT, and penetrate to second objective, Zero day to be 12 November, the advance to be on a two battalion front by two companies from each of 23rd and 24th Battalions. Zero would be around 1620, exact time to be set by GOC 142nd Brigade.[68] MSD 25 portrays the objectives. The barrage maps are not included. One shows the 18-pounder creeping barrage on the first objective, the lift to the intermediate line, the lift from there to the second objective and the final lift to a line halfway to the Gavrelle Support Trench. Another shows the howitzer barrage on the same lines at the same times. The third map shows the standing machine-gun barrages north and south of the raid area, on Crab Trench and on the support line and Stokes fire on selected targets. The artillery maps are interesting, but as they do not add appreciably to the story of this raid only the infantry map has been included.

On the 30th Lieutenant-Colonel Turner advised XIII Corps and flanking formations of the raid to be made on 4 November, Zero to be advised. The next day he followed up with additional information:

> General Programme. GOC 142nd Brigade to base his orders on the Preliminary Instructions.
>
> Preliminary Operations. Co-ordinating details with divisions providing support, wire-cutting and artillery assistance.
>
> Diversions. XVII Corps simulated attack, smoke and rocket signals, diversionary shoots.[69]

142nd Brigade issued two Operation Orders, 224 and 225, both on 29 October. The first appointed Lieutenant-Colonel Miller, CO 24th Battalion, OC Raid, issued maps and detailed

67 TNA: WO 95/2703: 47th Division General Staff, Operation Order 189, 30 September 1917.
68 *Ibid.*, 47th Division, Operation Order 189, 30 September 1917.
69 *Ibid.*, Operation Order 195, 30 October, letter G.90/1/65, 31 October.

signal communications, smoke arrangements and rocket signals. An appendix "Timetable" set out chronologically actions Zero to Zero plus 60 to be taken by infantry, artillery, Stokes and machine-guns. Appendix II, Administrative Instructions, specified medical support, prisoner handling, rations and rum and other administrative matters. The second Operation Order detailed arrangements for the move forward into assembly trenches at the conclusion of the training period and for the holding of the line while the assault companies were training.[70]

Battalion Operations orders are very similar, each including a Timetable and Administrative Instructions. The right assault battalion, the 24th, would assault on a 400 yard front, the two companies in two waves arranged pretty much as per *Normal Formation for Attack*. Wave One in addition to securing the first objective would also be responsible for clearing CT Chink. The second wave was the stronger of the two as it was anticipated that it would face the strongest opposition. 23rd Battalion, left assault, on a 300 yard front, adopted a similar formation, A Company on the left responsible to clear CT Carp and C Company on the left to clear CT Chaff. In the Operation Orders of both battalions arrangements for the assembly areas, for action in enemy trenches and for the withdrawal were carefully spelled out.[71]

There can be no better account of how the raid went than that of the brigade commander, V.T. Bailey. His is probably the best brigade report seen in all of the research for this present book, but it should be said that when everything comes up roses report writing becomes far easier. First, the assault force assembled forward of British wire without hindrance. Enemy wire then proved no obstacle. At Zero plus five the raiders carried the first objective, some opposition met, but most enemy had quickly headed rearward instead. Carp, too, was easily cleared. Enemy in Chaff also cleared out quickly taking most of their machine-guns ands light mortars along. At Zero plus 12 the second objective was carried, a garrison of about 100 seen well on its way to the rear to avoid contact. Sixteen prisoners were taken, plus five machine-guns and one light mortar. Throughout enemy trenches were found in bad condition, mostly unrevetted and without duckboards, very few traverses and in some stretches resembling nothing more than a "V" shaped ditch. Casualties were very light, four ORs killed and three officers and 29 ORs wounded. All in all, said Bailey, the enemy offered "very little fight." According to prisoners, at the time of the raid preparations for relief were underway. Maude summed the raid up this way: "Everybody was very much pleased with everybody else, including the Army, Corps, Division and Brigade commanders." Bailey and Maude both give much of the credit for the success to division and brigade staff.[72]

This pattern in furtherance of a policy of constant activity to sap enemy confidence continued in November and December 1917. 31st and 46th Divisions, for example, conducted raids in December, each in two or three company strength, both finding opposition in enemy first and support lines slight, the 46th Division's raiders encountering very few Germans even in their third line trenches. The gain in both these raids was a few prisoners at a cost of a few casualties. As 1917 drew to a close 8th British Division's experience was common:

70 *Ibid.*, Brigade Operation Orders, 29 October.
71 *Ibid.*, Operation Order 196 (24th Battalion) and Operation Order 73 (23rd Battalion), 1 and 2 November respectively.
72 TNA: WO 95/2742: raid report 142nd Brigade 4 November; Maude, *47th Division*, p. 117.

> His [German] infantry dispositions were indeed highly favourable for the exploitation of minor openings for aggression by our junior commanders. His troops were distributed between a forward line of outposts for observation; an intermediary, or covering, line through which the forward troops would drop back, their retreat covered by its fire; and finally a main line of resistance to which both the former lines would eventually retire. The forward line, consisting of isolated posts, held in some cases by half a dozen men or less and well in advance even of the second or covering line, offered obvious opportunities and these were not neglected. The capture of two or three prisoners became almost a regular feature of the daily reports.[73]

In Sir Arthur Currie's papers resides an undated 38 page document entitled "Lectures" compiled by 47th Battalion of 4th Canadian Division probably late in the winter of 1917/1918, or so the content suggests. Currie obviously thought highly of it since it is the only document of its kind in his papers. It covers many of the facets of trench warfare from development of esprit de corps to officer responsibilities, work parties, discipline and trench stores. The document begins with its purposes: "to foster esprit de corps and to place within the reach of officers recently joined the accumulated knowledge of nearly three years experience in France."

The last nine pages of the "Lectures," almost a quarter of it, focus on raids and patrols. Four of the nine reflect what the 47th Battalion considered the essentials of raiding as derived from battalion experience and, no doubt, enriched by the experience of other battalions, Canadian and British. Much of what is in the document could be said to be universal. To the 47th Battalion at this stage of the war the purpose of a raid was to gain information which was, admittedly, more restrictive than the view expounded by the higher end of the chain of command. The 47th believed there were only two types of raid, the first a "stealth raid" which was small scale, a section or little better, able to enter enemy trenches unseen and snatch prisoners or identifications, and artillery need not apply, nor was a strafe intended. Otherwise, one went about an "ordinary raid" which was much larger, maybe 50 to a thousand men, bags of artillery hammering away. The 47th thought that organizationally planners should build on the bombing section of a platoon as in *SS 143 Instructions for the Training of a Platoon for Offensive Action*. This applied to either type of raid. But the section had to be all-arms, able to manoeuvre quickly, able to bomb a trench, make a frontal attack or block a trench. As for equipment, the rule should be go light: bombs, rifle and bayonet and a bandolier of ammunition. Recce had to be more than just a "dekko" (a look-see) at enemy wire; it meant recce of own trenches, jumping off position, approaches to it, own wire and no man's land. Artillery was critical, success depending on their fire support: keep enemy heads down until the enemy trenches are reached, keep enemy fire down while raiders are in them, box barrages, creeping barrages: get the infantry in, help them get about and then get them out. Once in the enemy trenches beware his tricks, such as leaving his trenches and getting into shell holes from which to bomb intruders, or pulling down a knife rest to block a trench and then bombing you from above. As for dug-outs, the 47th had learned that once bombed the occupants become "congenial," except officers. With those who still appeared in fighting humour take no chances, make it "short and sweet" for they usually

73 TNA: WO 95/2342 and 2665: 31st and 46th Divisions, General Staff, November/December 1917; Boraston and Bax, *Eighth Division*, p. 162.

caused more trouble than 20 or 30 men put together. Regarding identifications of the enemy, be thorough, turn in all printed matter at once and do not "fleece" prisoners in the trenches where much may be lost or held back. This summation of one battalion's experience cannot be comprehensive without including the entire text, but it does convey a sample of what actual experience had taught. There is, of course, no substitute for experience. Much of this had direct relevance to doctrinal development of both sides.[74]

This, then, marks the end of raiding in 1917, the third full year of the Great War. The next chapter examines raiding during the first half of 1918.

74 LAC, MG30E100 (Currie Papers), Volume 35, 'Lectures' 47th Canadian Infantry Battalion; *SS 143 Instructions for the Training of Platoons for Offensive Action* (London: HMSO, December 1916, February 1917 and September 1917).

15

1918 – Winter Changed to Spring

Patrolling ranks most things above,
Or better still a cheery raid
My bosom swells with martial glee
When told that Zero is at three.
The Daily Dump, Scots Guards Trench Journal

Come New Year 1918 the dogs of war had been running hard for over three years. After Passchendaele many had been nearing exhaustion, their morale at a low point, the war seemingly endless and a sense of failure troubling the officers and men in both sets of trenches. The historian of the KRRC very aptly summed up this situation:

> Both sides … may fairly be said to have been thoroughly war-worn. It is no doubt perfectly true that the Allied armies, as a whole, never lost heart, but that does not say that they did not feel despondent and 'fed up.' It would be fair to say that the view of the individual was that … the Allies would win in time, but that he personally was not likely to see the end of it [1]

But in the weeks afterward morale rebounded, well on the upswing before very long. The Germans had the benefit of certain encouraging tangibles, for one the total collapse of the Russians and for another a successful campaign with their Austrian ally against Italy. The first would release many divisions that would bolster Operation Michael, the start of a massive *Kaiserschlacht* that would, they thought, bring victory to Germany on the Western Front.[2]

1 Major-General Sir Stewart Hare, *The Annals of the King's Royal Rifle Corps: Volume V. The Great War* (London: John Murray, 1932), pp. 276-77.
2 Edmonds, *German March Offensive*, p. 142. By end-January 175 German divisions were on the Western Front, 180 by end-February and 192 plus three brigades by 21 March. The Chief of Staff of the German First Army stated that eight divisions had come from Italy and 40 from the East, but as six had gone West to East in the last months of 1916 the net gain was 42, this making German Western Front strength 136,618 officers and 3,438,288 ORs. Edmonds says their officer strength alone exceed the whole of the BEF as it was in August 1914!

German offensive preparations included very active raiding. For the BEF standing on the defensive did not mean standing down. Consequently, the policy was active defence. Knowing that a major offensive in the near future was virtually certain, and likely would come with "little or no preliminary advertisement," GHQ recognized "the urgent importance of keeping a close watch upon the enemy's movements so … as [to obtain] as much warning as possible." Haig's despatches covering late 1917 related this situation and included a comparison. Between early December and the opening of their offensive the Germans made 225 raids, of which 62 were successful. Of the 125 raids by the BEF during the same period 77 were successful.[3] This success rate show that raids had not become careless in planning and execution; they had, perforce, been properly prepared and organized.

The imbalance in the number of raids is easily explained. For one thing, enormous work had to be put into improving defences in accordance with the new British defence in depth system. Second, this defence would be conducted by three-battalion brigades, not the four-battalion brigades that has been the mainstay of British tactical thinking and outlook. Finally, the reasons for raiding had shifted due in no small part to the change from linear defence. On the one hand, enemy posts, much easier to approach and requiring fewer numbers to take them on, meant smaller raiding parties, but, conversely, these could not be expected to penetrate and damage main lines of defence as they simply lacked the strength to do so. An example of what could happen when smaller parties attempted deeper penetration was the experience of 3rd Battalion The Rifle Brigade (24th British Division) on 21 January. Parties of raiders tasked to secure the objective front line and establish blocks found only four Germans, two being killed and two taken prisoner. The third party tasked to penetrate to the support line, Second Lieutenant J. Munday and 10 men, "turned to the right … and were not seen again." Nor did they turn up before the battalion moved to a new area. Outposts also made achieving surprise more difficult in that in acting as a filter they often alerted main line defenders. With experience, though, the junior officers leading raids became adept at surprising posts and preventing the occupants sounding the alarm. Another factor was the shift in focus, raids no longer being geared primarily or generally on harassment, demolition and attrition, which is not to say that such intentions ceased, but given the fact that "something wicked this way comes," i.e. Operation Michael, the purpose of many raids became more focussed on obtaining and/or confirming the identity of opposing troops and information generally about what was coming. As Lieutenant-Colonel G.E.C. Rasch, DSO, CO 2nd Grenadier Guards, would say before a raid in early March, "Raids lately have become regrettably fashionable owing to the anxiety of the Higher Command to obtain a constant supply of prisoners who may give them information of the German offensive which is expected."[4]

Conversely, the German concern was keeping secret the when, where and in what strength the "something wicked" would come. The aim was not to lose men to raiders. In practise, this usually meant inflict damage as much as possible, and resist for a time, but know when to get out. Earlier chapters and this one, too, offer examples of raids where empty trenches, or "slight" resistance by a few men and the sight of enemy backs as they scurried rearward, was all that

3 Headlam, *Guards Division,* Volume II, p. 125; Boraston, ed., *Haig's Despatches,* p. 181.
4 TNA: WO 95/2206: 3rd Battalion, The Rifle Brigade, February 1918, raid report, and TNA: WO 95/1215: 2nd Grenadier Guards, March 1918,'Narrative of Raid March 5th'.

greeted raiding parties as they entered enemy trenches. Nevertheless, the Germans knew that raiders would take prisoners and some would prove talkative.

In a pattern reminiscent of the previous winter the Germans persistently raided in January 1918, almost nightly in fact, commencing on 1 January with a 100-man raid on 54th Canadian Battalion (4th Division) in the Lens area. This raid netted four prisoners. A few days later they struck at 50th Canadian Battalion, also 4th Division, in the early morning. One German party moving undetected between two posts took one prisoner. A second party, having gotten through Canadian wire undetected, encountered by chance an outgoing Canadian patrol led by Lieutenant J.A. MacDonald who took them on and prevented any further penetration. A third party failed to take a third post, several raiders the victim of Lewis guns. One wounded German left behind later that day revealed that the three parties had totalled 60 men, their failure to achieve more significant gain due to the surprise encounter with MacDonald and his patrol who broke up, according to the prisoner, a well-organized and rehearsed raid.[5]

Another 4th Division unit, 44th Battalion, attempted a retaliatory raid two days later, but found the objective, a sap and a length of connecting trench, completely empty. Some machine-gun fire from a trench to the rear commenced, but caused only one casualty, the fire erratic and short-lived. That same day (the 13th) 58th Battalion of 3rd Canadian Division had a very different experience, the two officers and 42 men of the raiding party finding themselves in a stiff fight, but they prevailed, then established a block either side of the objective and during the subsequent trench clearing captured 11 prisoners. This raid was said to have achieved complete surprise because no artillery bombardment had announced it. Instead, Stokes mortars put down intense fire at the moment the assault began. No Canadian casualties were suffered. The OC received the MC and several MMs were awarded.[6]

8th Brigade, 3rd Canadian Division, launched three raids during the week 7-14 January. On the 5th, brigade HQ issued Operation Order 153 for the first of these, this going to Major G.F. MacFarland's 4CMR. The primary purpose of the OC Raid, Lieutenant Leslie Bumstead, and his 30 men, as brigade described it, was securing prisoners and identifications. At a conference that same day brigade specified the point of entry and the section of the trench to be raided, but when air photographs received the next day revealed changes in enemy dispositions the Battalion Scout Officer, Lieutenant Arthur Clarke and one man reconnoitred that afternoon. They discovered the enemy sap passable at its head, but about 30 yards short of the main trench it had been filled with wire. Knowing that the raiders intended to use the sap, it being a covered approach, Clarke had paid close attention to it. His report led to a decision to cut the wire manually as much as possible, then use a Bangalore to finish the job. In addition, the raiders would carry duckboards just in case wire had to be bridged to allow passage.[7]

5 Nicholson, *Canadian Expeditionary Force,* p. 338; LAC, War Diary, 50th Battalion, January 1918.

6 LAC, War Diaries, 44th and 58th Battalions. The OC of the latter raid, Lieutenant Arnold Jucksch, would a month later be awarded the DSO for directing the assembly of the battalion for an attack under heavy fire and then leading a company in a counter-attack during which 50 prisoners were taken. In August he received a Bar to his MC for another raid during which 12 prisoners were taken and the raiders did not lose a man. His 2IC during the January raid, Lieutenant Walter Johnson, was awarded his first MC in July and a Bar in August, His DSO came in 58th Battalion's attack. See Riddle and Mitchell, *Military Cross* and *Distinguished Service Order.*

7 Bennett, *4th Canadian Mounted Rifles 1914-1919,* p. 95; LAC, War Diary, 4CMR, January 1918.

At 1700 Bumstead and his men made their way to the sap where they began wire-cutting. For three hours they toiled, quite undetected by the enemy, the result being 10 yards of wire gapped. In went the Bangalore, but no explosion, nor any after four more attempts, despite checking and re-checking the detonator and the connections. When the party then tried to remove the Bangalore it could not be extracted from under the wire. On resorting to using the duckboards, the first man up fell into the wire and a 30-minute struggle began to free him, this interrupted by the enemy who had finally woken up to the events underway. As bombs began arriving, withdrawal became the only option. Perhaps there should have been a sapper or two along to manage the Bangalore, but as the raiders had some expertise sappers had not been requested. As for the wire, there being 30 yards of it to cut, the time allotted to do that was probably overly optimistic. Twenty yards may have been asking too much of a Bangalore. Notwithstanding, the GOC, Louis Lipsett, expressed appreciation of a good try and blamed "bad luck" for the outcome.[8]

On the 10th, 8th Brigade issued its Operation Order for a raid by 2CMR on 12 January. In his Operation Order the CO, Lieutenant-Colonel George Johnston, DSO, MC, ordered two small raids, their entry points separated by about 900 yards, this plan based on two patrols made in late December by Lieutenant John MacGregor. On the left of the battalion front where the trenches were only 50 yards apart, MacGregor would assault with 20 men covered by a party of 10 men in a sap. On the right Lieutenant Humphrey Williams with 15 men, plus a covering party, faced an advance of 500 yards to the enemy trenches. Artillery would box the objective areas at the same time as the raiding parties were to enter the enemy trenches. In Johnston's account of the raids privately printed shortly after the war he wrote that on 10 January despite the enemy having registered all the battalion CTs he decided to launch the raids at 0210 the next morning (11 January), a time at which the enemy might not expect a raid.[9]

Because of the distance that had to be covered Williams and party left battalion trenches before midnight and reached the enemy wire without incident or delay. At Zero his covering party unleashed rifle grenades and smoke bombs into the enemy line, these apparently causing the enemy to think they were gas since on entry the raiders found the defenders wearing gas masks. Except for the entry point, where a hard fight ensued, the trench was only lightly held. With no dug-outs to shelter in, those enemy who chose not to fight had nowhere to go but over the parados to the rear. At the 30-minute mark Williams withdrew his party, all being home by 0320.[10]

MacGregor's party was less fortunate, it being spotted prior to Zero. However, he got the party to ground, the ensuing silence and lack of response causing the enemy to cease firing, probably thinking no movement had actually occurred. At Zero, having found a new entry point, and despite the resumption of enemy fire, MacGregor and his men got the duckboards onto the wire and entered the enemy trench. They found it quite heavily manned, but secured it once the enemy machine-guns made off to the rear. Two prisoners accompanied the raiders home, which they reached by 0230. Casualties for the two raids were one officer and three ORs wounded and one OR wounded and subsequently died of wounds. Both officers received the MC and five MMs were awarded.[11]

8 *Ibid.*
9 *Ibid.*, 2CMR, Operation Order 99; Johnston, *2nd Canadian Mounted Rifles,* p. 61.
10 *Ibid.,* 2CMR, report on raids 12 January 1918.
11 *Ibid.*, Bishop, *Our Bravest and Our Best,* pp. 136-37. MacGregor, born in Scotland in 1888, emigrated to Canada in 1909. In March 1915 he enlisted as an ordinary soldier. September marked his

A night raid on 14 January by 5CMR (Lieutenant-Colonel Denis Draper, DSO) was the last of this 3rd Division troika. This raid, the smallest of the three, ran into wire, but duckboards got the raiders through and into the enemy trench coincidental with a box barrage placed around the objective. The party was only discovered after it entered the trench. During an 11-minute stay the raiders killed 14 Germans and captured two. Only one Canadian was wounded.[12]

4th Division, too, sought prisoners and identifications. On Friday 4 January Victor Odlum, GOC 11th Brigade, advised his four battalion commanders that he had received orders to raid before the brigade left the line. What he had decided upon was retaliation for the enemy raid on 54th Battalion on 1 January (see earlier). He listed raid purposes as domination of no man's land and securing prisoners. Each of 54th, 75th and 87th Battalions would raid separately in one platoon strength on the coming Tuesday, 8 January. The raid by 75th Battalion would go in early evening on the 8th followed by 87th Battalion on the same objective later during the night. That battalion's War Diary reveals that neither CO was keen: "No one was anxious for the raid to be put on, owing to the ground not being suitable, no man's land at the nearest point being over 800 yards wide." When he gave his orders Odlum offered an alternative. If fighting patrols could satisfy orders then the raid would not proceed.[13]

The CO 54th Battalion decided on a raid. Afterward the two officers and 28 men of the battalion complained that the short duration of the artillery barrage gave "Fritz a chance to vacate his front line which he lost no time in doing. Our raiding party entered his front line but found nobody there." The COs of the 75th and the 87th Battalions, Lieutenant-Colonels C.C. Harbottle, DSO, and J.V.P. O'Donahoe, DSO, agreed that instead of raiding the enemy fighting patrols on alternate nights would seek identifications in no man's land, but when patrols on 4, 5, 6 and 7 January met no enemy final preparations commenced for a double raid. However, when 87th Battalion patrols on the night of the 7th found that enemy wire had not been sufficiently cut the two COs reconsidered. As it was 75th Battalion's turn to patrol, and given the fact that even if an adequate gap was found it was likely that more wire would be encountered, perhaps in the form of concertina or low-wire entanglements, they decided that the best course was to make only one raid and the 75th would do it.

At 1700 on the 8th, Lieutenant John Leonard of the 75th set out to check the state of the wire. Two hours later he and his two men returned. Having found a good gap in the wire the three had entered the enemy trench and searched it for about 125 yards. No enemy were present. On moving to the enemy support line they found the wire intact with no gaps. Brigade when advised of this ordered the raid to try snatching the occupants of an outpost. At 2130 Leonard's observer party in no man's land was relieved by a similar sized party to continue watching the gap he had found. Meanwhile, the raiding party of 55 men under Lieutenant Thomas Tilly had reached the battalion front line and then began moving into assembly position in no man's land

promotion to Sergeant and the award of the DCM. Commissioned in May 1917 he won his first MC in January 1918 (for the raid described here), his second coming soon after. His VC was won in late September 1918. During the Second World War as a Lieutenant-Colonel he commanded the Training Centre at Wainwright, Alberta. The Western Front Association website calls him Canada's most highly decorated soldier.

12 LAC, War Diary, 8th Brigade, report on raid.

13 LAC, War Diaries, 54th, 75th, 82nd and 102nd Battalions. The quoted sentence is in the diary of the 75th.

at 0130. When ready the five groups of the party advanced in diamond formation with Tilly in the centre and a Lewis gun with each of the sections left and right:

X
X T X
X

At 0200 the barrage opened on the enemy front line. At this time nothing had been seen or heard of the raiders, which is not surprising given the width of no man's land. Thirty minutes later the raiders were back, no enemy having been encountered, but they had the shoulder straps of a greatcoat belonging to a man of the 156th Regiment. Identification secured! The only casualty was Tilly slightly wounded. Leonard and Tilly each received the MC. Leonard's CO described his patrol as "the best seen in the Battalion for a very long time."[14]

7th and 8th Battalions of 1st Division made one of the last Canadian raids of January on the 30th. It being suspected that the enemy opposite had just been relieved the raid was ordered to identify the newcomers. This endeavour actually involved three raids: Raid "B" by the 7th at 1230, Raid "A" also by the 7th at 1945 and Raid "C" by the 8th at 1815. If "B" secured the required identifications then "A" and "C" would not be done. "B" raiders entered the objective trench after cutting wire for 90 minutes, but found it blocked with new wire 20 yards either side of their entry point. No identifications were secured. Raid "C" likewise failed, the party coming under fire immediately it crossed the first wire belt, and there being no gaps in the second, the party had to withdraw. Raid "A" was then cancelled. While these raids were very small, one officer and 10 men each, and all failed, the CO of the 7th, Lieutenant-Colonel W.F. Gilson, thought Raid "B" valuable in one respect: "The feasibility of entering enemy trenches by stealth was amply demonstrated by the fact that wire-cutting for one and one-half hours was carried on without the enemy being alarmed prior to the trench being entered." In fact, the enemy had manned only one of the wire-blocks in the trench and its sentries were surprised. While daylight stealth and protracted wire-cutting had been feasible in this instance the "B" raiders were also most fortunate. It should be noted that the entry point at a sap/trench junction on a small salient probably struck the enemy as a vulnerable point, hence the wire blocks either side. The reality, according to the brigade report (2nd Brigade), was "successful stealth raid practically impossible."[15]

14 LAC, War Diary, 75th Battalion; *SS 143 Instructions for the Training of Platoons for Offensive Action*, Appendix II The Platoon in Artillery Formation. This formation was commonly referred to as Diamond Formation because of its shape. Each "X" represents a section, its men moving in fours or pairs or in single file depending on ground and other factors. The intervals also depended on circumstances. One of the numerous, indeed multitudinous "Training Leaflets" issued by the "IG [Inspector General] Training, BEF, France," outlines the advantages and disadvantages of this formation, the former boiling down to the better control gained by the OC by being in the centre. The leaflet, "Training Leaflet No. 4 Attack Formation for Small Units" cautions that diamond formation will "as a rule disappear when contact is reached and rushes are made." The reason for this is obvious. For a detailed account of diamond formation see Nicol, *Till the Trumpet Sounds Again*, p. 50.

15 LAC, War Diaries, 7th and 8th Battalions, 2nd Brigade. William Forbes Gilson, age 40 in 1917, was CO of the 7th from October 1916 to demobilization. Only four other officers commanded Canadian

Canadian raids in January were at the lower end of the scale, most one platoon or less. Likewise, British raids. Often their results were similar, the enemy being light on defence of forward lines and preferring to shun contact. In fact, January, when it comes to raiding, was rather quiet: "Nothing to report" is a summation that appears in many of the British divisional histories. 20th Division's historian noted that "Almost the only fighting [that month] occurred on 9/10 January when the 20th did a demonstration in support of a 37th Division raid." Patrol activity, on the other hand, and not surprisingly, was at a high level.[16]

This 37th Division raid was actually two raids founded by 111th Brigade: Raid "B" by the 13th Battalion, The Rifle Brigade, followed by Raid "A", a much larger operation by the 13th KRRC, both on the night 9/10 January. All went well for "B" until the raiders penetrated the enemy wire where they were greeted with heavy machine-gun fire and a strong garrison. Being unable to enter the trench the raiders withdrew. Raid "A" (six officers and 100 ORs) aimed to obtain prisoners. The raiders were in three parties: a storming party of two officers and 30 ORs and left and right flank parties each of an officer and 30 ORs. The OC Raid, Major P.N. Russell, and the raid 2IC would remain at a point just outside the objective. With them a small party would await and manage any prisoners. The stormers would attack six pill-boxes, five men to each, covered by the flank parties during their attacks and subsequent withdrawal. When Pill Box 1 was bombed and entered three of the six occupants were dead and three unwounded. One of the latter shouted in English to the party leader, Lieutenant Low, "Look out, there is another behind you" and when Low turned another German fired from behind one of the men who had his hands up and killed Low. All three Germans then paid the price. Unfortunately, the shoulder straps taken went astray during the withdrawal. The German ruse was not the only example of what the GOC 36th (Ulster) Division called "battlefield brutality." In a letter home he related what had happened and how one "brutality" leads to another:

> We did a highly successful raid the other day, broke into German trenches in 3 places, took several prisoners and killed nearly fifty, I was rather annoyed that the parties did not take more prisoners, but our men wouldn't trust them. They had been had before by Boches holding up their hands and shouting 'Kamerad' while another man took a pot shot from behind him, so they killed everyone that they met. They left behind a number of booby traps for the Boches when they returned. They pulled the pins out of Mills grenades and put them under the dead Boches in the trenches, so that the weight of the body keeps the lever down, in the hope that when the Boches came back and lifted up their defunct comrades, they would explode violently. I did not hear whether the traps worked, but they deserved to.

battalions for longer than that. Born in Britain Gilson had pre-war service with three British regiments. He began the war as an NCO with the 7th. During his time in command Gilson was awarded three DSOs. The citations in Riddle and Mitchell, *Distinguished Service Order,* show what a fine CO he was. See W. Stewart, '"Byng's Boys": A Profile of Senior Commanders of Canadian Combat Units on the Somme, 1916', *War in History,* 23.1, p. 77.

16 Inglefield, *20th (Light) Division,* p. 213. Of the British divisional histories 28 offer only a para or two on January 1918, most relating the tribulations of bad weather, urgent defensive preparations and especially the painful adjustments in going from four-battalion brigades to three-battalion brigades. In only two of these 28 histories is the word "raid" even mentioned during the coverage of January. Of course, these books relate selected raids, raids that were thought deserving of comment, so it is possible that more raids were made but were excluded for one reason or another.

An illustration of this German ruse appeared on the cover of a March 1916 issue of *The War Illustrated.* The caption reads

> A favourite ruse of the treacherously-inclined Hun is to hide behind a comrade who apparently is surrendering himself prisoner. With rifle ready and loaded, he is able to take in cold blood the life of the hesitant Briton. This cowardly conduct occurred recently during a Canadian [raid] on the Prussian Guard. Fortunately, the Maple Leaf man was too quick for the Prussians, and managed to get a revolver bullet and bayonet thrust in first. In this engagement the Canadians took the enemy by surprise, and succeeded in wreaking considerable damage with bombs.

A second pill-box was found empty. The other four could not be reached due to extremely heavy machine-gun fire. Raider casualties totalled two officers and two ORs killed, seven wounded and five missing.[17]

Much the same pattern prevailed during February. The re-organization forced upon the British divisions occupied every brigade and the many battalions that had to be shuffled about. For that month the published histories of the Guards, 12th, 15th, 35th and 42nd Divisions, briefly describe in a paragraph or two one raid by each division. Each of these raids, none exceeding a company in strength, secured identifications, taking between one and 11 prisoners, all at very low cost, three of the five raids suffering no casualties at all. 2nd Division's history summed up February thus: incessant patrolling, over 120 recce and fighting patrols, and a "certain number" of raids (no details of any kind offered).[18] Incessant patrolling was the regime in all five divisions. 11th Division's War Diary (this division has no published history) reported on a small daylight raid, 21 all ranks, by 8th Northumberland Fusiliers on 24 February. Like the Canadian raid by 7th and 8th Battalions in January (see above) the raiders once in the enemy trench encountered blocks left and right a short distance from their entry point. Again, only one of the blocks was manned. The only Germans encountered were two killed outside a dug-out, one being relieved of his shoulder straps. Of the raiders, only the OC Raid had previously raided, the rest being new arrivals. The CO, Lieutenant-Colonel V.R. Ford, commented in similar vein to what the CO of the 7th Canadian Battalion, Lieutenant-Colonel Gilson, had said:

> When the opportunity permits, small and carefully practised enterprises, carried out boldly and silently as far as possible, even with a moderate degree of success, have a very stimulating effect, not only on those who take part in them, but also on the remainder, as the men gain confidence in themselves and their leaders without undue casualties.[19]

During the previous week 32nd British Division in the Ypres sector had launched a raid consisting of elements of two brigades. Even before returning to the line in early February the GOC,

17 TNA: WO 95/2531: 111th Brigade Operation Order 184 and "Lessons"; WO 95/2531: Operation No. 2 (Raid B), 13th KRRC and 13th The Rifle Brigade; David R. Orr and David Truesdale, *"Ulster will Fight ... " Volume 2: The 36th (Ulster) Division from Formation to the Armistice* (Solihull: Helion & Company, 2016), p. 243; *The War Illustrated,* 11th March 1916.

18 Wyrall, *Second Division,* Volume II, p. 524.

19 TNA: WO 95/1821: 11th Division General Staff, Intelligence Summary 25 February.

Major-General C.D. Shute, had ordered brigades to prepare and submit plans for raids as soon as possible. Once the 96th and 97th Brigades had taken over their frontages on the 7th and the 4th of February respectively they immediately commenced recce of enemy wire and defences. The four battalions taking part – 2nd King's Own Yorkshire Light Infantry (KOYLI) and 11th Border Regiment, both in 97th Brigade, and the 15th and 16th Lancashire Fusiliers (96th Brigade) – were required to patrol nightly in accordance with instructions issued and co-ordinated by the two Brigade HQs. Patrol reports, noted Shute, were "carefully read and sifted" at brigade and at division. Any "uncertain points" had to be cleared up by additional patrols. All information so gained, plus reports by observation posts, infantry and artillery, were correlated and marked on operational maps at the two brigade HQs and at division. These assisted in formulating brigade plans, these being complete by 15 February. It is evident throughout the preparations that the division and brigade commanders were heavily involved in every aspect.

Shute initially intended each brigade to carry out one raid on different nights, but he then did an Appreciation to determine the best option. Since the division had not raided for "many weeks", its artillery having been quiet and its attitude generally unaggressive, it seemed reasonable to think that a first raid would achieve surprise, but as it would stir up the enemy the success of a second raid would be considerably less. He knew that a raid on a narrow front would tell the enemy that the enterprise was merely local and he could safely turn all his firepower on the narrow area. Conversely, the wider the area the more likely it was that the enemy would think it a major operation. This would create doubt in his mind about where to concentrate. Shute's Appreciation convinced him that the raid by the two brigades should be simultaneous on a front of 1,500 yards, Zero at 2300 on 18 February.[20]

The plan had 97th Brigade as left assault and 96th Brigade as right assault. The 97th had three objectives: on the left a series of posts along a road, in the centre pill-boxes near farm buildings and on the right outposts along a tree line. B Company of the 2nd KOYLI (five officers and 108 ORs) would raid on the left, D Company in the same strength in the centre would hit the farm and three officers and 60 men of the 11th Borderers would tackle the outposts on the right. 96th Brigade, to the right of the 97th, would raid in somewhat smaller numbers, a total of eight officers and 119 ORs. On the left (next to the 11th Borderers) No. 3 Party had several pill-boxes as its objective. Its neighbour, No. 2 Party, had another group of pill-boxes to deal with. These two parties, each of two officers and 27 ORS including two sappers, were founded by 16th Lancashires. No. 1 Party to the right, five officers and 55 ORs plus two sappers, were from 15th Lancashires. This party would raid some farm buildings. The primary objective of all parties was prisoners and/or identifications.[21]

Divisional artillery reinforced by one field artillery brigade plus a brigade of 35th Divisional Artillery and three Belgian batteries, would support the raids. Heavy Artillery would fire counter-battery exclusively, primarily gas shells since neutralization rather than destruction was the aim. Stokes mortars would target the objectives at Zero for 10 minutes. Recce having earlier reported weak points in enemy wire, and it being calculated that divisional artillery at intense rate and hurricane Stokes fire at Zero would clear the way, no wire-cutting was done before

20 TNA: WO 95/2371: 32nd Division report on raid south of Houthulst Forest, 18/19 February 1918.
21 TNA: WO 95/2371: 32nd Division General Staff, Operation Order 158; WO 95/2400 97th Brigade Operation Order 203; WO 95/2396: 96th Brigade Operation Order 426.

the raid. Given the width of the raid, the guns available were not sufficient to form an artillery curtain to shut in the enemy. However, divisional artillery would provide what fire it could on a line 250 yards behind the objectives for up to 45 minutes after zero.[22]

No. 1 Party of 96th Brigade's raiders under Captain Arthur Cantwell, MC, had been organized in several discrete sub-parties to handle particular roles such as wire-cutting, laying tapes and carrying Bangalores. As it turned out, only one Bangalore had to be used, wire elsewhere proving no obstacle. As Cantwell went about clearing pill-boxes 15 prisoners were taken, including one officer who subsequently died of wounds. His papers and effects were brought in. No. 2 Party had no difficulty with wire either and in quickly mopping up its assigned objective took four prisoners, killed one enemy officer and secured his papers. No. 3 Party, which was delayed by a few shorts of friendly artillery, found on reaching its objective that the 11th Border Regiment had already cleared the area. Enemy resistance throughout varied, some men choosing to make a good fight of it, but more got out of the way as quickly as possible.[23]

Of the 11th Borderers' three parties one encountered no enemy, one could not reach its objective due to machine-gun fire that killed the officer leading the party and the third took one prisoner during a brief skirmish, killing 12 others. Of the two KOYLI companies D Company captured three pill-boxes, killed 28 Germans and captured 13 and B Company, whose objective was enemy dug-outs, secured identifications from the two Germans they killed. No other enemy were seen within their objective area.[24]

Determined to ascertain "a fair estimate" of total enemy losses Shute personally interviewed "all" (quite an undertaking) the officers and men who had raided and came up with these figures: 38 prisoners, 40 Germans bombed and seen dead or wounded, 120 Germans seen dead or wounded by artillery or rifle fire, and 38 Germans actually killed by individuals. The raiders lost four killed including one officer, 32 wounded including three officers and one OR missing. Commenting on the difference in the third category – 96th Brigade, 115 Germans; 97th Brigade, five Germans – Shute attributed this to the many pill-boxes the enemy sheltered in at 97th Brigade's objective and the scarcity of same in 96th Brigade's area. Also, 97th Brigade's objective was lightly held.[25]

The GOC 97th Brigade, Brigadier-General C.A. Blacklock, summing up his brigade's raid, said "Everything went according to plan," this gratifying indeed, and a tribute to those who had planned and executed the raid since "there was no opportunity of taking the raiders out of the line to train." In lieu, the careful instruction of every man was stressed: "Brigadiers saw each man … on the day … [of] the raid, and received a personal assurance from every man that he knew his particular role. Many points were discussed and a final coaching given on how to deal with possible eventualities." Shute does not explain why there was no opportunity to train, but he noted that in his opinion "drill and practice out of the line … is apt to be overdone and men get stale and their enthusiasm wanes." He then recorded that a third of the raiders were men who had not been in the line before and "many tips had to be explained

22 *Ibid.*, report on raids south of Houthulst Forrest, 18/19 February. For rates of fire see Chapter 2, footnote 27 and Chapter 14, footnote 34.
23 *Ibid.*
24 *Ibid.*, 97th Brigade report.
25 *Ibid.*

to them as to the conditions they might expect." Because of this, and it being a night raid, special care had also to be been taken to ensure the raiding parties kept direction out and back, including the usual white tapes plus red signalling flashlights and "checking in" stations out and back, these manned by officers. Blacklock attributed success to extensive pre-raid recce, excellent planning and the work of the OC 97th Trench Mortar Battery who on very short notice had to get his Stokes and ammunition to eight firing positions, accurately plot them and produce exact bearings and distances based on triangulation, no registration being allowed. Over 1,700 bombs had been distributed to the eight positions, one infantry company being given to the battery to get the ammunition into place. The battalion reports include unanimous praise of the Stokes support.[26]

A third of Shute's 10-page report concerns "Notes and Lessons." It can be difficult to separate these since one man's note is another man's lesson and one or the other or both may elicit the question "Doesn't everyone do that?" Six of the 15 numbered paragraphs pertain specifically to this raid and are not further discussed. While this or that paragraph of the remaining nine may be both note and lesson they are universal and bear reiteration. First, Shute considered recce fundamental in the careful choice of objectives and in the success of any raid. Second, artillery officers should be shown the actual objectives so that no errors in targetting would be made. Third, the reason that enemy artillery did not respond was gas shells: neutralization not destruction. Fourth, one had to realize that machine-gun barrages were speculative, their effectiveness impossible to estimate; all that could be said was that some of their fire may have found a mark. Fifth, maintaining direction was so critical that measures designed to ensure keeping on course warranted the closest attention especially when inexperienced troops were participating. Sixth, "checking in stations" had to be redundant since they were apt to get shelled. Next, raiding on a wide front had many advantages. Eighth, while the one Bangalore fired properly as a rule RE should handle them as previous infantry experience with them had often been far less than happy. Finally, blankets rather than mats or duckboards were the better option for crossing wire they being lighter and less awkward.[27]

What makes this raid all the more interesting is that Major-General Cameron Shute ordered it. He joined the 32nd from the Royal Naval Division (RND) where his tenure had not proven satisfactory to him or the division, a relationship made famous, or rather infamous, by A.P. Herbert who penned a rather unflattering poem about Shute, a poem beautiful in its rhythm and alliteration, near genius, but one unlikely to please the subject. Herbert's inspiration came when Shute on assuming command of the RND vehemently criticized just about everything he saw including what he considered the division's inadequate attention to sanitation. Granted the poem does not mention raiding, but having raised the reader's curiosity it seems only fair to tender the last stanza:

26 *Ibid.*, University of Birmingham, War Studies Research project, "Lions Led By Donkeys." Blacklock was commissioned in the KRRC in 1901. After service during the South African War he emigrated to Canada in 1904. He rejoined his regiment in 1914 and took command of 10th KRRC in December 1915. Promoted to Brigadier-General in January 1917 he served briefly as GOC 182nd Brigade (2nd Division) before moving to 97th Brigade in March 1917. On 30 August on promotion he took command of 63rd Division (Royal Naval Division). In 1920 he resigned and returned to Canada. British War Diary, 32nd Division General Staff, February 1918, 'Report of Raids South of Houthulst Forest'.

27 *Ibid.*

For shit may be shot at odd corners
And paper supplied there to suit,
But a shit would be shot without mourners
If somebody shot that shit Shute.

What is relevant is that Shute, a pre-war regular and battalion CO, then a competent brigade commander, was now commanding 32nd Division, where he would thrive sufficiently to go on to command V Corps. In the way of such things he likely would not now be remembered were it not for the poem.[28]

A week later (27/28 February) 32nd British Division would raid again, this time in double the strength of the earlier effort, the new endeavour featuring 597 all ranks of Brigadier-General F.W. Lumsden's 14th Brigade and 210 all ranks of L.F. Ashburner's 96th Brigade. Once again Shute's report on the raid reflects the great care taken in the selection of objectives, recce and planning and his desire to exercise firm control. Once again Shute begins with his pre-raid Appreciation in which, not surprisingly, the focus is on 14th Brigade since it would execute the primary part of the raid. What he offers is comprehensive including summations of the results of the earlier raid, what was known of enemy dispositions, what he expected the raids to achieve (prisoners and/or identifications), consideration of the ground and an assessment of the advantages and disadvantages of the proposals for the primary operation by 14th Brigade on the left, an operation on a wide frontage (600 yards) with multiple objectives. He passes very lightly over the secondary role 96th Brigade would play, its strength being one-third that of 14th Brigade and its task being much simpler as its objectives were more in the nature of specific points (two), although, of course, contiguous real estate could not be ignored.

The earlier raid had established that the enemy outpost line was only lightly held and its defences and wire could be easily penetrated. Enemy morale had been assessed as somewhat less than high, the enemy seemingly lacking any inclination to retaliate. Information gained from prisoners and study of air photographs indicated that the enemy main line of resistance rested on a disused railway running east to west south of a creek with the west end of track a strongly defended locality consisting of a group of pill-boxes. As for the outpost line, it had been strengthened by strong points immediately behind it at several farms and groups of pill-boxes. Shute intended to raid soon and penetrate more deeply than the earlier raid had in order to more precisely define the enemy main line. The minor operation by 96th Brigade on the right would not only confirm enemy strength at known points such as the farm, but would divert enemy attention from 14th Brigade's operation. It had been suggested that the division on the right of the 32nd would also raid at the same time, but lack of artillery support made this impossible. However, a diversion in the form of a "Chinese Attack" using dummy figures between the two operational areas would be arranged.[29]

28 Where this poem was first set down is unrecorded. The state of the relationship between Shute and the RND was such that Shute is not mentioned even once in a comparison of Shute and his predecessor at pages 185-87 in Douglas Jerrold, *The Royal Naval Division,* nor does a photograph of him appear in that book. This in itself is telling.

29 TNA: WO 95/2391: 32nd Division General Staff, 14th Brigade report on raid 27/28 February. Lumsden, GOC 14th Brigade, was the recipient of the VC and the DSO and three Bars. University of Birmingham, War Studies Research Project, "Lions Led By Donkeys." Ashburner, a South

The essence of 14th Brigade's plan was an advance in a north-easterly direction starting from assembly positions about 200 yards forward of brigade trenches. Shute had three objections to this: first, it demanded a "considerable" force; second, since the direction of attack would be diagonally across the divisional front its left flank would be vulnerable; and, finally, assembly of the large raiding force in no man's land might be detected. However, he accepted Lumsden's assessment that three assault companies sufficed, a conclusion drawn by Lumsden after careful personal recce had revealed three distinct advantages of his plan: first, enemy defences, including his machine-guns, were organized to meet attack from the south; second, the ground between the assembly positions and the objective was more open than anywhere else on the brigade front; and, finally, the direction of the attack would come as a surprise. As to possible detection in no man's land, Lumsden believed that careful arrangements for assembly during the darkest hours would lessen the risk. Shute agreed, but to further lessen the risk he ordered nightly patrols to warn of any new enemy posts being established at points where observation of the assembly positions was possible and also to warn of any new wire. The choice of Zero Hour had also to be weighed against the need for as much light as possible during the actual operation. Shute did not mention the problem of keeping direction probably because Lumsden's Operation Order 191, given the wide frontage and the fairly long approach, paid navigation close attention, which was fortunate since during the raid "some difficulty was experienced … due in part to the darkness of the night and the difficult nature of the ground." As for left flank vulnerability, the artillery fire plan included a standing barrage on that flank from Zero onward.[30]

The detailed plan called for one company of the 2nd Manchesters on the right to raid a particular farm complex plus clear the immediate area assisted by 16th Lancashire Fusiliers which would furnish four platoon sized patrols as protection on the Manchesters right flank. To their left would be three and one-half companies of the 6th Royal Scots and then to their left one company of the 1st Dorsets. Artillery support would include field artillery, 18-pounders (66) and 4.5-inch howitzers (21), plus 12 Belgian field guns and 10 "heavies" (6-inch howitzers) of Corps Artillery, most of this allocated to the primary operation, and eight Stokes. Zero was set for 1932 on the 27th, this time seeming a good balance, it being predicted that the light would improve around 2000. In fact, no improvement was obvious until about 2200.[31]

As Lumsden had promised, the raiders remained undetected in their assembly positions. The assault went in at Zero, the creeping barrage being good although somewhat thin, and direction keeping proved no difficulty. The eight equally sized parties of the Manchesters kept close to the barrage during the assault. Trip wires were found on all roads, more so on the main west-east road. Loose concertina had been placed in several areas. At the main objective (the farm complex), which had been thoroughly wrecked by artillery, the raiders met no opposition. Two machine-gun posts at the farm were attacked and both guns captured, plus eight prisoners, some of whom were "discovered shamming death, but on inserting a bayonet they were found to

African War veteran, was appointed BM of a brigade in December 1914, in due course moving to 1st Australian Division as GSO2. He did not command a battalion before his promotion to Brigadier-General and appointment to command of 96th Brigade in December 1916. In August 1917 after nine months in command he was dismissed and returned to England where he served with the Territorials. He did not again hold field command.

30 *Ibid.*, 14th Brigade Operation Order 191, 25 February 1918.

31 *Ibid.*, 32nd Division General Staff, 14th Brigade Operation Order 159 and report on raid.

be alive." The patrols furnished by the Lancashires found no enemy, but received some fire from wire-protected posts located north of the objective. The Manchesters experienced machine-gun fire from positions well beyond their objectives.

Once on the objective the 6th Royal Scots brought rifle fire to bear on the enemy fleeing into the forest to which patrols then advanced, but found no enemy on its edge or close to it. The Dorsets on the left being unable to keep up to the barrage met with considerable enemy fire at the main objective. At the railway siding the assault troops used the embankment as a covered forming up place for taking on the five pill-boxes. Most of the enemy, however, fell back from pill-box to pill-box as the raiders worked eastward, At Zero plus 100 withdrawal commenced, no interference being offered.

Between the two raids the diversionary "Chinese Attack" by the neighbouring division consisting of 24 figures to simulate advancing troops apparently drew "considerable" fire (such always hard to quantify) thus sparing the right of the main raiding party some casualties. However, the dummies once raised were soon destroyed by shelling.[32]

Once again Shute personally interviewed participants and grouped enemy casualties in categories similar to what he had done previously: 15 prisoners, 48 enemy killed by artillery or machine-guns, and 105 killed by raiders or seen dead or wounded. 14th Brigade did most of the damage and suffered most of the casualties, 90 of 137, half of these described as very slightly wounded. This raid offered fewer lessons than the one on 18/19 February for several reasons. First, insufficient guns in support meant that the enemy could not be penned and were able to withdraw at will. Second, time spent in enemy trenches was too short to do as much damage as desired. Third, it had again been shown that the wider the attack frontage the less the amount of enemy fire that had to be faced. Finally, the raid demonstrated not so much a lesson as a confirmation of the effectiveness of the rifle, this very apparent when the enemy started bolting: "There was no reliance on bombs, men got into firing positions and used their rifles with a conviction that they were employing a most effective weapon." This reiterated what "Alf" knew: "the rifle will pull you through."[33]

By the beginning of February it was obvious to 1st Canadian Division that the enemy was of an aggressive mindset. All along the divisional front low flying aircraft ranged overhead and at night motor vehicles and wagons could be heard coming forward and then back, the frequency and volume of the traffic clearly well beyond normal nightly activity. Troops in the front line had first hand experience of enemy fighting spirit. One the night of 1 February, for example, fighting patrols from 3rd Battalion were brought up hard in the face of an alert and active enemy, his trenches ablaze with fire at the onset of patrol movement. In no man's land, too, the enemy seemed out for blood; 4th Battalion, for one, lost men to the enemy in one savage encounter. While these events gave pause for thought, they did not deter equally aggressive raids.

On 3 February 3rd Battalion embarked on a stealth raid, no preliminary bombardment.[34] Major H.S. Cooper, OC Raid, organized his raiders into two parties, each of one officer and 26 ORs, their purpose being to obtain information and prisoners. At 1830 the two parties, the left one under Lieutenant John Ramsden and the right one under Lieutenant Roy Bailey, moved into

32 *Ibid.*
33 *Ibid.* Alf's poem is at Chapter 11 of this present study.
34 Goodspeed, *Battle Royal*, pp. 216-17.

no man's land. Ramsden's party just over an hour later reached a point just 20 yards short of enemy wire. Upon coming under an intense bombing attack Ramsden ordered a rush forward, but only he and two men were able to enter the trench. On entry Ramsden disappeared. The two men then withdrew. Bailey's party had managed to get even closer to the enemy wire and in a rush the left half of his party was in and clearing the trench left and right, but the party being outmatched, and with no hope of the right half joining in, Bailey ordered withdrawal. The right half had lost most of its strength when a phosphorous bomb carried by one man exploded causing severe burns to several men. Total raid casualties included one officer missing and one wounded, plus two ORs missing and 11 wounded. No prisoners or identifications were secured. Officer patrols later that night did not find any of the missing. However, Lieutenant Ramsden came in the next night. Wounded, he had spent the whole of the day, the 4th, hidden just a few yards from enemy sentries and had then crawled, once it was dark, across no man's land.[35] The CO, Lieutenant-Colonel J. B. Rogers, DSO, MC, who ascribed failure to enemy alertness, saw the lesson as this: abandon stealth raids and precede all raids with artillery and trench mortar bombardment. Others shared his opinion. 47th Battalion's "Lectures" (see Chapter 14) had reached at about the same time a similar conclusion.[36] This is not to say that 3rd Battalion's experience ended the debate about the relationship between artillery and raids which has been discussed elsewhere.

47th Battalion's views on stealth raids and preliminary bombardments seem to have been shared by 46th Battalion, the two units both in 10th Brigade of 4th Division. On 14 February, it having been "intimated" to the CO on the 5th that "a raid on this front [Hill 70 area] was desired," two parties of the 46th, each of an officer and 37 ORs, raided enemy positions on a railway embankment, this objective having been selected after careful recce.[37] On the 10th and 11th all the raiders had ample opportunity to view the ground and the officers and NCOs joined patrols in order to become familiar with the approaches to the objective and to select the best assembly position for the raid. Concurrently, and into the 12th and 13th, 6-inch trench mortars worked hard at wire-cutting. By the afternoon of the 13th adequate gaps appeared to have been cut. At night, Stokes mortars negated repair attempts. It was noted, however, that the cutting had attracted enemy attention.

At Zero (0545) initial barrages – 18-pounders firing shrapnel on the front of the embankment, 4.5-inch howitzers on its rear and trench mortars on selected targets, plus searching machine-gun fire on rear lines of approach – commenced and at Zero plus three formed a box barrage. The right party on reaching the embankment became the target of such heavy machine-gun fire that it could not advance for some time until eventually one section got behind the machine-gun. One member of its crew was captured. At this time the party heard the signal for withdrawal and complied. The other party had no difficulty with wire and soon crossed over the embankment where it took four prisoners and bombed several dug-outs. This party reported the embankment as lightly held. Total battalion casualties were light, two missing and three wounded.[38] Clearly, preliminary bombardment had been no guarantee of success, at least for

35 LAC, War Diary, 3rd Battalion, Operation Order 136 and raid report on 5 February.
36 LAC, MG30E100 (Currie Papers), Volume 35.
37 LAC, War Diary, 46th Battalion, report on raid by Lieutenant-Colonel H.J. Dawson. Brigade's comments on the raid were brief, the most significant concerning the need for careful training and the great effectiveness of the 6-inch mortar in cutting wire.
38 *Ibid.*

half the raiders. However, the wire-cutting that had seemed adequate proved not as thorough as had been supposed. The cutting had been noticed and surprise was lost.

Even before George Tuxford's 3rd Canadian Brigade took over the Hill 70 sector of the Canadian front, 1st Division's urgent need for identifications resulted in an order to raid and get prisoners. Immediately the brigade was on the ground it commenced recce with a view to selecting an objective. In his report on the raid Tuxford began with some recent history that had convinced him not to imitate 46th Battalion's raid:

> Several unsuccessful attempts had been made by units of other brigades during the last week of January and the first week in February. All these raids had been attempted as 'stealth' raids without artillery co-operation, and it was clear that even where it was possible to cut the strong wire in front of enemy lines, he was too … alert and manned his trenches too strongly for this type of raid to have a possible chance of success. It was therefore decided to ask for artillery both to cut wire and to cover the raiding parties, and to attempt to enter enemy trenches at a number of points simultaneously.[39]

During several conferences with battalion commanders, 3rd Brigade's Staff Captain (Intelligence), artillery commanders and machine-gun and trench mortar officers, five raiding parties were decided upon, 13th, 14th and 15th Battalions to provide one each and 16th Battalion to provide two. Total strength would be 10 officers and 196 ORs. Eight entry points were selected, plus five others where wire would be cut to disguise the real points. Terrain put the entry points into two groups: 13th and 14th Battalion objectives in one and the 15th and 16th Battalion objectives in the other. Divisional 18-pounders, plus 18-pounders of 11th British Division, would lay down a box barrage around each group, 4.5-inch howitzers would fire on selected points and heavy artillery would provide counter-battery fire. Medium and heavy trench mortars plus Stokes would deal with wire. Zero was set for 0300 which would allow thorough recce to determine the state of the wire on the night of 13 February.

Wire-cutting began on the 7th. By the 11th it was clear to Tuxford that too much had been asked of the mortars and two batteries of heavy artillery began assisting. Even so, recce that night revealed that while entry points for the 13th Battalion and the northern objective of 16th Battalions were satisfactory, the latter battalion's second objective entry point was "doubtful" and 14th and 15th Battalion entry points were 'impassable." Consequently, Tuxford ordered a 24 hour postponement. Next day 18-pounders joined in the cutting. Recce that night reported the entry point at 16th Battalion's southern objective improved to a point that the remainder of the wire could be manually cut. 15th Battalion now had a satisfactory gap, but the 14th Battalion's remained impassable. On being so advised, Tuxford cancelled that battalion's raid.[40]

A mixed reception greeted the raiders. Such heavy machine-gun fire from both flanks hit the 13th Battalion's two officers and 39 ORs that only one officer and a few men actually entered the enemy trench. Fierce enemy opposition quickly drove the small party out. Clearly,

39 LAC, War Diary, 3rd Brigade, report on raid, Hill 70 sector, 13 February.

40 *Ibid.* It was an infantry responsibility to say whether or not wire-cutting was satisfactory. This had not always been the case and argument and complaint had often soured infantry-artillery relations. (LAC, RG9IIIC3, Volume 4063, Folder 13, File 1).

the entry point was covered and the enemy prepared.[41] 15th Battalion raiders found only one of their two entry points usable, but the whole party, one officer and 53 ORs, did enter the trench where they took one prisoner. Dubbed by his captors the "Heidelberg Professor," he had only been in the line one day: "He was very short-sighted, which fact, he explained, had prevented him from keeping up with the rest in their flight [which] ultimately led to his capture. He wasn't much of a prisoner, being very ingratiating and willing to please, but still, he was a prisoner."[42]

16th Battalion's northern party failed to enter enemy trenches, but the southern party did so without difficulty, took five prisoners, the capture of the first, even in the circumstances, quite amusing in the later recollections of the OC of the party, Lieutenant S.D. Johnston:

> I heard a tramping sound coming down the trench and thought 'Here they come.' We crouched down at the corner of a traverse, all ready for them and when we reckoned they were about on us I sprang out, revolver pointed … Behold a solitary Hun, who, when he saw us, threw down his rifle … off with his equipment like a flash, and up with his hands. 'Twas funny! He did it as if he was doing [it] by the numbers.

Dug-out wrecking commenced, but, as Johnston said, the focus had to be the preservation of prisoners "for what good would it be if we don't bring back prisoners, the staff would frown on us and doubt out stories." Brigade casualties were remarkably light, less than nine percent. Six prisoners in all were taken. 13th Battalion did not get one, but did so during a small raid the next night, thus all regiments facing 3rd Brigade were identified, this satisfying the primary purpose of the raids.[43]

As February closed additional indications of an early German offensive began to appear. Enemy air activity increased, air photographs revealed new roads and roads under repair behind enemy lines and ammunition dumps were detected forward. Raiding was also affected as this report by 51st (Highland) Division shows:

> It was noticed that the enemy was taking elaborate precautions to avoid any of the trench garrison being captured. Raiding parties either found his outpost line empty or the garrisons withdrew as soon as the raiders approached. His object doubtless was to prevent us from capturing a prisoner and extracting from him information regarding his preparations.[44]

56th Division, however, found that its opponent favoured aggressive precautions. The brigades were urged to do their utmost to secure prisoners, but found that every effort faced an enemy "more than ever on the alert, with parties lying out to catch intruders;" in modern terms, he was

41 LAC, War Diary, 13th Battalion, 'Special Operation Order', and raid report; Fetherstonhaugh, *13th Battalion*, pp. 221-22.
42 LAC, War Diary, 15th Battalion, Operation Order 5 and 'Notes on Raid'; Beattie, *48th Highlanders*, p. 290.
43 LAC, War Diary, 16th Battalion, 'Notes' on raid and 3rd Brigade report; Urquhart, *16th Battalion*, pp. 249-50 and Appendix II, 'Details of Battles and Raids Engaged in by 16th Canadian Battalion'.
44 Bewsher, *Fifty First (Highland) Division*, p. 270.

setting "standing patrols" to wreck "snatch" parties. Several small raids by 2nd British Division in early March produced only one prisoner.[45]

But despite precautions the enemy coughed up prisoners. 12th British Division launched several small raids, two on 1 and 8 March each took one prisoner, and a larger raid, 200 all ranks of the 6th Royal West Kents, made off with nine prisoners, these taken in the enemy support line, the raiders strength allowing deep penetration.[46] On 6 March a unit of 9th (Scottish) Division, raiding in a strength of 45 all ranks, had not a shot fired at it, the reason being the trench was empty. The night before, however, a raiding force of about 300 all ranks of the 16th Royal Fusiliers in penetrating enemy lines more deeply took 15 prisoners, the cost being 11 dead, five missing and 34 wounded. The published history of 2nd British Division refers to several raids in the first half of March, each seeking prisoners or identifications, but only one obtained an identification (epaulettes).[47] Also on the 6th, Lieutenant-Colonel Rasch's 2nd Grenadier Guards raided seeking information about the imminent offensive. The battalion War Diary called this raid north of the Scarpe River the only non-routine event, everything else being devoted to defensive preparations such as improving wire, erecting more wire, digging trenches and reserve units coming forward. As for the raid, at 0240 on the 6th artillery hit the German front line briefly before lifting to the support line and then falling on two other sides of the box. Three parties of raiders, under 50 all ranks, surprised the enemy completely, took two prisoners and withdrew within 10 minutes. The divisional historian declared the raid the only event of importance before the German attack on 21 March. Again, it was a case of the enemy not hanging about: as the raiders reached the enemy front line the Germans could be seen "running in all directions across the top to the support line." On the 9th, 12th British Division had the same experience, the Germans off to the rear as fast as they could go. However, nine stragglers were caught.[48]

The second week of March was much the same: small raids, a platoon or less, lightly-manned enemy front lines, a prisoner or two and while casualties were most often light, they could be costly; for example, during a night raid by the 9th Cameronians (14th British Division) the OC Raid, Major M.H. Forsyth, was killed. He had been acting CO for a brief time before the raid. On the 13th, 4th West Riding Regiment (49th Division) did very well despite coming under persistent "shorts" (18-pounders) coming from the right across the brigade front. This fire had begun even before Zero and caused several casualties, but the raid got on with attacking a pill-box. A bomb pushed through a loophole brought out 37 Germans with three machine-guns, this haul, less one killed by the "shorts," being escorted to battalion lines.[49]

45 Major C.H. Dudley Ward, *The Fifty-Sixth Division 1914-1918* (Uckfield, East Sussex: Naval and Military Press, n.d.), p. 223; Wyrall, *Second Division,* Volume 2, pp. 527-28.

46 Scott, *12th (Eastern) Division,* pp. 164-65.

47 Story, *Cameronians,* p. 198; TNA: WO 95/2554: 113th Brigade, 38th Division and WO 95/2556, 16th Royal Welsh Fusiliers); Wyrall, *Second Division,* Volume 2, p. 529.

48 Ponsonby, *The Grenadier Guards,* Volume II, p. 366: TNA: WO 95/1194: Guards Division, report on raid 5/6 March. Many British Divisions, according to their published divisional histories, did not raid in March or did not report making any raids including the 15th, 17th, 18th, 20th, 23rd, 25th, 29th, 34th, 35th, 36th, 50th and 51st. British War Diary, 6th Royal West Kents, report on raid.

49 TNA: WO 95/1772: 9th Cameronians; WO 95/2798: 4th West Riding Regiment and WO 95/2798: 147th Brigade, reports on raid.

This pattern continued during the week preceding the German offensive: small raids seeking prisoners and/or identifications, little opposition, occasional captures. 169th Brigade of 56th British Division made the most interesting of these raids on 16 March. While it was finely planned, it failed, "hung up by a mass of uncut wire" according to the divisional history. The objective of the raid was a 300-yard stretch of Crab Trench from its junction with Chaff Trench to the junction of Crab Trench and a trail.[50] None of the raiders, three officers and 70 ORs of the London Rifle Brigade, were able to enter the trench it being "closely packed" with defenders. Surprise may have been lost during the time the raiders were forming up forward of the battalion wire or possibly the deception during wire-cutting had failed to deceive the enemy. Captain J.S. Calder, MC, OC Raid, reported the first belt of wire cut to bits, but the second and third belts delayed and disorganized the raiders.[51] Nowhere in the documentation (proposal to raid, brigade training instructions, withdrawal instructions and raid reports) is there any indication that the state of wire was checked by recce at any time before the raid. Wire-cutting had begun on 12 March by divisional artillery, assisted by artillery of a flanking division, by Corps Heavy Artillery and by medium mortars.

It is a shame that the raid failed since with the exception of what seems to have been a lack of determined recce of the wire the planning was thorough. Deception features strongly in the plan especially in regard to wire-cutting where every possible means was implemented to divert enemy attention from the points of entry. It is clear that brigade was closely involved in the planning, even central, so much so that this seems to have marginalized the battalion commander, Major F.H. Wallis, MC. One example of this is the incredibly detailed step-by-step instruction on withdrawal, all the brigade commander's "ideas," that went to Wallis on the 12th. These included a complex and problematical system by which Captain Calder would advise the raiding parties to withdraw. On the 10th Wallis had received an equally lengthy step-by-step instruction specifying not only how he was to train and rehearse the raiders, but also how the raiding parties were to move, not only during the actual raid, but also precisely how they were to reach their assembly position forward of the battalion wire. These instructions came complete with diagrams, the whole leaving nothing to the imagination and little to be done.[52] Such over-direction must have been disheartening, likely leaving Wallis to wonder why he was there.

The "ideas" instructions were signed either by the brigade commander, E.S. Coke, or by his BM, Captain W. Carden Roe. But the ideas were obviously Coke's. True, Wallis was only acting CO, but he was an experienced company commander, the recipient of the MC (August 1916), another in September 1917 and yet another in January 1918! As to results of the raid, no prisoners, 13 wounded and the only gain confirmation that the enemy front line was strongly held and its garrison very much on the alert.[53]

"Some Notes on Raids" which the GSO1 of 19th Division, Lieutenant-Colonel Montgomery, issued to brigades on 15 February 1918 reflects command and control in that division at that

50 Dudley Ward, *Fifty-Sixth Division*, p. 219. Crab Trench had been raided by 47th Division in November 1916 (see MSD 24).

51 TNA: WO 95/2962: London Rifle Brigade, report on attempted raid.

52 *Ibid.*, brigade ideas on withdrawal and training, 10 March.

53 Wallis's awards are in Warrington, *Military Cross Register*, p. 704; Dudley Ward, *Fifty-Six Division*, pp. 3, 140. Coke became GOC 169th Brigade in early 1916 and held command to the Armistice. Roe became BM in June 1917.

time. It should not be supposed that its concept of "Guidance and Supervision by Higher Command" was peculiar to that division:

> Whilst it is very desirable that the plan should conform as far as possible to the wishes of the unit detailed to carry it out, it is at the same time essential that the higher commanders should exercise to the full their functions of guidance and supervision, so as to ensure that no available means are overlooked which might increase the chances of success or diminish the risk of failure.[54]

Of the six pages of Montgomery's Notes, the last three list 20 lessons about raids that applied universally. One would have thought that by this point of the war (February 1918) and the division having been in France for about 30 months, some would not need reiteration, but the fact they are included does suggest doubt and/or concern that they were not yet generally realized within the 19th Division. It was a fact, too, that one had always to think of the officers and men who were new to the division and to combat and required guidance. The most important of the 20 are listed here, additional comment in square brackets:

> Weather. Unless other considerations are paramount a raid should not take place under unfavourable weather conditions.
>
> Wire Cutting. Officers supervising arrangements or participating in the raid should examine the progress of wire cutting in company with battery commanders or FOOs. OC Raid must satisfy himself that gaps are sufficient and report to that effect prior to the raid. [Controversy about what was sufficient had negatively coloured infantry-artillery co-operation and eventually led to agreement that the infantry would determine sufficiency].
>
> Rehearsals. Raiding parties should practise for at least 2 or 3 days, better a week, including careful attention to the formation to be used in the advance.
>
> Assembly. The CO should be present when the raiders assembled before being taken to the front line trench; company commanders likewise when the raid is small.
>
> Landmarks. Raiders who accompany pre-raid patrols should be warned to note the appearance of our own lines when looking back from the enemy lines to pick up landmarks that may be of use.
>
> Compass Bearings. Bearing of the objective should be carefully taken. All officers should be provided with compasses. [Distances between the lines had become greater generally by 1918].

54 TNA: WO 95/2056: 19th Division General Staff, 'Some Notes on Raids', 15 February 1918. Chapter 6 includes a summary of what Montgomery considered were the criteria involved in the selection of the objective of a raid.

Secrecy. Date and Zero should not be disclosed until the last possible moment. A raid must not be referred to on the telephone.

Flank Protection. Lewis guns to cover flanks on reaching enemy lines and during crossing of No Man's Land.

Dug-out Bombing. Dug-outs must where possible be searched prior to destruction and entrances guarded as soon after entering the trench as possible.

Identifications. Some members of raiding parties should be specifically tasked to obtain identifications. In the excitement of fighting this often gets forgotten.[55]

A smaller raid, one officer and 26 men, later that month also failed to take prisoners or secure identifications. It is mentioned here only for the summation by Lieutenant-Colonel S. Rhodes, the CO of the raiding unit: "had the party gone with the bayonet instead of resorting to bombs, a different result might have been obtained." Even at this late stage of the war it seems that the cult of the bomb had not quite released its grip and given way entirely to the rifle and bayonet, which tools had begun to reassert themselves more than a year earlier.[56]

Several Canadian raids were carried out in March, but fewer than in February. On the 6th 21st Battalion (4th Brigade) launched a raid (two officers and 70 ORs) in the Lens area in retaliation for a raid on the 4th during which the enemy, 280 strong, penetrated Canadian lines, killed four men and wounded 38, including two officers, before being driven out, two of their wounded left behind. The retaliation did not get all the revenge that was desired. Only "slight" resistance met the raiders, one prisoner nabbed and 13 Germans killed. Casualties came to two killed and 10 wounded. The OC Raid, Lieutenant Arthur May, received a Bar to his MC, the prisoner being personally taken by him and five enemy falling to his revolver.[57] Six days later 7th and 10th Battalions (1st Division) made two simultaneous night raids in the Lens area, each battalion fielding about 70 all ranks, the purposes of both raids being prisoners and/or identifications. Raid "A" (7th Battalion) on the left of the objective followed the barrage immediately as it lifted from the enemy front line. The wire having been well cut one group of its northern (left) party began clearing the trench to the left boundary of the objective area. An enemy machine-gun that had put some fire onto the entry point retired quickly as the raiders progressed. One German was killed and one captured. A second group, which entered the trench just behind the first turned right. No enemy were encountered as the group worked along blowing up dug-outs. As planned, it met the left party of the southern group. Its right hand party on entry met no enemy. Withdrawal began at 2120 after 20 minutes in the trench. 10th Battalion raiders on the right fared similarly,

55 TNA: WO 95/2056: 19th Division General Staff, 'Some Notes on Raids'.
56 TNA: WO 95/2804: 49th Division, CO's report on raid by 5th York and Lancaster Regiment, 25 March 1918.
57 LAC, War Diaries, 21st Battalion and 4th Brigade. Brigade made only one change to the plan, increasing raiding strength from 40 to 70 based on an assessment that 40 would not be enough to deal with the probable garrison at the objective, an assessment that proved erroneous.

killing five Germans and capturing one. Raider casualties included one officer and one OR killed and one officer and eight ORs wounded.[58]

The most successful Canadian raiders in March were the five officers and 151 ORs of 5CMR (3rd Division). Their raid, two miles southeast of Mericourt, began at 0530 on the 15th. The battalion's proposal for a raid had been accepted two weeks earlier whereupon preparations began immediately including training under the OC Raid, Major Thomas Sneath, MC. This raid is interesting for a number of reasons. First, the CO of 5CMR, Lieutenant-Colonel Draper, decided not to take a rifle company, asking instead for volunteers, both officers and men, and then selected the raiders from the volunteers. At this stage of the war most Canadian battalions preferred to raid with established companies and platoons, the latter having become the "unit" of assault and known commanders being a fundamental advantage of that fact. Second, the raiders would have a long way to go, it being 700 yards to the chosen assembly positions and 200 yards more to enemy lines. Careful movement and silence would be critical. Third, very thorough pre-raid recce was insisted upon right from the time of the selection of objectives, which had been determined by careful monitoring of enemy wire, gaps and locations of machine-guns and confirmation by a patrol that the enemy manned the outpost line. Enemy wire had been seen to consist of an outer band of concertina with five gaps and an inner barbed wire belt with two gaps. Recce continued right up to Zero day and into the evening of the raid when an officer's patrol went out to check wire. On return it reported finding the wire unchanged, not strengthened in any way and "not much of an obstacle." This patrol then went out again, this time "sweeping No Man's Land … for the purpose of denying [it] to the enemy until the raiders were complete in their assembly position at 0445." A patrol by the neighbouring battalion did encounter an enemy patrol, but it did not move far enough to the south to come into contact with 5CMR. Finally, the organization of the raiders indicated careful thought. Each of the three parties was divided into a number of sections, the number corresponding to the number of specific tasks of each party and the strength of each section tailored to its task. This was one reason why Draper had decided not to take an established company. Each party and each section were allocated to a specific gap in the wire depending on their tasks and on enemy locations. Careful writing of the organization in 5CMR's Operation Order and in training ensured that every participant knew how he was to move and where and what his tasks was. Prior to the raiding parties leaving the assembly position, left and right flanking parties, each of 20 ORs under an officer, established positions in order to provide cover on the withdrawal, plus guides to ensure direction was maintained. 5CMR described the artillery and machine-gun barrages that erupted at Zero as splendid.

The raid itself, in the opinion of the participants, met "feeble' opposition, some parties meeting no enemy at all. In all, 19 prisoners were taken. Casualties were one officer and four ORs killed and 22 wounded. Sadly, the officer killed was Major Sneath, a matter of great regret to battalion and brigade alike.[59]

April was not as a whole a raiding month for most British Divisions, which is not surprising given the start of the German offensive that began at dawn on 21 March. The problem became not so much identification of what was in front, but how to stop it, or at least wear it down.

58 LAC, War Diaries, 2nd Brigade, 7th and 10th Battalions, reports on raids; Dancocks, *Gallant Canadians*, p. 159.

59 LAC, War Diary, 5CMR, Operation Order 95 and CO's report.

However, First Army in which the Canadian Corps was for a time, was outside the German line of march. The four Canadian division commanders expected brigades, as GOC 4th Division, David Watson, put it, "to make every effort to secure identifications."[60] Watson's 10th and 11th Brigades raided several times during the first half of April.

The first of these occurred on the 3rd when a small party, one officers and 30 ORs, of 54th Battalion (11th Brigade) made a stealth raid during which three prisoners were taken. While it did not raid again that month the 54th conducted numerous patrols. On the 9th "in accordance with the division commander's wishes" three platoons from each of the 87th and 102nd Battalions, 11th Brigade, raided the enemy, Zero at 0500 on the 10th. One party of the 87th found the objective deserted, this a surprise since the area had been closely observed for several days and had seemed to be constantly occupied. The other party, which was soon joined by the first one, found the enemy rapidly retiring and a running bombing fight ensured during which an officer and an NCO were reported missing. No prisoners or identifications were secured, this due to overzealousness to kill. The battalion commander thought the unsatisfactory result "taught us several very good lessons, the main one being the inferiority of the bomb to the rifle and bayonet during such an operation." Canadians, too, were slow to abandon the cult of the bomb. The 102nd found its objective heavily manned. Delay in entering the trench due to difficulty locating gaps in the wire ate heavily into the time allotted and when the withdrawal signal sounded one party of the 102nd had not taken any prisoners. The other party, which experienced considerably more fighting, did take 10.[61] Finally, on the 9th the 46th and 47th Battalions, one company each, made a joint raid. The 46th met no opposition. 47th Battalion had "a good scrap" briefly, but their opponents broke off and ran rearward. The only prisoner fell victim to artillery during the return to battalion lines.[62]

A joint raid in April by 14th and 16th Battalions merits mention since it was, as Hugh Urquhart said, the most successful raid ever done by the 16th.[63] On 25 April, three days before the raid, George Tuxford, GOC 3rd Brigade, had proposed it to HQ 1st Division, beginning with a description of the difficulties attending a raid in the Gavrelle sector. First, no man's land in that area being very wide, ranging from 500 to 1,400 yards, a daylight raid was precluded since it would make a clean withdrawal problematic. Consequently, he had decided upon 0100 as Zero, a time that granted the assault and the withdrawal the cloak of darkness. Second, distance also meant that the assembly position would have to be close to the enemy outpost line. If the raiders were to avoid detection the greatest care would have to be taken. Third, it was known that the enemy held a main line with an outpost line in front and, as usual, the outpost line would withdraw immediately the posts were approached in strength in order to warn the main line garrison. Protecting the outpost line were three belts of wire which would be cut manually. Finally, wire also featured between the first objective, the enemy front line, and the support line, the final objective. Tuxford planned a two-battalion raid on a 500 yard front, 16th Battalion left, 14th Battalion right, each to provide not less than 100 all ranks.

60 LAC, War Diary, 11th Brigade, 1 April 1918.
61 LAC, War Diaries, 54th, 87th and 102nd Battalions. The missing of the 87th returned later.
62 LAC, War Diaries, 46th and 47th Battalions. The 46th raided the same area on 22 April. The raid failed due to the high state of alert of the Germans and the presence of a working party.
63 Urquhart, *16th Battalion*, p. 258.

About 50 guns (18-pounders) and 18 4.5-inch howitzers would cover the whole of the brigade front (1,500 yards) concentrating on the objective, but circumspectly so as not to draw attention to the area. The preliminary barrage would remain on the enemy front line from Zero to Zero plus 10 during which time the raiders would close up tight to the barrage and rush the outposts. As always, Tuxford was innovative: "I intend trying the effect of rifle grenades filled with lachrymatory gas during the preliminary bombardment … which may induce the enemy to put on his gas masks." Experiments by his staff obtained good results with this. The howitzers would switch fire to selected targets at Zero plus five. At Zero plus 10 guns and howitzers would lift to the support line. Stokes and medium mortars would also shoot at selected targets. Heavy artillery would focus on counter-battery. Afterward the 14th Battalion's historian described the preliminary barrage as so accurate the raiders "leaned on it," many calling it the best they had ever seen. At Zero plus 30 the barrage would form a box. Ten minutes later withdrawal would begin.[64]

Two days later Tuxford issued an amendment in consequence of recce by Captain James Scroggie who would lead the 16th Battalion raiders. Scroggie had observed that an enemy working party engaged in digging a trench on the outpost line was already two feet down, a machine-gun providing cover, and the men digging as fast as they could go. Tuxford then pronounced the new trench the first objective and the front line the second, dropping the support line as an objective. At Zero the artillery would hammer the front line for 20 minutes and then place the box barrage. The infantry at zero would fire one rifle grenade per man, 120 in all on the new trench and immediately rush it, having 20 minutes in which to do so, then go to ground under cover of the barrage before it shifted.[65]

Captain Scroggie, 16th Battalion, organized his eight officers and 150 ORs, including two Lewis gun teams, into three parties and a small reserve. Party "B" (five and 103 and the Lewis guns) would assault the first objective. Party "C" (two officers and 19 ORs) and Party "D" (one officer and 16 ORs) were to clear two outposts that could, were they to survive, adversely affect the withdrawal. Also, the assaults on these two posts, which were about 500 yards from the primary raiding party ("B"), would serve as a diversion. Lieutenant John Patterson, OC 14th Battalion raiders, organized his men into six parties since his objectives were somewhat more involved. "A" and "B" Groups, each of an officer and 25 men and a Lewis gun, would mop up enemy posts and then enter the trench as soon as the barrage lifted. There the two Groups would destroy dug-outs that had been marked on a chart Patterson would carry and also establish a block with a Lewis gun on the right (southern) flank. "C" Group, one officer and 20 men, would provide two covering parties to support other groups as necessary, and prepare to receive wounded and prisoners. "D" and "E" Groups, one officer and 10 men each, would tackle enemy blocks on CTs and destroy a suspected large dug-out and post. "F" Group, one officer and 25 men plus a Lewis gun, would be in reserve.[66]

"A" Group, Lieutenant B.A. Neville, had no difficulty with the posts, but on entering the trench met strong opposition led by an officer. When he was killed the enemy wilted. Three

64 LAC, War Diary, 3rd Brigade. All documentation for this raid is at Appendix 26: plan and amendments, brigade and battalion orders, artillery orders, diary of events and reports by brigade and the battalions. Fetherstonhaugh, *14th Battalion,* p. 206.

65 LAC, War Diary, 3rd Brigade amended plan.

66 LAC, War Diaries, 14th and 16th Battalion Operation Orders.

dug-outs were blown up. An enemy counter-attack came rapidly to ruin, bombs finishing off the attackers less two who surrendered. "B" Group, Lieutenant H.E. Beckett, had a very similar experience. A machine-gun crew trying to get into action was bombed, the crew being killed personally by Beckett. "C" Group, Lieutenant G. Beattie, joined in the "general free for all." Lieutenant R.G. Allen and his "D" Group met strong opposition at the CT blocks, but prevailed, capturing several prisoners plus a machine-gun. "E" Group under Lieutenant G.B. McKean had the hardest fight, so hard that three times the party had to send for more bombs. McKean so distinguished himself, his bravery instrumental in defeat of the enemy, that he was recommended for and received the VC. His actions were described in Chapter 6. "F" Group, Lieutenant S.J. McEwen, played a significant role in the successes of "D" and "E" Groups. Each of the six Group commanders killed at least one German. In all, 24 prisoners and two machine-guns were seized. Casualties were very light: two ORs killed, one accidentally, and 11 wounded.[67]

Three MCs were awarded: Lieutenants Neville, Allan and McEwen. Lieutenant McKean's citation for the VC read: "This officer's bravery and dash undoubtedly saved many lives for had this position not been captured the raiding party would have been exposed to dangerous enfilade fire during the withdrawal."[68]

Captain Scroggie and his 16th Battalion raiders of Party "C" had the misfortune early on to be hit with some "shorts" during the preliminary bombardment, but they rushed the outpost line only to find the occupants gone. Both officers with the party were wounded. Party "D" was hit by heavy machine-gun fire, but reached the gun, its crew abandoning it as the raiders were nearly on top of them. The officer commanding this party was killed. Party "B" was discovered early by the enemy, but held on despite heavy enemy fire and at Zero rushed forward to their objective, securing it and receiving the other parties as they arrived. The take during the raid was 28 prisoners and three machine-guns. Casualties totalled 10. Scroggie and Lieutenants A.M. MacLennan and J.A. Tuxford received the MC.[69]

In all, 52 prisoners, including one officer, were taken and as many as 80 Germans were killed. The enemy had fought well under their officers, but lost heart when they were killed. Tuxford noted that rifle grenades had been very effective. He thought Scroggie's thorough planning has spelled success. The artillery had played a major part in this, Tuxford echoing what one raider said about the guns; their fire was like "a knife sharp and even." Hugh Urquhart, 16th Battalion's historian, gave a lot of the credit to recce: every one of the officers on the raid had been out on patrols before it and all NCOs and one-third of the raiders had been taken out to the assembly area where their objectives were pointed out. Urquhart also praises Scroggie, his plan such that it deserved success.[70]

Thus ended the last April in this war. Much had changed in times past when it came to raiding. In the half-year that remained more raids would be executed, more challenges would be faced and more changes would bring more adjustments. These are the subject of the next chapter.

67 LAC, War Diary, 14th Battalion report on raid; Fetherstonhaugh, *14th Battalion,* pp. 206-209; "Murray, 'Raids', p. 338.
68 Bishop, *Our Bravest and Our Best,* p. 87.
69 LAC, War Diary, 16th Battalion, report on raid. Scroggie took command of the 16th in early 1919.
70 LAC, War Diary, 3rd Brigade report; Urquhart, *16th Battalion,* p. 258.

16

To The Armistice

> Be sure – be sure, we're going to do some splendid things.
> Rudyard Kipling. "Road-Song of the Bander-Log"

On 21 March the Germans commenced their massive offensive. It was to continue virtually non-stop until the end of April:

> On the 4th and 5th the enemy made a final effort to prevent the French and British line becoming stable. The principal attack … was made south of the Somme, and involved the whole of the British front between the river and where we joined the French, and also the French on our right.

On the front from Lens to Armentieres the British First and Second Armies became heavily engaged. In the Lys battle prior to the end of April the enemy wagered 42 divisions against 25 British divisions. In the six weeks from 21 March to 30 April 55 British infantry divisions and three cavalry divisions faced 109 different German Divisions.[1] Given the situation Canadian Divisions for a time would be deployed on a divisional rather than on a Corps basis. This began on 23 March when GHQ ordered 1st Canadian Division into First Army Reserve and 2nd Canadian Division into GHQ Reserve. Four days later 3rd Canadian Division was re-allocated to XIII Corps and 4th Canadian Division went into GHQ Reserve. That same day 1st Division was allocated to XVII Corps and 2nd Division to VI Corps in the Neuville-Vitasse sector. On 30 March 3rd and 4th Divisions returned to the Canadian Corps, likewise the 1st Division on 8 April, but it would be the end of June before 2nd Division rejoined the Corps, just in time to enjoy the 1 July Dominion Day celebrations at Tinques.

Once the offensive had run its course normal trench warfare resumed: sniping, shelling, occasional local attacks and, of course, patrolling and raiding, the latter as always seeking prisoners and/or identifications. Such activities would be the norm in May and June, followed by a pair of months preparing and executing the return volley, the Amiens offensive, and then late summer during which something similar to raiding, but with a twist, would resume.

1 Boraston, *Haig's Despatches,* pp. 215, 220, 235.

In early May 56th British Division held a sector immediately north of the Arras-Cambrai road. On the 4th the new GOC, Major-General Sir Amyatt Hull, arrived. He, like every General, wished to know who the enemy was and what he was doing, or was going to do. After 10 days study of his sector Hull ordered a "whole series" of raids, at the end of which the Germans, according to the divisional historian, raised a board above their line on which was chalked "Please don't raid us any more!"[2]

One of the first in Hull's series was a small raid by 8th Middlesex that identified the just arrived division opposite the 56th. Six days later 7th Middlesex, also of 167th Brigade, encountered strong enemy posts covering large working parties wiring their front and working at something in front of the wire. This news drew an immediate demand for a raid as soon as possible. The usual pre-raid activities commenced forthwith, objective selection and planning, recce and training being the focus. On the 25th the two units that would raid – it had become a joint raid – received the brigade Operation Order and prepared their own from it. Zero day was set as the 28th.[3]

The raiders consisted of a right and a left assault group, the former consisting of two platoons of the 1st London Regiment under Lieutenant Bernard Preedy and the latter three platoons of the 7th Middlesex under Captain Duncan Shiell, MC. The Londoners' effort had mixed results. Their right platoon found enemy wire well cut, the trench almost obliterated and full of dead, the only live enemy heading rapidly to the rear before the platoon entered their line. However, the platoon commander then advanced his party beyond the objective where his men killed several Germans. The other platoon suffered a loss of direction due, it seemed, to the fact that the enemy trench that was its objective did not run across the line of attack. The brigade report noted considerable difficulty in tracing the movement of this platoon. Its commander had been killed very soon after the raid began. Some of the platoon did enter the trench, but how far they got beyond it could not be accurately plotted, nor did a link-up with the 7th Middlesex occur. Here, too, most of the enemy quickly withdrew, no prisoners being secured. Casualties included one officer and one OR killed, plus 11 wounded.

The left assault group, the 7th Middlesex, met with stronger opposition. The right platoon took out a machine-gun, but could not overcome the enemy. Less opposition faced the centre platoon since many of the enemy were withdrawing. One prisoner was taken. On the left the third platoon had to deal with strong enemy parties firing from shellholes. Once in the trench the raiders moved up a CT where they became heavily engaged in bombing fights. In one area 10 prisoners were only briefly a prize since they were all killed by another party that did not realize that they had surrendered. Casualties totalled one man missing and 23 wounded, testimony to the harder fight the men of the 7th had.[4]

Both groups of raiders praised the artillery fire that had cut the wire so well and so severely damaged enemy trenches. All the fire being enfilade, the raiders could get very close to it and reached the objective before many of the enemy were prepared. The divisional historian thought the raid "somewhat ambitious," but did not elaborate.[5] Fortunately, the brigade report is comprehensive. First, the raid encompassed a thousand-yard front and aimed to penetrate to a depth of

2 Dudley Ward, *Fifty-Sixth Division,* p. 249.
3 TNA: WO 95/2948: 167th Brigade, Operation Order 213 and brigade report.
4 *Ibid.*
5 Dudley Ward, *Fifty-Sixth Division,* p. 249.

300 yards. Second, a Zero hour at 2300 meant "none too much light," this making matters more difficult for a raiding force of mostly "officers and men [going] over for the first time." Third, the raiders had "no opportunity of practising the raid out of the line," an omission not explained and surprising since three days stood between receipt of the brigade Operation Order and Zero day. Fourth, given the wide frontage, and the patrols that reported the presence of strong enemy working parties, the strength of the raiding force seems inadequate. The raid report notes "numbers of the enemy ... were much more than was anticipated" and the division historian writes of long stretches of the enemy lines north of the road being "packed." Brigade also thought the withdrawal "perfectly" executed, but the question of the efficacy of the signal to withdraw had been "as difficult as ever." However, none of the platoons complained of any difficulties during the withdrawal.[6] Despite the somewhat disappointing results – one prisoner – the brigade report and the postwar divisional history called the raid a success. Claims of 200 enemy casualties could not be confirmed and were, no doubt, exaggerated. Raider casualties included two officers killed and two wounded, two ORs killed and 49 wounded. The profit is debatable.

Four days earlier 18th Brigade of 6th British Division had made a similar sized raid southeast of Ypres. The unit involved, 2nd Durham Light Infantry, Lieutenant-Colonel D.L. Brereton, DSO, raided with two companies, right assault five officers and 77 ORs of Captain R. Hazlett's A Company, and left assault an identical number of Captain C.G. Handcock's C Company. Zero was set for midnight. Of Hazlett's three platoons, 2 Platoon on reaching the objective found no enemy whereupon the platoon commander took his platoon straight to 1 Platoon's objective. That objective also being unmanned all three platoons then proceeded to 3 Platoon's objective, a large pill-box, well-wired in and occupied. A bomb wounded all six occupants, but as entry was being made the raiders suddenly found themselves under attack by a second enemy party. Once this was repulsed the six wounded enemy were escorted to battalion lines. Hazlett on moving further northeast encountered an outpost, the four occupants being surprised and captured, raising the catch to 10. Losses were negligible. Two of Handcock's platoons assigned to take a farm building had a rougher time on encountering about 20 enemy, who were dispersed, six prisoners being captured. Movement beyond the farm buildings ceased, however, when it became obvious that raider strength was insufficient to contend with a strongly held complex. Total raider casualties were only three wounded and two missing. All 16 prisoners made it to battalion lines.[7]

Battalion and brigade reports on the raid commended the officers for their initiative in going beyond their objectives to get prisoners. The GOC did not explain why the raiders had not practised on taped ground. Moreover, "officers and men had little opportunity of discovering each other's worth," a reference to the casualties taken during the German offensive and the many new reinforcements. Major-General T.O. Marden, GOC 6th Division, thought the success of the raid largely due to careful recce during a two-week period before the raid, but gives no details as to how frequent recce was and at what times the enemy trenches appeared manned. The report also noted that this was the first experience the battalion commander had of organizing a raid on a larger scale. Without anything more this comment is rather ambiguous. In passing on the remarks of the Corps Commander on 23 May the BGGS praised all the arrangements that had

6 *Ibid.*, p. 250; TNA: WO 95/2948: 167th Brigade, report on raid.
7 TNA: WO 95/1615: 18th Brigade, Durhams Operation Order 2 and raid report.

been made for the raid. A day earlier he had forwarded other Corps Commander comments to all division commanders in II Corps including Marden, ones that would not have pleased him and which, no doubt, became the subject of discussion with his GSO1, Lieutenant-Colonel T.T. Grove. The BGGS began by saying that while the Corps Commander had no wish to discourage division commanders from acting on their own initiative when favourable opportunities arose, there had to be a preamble:

> When such operations are contemplated he wishes in all cases to be informed either verbally or in writing of the scope, place and time of the operation. II Corps has to warn Corps on the flanks … when any minor operation such as a raid is contemplated which may cause abnormal artillery fire and this cannot be done unless information … is received from Divisions.
>
> Similarly, Divisions must invariably inform Divisions on their flanks of any proposed operation, which is likely to cause abnormal artillery fire or affect flank formations in any way.
>
> Further, if for any minor operation, Division Commanders arrange to give artillery assistance to, or get artillery assistance from, the Divisions on their flanks, the Corps Commander wishes to be informed of the arrangements.

Red hat bands, red tabs and red faces here, but it had been a long war and senior HQs and senior staffs do make mistakes. All Marden could do in reply was express his regrets.[8]

One of the first Canadian raids in May came on the 3rd when 28th and 31st Battalions of 6th Brigade (2nd Division) raided near Mercatel on the Arras-Bapaume Road (see MSD 26, Neuville-Vitasse). Two officers and 45 ORs of 31st Battalion struck at an enemy outpost separate from and to the left of the primary objective area. The intent was diversion and in this it achieved some success. On reaching the post the raiders under Lieutenant G.A. Cunliffe found it unoccupied. On moving down the trench two men were slightly wounded by a booby trap. When it detonated enemy artillery immediately placed a box barrage around the outpost. This lasted only briefly and the raiding party withdrew, no attempt to hinder them being made.[9]

For the main raid 28th Battalion had two objectives, the first being the outpost line on the Arras-Baupaume Road and the second the close support positions 100-150 yards to the enemy rear. Three platoons of B Company under Captain Reginald Blackburn, MC, formed the right assault company and three platoons of D Company under Captain Harry Salmon, MC, formed the left assault company, the total frontage being 600 yards.[10] Both companies were to advance in two waves, two platoons in the first and one in the second, the waves not of conventional lines, but of loose sections or "blobs." The first wave would go directly through to

8 *Ibid.*, 6th Division, correspondence on the raid 21-24 May.
9 LAC, War Diary, 31st Battalion and 6th Brigade reports on raid.
10 LAC, War Diary, 6th Brigade, Instructions for Minor Operation, 2 May; Calder, *28th (Northwest) Battalion*, p. 161. As a Lieutenant and platoon commander Salmon had been severely wounded on the Somme in September 1916. Every survivor of his platoon signed a letter to the battalion commander requesting that Salmon's gallantry be recognized. He subsequently received the MC. He received a Bar to it in January 1918. During the Second World War he commanded 7th Brigade and then 3rd Division.

the second objective, the second wave following up to the first objective acting as moppers up and taking responsibility for escorting prisoners and evacuating wounded.[11] Considering that it was 800 yards to the first objective and the second another 150 beyond that, and the jumping off position would be 500-600 yards in front of the battalion front line, aggressive pre-raid patrolling reached right up to the enemy outpost line. The night before the raid the Battalion Scout Officer, Lieutenant J. Bell, and party, while taping the jumping off line, had established a screen of scouts to prevent any enemy patrols chancing upon the preparations.[12] Timing would be crucial given the light conditions, the size of the raiding force, the distance involved and the difficulty of evacuating casualties. To ensure all would be completed before daylight Zero was set at 0230. Given the narrow time window and the circumstances raid leaders realized that the raid "was attended by no small difficulties."[13]

Blackburn's company on the right met only light resistance, the enemy having largely withdrawn when the barrage opened. The enemy outpost line, which had suffered severely from the barrage, offered no fight: "great difficulty catching up to the enemy who ran from their shell hole positions." Four machine-guns, two light and two heavy, were captured along with nine prisoners. Blackburn, an officer who had seen a lot of fighting, personally killed two Germans and reported that he had never "seen (proportionally) so many dead." Most had been killed by artillery, perhaps 100 or so in all.[14] Salmon's company on the left met "a great deal of resistance," a bomb and fire fight ensuing and halting the left of the company assault until one platoon got in behind the enemy trench. Another platoon went quickly through to the second objective there taking one prisoner and a machine-gun. Withdrawal began soon after and by 0315 all the raiders had cleared through a check point. 28th Battalion casualties were four killed and 42 wounded, mostly walking cases.

The GOC 6th Brigade, A.H. Bell, expressed his satisfaction with the raid in a personal letter to the CO of the 28th, Lieutenant-Colonel Alexander Ross, DSO, crediting the success of the raid to "careful organization."[15] The instructions and orders for the raid give every indication of the most thorough planning throughout with special attention to the withdrawal, which was always an awkward time. Battalion instructions for the raid reiterated guidance regarding weapons: "in the actual attack only the rifle and bayonet should be used … bombs [only] for driving the enemy from dug-outs." The brigade report in referring to use of the rifle noted the "great tendency on the part of men who had not been over the top before to stop and fire on them [the retreating enemy] which no doubt deprived us of many more prisoners."[16] As always, no matter how good the training only experience could validate it.[17]

11 LAC, War Diary, 6th Brigade. The assault was in accordance with *WO 3995 The Organization of an Infantry Battalion and The Normal Formation for the Attack* in that the first wave was to go to the furthest objective, but the "blobs" referred to were a refinement for the raid.

12 LAC, War Diary 6th Brigade, report on raid; 28th Battalion War Diary, entry for 2 May.

13 *Ibid.*

14 *Ibid.*

15 LAC, War Diary, 28th Battalion, Appendix to battalion report on raid.

16 LAC, War Diary, 28th Battalion, report on raid; *WO 3995 The Organization of an Infantry Battalion and The Normal Formation for the Attack,* Amendment, Section 7, sub-paragraph (d), p. 3: "the rifle and the bayonet is the first and the hand grenade the second weapon of every soldier."

17 *SS 152 Instructions for the Training of the British Armies in France (Provisional)* (London: HMSO, June 1917). During recruit training, which had been reduced to 14 weeks, a step that made a gradual

About three weeks later 31st Battalion had centre stage. The raid it would launch would prove more challenging because the objective would be Neuville Vitasse which 5th Brigade had raided on 7 May. At that time only half of the 11 officers and 219 ORs of 25th Battalion had crossed through enemy wire and that half found the trenches empty. Only two prisoners were taken. 5th Brigade blamed the weather for these meagre results which leaves one to think that a postponement would have been better. But when recce on 18 May of the front directly opposite the village identified it as a good target, preparations for another raid began. The night chosen for the raid by 31st Battalion was 21/22 May. B Company and C Company under, respectively, Captain David Robertson and Captain Herbert Norris, DSO, would execute the raid. Raid "A" under Norris would attack the southwest part of the village. Raid "B" and sappers under Robertson would assault the centre of the village on a 300 yard front. The final objective for both would be the major street running north-south along the eastern edge of the village (see MSD 26). The attack would be supported by a creeping barrage of 18-pounders, three lifts being made. Selected targets would be left to 4.5-inch and 6-inch howitzers and Stokes and machine-guns. On the 19th the two companies left the line to commence training on a taped course, training continuing on the 20th. That night 6-inch howitzers began wire-cutting.[18]

During the night of the 21st the raiding parties moved to assembly positions opposite the village, pausing briefly there and then moving forward into jumping off positions, all being in place just after midnight. Zero was set for 0045. Robertson had organized his "B" raiders, four officers and 115 men, into two waves, two platoons in the first and one platoon, plus scouts and sappers in the second. The first wave would go directly to the final objective followed by the second wave acting as moppers up. On sighting the first wave, the enemy fell back to a position about midway between the two objectives, their stand there brief, the raiders, in bouncing them out, killed five and captured five others, and then pushed on quickly to the second objective. There sappers destroyed the observation post and dug-out that had been one of the purposes of the raid. Robertson then took his men and the prisoners back to battalion lines.[19]

The "A" raiders under Captain Norris, three officers and 104 ORs, had, as the battalion history says, "more spectacular and comprehensive" tasks. Consequently, Norris had formed five parties, each assigned specific tasks:

> Number One. Lieutenant J. O'Hara and 25 ORs. Rush up the south arm of the "U" road to the main east-west road, establish a block at that junction and then clean-up dug-outs and shelters south of the "U" road.

decline in standards inevitable, 155 hours were spent on musketry, giving the subject the largest slice of the training hours available. In *Training in Canadian Reserve Battalions* (London: Harrison And Sons, January and October 1917) musketry also consumed the largest part of the curriculum. For more information on training see Radley, *We Lead Others Follow.*

18 LAC, War Diaries, 5th Brigade report on raid 7 May; 6th Brigade, instructions for raid and Operation Order 257; 31st Battalion, entries for 18 and 20 May; Riddle and Mitchell, *The Distinguished Service Order.* The then Lieutenant Norris was awarded the DSO in December 1916: "The officers of the battalion having become casualties he took command and under very heavy fire organized and consolidated the position. He displayed high qualities of initiative and command."

19 LAC, War Diary, 6th Brigade, 20 May; Singer, *31st Battalion,* pp. 313-14.

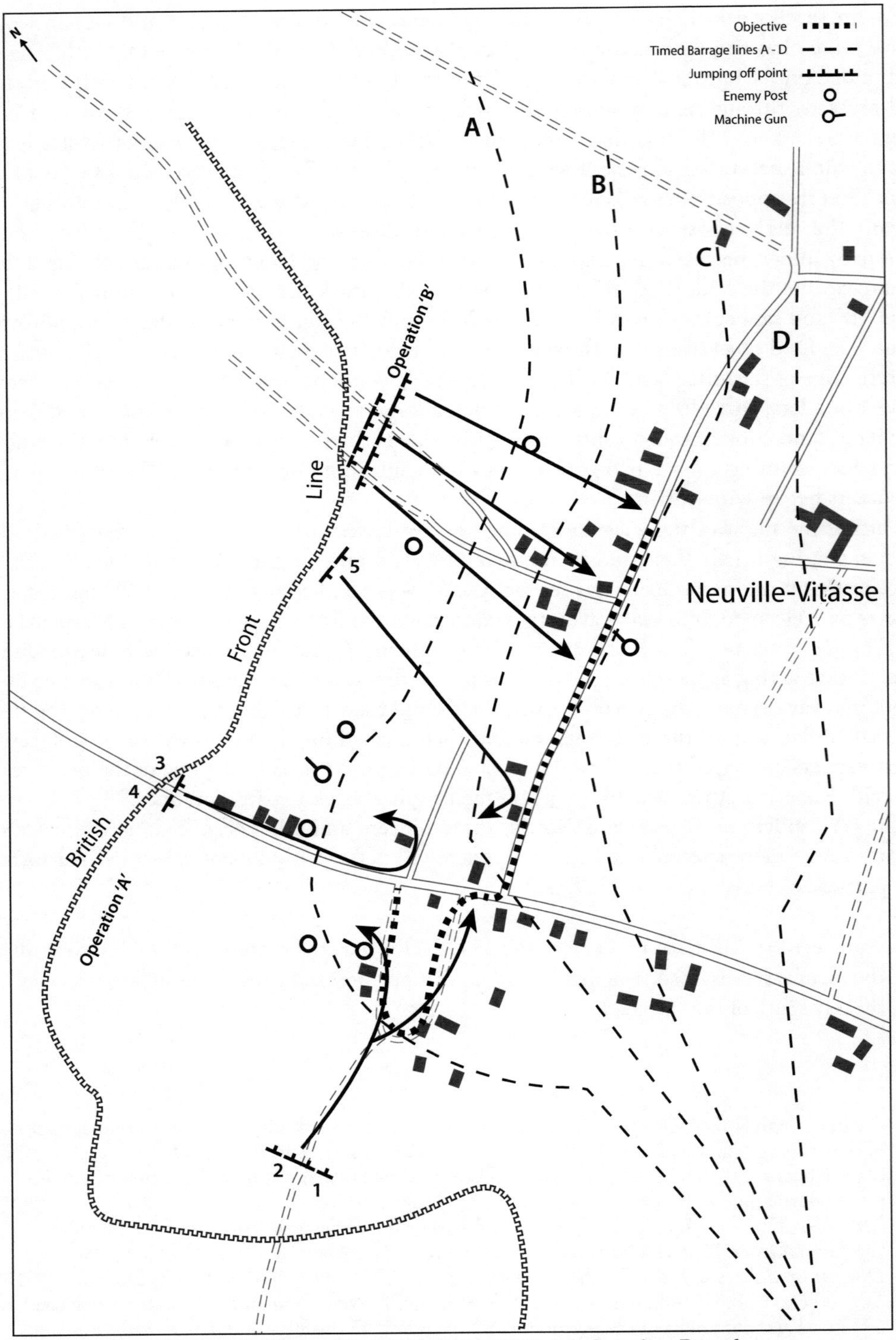

26 Neuville-Vitasse Raid, 21/22 May 1918, 6th Canadian Brigade.

Number Two. NCO and 15 men. Rush up the north arm of the "U" and clear north of the "U" and west of the main road.

Number Three. NCO and 12 men. Rush up both sides of the main road clearing posts and barriers so Number Four can go through to its target. Then follow Number Four and clear the orchard.

Number Four. Captain W. Graham and 25 men. Follow Three, turn left at junction and to orchard to mop up.

Number Five. Lieutenant W.T. Bannan and 25 ORs. Cross the open area to main street and deal with any works adjoining the road.[20]

Of the five parties, the three largest were commanded by an officer. Add Captain Norris and that represents the employment on the raid of four of a company's six officers. The two not involved were the company commander, a Major (officers of this rank did not normally or routinely command actual assault parties during raids) and one Subaltern who would not have been available since each company had to have a Duty Officer in the trenches at all times, or he may have been absent on other duties. This is why two of the parties on the raid, the smallest ones, are commanded by NCOs. For further discussion on the employment of officers and NCOs on raids see Chapter 7, specifically the text starting at footnote 10, which highlights how inadequate research caused one author to make assertions he cannot substantiate or defend.

The two parties assaulting from the southwest (No. 1 and No. 2) met very strong opposition including cross machine-gun fire from posts north and south of the junction of the "U" road and the main street. New wire across the junction covered a barrier which proved extremely difficult to surmount. Repeated attempts put Lieutenant O'Hara and a few men over it, but they were very soon forced out. The two parties could get no further. Parties 3 and 4 proceeded along the main east-west road, the first eliminating an enemy post after hand-to-hand fighting and the second then continuing along that road. A prize of 10 francs had been offered for prisoners. Private Mitchell, having collared one of the two prisoners, loudly stated his claim: "My name is Mitchell and the 10 francs is mine." As the party moved on a bombing attack caused several casualties including Captain Graham. When it became clear that a large enemy party had gained their rear, and would soon cut the party off, the NCO who had taken command of No. 4 wisely ordered withdrawal. In the meantime, No. 5 Party had reached its objective, discovering on the way a new trench parallel to the main north-south street and north of the east-west road. As the party moved past this this trench suddenly an enemy group erupted from it, but before they could engage a Lewis gun virtually gutted the party. On looking into the trench Lieutenant Bannan saw more Germans lying in it. They did not respond to commands and were shot. Two were taken prisoner. Bannan then ordered withdrawal, which had to be shell hole to shell hole due to enemy fire. Parties 3 and 4 also had a difficult time during their withdrawal. Nevertheless, all parties, their casualties and 11 prisoners, got clear and returned to battalion lines. Casualties included six men killed, two missing (believed killed) and 38 wounded. Of the

20 Singer, *31st Battalion*, p. 314; LAC, War Diary, 31st Battalion, Operation Order 252.

two officers wounded, Captain Graham later died. Battalion and brigade reports indicate that fighting during the raid was savage, the Germans appearing determined to punish the raiders severely. The prisoners had yielded only grudgingly after stubborn and protracted resistance.[21]

Other Canadian raids during May were mostly smaller in size and scope and none warranting more than mention, if that, in battalion histories. This is not to say that such minor enterprises were unimportant for they kept the pressure on and along with losses there were some gains. In many of these "ordinary" raids it is striking how often good recce got credit for success. Some of these raids were strictly "in-house," too. On 26 May, for example, three officers and 49 ORs of 24th Battalion (5th Brigade) raided enemy posts along the Arras-Baupaume road. As it was a stealth raid no fire support was involved, nor was any deception arranged. Planning was sound, all going smoothly, three Germans were captured and perhaps 20 killed; in short, a raid well-executed, the result of training and years of experience of what raids entailed and demanded of participants. A raid the next day by 22nd Battalion, also 5th Brigade, two officers and 41 ORs, while involving "outsiders" – artillery, mortars and machine-guns – ended in similar fashion: three prisoners, 20 or so enemy dead, in all, a classic "smack and back." It could even be said at this stage of the war that success was "usual" and expected; otherwise, scarcely concealed disappointment arose.[22]

In June the area opposite Beaumont Hamel (MSD 27) saw V Corps (C.D. Shute) make the largest British raid during that month. 50th Brigade, Brigadier-General G. Gwyn-Thomas, of P.R. Robertson's 17th Division put more than 1,000 all ranks into the enterprise, 18 officers and 500 ORs from each of the 7th East Yorkshires and the 6th Dorsetshires. While successful, this raid is notable not only for its size, but for the casualties (23 percent), and for another example of Shute's continuing "hands-on" approach to raiding. In this instance, the brigade commander, Gwyn-Thomas, was very much the "new boy," having only been in command of 50th Brigade since 20 April.[23]

On 3 June the divisional commander (Robertson) submitted to Corps his plan for the raid to be carried out in early June. The copy in the 17th Division General Staff War Diary is copiously annotated in manuscript personally by Shute, his hand-writing unmistakable since more manuscript comments by him appear on the bottom of Robertson's memorandum covering 50th Brigade's report, this signed "C.D. Shute, Lt. Genl." His manuscript comments, which were typed and then signed by him and sent to Third Army on 12 June, cannot be included here since to do so would obviously require 50th Brigade's fulsome report as well. However, a summary can be offered. Throughout the main body of the plan are nearly 20 comments, these relating to assembly of the raiders, deception, four comments on attack formations, four on the withdrawal (two others are illegible) and six general remarks, perhaps seven, but the last illegible and possibly part of the sixth. The appendices concerning machine-guns, trench mortars and Stokes also got a thorough review and numerous comments, some beginning "surely better to … " "Surely" has its own peculiar and

21 LAC, 6th Brigade and 31st Battalion, reports on raid.

22 LAC, War Diaries, 22nd and 24th Battalions, Operation Orders and raid reports; R.C. Fetherstonhaugh, *The 24th Battalion, C.E.F., Victoria Rifles of Canada 1914-1919* (Montreal: Gazette Printing Company, 1930), pp. 212-13.

23 On Shute and raiding while he was GOC 32nd Division see Chapter 15. Gwyn-Thomas was Indian Army (2nd Lancers). He was appointed a BM in November 1916. While with the Bengal Lancers in November 1916 he was awarded the DSO for conspicuous gallantry. He was promoted Lieutenant-Colonel in February 1917 and early in 1918 Brigadier-General Indian Cavalry. According to the entry for 20 April in the War Diary of 50th Brigade he arrived at brigade HQ that day.

particular military provenance and nuance! This is not to imply that the comments lacked merit or value; Shute was, after all, an experienced and able senior officer, despite a somewhat tarnished reputation that followed him on leaving the RND. He had only two comments on the artillery fire plan, which had already been carefully reviewed and annotated by the CRA 17th Division. What all this review and amendment resulted in was a plan as good as one could possibly be. The results say so.[24]

Given the width of their objectives the right assault battalion, the Dorsetshires, advanced on a frontage of three platoons and to the left the East Yorks advanced six "up" (see MSD 27). As per the plan as amended by Shute the Dorsetshires would assault in four waves of one company each, each wave of four platoons:

> First Wave. Fourth platoon to follow right platoon in file. Wave tasks to secure first objective and establish a block at right of battalion area. Fourth platoon to establish defence at eastern end of "Y" Ravine.
>
> Second Wave. Pass though First Wave and move direct to final objective following barrage closely. Fourth platoon to establish defence flank on northern edge of "Y" Ravine.
>
> Third Wave. Follow Second Wave. Capture third objective. Support Second Wave. Fourth platoon as above.
>
> Fourth Wave. Follow Third wave. Mop-up areas between first and final Objective. Fourth platoon as shown.
>
> Lewis Guns. Deploy across no man's land during the assault, act as right flank guard and be able to fire up "Y" Ravine and up branches that project southward.

The assault formation and tasks of the East Yorks were as follows:

> First Wave. Six platoons. Secure first objective. Two northern-most platoons to deal with the Crater and protect left flank.
>
> Second Wave. Five platoons, one north of the Crater. Capture final objective. Provide left flank protection.
>
> Third wave, Five platoons, northern-most to secure gap between first and final objectives and prepare to defeat any counter-attack from the north.
>
> Lewis Guns. Left flank protection.

24 TNA: WO 95/1984: 17th Division General Staff, G.970, 3 June, plan for raid on 9 June; Gordon Corrigan, *Mud, Blood and Poppycock: Britain and the First World War* (London: Cassell, 2003), p. 87. Shute, a Staff College graduate, had been Brigadier General Staff Aldershot, "one of the really taxing, and important, pre-war staff jobs dealing with troops," As a graduate, Shute was entitled to put after his name the letters "psc," an indication of qualification not so important as the time he graduated, but one that would become pure gold during the war when graduates were in high demand at every formation from brigade up.

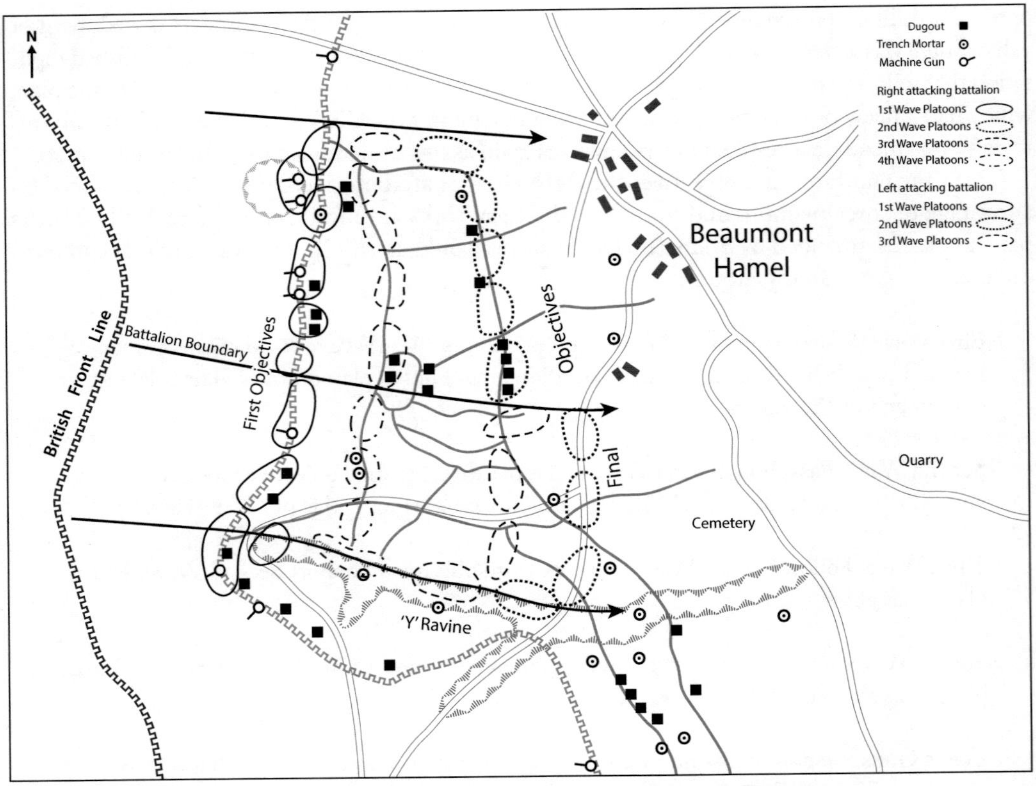

27 Beaumont Hamel Raid, 6/7 June 1918, 17th British Division.

The artillery would begin a creeping barrage on a line 100 yards west of the enemy front line, lifting at Zero plus five and creeping back in lifts of 100 yards per four minutes. Trench mortars and machine-guns would fire on selected targets.[25]

In execution the raid was faultless, both battalions achieving all objectives. Assault companies kept close to the barrages, crossed no man's land quickly and just as quickly were in the enemy trenches where they met little opposition. What little there was displayed no will to fight. Some machine-gun fire from south of the "Y" Ravine was ineffective. In all, 30 prisoners were seized. Casualties totalled 240 including 16 killed, overall a 23 percent rate. All reports from brigade up credited sound planning and preparation for success. It would be hard to argue with that conclusion. Some "things," including artillery shells, went astray, "shorts" always controversial and usually followed by investigation. Gwyn-Thomas referred to "individual guns which fired consistently short." Robertson's report elaborated:

> Losses were undoubtedly caused by short shooting of individual guns, despite the most careful registration, but I am satisfied that excess of zeal caused leading lines to run into

25 TNA: WO 95/1984: 19th Division General Staff, 50th Brigade Operation Order 53, 7 June.

> the barrage and that a proportion of the casualties were caused through this. The question of short shooting is under investigation.

Wanting to put the best face on it, Robertson concluded that the severity of the casualties might appear out of proportion to the results, but he believed that the enemy had suffered more and that morale "which perpetual trench warfare stagnates, has been enhanced." At HQ V Corps, Shute summarized events for Third Army. He stated that while friendly fire has caused some casualties this was unavoidable. However, there were more than previously "due to the men closing up more on the barrage and to worn guns and a less deliberate type of warfare." He concluded that the enemy was relying more on machine-guns to hold his forward zone and less on riflemen.[26]

Several of the other British raids in June were in roughly company strength. A very well-planned raid on 19/20 June by five officers and 138 ORs of the 2nd Worcestershires (33rd Division) southeast of Ypres targeted the southern shore of Zillabeke Lake (see MSD 28). The idea for this raid had surfaced immediately after the battalion returned to the line four days earlier. The objective was to identify the unit holding the area around Manor Farm, including several dug-outs and small buildings and an outpost at point I. The assault would be in conjunction with a rolling barrage moving from the southeastern shore of the lake at 50 yards per minute until it reached a line 200 yards south of the road and rail junction near the "22" line. There it would stand until withdrawal and then join in the box barrage along the edge of Zillebeke. The OC Raid, Lieutenant Harold Boswell, organized the raiders, B Company reinforced by one platoon of D Company, into six groups, each of the three largest under an officer and the others under an NCO (see 31st Canadian Battalion raid earlier in this chapter). Each group, I to VI, was allotted a specific area and each section had a specific objective. Group I, two sections under an NCO, would clear Objective I and then take up a position to cover the line of withdrawal. Group II under Second Lieutenant F. Barnard would clear II, including the machine-gun at "X" and then form a defensive front facing east. Once it had cleared III, Group III under an NCO would take up a position at "Y" to cover the withdrawal. The nine sections of Group IV under Second Lieutenant H.G. Hill would clear the farm itself. Groups V and VI, V under an officer, would clear objectives V and VI.

As it turned out, objectives I, III and IV were unoccupied. In the V and VI areas all dug-outs were found occupied and all were destroyed with Stokes bombs. Group II in taking the machine-gun at "X" seized two prisoners and then three more at a separate post. The withdrawal worked perfectly, the forward groups filtering back through objective III to objective I and then home with the prisoners. The cost of the raid was two wounded. The very neat evening's work earned Boswell the MC.[27]

One special raid in June may have been, if not the first, certainly one of the few involving tanks, in this instance five female tanks of 10th Tank Battalion accompanied a few sappers and five platoons of 5th KOYLI in a raid on 22/23 June on enemy lines opposite Bucquoy north of the Somme. According to the brigade report everything went well until the lead tank with the sapper detachment and one KOYLI platoon came under intense trench mortar fire. Owing

26 *Ibid.*, 50th Brigade report with covering memorandum to V Corps and V Corps to Third Army.
27 TNA: WO 95/2407: 2nd Worcestershires, 33rd Division, raid report; Stacke, *The Worcestershire Regiment*, p. 407.

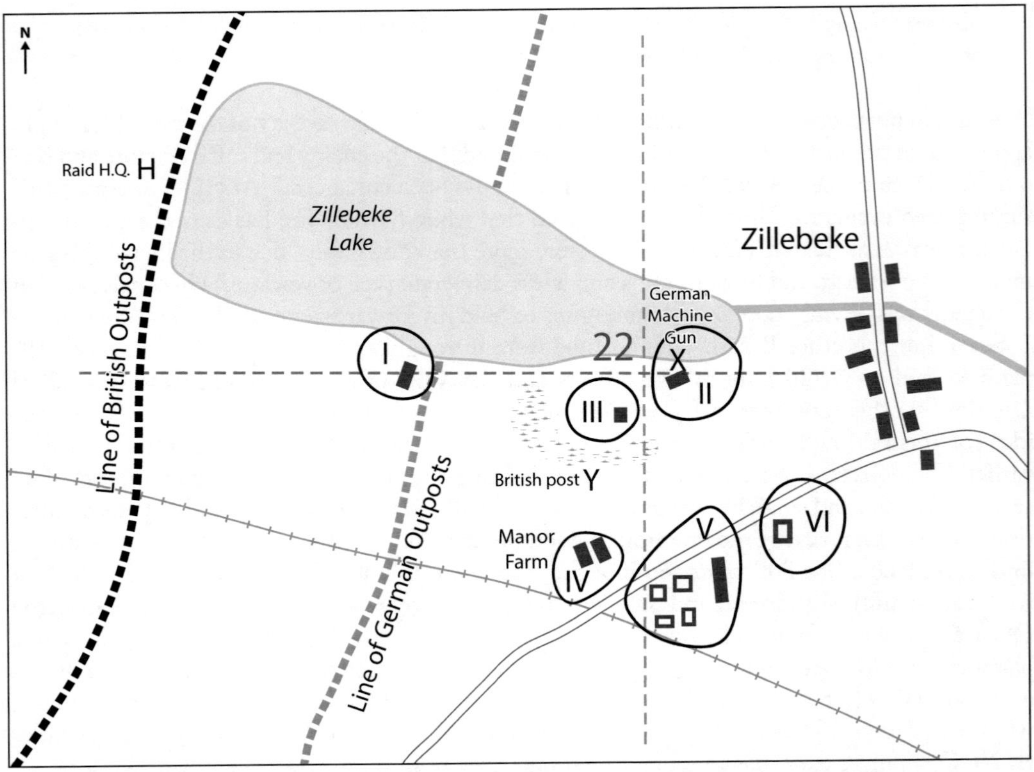

28 Manor Farm (Zillebeke) Raid, 19/20 June 1918, 33rd British Division.

to a thick band of mature trees facing the road the lead tank could not go straight ahead in accordance with the plan, but instead had to turn to the right, this exposing the lead KOYLI platoon to machine-gun fire from the trees and from the flanks. Most of the platoon fell victim to this fire. The next platoon, not knowing what had happened, also suffered heavily, including its commander who could not then give instructions to the accompanying tank. Unable to get forward, and now disorganized, the infantry withdrew. Once re-organized the raiders again moved forward, but mortar and machine-gun fire prevented further progress. The tanks, despite now being without the infantry and sappers, proceeded to the objectives, but being on their own were "unable to show any tangible result." No prisoners were taken. Tank crew casualties were one officer and three ORs wounded. Infantry casualties were four killed and 44 wounded. The GOC 4th Tank Brigade suggested that in any future joint raids the infantry should only join the tanks once the enemy outpost line had been crossed. What had looked to be a promising venture became in the end a disappointment. Good enemy use of ground and his support weapons to dominate the area by fire had separated tanks from infantry and caused the failure.[28]

28 TNA: WO 95/3070: 62nd Division General Staff, 187th Brigade and 10th Tank Battalion, 4th Tank Brigade reports on raid.

Most Canadian raids in June were also in roughly company strength. One of the first involved two platoons of A Company (Major William Maclean, MC) and two platoons of C Company (Captain Oswald Hepworth) of 29th Battalion (2nd Division). The objectives were the enemy outpost line along the Arras-Baupaume road and the bank 100 yards in rear of that. The assault formation decided upon was four platoons in two waves, the first to deal with the outposts and the second to go through to the bank, clearing as it went. Each flank would have a covering party for protection during the raid and the withdrawal. Maclean's company on the right consisted of 1 and 2 Platoons under Lieutenants C.E. Smith and H.E. Jekill. On the left were 11 and 12 Platoons of C Company under Lieutenants S.H. Jefferis and George Cruikshank, MC. The whole raiding party totalled seven officers and 175 men. Artillery support was limited to a "crash" lasting 30 seconds on known enemy posts and the outpost line, then a shift to the road line for three minutes before ending on the final objective. Prior to the raid officers and some of the NCOs participated in recce of the area over two nights. From this, plus careful study of intelligence maps and air photographs, each section was allocated a specific objective.[29]

Zero was set for 0045 on 3 June. Both companies left their trenches for the jumping off line about 500 yards distant almost three hours before Zero. C Company reached the line at 0015, A Company not until three minutes before Zero. At this time a nervous enemy put down machine-gun fire on the area and periodically bombed areas in front of his posts. Smith's platoon of A Company on reaching the outpost line could only watch as the enemy made good his escape. Nor did the rest of A Company find any enemy. The second wave once at the final objective picked up one prisoner wearing a Red Cross brassard, but also carrying a bayonet. None of the enemy posts along the bank, which were marked on the intelligence map, were occupied. These posts proved hard to find due to the darkness and long grass which hid many of them. At the final objective Jekill's platoon took two prisoners. Only the trench along the bank showed any signs of recent occupation.

Number 11 Platoon of C Company (Jefferis) was bombed briefly by a few enemy who then retreated to a tunnel along the road. The platoon took two prisoners near the tunnel, adding one another at the final objective. One man of the platoon went missing and could not be found. In all, the two companies took six prisoners. The cost was less than a dozen wounded. Maclean and Hepworth received the MC. Considering the effort made in planning and preparation little was achieved, most of the enemy evacuating at the first sign of trouble. Those that did stay to fight did so in a most determined manner, this not apparent in the casualty figures, but obvious in descriptions of the fighting.[30]

In late May a large-scale raid by three battalions of 4th Canadian Division on Neuville-Vitasse had been proposed, but when this was cancelled 20th Battalion of 2nd Division received orders to make a smaller raid on 2/3 June on the Maze, a series of enemy trenches southwest of the village. Raiding strength, initially 150, was reduced to four officers and 120 ORs in four equally sized platoons. While the raiders did not get to practise on a taped course, recce continued over six days during which patrols found enemy wire too thin to pose much of an obstacle. Preliminary barrage not being considered necessary the raid proceeded on the basis that surprise could be achieved, a supposition that came true. The raid went without a hitch.

29 LAC, War Diary, 29th Battalion, Operation Order 152, Lieutenant-Colonel W.S. Latte, DSO.
30 *Ibid.*, report by Lieutenant-Colonel Latte.

During 30 minutes in the enemy position the raiders took 16 prisoners. While reports characterized enemy reaction as unorganized the enemy did inflict 20 casualties. All in all, the raid was dubbed a tidy piece of work.[31]

Captain Robert Clements, MC, recalling 2nd Canadian Division's time with VI British Corps, remembered how during the period April-June 1918 in the Mercatel and Neuville-Vitasse sector of VI Corps front "Every 2nd Division battalion took a hand at raiding enemy front line outposts … the Germans being kept under continual pressure." The last raid by the 25th Battalion during this period came on 13 June when six officers and 140 ORs under Captain G.W. Anderson raided the "Maze," which 20th Battalion had hit 10 days earlier. The two raids were very alike, each deploying four parties of 25-30 men, each under an officer, and a covering party. Field and heavy artillery provided support, as did trench mortars. On the whole, the enemy offered little resistance. One of the parties, meeting about 20 Germans just coming into the line on relief, hit these hard, five of them including two officers becoming prisoners. One of these officers and Captain Anderson were killed during the withdrawal by German artillery. Other Canadian casualties included one OR killed, three missing and 22 wounded.[32]

2nd Division's last raid during its time with VI Corps was grander; it was, in fact, the largest 2nd Division raid of the month, 18 officers and 490 men of the 27th and 31st Battalions (6th Brigade), the raiders having a go at Neuville-Vitasse itself (see MSD 29). Alexander Ross, who became GOC 6th Brigade in October 1918, described the raid as larger than any raid previously made by the brigade. One of the early preparations included a special recce on 16 June by the BM, Major The Hon. F.E. Grosvenor, DSO, MC and Bar, and Staff Captain (Intelligence), followed by a conference of the brigade commander, A.H. Bell, the two COs, Lieutenant-Colonels H.J. Riley, DSO (27th Battalion) and E.S. Doughty, DSO (31st Battalion) and others. [33] On the 21st, 6th Brigade issued Instruction No. 1 for the raid which would encompass the whole of the village, a frontage of about 1,000 yards, with the final objective being a north-south trench on the eastern edge of the village. Depth of the raid would be about 500 yards. Zero was set for 0115 on 25 June. The right assault battalion (four companies) would be the 27th with two companies of the 31st on the left. The latter, plus a sapper demolition party, would also advance to the limit shown on both legs of the "Y" junction in D Company's area and destroy any dug-outs. The assault would be in two waves, the leading wave keeping tucked up to the barrage, followed by moppers up, some tasked to clear known enemy posts. On reaching the final objective blocks would be set in trenches leading rearward. On the night of 22/23 June at Zero plus one "J" Special Company RE would project 200 oil drums into enemy lines, 40 on the Sugar factory, 100 on the area of the large building immediately above the "V" in Vitasse and on the Maze trenches southeast of the village (the Maze is not shown on MSD 29). Fire support included a preliminary barrage lifting four times, 100 yards per lift, on a timed schedule, and fire on selected targets by heavy artillery and 6-inch trench mortars.[34]

Prior to the raid recce was extensive: 18 daylight patrols in which eight officers and 38 ORs of the raiding force participated and 24 night patrols that included 24 officers and 250 of the

31 LAC, War Diaries 20th Battalion and 4th Brigade, raid reports.
32 Tennyson (ed.), *Merry Hell*, p. 202; LAC, War Diaries, 5th Brigade and 25th Battalion, Operation Orders 237 and 176 and reports on raid.
33 *Ibid.*, 6th Brigade.
34 *Ibid.*, 6th Brigade Instructions No. 1 (21 June) and No. 2 (23 June).

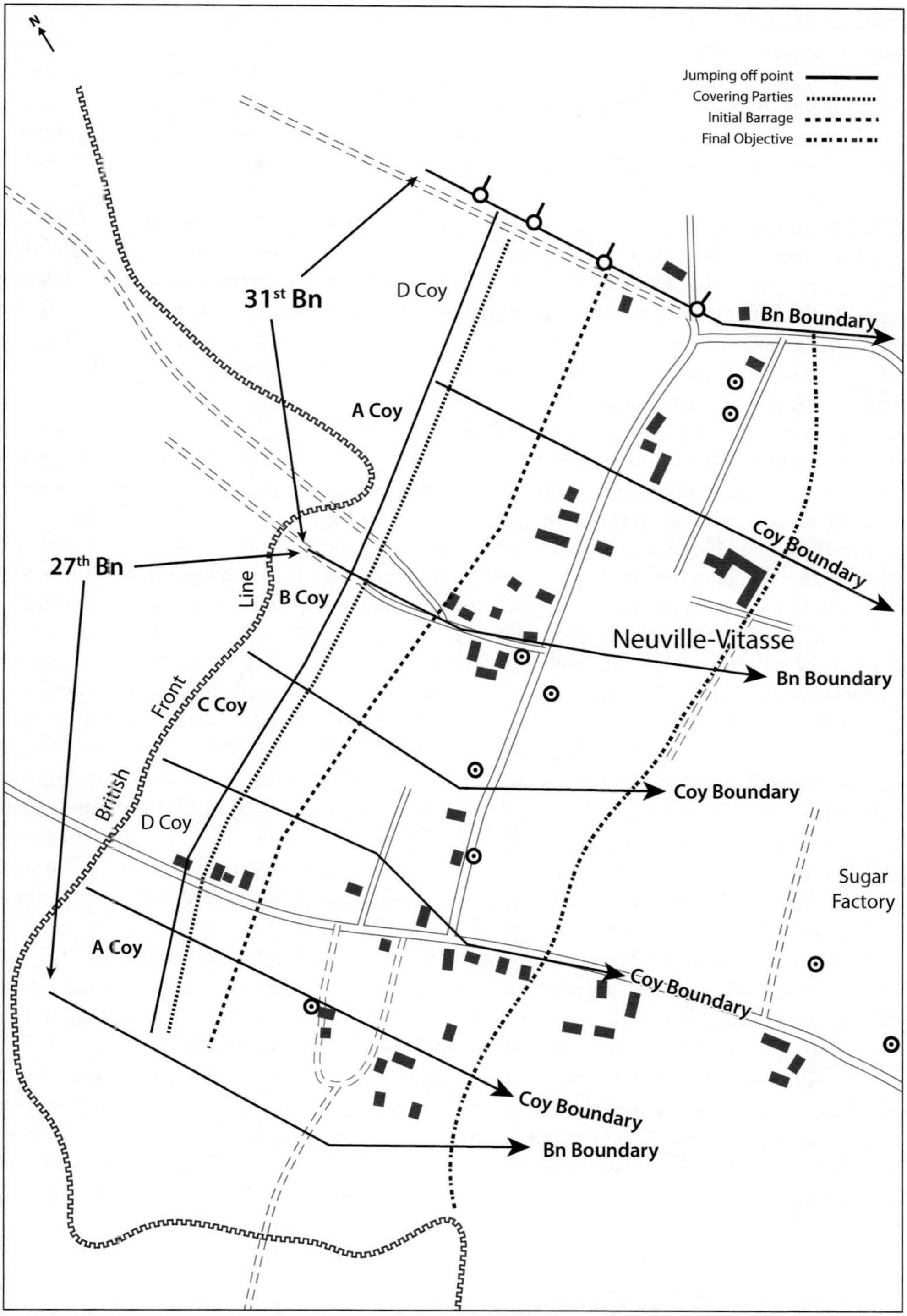

29 Neuville-Vitasse Raid, 13 June 1918, 2nd Canadian Division.

raiders. Given the conformation of battalion lines in 31st Battalion's area no man's land became progressively wider as the front moved northward. The battalion front was monitored each night before the raid by a line of outposts along the jumping off line that ran parallel to the enemy lines. Fighting Patrols from 28th Battalion operating from this outpost line swept the open areas engaging enemy patrols and in so doing kept the area free of enemy. Covering parties of the 28th remained in place on the night of the raid until relieved by the assault troops shortly before Zero.

On the night of the raid weather did not co-operate as well as it might have. A fresh and favourable wind that had persisted for some days, and well into the night of the 25th, suddenly dropped, the result being that smoke from "J" Company's oil drums when added to a thick mist increased the difficulties of taping the jumping off line and the guide lines back to battalion trenches. Lieutenant Gainor, the officer doing these tasks, later described anxious moments locating himself and laying the tapes accurately, despite his great familiarity with the ground, but he had all in place before Zero.[35]

On the right 27th Battalion experienced delay due to the "fog" caused by the oil, but the assault still began well, each company moving in a formation of parties and sections tailored to the nature of the various company objectives, each company having its own covering party. A Company, meeting almost no opposition, followed the barrage right through to the final objective. The right of D Company also met little opposition, there being no trace of any enemy to the left of the "U" loop joining the east-west main road. Searches of dug-outs along this road found only three enemy, all lying in a ditch with gas masks on. These were quickly hustled off to battalion lines. North of the road, however, strong opposition inflicted such heavy casualties that the raiders could not reach the final objective. When Lieutenant Scott Cameron, commanding the right of C Company, was seriously wounded the NCO who took over followed the retreating enemy into the friendly barrage, a decision that left only four of his 23 men unwounded. None of this party reached the final objective. The half of C Company on the left came under direct machine-gun fire, but despite this, the wire and the dense smoke, it destroyed the machine-gun and reached the final objective where it took a pill-box. Mills grenades were used to damage every dug-out found. B Company destroyed one machine-gun post on its way to the final objective where it had a bitter fight with a large enemy party which eventually withdrew. Two prisoners were taken by the battalion. Casualties were four killed, six missing and 47 wounded including three officers.[36]

31st Battalion attacked with two companies, A Company right and D Company left. Captain Park Tucker, OC A Company, although wounded almost immediately, continued in command. Stiff opposition, including machine-gun fire continued throughout the raid. The right of A Company on reaching the final objective blocked enemy trenches leading rearward. Of the Germans taken by A Company some were wearing gas masks, one strongly resisting having his mask removed until he realized that his captors were not wearing masks. This party suffered several casualties when a trench mortar ammunition dump blew up. The left party of A Company also endured considerable machine-gun fire, being unable to return it because of the mist. One of the officers with this party was wounded and then went missing, but returned to battalion

35 LAC, War Diary, 6th Brigade report on raid.
36 *Ibid.*, 6th Brigade and 27th Battalion reports.

lines shortly before daylight. Several prisoners were seized by this party. D Company on the left also faced a hard fight, four of the five officers becoming casualties, including Captain Herbert Norris, DSO, who was killed (see 31st Battalion's raid in May above). However, all parties of the company reached the final objectives. Lieutenant J. Mee, leading the party that was to explore the "Y" junction, deployed a covering group at the junction before sending a section down each leg of the "Y." One section soon met a large enemy party coming on the run up the leg. While heavily outnumbered this section slowed the enemy advance inflicting substantial casualties during the process. On a signal from Lieutenant Mee at the junction it returned to his location. Captain Tucker received the MC for the raid.[37]

The withdrawal of all companies involved in the raid went well, covering parties carrying out their function effectively despite light machine-gun fire from guns that the Germans had pushed forward. The brigade report made mention of the obvious difference observed by the raiders in the morale of the opposition, 12th and 10th Companies of 3rd Battalion, 85th Infantry Regiment. The 27th Battalion had been opposed by the 12th Company, which offered such strong opposition that the 27th was "unable to capture many prisoners [only two] and [was] deprived of any adequate reward or compensation." 31st Battalion, confronted by the 10th Company, took 21 prisoners, including one officer, but paid a higher price, a fact not realized apparently by Lieutenant Gainor, the officer who had laid out the tapes before the raid. He had then joined the raiders taking with him a long pole with a Canadian flag attached. This he left in the most conspicuous place he could find. On it he had pinned a communique announcing an Austrian defeat and below that had added a note addressed "To OC 10th Company, 3rd Battalion, 85th IR. Next time we raid you we will go through to your battalion HQ. The morale of your company is damn rotten."[38] The raiders received much praise for the raid, including a greatly appreciated letter from General Byng, a former GOC the Canadian Corps.

Even before 1918 it had been well-established that when it came to raiding artillery was a mixed blessing. One example earlier in this chapter was the 8/9 June raid by 17th British Division. This also applied to operations other than raids, the extent and efficacy of artillery support at times exciting controversy and heated argument; for example, in June 1915 the GOC 1st Canadian Division, Arthur Currie, had complained that "every time we have been in trenches lately we have suffered more or less from the fire of our own guns." Henry Burstall, then CRA, had been incensed by this comment, which he considered "absurd and improbable." Wire-cutting proved another difficult aspect of infantry-artillery co-operation. Before Givenchy in June 1915 Burstall had insisted, in order to avoid criticism afterward, that the infantry must "express themselves as satisfied" with the cutting before the assault. This was taken up and became the rule. But "shorts" proved a problem never completely resolved.[39]

37 *Ibid.*, 6th Brigade and 31st Battalion reports; Singer, *31st Battalion*, pp. 324-32.

38 Singer, *31st Battalion*, p. 330.

39 Major-General Sir Henry Burstall (as he became) was a Regular artillery officer, a South African War veteran and one of only two Canadian division commanders who were Staff College graduates. Until September 1915 he was CRA 1st Division. He then became GOCRA Canadian Corps. In December 1916 he became GOC 2nd Division. Blunt and forthright (like Currie) Burstall was a master gunner, a good tactician and a good division commander. His and Currie's remarks on gunnery are at LAC, 1st Division General Staff War Dairy, June 1915, Appendix VII.

A good number of raid reports between May and August 1918 reflect the continuing problem of "shorts," which had damaged and even wrecked some raids. In May immediately after a raid by 13th Royal Scots (15th British Division), the CO recommended no harassing fire before a raid on the area in front of the assembly position because it increased the difficulties of assembling and "in this case one unlucky short knocked out a complete bombing party that was to have taken part." 1st King's Own Scottish Borderers (29th Division), raiding four days later, reported that raiding parties while in the enemy trenches were struck by five or six mortar bombs, five men being wounded. Then "our own guns started a barrage on the trench we were in … after we had nine casualties I ordered the party to retire." The angry battalion commander described the whole raid "much hindered and harassed by our own artillery fire and also by a few trench mortar shells. All our casualties apparently caused by our own fire." On 20/21 May 1st Dorsets (32nd Division) reported how:

> the barrage opened at Zero, but was not correctly placed … on the Centre … guns were firing very short. On the left the barrage was good, except on the railway embankment, where again it was short. Besides inflicting numerous casualties on the troops at the very outset the barrage tended to cause confusion … the right company instead of being able to move forward had to take cover.

The shorts at centre caused the centre raiding party to slide off to the flanks meaning that at the objective a gap about 80 yards wide existed between the parties. Clearly, shorts were a serious matter. In any case, the brigade commander (14th Brigade) blamed friendly artillery for 90 percent of the casualties. Shorts were trouble for Canadians, too. In July 85th Canadian Battalion (4th Division) complained that inaccurate fire had wrecked its raid, the CO stating that friendly fire, which he personally observed, had made it impossible for the raiding parties to enter enemy trenches. The OC Raid commented that friendly fire had come down ahead of, on and even behind his assault line.

Such reports could result not only in infantry-artillery tension, but also add to disagreements between levels of command, an example being the raid by 1st Essex (37th Division) on 30 July 1918. On the receipt of an initial report about shorts, the GOC demanded a second report from the battalion and directed his CRA to investigate. As all the reports concerning the complaint are very lengthy only the conclusions are included here. The CRA concluded that the casualties were caused by enemy artillery, not friendly, a conclusion the GOC shared. The battalion commander thought it "a matter of opinion" whose fire had done the damage, but admitted it was possible that the raiders ran into the barrage, "be that as it may, no blame is attached to the artillery." All the reports having been studied, the BGGS IV Corps reported the Corps Commander's view, based in part on consultation with the GOCRA: "the failure of the raid was due to the short shooting of some of the supporting batteries rather than to enemy artillery."[40]

Turning now to July, on the night 2/3 July 96th and 97th Brigades of 32nd British Division launched raids, the 96th being the left brigade and the 97th the right brigade of the divisional

40 TNA: WO 95/2515: 13th Royal Scots, 1st King's Own Scottish Borderers and 86th Brigade, 14th Brigade and 32nd Division General Staff and 1st Essex, 112th Brigade and 37th Division General Staff; LAC, War Diaries, 12th Canadian Brigade and 85th Battalion.

frontage. The 16th Lancashire Fusiliers, 312 all ranks, made the raid on the left and the 10th Argyll and Sutherland Highlanders, 144 all ranks, the one on the right. Zero for both raids was 0100 on 3 July.[41]

The Lancashires raid, in the words of the division's report, "did not meet with the success hoped for owing to the volume of machine-gun fire met with," this fire coming from points beyond the artillery barrage. One of the raiding parties found few Germans, only five seen and killed. The volume of enemy fire became such that during the withdrawal both parties suffered many casualties. The sole accomplishment was one prisoner brought home. Casualties included one officer missing and two wounded, 18 ORs missing, most believed killed, and 55 wounded. C.D. Shute's comment on the earlier raid by 17th Division (8/9 June) as to how the enemy held his line also apply here. The 10th Argylls did rather better, reaching all their objectives. One of the three prisoners stated that relief of posts was in progress and the newcomers were caught in the barrage. Enemy dead from artillery fire were estimated at about 40. A further dozen Germans (by actual count) were killed by the bayonets of raiders. No bombs were thrown during the raid. Objectives were not held in strength, nor did the enemy make much of a fight.[42]

97th Brigade's War Diary entries on the raid also contain an Appreciation by the brigade commander, J.R.M. Minshull-Ford, and comments made upon it by division HQ. First, the GOC, T.S. Lambert, approved the scheme providing "recce establishes that there is something definite to raid" at the chosen objective. Such an admonition was not inappropriate or uncommon given the changes in enemy defensive doctrine. A good number of raid reports relate how the raiders at this time and earlier came up against nothing. Minshull-Ford's Appreciation acknowledged "the risk of finding the Outpost Line empty," but in this case observation and prisoner interrogations confirmed that it was manned day and night. Second, Lambert did not think the forming up place suitable, but he did not insist on a change. Also, he thought the brigade Appreciation exaggerated the extent to which fire from brigade lines could protect the flanks of the assault, but here, too, he did not demand a change. He did "wish" machine-guns to be placed in no man's land (locations were specified) to provide additional protection. The subsequent Operation Order complied. Finally, he thought 15 minutes in enemy lines sufficient. Events would prove otherwise. Afterward, Minshull-Ford called the raid "happy and fortunate," this for him, too, since his Appreciation, which drove the plan, was a primary element in the raid's success.[43]

The next night, 4/5 July,7th Royal Fusiliers, 190th Brigade, RND (63rd Division), executed what the GOC called a "nice clean little bit of work," two officers and 52 ORs raiding three posts south of the "Y" Ravine (see MSD 27) and then moving up the enemy trench, but not as far as the head of the ravine.[44]

Captain W.H. Nicholson, MC, OC Raid, divided the raiders into five sections, one under an officer to take the northern post, two for the central post and the last two for the southern post. His HQ remained in the battalion front line. As the barrage opened, the three groups

41 TNA: WO 95/2372: 32nd Division General Staff, G.S. 1719/27/1, 30 June; VI Corps G.S. 50/127, to Third Army, 30 June.
42 *Ibid.* Shute had said the enemy was relying on machine-guns, not riflemen, to hold his forward zone.
43 TNA: WO 95/2401: 97th Brigade, 'Appreciation for a Raid on the Enemy's Position in Front of the Right Brigade (87th Brigade)', 12 June, and comments by GOC 32nd Division; 10th Argylls raid report; letter 97th Brigade to division, 3 July.
44 TNA: WO 95/3117: RND General Staff, report on raid.

advanced to their objectives. On finding the northern post destroyed the party moved immediately into the trench where it took three prisoners. The central post was not occupied, nor were any Germans about. The right party, after killing the occupants of the southern post, pushed up the trench, but after a time the NCO in charge became separated and did not hear the withdrawal signal. He later returned with one prisoner, making four in all. The only casualty was one man wounded.

Despite its undramatic course this raid offered a number of good lessons. First, the brigade commander, stressing the necessity of close co-ordination between the sections of a raiding party, thought that had the OC of the northern party been aware of the situation of the other parties he would probably have delayed ordering withdrawal, thereby making an advance to the head of the ravine possible. Had he been centrally located he would have realized the situation. Moreover, a commander being necessarily involved in directing the party he is with almost always becomes completely engaged in that and he should not be responsible for that which he cannot see or control. Both C.E. Lawrie, the divisional commander, and C.D. Shute, GOC VI Corps, agreed. Two other lessons were relevant. First, the consensus said raiding parties should not be selected from volunteers, but should be members of an existing platoon or company. This was the usual practice in the Canadian Corps, too, although there had been exceptions. Lawrie also preferred the use of rockets fired in friendly lines to signal withdrawal, a course not favoured universally since rockets were not always seen or distinguishable. Finally, there was the difficulty in direction keeping. The NCO who became separated and lost his way had the good fortunate to be in charge of a prisoner who did not lie when asked the way to battalion lines. "Raiders," wrote Lawrie, "invariably are liable to get turned around and lose their way."[45]

A novel means of indicating and keeping direction featured during a raid by a unit of W.E. Ironside's 99th Brigade (2nd British Division) on 22/23 July. The brigade War Diary for that month shows that Ironside was closely involved in the planning and preparation of this raid. One reason for this was that the CO of the unit doing the raid, Lieutenant-Colonel D.W. Powell, 1st Royal Berkshires, had only been in command since 11 June and he had only been in rank since late February. Moreover, the unit had not raided after the arrival of Powell since for a time it had been in brigade reserve where it had experienced the impact of the flu that was then rampant. These facts explain why Powell received on 7 July a very detailed two-page instruction from brigade consisting of a 29 point guide on how to plan a raid. Powell would surely have appreciated this carefully thought out and well-written guide. Despite Powell's inexperience with raiding, Ironside in his report on the raid stated that he had chosen the 1st as it was the strongest battalion in the brigade and "best able to afford casualties."[46]

Ironside's interest also stemmed from his personality which influenced his style of command and his views on control. As a relatively new brigade commander (he took command of the 99th on 27 March), he was, no doubt, inclined to be extra watchful. Another element in his mind may have been his part as GSO1 in the planning of the disastrous raid by 4th Canadian Division shortly before Vimy Ridge. Several aspects of that plan simply did not receive the attention they should have, which is not to say that Ironside alone should be blamed for what

45 *Ibid.*, 190th Brigade, report on raid and manuscript comments by Shute. There is nothing in Jerrold, *Royal Naval Division*, on this raid.

46 TNA: WO 95/1370: 1st Royal Berkshires, memorandum Ironside to CO, 7 July and 99th Brigade report on raid.

transpired, but given his appointment and his influence over the division commander (Watson) he must be accorded a considerable share of the blame. But in view of Brian Bond's accurate assessment of Ironside as "supremely self-confident, forceful and opinionated" that bad experience in early 1917 probably did not weigh heavily on him. He could not allow such retrospection for he had to get on with commanding his brigade and not dwell on the past. Perhaps the bad experience made him mindful to ensure that no detail of the upcoming raid had been missed or neglected. In any case, on 3 July he issued what amounts to a warning order to Powell: raid on a large scale (not less than 200 all ranks), "clean up" the objective and do so on or about 16 days hence. Two days later an outline of the raid went to 2nd Division and to the 1st Berkshires: raid to take place about 22 July, two-company strength – "these may be composite" – night or early morning, artillery barrage to support, probably heavy artillery as well.[47]

The raiders, six officers and 203 ORs of B and C Companies under Captain V.G. Stokes, MC, would raid in three waves, supported by a reserve and a covering party on each flank, on 23 July at 0030. The raid would be supported by a creeping field artillery barrage and protected by a box barrage laid down by heavy artillery, trench mortars and machine-guns. All preparations before Zero went smoothly, all assault troops being in position by midnight. When the barrage opened at Zero the waves moved forward on the tapes previously laid. On the right the raiders pushed forward too fast, an officer and two men being killed having gotten too close to the barrage. Both flank parties and the party responsible for the first objective were on it very quickly and without appreciable opposition. Two prisoners were sent rearward under guard. By Zero plus 26 all parties were clearing the final objective. No enemy were found on the right, but elsewhere they could be seen withdrawing, several falling victim to rifle fire and three stragglers captured. At Zero plus 30 withdrawal commenced and continued without interference. Direction keeping was easy thanks to a searchlight providing a clear mark on which to focus, its beam being in Captain Stokes' words "easily distinguishable." Casualties included one officer killed and one wounded, plus three ORs killed and 30 wounded, many being suffered in no man's land and a large proportion due to following too closely to the barrage during the advance.

Ironside's report on the raid went beyond the usual. For one thing, it began with a precise account of all that was known and unknown about the enemy defence and his dispositions, including what was most likely his night posture. Then the plan for the raid was covered in one paragraph followed by a point form chronology of raid preparations from 5-22 July ending with the highlights summarized by time. The result is a very clear and concise account.[48]

On 26/27 July elements of 10th Canadian Brigade, Brigadier-General R.J. Hayter, DSO, psc, an officer Ironside knew from his time as GSO1 4th Canadian Division, raided enemy trenches near Willerval east of Vimy.[49] Bad weather the night of the raid, frequent heavy rain showers

47 *Ibid.*, 99th Brigade, instructions and memorandum.

48 *Ibid.*, 99th Brigade, raid reports of CO 1st Berkshires and OC Raid; Wyrall, *Second Division,* Volume 2, p. 597.

49 Ross Hayter was born in India in 1875. After graduating from Royal Military College he was commissioned into The Cheshire Regiment. He graduated from Staff College in 1905. Attached to the Canadian Militia in 1914, he became BM 1st Canadian Brigade at the outbreak of war. He remained in that post until September 1915 when he became GSO2 1st Division, moving on in January 1916 to GSO1, 3rd Division and then in August of that year to 1st Division as GSO1. Promoted Brigadier-General at the end of 1917, he took command of 10th Brigade. In October 1918 he became BGGS of the Canadian Corps. It is noteworthy that Hayter did not command a

pelting down, added to the difficulties inherent in an approach march to the jumping off line a thousand yards distant. Given this, and the need for great caution in order to avoid detection, the two officers and 60 men of the raiding party of the 46th Battalion began the trek forward at 2130, five and one-half hours before Zero. Battalion scouts had earlier laid tapes out to the jumping off line. Concurrently, carrying parties had established two 6-inch mortars and two Stokes in firing positions in no man's land from which these would join in the artillery barrage. Heavy artillery would engage selected targets in the enemy rear and on trench junctions.

The raiders at Zero advanced in eight groups. Wire presented no obstacle. At the initial objective the enemy machine-gun post reported by patrols could not be found despite a careful search. Few enemy were seen, only two being captured 200 yards behind the outpost line. Withdrawal was unhindered, enemy artillery very slow to respond. Casualties were four wounded and one missing. In his report the CO, Lieutenant-Colonel H.J. Dawson, attributed success to careful pre-raid recce. Hayter in his report referred to the unusual distance, about a thousand yards that the raiders had to cover, a trek whose difficulties could "not to be underrated."[50]

That same night (26 July) 2nd Canadian Brigade (1st Division) had launched a large-scale raid in the Arras sector, in all 14 officers and 389 ORs from 5th and 10th Battalions plus sappers of 3rd Engineer Battalion. The purposes were to foster in the mind of the enemy a belief that an attack on this front was imminent (the Amiens offensive was only days away) and to take prisoners. Pre-raid recce had established that the enemy did not occupy the same strong points at night as the day shift did and that at night an advanced fringe of riflemen and machine-gunners protected the garrison. Consequently, Zero was set for 2100, the thinking being to hit the enemy before he had taken up his night deployment. This, in fact, was what occurred. In this raid, too, the objective was about a thousand yards away. To reduce this distance some old trenches and dug-outs about 300 yards out in no man's land were selected as the jumping off position. The move there would be made during darkness. Before daybreak on Zero day the raiders were firm in the old trench where, in the words of the brigade report, "all ranks conducted themselves with admirable discretion during the twenty hours prior to Zero." Lieutenant-Colonel P.O. Tudor, DSO, CO 5th Battalion, gave credit where credit was due: "success depended on getting into [position] the previous night and remaining concealed all day … though the shelters were in full view of the enemy he was given no sign of the presence of the raiders."[51] This was quite a feat considering the numbers of men involved and the lengthy waiting time. It says much about the state of battle discipline in 2nd Brigade.

Of the two raiding parties the nine officers and 242 ORs of Party "A" (5th Battalion) had the primary role. Party "B" five officers and 147 ORs of 10th Battalion, would provide flank protection. As the barrage burst overhead at Zero Major P. Walker took "B" forward through gaps in the enemy wire and into a position in the enemy lines from which any enemy reinforcements trying to come forward could be prevented from doing so. As it turned out, no enemy appeared at all. One man was slightly wounded during the 10th Battalion's time in enemy lines.[52] Major C. Pyman, OC 5th Battalion raiders, took his three assault parties and three covering parties,

battalion before becoming GOC 10th Brigade. This did not hurt him or his brigade for both had a fine reputation.

50 LAC, War Diaries 46th Battalion, Operation Order 157 and report on raid, and 10th Brigade report.

51 LAC, War Diaries 10th Brigade and 5th Battalion.

52 Dancocks, *Gallant Canadians*, p. 165.

each of one officer and 40 ORs, into enemy lines where no appreciable enemy were encountered. Seven stragglers were picked up. Casualties included eight ORs killed and 38 wounded, almost all caused by enemy artillery: "owing to many previous raids and our preliminary barrage the enemy anticipated a raid … His plan [was] to withdraw his posts and then shell the locality."[53]

While Canadian raids continued well into July, getting the last kick in before 8 August, the first day of the Amiens offensive, and of The Hundred Days, what raids were made were small-scale and less ambitious. At midnight on 22 July elements of two battalions of Victor Odlum's 11th Brigade raided in the Maroeuil area, two platoons per battalion. Little was achieved. On detecting one of the platoons the enemy withdrew. Mislead by a trench not shown on the map, the platoon did not reach its objective and could not gain contact with the second platoon which met with no enemy. Both platoons of the other battalion, the 102nd, encountered more wire than had been anticipated and one platoon on getting through it found itself in trenches that were not on the map. Here confusion reigned giving the enemy time to scram. Three stragglers were picked up. The second platoon, after similar delay in getting oriented, turned right and met with considerable wire and enemy, the result being a severe bombing fight. Again, delay gave the enemy time to withdraw. This platoon took six prisoners, making nine in all for the battalion. Brigade casualties came to one killed and 20 wounded. Odlum, an experienced raider himself, gave all credit to the two COs whose "operations were entirely their own. I was kept informed but apart from co-ordinating time and artillery I did not interfere." But then his focus was the main event, the Amiens offensive.[54]

The other two battalions of 11th Brigade were preparing a raid for 28/29 July, recce commencing on the 24th. Each battalion would field two platoons to strike immediately south of the area raided on 22 July. Captain M.A. Neelon and Lieutenant A.E. Holmes commanded the platoons of 75th Battalion. At Zero (2300) Neelon's platoon rushed the enemy trench. On leaping into it Neelon landed on three Germans, one being killed as he attempted to run. One of the others fell to his knees, clasped his hands together and muttered "Good God! Mercy!" Neelon, who had been studying German for some time, replied. "Certainly!" The purpose of the raid – prisoners – thereby easily achieved! The other platoon met no enemy at all. After the raid Neelon's tunic would sport the purple and white ribbon of the MC. The raiders of 87th Battalion had harder fighting, killing 28 Germans and capturing two at a cost of five wounded and one missing, the latter not found before withdrawal.[55]

References to raiding and raids during the last three months of the war are uncommon in the published histories of British Great War divisions. The same is true of Canadian battalion histories. The Amiens Offensive, during which the war marched steadily and relatively rapidly eastward, was centre stage starting in August, everything else pushed to the wings and scarcely in mind. With things moving along trench warfare became open warfare. Many things, including raiding, changed.

This is not to say that raids entirely ended, but the really big "shows" were a thing of the past. The strongest British raids in the whole of the period after 8 August were two-company raids, or more accurately elements of two companies; for example, 2nd British Division's two-company

53 LAC, War Diary, 5th Battalion, report on raid.
54 LAC, War Diaries, 11th Brigade and both battalions and brigade reports.
55 *Ibid.*

raid on 14 August, the largest it made after the 8th, was noted by the divisional historian as the division's "culminating effort in trench warfare." 12th Division's history marked August as the "end of tedious trench warfare." In September there were instances where the two-company raids simply could not get beyond enemy reserve lines, resistance too strong for two companies to overcome. One battalion of 15th Division, for example, raiding in two companies had in fierce hand-to-hand fighting three officers killed and three wounded, plus 10 ORs killed, 30 wounded and five missing. Three other two-company raids by this division in September failed to get a single prisoner and suffered many casualties.[56] Smaller raids, usually platoon size, became the norm. Objectives changed, too, no longer lines (plural) of trenches, with parties and waves, sometimes as many as four, going left, right and rearward, with often complex fire plans of field and heavy artillery, trench mortars and Stokes and machine-guns. Instead, raids went against a point or points such as single outposts or weapons emplacements which a platoon could handle silently without elaborate fire plans because everything needed, the "readies," was in-house, including Lewis guns and rifle grenades (the platoon had been for some time the "unit of assault" and its rifle-grenadiers the infantry's artillery). Stokes 3-inchers could be easily added if a little more "oomph" was required.

With the enemy in retreat, evacuating position after position, the new warfare often became running the enemy down in the open. Pursuers had to be "especially active in patrolling and prepared to follow up any retirement at once."[57] Pursuit demanded that the hounds be at least as fast as the fox for he usually had a head start. This could be obviated somewhat by early knowledge gained from constant patrolling, both recce and fighting patrols. Given such fluidity, who now had time to plan fancy raids? In any case, given the new style of warfare they were no longer appropriate. The wheel, as it usually does, had come full circle. The pre-war "Reconnaissance in Force," a concept defined and explained in *Combined Training (Provisional.)*, which had persisted into the early part of the war, had then ended as the spade became a second "best friend" to the soldier and raids became the mode. It now returned in the guise of patrols in various forms: recce, "snatch," standing and fighting. The War Diary for 25 September of the 1st Royal Warwickshire Regiment (10th Brigade, 4th British Division), for example, includes an order to "make a recce in force" that night. The CO objected since no recce by day had been made, but in the end complied, of course.[58]

Experience drove doctrine and doctrine drove training and organization. Part of the turning of slow to fast, or faster, was organizational change. In preparation for pursuit 15th British Division, for example, formed "Brigade Groups," each with artillery and engineers, making what were all-arms entities capable of rapid movement and a degree of independent action. 42nd Division, seeking more effective co-operation of all-arms under "the new conditions of open warfare," formed groups consisting of an infantry brigade, an artillery brigade, a machine-gun company (or more), sappers and cavalry (or tanks if available). Such changes were on pace within the BEF as a whole. Unfortunately, much of this did not survive the war.

56 Wyrall, *Second Division,* Volume 2, p. 597; Scott, *12th (Eastern) Division,* p. 190; Stewart, *Fifteenth (Scottish) Division,* p. 264.

57 Scott, *12th (Eastern) Division,* p. 215.

58 TNA: WO 95/1484: 1st Royal Warwickshire Regiment, 25 September 1918; *Combined Training,* p. 77.

November brought an Armistice. On learning of it Andrew McNaughton, GOC Canadian Corps Heavy Artillery, expressed complete disgust: "Bloody fools, we have them on the run. That means that we shall have to do it all over again in another twenty-five years."[59]

Renewed hostilities, when they came, would include raids.

59 Swettenham, *McNaughton,* Volume 1, p. 168.

17

Finis

> 'Tis all a Chequer-board of Nights and Days
> Where Destiny with men for Pieces plays:
> Hither and thither moves, mates and slays,
> And one by one back in the Closet lays.
> The Rubaiyat of Omar Khayyam

The Closet door came whipping open 25 years later and then again in Korea where there was "pressure on the Commonwealth Division for more large raids to show the enemy we can still be offensive and to keep our soldiers sharp." And yet again during the Falklands War in 1982 (hard to keep that Closet closed): "Special Forces would carry out a diversionary raid. 40 Commando would land at San Carlos Settlement. The Commando was also warned to be ready to conduct raids after the landings." 40 Commando was no stranger to raiding. At Anzio in March 1944 it had raided the Germans. This all sounds very familiar. In reading accounts of the Korean and Falklands Wars, and noting especially patrolling and raiding, it is as if no time has passed at all, seemingly more episodes in a continuing, long-running series of raids, their policy, purposes, planning, pressures, education and execution being related in terms, sequencing and results now not unknown to us.[1] Any new war will see more patrols and raids since commanders firmly believe, and with cause, that "Time spent in recce is seldom wasted." Look-see will invariably, as of old, become see and savage, war being a process of inculcating and practising aggression: "bees for flies, and hornets … for bees."[2]

But to return to the Great War much changed between 1915, when raiding captured the imagination of senior commanders and offered a means to strike at the enemy, thereby maintaining offensive spirit, keeping and testing skills and training junior officers, at a time when

1 Lieutenant-Colonel Herbert Fairlie Wood, *Strange Battleground: The Operations in Korea and Their Effects on the Defence Policy of Canada* (Ottawa: Queen's Printer, 1966), p. 173; Anthony Farrar-Hockley, *Official History: The British Part in the Korean War. Volume II. An Honourable Discharge* (London: HMSO, 1995) and William Johnston, *A War of Patrols: Canadian Army Operations in Korea* (Vancouver: UBC Press, 2003. See also Ian Gardiner, *The Yompers: With 45 Commando in the Falklands War* (Barnsley: Pen & Sword, 2012), p. 63; Carlo D'Este, *Fatal Decision: Anzio and the Battle for Rome* (New York: Harper, 1991), p. 296.

2 Martin Luther, *Whether Soldiers Can Also Be In a State of Grace* (1526).

limited resources did not permit larger "shows," and the summer of 1918 when a new style of warfare made raiding a poor fit. *On The Dangerous Edge* has shown how raiding went through stages, these not always discrete, lacking in some ways sharply defined edges, but the pattern clear enough during the cycle. First came the beginnings, small, amateurish and simple, sometimes just a few men under a Subaltern, a mad dash across no man's land, winkle a Hun, then "through the wire and home and [get] our rum."[3] Then since expectation never ends came raids larger, professional, sophisticated and complex, now companies, hundreds of men, often hundreds of guns in support and prodigious ammunition expenditure, all this indicative of a striving for bigger and better, maximum damage, *"Klotzen, Nicht Kleckern,"* the most apropos translation being "Kick, Don't Tickle."[4] Next was a transitory stage, a mix of large and small, reflecting the changes in defensive doctrine. Finally, all come round again, full circle, open warfare, not seen since 1914, truly broke out in mid-1918, and raids became something else.

The drivers for raids, just as in everything else, were experience and technology. The first included learning how to integrate and make best use of the second including trench mortars (light, medium and heavy), grenades, rifle grenades, machine-guns, Lewis guns, gas, smoke, even aircraft and in at least one instance a tank. The light mortar, the Stokes (3-inch and 4-inch) was probably the outstanding invention of the war. Remarkably simple and inexpensive, it vastly increased the firepower available to the infantry, but not under battalion control which meant availability could not be guaranteed. A primary factor in integration of mortars and machine-guns was the question of which Arm and which level of command would exercise control. Control meant not only immediate and guaranteed response, but augmentation of manpower, resources and influence. In May 1918 Brigadier-General Frederick Loomis, GOC 2nd Canadian Brigade, recommended that "two Stokes guns and one-quarter of personnel [of a Stokes battery] be transferred to each infantry battalion, becoming an integral part of the battalion." Loomis, as some others had, grasped the necessity for each battalion to be a balanced, all-arms team capable of providing its own close support. Rifle grenades were another means of immediate infantry-controlled close support and these are sometimes neglected in modern studies; not so by the infantry of the time who referred to rifle grenades as the infantry's artillery.[5] Operationally the Stokes provided very rapid fire, it could be quickly set up to fire and its relatively light weight made it more easily portable. Soldiers may have initially disliked the Stokes because they drew retaliatory fire, but they soon realized and appreciated their enormous destructive power. Not for nothing did Mister Wilfred Stokes become Sir Wilfred Stokes. Various explosive devices such as Bangalores, oil cylinders, thermit shells, flame projectors and gas of all types gave the sappers a solid niche in raiding and solidified their role in warfare as a whole. Artillery, too, underwent substantial change. As better fuses and ammunition came into general use, more sophisticated and effective fire support resulted.

Experience and technology wrought new defensive doctrine, depth, not linear, and offensively, worms and waves, moppers up, the platoon as the "unit of assault" as per *The Normal Formation for the Attack* and other manuals in the SS series. Raider and defender alike developed

3 Arthur Graeme West, 'The Night Patrol' in Stephen (ed.), *Poems of the First World War: 'Never Such Innocence'*, p. 95.
4 Kenneth Macksey, *Guderian: Panzer General* (London: MacDonald and Janes, 1975), p. 100.
5 LAC, RG9IIIC3, Volume 4053, Folder 24, File 16, Loomis to GOC 1st Canadian Division, 21 May 1918.

new trench fighting tactics, the Germans adopting measures such as loopholes in traverses and hidden entrances to dug-outs. Such measures, plus blocks in trenches, could box attackers into killing zones. To counter these tactics raiders often resorted to raiding parties clearing from above ground as well as clearing along trenches. Effective German use of artillery and especially mortars made counter-battery fire more important and often resulted in a greater "slice" of available guns being dedicated to counter-battery. Other new tactics surfaced such as deception measures like "Chinese attacks," use of dummies and complex fire plans designed to deceive. All of these had great impact not only in raids, but in the development of doctrine for larger operations. Learning involves how best to manage and use all this, and learning is not always a gentle, precise and ever-upward slope, but rather a jagged line with highs and lows along which misapprehensions can arise and confusion, too, between the peculiar and the universal. Raiding also offered a means to improve individual battle skills, to instill new skills and to increase confidence and "tactical awareness." One contemporary account expressed concern that because training for raids had become so much a drill "the slightest departure from the programme, the tiniest touch of spontaneity, would be fatal … the raid became an elaborate staff exercise, and the practice even grew up of the raiding party coming up to the line specially for the raid, while the line was held by some other battalion who knew little or nothing of the purpose of the operation." Given the record the first part of this exaggerates and while there were instances of the technique then described, such did not become general and when it was employed units compensated, for example, by temporary re-allocation of sub-units and units.[6]

Successes came, but so did failures and from both, but primarily from the latter, lessons that had to be recognized and implemented in planning and conducting raids and, indeed, in all operations. Seeing a lesson did not mean it would be interpreted and implemented as well as it should be. Lessons highlighted certain essentials upon which success depended. The short list that follows does not imply relative importance; rather it is simply sequenced as a raid was. First came thorough recce of ground and enemy. Second was careful planning and preparation. Third was execution. In the end it was the officers, usually young Subalterns, and their men that were successful or not. Lieutenant-Colonel Winston Churchill's remark about living on the brink of the abyss applied in spades to raiders who had perforce to leap from that brink, usually in the dark, fall 10 feet or so, no knowledge of what lay below, and be instantly ready to engage in savage fighting, life or death the result. While all who wore the King's uniform and served in the trenches can and should be considered members of an extraordinary generation of men, raiders stand, perhaps, just a little taller.

Five of Kipling's six honest serving men relate to the method and techniques of raiding: what to raid (target), where (location), when (day or night and Zero), who (troops engaged) and how (strength, composition, tactics). The first and second, as this study has shown, involved a selection process involving ground study, including approaches and conformation, and recce of enemy dispositions and estimates of enemy strength. Recce was an essential and critical element of this process. "When" to raid had to be weighed very carefully for here it might be possible, if the right choice was made, to achieve some degree of surprise, which was always a key and desirable object. Initially, "who" might be volunteers or selected volunteers, officers usually tasked

6 Some instances of this are related in Jerrold, *Georgian Adventure*, p, 145. See also Connolly, *Steady the Buffs!*, p. 87.

or selected to lead the raids. Given the organizational changes made within infantry battalions, specifically to platoon organization and composition, and the acceptance of the platoon as the "unit" of assault, the preference became the tasking by COs of constituted companies and platoons, not the formation of new entities. Both options had disadvantages and advantages. "How" was the plan that had to contain all that was necessary to achieve the purpose(s) of the raid. The ideal included keeping the plan as simple as possible. If the "Intention" in an Appreciation (Intention being that which had to be achieved) was not clear then the plan would have the same flaw. It was a fact, too, that a plan that had in it an element of surprise stood a better chance of achieving success. These five serving men received, or should have received, their due in the documents relevant to battle procedure including the Appreciation, the proposed plan or "scheme," the Preliminary Instructions (in a few cases identified as a Warning Order), and in the Operation Order, Operation Instructions and finally in the Administrative Instructions that eventually became a part of pre-raid battle procedure.

A post-war inquiry originated at the highest level in June 1932 when the CIGS (Chief of the Imperial General Staff) read James Edmond's "Volume 5" of the British Official History. "So shocked," was the CIGS, "at the tactical ineptitude that it exposed" that he ordered Lieutenant-General Sir Walter Kirke to establish a committee of inquiry to report upon the lessons of the war.[7] "Volume 5" would be mentioned at least once in every paragraph of the section of Kirke's report dealing with raiding. Kirke's Terms of Reference were to investigate and report upon the principal lessons to be derived from experience in the theatres of war and determine whether or not these lessons had been incorporated in *FSR* and in training manuals.

Kirke's report came very quickly. In October 1932 the War Office published the findings of his committee of nine Brigadiers and Major-Generals. The findings consisted of a "General Report" covering four themes: peacetime preparation for war, strategy and tactics, equipment and organization and training. Submitted separately were two reports on the lessons of the Western Front and one each on Gallipoli, Palestine and Mesopotamia. The first of the two Western Front reports contained 19 lessons under the heading "Lesson 18 Minor Operations – Raids" focussing on "the advisability of minor offensives in the intervals between major operations." In just over a page raids were summarized as to four purposes or "intended results" – improving morale, lowering enemy morale, securing identifications and deceiving the enemy – and to what extent these were achieved. Lesson 18 categorized these "intended results" thus: one complete failure, one that in occasionally serving its purpose was justifiable and two achieving an unquantifiable degree of success, one of these two doing so at a cost higher than what the enemy had paid.[8]

Looking first at the two that defy precise quantification the difficulty, more often than not, was the absence of a means of measurement and credible observation. Lesson 18 says that raids "must have been wearying to the enemy," which is so, but they were also a weary road for the raiders and for those who planned and prepared raids. Those who believed that raids lowered enemy morale failed to convince front line troops, the officers and men that did the fighting,

7 David French, 'Sir James Edmonds and the Official History: France and Belgium' in *The First World War and British Military History*, Brian Bond (ed.) (Oxford: Clarendon Press, 1991), pp. 83-84. "Volume 5" was how the committee referred to *Haig's Command to the 1st July* published in June 1932.

8 *Report of the Committee on the Lessons of the Great War* (The War Office, October, 1932; reprint edn. (Uckfield, East Sussex: Naval and Military Press, n.d.), Appendix I, Lesson 18.

of the validity of their theory. Lieutenant-Colonel J.L. Jack, in 1917 CO 2nd West Yorkshires, replying to a claim that German morale had declined, observed that this was not his experience nor that of his officers and men. Nor was then Captain W.W. Murray, 2nd Canadian Battalion, convinced. Noting the emphasis placed upon the supposed and non-quantifiable degradation of enemy morale, he asked "How much so we wonder? How much did the raiding of a few yards of trench affect the morale of the German Army in the main?"[9] Raids, said Lesson 18, were "probably" costlier to the BEF than to the Germans. Keeping in mind that estimates of German casualties during raids were routinely too high, often more wish than fact, Lesson 18 seems accurate. When it came to comparing losses against numbers of prisoners Murray asked "Did this raid pay? Will somebody please pay the attritionist?" *FSR* would emphasize in the 1924 edition that "It is the first principle of a raid that it should result in greater losses to the enemy that to the troops which carry it out." William Philpott notes that by the end of 1915 "the guiding axiom of military operations in attritional warfare [said] armies ideally needed to inflict loss on the enemy at a rate that matched or exceeded that which they suffered."[10] The classic antonym was the largest Canadian raid of the war shortly before Vimy. It proved the costliest failure, so much so that it even elicited the compassion of the enemy. "One does not like to speak of this affair," wrote Colonel Murray in April 1933.[11] The other immeasurable (usually) was deception of the enemy. The committee referred to an example of "a measure of success on the Somme" mentioned in the "Volume 5" available to it, but also offered an example where deception did not appear to have "achieved [anything] commensurate with the hardships and casualties endured.[12] *On The Dangerous Edge* has offered examples where some benefit was seemingly provided by deception, even instances where the benefits were clearly evident and observable, but such were uncommon.

As for the third purpose – securing identifications – on occasion this was achieved, said Lesson 18, and raids for that purpose were therefore "fully justified." "Volume 5" described identifications as a "special" task. The other Volume 5, *26th September-11th November The Advance to Victory,* which Kirke's committee would not have seen (it was published in 1947), gave this task less emphasis saying only "A few [raids] were naturally required to take prisoners for identification." However, in the research for this present study it became clear how very uncommon it was not to see in the Operation Order for a raid, Canadian or British, "take prisoners" and/or "secure identifications." An account of the Korean War includes a sentence that applies in spades to those Great War raids whose purpose was prisoners: "As always when a war gets bogged down in static defence, regiments in the line were subjected to clamorous demands for prisoners, and a bottle of whisky or extra days leave were promised to all who could bring one in."[13] Douglas Jerrold believed that the cost of an average raid was without "counterbalancing gain except in the rare cases when an identification of the unit opposite was really required."

9 Terraine (ed.), *General Jack's Diary,* p. 191; Murray, "Raids," p. 337.

10 Murray, 'Raids', p. 337; *FSR,* 1924, Volume 2, p. 241. While in some cases an actual body count in a 10 or 20 minute stay in enemy trenches was possible the usual measuring stick was an estimate. William Philpott, *Attrition: Fighting the First World War* (London: Little, Brown, 2014), p. 162.

11 Murray, 'Raids', p. 338.

12 *Report of the Committee,* Lesson 18; Edmonds, *Haig's Command to the 1st July,* pp. 213, 310.

13 *Ibid.,* p. 156; Edmonds and Hyslop, *26th September-11th November The Advance to Victory,* p. 611; A.J. Barker, *Fortune Favours the Brave* (London: Leo Cooper, 1974), p. 51.

Colonel Murray was skeptical, remarking sarcastically about the "great object" of securing identification that "We never heard of this being put to much use. Perhaps it was, however." He was, of course, a junior officer during the war and probably not fully aware of the use and importance of accurate and timely information on the enemy order of battle.[14]

When it comes to the fourth "intended result," improvement of own troops morale, Kirke's Committee was forthright:

> If the primary object of raids was to improve the morale of our troops it may be at once admitted that, as conducted, they completely failed in their purpose. They were generally carried out with no definite object but to be frightful. They were often staged under conditions entirely detrimental to their success. (Volume 5, p. 156). The best leaders and the best men were necessarily selected for these operations, and irreplaceable material was thus expended for quite nebulous reasons, our casualties were great, everyone hated them, and their delivery for insufficient reason has left a bitterness among the fighting troops which is reflected in war literature and stage productions. As a morale raiser they may be definitely ruled out (at any rate as conducted on the Western Front).[15]

Whatever the benefits of raids they did not come cheaply. Lord Moran, commenting on the ways to create and maintain offensive spirit, wrote how "The Army was to be blooded in a hundred raids [which was] to dissipate like a spendthrift not only the lives but the moral heritage of the youth." What he refers to is the loss of many good lower and middle-ranking officers who in due course would have become battalion or brigade commanders. *Advance to Victory* adds that not only were many first class officers and men lost, but raids led to retaliation which meant more casualties. The real point is attrition. Raids for no good reason could be seen as akin to squeezing an orange. Keeping on means the juice will soon all be gone.[16]

The Committee's judgement on own morale is obviously an aggregate, an average of good, bad and indifferent raids. A good raid, provided it was not too costly, raised morale and helped build unit cohesion and esprit de corps. A bad raid brought depression, a sense of lesser worth and wonder about the state of leadership. The disastrous Canadian raid just before Vimy, which saw two commanding officers and several company commanders lost, is a salient example of the negative effects of a bad raid. On the other hand, Jerrold points out that while some raids were "brilliantly successful … they were costly and wholly bad for the morale of the troops involved." All too often it was plain to see that the balance of profit was with the enemy; raiders from 25th British Division in January 1916, for example, came away with 11 prisoners, but at a cost of four officers and 24 ORs killed, six officers and 95 ORs wounded. The balance here hardly seems favourable.

Quite contrary to the committee's assessment, Colonel Murray thought "the best result achieved by raids" was the raising of BEF morale and how raids built a "superiority complex" that was central in achieving domination of no man's land. "Too much emphasis cannot be placed upon this," he wrote, "a battalion which was not the boss of its own front was not a

14 Jerrold, *Georgian Adventure,* p. 145; Murray, 'Raids', p, 338.
15 *Report of the Committee,* Lesson 18(c); Edmonds, *Haig's Command to the 1st July,* pp. 156-57.
16 Lord Moran, *Anatomy of Courage,* p. 71; Edmonds, *26th September-11th November The Advance to Victory,* p. 611.

soundly disciplined unit." Here he echoes *SS 135 Instructions for the Training of Divisions for Offensive Action:* "control of No Man's Land … is of special importance for cultivating an offensive spirit.[17] A Second World War Subaltern reflecting upon offensive spirit said:

> The thinking behind this policy seemed to me … superficial and probably left over from the Great War. If young officers queried this wisdom the standard reply was 'I quite agree with you, but it all helps to dominate No Man's Land.' There is undoubtedly a certain validity to this argument but was it worth the consequent loss of good young officers and NCOs?
>
> I doubt it. One must admit, however, that [the process of establishing domination] did make the opposition jumpy.[18]

In the final paragraph of Lesson 18 the Kirke Committee stated the condition it thought justified raids:

> The conclusion would seem to be that minor offensives are justifiable only as a definite military operation for a specific purpose conducing to the success of the commander's plan. They have no place in the conduct of war when carried out merely as a sort of competition between formations with no specific military object, and when needlessly ordered they impair the confidence of the troops in their leaders and lower their morale.[19]

Colonel Murray concluded with this: "May we therefore sum up by saying that raids for the sake of raiding are useless and criminal, while a raid with a bonafide object, which is carefully planned and executed, may be justifiable and beneficial." A British officer believed that raids were bad for morale if they were seen to be "apparently, if not actually, devoid of any military purpose which could justify the inevitable loss of life." The "Retrospect" of *26th September–11th November Advance to Victory* concluded that "Probably very small lightning raids to obtain prisoners and large raids … for some definite purpose, would have been better than raiding for the sake of raiding."[20]

All of this is valid. Stephen Badsey in his article on the raid at Cherisy in September 1917 concluded that the raid was "too small and too normal … to have any lasting consequences." The same could be said of most such raids, but this is not to say that they had no impact or usefulness. Trench warfare lessened contact with the enemy, the unseen enemy, and it dulled one's senses in its monotony and tedium. Not for nothing did commanders see this as the "edge" being dulled, even lost. Raids, then, while certainly on the dangerous edge, were also diversion, excitement, adventure, opportunity, too, for a chance to be out and doing against a "live" enemy, a test, proof of one's training, knowledge, skill and worth in controlling and fighting his men and in the honing of soldierly and especially officer-like qualities. Writing in 1936 Lieutenant-Colonel M.K. Wardle, DSO, MC, reiterated a salient and unchallengeable fact about the Great War:

17 Murray, 'Raids', p. 337; *SS 135 Instructions for the Training of Divisions for Offensive Action.*
18 Jary, *18 Platoon,* p. 72.
19 *Report of the Committee,* p. 23.
20 Murray, 'Raids', p. 340; Jerrold, *Georgian Adventure,* p. 145; Edmonds, *26th September–11th November Advance to Victory,* p. 611.

> It is easy to see that the training of the platoon, and of its commander, is the central, all-important act. It is the platoon that gives and receives the blows … it is the platoon that renders a force slow or sticky … it is by the skill and courage of the platoon, in patrolling, in observation, … that senior commanders can build up that true picture of the course of battle … One of the lessons of the Great War was the capital importance to our Army of the young regimental officer.[21]

After every raid the OC Raid knew he would be asked "To what do you attribute success (or failure)? And "What are the lessons?" The answers were a vital part of the quest for the best vision of what to do and what not to do. Validation or rejection of prevailing practice became for every officer a major consideration in the exercise of command. None of this is mentioned in the Kirke Report, which is not to condemn it, or think it any less valid in what it says, but the aspect of train, test and validate confirms the simple fact that raids were an integral part of war on the Western Front, a front that was never quite "all quiet." Whether or not raids were worth the cost is as hard to judge now as it was then. Opinion remains divided. But we can see and understand why a judgement is so difficult.

The military fact is simply that raids were necessary and invaluable. It is hard to see any alternative given the nature of trench warfare and the technological limitations of the time. Looking ahead, for sure, we have not seen the end of situations where soldiers wait for action: "somewhere men with blackened faces and grim clubs and axes and bombs – men with knocking hearts, stifling the yawns of nervousness … knowing that the enemy are ready for them – knowing that they will probably be killed or wounded or caught like rats."[22] Making a judgement does not preclude admitting contradiction and anomaly. The evidence says one cannot do otherwise. What Charles Dickens said of an earlier time applies equally well to raiding:

> It was the best of times, it was the worst of times, it was the age of wisdom, it was the age of foolishness, it was the epoch of Belief, it was the season of light, it was the season of darkness, it was the spring of hope, it was the winter of despair.[23]

21 Stephen Badsey, 'The Trench Raid at Cherisy, 15 September 1917', *Imperial War Museum Review,* 4 (1989), p. 95; Lt.-Colonel M.K. Wardle, DSO, MC, *Foundations of Soldiering* (Aldershot: Gale & Polden Limited, 1936), pp. 2-3, 7.

22 Hart-Davis, *Siegfried Sassoon: Diaries 1915-1918,* p. 73.

23 Charles Dickens, *A Tale of Two Cities* (London: Penguin, 1988), p. 35.

Appendix

Canadian Corps Order of Battle

1st Division

1st Brigade	1st, 2nd, 3rd, 4th Battalions
2nd Brigade	5th, 7th, 8th, 10th Battalions
3rd Brigade	13th, 14th, 15th, 16th Battalions

2nd Division

4th Brigade	18th, 19th, 20th, 21st Battalions
5th Brigade	22nd, 24th, 25th, 26th Battalions
6th Brigade	27th, 28th, 29th, 31st Battalions

3rd Division

7th Brigade	RCR, PPCLI, 42nd, 49th Battalions
8th Brigade	1st, 2nd, 4th, 5th Canadian Mounted Rifles
9th Brigade	43rd, 52nd, 58th, 60th/116th* Battalions

4th Division

10th Brigade	44th, 46th, 47th, 50th Battalions
11th Brigade	54th, 75th, 87th, 102nd Battalions
12th Brigade	38th, 51st, 72nd/78th*, 73rd/85th* Battalions

(*denotes replacement battalion)

Bibliography

Archival

Library and Archives of Canada Record Groups 9, 24 and 41 and Service Records
Personal Papers and Unit Records – MG 30E: Baldwin, H.W. (65). Clements, R.N. (156). Creelman, John Jennings (8). Currie, Arthur W. (100). Griesbach, William Antrobus (15). Macdonell, Archibald Cameron (20). Macintyre, Duncan (241). MacPherson, Huntley (23). Matthews, Harold Halford (60). Mitchell, C.H. (61). Odlum, Victor Wentworth (300). Parrsons, Johnson Lindsay (117), Phelan, Frederick (54). Russell, E.W. (220). Sinclair, Ian MacIntosh Rae (432). Turner, Richard E.W. (46). Urquhart, Hugh MacIntyre (75). Villiers, Paul Frederick (236). Warden, J.W. (192). Watson, David (69). 3rd Battalion (318). 10th Battalion (349). Woods, William B. (MG 31 G29-31) Saskatchewan Provincial Archives
R.2.247, 'The Great War As I Saw It', Memoirs of Brigadier-General George Tuxford
Imperial War Museum
Personal and Other Papers: Stanley Brittain, William Kerr, E.A. McKechnie and E.W. Russell
Canadian Letters and Images Project
Papers of Corporal Alfred Andrews (10th Battalion)
University of Birmingham
War Studies Research Projects, "Lions Led By Donkeys"
The National Archives of the United Kingdom
Public Records Office, WO 95, War Diaries

Manuals and Instructions

Becke, Major A.F. (comp.), *History of the Great War By Direction of the Historical Section of the Committee of Imperial Defence: Order of Battle of Divisions. Part 1. The Regular British Divisions* (London: HMSO, 1935).
——. *Part 2A. The Territorial Force Mounted Divisions and the 1st-Line Territorial Force Divisions (42-56)* (London: HMSO, 1936).
——. *Part 2B. The 2nd-Line Territorial Force Divisions (57th-69th) With the Home-Service Divisions (71st-73rd) and 74th and 75th Divisions* (London: HMSO, 1937).
——. *Part 3A. New Army Divisions (9-26)* (London: HMSO, 1938).
——. *Part 3B. New Army Divisions (30-41) and 63rd (R.N.) Division* (London: HMSO, 1945).
——. *Part 4. The Army Council, G. H. Q.s, Armies and Corps 1914-1918* (London: HMSO, 1945).

Canadian Corps Trench Orders (London: Harrison And Sons, 21 October 1915).
Canadian Corps Trench Orders (N.p.: Army Printing and Stationary Services, July 1916).
Canadian Corps Trench Standing Orders. (N.p.: Army Printing and Stationary Services, 1917).
CDS 74 The Training and Employment of Grenadiers (GHQ: Stationary Service, 1915).
Combined Training (Provisional.) (London: War Office, 1902).
Field Service Pocket Book (London: General Staff, War Office, 1914).
Field Service Regulations Part I Operations (London: HMSO, 1909; reprint ed., 1912).
Field Service Regulations Volume II Operations 1924 (London: HMSO, 1924).
Field Service Regulations Volume II Operations 1929 (London: HMSO, 1929).
Field Service Regulations Volume II Operations 1932 (London: HMSO, 1932).
Canadian Army *Manual of Training (CAMT) 1-36 Staff Procedures Volume 3 Staff Duties in the Field* (Ottawa: Army Headquarters, 1963).
Infantry Training. (4-Company Organization).1914 (London: HMSO, 1914).
Infantry Training. Vol. I. Training, 1926 (London: HMSO, 1926).
Manual of Military Law (London: HMSO, 1914; reprint ed., 1917).
Notes for Commanding Officers (Aldershot: Gale and Polden, 1917 and 1918 editions).
Notes on Trench Routine and Discipline by a Second in Command (London: Forster Groom & Co., Ltd., 1916).
Platoon Organization (London: War Office, January 1917).
SS 98/5 Artillery Notes. No. 5 Wire-Cutting (GHQ, February and June 1916).
SS 101 Notes for Infantry Officers on Trench Warfare (London: HMSO, March 1916).
SS 103 Orders Regarding the Sending of Messages Within 1500 Yards of the Firing Line (GHQ, O.B./630, February 1916).
SS 107 Notes on Minor Enterprises (G.H.Q., March 1916).
SS 109 Training of Divisions for Offensive Action (GHQ, May 1916).
SS 119 Preliminary Notes on the Lessons of the Recent Operations (Army P&S, July 1916).
SS 126 Training and Employment of Bombers (London: HMSO, September 1916).
SS 135 Instructions for the Training of Divisions for Offensive Action (London: HMSO, December 1916).
SS 139/6 Artillery Notes No. 6. Trench Mortars (GHQ, June 1916 and March 1917).
SS 143 Instructions for the Training of Platoons for Offensive Action (London: HMSO, December 1916, February 1917 and September 1917).
SS 143 Training and Employment of Platoons (Army Printing and Stationary Services, February 1918).
SS 144 The Normal Formation for the Attack (London: HMSO, February 1917).
SS 152 Instructions for the Training of the British Armies in France (Provisional) (London: HMSO, June 1917).
SS 182 Instructions on Bombing Part II Training and Employment of Bombers (London: Harrison and Sons, November 1917).
SS 185 Assault Training (London: HMSO, November 1917).
SS 195 Scouting and Patrolling (GHQ, December 1917).
SS 381 Collection of Information Regarding the Enemy (GHQ "I", October 1915).
SS 391 Field General Courts-Martial Notes for Guidance of Presidents (N.p., n.p., 1916).
SS 398 The Training and Employment of Bombers (London: Harrison And Sons, March 1916).

SS 408 Some of the Many Questions a Platoon Commander Should Ask Himself on Taking Over a Trench and at Intervals Afterwards (N.p.: Stationary Services Press, April 1916).
SS 415 The Duties of An Officer. Knowledge and Character (London: HMSO, 1917).
SS 462 German Raid on British Trenches Near La Boisselle, 11th April, 1916 (GHQ, August 1916).
*The Complete Guide to Map Reading (*Aldershot: Gale and Polden Ltd., 1911).
Training in Canadian Reserve Battalions (London: Harrison And Sons, January and October 1917).
Training Leaflet No. 4 Attack Formations for Small Units (IG Training, BEF, France. 1918).
*WO 33/723 Notes on Close Shooting by Guns and Howitzers, Registration of Targets and Calibration (*H & S, August 1915).
WO 2313 Notes on Map Reading (London HMSO, 1915).
WO 3476 Notes on Trench Warfare for Infantry Officers. Revised Diagrams (London: Harrison and Sons, 1917).
WO 3995 The Organization of an Infantry Battalion and the Normal Formation for the Attack. GHQ, April 1917. Previously Issued as O.B./1919, 7 February 1917 (GHQ).
Report of the Committee on the Lessons of the Great War. London (The War Office, October 1932. reprint ed., Uckfield, East Sussex: Naval and Military Press, n.d).

TRENCH JOURNALS

A Christmas Garland From the Front
Another Garland From the Front
The B.E.F. Times
The Better Times
The Brazier
The Dead Horse Corner Gazette
The Fortyniner
The Kemmel Times
The Listening Post
The New Church Times
RMR Growler
The Twentieth Gazette
The Listening Post
The Wipers Times

BOOKS

Adams, Bernard, *Nothing of Importance: A Record of Eight Months at the Front With a Welsh Battalion October 1915 to June 1916* (London: Methuen, 1917; reprint ed., Uckfield, East Sussex: The Naval and Military Press, n.d.).
Adkin, Mark. *The Western Front Companion (*London: Aurum Press Ltd., 2013).
Aldington, Richard, *Death of a Hero.* London (The Hogarth Press, 1984).

Allen, E.P.S., *The 116th Battalion In France: By the Adjutant (*Toronto: Hunter-Ross Co. Ltd., 1921.

Allinson, Sidney, *The Bantams* (Oakville: Mosaic Press, 1982).

Andrews, William Linton, *Haunting Years* (London: Hutchinson & Co., n.d.).

Ashworth, Tony, *Trench Warfare 1914-1918: The Live and Let Live System* (New York: Holmes & Meier Publishers, Inc. 1980).

Astill, Edwin, *The Great War Diaries of Brigadier-General Alexander Johnston 1914-1917* (Barnsley: Pen & Sword, 2007).

Atkinson, C.T., *The Seventh Division, 1914-1918* (London: John Murray, 1927).

Atkinson, C.T., (comp.), *The Devonshire Regiment* (Exeter: Eland, 1926).

Atteridge, A. Hilliard, *A History of the 17th (Northern) Division* (Uckfield, East Sussex: Naval and Military Press, n.d.).

Bagnall, F.W., *Not Mentioned in Despatches: The Memoir of Fred Bagnall, 14th Battalion. C.E.F. 1914-1917* (Vancouver: North Shore Press, 1933; reprint ed., Ottawa: CEF Books, 2005).

Baldwin, Sergeant Harold, *"Holding the Line"* (Chicago: A.C. McClurg & Co., 1918).

Barnard, Lieutenant Colonel W.T., *The Queen's Own Rifles of Canada 1860-1960: One Hundred Years of Canada* (Don Mills: Ontario Publishing Company, 1960).

Barker, A.J., *Fortune Favours the Brave* (London: Leo Cooper, 1974).

Barrie, Alexander, *War Underground: The Tunnellers of the Great War* (London: Tom Donovan, 1961).

Barton, Peter, *The Battlefields of the First World War* (London: Constable In Association with the Imperial War Museum, 2005).

——. *Lost Legions of Fromelles* (London: Constable, 2014).

——. *The Somme: The Unseen Panoramas* (London: Constable In Association With the Imperial War Museum, 2011).

——. Peter Doyle and Johan Vandewall, *Beneath Flanders Fields: The Tunnellers' War 1914-18* (Stroud, Gloucestershire: Spellmount, 2004).

Baynes, John, *Far From a Donkey: The Life of General Sir Ivor Maxse* (London: Brasseys, 1995).

Bean, C.E.W., *The Official History of Australia in the War of 1914-1918.* Vol. III. *The A.I.F. in France 1916 (*St. Lucia, Queensland: University of Queensland Press, 1982).

Beattie, Kim, *48th Highlanders of Canada 1891-1928* (Toronto: 48th Highlanders of Canada, 1932).

Beaverbrook, Lord, *Canada in Flanders.* Volume II (Toronto: Hodder and Stoughton, 1917).

Beckett, Ian (ed.), *The Memoirs of Sir James Edmonds* (Brighton: Tom Donovan Editions, 2013).

Beckett, Ian F.W. and Steven J. Corvi, *Haig's Generals* (Barnsley: Pen & Sword, 2006).

Bennett, MC, Captain S.G., *The 4th Canadian Mounted Rifles 1914-1919.* (Toronto: Murray Printing Company Limited, 1926).

Beresford, Charles, *The Christian Soldier: The Life of Lt. Col. The Rev. Bernard William Vann, VC, MC & Bar, Croix de Guerre avec palme* (Solihull: Helion & Company Limited, 2017).

Berton, Pierre, *Vimy* (Toronto: McClelland & Stewart, 1986).

Bewsher, Major F.W., *The History of the Fifty First (Highland) Division 1914-1918* (Uckfield, East Sussex: Naval and Military Press, n.d.).

Bidwell, Shelford, *Gunners at War: A Tactical Study of the Royal Artillery in the Twentieth Century* (London: Arrow Books Ltd., 1972).

Bidwell, Shelford and Dominick Graham, *Firepower: British Army Weapons and Theories of War 1904-1945* (London: George Allen & Unwin, 1982).

Birchall, Captain A.P., *Rapid Training of a Company for War.* (London: Gale and Polden, 1915).

Bird, Will R., *Ghosts Have Warm Hands* (Toronto: Clark, Irwin & Company, 1968).

——. *The Communication Trench* (Ottawa: CEF Books, 2000).

Bishop, Arthur, *Our Bravest and Our Best: The Stories of Canada's Victoria Cross Winners* (Toronto: McGraw-Hill Ryerson, 1995).

Black, Ernest G., *I Want One Volunteer (*Toronto: Ryerson, 1965).

Blake, R. (ed.), *The Private Papers of Douglas Haig 1914-1919* (London: Eyre & Spottiswoode, 1952).

Blunden, Edmund, *Undertones of War.* (Harmondsworth, Middlesex: Penguin Books Ltd., 1982).

——. *The Mind's Eye (*London: Jonathan Cape, 1934).

Body, Major O.G., *Notes on Appreciations, Instructions, Operation Orders and Message Writing* (London: Hugh Rees Ltd., 1930).

Bond, Brian (ed.), *The First World War and British Military History* (Oxford: Clarendon Press, 1991).

Bond, Brian and Nigel Cave (eds.), *Haig: A Reappraisal 70 Years On* (Barnsley, South Yorkshire: Leo Cooper, 1999).

Boraston, Lieut.-Colonel J.H. (ed.), *Sir Douglas Haig's Despatches (December1915-April 1919)* (London: J.M. Dent & Sons Ltd., 1920).

Boraston, Lt.-Colonel. J.H. and Captain Cyril E.O. Bax, *The Eighth Division 1914-1918* (London: The Medici Society Limited, 1926).

Bowman, Timothy, *The Irish Regiments in the Great War: Discipline and Morale* (Manchester: Manchester University Press, 2005).

Bradbridge, Lt.-Col. E. U. (ed.), *59th Division 1915-1918* (Chesterfield: Wilfred Edmunds, Limited, Printers, 1928).

Brophy, John and Eric Partridge, *The Long Trail: What the British Soldier Sang and Said in the Great War of 1914-18* (London: Andre Deutsch, 1965).

Brown, Malcolm, *Tommy Goes to War* (London: J.M. Dent & Sons Ltd., 1978).

——. *The Imperial War Museum Book of the Western Front* (London: Pan Books, 2001).

Buckley, Francis, *Q.6.A And Other Places* (London: Spottiswoode, Ballantyne & Co. Ltd., 1920).

Burns, Lt.-Gen. E.L.M., *General Mud: Memoirs of Two World Wars* (Toronto: Clarke, Irwin and Company Limited, 1970).

Burrowes, Brigadier-General A.R., *The 1st Battalion The Faugh-A-Ballaghs in the Great War* (Uckfield, East Sussex: Naval and Military Press, n.d.).

Bush, Captain Eric Wheler (ed.), *Salute the Soldier: An Anthology of Quotations, Poems and Prose* (London: Allen & Unwin, 1966).

Calder, Major D.G. Scott, *The History of the 28th (Northwest) Battalion, C.E.F. (October 1914-June 1919)* (Regina: privately printed, 1961).

Cane, Bruce, *It Made You Think of Home. The Haunting Journal of Deward Barnes, Canadian Expeditionary Force: 1916-1919* (Toronto: The Dundurn Group, 2004).

Carrington, Charles, *Soldier From The Wars Returning* (London: Hutchinson, 1965).

——. (ed.), *The Complete Barrack-Room Ballads of Rudyard Kipling* (London: Methuen & Co. Ltd., 1974).

Carstairs, Carroll, *A Generation Missing* (London: William Heinemann Ltd., 1930; reprint ed., Stevenage, Herts: The Strong Oak Press Ltd., 1989).
Cassar, George, *Beyond Courage: The Canadians at the Second Battle of Ypres* (Ottawa: Oberon, 1985).
Chapman, Guy, *A Passionate Prodigality* (New York: Holt, Rinehart and Winston, 1965).
Chappell, Mike, *The Canadian Army at War.* Osprey Men-At-Arms Series, No. 164 (London: Osprey Publishing, 1985).
——. *British Battle Insignia 1 1914-18.* Osprey Men-At-Arms Series. No. 182 (Botley: Osprey Publishing, 1986).
Chasseaud, Peter, *Rats Alley: Trench Names of the Western Front 1914-1918* (Stroud, Gloucestershire: Spellmount, 2006).
Cinquante-Quatre: Being a Short History of the 54th Canadian Infantry Battalion By One of Them (N.p.: privately published, 1919).
Clausewitz, Carl von, *On War.* Michael Howard and Peter Paret, (ed. and trans.) (Princeton, N.J.: Princeton University Press, 1976).
Clifton, Ronald, *Staff Officers in the British Army 1914-1918: Military Fact Sheet No. 16* (Macclesfield: Western Front Association, February 2003).
Cloete, Stuart, *A Victorian Son: An Autobiography 1897-1922* (London: Collins, 1972).
Clyne, H.R.N., *Vancouver's 29th* (Vancouver: Tobin's Tigers Association, 1964).
Collyer, Brigadier-General J.J., *The Campaign in German South West Africa 1914-1915* (Pretoria: Government Printer, 1937).
Committee of Officers Who Served With the Battalion, *The War History of the Sixth Battalion The South Staffordshire Regiment (T.F.)* (London: William Heinemann Ltd., 1924).
Connelly, Mark, *Steady the Buffs!: A Regiment, a Region, and the Great War* (Oxford: University Press, 2006).
Cook, Tim, *At the Sharp End* (Toronto: Viking, 2007).
Cooksey, Jon (ed.), *Blood and Iron: Letters from the Western Front: Hugh Montagu Butterworth* (Barnsley: Pen and Sword, 2011).
Cooksey, Jon and David Griffiths (eds.), *Harry's War: The Great War Diary of Harry Drinkwater.* (St Ives: Ebury Press, 2013).
Coombs, Rose E.B., *Before Endeavours Fade* (London: Battle of Britain International Limited, 1983).
Coop, The Rev. J.O., *The Story of the 55th (West Lancashire) Division* (Uckfield, East Sussex: Naval and Military Press, n.d.).
Cooper, Duff, *Haig.* Volume I (Toronto: Macmillan, 1935).
Cooper, Eric Thirkell, *Soliloquies of a Subaltern: Somewhere in France* (London: Burns & Oates Ltd., 1915).
Coppard, George, *With a Machine Gun to Cambrai* (London: Papermac, 1980).
Corrigall, Major D.J., *The History of the Twentieth Canadian Battalion (Central Ontario Regiment): Canadian Expeditionary Force in the Great War, 1914-1918* (Toronto: Stone & Cox Limited, 1935).
Corrigan, Gordon, *Mud, Blood and Poppycock: Britain and the First World War* (London: Cassell, 2003).
Craig, Norman, *The Broken Plume* (London: Imperial War Museum, 1982).

Croft, Lieut.-Colonel W.D., *Three Years With the Ninth (Scottish) Division* (London: John Murray, 1919).

Crookenden, Col. Arthur, *The History of the Cheshire Regiment in the Great War* (Uckfield, East Sussex: Naval and Military Press, n.d).

Crozier, Brig. Gen. F.P., *A Brass Hat in No Man's Land* (Bath: Cedric Chivers Ltd., 1968).

Cruttwell, C.R.M.F., *A History of the Great War 1914-1918* (Oxford at the Clarendon Press, 1964).

Cuddeford, D.W.J., *And All For What?* (London: Heath Cranton Limited, 1933).

Currie, Lieut.-General Sir A.W., *Canadian Corps Operations During the Year 1918. Interim Report* (Ottawa: Department of Militia and Defence, 1919).

Dancocks, Daniel G., *Sir Arthur Currie: A Biography* (Toronto: McClelland & Stewart, 1985).

——. *Legacy of Valour: The Canadians at Passchendaele* (Edmonton: Hurtig, 1986).

——. *Spearhead to Victory: Canada and the Great War* (Edmonton: Hurtig, 1987).

——. *Welcome to Flanders Fields: The First Canadian Battle of the Great War: Ypres, 1915.* (Toronto: McClelland & Stewart, 1988).

——. *Gallant Canadians The Story of the Tenth Canadian Infantry Battalion 1914-1919* (Calgary: The Calgary Highlanders Regimental Funds Foundation, 1990).

Davies, Frank and Graham Maddocks, *Bloody Red Tabs: General Officer Casualties of the Great War 1914-1918* (London: Leo Cooper, 1995).

Davson, Lieutenant-Colonel H.M., *The History of the 35th Division in the Great War* (London: Sifton Praed & Co., Ltd., 1926).

Delaney, Douglas E. and Serge Marc Durflinger (eds.), *Capturing Hill 70: Canada's Forgotten Battle of the First World War* (Vancouver: UBC Press, 2016).

D'Este, Carlo, *Fatal Decisions: Anzio and the Battle for Rome* (New York: Harper, 1991).

de Wiart, Adrian Carton, *Happy Odyssey* (London: Jonathan Cape, 1950).

Dinesen, Thomas, *Merry Hell: A Dane With the Canadians* (London: Jarrolds, 1929).

Douie, Charles, *The Weary Road: Recollections of a Subaltern of Infantry* (Stevenage, Herts: Strong Oak Press Ltd., 1988).

Doyle, Peter, *Tommy's War: British Military Memorabilia 1914-1918* (Ramsbury, Wiltshire: The Crowood Press Ltd., 2008).

Doyle, Peter and Chris Foster, *Remembering Tommy: The British Soldier in the First World War* (Stroud: Spellmount, 2013).

Dudley Ward, Major C.H., *The Fifty-Sixth Division 1914-1918* (Uckfield, East Sussex: Naval and Military Press, n.d).

——. *History of the Welsh Guards* (London: London Stamp Exchange Ltd., 1988).

——. *The 74th Yeomanry Division in Syria and France* (Uckfield. East Sussex: Naval and Military Press, n.d.).

——. (comp.) *Regimental Records of the Royal Welch Fusiliers (23rd Foot).* Vol. III. *1914-1918 France and Flanders* (London: Forster Groom & Co. Ltd., 1928).

——. (comp). *Regimental Records of the Royal Welch Fusiliers (23rd Foot).* Vol. IV. *1915-1918 Turkey-Bulgaria-Austria* (London: Forster Groom & Co. Ltd., 1929).

Duffy, Christopher, *Through German Eyes: The British and the Somme 1916* (London: Weidenfeld and Nicolson, 2006).

Dugdale, Captain Geoffrey, *"Langemarck" and "Cambrai": A War Narrative 1914-1918* (Uckfield, East Sussex: Naval and Military Press, n.d.).

Duguid, Colonel A. Fortescue, *Official History of the Canadian Forces in the Great War 1914-1919* General Series Vol. I. *From the Outbreak of War to the Formation of the Canadian Corps August 1914 – September 1915* (Ottawa: King's Printer, 1938).
——. *Official History of the Canadian Forces in the Great War 1914-1919* General Series Vol. I *Chronology, Appendices and Maps* (Ottawa: King's Printer, 1938).
Dundas, R.N. (ed.), *Henry Dundas Scots Guards: A Memoir* (London: William Blackwood and Sons, 1921).
Dunn, Captain J.C., *The War the Infantry Knew 1914-1919: A Chronicle of Service in France and Belgium* (London: Jane's Publishing Company Limited, 1987).
Duty and Service: Letters From the Front From Lionel William Crouch (London: Printed for Private Circulation, 1917).
Eberle, V.F., *My Sapper Venture* (London: Pitman, 1973).
Eden, Anthony, *Another World 1897-1917* (London: Allen Lane, 1976).
Edmonds, Brigadier-General J.E. and Captain G.C. Wynne, *Military Operations France and Belgium, 1915: Winter 1914-15: Battle of Neuve Chapelle: Battle of Ypres* (London: Macmillan, 1927).
Edmonds, Brigadier-General J.E. and Lieut.-Colonel R. Maxwell-Hyslop, *Military Operations France and Belgium 1918: Volume V 26th September-11th November: The Advance to Victory* (London: Macmillan, 1947).
Edmonds, Brigadier-General J.E., *Military Operations France and Belgium, 1915: Battles of Aubers Ridge, Festubert, and Loos* (London: Macmillan, 1928).
——. *Military Operations France and Belgium, 1916: Sir Douglas Haig's Command to the 1st July: Battle of the Somme* (London: Macmillan, 1932).
——. *Military Operations France and Belgium, 1916: Sir Douglas Haig's Command to the 1st July: Battle of the Somme. Appendices* (London: Macmillan, 1932).
——. *Military Operations France and Belgium 1917: Volume II 7th June-10th November Messines and Third Ypres (Passchendaele)* (London: Macmillan, 1948).
——. *Military Operations France and Belgium, 1918: The German March Offensive and Its Preliminaries* (London: Macmillan, 1935).
——. *Military Operations France and Belgium, 1918: March-April: Continuation of the German Offensives* (London: Macmillan, 1937).
——. *Military Operations France and Belgium 1918: Volume IV 8th August-26th September The Franco-British Offensive* (London: Macmillan, 1947).
——. *Military Operations France and Belgium 1914: Mons, The Retreat to the Seine, The Marne and the Aisne. August-October 1914* (London: Macmillan, 1933).
Edmonds, Charles [Charles Carrington], *A Subaltern's War* (London: Peter Davies Ltd., 1929).
Egremont, Max, *Siegfried Sassoon: A Life* (New York: Farrar, Straus and Giroux, 2005).
Elliot, Major S.R., *Scarlet to Green: A History of Intelligence in the Canadian Army 1903-1963* (Toronto: Canadian Intelligence and Security Association, 1981).
Ellis, John, *Eye-Deep in Hell: The Western Front, 1914-1918* (London: Croom Helm, 1975).
——. *The Sharp End* (New York: Charles Scribners Sons, 1980).
Enser, A.G.S., *A Subject Bibliography of the First World War: Books in English 1914-1978* (London: Andre Deutsch, 1979).
Ex-Private X [Alfred McClelland Burrage], *War is War* (London: Victor Gollancz Ltd., 1930).

Ewing, John, *The History of the Ninth (Scottish) Division 1914-1919* (Uckfield, East Sussex: Naval and Military Press, n.d.).

Falls, Captain Cyril, *Military Operations France and Belgium, 1917: The German Retreat to the Hindenburg Line and the Battles of Arras* (London: Macmillan, 1940).

——. *Military Operations France and Belgium, 1917: The German Retreat to the Hindenburg Line and the Battles of Arras: Appendices* (London: Macmillan, 1940).

——. *War Books: An Annotated Bibliography of Books About the Great War* (London: Greenhill Books, 1989).

——. *The History of the 36th(Ulster)Division* (London: M'Caw, Stevenson & Orr, Ltd., 1922).

Farr, Don, *The Silent General: Horne of the First Army* (Solihull: Helion & Company Ltd., 2007).

Farrar-Hockley, Anthony, *Official History: The British Part in the Korean War. Volume II. An Honourable Discharge* (London: HMSO, 1995).

Feilding, Rowland, *War Letters to a Wife: France and Flanders, 1915-1919* (London: The Medici Company, 1929).

Fetherstonhaugh, R.C., *The 13th Battalion Royal Highlanders of Canada 1914-1919* (Montreal: The 13th Battalion Royal Highlanders of Canada, 1925).

——. *The Royal Montreal Regiment 14th Battalion, C.E.F. 1914-1925* (Montreal: The Gazette Publishing Co. Limited, 1927).

——. *The 24th Battalion, C.E.F., Victoria Rifles of Canada 1914-1919* (Montreal: Gazette Printing Company, 1930).

——. *The Royal Canadian Regiment 1883-1933* (Montreal: Gazette Printing Company, 1936).

Fewster. Kevin, *Gallipoli Correspondent: The Frontline Diary of C.E.W. Bean* (Sydney: George Allen & Unwin, 1983).

Fifth Battalion Year Book (Saskatoon: Fifth Battalion Association, n.d.).

Fischer, David Hackett, *Historians' Fallacies: Toward a Logic of Historical Thought* (New York: Harper Torchbooks, 1970).

Fletcher, Ian (ed.), *Letters from the Front: The Great War Correspondence of Lieutenant Brian Lawrence, 1916-1917* (Tunbridge Wells: Parapress, Ltd., 1993).

Fosten, D.S.V. and R.J. Marrion, *The British Army 1914-18* (London: Osprey Publishing, 1978).

Foster, Charles Lyon and William Smith Duthie (eds.), *Letters From the Front Being a Record of the Part Played By Officers of the Bank in the Great War.* Vols. 1 and 2 (Toronto: Canadian Bank of Commerce, 1920).

Foulkes, Major-General C.H., *"Gas!": The Story of the Special Brigade* (Edinburgh: Blackwood, 1934).

Fraser, David (ed.), *In Good Company: The First World War Letters and Diaries of The Hon. William Fraser Gordon Highlanders* (Salisbury, Wiltshire: Michael Russell, 1990).

Fraser, Edward and John Gibbons, *Soldier and Sailor Words and Phrases* (London: George Routledge and Sons Ltd., 1925).

French, Anthony, *Gone For a Soldier* (Kineton: The Roundwood Press, 1972).

Fyfe. Albert J., *Understanding the First World War: Illusions and Realities* (New York: Peter Lang, 1988).

Gallagher, Gary W. (ed.), *Lee and His Army in Confederate History.* (Chapel Hill: The University of North Carolina Press, 2001).

Gardiner, Ian, *The Yompers: With 45 Commando in the Falklands War* (Barnsley: Pen and Sword, 2112).

Gardner, Brian (ed.), *Up the Line to Death: The War Poets 1914-1918* (London: Magnum Books, 1976).

Gibbon, Frederick P., *The 42nd (East Lancashire) Division 1914-1918* (London: "Country Life," 1920).

Gilbert, Martin, *The Challenge of War: Winston S. Churchill 1914-1916* (London: William Heinemann Ltd., reprint ed., London: Mandarin, 1990).

Gillon, Captain Stair, *The Story of the 29th Division: A Record of Gallant Deeds* (London: Thomas Nelson & Sons Ltd., 1925).

Glover, Michael (ed.), *The Fateful Battle Line The Great War Journals and Sketches of Captain Henry Ogle, MC* (London: Leo Cooper, 1993).

Goodspeed, Major D. J., *Battle Royal: A History of the Royal Regiment of Canada 1862-1962* (Toronto: The Royal Regiment of Canada Association, 1962).

——. *The Road Past Vimy: The Canadian Corps, 1914-1918* (Toronto: Macmillan, 1969).

Gould, L. McLeod, *From B.C. to Baisieux: Being the Narrative History of the 102nd Canadian Infantry Battalion* (Victoria: Thos. R. Cusack Presses, 1919).

Graham, Stephen, *A Private in the Guards* (London: Macmillan, 1919).

Graves, Robert, *Goodbye to All That* (Harmondsworth, Middlesex: Penguin Books Ltd., 1960).

Grey, Jeffrey, *A Military History of Australia* (Sydney: Cambridge University Press, 1990).

Grey, Major W.E., *The 2nd City of London Regiment (Royal Fusiliers) in the Great War (1914-1919)* (London: Published from the Headquarters of the Regiment, 1929).

Greenhous, Brereton and Stephen J. Harris, *Canada and the Battle of Vimy Ridge: 9-12 April 1917* (Ottawa: Department of National Defence, 2004).

Greenwell, Graham H., *An Infant in Arms: War Letters of a Company Officer 1914-1918* (London: The Penguin Press, 1972).

Griffith, Paddy, *Battle Tactics of the Western Front: The British Army's Art of Attack 1916 -18* (New Haven: Yale University Press, 1994).

——. (ed.), *British Fighting Methods in the Great War* (London: Frank Cass, 1996).

Griffith, Wyn, *Up to Mametz* (London: Faber and Faber Limited, 1931).

——. *Up to Mametz and Beyond,* Jonathan Riley (ed.) (Barnsley: Pen & Sword, 2010).

Gullet, Henry (Jo), *Not As a Duty Only: An Infantryman's War* (Melbourne: University Press. 1976).

Haking, Brig.-General R.C.B., *Company Training* (London: Hugh Rees Limited, 1915).

Haldane, Lieut.-Colonel M.M., *History of the Fourth Battalion The Seaforth Highlanders* (Uckfield, East Sussex: Naval and Military Press, n.d.).

Hamilton, General Sir Ian, *The Soul and Body of an Army* (London: Edward Arnold & Co., 1921).

Hamilton, Master of Belhaven, Lieutenant-Colonel The Hon. Ralph, *The War Diary of the Master of Belhaven* (London: John Murray, 1924; reprint ed., Barnsley, South Yorkshire: Wharncliffe Publishing Limited, 1990).

Hanbury-Sparrow, Lt. Col. A.A., *The Land-Locked Lake* (London: Arthur Barker Ltd., 1932).

Hare, Major-General Sir Steuart, *The Annals of the King's Royal Rifle Corps: Volume V. The Great War* (London: John Murray, 1932).

Harris, Stephen, *Canadian Brass: The Making of a Professional Army, 1860-1939* (Toronto: University of Toronto Press, 1988).

Harrison, Charles Yale, *Generals Die in Bed* (Hamilton: Potlach Publications, 1975).

Harrison, Gary (ed.), *To Fight Alongside Friends: The First World War Diaries of Charlie May* (London: William Collins, 2014).
Hart, Peter, *The Somme* (London: Weidenfeld & Nicolson, 2005).
Hart-Davis, Rupert (ed.), *Siegfried Sassoon Diaries 1915-1918* (London: Faber & Faber, 1983).
Harvey, David, *Monuments to Courage Victoria Cross Headstones and Memorials. Volume One 1854-1916* and *Volume Two 1917-1982* (Bahrain: Published on behalf of the Author by Kevin and Kay Patience, 1999).
Harvey, Trevor, *An Army of Brigadiers: British Brigade Commanders at the Battle of Arras 1917* (Solihull: Helion & Company Limited, 2017).
Hay, Ian [Major-General John Hay Beith], *The First Hundred Thousand Being the Unofficial Chronicle of a Unit of "K(I)"*(Toronto: William Briggs, 1916).
Hayes, Lt. Col. Joseph, *The Eighty-Fifth In France and Flanders* (Halifax: Royal Print & Litho Limited, 1920).
Headlam, Lt. Col. Cuthbert, *History of the Guards Division in the Great War 1915 – 1918*. Vols. I. and II (Uckfield, East Sussex: Naval and Military Press, n.d.).
Hewett, Stephen H., *A Scholar's Letters From the Front* (London: Longmans, Green And Co., 1918).
Hindenburg, Paul von, *Out of My Life,* F. Holt. (trans.) (London: Cassell, 1920).
Hiscock, Eric, *The Bells of Hell Go Ting-A Ling-A Ling* (London: Arlington Books Ltd., 1976).
Hitchcock, Captain F.C., *"Stand To": A Diary of the Trenches 1915-1918* (Norwich, Norfolk: Gliddon Books, 1988).
Hodgkinson, Peter E., *British Infantry Battalion Commanders in the First World War* (Farnham: Ashgate Publishing Limited, 2015).
Holmes, Richard, *Firing Line* (Harmondsworth, Middlesex: Penguin Books, 1987).
——. *Tommy The British Soldier on the Western Front 1914-1918* (London: Harper Collins, 2004).
——. *Shots From the Front The British Soldier 1914-18* (London: Harper Press. 2008).
——. *Soldiers* (London: Harper Press, 2011).
Housman, L. (ed.), *War Letters of Fallen Englishmen* (London: Victor Gollancz, 1930).
Hussey, Brigadier-General A.H. and Major D.S. Inman, *The Fifth Division in the Great War* (London: Nisbet and Co. Ltd., 1921).
Hutchison, DSO, MC, Lieutenant-Colonel Graham Seton, *The Thirty-Third Division in France and Flanders 1915-1919* (Uckfield, East Sussex: Naval and Military Press, n.d.).
Hyatt, A.M.J., *General Sir Arthur Currie: A Military Biography* (Toronto: University of Toronto Press, 1987).
Inglefield, Captain V.E., *The History of the Twentieth (Light) Division* (Uckfield, East Sussex: Naval and Military Press, n.d.).
Iriam, Glenn R., *In the Trenches 1914-1918* (N.p.: Art Book Bindery, 2008).
Ivelaw-Chapman, John, *The Riddles of Wipers: An Appreciation of The Wipers Times, A Journal of the Trenches* (London: Leo Cooper, 1997).
James, Brig. E.A., *British Regiments 1914-1918* (Uckfield, East Sussex: Naval and Military Press, n.d.).
Jary, Sydney, *18 Platoon* (Carshalton Beeches, Surrey: Sydney Jary Limited, 1987).
Jerrold, Douglas, *Georgian Adventure* (New York: Charles Scribner's Sons, 1938).
——. *The Hawke Battalion* (Uckfield, East Sussex: Naval and Military Press, n.d.).
——. *The Royal Naval Division* (Uckfield, East Sussex: Naval and Military Press, n.d.).

Jessel, Major R.G., *G, A, and Q An Introduction to the Staff* (Aldershot: Gale and Polden, 1947).
Johnson, Douglas Wilson, *Battlefields of the World War, Western and Southern Fronts: A Study in Military Geography* (New York: Oxford University Press, 1921).
Johnston, Lt.-Col. G. Chalmers, *The 2nd Canadian Mounted Rifles (British Columbia Horse) in France and Flanders* (Vernon, B.C.: Vernon News, n.d.).
Johnston, William, *A War of Patrols: Canadian Army Operations in Korea* (Vancouver: UBC Press, 2003).
Junger, Ernst, *The Storm of Steel* (London: Chatto and Windus, 1929; reprint ed., London: Constable, 1994).
——. *Copse 125,* Basil Creighton (trans.) (London: Chatto and Windus, 1930; reprint ed., N.p. Zimmermann and Zimmermann, 1985).
Kelly, D.V., *39 Months With the "Tigers" 1915-1918* (London: Ernest Benn Limited, 1930).
Kelly, R.B. Talbot, *A Subaltern's Odyssey: A Memoir of the Great War 1915-1917* (London: William Kimber, 1980).
Kerr, Wilfred Brenton, *Arms and the Maple Leaf: Memories of Canada's Corps 1918* (Seaforth, Ontario: Huron Expositor Press, 1943).
——. *Shrieks and Crashes* (Toronto: Hunter-Rose Company, 1929).
Kincaid-Smith, M., *The 25th Division in France and Flanders* (London: Harrison, 1920).
Kipling, Rudyard, *The Irish Guards in the Great War: The First Battalion* (New York: Sarpedon, 1997).
Laffin, John, *On the Western Front: Soldiers' Stories From France and Flanders 1914-1918* (Brunswick Road, Gloucester: Alan Sutton Publishing Limited, 1985).
Leader, Major W.K.M., *An Elementary Study of Appreciations, Orders and Messages* (London: Sifton, Praed & Co. Ltd., 1936).
Lewis, Lieut. R., *Over the Top With the 25th* (Halifax: H.H. Marshall Limited, 1918).
Lewis-Stempel, John, *Six Weeks: The Short and Gallant Life of the British Officer in the First World War* (London: Weidenfeld & Nicolson, 2010).
Liddell Hart, Captain B.H., *The Real War 1914-1918* (Toronto: Little, Brown & Company, 1930).
Liddle, Peter H. (ed.), *Passchendaele In Perspective: The Third Battle of Ypres* (London: Leo Cooper,1997).
Lipscomb, Captain W.P., *Staff Tales* (London: Constable, 1920).
Livesay, J.F.B., *Canada's Hundred Days: With the Canadian Corps from Amiens to Mons, Aug. 8-Nov. 11, 1918* (Toronto: Thomas Allen, 1919).
Love, David W., *"A Call to Arms": The Organization and Administration of Canada's Military in World War One* (Calgary: Bunker to Bunker Books, 1999).
Lucas, Michael, *The Journey's End Battalion: The 9th East Surrey in the Great War* (Barnsley: Pen & Sword, 2012).
Lucas, Sir Charles (gen. ed.), *The Empire at War.* 5 vols (Oxford: OUP: 1921-26), Vol. 2 *Canada* by F.H. Underhill. London: Clarendon Press, 1923.
Lucy, John F., *There's a Devil in the Drum* (London: Faber & Faber Limited, 1938).
Ludendorff, Field-Marshal Erich, *My War Memories, 1914-1918* (London: Hutchinson, 1919).
Lytton, Major The Hon. N.S., *The Press and the General Staff* (London: Collins, 1920).
MacDonald, F.B. and John J. Gardiner, *The Twenty-Fifth Battalion Canadian Expeditionary Force (*Sydney, N.S.: City Printers Limited, 1983).

Macdonald, Lyn, *They Called it Passchendaele: The Story of the Third Battle of Ypres and the Men Who Fought In It* (London: Michael Joseph, 1978).

——. *Somme* (London: Michael Joseph, 1981).

——. (ed.), *Anthem for Doomed Youth: Poets of the Great War* (London: Folio Society, 2000).

MacGowan, S. Douglas, Harry (Mac) Heckbert, M.M. and Byron E. O'Leary, *New Brunswick's "Fighting 26th": A History of the 26th New Brunswick Battalion, C.E.F. 1914-1919* (Saint John, N.B.: Neptune Publishing Company Limited, 1995).

MacGregor, James, *MacGregor V.C.: Goodbye Dad* (Victoria, B.C.: Victoria Publishing Company, 2002).

McClintock, Alexander, *Best O'Luck* (Toronto: McClelland, Goodchild & Stewart, 1917).

McEvoy, Bernard and Capt. A.H. Finlay, MC, *History of the 72nd Canadian Infantry Battalion Seaforth Highlanders of Canada* (Vancouver: Cowan & Brookhouse, 1920).

McKee, Alexander, *Vimy Ridge* (London: Souvenir Press, 1966).

McKean, George B., *Scouting Thrills: The Memoir of a Scout Officer in the Great War* (Oxford: Oxford University Press, 1919).

McPhail, Helen and Philip Guest, *On the Trail of the Poets of the Great War: Robert Graves and Siegfried Sassoon* (Barnsley, South Yorkshire: Pen and Sword Books Limited, 2001).

——. *On the Trail of the Poets of the Great War: Wilfred Owen* (Barnsley, South Yorkshire: Pen and Sword Books Limited, 1998).

McWilliams, James L. and R. James Steel, *Gas!* (St. Catherines: Vanwell Publishing, 1985).

Macintyre, D.E., *Canada at Vimy* (Toronto: Peter Martin Associates Limited, 1967).

Macklin, Major-General W.H.S., *An Introduction to the Study of the Principles of War* (Ottawa: King's Printer, 1954).

Macksey, Kenneth, *Guderian: Panzer General* (London: Macdonald And Janes, 1975).

Manning, Frederick, *The Middle Parts of Fortune* (London: Peter Davies, 1929).

Mark VII [Max Plowman], *A Subaltern on the Somme* (London: Chatto and Windus, 1929; reprint., Uckfield, East Sussex: Naval and Military Press, n.d.).

Martin, Bernard, *Poor Bloody Infantry: A Subaltern on the Western Front 1916-1917* (London: John Murray, 1987).

Maude, Alan H., *The History of the 47th (London) Division 1914-1919* (London: Amalgamated Press Ltd., 1922).

Maxwell, Mrs. Charlotte (ed.), *Frank Maxwell Brig.-General, VC, CSI, DSO: A Memoir and Some Letters* (London: John Murray, 1921).

Maxwell, Robert, *Villiers-Stuart Goes to War* (Edinburgh: The Pentland Press, 1990).

Meek, John F., *Over the Top! The Canadian Infantry in the First World War* (Orangeville, Ontario: n.p., 1971).

Messenger, Charles, *Call to Arms: The British Army 1914-18* (London: Weidenfeld & Nicolson, 2005).

Middlebrook, Martin, *The First Day on the Somme: 1 July 1916* (London: Purnell, 1971).

Miles, Captain Wilfred, *Military Operations France and Belgium, 1916: 2nd July 1916 to the End of the Battles of the Somme* (London: Macmillan, 1938).

Military Advisory Board, *Canada in the Great World War; an Authentic Account of the Military History of Canada from the Earliest Days to the Close of the War of the Nations.* Vol. II: *Days of Preparation* (Toronto: United Publishers of Canada Limited, 1917).

——. Vol. III: *Guarding the Channel Ports* (Toronto: United Publishers of Canada Limited, 1919).

——. Vol. IV: *The Turn of the Tide* (Toronto: United Publishers of Canada Limited, 1920).

——. Vol. V: *The Triumph of the Allies* (Toronto: United Publishers of Canada Limited, 1920).

——. Vol. VI: *Special Services Heroic Deeds Etc.* (Toronto: United Publishers of Canada Limited, 1921).

Miller, Carman, *Painting the Map Red: Canada and the South African War* (Montreal: McGill-Queen's University, 1993).

Molony, Major C.V., *"Invicta": With the First Battalion The Queen's Royal West Kent Regiment in the Great War* (London: Nisbet & Co. Ltd., 1923).

Monroe, Catherine Becker (ed.), *Silhouettes of the Great War: The Memoir of John Harold Becker 1915-1919* (Ottawa: CEF Books, 2001).

Montague, C.E., *Disenchantment* (London: Chatto and Windus, 1922).

Moody, Colonel R.S.H., *Historical Records of The Buffs East Kent Regiment 1914-1919* (Uckfield, East Sussex: Naval and Military Press, n.d.).

Moorhouse, Brendon, *Forged by Fire: The Battle Tactics and Soldiers of a World War One Battalion: The 7th Somerset Light Infantry* (Staplehurst: Spellmount Limited, 2003).

Moore-Bick, Christopher, *Playing the Game: The British Junior Infantry Officer on the Western Front 1914-18* (Solihull, West Midlands: Helion & Company Limited, 2011).

Moran, Lord, *The Anatomy of Courage* (London: Constable, 1945).

Morton, Desmond, *When Your Number's Up: The Canadian Soldier in the First World War* (Toronto: Random House, 1993).

Moss, Robert F., (ed.) *Raymond Chandler: A Literary Reference* (New York: Carroll and Graf Publishers, 2002).

Murphy, C.C.R., *The History of the Suffolk Regiment 1914-1927* (London: Hutchinson, 1928).

Murray, Colonel W.W., *The History of the 2nd Canadian Battalion (East Ontario Regiment) Canadian Expeditionary Force* (Ottawa: Mortimer Ltd., 1947).

Nash, N.S., *Valour in the Trenches "Bombo" Pollard VC MC* DCM HAC In the Great War* (Barnsley, South Yorkshire: Pen & Sword Books Ltd., 2011).

Nason, Anne, (ed.), *For Love and Courage: The Letters of Lieutenant-Colonel E.W. Hermon from the Western Front 1914-1917* (London: Preface Publishing, 2008).

Needham, Lieutenant-Colonel J. Layland, *The Solution to Tactical Problems* (London: Hugh Rees, Ltd., 1916).

Neillands, Robin, *The Great War Generals on the Western Front 1914-1918* (London: Magpie Books, 2004).

Neville, Lt. Col. Sir James, *War Letters of a Light Infantryman* (London: Sifton, Praed & Co., 1930).

Nevins, Thomas, *Ernst Junger and Germany: Into the Abyss, 1914-1945* (Durham: Duke University Press, 1996).

Nichols, Captain G.H.F., *The 18th Division in the Great War* (London: William Blackwood and Sons, 1922).

Nicholson, Colonel G.W.L., *Official History of the Canadian Army in the First World War: Canadian Expeditionary Force, 1914-1919* (Ottawa: Queen's Printer, 1962).

Nicholson, Col. W.N., *Behind the Lines: An Account of Administrative Staffwork in the British Army 1914-1918* (London: Jonathan Cape, 1939).

Nicol, Randall, *Till the Trumpet Sounds Again-The Scots Guards 1914-1919 In Their Own Words Volume I: 'Great Shadows' August 1914–July 1916* (Solihull: Helion & Company Limited, 2016).

Nicolai, Colonel W., *The German Secret Service,* George Renwick (trans.) (London: Stanley Paul & Co., Ltd., 1924).

Noakes, F.E. *The Distant Drum: A Memoir of a Guardsman in the Great War.* London: Frontline Books, 2010.

Noakes, Vivien, *Voices of Silence: The Alternative Book of First World War Poetry* (Stroud: Sutton Publishing Ltd., 2006).

Norris, Lieutenant Armine, *"Mainly for Mother"* (Toronto: The Ryerson Press, 1917).

Orr, David R. and David Trusedale, *"Ulster Will Fight ... " Volume 2: The 36th Ulster Division from Formation to Armistice* (Solihull: Helion & Company, 2016).

Orwell, George, *Nineteen Eighty-Four* (London: Penguin Books, 1987).

Pagan, Brig.-Gen. A. W., *Infantry: An Account of the 1st Gloucestershire Regiment During the War 1914-1918* (Aldershot: Gale & Polden Ltd., 1951).

Page, Christopher, *Command in the Royal Naval Division: A Military Biography of Brigadier General A.M. Asquith DSO* (Staplehurst: Spellmount, 1999).

Pearse, Colonel H.W. and Brigadier-General H.S. Sloman, *History of the East Surrey Regiment 1914-1917.* Vol. II (London: The Medici Society, 1923).

Peat, Harold R., *Private Peat* (Indianapolis: Bobbs-Merill Co., 1917).

Peck. Edward, *Cy Peck, VC: A Biography of a Legendary Canadian* (Winnipeg: privately printed, 2008).

Pedley, James H., *Only This A War Retrospect* (Ottawa: Graphic Publishers, 1927).

Perry, F.W., *History of the Great War Order of Battle of Divisions Part 5A. The Divisions of Australia, Canada and New Zealand And Those in East Africa* (Newport, Gwent: Ray Westlake, 1992).

Petre, F. Loraine, Wilfred Ewart and Major-General Sir Cecil Lowther, *The Scots Guards in the Great War 1914-1918* (London: John Murray, 1925).

Philpott, William, *Bloody Victory: The Sacrifice on the Somme and the Making of the Twentieth Century* (London: Little, Brown, 2009).

——. *Attrition: Fighting the First World War* (London: Little, Brown, 2014).

Pinney, Thomas (ed.), *The Cambridge Edition of the Poems of Rudyard Kipling Volume II Collected Poems* (Cambridge: Cambridge University Press, 2013).

——. *The Cambridge Edition of the Poems of Rudyard Kipling Volume III The Uncollected Poems* (Cambridge: Cambridge University Press, 2013).

Pollard, Captain A.O., *Fire-Eater: The Memoirs of a V.C.* (Uckfield, East Sussex: The Naval and Military Press Ltd., n.d.).

Ponsonby, The Right Hon. Sir Frederick, *The Grenadier Guards in the Great War of 1914-1918.* Vol. I and Vol. II. (London: Macmillan, 1920).

Powell, Geoffrey, *Plumer The Soldier's General* (London: Leo Cooper, 1990).

Priestley, Major R.E., *Breaking the Hindenburg Line: The Story of the 46th (North Midland) Division* (London: T. Fisher Unwin Ltd., 1919).

Pugsley, Christopher, *On the Fringe of Hell: New Zealanders and Military Discipline in the First World War* (Auckland: Hodder & Stoughton, 1991).

Radley, Kenneth, *We Lead Others Follow: First Canadian Division 1914-1918* (St. Catharines: Vanwell Publishing Limited, 2006).

——. *Get Tough, Stay Tough: Shaping the Canadian Corps 1914-1918* (Solihull: Helion & Company Limited, 2014).
Rae, Herbert, *Maple Leaves in Flanders Fields* (Toronto: William Briggs, 1916).
Rawling, Bill, *Surviving Trench Warfare: Technology and the Canadian Corps, 1914-1918* (Toronto: University of Toronto Press, 1992).
Rawson, Andrew, *British Army Handbook 1914-1918* (Stroud, Gloucestershire: Sutton Publishing Limited, 2006).
Read, Herbert, *Annals of Innocence and Experience* (London: Faber and Faber Ltd., 1956).
——. *The Contrary Experience* (London: Faber, 1963).
Rees, Major R.T., *A Schoolmaster at War* (London: Haycock Press, 1936).
Reid, Gordon (ed.), *Poor Bloody Murder* (Oakville: Mosaic Press, 1980).
Richards, Frank, *Old Soldiers Never Die* (London: Faber and Faber, 1933; reprint ed., Baston, England: H.J. Krijnen and D.E. Langley, 2004).
Riddle, David K. and Donald G. Mitchell (comps.), *The Distinguished Service Order Awarded to Members of the Canadian Expeditionary Force and Canadians in the Royal Naval Air Service, The Royal Flying Corps and Royal Air Force 1915-1920* (Winnipeg: Kirkby-Marlton Press, 1991).
——. *The Military Cross Awarded to Members of the Canadian Expeditionary Force 1915-1921* (Winnipeg: Kirkby-Marlton Press, 1991).
Roberts, John Stuart, *Siegfried Sassoon* (London: Metro Publishing, 2014).
Rogerson, Sidney, *Twelve Days* (London: Arthur Barker Ltd., 1933).
Ross of Bladensburg, Lieutenant-Colonel Sir John, *The Coldstream Guards 1914-1918* (London: Oxford University Press, 1928).
Rostron, Peter, *Gloucestershire Hero: Brigadier Patsy Pagan's Great War Experiences* (Barnsley: Pen & Sword Books Ltd., 2015).
Roy, Fred L., *Shock Troops of the Confederacy: The Sharpshooter Battalions of the Army of Northern Virginia* (Asheville: CFS Press, 2006).
Roy, Reginald H., *For Most Conspicuous Bravery: A Biography of Major-General George R. Pearkes, V.C., Through Two World Wars* (Vancouver: University of British Columbia Press, 1977).
——. (ed.) *The Journal of Private Fraser 1914-1918 Canadian Expeditionary Force* (Victoria: Sono Nis Press, 1985).
Royle, Trevor, *A Dictionary of Military Quotations* (London: Routledge, 1990).
——. (ed.) *In Flanders Fields: Scottish Prose and Poetry of the First World War* (Edinburgh: Mainstream Publishing, 1991).
Russenholt, E.S., *Six Thousand Canadian Men: Being the History of the 44th Battalion Canadian Infantry 1914-1919* (Winnipeg: The Forty-Fourth Battalion Association, 1932).
Samuels, Martin, *Command or Control? Command, Training and Tactics in the British and German Armies, 1888-1918* (London: Frank Cass, 1995).
——. *Doctrine and Dogma: German and British Infantry Tactics in the First World War* (Westport: Greenwood Press, 1992).
Sandilands, Lieut.-Colonel H.R., *The 23rd Division 1914-1919* (Edinburgh: William Blackwood And Sons, 1925).
Saunders, Anthony, *Weapons of the Trench War 1914-1918* (Stroud: Sutton Publishing, 1999).
——. *Raiding on the Western Front* (Barnsley: Pen and Sword, 2012).
Sassoon, Siegfried, *Memoirs of an Infantry Officer* (London: Faber and Faber, 1965).

——. *The War Poems* (London: Faber and Faber, 1983).

Scott, Major-General Sir Arthur B. (ed.), *The History of the 12th (Eastern) Division in the Great War 1914-191.* (London: Nisbet & Co. Ltd., 1923).

Scudamore, Major T.V., *A Short History of the 7th Battalion, C.E.F.* (Vancouver: Anderson & Odlum, 1930).

Senior, Michael, *Haking: A Dutiful Soldier. Lt General Sir Richard Haking, XI Corps Commander 1915-18 - A Study in Corps Command* (Barnsley, South Yorkshire: Pen & Sword Books Ltd., 2012).

Shackleton, Kevin R., *Second to None: The Fighting 58th Battalion of the Canadian Expeditionary Force* (Toronto: The Dundern Group, 2002).

Shakespear, Lieut.-Colonel J., *The Thirty-Fourth Division 1915-1919* (London: H.F. & G. Witherby, 1921).

Shannon, Kevin, *The Lion and the Rose: The 4th Battalion The King's Own Royal Lancaster Regiment 1914-1919* (Croydon: Fonthill, 2015).

Sheffield, G.D., *Leadership in the Trenches: Officer-Man Relations, Morale and Discipline in the British Army in the Era of the First World War* (Houndmills, Basingstoke: MacMillan Press Ltd., 2000).

Sheffield, Gary and John Bourne, *Douglas Haig: War Diaries and Letters 1914-1918* (London: Weidenfeld & Nicolson, 2005).

Sheldon, Jack, *The German Army on the Somme 1914-1916* (Barnsley, South Yorkshire: Pen and Sword, 2005).

——. *The German Army at Passchendaele* (Barnsley, South Yorkshire: Pen and Sword, 2007).

——. *The German Army on Vimy Ridge 1914-1917* (Barnsley, South Yorkshire: Pen & Sword, 2008).

Sheldon-Williams, Inglis and Ralf Frederic Lardy Sheldon-Williams, *The Canadian Front in France and Flanders,* (London: A & C Black Ltd., 1920).

Sherriff, R.C., *Journey's End: A Play in Three Acts* (London: Victor Gollancz Ltd., 1929).

Silkin, Jon, *Out of Battle: The Poetry of the Great War* (Oxford: Oxford University Press, 1978).

Simpson, Andy, *Hot Blood & Cold Steel: Life and Death in the Trenches of the First World War* (Staplehurst, Kent: Spellmount, 2002).

Singer, Major H.C., *History of the 31st Canadian Infantry Battalion C.E.F.* (Calgary: privately printed, [1939]).

Slim, Field-Marshal Sir William, *Defeat Into Victory* (London: Cassell And Company Ltd., 1956).

Spagnoly, Tony, *The Anatomy of a Raid: Australians at Celtic Wood 9th October 1917* (London: Multidream Publications Ltd., 1991).

Spaight, Robin, *British Army Divisions in the Great War, 1914-1918: A Checklist* (Richmond, Surrey: Robin Spaight, 1978).

Spencer, Tony (ed.), *Stanley Spencer's Great War Diary: 1915-1918* (Barnsley: Pen and Sword, 2008).

Stacey, C.P., *A Date With History* (Ottawa: Deneau, 1983).

Stacke, Captain H. FitzM, *The Worcestershire Regiment in the Great War.* Volume One and Volume Two (Uckfield, East Sussex: Naval and Military Press, n.d.).

Statistics of the Military Effort of the British Empire During the Great War 1914-1920 (London: HMSO, March 1922).

Stevens, G.R., *A City Goes to War* (Brampton, Ont.: Charters Publishing Company, 1964).
Stewart, Lieut.-Colonel J. and John Buchan, *The Fifteenth (Scottish) Division 1914-1919* (Edinburgh: William Blackwood And Sons, 1926).
Story, Colonel H.H., *History of the Cameronians (Scottish Rifles) 1910-1933* (Aylesbury: Hazell Watson & Viney Ltd., 1961).
Swettenham, John, *McNaughton*. Volume 1: *1887-1939* (Toronto: The Ryerson Press, 1968).
Swinton, R.E. Major-General Sir Ernest (ed.), *Twenty Years After. The Battlefields of 1914-18: Then And Now* (A George Newnes Publication, Parts 14, 32 and 36 and Supplementary Volume Parts 7, 11, 12, 16 and 17, 1936-38).
——. *The Defence of Duffer's Drift* (Oxford: George Ronald, 1949).
Talbot Kelly, R.B., *A Subaltern's Odyssey: A Memoir of the Great War 1915-1917* (London: William Kimber, 1980).
Tascona, Bruce and Eric Wells, *Little Black Devils: A History of the Royal Winnipeg Rifles* Winnipeg: Frye Publishing, 1983).
Tawney, R.H., *The Attack and Other Papers* (Nottingham: Spokesman, 1981).
Tennyson, Brian Douglas (ed.), *Merry Hell: The Story of the 25th Battalion (Nova Scotia Regiment) Canadian Expeditionary Force 1914-1919: Captain Robert N. Clements, MC* (Toronto: University of Toronto Press, 2013).
Terraine, John, *The Smoke and the Fire: Myths and Anti-Myths of War, 1861-1945* (London: Sidgwick & Jackson, 1980).
——. (ed.), *General Jack's Diary 1914-1918: The Trench Diary of Brigadier-General J.L. Jack, DSO* (London: Cassell, 2003).
Thomas, Alan, *A Life Apart* (London: Victor Gollancz Ltd., 1968).
Thompson, Julian, *The 1916 Experience: Verdun and the Somme* (London: Sevenoaks, 2009).
Thucydides, *History of the Peloponnesian War.* Rex Warner (trans.) (Harmondsworth: Penguin Books Ltd., 1954).
Tilsley, W.V., *Other Ranks* (London: Cobden-Sanderson, 1931).
Tompkins, Stuart Ramsay, *A Canadian's Road to Russia: Letters from the Great War Decade* (Edmonton: University of Alberta Press. 1989).
Topp, Lieut.-Colonel C. Beresford, *The 42nd Battalion, C.E. F. Royal Highlanders of Canada* (Montreal: Gazette Printing Co. Limited, 1931).
Urquhart, Hugh M., *The History of the 16th Battalion (The Canadian Scottish Regiment) Canadian Expeditionary Force in the Great War, 1914-1919* (Toronto: Macmillan, 1932).
——. *Arthur Currie: The Biography of a Great Canadian* (Toronto: Macmillan, 1950).
Vaughan, Edwin Campion, *Some Desperate Glory* (London: Papermac, 1985).
Vokes, Major-General Chris, *Vokes: My Story* (Ottawa: Gallery Books, 1985).
Wallace, O.C.S. (ed.), *From Montreal to Vimy Ridge and Beyond: The Correspondence of Lieut. Clifford Almon Wallace, B.A. of the 8th Battalion, Canadians, B.E.F., November 1915-April 1917* (Toronto: McClelland, Goodchild and Stewart, 1917).
Walsh, Milly and John Callan, *We're Not Dead Yet: The First World War Diary of Private Bert Cooke* (St. Catharines: Vanwell Publishing Limited, 2004).
Wardle, Lt.-Colonel M.K., *Foundations of Soldiering* (Aldershot: Gale & Polden Limited, 1936).
Warrington, Peter, *For Distinguished and Meritorious Services in Time of War: The Great War Recipients of the Military Cross 1914-1920: A Register British and Empire* (Uckfield, East Sussex: Naval and Military Press, 2015).

Watson, Alexander, *Enduring the Great War: Combat, Morale and Collapse in the German and British Armies, 1914-1918* (Cambridge: Cambridge University Press, 2008).

Wauchope, Major-General A.G., *A History of the Black Watch (Royal Highlanders) in the Great War, 1914-1918. Volume Two: Territorial Force* (London: The Medici Society Limited, 1926).

Wavell, Field-Marshal Earl, *Soldiers and Soldiering or Epithets of War* (London: Jonathan Cape, 1953).

Wheeler, Victor, *The 50th Battalion in No Man's Land* (Calgary: Alberta Historical Resources Foundation, 1980).

Wheeler-Holohan, V., *Divisional and Other Signs.* (London: John Murray, 1920).

Whitton, Lieut.-Col. F.E., *History of the 40th Division* (Uckfield, East Sussex: Naval and Military Press, n.d.)

Wigney, Edward H., *Serial Numbers of the CEF* (Nepean, Ontario: privately published. 1996).

Williams, Jeffery, *Byng of Vimy: General and Governor General* (London: Leo Cooper, 1983).

Wilson, Jean Moorcroft, *Siegfried Sassoon: Soldier, Poet, Lover, Friend* (New York: Overlook Books, 2014).

Winter, Denis, *Death's Men: Soldiers of the Great War* (Harmondsworth: Penguin, 1985).

Wipers Times: The Complete Series of the Famous Wartime Trench Newspaper (London: Little Books Ltd., 2006).

Wood, Herbert Fairlie, *Vimy!* (London: Corgi Books, 1972).

——. *Strange Battleground: The Operations in Korea and Their Effects on the Defence Policy of Canada* (Ottawa: Queen's Printer, 1966).

Worthington, Larry, *Amid the Guns Below* (Toronto: McClelland and Stewart, 1965).

Wylly, Colonel H.C., *The 1st and 2nd Battalions The Sherwood Foresters (Nottinghamshire and Derbyshire Regiment) In the Great War* (Aldershot: Gale & Polden, Ltd., 1925).

——. *The Loyal North Lancashire Regiment. Vol. II. 1914-1919* (London: Royal United Services Institution, 1933).

Wyrall, Everard, *The Story of the 62nd (West Riding) Division 1914-1919.* Volume One (Uckfield, East Sussex: Naval and Military Press, n.d.).

——. *The Fiftieth Division 1914-1919* (Uckfield, East Sussex: Naval and Military Press, n.d.).

——. *The Nineteenth Division 1914-1918* (Uckfield, East Sussex: Naval and Military Press, n.d.).

——. *The History of the Second Division. Vol. II. 1914-1918* (Uckfield, East Sussex: Naval and Military Press, n.d.).

Young, Brigadier Peter, *Marston Moor 1644: The Campaign and the Battle* (Kineton: The Roundwood Press, 1970).

THESIS

Jenkins, Dan Richard, 'Winning Trench Warfare: Battlefield Intelligence in the Canadian Corps, 1914-1918'. (Carleton University, Ottawa, 1999).

ARTICLES

Badsey, Stephen, 'The Trench Raid at Cherisy, 15 September 1917', *Imperial War Museum Review,* 4 (1989), pp. 87-95.

Bailey, Jonathan, 'British Artillery in the Great War', in Paddy Griffith (ed.), *British Fighting Methods in the Great War* (London: Frank Cass, 1996).

Barclay, Brigadier C.N., 'Discipline and Morale in a Changing World', *Army Quarterly* (October 1964), pp. 96-99.

Barnes, Leonard, 'Youth at Arms', in Brian Gardner (ed.), *Up the Line to Death: The War Poets 1914-1918* (London: Magnum Books, 1976).

Baynes, John, 'The Officer-Other Rank Relationship in the British Army in the First World War', *Quarterly Review* (October 1966), pp. 442-52.

Becke, Major A.F., 'The Coming of the Creeping Barrage', *Journal of the Royal Artillery,* 58 (January 1932), pp. 19-42.

Bidwell, Major R.G.S., 'An Approach to Military History', *Army Quarterly* (January 1949), pp. 243-46.

Blunden, Edmund, 'The Watchers', in *Undertones of War (*Harmondsworth, Middlesex: Penguin Books Ltd., 1982).

Bond, Brian, 'Ironside', in John Keegan (ed.), *Churchill's Generals* (London: Warner Books, 1992).

Bourne, John, 'Charles Monro', in Ian F.W. Beckett and Steven J. Corvi (eds.), *Haig's Generals* (Barnsley: Pen and Sword, 2006).

Brennan, Patrick H., 'Byng's and Currie's Commanders: A Still Untold Story of the Canadian Corps', *Canadian Military History,* 11 (Spring 2002), pp. 15-16.

Broad, Lt.-Col. C.N.F., 'The Development of Artillery Tactics – 1914-1918', *Journal of the Royal Artillery,* 49.2 (1922-1923), pp. 62-81.

——. 'The Development of Artillery Tactics – 1914-1918', *Journal of the Royal Artillery, 4*9.3 (October 1922), pp. 127-48.

Carmichael, Jane, 'Photographers at Passchendaele', *Imperial War Museum Review,* 2 (1987), pp. 4-14.

Carrington, C.E., 'Kitchener's Army: The Somme and After', *Journal of the Royal United Services Institute* (March 1978), pp. 15-20.

Carroll, Terry, 'A Wexford Soldier Dies With the Canadians at Vimy Ridge', Western Front Association *Bulletin,* 98 (March 2014), pp. 15-17.

Chorley, Matthew, "'Learning Curve" at Divisional Level Between August 1916 – August 1917: The Case of the 29th Division', *Stand To!,* 94 (May 2012), pp. 18-28.

Clifton, Ronald, 'What is an Artillery Brigade?', *Stand To!,* 31 (Spring 1991), p. 34.

——. "What is a Heavy Battery?', *Stand To!,* 35 (Summer 1992), p. 32.

Dawnay, G.P., 'A German Trench Raid', *Army Quarterly,* XXX (April 1935), pp. 86-93.

Dorrington, Nigel, "'Live and Let Die" – The British Army's Experience of Trench Raiding 1915-1918', *Journal of the Centre for First World War Studies,* 3.1 (September 2007), pp. 1-31.

Durey, Michael, "'Two Minor Demonstrations": The 1/1st Cambridgeshire Battalion's Raid on the Ancre, 16-17 September 1916'. *Stand To!.* 91 (April/May 2011), pp. 5-9.

Eady, Major H.G., 'On Writing Appreciations', *RUSI Journal,* 484 (November 1926), pp. 684-92.

Englander, David, 'Discipline and Morale in the British Army, 1917-1918', in *State, Society and Mobilization in Europe During the First World War*, J. Horne (ed.) (Cambridge: Cambridge University Press, 1997).

Essame, Major-General H., 'Second Lieutenants Unless Otherwise Stated', *Military Review* (May 1964), pp. 86-97.

Falls, Cyril, 'The Best of My War', in *Promise of Greatness: The War of 1914-1918*, George A. Panichas (ed.) (London: Cassell, 1968).

Fellowes, Sgt. H., 'Zero Hour', in *Voices and Images of the Great War*, Lyn Macdonald (ed.) (London: Michael Joseph, 1988).

Frame W. Alex and S.D. Badsey, 'Unknown Raiders? Or, Not Every Picture Tells a Story', *Stand To!*, 4 (Spring 1982), pp. 9-13.

French, David, 'Sir James Edmonds and the Official History: France and Belgium', in *The First World War and British Military History*, Brian Bond (ed.) (Oxford: Clarendon Press, 1991).

Garnett, Colin, 'The Art of Minor Operations: Canadian Trench Raiding, 1915-1918', *Canadian Military History*, 24 (Winter/Spring 2015), pp. 249-282.

Godefroy, Andrew, 'Daring Innovation: The Canadian Corps and Trench Raiding on the Western Front', in *Show No Fear: Daring Actions in Canadian Military History'*, Colonel Bernd Horn (ed.) (Toronto: Dundurn Press, 2008).

——. 'A Lesson in Success: The Calonne Trench Raid, 17 January 1917', *Canadian Military History*, 8 (Spring 1999), pp. 25-34.

Griesbach, Major-General The Honourable W.A., 'Military Studies'," *Canadian Defence Quarterly*, 7 (October 1929), pp. 19-28.

Gurney, Ivor 'The Stokes Gunners', in *Poetry of the First World War: An Anthology*, Tim Kendall (ed.) (Oxford: University Press, 2013).

Hanbury-Sparrow, Lt-Col A.A, 'Discipline or Enthusiasm', *British Army Review*, 20 (April 1965), pp. 8-13.

Hardy, Captain Richard Luard, 'The Ideal Subaltern', The King's Royal Rifle Corps Association *Journal* (1998), pp. 73-75.

Hodgson, Lieut. William Noel, 'The Raid', in *Verse and Prose in Peace and War* (London: John Murray, 1917.

——. 'Back to Rest', in *Verse and Prose in Peace and War* (London: John Murray, 1917).

Hopkinson, Laurence, 'Night Raid on the Hollandscheschuur Salient', *Stand To!*, 102 (January 2015), pp. 3-6.

Hudson, Major N., 'Trench Mortars in the Great War', *Journal of the Royal Artillery*, 47 (April 1920), pp. 17-29.

Jackson, Geoffrey, 'What was the point? Raiding in the Summer of 1917', *Canadian Military History*, 19 (Autumn 2010), pp. 31-40.

Keegan, John, 'Towards a Theory of Motivation', in *Time to Kill The Soldier's Experience of War in the West 1939-1945*, Paul Addison and Angus Calder (eds.) (London: Pimlico, 1997).

Kipling, Rudyard, 'The Wishing Caps', in *The Cambridge Edition of the Poems of Rudyard Kipling Volume II Collected Poems II*, Thomas Pinney (ed.) (Cambridge: Cambridge University Press, 2013).

——. 'The Lesson', in *The Cambridge Edition of the Poems of Rudyard Kipling Volume I Collected Poems I*, Thomas Pinney (ed.) (Cambridge: Cambridge University Press, 2013).

——. 'Ubique', in *Kipling's Soldiers,* George and Christian Newark (comps.) (Romford: The Pompadour Gallery, 1993).

——. 'Shadow and Sun', in *The Cambridge Edition of the Poems of Rudyard Kipling Volume III The Uncollected Poems,* Thomas Pinney (ed.) (Cambridge: Cambridge University Press, 2013).

——. 'The Man Who Was', in *The Cambridge Edition of the Poems of Rudyard Kipling Volume II Collected Poems II,* Thomas Pinney (ed.) (Cambridge: Cambridge University Press, 2013).

Lee, John, 'Some Lessons of the Somme: The British Infantry in 1917', in *Look to Your Front: Studies in the First World War by the British Commission for Military History,* Brian Bond et al. Staplehurst: Spellmount, 1999.

Lewendon, Brigadier R.J., 'The Cutting of Barbed Wire Entanglements by Artillery Fire in World War 1', *Journal of the Royal Artillery,* 112 (September 1985), pp. 115-16.

Liddle, Peter A., 'The Battle of the Somme: Image and Reality', *Stand To!,* 39 (Winter 1993), pp. 11-17.

Lynch, Tim, 'Not Just a Name on a Wall: Finding George Galloway', *Stand To!,* 82 (April/May 2008), pp. 46-53.

Macintyre, Duncan, 'The Trench Raiders', in *War Studies Legion Magazine,* 2016).

MacKenzie, Donald A., 'Bogie Raids on Winter Nights', in *From All the Fronts.* (Glasgow: Blackie and Son Limited, 1917).

MacKenzie, S.P., 'Morale and the Cause: The Campaign to Shape the Outlook of Soldiers in the British Expeditionary Force, 1914-1918', *Canadian Journal of History,* XXV (August 1990), pp. 215-32.

McAndrew, Bill, 'The Soldier and the Battle', in *Military History and the Military Profession,* David A. Charters, Marc Milner and J. Brent Wilson (eds.) (Westport, Conn.: Praeger, 1992).

McCarthy, Chris, 'Queen of the Battlefield: The Development of Command, Organization and Tactics in the British Infantry Battalion During the Great War', in *Command and Control on the Western Front,* Gary Sheffield and Dan Todman (eds.) (Staplehurst: Spellmount, 2004).

McNaughton, Brigadier-General A.G.L., 'The Development of Artillery in the Great War', *Canadian Defence Quarterly,* 6 (January 1929), pp. 160-71.

'Major-General Louis James Lipsett, C.B., C.M.G.', *Canadian Defence Quarterly,* 6 (April 1929), pp. 293-300.

Messenger, Charles, 'Trench Raiding', in *History of the First World War* (London: Purnell for BPC Publishing Ltd., n.d.).

Montgomery, Field-Marshal Viscount, 'Morale in Battle', *British Medical Journal,* 2 (9 November 1946), pp. 702-704.

Murray, Captain W.W., 'The Trench Magazine', *Canadian Defence Quarterly* (April 1928), pp. 329-32.

Murray, Colonel W.W. [Kultus Nanich], 'Raids', *Canadian Defence Quarterly* April 1933), pp. 336-40.

Nichols, Robert, 'Assault', in *Ardours and Endurances* (London: Chatto & Windus, 1918).

Obturator [pseud.], 'Garrison Library', *Stand To!,* 1 (Spring 1981), p. 13.

Peacock, Dr. A.J., 'Evidence in Camera: A Cautionary Tale', *Stand To!*3 (Winter 1981), pp. 3-13.

Pegram, Aaron, '"The Bosches seem to have done pretty well what they intended to do"– I ANZAC Corps and the German Raid on the Bridoux Salient, May 1916', *Stand To!*, 97 (May 2013), pp. 4-7.

Pugsley, Christopher, 'Learning from the Canadian Corps on the Western Front', *Canadian Military History*, 15.1 (Winter 2006), pp. 5-32.

Radley, Kenneth, 'Inescapable Realities: Canadian Command, Spring 1915', in *Courage Without Glory*, Spencer Jones (ed.) (Solihull: Helion Publishing, 2015).

Reynolds, Ken, '"Under the Cover of Darkness": The Canadian Trench Raid of 8-9 June 1917', in *Fortune Favours the Brave: Tales of Courage and Tenacity in Canadian Military History*, Colonel Bernd Horn (ed.) (Toronto: Dundurn Press, 2009).

Richardson, Matthew, 'The Ypres Raid – 7 April 1917', *Stand To!*, 44 (September 1995), pp. 10-12.

Roberts, James, 'Making the Butterflies Kill', *Stand To!*, 68 (September 2003), pp. 38-44.

Sassoon, Siegfried, 'The Kiss', in *The War Poems* (London: Faber and Faber Ltd., 1983).

Saville, Graham, 'Night Attack: 2/Royal Munster Fusiliers at Cite Calonne 25 June 1916', *Stand To!*, 56 (September 1999), pp. 25-26.

Scott, Peter T., 'The CDS/SS Series of Manuals & Instructions A Numerical Checklist', *The Great War 1914-1918* 1 (February 1989), pp. 50-54; (May 1989), pp. 115-16; (August 1989), pp. 155-57; 2 (February 1990), pp. 70-71; (May 1990), pp. 106-107; (August 1990), pp. 153-54; 3 (November 1990), pp. 33-35; (February 1991), pp. 68-70; (May 1991), pp. 100-101; (September 1991), pp. 134-36.

——. 'Mr. Stokes and His Educated Drainpipe', *The Great War 1914-1918*, 2 (May 1990), pp. 80-95.

——. 'Trench Weaponry: 3 The West Spring Gun', *Stand To!*, 5 (Summer 1982), p. 16.

Senior, Mike, 'Raids and Patrols: What's the Difference?' *Stand To!*, 89 (August/September 2010), pp. 9-11.

Sheffield, Gary, 'Officer-Man Relations, Discipline and Morale in the British Army in the Great War', in *Facing Armageddon The First World War Experience*, Hugh Cecil and Peter H. Liddle (eds.) (London: Leo Cooper, 1997).

Sheffield, G. D., 'The Morale of the British Army on the Western Front, 1914-1918', in *War in the Age of Technology*, Geoffrey Jensen and Andrew Wiest (eds.) (New York: New York University Press, 2001).

——. 'How Even Was the Learning Curve? Reflections on the British and Dominion Armies on the Western Front 1916-1918', in *1918 Defining Victory. Proceedings of the Chief of Army's History Conference 29 September 1998*, Peter Dennis and Jeffrey Grey (eds.) (Canberra: Army History Unit, Department of Defence, 1999).

Simpson, Keith R., 'Capper and the Offensive Spirit', *RUSI Journal* (June 1973), p. 55.

Sixsmith, Major-General E.K.G., 'Morale and Discipline', in *History of the First World War*, 6.4, Brigadier Peter Young (ed.).

Spagnoly, Tony, 'Canada at Ypres: La Petite Douve Farm, Messines, November 1915', *Stand To!*, 39 (Winter 1993), pp. 23-25.

——. 'Australians at Broodseinde (Ypres) The Raid at Celtic Wood, 9 October 1917', *Stand To!*, 25 (Spring 1989), pp. 6-12.

Spartacus, 'Simplicity', *British Army Review*, 98 (August 1991), pp. 48-52.

Stewart, W., "'Byng Boys': A Profile of Senior Commanders of Canadian Combat Units on the Somme, 1916', *War in History,* 23 (1) (2016), pp. 55-78.
Swinton, Major-General Sir Ernest, 'Concerning Officers and N.C.O.s', *Twenty Years After.* Supplementary Volume, Chapter XXIII, p. 372.
——. [Old Luk-Oie] 'The Point of View', in *The Green Curve* (London: William Blackwood & Sons, 1909).
Sykes, Julian, 'A Trench Raid Near Arras. June 1916', *Gun Fire,* 6, pp. 42-50.
Taylor, Martin, '*The Open Exhaust* and Some Other Trench Journals of the First World War', *Imperial War Museum Review,* 5 (1990), pp.18-27.
Terraine, J.A., 'The Texture of the Somme, 1916', *History Today* (October 1976), pp. 559-68.
Todman, Dan and Gary Sheffield, 'Command and Control in the British Army on the Western Front', in *Command and Control on the Western Front: The British Army's Experience 1914-1918,* Gary Sheffield and Dan Todman (eds,) (Staplehurst: Spellmount, 2004).
Travers, Tim, 'Currie and 1st Canadian Division at Second Ypres, April 1915: Controversy, Criticism and Official History', *Canadian Military History* 5 (Autumn 1996): 7-15.
West, Arthur Graeme, 'The Night Patrol', in *Poems of the First World War:'Never Such Innocence',* Martin Stephen (ed.) (London: J.M. Dent, 1993).
Whitehead, Ralph, 'The Raid', *Stand To!,* 50 (September 1997), pp. 26-28.
Woodward, Lieutenant-Colonel Walden, 'The British Army Staff', *Military Review* (April 1952), pp. 3-13.
Wyrall, Everard, 'On the Writing of "Unit" War Histories', *Army Quarterly* (July 1923), pp. 386-90.
Young, W.T., 'An Officer's Notebook', *Stand To!,* 20 (Summer 1987), pp. 21-22.

Index

Officers and ORs

Officers

ORs

Places

Index of Formations and Units